MW01167327

The B.
Dictionary
of Religion

The Brill
Dictionary
of Religion

Edited by Kocku von Stuckrad

Revised edition of Metzler Lexikon Religion
*edited by Christoph Auffarth, Jutta Bernard
and Hubert Mohr
Translated from the German by Robert R. Barr*

Volume IV

S-Z

BRILL   Leiden · Boston 2007

This book is printed on acid-free paper.

Cover design and photography by Celine Ostendorf and Ivo Romein.

Despite our efforts we have not been able to trace all rights holders to some copyrighted material. The publisher welcomes communications from copyright holders, so that the appropriate acknowledgements can be made in future editions, and to settle other permission matters.

Original German language edition: *Metzler Lexikon Religion*, vol. 1-4. Stuttgart, Germany. Copyright © J. B. Metzlersche Verlagsbuchhandlung und Carl Ernst Poeschel Verlag 2000.
Vol. 1 published 1999 as: *Metzler Lexikon Religion*. Gegenwart – Alltag – Medien. Band 1: Abendmahl – Guru. Herausgegeben von Christoph Auffarth, Jutta Bernard, Hubert Mohr, unter Mitarbeit von Agnes Imhof und Silvia Kurre. Stuttgart · Weimar, 1999. ISBN 3-476-01551-3.
Vol. 2 published 1999 as: *Metzler Lexikon Religion*. Gegenwart – Alltag – Medien. Band 2: Haar – Osho-Bewegung. Herausgegeben von Christoph Auffarth, Jutta Bernard, Hubert Mohr, unter Mitarbeit von Agnes Imhof und Silvia Kurre. Stuttgart · Weimar, 1999. ISBN 3-476-01552-1.
Vol. 3 published 2000 as: *Metzler Lexikon Religion*. Gegenwart – Alltag – Medien. Band 3: Paganismus – Zombie. Herausgegeben von Christoph Auffarth, Jutta Bernard, Hubert Mohr, unter Mitarbeit von Agnes Imhof und Silvia Kurre. Stuttgart · Weimar, 2000. ISBN 3-476-01553-X.
Vol. 4 published 2002 as: *Metzler Lexikon Religion*. Gegenwart – Alltag – Medien. Band 4: Text- und Bildquellen, Filmographie, Zeittafeln, Gesamtregister. Herausgegeben von Christoph Auffarth und Hubert Mohr, unter Mitarbeit von Benita von Behr, Jutta Bernard und Kirsten Holzapfel. Stuttgart · Weimar, 2002. ISBN 3-476-01554-8.

Library of Congress Cataloging-in-Publication-data
LC Control Number

ISBN (*Vol.* 1): 978 90 04 16281 5
ISBN (*Vol.* 2): 978 90 04 16282 2
ISBN (*Vol.* 3): 978 90 04 16283 9
ISBN (*Vol.* 4): 978 90 04 16284 6
ISBN (*Set*): 978 90 04 15100 0

Copyright 2007 by Koninklijke Brill NV, Leiden, The Netherlands.
Koninklijke Brill NV incorporates the imprints Brill, Hotei Publishers, IDC Publishers, Martinus Nijhoff Publishers and VSP.

Printed in The Netherlands

CONTENTS

Sabbath → Sunday/Sabbath

Sacrifice

1. On New Year's Eve, on the beaches of Rio de Janeiro, toilet articles for women, champagne, mineral water, white corn pudding, or flowers are placed in the water. It is the festival of the Sea Goddess Yamanjá (see picture), one of the most meaningful feasts in the life of the Afro-Brazilian population. The breakers carry the gifts out to sea, and then the people have assurance that their gifts have been acceptable to the goddess, and that their hope for the granting of their requests is justified.[1] Still more 'exciting,' however, to the Western observer and the media, are the rituals of slaughter in the Afro-American religions, that arouse such spectacle, shudder, fascination—and perplexity. In the course of a divine service that may last several days, sanctuaries are transformed into 'slaughterhouses' (G. Bataille). Many and varied rites of consecration impart a divine character to the sacrificial animals: the latter are washed, perfumed, and powdered. Bulls and goats are draped in splendid attire, of velvet or silk, in a color symbolizing the divinity to whom sacrifice is being made. The horns of bulls are decorated with lighted candles; fluids (water, rum) and foods are set on the backs of animals in the form of a cross. Now they are offered their consecrated nourishment, and by way of being consumed themselves, they become the irrevocable property of the deity. If they decline the meal, they must be replaced with other animals—the god would not accept the sacrifice ('topos of voluntareity'). Participants stroke, embrace, and kiss the animals, which stand symbolically facing the four directions of heaven. Detailed regulations determine the killing of the sacrificial animals. By way of a preternatural → possession of the slaughterer, the divinity itself slays the victim. In → voodoo, the participants drink the blood of the sacrifice, or preserve it for ritual actions, while in Afro-American religions the 'divine seats' are steeped in the 'emission of blood.' Blood contains 'sacred power' (*ashé*) in a high measure. The carcasses are distributed: the portions for the deity—blood, head, ears, tongue, feet, and tail—are set down on the altar. Bones are sometimes buried separately. The best of what remains goes to the community members present. Believers then consume the meat in the festal meal—sacrificial festivals are 'good for eating.'

2. Sacrificial actions play a key role in the religions of humanity. Sacrifices are often very complex ritual actions, in the course of which communication between human beings and spirits is thought to be produced or broken off, as participants part with an object (statue or figure, food item, liquid, inscribed paper) or living being. A definition of the concept is problematic, since such different kinds of religious phenomena are understood under 'sacrifice' as Jesus's sacrifice of atonement, votive gifts, and animal sacrifices, that are basically distinct, in the intentions of actors as well as in the principal theological world pictures and faith systems.

3. The concepts that denote 'sacrifice' (in English and French) are unclear and polyvalent. In other modern languages, the word for 'sacrifice' (German *Opfer*, Dutch *offer*, etc.; cf. the English 'offer') is not a scientific concept, but

Clarification of Concepts

Pilgrims from Iraq sacrifice a sheep before the journey to Mecca. At the right, in the picture, a man is already wearing the *ihram* garment (pilgrim's attire). Animal sacrifices, in Islam, can be offered at various occasions; the most frequent are the two great Islamic festivals, the breaking of the fast at the end of Ramadan, and the sacrificial festival during the month of pilgrimage. Classic sacrificial animals are camels and sheep. The ceremony consists of prayer, and the recitation of certain formulae, at which the animal is laid in the direction of Mecca, and sacrificed. Except in the case of a vow, the flesh is partly consumed by the participants and partly distributed to the

a loan word, formed from the church Latin *operari*, 'to serve God through works' (concretely, since Church Father Cyprian, 'to give alms'). The concept of *Opfer*, 'sacrifice', in German, falls in both an active ('renounce') and a passive ('victim', someone 'suffers an evil'; cf. the Dutch *slachtoffer*) region of meaning. Modern everyday speech, therefore, applies the word 'sacrifice', on the one side, in keeping with Christian moral conceptualizations for the designation of non-ritualized, ethical activity, distinguished by 'renunciation', by 'painful loss for a higher end': one 'sacrifices a day for one's family'. Theological ideologies of renunciation can be re-formed and harnessed for political ends. In the sacrificial ideology of the National Socialists the 'sense and meaning of cultic sacrifice' lay in the idea that soldiers of the German Wehrmacht offered themselves 'for the good of the community' ('sacrifice for the Fatherland', 'victims of war').[2] On the other side, the meaning of the Latin word *victima* echoes in the passive region of meaning—the 'sacrificial animal' that is delivered up apart from its own will, that is led to the now metaphorical altar of slaughter—as 'road casualty', or, indeed, that is produced as a sacrifice of the *Holocaust* (from the Greek, *holokaútoma*, 'whole burnt offering'). This double meaning was composed against a background of the Christian theology of sacrifice. These ambivalent uses and subtexts of the words used for 'sacrifice' have led to conceptual confusion. Hence, modern religious studies takes its orientation more precisely in the content of the Latin concept *sacrificium* ('sacred action'). However, no unitary scientific usage prevails.

4. Descriptive classifications of sacrificial rituals are differentiated according to the composition or the handling of the sacrificial material. Nevertheless, one can distinguish vegetable sacrifices, animal sacrifices, human sacrifices, bloody and unbloody sacrifices, or, again, burnt offerings, sacrifice in which the victim is slain, immersion sacrifices, drink offerings ('libations'), and sacrifices of annihilation. *Typologies* regard rather the actors' intentions that underlie the sacrificial rituals: the traditional categories of praise, thanksgiving, impetration, and satisfaction would correspond here. In theoretical and descriptive works, classifications and sacrificial types frequently overlap. If sacrifice is conceptualized as an action performed by human beings, one effectuating a symbolic exchange with gods or spirits—thus, in a communicative structure—then the 'connecting' type of sacrifice versus the 'dividing' will be conceived as follows: sacrifices are then rituals performed by the actors in order to produce or discontinue a communication with the sacred region, the divine powers. To the connecting type of sacrifice correspond the sacrifices of praise, thanksgiving, and impetration. It is especially the material of the sacrifice that produces connections between human and spirit beings, and, in the course of the communicative process, human intercourse is withdrawn, 'destroyed.'[3] Examples of a *connecting* aspect would be the 'food sacrifices' of Afro-American religions, or votive gifts modeled on the *Do ut des* concept—"I give in order that you give." In the *dividing* type of sacrifice, the ritual process is set in motion in order to break off contact with spiritual beings, by means of a communicative act. Thus, in the Afro-Brazilian rite of the 'exchange of heads,' the evil or the psychic or physical infirmity is transferred from the head of the patient to that of the sacrificial cock—it is interpreted as a 'quest for a homecoming' on the part of the malevolent spiritual being. The animal is then exposed or slain—that is, offered as a whole to the deity in question.[4] In the 'scapegoat rituals,' the meal to be eaten by human beings is absent (in Israel, a buck was slain, or driven into the wilderness, as a 'sin offering' for the community; cf. Lev 16).

needy. At the sacrificial festival in Mina, there is usually more meat left over than can be distributed, which, earlier, would have led to problematic hygienic circumstances. Today, therefore, sacrifice is no longer offered by individuals. Instead, a contribution, in a specified amount, is made with the Islamic Bank for Development, and then the slaughtering is done by butchers, while the meat is put in deep freeze and sent to needy persons in the Islamic world. (Agnes Imhof)

5. Practical occasions of sacrifice that arise in 'everyday' life are as manifold as are the situations in which human beings must live: here, sacrifice is offered in order to 'impetrate' the benefaction of the deity in existential need (the 'impetratory sacrifice'), to render thanks to it ('sacrifice of thanksgiving,' 'firstfruits,' thanksgiving festival after the harvest), to foster the fertility of the fields by means of sacrificial blood and other sacrificial matter (→ Agrarian Religion/Agrarian Magic), to placate the wrath of the deity or to purify the community ('scapegoat'), or to render the dead sympathetic by placing offerings of nourishment on graves (sacrifices to the dead). Sacrificial acts can also form components of complex rituals, for instance of → prophecy (the sacrificial 'reading' of the innards of the slain animal), → initiation (V. Turner 1977), or → feast.

Occasions Arising in the Practical World

6. As for the handling of the sacrificial material, theories of sacrifice usually underscore the economic aspects of sacrificial rituals: hunting rituals, with hunting peoples, guarantee the continuity of the scarce, valuable, nourishment by meat, and the "symbolical surplus value of the meat" (G. Baudy) is reflected in the code of distribution. Originally, even the slaying of the animal may always have been accomplished only in the course of a religious ritual—in the course of a 'sacrifice,' then—and thereby publicly 'checked' and controlled (W. Burkert). In the Hebrew Bible, however, a distinction was drawn between

Economy of Sacrifice

At the celebration of the New Year, the Afro-Brazilian population offer sacrifice to the goddess Yemanjá, on the banks of the Rio de Janeiro: flowers, dolls, and other gifts especially dear to the goddess are committed to the sea. In their sacrificial prayers, believers beg of Yemanjá the granting of their requests and wishes. (J. Drexler)

A special sacrifice, under the all-seeing eyes of the Buddha, at the ornamented stupa of Bodnath (Katmandu, in Nepal). At this Tibetan Buddhist sanctuary, it is seen as spiritually meritorious to have limewater poured from the edge of the one-meter-high hemisphere by temple workers, in exchange for a monetary contribution. The action is performed several times a day, so that, in the some five centuries of its existence, the monument has materially expanded. A second form of ritual libation is more expensive: from the base of the hemisphere, in high bows, saffron water is cast up upon the limestone to make dark stains, from which emerges the pattern of a lotus blossom—a sacred symbol in Buddhism. (E. Stapelfeldt)

In many religions, the burning of sweet-scented essences (incense, rosin, sandalwood, aloes, myrrh, camphor, cedar, etc.) constitutes an important component of worship or cult. In Catholicism, for example, the burning of incense (or 'incensation') has been practiced since the fourth century, and stands as an image and symbol of the prayer that ascends to God. The sacrifice of smoke and fragrances serves for the consecration or dedication of places, for ritual purification, to dispel demons, and to rejoice the gods by the ascending fragrance. Especially in → Daoism, the burning of incense sticks plays an important role in ritual, and in the everyday practice of believers: the vessels for sacrifices of smoke are key components of the temple. Here a young mother in Hong Kong offers a bundle of incense sticks in a Daoist temple, dedicated to the gods Man and Mo. Both deities go back to persons who, according to legend, lived some 1,500 years ago. Man, the God of Literature, is the patron of government officials, while Mo, the God of Martial Arts, is venerated by both police officers and the criminal milieu. (Benita von Behr)

cultic slaughter that was concentrated in Jerusalem after King Josiah (cf. Lev 17:3-4, from the post-Exilic law of holiness), and profane slaughter that was entirely permitted. Furthermore, there are types of sacrifice, such as the sacrifice of nourishment for the gods in the Sumerian-Babylonian, Egyptian, or Greco-Roman regions, which are compatible with a broader application of the sacrificial material. Indeed, it was the distribution of the nourishment—grain, or the meat of the animals that had been slaughtered—that belonged to the main tasks of ancient temple complexes. The Greeks used sacrificial implements, such as the sacrificial spear (in Gk., *obelós*), before the seventh century BCE, as a kind of 'tool money.' The 'sacrificial stock' developed from the sacred grain supply (in Gk., *thesaurós*). Again, the German/Dutch word *Geld* ('money') derives from the Old High German, a 'sacrifice to the gods.'[5]

Human and Divine Benefits of Sacrifice

But sacrificial gifts are distributed not only literally among participants, but also symbolically between believers and mythic powers. In Greek myth, the 'unjust' distribution of sacrifices between or among human beings and gods is, proverbially, the 'betrayal of → Prometheus': the gift that the Greek gods received was only the smoke of burnt thighbones, while human beings would take all of the flesh.[6] It has been observed that, among hunters of the Old Stone Age as well as of today, there are comparable hunting rituals: burnt thighbones, preservation of skulls (*boukránia*) and horns of sacrificial animals at the sacred place were said to have been undertaken as hunting rites of regeneration, in order that new life be restored to the animal. Again, the ritual topos of voluntary slaying ('comedy of innocence') probably has its origin in hunters' hesitation to kill. Homeric offerings of nourishment, then, would have been the "ritual slaughter" of an animal, "that the human beings might eat it."[7] Finally, economic considerations enter into the distribution practice. When the African Nuer have no bullocks to sacrifice, they sacrifice a cucumber, called a 'bullock' in the ritual context. 'Renunciation' from the side of those sacrificing is thereby reduced to a minimum. In the extreme case, in serious crises (drought, hunger, war), the distribution can take on the form of unilateral 'eradication sacrifice': Nuer slaughter bullocks in the bush, where the sacrificial meat is entirely surrendered to spirit beings who are hostilely disposed. Here, renunciation becomes painful loss. Gifts are then not only *for* the gods, but also *against* them, so that they are kept at a distance; dispelled, reconciled, accorded sacrifices. In such a ritual, with the assistance of this 'sacrifice of satisfaction,' or a 'sacrifice of firstfruits' offered in some other way, situations of fear are subjected to control: they are dampened, as the inimical spirits are demonstratively awarded the best or first portion (and therefore the 'alpha position'; B. Gladigow 1984).

Sacrificial Ideologies

7. A diversity of religious worldviews underlies sacrificial rituals. Thus, the word for sacrifice used by the African Dogon is *bulu*, 'to restore to life': the reference is to the idea of the bloody sacrifice as a ritual technique leading to a new distribution of the power of life, *nyama*. The different linguistic usages betray culture-specific conceptual worlds, and sacrificial ideologies, that cannot be brought over a common denominator. This diversity is what caused the older scientific theories of sacrifice to fail, to the extent that they sought to formulate a general 'theory of sacrifice' according to a unitary 'meaning and end of sacrifice.' The unitary nature of sacrifice emerged as an illusion; the theoretical constructions had been especially infiltrated by Christian conceptions.[8] Just so, ethnographic observation in no way justifies

the emphasis on bloody, or even 'bloodthirsty' rites of sacrifice that occurs in recent theories (R. Girard, W. Burkert): in this perspective, the latter must be interpreted as exoticising reception of the 'other.'

Sacrificial Interpretations

8. Scientific theories usually emphasize partial aspects of sacrificial rituals: the slaying, distribution, and eating of the material of the sacrifice. As a rule, these aspects form components of the 'bloody-sacrifice complex.'

Sacrifice as Gift Exchange and Renunciation

(a) Building upon his concept of → animism, evolutionist E. B. Tylor (1871) defined sacrifice as gift, formed on the exemplar of human social relations: 'originally,' sacrifice was not a selfless gift, but a 'bribe'; in higher evolutionary development, gifts were offered out of 'homage,' or, in the properly ethical form, out of 'renunciation.' In the animistic view of sacrifice, deities take their nourishment from the 'substance,' 'essence,' or 'soul' of the sacrificial material. Afro-American sacrificial rites confirm this view in that, here, the duty of the believer consists in 'giving the gods to eat.'[9] Blood, innards, extremities of slain animals, are set before the images of the gods, that the gods may consume their 'essence.' In ethnographic literature, the 'dynamistic' interpretational variant occurred as well, i.e. that this kind of sacrifice of foodstuffs is a matter of a reciprocal magical exchange of power (G. van der Leeuw; → Power) between gods and believers: thus, the sacrificial acts of Afro-Americans or Dogon are ritual techniques of the redistribution of life power, so that the theoretical model in the sense of dynamistic tendencies remains disputable.

The Sacramental Sacrificial Meal

(b) Scots theologian and oriental scholar William Robertson Smith recognized the importance of the sacrificial meal ('communion') for the founding of community. Here, holds Smith, by way of the consumption of the collectively slain animal, mystical unification is realized with the deity being honored. Smith's speculative theory of the origin of the sacrificial meal influenced Freud's psychoanalytical interpretations of sacrifice as the murder of one's father, and anthropophagous sacrificial meal. Smith's understanding also influenced the sociological approach of Émile Durkheim, who, like Smith, saw the animal totem as a symbol of society. Of course, the 'sacramental' eating of God at the → Lord's Supper, that doubtless acted as patron of Smith's theory, is to be distinguished from the eating *with* the god of the Afro-American festival of sacrificial food.

Sacrifice as Communicative Act

(c) In 1899, French sociologists Henri Hubert and Marcel Mauss, close collaborators of Émile Durkheim, created the interpretation of sacrifice that has been most important ever since. In their analysis of the structure of the ancient Indian, Vedic animal sacrifice, they defined sacrifice itself as a mediated *communication between the profane and the sacred world*: the sacrificial animal, which must first be sacralized, is a means of communication, and the sacrifice itself is a → rite of passage between the two worlds. Rites of entry and exit, or sanctification and de-sanctification, place a framework around the actual sacrificial act, whose climax, held Hubert and Mauss, was formed by the slaying of the animal. With the act of slaying, the sacred and dangerous 'energies' have been released, which now flow out both to the Holy and to the persons performing the sacrifice. The social function of sacrifice consists in the reconciliation of those making the sacrifice, and the society represented by the gods for whom the sacrifice is intended: the person performing the sacrifice presents society with its concept as a 'gift.'

(d) If, for J. G. Frazer (around 1900) scapegoat rites rested on the 'magic' transfer/conveyance of the insalubrious to the matter or material of the offering (animal, human being), René Girard saw (in 1972), in the mechanism of the scapegoat procedure, *the* means used by society for controlling the threat of the violence that ever looms in its inmost being, by projecting it onto a surrogate sacrifice. In the dismal, gloomily archaic, vision of *homo necans* (Lat. 'human being who slaughters'), entertained by scholar of antiquity Walter Burkert in the same year, interhuman aggressions are liberatingly ('cathartically') called on to invest the sacrificial animal in the sacred act of slaying, in a fashion that is harmless for society. This manner of '→ catharsis theory' entertained by sociology of religion can be understood as a quest for a psychically hygienic escape from the societal violence being recognized as the "key problem of the present."[10]

Sacrifice as Purifying Power

9. *Crisis* of sacrifice:[11] In the Christian theology of sacrifice, Jesus's eschatological sacrifice of atonement ends the biblical practice of the bloody sacrifice, criticized by the prophets themselves as external ritualism. The concentration of the Israelitic sacrificial system in Jerusalem had the effect that, after the destruction of the Temple there (70 CE), the institutionalized cult of sacrifice by slaughter had ended. The 'divine services of the word,' celebrated in the synagogues, replaced the Temple of sacrifice; spiritualized and imagined modes of sacrifice replaced the bloody cult; humility and prayer replaced burning flesh. The metaphorization and spiritualization of the Hebrew biblical concept of sacrifice progressed in Christianity with even more force than it had before: human beings are to offer themselves as a "living, holy, sacrifice pleasing to God" (Rom 12:1). The 'spiritual sacrifices' of Christians include all acts of self-giving and surrender to God, all ascetical self-denial, all altruistic works of love of neighbor. In the Western Christian tradition, phenomenal modes of sacrifice that are material are ascribed to early, 'unenlightened' stages of humanity: societies bearing a Christian stamp know only profane slaughterhouses—unlike Judaism, in which any killing of an animal is still ritualized. Anti-cultic tendencies are also observable in other religions: pre-Socratic philosophers, or Pythagoras (→ Vegetarianism), criticized the practice of the bloody sacrifice; Buddhism sharply rejects the Vedic animal sacrifices.

Spiritualized Modes of Sacrifice

10. Modern observation, as practiced by cultural studies, ought to be concerned not with formulating a general theory of sacrifice, but with a consideration of the imbedding of sacrificial rituals in particular cultures. Instead of the essentialist, theological question of the meaning of sacrifice in itself, concrete sacrificial rites should be investigated and researched as components of religious practice and of a symbolical worldview.

In the multi-religious common life of Western post-modernity, as in the undertow of current globalization, state religions with binding monopolies on norms and belief are cast adrift, at an obviously accelerating rate, from a basic plurality of worldviews and religious communities. However, precisely in the practice of bloody animal sacrifice, conflicts can germinate: thus, recently, in the "Orgies-Mysteries Theater" of action artist Hermann Nitsch (→ Blasphemy, ill.), whose 'Dionysan' private cult, despite correct professionally executed slaughters, called forth raging protests from animal

Modernity

protectionists and Catholic officials—who, granted, are rarely willing to re-nounce their hot dogs!

1. FIGGE, Horst, Geisterkult, Besessenheit und Magie in der Umbanda-Religion Brasi-liens, Munich 1973.
2. Cf. BERTHOLET, Alfred, Der Sinn des kultischen Opfers, Berlin 1942, 27.
3. HUBERT/MAUSS 1968, 11ff.
4. FIGGE (as in note 1) 1973, 131f.
5. Cf. BAUDY 1983, 150f.; GLADIGOW 1984.
6. Hesiod, Theogony V, 535ff.
7. MEULI 1946, 281f.
8. DETIENNE 1986; DREXLER 1993.
9. Cf. FIGGE 1973, 90; MÉTRAUX 1959, 168.
10. BURKERT, Walter, Homo necans. Interpretationen altgriechischer Opferriten und Mythen, Berlin 1972, 8 (Engl. version BURKERT 1983).
11. GIRARD 1977.

Literature

ANDERSON, G. A., Sacrifices and Offerings in Ancient Israel: Studies in Their Social and Political Importance, Ann Arbor 1986; BAUDY, G., "Hierarchie oder: Die Verteilung des Fleisches," in: GLADIGOW, B./KIPPENBERG, H. G. (eds.), Neue Ansätze in der Religions-wissenschaft, Munich 1983, 131-174; BURKERT, W., Homo Necans: The Anthropology of Ancient Greek Sacrificial Ritual and Myth, Berkeley 1983; DETIENNE, M./VERNANT, J.-P. (eds.), The Cuisine of Sacrifice among the Greeks, Chicago 1986 (Fr. 1979); DREXLER, J., Die Illusion des Opfers: Ein wissenschaftlicher Überblick über die wichtigsten Opfertheo-rien ausgehend vom deleuzianischen Polyperspektivismusmodell, Munich 1993; FIRTH, R., "Offering and Sacrifice: Problems of Organization," in: Royal Anthropological Institute of Great Britain and Ireland 93,1 (1963), 12-24; GIRARD, R., Violence and the Sacred, Baltimore 1977; GLADIGOW, B., "Die Teilung des Opfers," in: Frühmittelalterliche Studien 18 (1984), 19-43; HAMERTON-KELLY, R. G. (ed.), Violent Origins: Walter Burkert, René Girard, and Jonathan Z. Smith on Ritual Killing and Cultural Formation, Stanford 1987; HUBERT, H./MAUSS, M., Essai sur la nature et la function du sacrifice (1899), in: MAUSS, M., Oeuvres I, Les fonctions socials du sacré, Paris 1968, 191-307; MÉTRAUX, A., Voodoo in Haiti, London 1959; MEULI, K., Griechische Opferbräuche, Basle 1946, 185-288; READ, K. A., Time and Sacrifice in the Aztec Cosmos, Bloomington/Indianapolis 1998; TURNER, V., "Sacrifice as Quintessential Process: Prophylaxis or Abandonment?," in: History of Religions 16,3 (1977), 189-215.

→ *Afro-American Religions, Agrarian Religion/Agrarian Magic, Animal, Animism, Blood, Communication, Eating/Nourishment, Exchange/Gift, Human Sacrifice, Lord's Supper/ Eucharist, Materiality, Ritual, Suicide, Vegetarianism, Voodoo*

Josef Drexler

Sadhu

1. Derived from the Sanskrit verb *sadh* ('to attain,' 'to perfect' or 'to im-prove'), *sadhu* is the designation for holy men (and/or, rarely, women) in In-dia. Any religious ascetic or holy person can be called a sadhu. In the more proper sense, sadhus are initiates of various ascetical orders, who either live in settlements (*matha*) similar to monasteries, or wander about homeless. Although most of these orders, like Indian religions across the board (→

In India, a multiplicity of ascetical groups exist, all having different orientations, practices, and distinctive traits. This Hindu sadhu, in the vicinity of Rishikesh (Uttar Pradesh), is identifiable as a follower of Shiva, by the trident in the corner. However, the representations above his home shrine show that the veneration of other Hindu divinities (e.g., of flute-playing Krishna, or of ten-armed goddess Durga riding on the lion), with the bell, oil lamp, and mussel horn is entirely a part of his spiritual practice. Other photographs testify to the meaning for the group of the personalities of founders and teachers. Staff and wooden shoes indicate the tradition of the overland traveler; the water pot recalls the vow of mendicancy. His cabin is itself an expression of the ideal of poverty. (E. Stapelfeldt)

Hinduism), can be considered as Shivaites or Vishnuites, in their religious practices many traits of Tantrism (→ Tantra) are found, as well. In addition, ascetics of other Indian religions—such as Jainism and → Buddhism, along with even the followers of North Indian mystic Kabir (fifteenth century), who is reverenced by Hindus and Muslims alike—are called sadhus. Ascetics of Islamic currents, on the other hand, similar to the sadhus, are called fakirs (Ar. *faqir*, 'poor').

2. To the Vishnuite sadhus, also called vairagins (Skt. 'passionless'), belong the Shri-Vaishnavas, Ramanandins, and followers of philosopher Vallabha (1479–1531) or mystic Caitanya (1486–1533; → Hare Krishna Movement). Shivaitic sadhus descend from the famous philosopher Shankara (788–820), to a certain extent, who is supposed to have founded the four orders of the Samyasins, Dandins, Paramahamsas, and Brahmacarins; or else they belong to other, rather heterodox currents, such as the Lin-

gayats, the tantric Aghoris (→ Tantra), or Alakhnamis. Acceptance into these orders is joined to rituals of initiation, at which the sadhu receives a new name, one typical of the order. Sadhus are addressed with the term of respect *baba* ('Father'), often despite their age. Especially at great religious festivals, sadhus of the various denominations join larger groups, in which they then enjoy privileges. Thus, at the Kumbha Mela festival, celebrated every six years, the various groups of sadhus may bathe first in the sacred river (→ Feasts and Celebrations, with ill.). Often, the order of honor assumed by the respective religious orders is disputed, even to the point of martial violence. Even apart from this, sadhu groups often demonstrate pretentious, outright bellicose attitudes and deportment.

Nudity and Fasting

3. If indeed they do not go naked, as some do, sadhus are most often clad only in loincloths. Their possessions are often limited to a begging bowl, and a few objects typical of their order. Thus, Shivaite sadhus, as a rule, have an animal skin to sit on, a trident (*trishul*) or staff (*danda*), used as a hiking stick as well as a weapon, and a small, double drum called a *damaru*. Their respective denominations are indicated by signs painted on their foreheads and upper arms, (*tilak*: Shivaites mostly three diagonal lines, Vishnuites a *U*), as well as by adornments about the neck (Shivaites wear a chain, *mala*, of rudraksa kernels, Vishnaites one of Tulsi wood). Shivaitic sadhus are often seen performing the chillum ritual, at which cannabis products are smoked (→ Intoxication/Drugs/Hallucinogens). Many sadhus hold themselves to strict prescriptions of fasting and diet, others observe no sort of dietary limitations, and eat even cat and rat meat. Most sadhus live in celibacy.

Vows

4. Sadhus sometimes keep incredibly strict vows (*trata*): on pilgrimages, they draw weights behind them, or lie down and roll for hundreds of miles; they lie on the celebrated bed of nails, or stand for years under a tree. 'Standers' are recognized by their typical rack construction, with the help of which they can even sleep standing. Frequently, observance of such vows has an extremely deleterious effect on the ascetic's body; on the other hand, the sadhus, who support all torments with such iron consistency, are credited with immense supra-sensory powers, so that people are afraid of them, besides revering them and supplying them with food. In rural areas, through virtuosic accomplishments, a sadhu can achieve considerable social prestige, and a position of local authority. Sadhus, who at times preach publicly, constitute an ever-present counterbalance to the conservative, ritualistic Brahmans and temple priests. It is obvious, of course, that only some sadhus are actual practitioners of the spiritual disciplines; others are simple beggars, who cause wonderment and 'earn' money with pocket tricks. Persons, who would be classified as mentally ill by Western criteria, are venerated in India as saints, indeed, as sadhus. The institution of the sadhu offers the opportunity of rising above the caste-oriented societal system in India, and acquiring great social prestige.

Adepts from the West

5. The sadhu movements have received adepts from the West, some of whom wander about with the Indian orders or brotherhoods, and are scarcely distinguishable from them. Others return to the West, to lead an ascetic life there in reclusion.

Literature

BHAGAT, M. G., Ancient Indian Asceticism, New Delhi 1976; DAVIS, Martin P., Sadhu Hagenstein: A White Man among the Brown. The Record of a Man of God, Washington 1930; GROSS, R. L., A Study of the Sadhus of North India, Berkeley 1979; HARTSUIKER, Dolf, Sadhus: India's Mystic Holy Men, Rochester 1993 (photographs); STREETER, B. H./ APPASAMY, A. J., The Sadhu: A Study in Mysticism and Practical Religion, Delhi 1987.

→ *Asceticism, Guru, Hinduism, Indian Subcontinent, Tantra, Veneration of the Saints*

Karl-Peter Gietz

Salvation Army

1. The Salvation Army goes back to the former Methodist preacher William Booth (1829–1912). In view of the enormous misery—including moral misery—and great alienation from religion, of the inhabitants of the poor quarters of East London, Booth saw the need for a radical spiritual conversion. Economic and social circumstances were depressing, especially in districts of industrial concentration, and were characterized by great material poverty. Large areas of the population were plunged in misery. Wages were ordinarily beneath subsistence level, and life expectancy was short. Diseases were numerous.

William Booth

Booth's Christianity was that of the Methodist direction, with its emphasis on a tireless missionary toil. However, he soon recognized that the destitute classes would be little open to the Christian gospel without social welfare. Therefore, his work purely for the conversion of the people would have to be complemented by activity that was social in a religious way (→ Charitable Organizations).

2. As an organization, the Salvation Army emerged in 1865 from the "Christian Mission"—a work constituted by then of over one hundred missionary societies of East London, for which Booth worked as a preacher. The organization bore the name "Salvation Army" only from 1880 on. Gradually, Booth succeeded in winning ever more influence over the Christian Mission, and establishing his ideas. Although he was confronted with more and more hostility, he had great success with his missionary work. Of particular concern to him here were the collaboration of the laity, and the public profession of the newly converted. Booth also gained respect by his street sermons, and by the processions that he held to attract the curious and convert them. These marches were later to become characteristic of the Salvation Army.

By 1877, Booth had succeeded in bringing the Christian Mission entirely under his influence, and all instances of control and all groups that had hindered him in the implementation of his concepts had been dissolved. Now he had realized his goal of a powerful salvation movement. Hand in hand with this phenomenon went a strong hierarchization, with a quasi-military apparatus at whose summit stood 'General' William Booth. Booth was chosen for life, and might designate his successor himself. Not only did he dispose of the Salvation Army's entire fortune, but he also enjoyed extensive powers of decision. Again, the great financial success of his book, *In Darkest England and the Way Out* (1890), in which Booth castigated the deplorable state of social affairs and called for a remedy, gave him the financial means to lend his activities a greater force. The concept set up 'urban colonies' and 'land colonies,' whose personnel had been provided with training as farmers, against the flight from the land, as well as against organized emigration to the United States or to British colonies overseas. The social program was innovative. Among other things, it provided attorneys for the poor, 'poor man's banks,' clinics, search services for missing persons, and a social service of its own for sailors (Whitechapel-by-the-Sea).

Army of God

Conceptual and organizational elements from the area of the military became characteristic of the Salvation Army. It is organized as the 'Army of God.' At the side of the General, who has been elected every five years since 1929, and who is at the top, stands a staff of collaborators, the Staff. Under the General are the Superintendents—the district leaders—followed by the high-ranking collaborators of a mission station. Unlike the 'Officers,' whose main occupation is with the Salvation Army, are the lay assistants, the 'soldiers,' who practice a civil profession. The Officers are prepared for their later profession in a school for cadets. All of the offices, including that of General, are open to women. The countries in which the Salvation Army is active are divided into various 'corps.' The members wear a uniform, and carry a flag. Beginning in 1887, choruses were established: spiritual texts were set to the melodies of popular songs, and this greatly contributed to the popularity of the movement. A weekly organ *The War Cry* appeared, which is still distributed today.

Belief and Religious Practice

3. In 1878, the Profession of the Salvation Army was formulated as eleven binding articles of faith. Special importance attaches to repentance and conversion to God, which are regarded as prerequisite for personal salvation. The Salvation Army does not hold sacraments, such as Baptism or the Lord's Supper, to be necessary. There is no regulated formula of worship, not even for weddings or the dedication of children. Rather, the Holy Spirit should be permitted to work freely: rigid precepts would only be a hindrance here. What is important, instead, are public proclamation and the salvation assemblies, which serve to bring the unconverted to the table of repentance and thus to move them to conversion. Members of the Salvation Army oblige themselves to renunciation of the use of alcohol and tobacco. A double membership in the Salvation Army and in another church is possible.

Great worth was ascribed to the Salvation Army through its works of charity (→ Charitable Organizations). These shifted more and more into the foreground even during Booth's lifetime—altogether against his personal convictions, as the religious aspect was far more important to him. Members have always focused their work on the most urgent social problems of large cities' slums, city centers, and red light districts. Thus, for example, Booth's spouse and fellow combatant Catherine (1829–1890) worked for the establishment of houses for prostitutes. The Salvation Army managed, besides, to have the minimum age of emancipation for girls raised from thirteen to sixteen. Through the creation of soup kitchens and shelters for drinkers, women, the homeless, sailors, prisoners of war who had been released, and much more, the Salvation Army extended its charitable services.

Although the Salvation Army was first active in London, it spread throughout England and nearly the entire world, while its founder was still alive. In 1880 work began in the United States, Ireland, and Australia, a year later in France, and in 1886 in Germany. Worldwide, the Salvation Army counts circa three million members and friends (including 17,000 active 'Officers'), and exists in ninety-three countries, divided into 14,428 'corps.'

Literature

EASON, Andrew Mark, Women in God's Army: Gender and Equality in the Early Salvation Army, Waterloo 2003; HATTERSLEY, Roy, Blood and Fire: William and Catherine Booth and Their Salvation Army, London 1999; MURDOCH, Norman H., The Origins of the Salvation Army, Knoxville 1994; SANDALL, Robert, The History of the Salvation Army, 4 vols., London 1947–1964; TAIZ, Lillian, Halleluja Lads and Lasses: Remaking the Salvation Army in America, 1880–1930, Chapel Hill 2001; WINSTON, Diane, Red-Hot and Righteous: The Urban Religion of the Salvation Army, Cambridge 1999.

→ *Charitable Organizations, Charismatic Movement, Industrial Society, Mission*

Astrid Czerny

Salvation / Redemption

1. a) *Extra-worldly and intra-worldly salvation:* Any striving for salvation is a quest for an ideal condition, a 'better world.' It presupposes the experience of the contrary, of 'disaster,' as with war, imprisonment, sickness, or even simply the finitude, the limitedness, of life. One hopes to be freed, rescued, or redeemed, in a lasting or eternal condition delivered from such disaster. Over against a reality felt and experienced as imperfect, a perfect world is set, (1) which, in the future, will replace the negative state of the present and its misery—or which is already reality, but (2) which, either only in the community of believers, is realized formatively or as an exemplar, or (3) which is at hand only in another world—for instance in a → hereafter—as the ideal (because not experiential) counter-model. Thus, all divinities are 'perfect'; even future, or imaginary, persons can model the redeemed state, from the mythical, fabled peoples such as Homer's 'righteous Abians,' to → Nietzsche's Hyperboreans, to extraterrestrials. All of the sufferings of the 'here' or 'here below' receive a higher, ultimate sense and meaning, as believers interpret them as heralding signs of an approaching salvation. Here, the more helpless the situation of the moment, the greater seems the need for salvation. The less one has the powers and means to avert the cataclysm, the more one will hope for another, mightier power, such as a political leader, or a superhuman messiah or god, as a replacement for this purpose. Since the → Enlightenment, the idea of the improvement of human beings (through repentance and redemption) in the future has been connected with the development by which they gain their highest stage or perfection in the further course of evolution, and thus also perfect themselves: the new person, the new human being.

Salvation and Disaster

b) But in so doing, the traditional pattern of redemption awaiting a *drama of salvation* is transformed. When redemption seems very improbable, one hopes for a 'miracle.' Before the advent of the new 'realm of salvation,' or new age—to come by way of a global reckoning, and the annihilation of the wicked—a final battle is usually expected between two opposed powers or

Drama of Salvation

poles (along with a kind of world judgment, or divine judgment) such as be-tween good and evil. Traditional as well as modern concepts of redemption build on a three-step model, which begins with a 'Golden Age,' followed by the 'fall' of the human being (as, in Christianity, the expulsion of Adam and Eve from Paradise after the 'original sin'), and then salvation: the reconstitu-tion of the primordial mythical, 'paradisiacal,' condition.

Ways to Salvation

2. a) *Salvific life and rituals:* In religious concepts, a person can share in salvation by way of surrender and offering oneself to the deity or the highest being, the absolute; by following the respective foundations of faith, various ritual practices such as prayer, meditation, veneration of images of gods; as well as by asceticism and the renunciation of certain profane pleasures. Believers expect salvation as a 'reward,' often only in the life hereafter, for their efforts, but cannot attain it solely from and by themselves. By Jesus's vicarious death on the cross, Christians stand even now redeemed from their sins, if they confess them before him. The goal is the immortality of the soul and eternal community with God; in Hinduism, to become one with Brahman by escaping the cycle of → rebirths, and thereby ending earthly → sufferings. Buddhists strive for an 'extinction' of individuation or individuality, by becoming one with what is actually real as opposed to what seems real in the present in life. Buddhists can receive assistance from bodhisattvas, who have renounced entering nirvana even now, in favor of the beings living on the earth. The starting point for a *collective* expectation of salvation, such as is maintained by → Jehovah's witnesses, takes its point of departure in the concept that the totality of the members of the faith com-munity will be redeemed, ordinarily as individuals. By a contract or covenant with God, Jews, too, are the chosen, the called, a people redeemed only in the 'heavenly' Jerusalem. *Individual* salvation places the redemption of the individuated person in the foreground, who need not be definitively bound to a community. Thus, many Christians strive for the 'redemption' of their own souls, rather than, mainly, for the salvation of the entire community of Christians. In modern esotericism (→ New Age), people might strive for an individual salvation through reuniting with a primordial life force, through meditation or ritual practice that fosters a process of individual and collec-tive redemption.

b) *Intermediaries of salvation:* Here, mediators of salvation or gurus tend to play a significant role. They are ascribed a → charisma, superhuman ca-pacities, and, especially, the power to guarantee salvation for their followers. After all, they share in the divine power themselves, often even as 'half God, half man.' Especially with leaders of a political religion (e.g., Hitler, Mus-solini, Lenin), it is not infrequently they themselves who lead their faith community into misery, after which they are elevated to the status of the redeeming figure seen as precisely the one to show the way out of that mis-ery. Modern mediators of salvation include extraterrestrials, who, on the strength of both their intellectual and their technological superiority, are seen as being capable of redeeming the earth, or of solving the problems that lie at the root of human failing.

Concepts of Redemption

3. The aim of *this-worldly concepts of redemption* is the future perfection of all humanity, and a happy life here on earth. The transformation of the human being into the superhuman being in Nietzsche, for instance, takes up the idea of a spiritual and intellectual rebirth. Human beings reach per-

fection 'on their own', without the intervention of an other-worldly power, although often by means of a secular leader who manifests strong parallelisms with the type of the religious leader. 'Worldly believers' insist on actually experiencing their desired salvation themselves, and in the near future, precisely because, in their vision, it can take place only in this life, and this life is the 'only one there is.' In → National Socialism, Adolf Hitler came forward as eschatological intermediary of salvation, who was to rescue, i.e. redeem, the entire German nation from threatening collapse and ruin. From the Thousand-Year Reich a 'New Germany' was to emerge, like a 'New Earth' (cf. Rev 21). Parallels with Jewish → Zionism are manifested in → Marxism, with its ideal of the equality of all human beings. Its prophet is Marx: the historically elect people, called to world revolution, are at the same time the most powerfully oppressed proletariat, which now introduces global, perfected humanism. A counter-sketch is offered by the → Unification Church: it awaits an anti-Marxist final battle, in the form of a Third World War, 'necessary for salvation', in which, under the leadership of the founder of the Church, Sun Myung Moon, the democratic world will exterminate the 'Communist world of Satan.'

4. Beginning in the 1970s, the goal of the currents outside established psychotherapy has been self-knowledge, or the 'finding of oneself', which could be regarded as equivalent to a 'spiritual rebirth', or redemption of those undergoing the 'therapy.' In many → New Age contexts, the goal is referred to as 'whole(ness)', 'being one', and the attainment of a 'cosmic consciousness.' An attitude toward modern medicine, and to → genetic engineering can also bear a religious stamp. The medical 'Gods in White' lead a battle against the evil of the world, seen especially in the incurable illnesses that are the 'scourges of humanity.' An ultra-refined medical technology rescues ever more persons from the threshold of death—for example, out of a coma—and brings them back into life. Human beings replace God, create new living beings by way of genetic engineering, reproduce themselves as clones, and thus eternalize themselves. The quest for the gene that is responsible for aging, and finally for death, promises nothing less than the abolition of death, a beauty that remains, and everlasting life. Human beings produce a "brave new world" (Aldous Huxley) on earth itself, and ensure their own immortality.

Modern Paths of Salvation

Literature

BRAATEN, Carl E., History and Hermeneutics, Philadelphia 1966; BUCHANAN, George Wesley, Revelation and Redemption: Jewish Documents of Deliverance from the Fall of Jerusalem to the Death of Nahmanides, Dillsboro 1978; LÖWITH, Karl, Weltgeschichte und Heilsgeschehen, Stuttgart 1953; Idem, Meaning in History, Chicago 1970 (¹1949); KÜENZLEN, Gottfried, Der Neue Mensch: Eine Untersuchung zur säkularen Religionsgeschichte der Moderne, Frankfurt/M. 1997; RUETHER, Rosemary Radford, Women and Redemption: A Theological History, Minneapolis 1998.

→ *Cross/Crucifixion, End/Eschaton, Hereafter, Jesus, Light/Enlightenment, Luck/Happiness, New Age, Socialism, Suffering, Utopia*

Gabi Brodbeck

Santiago de Compostela

Center of Europe at the End of the World

1. As a place of pilgrimage, a city, a diocese, and later, an archdiocese, in Galicia in the Northwest of Spain, Santiago de Compostela, along with and in rivalry with the far older centers of Rome and Jerusalem, is to be numbered among the three most important centers of extended pilgrimage (*peregrinatio maior*) of Western Christianity. The pilgrims' goal is the supposed tomb of Apostle James the Greater, who as 'Sant'Yago' gives his name to the city of Santiago. The legendary discovery/creation of the Apostle's grave in the early ninth century was extraordinarily appropriate when it came to contemporary mentalities: as a response to the complex situation resulting from (1) the Crusades of extra-European expansive medieval Christianity (2), the conditions of the special Spanish situation of the intra-European reconquest of areas and regions occupied by the Arabs (*reconquista*), and (3) their Christian *repoblación* ('re-population'). In the highly ideologized battle against Islam, the imbedding and foundation of the new local grave-cult was so successful that, in a short time, Compostela and the pilgrimage to Sant'Yago became an outstanding instance of European migration.[1] From all over Europe, including England and Scandinavia, the Baltic region, Poland, and Hungary, the network of 'James's roads' and 'ways,' with their churches, monasteries, and hospices of Saint James, leads to both of the passes of the Pyrenees, behind which, in Puente la Reina, all routes flow into the one common, royal way (*Camino Real*) to Compostela. Fascination and semantic depth of the cult and cult center of the phenomenon 'Santiago' are all the more present, inasmuch as, with the tradition of Charlemagne and Roland, they are coupled with European foundational myths. Connection with the place is no longer necessary. As a sword-swinging 'Moor-slayer' on his white horse in heaven (*matamoros*), James the Elder is patron of the troops of the Reconquista. Like the Cid in the Spanish national epic, they take the field with their battle cry "Santiago!" against the Arabs and their "Mohammed!" As the Apostle with the Scripture scroll, the saint, in unverified, but extremely popular, tradition, had his mission and martyr's death in Spain. He bears the responsibility and title of Spanish National Patron—*Patrón de España*. As *Santiago Peregrino* (Sp. "Santiago the Pilgrim") in pilgrim attire, and with the James shell, he represents not only himself, but all pilgrims and travelers. His name attaches to the phenomenon of the 'James pilgrim.' Thus, despite powerful swings and conversions of meaning over the course of the twelve-hundred-year-old cultic tradition, the enormous, and now so long effective, political, economic, juridical, artistic, religious, and spiritual dimension of the phenomenon provides the basis that the European Council today classifies Compostela as a European cultural capital, and the Camino Real as a European cultural memorial.[2]

The Three Great Places of Pilgrimage

2. a) The *history* of the Santiago pilgrimage, after its first beginnings at the start of the ninth century, is characterized by an extraordinarily speedy expansion. In its heyday, between the twelfth and fifteenth centuries, the Camino Real outdid both the pilgrimage to Rome, to the grave of Saint Peter and the seat of his successor the Pope, and the pilgrimage to Jerusalem and the sacred sites of Jesus.

b) With the replacement of the original local West Gothic Reconquista in Spain by a pan-European one, Santiago de Compostela, instead of a mar-

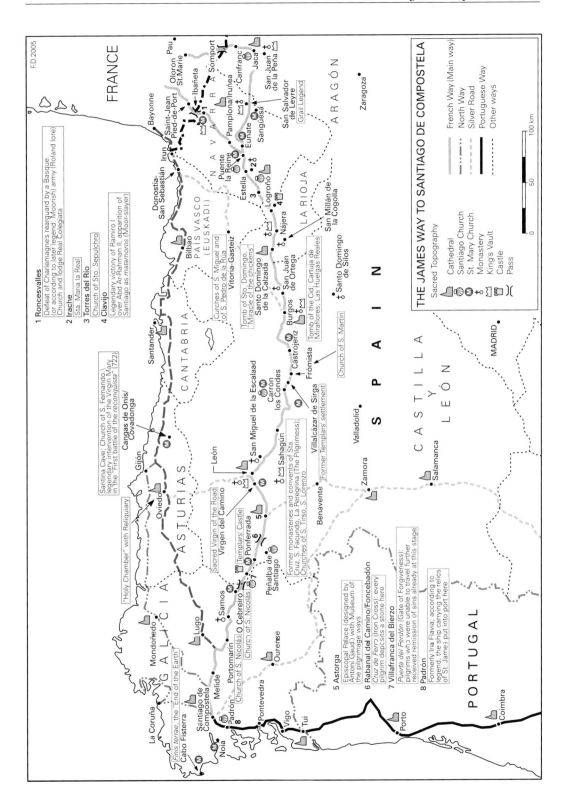

ginal locale at the "end of the known world" (*Finis Terrae*), became a European center of the Western periphery. Thus, the twelfth century marks the
fall of the West Gothic fractional tradition, against the pressure for gen-
eralization and 'internationalization': successfully initiated by the Spanish
kings, completed by the Cluniacs brought into the country, attended by the
imported French knights, and supported by the architectural cottages—that
is, the Latinization of West Gothic script and the Mozarabic rite of the Mass;
the Romanization of sacred architecture (a pilgrim basilica), sculpture and
painting style, which now became obligatory throughout Europe.

Levels of Mediation   c) The *Camino de Santiago* became a space of communication as privileged
as it was programmatic. A number of concrete cultural factors contributed to
that status: (1) It was spiritually bolstered in/by pre-Christian backgrounds
of Teutonic and Roman religions of light—semantically charged by Christian cosmology through the concept of the West as the Way to the End,
and thereby to the future of the world; (2) it was juridically defined by the
development of legislation for pilgrimage; (3) it was infrastructurally fixed
by the construction of bridges, roads, hospices, and cathedrals, and by policies of settlement and privileges of city and trade; (4) it was overspread by
a media-combination of oral, written, and iconic programs of the meaning
of the James cult. The highly continuous and massive execution of the act
of pilgrimage in this space of communication generated the James Way as a
memorial space of Christian expansion westward and thereby as an "iden-
tity-conferring space of self-reassurance."[3] At the same time, in this function,
it was an aggressively monocultural corridor—delimited by conflict with the
zones of cultural contact surrounding it—in a Spain of the three cultures
(Jewish, Arabic, Christian), with its defined manners of coexistence (*con-
vivencia*), far beyond 1492. Despite their fascination for doggedly increasing
quantities of pilgrims, the comprehensive literature of pilgrim reportage
documents a qualitative 'decline' of the James Ways, i.e., a transformation of
function. It was in a framework of the conversion to the 'new styles of piety'
of the *devotio moderna*, that a 'credence in wonders,' and conceptualizations
of self-sanctification through '(merely) bodily pilgrimage,' fell irredeemably
under suspicion of an 'exteriorism' of ritual that could no longer endure in
the face of the guarantee of justification of an interiority-orientated *devotio
spiritualis*. Thus, with Luther's sermon on Saint James's Day, July 15, 1522,
the Protestant polemic assaulted the James pilgrimage, as well: "Do not go
there, then, for it is unknown whether what lies there is Saint James or a dead
dog or a dead horse."

   The secularized *curiositas* that marks modern times where geographical
and ethnological otherness is concerned has long since permitted the religious pilgrimage to turn into an educational trip. Further, the 'receptacle' of
the James Ways accommodates the most wide-ranging varieties of migration, due to poverty, mendicancy, and worker migration. In the seventeenth
and eighteenth centuries it lost quantitative attraction, as well. Without an
independent dynamics as an area for trade, fairs, and finance, and with its
secondary market-trade, tailored only to service to pilgrims, Compostela
has sunken back into the marginality of the periphery.

New Meanings   d) With the appearance of the new Marian pilgrimages of the nineteenth
century, and with the transition of the function of patronage of travelers
to Saint Christopher, Saint James is disappearing from the extra-Spanish

'little tradition' of the popular practice of veneration of the saints, although, naturally, the 'great tradition' of a theology of history continues to 'archive' it. Only since the beginning of the 1980s is Santiago de Compostela coming to be included among the destinations of an organized tourism of pilgrimage and study, which is opening the *Camino* to experiences having dimensions of spiritual meditation, as well as making it available to historical formation in art and architecture.

1. Belonging to the type "temporary religious mass mobility"; see JARITZ/MÜLLER 1988.
2. "A highly symbolic and significant European cultural route," "a representative symbol of our identity." See the documentation in HASSAUER 1993, 80-93.
3. HASSAUER 1993.

Literature

DUNN, Maryjane/DAVIDSON, Linda Kay (eds.), The Pilgrimage to Compostela in the Middle Ages: A Book of Essays, New York 1996; FREY, Nancy Louise, Pilgrim Stories: On and Off the Road to Santiago, Berkeley 1998; HASSAUER, Friederike, Santiago—Schrift. Körper. Raum. Reise, Munich 1993; JARITZ, Gerhard/MÜLLER, Albert (eds.), Migration in der Feudalgesellschaft, Frankfurt/M. 1988; MYERS, Joan et al., Santiago: Saint of Two Worlds, Albuquerque 1991 (photographs); RUDOLPH, Conrad, Pilgrimage to the End of the World: The Road to Santiago de Compostela, Chicago 2004.

→ *Pilgrimage, Procession, Road/Path/Journey, Tourism, Veneration of Saints*

Friederike Hassauer

Satanism

1. The notion of Satan was coined by Christian theology; in the course of the last two centuries, however, an independent Satanism has developed that can no longer adequately be described through only theological approaches. In terms of religious history, the forerunners of the Christian doctrine of Satan, as well as of explicit Satanism, can be considered to be Iranian → dualism, ancient Hebrew demonology (→ Demon/Demonology), and → gnosticism. The Christian image of Satan emerged in the first centuries of the calendar. Here, Satan, who, in the Hebrew Bible, was still a plaintiff in the heavenly court, became God's extra-celestial adversary. In the apologetics of that time, competing cults were at times regarded as inspired by Satan; but the reproach of an authentic veneration of Satan was leveled only in the eleventh century. The ecclesial conception of Satanism, which would be valid for centuries, was produced in a framework of the persecution of witches and of the confrontation with the Enlightenment.

2. The actual basis for the modern variations of Satanism was created by the demonization, and at times explicit 'Satanization,' of individual striving for freedom that emerged in the times of the Counter-Reformation. The verso of this process was the stylization of Satan as the prototype of the free individual, which found its climax in the works of Milton and Blake. Beginning in the seventeenth century, if not before, Satan was no longer merely an incarnate catalog of vices, but a rebel against the old order, that placed limits on the individual. The literary Satanism of the nineteenth century,

Satan in Christian Theology

When British rock-group Venom brought out its second album, "Black Metal," the name of a new sub-genre of rock music was born. In 'black metal'—an especially extreme form of 'heavy metal'—demons, spirits, and witches come together. → Paganism, → atheism, or Satanism are personally professed, and polemics are raised against Christianity, which is looked upon as wishy-washy, and destructive of instinct and therefore of nature. Frequently, cover designs and texts, in the form of the corrupted cultural content of black Romanticism, bring Christian conceptualizations to life, as shown here. A black-robed figure in an apparently subterranean setting, offers buck-headed Satan a stone head—perhaps inspired by the Knights Templars' reputed *Caput LVIIIm*. This reactive, paradigmatically conformist Satanism finds application in areas of the 'heavy' scene, for the purpose of lending a particularly plastic shape to rebellion, machoism, and strivings for freedom. A separation from the values of a society or adult world, apostrophized as hypocritical, is just as intentional as the division from everything effeminate and powerless: things that the fan of such music may just as especially fear. Earnest confrontation with Satanist groups like the Church of Satan, or Temple of Set, takes place only rarely, or in phases. Musicians like Christofer Johnson, of Therion, one of the co-founders of the occult order, Dragon Rouge (Fr., "Red Dragon"), as well as the

which had its point of departure in poets like Lord Byron, and which influenced 'black Romanticism' especially, has its roots in the processes described above. Artistic Satanism is still at work in the present, for example in the performances of "Vienna Actionism," and in the 'black metal' style of heavy-metal rock music (see illustration).

3. An explicit (cultic) Satanism has finally grown larger only in the second half of the twentieth century and the first years of the twenty-first. A binding dogmatics of Satanism has never existed. Thus, not surprisingly, numerous, sometimes contradictory forms of the Satanistic phenomenon are to be distinguished.

- *Reactive Satanism* takes its point of departure in an unbroken theological Satanic image. Here, Satan is considered as the personification of evil, and venerated as such. Corresponding conceptualizations of Satan are found in, for example, 'youth Satanism.'
- In *'gnostically reassessed' Satanism*, Satan is seen as the calumniated God, well-disposed to human beings, while the Christian God is the deceiver and oppressor of human beings.
- *Integrative Satanism* seeks to transcend the boundaries between the Christian God and Satan, and to see the two as, for example, two collaborating poles of a single unity.
- *Syncretistically broken Satanism* embraces all of the occultist currents in which Satan does play a role (→ Occultism), but does not stand at the focus of the cult or of the doctrinal system. As a particularly salient example, we may cite the 'Thelemic' cults of Aleister Crowley (1875–1947). It may be questioned, of course, if this still belongs to "Satanism" at all.
- *Autarkic a-Christian Satanism* describes a Satanism that does derive from Christian teachings, but in its current phenomenal form developed into a 'positive' religion in the full sense of the word, and extensively abandoned Christian relationships.

events surrounding the Black Circle in Norway, are exceptions in a variegated scene. It should be noted that ideological warnings that youth are turning into brainwashed minions of Satan, betray the disposition of the respective authors or speakers more than they do that of heavy-metal fans. Furthermore, it is counter-productive to mix up the causes and effects of youthful behavior and to veil complex social and industrial problems by demonizing a subculture that is actually more harmless than it is pernicious. (Anselm Neft)

4. All organized Satanistic groups important today haven an inclination to autarkic a-Christian Satanism. Here, first and foremost, we should cite Anton Szander La Vey's First Church of Satan, Michael Aquino's Temple of Set, as well as Paul Douglas Valentine's Church of Satanic Liberation. The worldwide membership of these associations ranges from perhaps 300 to 3,000 members each, most of these being members of the upper middle class, with an education above the average. In the United States, these associations are officially recognized as churches; European branches are, as a rule, organized as incorporated association. Politically, a tolerant libertarianism, bordering on social Darwinism, is preferred. Contraventions of the existing laws of society are, in general, rejected.

Organizations

3. Spectacular cultic practices (→ Cult), usually covered by the media in exaggerated form, are, of course, found less in organized groups than in marginal ones, or in what is often referred to as 'youth Satanism.' According to recent research, however, this usually represents a transitory phase of protest and self-discovery. Helsper sees, as the main characteristic of youth occultism, not the quest for a new system of meaning, but a new intercourse with everywhere available bits and pieces of various *Weltanschauungen*. Helsper describes this as "Bricolage of meaning" ("*Sinn-Bastelei*"). Finally, Helsper holds that all of this reflects a loss of meaning in the religious itself. Many of the concrete practices repeatedly reported, as, for example, the desecration of cemeteries, are essentially inspired by such media reports themselves, which at times are even dramatized for fictional media 'presentations.'[1] In the individual cases in which this 'youth Satanism' takes extreme forms, these forms cannot be reduced to the causality of one element. Rather, an investigation must be made into the interplay of a plurality of causes.

Youth Satanism?

6. Up until now, public perception of Satanism has been dominated, first and foremost, by traditional church conceptions of Satanism, as fructified by media sensationalism. In this sense, Satanism is a projection screen for all of those moral abysses that the shadow side of society supposes it to contain—or that are actually to be met on that shadow side itself. Explicit,

Media Sensationalism

organized Satanism will probably continue to be an insignificant marginal phenomenon in the future, as well, although, in recent decades, an astonishing consolidation of the basic *Weltanschauung* of a Satanistic mainstream is to be observed. Finally, in these conceptions, the actual reality of modern neo-liberal societies, so marked by their individualism, is reflected in all but blinding clarity.

1. See HELSPER, Werner, Okkultismus—Die neue Jugendreligion?, Opladen 1992; MÜLLER, Ulrich, Das Leben und Wirken des Satanisten T., Regensburg 1989.

Literature

Source: LA VEY, Anton Szandor, The Satanic Bible, New York 1969.
  Secondary Literature: ELLIS, Bill, Raising the Devil: Satanism, New Religions, and the Media, Lexington 2000; Idem, Lucifer Ascending: The Occult in Folklore and Popular Culture, Lexington 2004; LEWIS, James R., Satanism Today: An Encyclopedia of Religion, Folklore, and Popular Culture, Santa Barbara 2001; MEDWAY, Gareth J., Lure of the Sinister: The Unnatural History of Satanism, New York 2001; OTTENS, Allen/MYER, Rick, Coping with Satanism: Rumor, Reality, and Controversy, New York ²1998; RICHARDSON, James T. et al. (eds.), The Satanism Scare, New York 1991; SCHOCK, Peter A., Romantic Satanism: Myth and the Historical Moment in Blake, Shelley, and Byron, Basingstoke 2003; VICTOR, Jeffrey S., Satanic Panic: The Creation of a Contemporary Legend, Chicago 1993.

→ *Anti-Cult Movements, Blasphemy, Cult, Devil, Demon/Demonology, Dualism, Evil/Evil One, Exorcism, Occultism*

Joachim Schmidt

Scholasticism

Faith/Reason

1. *Definition, eras, and main currents:* a) In the abstract, the principal theme of scholasticism (from Lat. *schola*, 'school') may be regarded to be the relationship between 'reason' and 'Christian faith', or, better, the tension between the principles of faith and the requirements of rationality. A comprehensive material definition understands scholasticism as the totality of the sciences established in the European Middle Ages, which, with theology and philosophy, also included mathematics and the science of nature. Ultimately, then, only the counter-movement of mysticism (such as with Bernard of Clairvaux, → Hildegard of Bingen, or → Meister Eckhart) remains outside of scholasticism. But scholastic analyses—in terms of the ideal of their own understanding—are not ultimately premise-free knowledge. Rationality, or reason, the *lumen rationale* (Lat., the 'light of reason'), must restrict itself to legitimating and illustrating what a Bible-based faith in revelation complements by way of a comprehension of the patristic Church Fathers. After all, their doctrine is itself regarded as 'assured truth.' Creativity does not correspond to the spirit of the Middle Ages.

Nevertheless, with early scholasticism, there emerged, for the first time since antiquity, in the history of the Christian West, a scientific culture. The latter relies no longer only on the 'recitation' of Biblical revelation and patrology: it seeks, rather, by means of a 'new,' logical dialectical method, to further a discussion of the faith. The *fides quaerens intellectum* ("faith should be insightful") of early representative Anselm of Canterbury (1033–1109) could be installed as the comprehensive motto.

b) In the scholarly literature, a tripartite division of the era has prevailed. Thus, in the early age of scholasticism (the tenth to the twelfth centuries), a development of the doctrine of method stands in the foreground. In Peter Lombard's *Sic et Non* (Lat., 'Yes and No'), voices of authorities pro and contra on basic questions, are understood as dialectical poles, weighed against one another in analysis, and—ideally—decided. The other standard work for basic scholastic training is Peter of Spain's (d. 1277) *Introduction to Logic for Beginners.*

Three Ages

The development of the great *Summas* (Lat., 'Compendiums') of Albertus Magnus (1193–1280) and Thomas Aquinas (1225–1274) marks the center of high scholasticism (thirteenth century). The goal of those self-conscious and ambitious projects was the systematic summary of all of the areas of knowledge, and research of the enthusiastic 'discovery' of the works of Aristotle—not least through the intermediary of Arab Islamic commentators (Averroes, Avicenna)—which flows into a far-reaching amalgamation of church doctrine and Aristotelianism.

Frequently, late scholasticism (the fourteenth to the fifteenth centuries) is wrongly interpreted as a time of decline and fall, in and by virtue of the phase of nominalism, connected especially with William of Occam (1300–1350). Standing in focus here is the debate over the universals—already discussed in the strict sense since the twelfth century: nominalism versus realism in the question of the reality of universals, that is, of general concepts. Realism, whose ultimate source is Plato, attributes a comparatively higher reality to general ideas and concepts than attaches to individual things. For extreme nominalism—which names Aristotle as its authority—only the individual is real: universals are not actually real, but are available only in the intellect.

2. *Social and political aspects of scholasticism:* a) The tradition of the philosophico-theological interpretation of scholasticism is genuinely concentrated on the reconstruction of intellectual questions. But this emphasis on rationality, on argumentative discussion, must not be allowed to conceal the fact that the theologico-philosophical confrontations of the Middle Ages are not conducted exclusively in terms of reasoned disputation.

Society: "What is Christian?"

The establishment, in theological disputations defining which positions are orthodox in terms of church policy, always serves factually the discrimination, the exclusion, of heterodox, 'not right believing,' positions. The definition of what is Christian makes possible, correspondingly, the delineation of heresy, the regulation and elimination of heretical individuals and groups that transgress the determined framework of theological acceptability.

To be sure, the question of 'orthodoxy' versus 'heterodoxy,' asked again and again, was not raised against outsiders alone, such as the heretical groups, but also outstanding participants in scholastic discourse itself. Even Thomas Aquinas fell under posthumous suspicion of heresy. Only the determined opposition of his Dominican Order preserved his writings from the bonfire, and then made possible, on the contrary, his canonization (1332). Roger Bacon (1214–1294) spent the last fourteen years of his life in monastic imprisonment. William of Occam only managed through flight to escape his condemnation before a papal court at Avignon (1324). Examples such as these illustrate the power politics on/of the verso of the learned, methodically rational discussion that marks our modern picture of scholasticism.

b) Thus, the background of the conflict over universals, which today is interpreted principally as an abstract philosophical discussion concerning the epistemological status of concepts, also calls attention to the question of the power politics of the Roman Church, which defines itself as 'catholic'—universal, all-comprehensive. Nominalism's position formulated a frontal attack on the theological monopoly of the papal Church. If the individual alone is real, then the universal Church can lodge no claim to the higher evidence of its dogmas and teachings. The Church is therefore only the voice of its individual believers, without claim to higher eminence. Medieval contemporaries—unlike today's researchers—saw very clearly that connection between the philosophical position and the politics of the real. Thus, a radical nominalist like William of Occam had to flee Cambridge, with its loyalty to the pope, to Munich: there, precisely by reason of the political volatility of his nominalism, he found asylum with papal enemy Louis the Bavarian. "Defend thou me with the sword, I shall defend thee with the word," William is said to have demanded of Louis.

Although on the basis of its effect on medieval thought and activity, scholasticism's influences on intellectual history, politics, and law must be regarded as dominant, one should not forget that, ultimately, the vehicle of scholasticism was but one, very small, elite circle—a literary and intellectual minority at the few universities then in existence (Bologna, Oxford, Paris), as well as at the urban cathedral schools (Chartres, Lyon, Cologne, Cambridge). Neither the secular princely courts, nor the traditional monasteries, played any decisive role in its development. In a time of restricted communication, the content of scholastic thought spread among the centers of scholastic research by way of the travels and international mobility of scholars, in the facilitating presence of Latin as the universal scholarly and scientific language.

Reformation

3. *Protestantism and Neo-Scholasticism:* a) Right in the face of "the whore that is reason," Martin → Luther's Protestant theology rejected a certain type of scholasticism—one which, with the help of logic, formulates propositions of faith from the premise of a basic principle. Nominalistically educated, Luther insisted on grounding faith on the Bible. By way of nominalism, the individual sciences, too, became independent of divine teaching. Luther's noisy fight with "the whore that is reason" was directed only against Thomists.

Neo-Scholasticism

b) The application of the designation 'scholasticism' was transformed beginning in the sixteenth century into a pejorative, upbraiding usage. The (often complicated) methodological stringency with which problems were analyzed was then disqualified as a 'how many angels on the head of a pin' or nit-picking type of 'argumentation.' Reduced to the exclusively theological area, scholasticism found its continuation in the works of Francisco Suarez (1548–1617), until it experienced a renaissance as neo-scholasticism in the second half of the nineteenth century, with, among others, Josef Geyser (1869–1948). Neo-scholasticism emphasizes the primacy of Christian theology vis-à-vis the currents of modern-age atheistic philosophies and sciences. It is also imbedded in an ecclesial attempt to ward off modernism,[1] against which a return to the theology of Thomas Aquinas (Neo-Thomism) was mounted. As recent representatives, we may cite Jacques Maritain (1882–1973), Joseph Bochenski (1902–1995), and Étienne Gilson.

1. Every Catholic priest, upon taking office, had to abjure modern theology. The requirement of the anti-modernist oath of 1910 was rescinded after the Second Council of the Vatican, in 1967 (see Denzinger, H., Enchiridion, Freiburg 1976, nos. 3537-3550; → Laicism).

Literature

Kretzmann, Norman et al. (eds.), The Cambridge History of Later Medieval Philosophy: From the Rediscovery of Aristotle to the Disintegration of Scholasticism, 1100–1600, Cambridge 1982; LeGoff, Jacques, Intellectuals in the Middle Ages, Cambridge 1993 (French ¹1957); Russell, Bertrand, Wisdom of the West: A Historical Survey of Western Philosophy in Its Social and Political Setting, New York 1959; Secada, Jorge, Cartesian Metaphysics: The Late Scholastic Origins of Modern Philosophy, Cambridge 2000.

→ *Aristotelianism, European History of Religion, Middle Ages, Mysticism, Platonism, Science*

Stefan Hartmann

Science

1. 'Science' (from Lat., *scientia* 'knowledge'; cf. German *Wissenschaft*, Dutch *wetenschap*, etc.) is a form of → knowledge, distinguished from everyday knowledge, the knowledge of the 'ordinary man,' in two respects. For one, it is systematic: that is, it orders knowledge, creates connections, and promotes it to a completeness and integrity. For another, it reflects upon the conditions of its knowledge. In the history of cultures, including those of the European West, there are several forms of science (§ 3a). One of them, dating from the nineteenth century, is science as research. 'Research' or 'scholarship' is defined by the assumption that its object, the empirically cognoscible world, is 'endless,'—that the process of research into this world can never reach an end, because any conclusion generates new problems (§ 3d). *Knowledge, Science, Research*

2. The notion of science held by scientists and among the public is often molded by historical conceptualizations. One instance of the latter is that science is the only rational, indeed even the only 'true' knowledge of the world, and therefore stands in competition to any kind of religion. Here, religion is 'irrational,' and, at best, a 'stopgap,' responsible for the (still) unexplained, and, for that matter, unexplainable. This manner of understanding represents *scientism*, as it elevates science to the status of touchstone of all knowledge. It stems from the (self-) interpretations of nineteenth-century scientists, or at least appeals to them. Other varieties of the relativization of religion rest on *historicism*, which hails from the end of the eighteenth century, and which proclaims that all that exists is a product of → history and conveyed by history. This implies the problem of the relativization of norms and values in any 'present age.' As early as the first half of the nineteenth century, the question arose of the validity of the Christian proclamation in its historical foundations (research into the 'life of Jesus,' history of dogma, issues of religious studies). But not even science could escape the effects of historicism. The claim of the science of history, of the early nineteenth century, to be able to show 'how it actually was' (Leopold von Ranke) had to *Truth, Scientism, Historicism*

face the recognition that even the content of our 'I' is a 'historical result,' as historian Johann Gustav Droysen formulated it as early as the middle of the nineteenth century. The question of whether scientific knowledge is supra-temporally true, or whether it is also culturally and therefore historically conditioned, recently ignited a 'science war' in the United States between physicists and historians of science.

Stages

3. For the sake of a relativization of reductionistic concepts of science, it will be useful to look back at certain stages of the history of science in the European West.

Scholasticism

a) High medieval science presents an independent form of science that rests on the basic premise of a recognizable order in the world as an order created by God (→ Scholasticism). The world is a cosmos, a beautiful and inwardly ordered shape and arrangement, created by God, in the super- and subordination of the things pre-thought by the intellect of the divine creator and created in perfection. After all, God is spirit—intellect and knowledge—and thus the order of the world is recognizable in its truth: the human intellect shares in the divine intellect as an intellect created to be similar. Recognition, knowledge, attains being, it is an "agreement between things and the recognizing spirit" or intellect (*adaequatio rei et intellectus*), as Thomas Aquinas's famous formula runs. A problem of knowledge in the modern sense is absent here. It is the task of science to collect all available knowledge of the world and all available book learning (including pre-Christian science and philosophy) and to present it in grand *summa*s.

Nominalism

b) The problem of knowledge in the modern sense, and hence a new form of science, enters the scene with the nominalism of the fourteenth-century (William of Occam, d. 1348), with the dawn of to the modern age and the constitution of the key problems of modern science. The primary problem is of a theological kind. If the world in its order can be known, then it follows that God must have created this world in such a way that he would be the 'servitor' of the world. This arrangement is irreconcilable with the notion of God's omnipotence. The only possible consequence to be drawn for the solution of the problem (while saving the concept of God's omnipotence) is the sacrifice of a cognoscibility of the world as a cosmos, and in its truth. All that is, can no longer be known as a whole, but now occurs only as an individual thing. Nothing any longer provides testimony concerning the order of the world as a whole through the means of science. Scientifically, the world is now to be grasped only as a 'mixtum-gatherum' of occurring things. Its form and style are unknown. And this includes its frontiers, so that the world itself is 'endless'—of course, in an immanent sense. The individual *res* ('thing') is not absolute, but is henceforward to be known only in its allusion to something else. The concept of 'substance' (the existent conceptualized as existing for itself, and at the same time at its specific place in an ordered whole) is replaced by the idea of function and relation. The consequences of this epistemological revolution are visible in all areas. The whole, and the sense of the world, can now only be spoken of in faith. Science must surrender its notion of a knowledge of the whole. The position of the person in the world becomes a matter of question. The question of the human being, and what she and he ought to do, becomes a problem. Theology can no longer be a science. Science is now merely knowledge of the individual. The question of the 'essence' of things is replaced by the question of the 'empirical' propositions, to be conveyed by experience and in experiment, upon the individual, and upon its functional connections with other individual things. Henceforward, knowledge needs foundation: epistemology. The question arises of the 'objectivity' of knowledge, and of its subjective conditions and limits.

c) During succeeding centuries, the basic premise of nominalism continued to prevail. For theologian Nicolas of Cusa (d. 1464), 'negative theology' and physics stand over against each other as modes of knowledge. Human knowledge is *docta ignorantia*—a 'knowing non-knowing,' or 'knowing of not knowing.' It knows something—indeed, a great deal, and knows ever more, but knows nothing in truth. It even knows why it ultimately knows nothing. Here are its capacities, as well as its boundaries. With similar intent, mathematician and physicist Blaise Pascal (d. 1662) offers a foundation for human science as an *ignorance savante*, and formulates his thesis of the plurality of 'knowledges': there are everyday knowledge (*esprit de finesse*), which understands decision and action, scientific knowledge (*esprit de géométrie*), and faith (*l'ordre du coeur*). As scientist, says Pascal, the human being must understand how to live at one and the same time in all three forms of knowledge, without being able to refer them to one another.

Knowledge without a Claim to Truth?

d) At the end of the eighteenth century, Immanuel Kant (d. 1804; *Kritik der reinen Vernunft*, "Critique of Pure Reason"; 1781) defined the capacities and boundaries of knowledge by positing the determination of the objects of knowledge by the condition of the knowing mind. It is not knowledge that conforms to objects, but objects that conform to knowledge: "The understanding grasps only that which it itself produces according to its composition."[1] Human knowledge is therefore empirical—directed upon experience, but at the same time determined by conditions that themselves do not have the character of experience. Absolute knowledge is impossible for human beings: they will never know 'things in themselves,' but only what is accessible in the light of their questions and sketches ('appearances,' 'phenomena'). The phenomenon gained through empirical work *is* the reality graspable by knowledge. Scientists find themselves in the position of judges of investigation, who listen to witnesses in order to experience something about an event at which they themselves were not even present. They come to know something, but not in the mode of 'truth,' although 'truth' must be the 'regulative idea' of their activity. Since the field of experience stretches to an indeterminable breadth, and the number of possible questions is unlimited, science is a process that runs *ad infinitum*: any outcome leads to new questions. This is science as investigation. No judgment as to the sense and meaning of this science-process is available through the means of science itself. The range of knowledge is therefore limited. However, this constraint is offset by the certitude that lies in the knowledge of precisely this limitation, and by the insight that knowledge is now a creative act. The reflection of 'subjectivity' belongs to the essential conditions of any 'objectivity.'

Critique of Knowledge

4. In spite of the extraordinary effects of Kant's critical theory of knowledge, the 'naïve' concept of science, the concept shaped by everyday knowledge, as a true reflection (at least as nearly as possible) of outer reality, becomes

Positivism

determinative again and again, and has led to a claim mounted in the most varied forms in the nineteenth century and until today. This objectivistic idealism is represented by historian Ranke (history as a narrative presentation of 'how it really was'), or in the form of materialistic 'image theories' in historical materialism since Karl Marx and Friedrich Engels (→ Marxism), or in the form of a positivistic scientism.

Historicism

5. Beginning in the 1830s and 1840s, science has been more and more determined by the purpose of the acquisition of 'facts,' now historical or scientific. As to what a 'fact' is, however, and what epistemological status it enjoys, no agreement prevails.

The scientific development of the nineteenth century took place under the sign of the notion that everything that is, is historically generated and conditioned. The same development basically determines the specific way in which the modern age constructs history. This *historicism* constitutes the rise of historical science as one of the principal sciences of the century, as well as involving a historicization of other, systematic areas such as theology, juridical science, and national economics. At the same time, around 1840, with the discovery of the cell, and of the functions of the nucleus as the basic unity of vegetable, animal, and human life, the modern, empirically based natural or physical sciences emerged.

Natural Science

a) From this point onward, the epistemic method of the empirical sciences—observation as the exclusive method of scientific knowledge in the area of natural or physical science (represented by outstanding scientists such as Rudolf Virchow, Hermann von Helmholtz, and Emil Du Bois-Reymond)—was represented as enjoying unlimited validity. Here it was a matter of the knowledge of unassailable ('hard') facts, and of the ('eternal') 'laws' demonstrated by the same. All progress, it was assumed (R. Virchow), rested only and solely on these eternal laws of nature having been established more precisely through a constantly advancing empirical observation. Natural or physical science, accordingly, was seen more and more as the "absolute organ of culture," and the history of natural science as the "authentic history of humanity" (E. Du Bois-Reymond). The triumph of the 'authority of the facts,' and the 'sovereignty' of the laws of science, must therefore extend, as well, beyond natural science, and form the totality of society and politics. Science must become the "method of the entire nation," and constitute the "authentic maxim of thought, of the moral act" (R. Virchow). At the close of the century, in his *Welträthsel* (1899; Eng. as "The Riddle of the Universe"), zoologist Ernst Haeckel explained that all open questions had been solved, or at least were soluble in principle, that 'culture' was reducible to 'nature,' and that it was the laws of nature that must create the basis of a new 'moral teaching.'

Experience and Understanding

b) What responses are appropriate from those sciences that are concerned with culture? One response was in their subjection to the arguments of the physical sciences, so that historical science was to be defined as a natural science. On the model of Newton's physics, likewise in history the erection of the historical totality must be presented as a recognition of law, developed from a gradual recognition of individual facts. Over against this scientific positivism, historian Johann Gustav Droysen called for an independent theory of historical knowledge (*Historik*, 'historics') that did not yet exist by any means. In this *Wissenschaftslehre der Geschichte* (Ger., "Scientific Doctrine of History"), developed from 1857 onward, it was on the foundation of the Kantian transcendental philosophy that Droysen defined the historical science as an empirical science, and therefore precisely as scholarship and investigation. But the given by which this empirical investigation was directed was not the 'past that was,' which after all is past, but the historical material at hand, the remnants and testimonials of that which has been. What is called 'history,' then, is not a model or reflection of 'the past event' (which, for that matter, is impossible), but a mental construct—not an arbitrary one, of course, but one gained by empirical investigation on historical material. The character of that material, according to Droysen, determines the difference, here, from natural or physical science, as the "other major method of empirical investigation." After all, the research of the investigating historian (and this distinguishes the latter from the investigating natural scientist) finds, within, the same ethical and intellectual categories as confront him and her in the actual objects of their episteme: thus their research is an 'understanding.' Furthermore, insists Droysen, even this 'understanding' is historically conditioned, since historical investigation "presupposes the insight that even the content of our ego is a historical result, an outcome, conveyed in many ways" (Droysen).

In contraposition to Droysen, philosopher Wilhelm Dilthey, in his *Einleitung in die Geisteswissenschaften* (1883; Eng. as "Introduction to the Human Sciences"), while defining all science as science of experience, nevertheless derives all experience essentially from the 'inner experience' of the individual, and there grounds the independence of the *Geisteswissenschaften* ('human sciences,' 'humanities'). It is the inner experience of the latter that means actual 'reality as it is,' and not only, as in the case of physical science, as the shadow of an outer, and ultimately concealed, reality. The 'understanding' (*Verstehen*) of the humanities has therefore a higher dignity than that of the mere 'explanation' (*Erklären*) produced by the natural or physical sciences. Natural sciences are only "sensual experiences about nature," while human sciences are the "comprehensive experience of the mental and spiritual world." There are two classes of sciences, then, and they are of very different kinds.

c) Meanwhile, an embittered adversary of both historical science and natural science had arisen: Friedrich → Nietzsche (d. 1900), who called into essential and crucial question any science, and any claim to scientific objectivity, on both sides. As early as 1874 (*Vom Nutzen und Nachteil der Historie für das Leben* (Ger., "Usefulness and Disadvantage of History for Life"),[2] Nietzsche delivered a fulminating indictment of historicism, and of a history that had 'spread out' and become science. History was destructive, an 'illness,' that destroyed 'life,' because of its indefatigable construction of historical facts that could no longer be brought into any connection; because the scientific objectivity to which it appealed was a fiction; and, above all, because this historical knowledge showed all things and each in their emergence, and thereby also in their expiration, and thus historically relativized them. This knowledge had a paralytic effect on life powers, on decision, and action. Accordingly Nietzsche argued for a new validation of the 'unhistorical'—namely, of the forgotten—and of the 'supra-historical'—namely, of art and religion, and would now only validate a history that sought to serve 'life,' and had therefore left off being a science. 'Scientific objectivity'

'Paralysis of Life'

was something altogether different from what it held itself out to be: it was nothing but an expression of the 'will to power.' This is also the reproach that Nietzsche leveled against the natural science of his time: it was something 'fearful and menacing,' a 'problem with horns' (as Nietzsche formulated it in 1886), since, here again, was the claim to universal validity and acceptance of this knowledge with all of its consequences, the "unbridled, fanciful optimism" of modern science, "faith in everyone's beatitude on earth itself," a seed of annihilation, an insane conceptualization, which, abetted by claim to reach objective causality, arrogates unto itself the capacity to "base and establish the innermost essence of things." But: there *are* simply no 'facts,' only interpretations, and, of course, the 'will to power,' that 'interprets.' Thus, on the occasion of the pretenses of the historical sciences, as of physical science, and of the motto that knowledge is power, Nietzsche rips the mask from science as a fiction, as an appearance, behind which lurks a will to power of an altogether different kind, a will to power for its own sake.

Kulturwissenschaft,
Cultural Studies

6. At the close of the nineteenth century, then, the grounding of science must be achieved anew. For historical science, this was done by the representatives of a historical *Kulturwissenschaft* (Georg Simmel, Max Weber), who once more sought to return to Kant's criticism and thereby at the same time to answer Nietzsche's question of the relationship between science and 'life.'

a) Max → Weber, especially, defines historical science as a 'reality science,' and 'experience-science,' which, of course, does not simply go around copying historical reality, but which presses forward in concepts and judgments "that are not empirical reality, nor copies of historical reality, but occasions of the ordering of reality in valid fashion." There is no such thing, says Weber, as to copy historical reality without premises. Science is empirically based science with hypotheses. Weber determines it (once again) as research and investigation, namely, as a process that cannot be closed or sealed, a process that proceeds *ad infinitum*, as Kant had explicated, because every result or conclusion at once raises new questions, and because, at least in the historical disciplines, the "eternally proceeding flow of culture ever introduces new problems to be solved." In this "proceeding into the indefinite," in this infinitude and endlessness of possible problems, as well as of possible objects, the range of science is grounded, as are at the same time, its limits. A science that always receives its questions from the contemporary 'culture' (which is why it also has something to say to its respective present) replaces a science with an absolute claim to knowledge, as well as the contrary, a science that ceases to be science 'in order to serve life,' as Nietzsche had demanded. That kind of historical science also has a different relation to physical science, than it had been defined in the nineteenth century. It understands itself in the sense of a complementarity of both areas of science. If, as Weber established, *Begriff* ('concept') and 'experiment' are in the same way the "great means of all scientific knowledge," then this also means an indication of the 'conceptual' in the 'experiment' of natural science, and the 'experimental' in the 'concept' of the cultural sciences.

Natural Knowledge
as Conditioned by the
Question Posed

b) It striking that, since about 1900, similar events in the natural sciences correspond to the new definition of historical knowledge in a framework of 'historical cultural science,' inasmuch as an analogous break occurred with the objectivism, scientism, and positivism of the nineteenth century. In physics, this 'revolution of the way of thinking' was significantly expressed in Werner Heisenberg's 'principle of indeterminacy,' as well as in Niels Bohr's concept of 'complementarity.' Heisenberg's famous formulation (1927) of the 'track' or 'path' of a particle, that comes into existence "only by virtue of our observing it," expresses the fact that the objectivistic subject-object model is inaccessible, because, in the world of the smallest particles, observed phenomena are constituted through, and only through, the observer and the event of the observation. Not even physical cognition, therefore, has an absolute character, but only a relational one. This physical science describes nature not as it is 'in itself'; rather it describes "the nature that is exposed to our question(ings) and our methods," and therefore understands itself as "a part of the oscillation between nature and ourselves." Atoms, therefore, are no longer 'things' or 'objects,' but are "components of situations of observation," which, for a physical analysis of phenomena, possess a "high explanatory value." This new physics, then, has taken hold of hitherto fully unknown worlds, and has, at the same time, reflected upon what it does, in the sense of a self-limitation. It is a "theory of possible knowledge of reality, not a theory of reality as such" (A. Gierer).

7. This manner of historical recapitulation of science in history may contribute to an assessment of the dimensions of science in today's society. A modern grasp of science can afford an unrestricted indication of the range of scientific cognition, although it should also be aware of its limits. Historians of today at times still claim of true knowledge of facts, and of the past 'as it actually was.' On the side of the natural or physical sciences, this position corresponds to a 'naturalistic' claim, with the thesis that any event is an authentically physical event, which can be completely described and explained with the means of physical science, and that it is possible to physical science to take an absolute observational perspective, and give causally complete explanations of total reality. Contrariwise, the question must be asked whether and to what extent even natural science, for its part, is conditioned by cultural history, which limits, not the range of its conclusions, but doubtless a possible universal claim to validity in all areas of life. Of natural scientists themselves, the question is being asked to what extent even physical science moves within very strict boundaries, set, on the one hand, by nature, and, on the other, by the structure of human thought (F. Jacob)—as well as whether there even is a precise theory of science, and a complete guarantee of science through its own means—thus, whether natural science can itself actually demonstrate its own completeness and freedom from contradiction (A. Gierer).

Science Today

The relationship between science and religion, so antagonistically conceptualized, especially in the nineteenth century, can be otherwise defined on such a basis. Competition in a bestowal of meaning with a monopolistic claim to truth is a thing of the past. One might even ask whether it is a matter of persons' having to learn to live once more in one world (J. Mittelstrass), or whether the philosophical excitement of modernity does not consist precisely in the fact that the human being has learned to live in many worlds at once (H. Blumenberg). Religion and science are then no longer antagonists, but dimensions of reality that can enter into a multiplex relationship to one another.

---

1. Preface to the 2nd ed., 1787.
2. "Unzeitgemäße Betrachtungen," 2nd piece (KSA 1:243-334).

Literature

BLUMENBERG, Hans, Wirklichkeiten, in denen wir leben, Stuttgart 1981; DASTON, Lorraine, "Fear and Loathing of the Imagination in Science," in: Daedalus (Winter 1998), 73-95; GIERER, Alfred, Im Spiegel der Natur erkennen wir uns selbst. Wissenschaft und Menschenbild, Reinbek 1998; GODFREY-SMITH, Peter, Theory and Reality: An Introduction to the Philosophy of Science, Chicago 2003; GOLDSTEIN, Jürgen, Nominalismus und Moderne: Zur Konstitution neuzeitlicher Subjektivität bei Hans Blumenberg und Wilhelm von Ockham, Freiburg 1998; HACKING, Ian, Representing and Intervening: Introductory Topics in the Philosophy of Natural Science, Cambridge 1983; HEISENBERG, Werner, Physics and Philosophy: The Revolution in Modern Science, New York 1961; KANITSCHEIDER, Bernulf/WETZ, Franz-Josef (eds.), Hermeneutik und Naturalismus, Tübingen 1998; LOSEE, John, A Historical Introduction to the Philosophy of Science, Oxford ^{4}2001; LATOUR, Bruno/WOOLGAR, Steve, Laboratory Life: The Social Construction of Scientific Facts, Princeton 1986; MITTELSTRASS, Jürgen, "Das ethische Maß der Wissenschaft," in: Rechtshistorisches Journal 7 (1988), 193-210; OEXLE, Otto Gerhard, Geschichtswissenschaft im Zeichen des Historismus. Studien zu Problemgeschichten der Moderne, Göttingen 1996; Idem (ed.), Naturwissenschaft, Geisteswissenschaft, Kulturwissenschaft. Einheit—Gegensatz—Komplementarität, Göttingen ^{2}2000; RHEINBERGER, Jans-Jörg, Toward a History of Epistemic Things: Synthesizing Proteins in the Test Tube, Stanford 1997; SHAPIN, Steven/SCHAFFER, Simon, Leviathan and the Air-Pump: Hobbes, Boyle, and the Experimental Life, Princeton 1989.

→ *Criticism of Religion, Enlightenment, History, Knowledge, Natural Science, Rationalism/ Irrationalism, Reason, Theology*

Otto Gerhard Oexle

Science Fiction

Mythic Reports

1. Mythic reports of gods and heroes, such as Gilgamesh, Odysseus, or Thoth, who had come to the boundaries of the world and of their own existence, have, over millennia, formed the narrative style that connects a mythic geography with reflections on 'other gods and other persons.' The fundamental enclosure of the traditional world thus remains preserved, even if, in journeys to the beyond, and heaven, or to 'new realms,' frontiers are overcome in narrative, and new spaces of existence are unlocked. Only with the 'open universe' of the Copernican world did the discussion on the 'plurality of worlds' gain currency—for which Bernard de Fontenelles's *Entretiens sur la pluralité des mondes* (Fr., "Conversations on the Plurality of the Worlds") provided the heading—and become a problem for philosophy and Christian theology. With the threat of the loss of the geocentric system, even original → sin and redemption become precarious in a new way. Furthermore, the discovery of a 'new world,' America, altogether concretized the problem. Since original sin was visualized as being 'transmitted by sexual generation,' were the Indians then without any sin, and therefore not needful of redemption?[1]

Mythic Geographies

2. The close connection between a mythic geography and a quest for salvation in the distance, or the idea of an alien god who comes from afar, entailed the concept that science-fiction literature, arising with the dawn of the twentieth century, has brought along religious lines of questions from

the beginning. → Utopias and *voyages imaginaires* are the literary (and critical of its respective 'present times') common background of science-fiction literature and its forerunners, while the 'entertaining' → fantasy literature connected, instead, to sagas, folktales, and romances of chivalry. After the technological problems of space travel and time journeys had been 'solved,' relatively quickly, by the leading authors, in 'fantastic' recourses to science, the questions arising in the point of departure were very promptly transformed, after a presentation of the conquest of time and space, into anthropological discourse. (The modern science-fiction literature of magazines, which spread during the 1920s in the "Bible Belt" of the United States, emerged at first as technological and moral instruction.[2]) The 'tremendous moment,' in another world, of encounter with an 'other' (an alien), summoned up in science-fiction literature practically all basic religious patterns. In terms of the latter, contacts with the 'other' could be dramatized: superiority and 'cosmic brotherhood,' dependency and need for redemption. The science-fiction genre acquired a special power after the Second World War, through the partial switch of media from literature to film. In films like Stanley Kubrick's "2001—A Space Odyssey" (1968; see photograph), or Steven Spielberg's "Close Encounters of the Third Kind" (1977), the contrary motifs of galactic colonization and of an invasion from Outer Space were transposed with graphic effect. The mobilizing fantasies of a 'flight from the world,' and those of a menace or rescue from the All, for decades determined the psychodynamics of science-fiction reading. After real space travel began to be routine in the 1980s, new frontiers and limit regions were thematized. In William Gibson's novel, *Neuromancer* (1984), the interface of computer systems with the human brain (and vice versa) led to a new 'beyond,' in which, and behind which, tremendous opportunities emerge. *Neuromantics* and *Cyberpunks* are the Argonauts of a new mythology.

3. In the general reception of science-fiction literature, three fundamental motifs overlap, and at the same time support one another.

- One motif takes its point of departure in the present stance of the world, and has foreign, strange worlds and 'gods' *entering into contact* with it, or having already done so. Thus, the schemata of epiphany and redemption, of appearance and rescue, are taken up into an intergalactic communication, and included in, transferred to, the sequence of an earlier presence ('parousia'), and possible return of the gods—the *delay of a parousia*. Working from this view, C. G. Jung and E. Benz have designated 'UFOlogy' (→ UFO) a modern religion of redemption ('soteriology'; → Salvation/Redemption).

- Another motif, like the first, begins with the existence of foreign worlds, but postpones contact with them to a distant future. Earth then frequently exists no more. The key soteriological pattern is then no longer a rescue from the All, but is a *new manner of human existence*, in the spaceship or in new frameworks. After the loss of the 'old world,' the question of meaning accompanies the spaceship, even under the new conditions of an 'astro-escapism,' in undiminished brutality. Dramaturgically, what unfolds is tantamount a series of pastoral conversations with the 'ship's chaplain.'

- A third motif, finally, develops something like a *religious anthropology of space*. In the foreign worlds (or even on the spaceship, as its own 'new world') are found the most diverse types and 'variants' of religion: ascetical (H. Harrison) or Hindu (R. Zelazny) 'gods,' for example, who

Stanley Kubrick's film epic, "2001—A Space Odyssey" (1968), can be regarded as one of the most important science-fiction films of the twentieth century. Its importance rests not only on its innovations in film and technological tricks, and in the visual power of its scenarios, but also, and especially, on its mythic and metaphysical quality. Arthur C. Clarke's and Kubrick's plot covers the whole history of human-ity—from the prehistoric generation by way of a 'primordial murder', in the prologue, to the era of the space travel of the near future, with a stop on the moon and space flight. It contains a parallel history of technology—or better, of the human confronta-tion with the tools and instruments gradually conducting their self-emancipation, from the deadly tool of the 'bone', to an intelligent, sensate ma-chine, the computer HAL

have determinate functions for that world, or who lead a euhemerism further through to 'god programs' that can be played by human beings. Besides, monotheism, as the traditional religion 'on board' the spaceship, often collides with an opaque cult of persons; or else super-systems, in dramatic interpretation 'ships' (as in Frank Herbert's "Dune Chronicles," 1965ff.), are transformed into gods. In this case, the latter produce 'abso-lute dependency' (Schleiermacher) and tolerate no other 'subjects' beside themselves.

4. As a mythology of the 'age of space travel' (→ New Myths/New Mytholo-gies), science fiction posits the traditional questions of meaning under the pressure of a new demand: What remains, if the salvation history of the demolished earth has been abandoned? What founds → 'values' and → 'meaning,' if the 'priests' are only functionaries of a pragmatic system of government? Despite all of the passages of religious criticism in this genre, there remains an element of religious reflection that comes forward all the more clearly, the more consistently the traditional religious convictions, in their spatial and temporal removal from *Terra*, are abandoned. Read-ing groups focusing on certain science-fiction authors and cult films ("Star Trek—Spaceship Enterprise") proclaim modern interfaces between reflected fiction and imagined reality.

1. On the motif of 'sin' in 'other worlds,' see GLADIGOW 1988, 255ff.
2. For the development of the genre, and thematic areas: ALPERS et al. 1988, 26ff.

Literature

ALPERS, Hans J. et al. (eds.), Lexikon der Science Fiction Literatur, Munich ²1988; GALIPEAU, Steven A., The Journey of Luke Skywaker: An Analysis of Modern Myth and Symbol, Chicago 2001; GLADIGOW, Burkhard, "Andere Welten – andere Religionen?," in: STOLZ, Fritz, (ed.), Religiöse Wahrnehmung der Welt, Zurich 1988, 245-273; Idem, "Welche Welt paßt zu welchen Religionen? Zur Konkurrenz von 'religiösen Weltbildern' und 'säkularen Religionen,'" in: ZELLER, Dieter (ed.), Religion im Wandel der Kosmologien, Frankfurt/M. 1999, 13-31; GUNN, James (ed.), The New Encyclopedia of Science Fiction, New York 1988; JAMES, Edward/MENDLESOHN, Farah (eds.), The Cambridge Companion to Science Fiction, Cambridge 2003; PEDERSON, Jay P. (ed.), St. James Guide to Science Fiction Writers, ⁴1996; PORTER, Jennifer E./McLAREN, Darcee L. (ed.), Star Trek and Sacred Ground: Explorations of Star Trek, Religion, and American Culture, Albany 1999; REILLY, Robert (ed.), The Transcendent Adventure: Studies of Religion in Science Fiction/Fantasy, Westport 1985; YEFFETH, Glenn (ed.), Taking the Red Pill: Science, Philosophy and Religion in The Matrix, Dallas 2003.

→ *Cosmology/Cosmogony, Fantasy (Genre), Machine, Natural Science, New Myths/New Mythologies, UFO, Utopia*

Burkhard Gladigow

9000. And finally, there is a fragmentary heroic history here, as well—the expedition to Jupiter, with departure, danger, battle, tragedy, death, and rebirth: with Kubrik, science fiction crosses over into anthropo-fiction. The unifying element is the → epiphany of a supra-dimensional, flawless metal monolith at the turning point of human and individual development—the materialization of a world soul, divine principle, or collective will to progress. In a decisive scene, a team of scientists inspects the monolith (center of the photograph), after it has been found on the moon by excavation. Kubrick stages the investigation of the artifact as a ritual circling 'approach to the Holy,' to the *fascinosum*, the *tremendum* (Rudolf Otto). The beams of light that emerge from the monolith point to Jupiter—and beyond. The final image shows an embryo wafting in the universe—symbol of the reincarnation or transformation of the human being into the Nietzschean 'superman'? (Hubert Mohr)

Scientology

1. Lafayette Ron Hubbard (1911–1984), active in the 1940s as a → science-fiction writer, in 1950 published a bestselling book *Dianetics: The Modern Science of Mental Health*, in which he set forth a model for the analysis and healing of psychic sufferings. It has remained a component of Scientology to this day.

According to the (etymologically erroneous) asseverations of Scientology, dianetics derives from the Greek *dia-*, 'through,' and *nous*, 'soul,' 'mind.' The aim of dianetics is to detect and remove 'engrams'—mental/spiritual images impressed into the soul/mind. Engrams arise through negative experiences stored in the 'reactive mind.' In situations that can be brought into connection with the sensations or feelings of an engram, the original pattern of defense or repulsion is once more activated. This mechanism, according to Hubbard, is responsible for bodily malfunctions and the impairment of the human psyche. Once all engrams are extinguished, persons find themselves in the condition of the 'clear.' The reactive mind then no longer exists. Guided by the analytical mind, which is in a position to deal with the consequences of the engrams, persons, in their actions, can follow the basic 'command' at the basis of all life: "Survive!" They are healthy and successful because they can use their abilities in optimal fashion.

Extinguishing the engrams becomes possible through 'auditing' (from Lat., *audire*, 'listen to'). By purposeful questions, an 'auditor' hunts out the engrams, which are thereupon extinguished through the conscious recall of the occurrences that underlie them. An important tool in this process is the 'electropsychometer,' developed by Hubbard, which indicates to the auditor the existence of engrams.

Auditing

Members of the Church of Scientology demonstrate in Berlin, on October 27, 1997, before a very historic background: the Kaiser Wilhelm Memorial Church. They make an appeal for public acknowledgment with an American flag, as well as German and Swiss flags, and a 'living image' of the Statue of Liberty. In her hand, the white-clad woman holds not only the obligatory torch, but also the original American edition of *What Is Scientology?*, which is an official presentation of the Church of Scientology. If we were to combine the signs used associatively, the intended message would be formulated somewhat as follows. The European states, too, are summoned to exalt religious freedom, after the example of the United States, and accord Scientology formal legal status as a religious community. Simultaneously, the appropriation, here, of the national symbols of the United States conveys a missionary thought: only with Scientology will one really be a participant in the liberty and freedom promised by the dream of the 'land of the free.' For those with whom this message has no success, Scientology is a spark that, at present, is igniting vigorous discussions on the definition of the concept of religion, and on the relative importance of state-guaranteed religious freedom as weighed against other goods. (Kirsten Holzapfel)

'Scientology,' derived from the Latin *scire/scientia* ('know/knowledge') and the Greek *logos*, is understood internally as 'knowledge, how one knows.' It broadens the dianetic model to include a mental component. The human being is no longer only body and mind, but a spiritual being ('thetan,' from the Greek letter *theta*). A thetan uses body and mind as a connective member to the physical universe, with the purpose of creating and controlling her own universe, consisting of matter, energy, space, and time (MEST). A thetan is immortal. When someone dies, the thetan leaves that body, and enters one of a new person being born. Having available a human body and understanding that work ever more optimally, without engrams, the thetan develops his spiritual and mental liberty and freedom in the MEST universe, and becomes an 'operating thetan' (OT).

2. In the framework of Scientology, the partial aspects (dynamics) constitutive of the "command: Survive!" were broadened. To the four dynamics in the concept of dianetics (self, procreation, group, humanity) were added four more (whole of life, material universe, spiritual being, infinity). The thrust to survival in the eighth dynamic (infinity) marks the point of intersection with the Divine, which is not enlarged upon in the Scientology literature: the eighth dynamic is also designated as the Supreme Being. In a framework of her spiritual development, the person or thetan must aim at progress in all dynamics.

Ethics and Practice

The path to spiritual freedom is called a 'bridge,' and is to be walked through numerous courses that build upon and complement one another. In terms of its structure, the bridge resembles occult systems of initiation. The path on the bridge can be traversed by way of either the pure use of the corresponding course, or the attendant training to the status of auditor. While the first courses exact a high price, the training generates a stronger integration into Scientology. Then comes a further conclusion: that the teachings of Scientology are imbedded in a rigid ethics, in which all those activities are labeled good that are serviceable as "constructive survival activities" of the development of the individual Scientologist or of his or her own group. Evil, accordingly, is everything harmful for Scientology. Critics, within its own ranks or from without, are seen as 'repressive persons' or 'anti-social personalities,' against whom a battle is to be waged.

The Scientologist's everyday is determined by the pursuit of the course, and by working in the organizations. Higher stages of the 'bridge' can only be traversed in seeking out churches. The outlay of time is great, so that social relations with non-Scientologists are scarcely possible. Hubbard established procedures for the celebration of naming, marriage, and death. The extent to which such celebrations are held is unclear. The weekly Sunday service is not held in all churches. For other feast days, as for Hubbard's birthday, or the anniversary of the publication of *Dianetics*, there is no established ceremonial: by and large, they have the character of a secular event.

3. a) The development of Scientology came in large part as a reaction to external influences. Originally, Hubbard wished to reform the psychology of his time. As the professional community rejected his Dianetics, and the stream of the Dianetics self-help groups dwindled, the foundation established by Hubbard in 1952 was met with competition, and he lost his copyright to *Dianetics*. It was at this point that he expanded his Dianetics into Scientology. In 1953, the first church was founded. The 1960s marked the appearance of Narconon, an organization to combat drug-addiction and offer rehabilitation, along with the Citizens' Commission for Human Rights (CCHR), for the discovery of abuses of received psychiatry. Both organizations cultivate a negative image of pharmaco-psychiatry. With the close of the 1970s, Scientology was reconstructed as a universal service organization. The existing Scientological principles of the perception of reality and communication, as well as the chief structures of the organizations themselves, were extended to the areas of economics, training, and education. With special organizations for persons in public life (Celebrity Centers), the credibility of popular members is utilized in order to correct the negative image arisen since the 1960s. Since 1982, the headquarters of Scientology are maintained at the

Organization

Religious Technology Center in Los Angeles, which administers the materials of Scientology, and licenses the respective organizations and clients.

Self-Image

In Scientology's self-image, on the other hand, history since 1950 has been the experience of a progressive knowledge and understanding concerning the universal validity of its own principles. With the purpose of building "a world without war and violence," and to "be able to have the rights pertaining to its competency, and to ascend to spiritual heights," it sees itself as standing in the tradition of the great religions of redemption. The knowledge contained in these religions is viewed as subsumed in Scientology, and complemented there with new elements of knowledge. Hubbard is honored as the founder of Scientology, and as a great scientist and philosopher.

Is Scientology a Religion?

c) Conflicts still prevail over the character of Scientology as a religion. While, for some, auditing is a religious act comparable to confession, critics regard it as psycho-manipulation ('brain-washing'; → Anti-Cult Movements). The perspective of a need for financing on the part of religions is opposed by the picture of an organization existing solely for profit. Scientology's legal recognition as a religious community is not uniform worldwide, and has repeatedly been the object of legal proceedings. In the United States, in 1993, it was recognized as a religious community by the tax offices with de facto responsibility for this determination. The decision was preceded by years of quarrel, and political influence is suspected. In Germany, on the other hand, in 1955, the Federal Labor Court decided that—at least where labor laws are concerned—Scientology is to be treated as a commercial business. But a definitive clarification is still pending. Appraisals of the character of Scientology as a religion are also always connected with the traditions of the respective countries, not least of all with public debate over alternative religion.

Pending further research, religious or spiritual references in the core area described in the beginning can be established. Independently of this, Scientology is the object of criticism on grounds of its particular hierarchical structures of leadership, the close control of its members, and acts of individual Scientologists in the gray areas of lawful permissibility. But there has been no proof of the allegation that Scientology is a Mafia-type organization that strives for world rule, and that systematically infiltrates politics and the economy.

For several decades now, Scientology has counted its own world membership at 8,000,000. Although as yet no independent reliable data is available on a global scale, it can be assumed that the actual membership is considerably smaller.

Literature

Sources: HUBBARD, Ron L., Dianetics: The Modern Science of Mental Health, Los Angeles 1950; NEW ERA PUBLICATIONS INTERNATIONAL, What Is Scientology?, Los Angeles 1992.

Secondary Literature: CHRISTENSEN, Dorthe Refslund, Rethinking Scientology: Cognition and Representation in Religion, Therapy and Soteriology, forthcoming; LAMONT, Stewart, Religion Inc.: The Church of Scientology, London 1986; MELTON, J. Gordon, The Church of Scientology, Salt Lake City 2000; WALLIS, Roy, The Road to Total Freedom: A

Sociological Analysis of Scientology, New York 1977; WHITEHEAD, Harriet, Renunciation and Reformulation: A Study of Conversion in an American Sect, Ithaca 1987; WINTHER, Joseph A., Dianetics: A Doctor's Report, New York 1951.

→ *Anti-Cult Movements, Church, Esotericism, New Religions, Occultism, Purification/ Hygiene/Bodily Grooming*

Steffen Rink

Secrecy

1. Secrecy is a *strategy developed by evolution*, in the case of beast and human alike within the biological food chain, that attains an elevated degree of individual opportunities and possibilities for survival and reproduction by way of the accumulation of various informational prospects. The person or animal with a successful disguise does not become prey, the one that hides his/her/its food survives times of want, the creature of restrained impulses and hidden intents can secretly dodge competitors for nourishment, sexual partners, and territory, and the one that protects progeny to the third generation ensures the safe transport of her/his/its genes. The greater the concealment and silence vis-à-vis the competing side ('information reduction'), or the more that that side is deceived and 'tricked' ('disinformation'), the greater the chances of reproduction on one's own side. A shortcoming with regard to secrecy can mean death. Fear and triumph, therefore, are the constant companions of secrecy. The invisibility of one is the insecurity of the other.

Secrecy as an Evolutionary Strategy

2. Explicit pleasure in the generation of secrecy that can become a craving or addiction appears only with the human being. Discovery in a game of hide-and-seek arouses squeals of delight in a child, even a very young one, the dissolution of the state of tension between hiding and showing oneself is enjoyed in all merriment, stubborn silence out of spite signs a new stage of development, and re-interpreting reality with words is the lovely ruse of others, not only for Huckleberry Finn.

Human Secrecy Intelligence

a) The basis of all of these phenomena is that, through cultural evolution, the human brain has become specialized in the practice of signs, and in intelligent, secretive ways of dealing with reality. Signs stand for something that, in itself, is invisible, insensible, and inaudible. Olfactory, optical, and acoustical behavior, in the sense of positing markers, here forms the evolutionary basis, but is the prisoner of the materiality of things. Only the achievement of a transformation from the openly communicative marking to the exclusive *secret sign* sparks the evolutionary breakthrough. In order to introduce the sign durably and reliably, a practice of secrecy, by means of a positing of signs, must represent the absent, secret thing in the present sign in such wise that it is *double-coded*—coded as an 'open secret sign.' All see or hear the sign; however, only some recognize, know, and take charge of that which the sign indicates (wild game depicted on rocks, the early Christian fish symbol, the Zen garden).

Double-Coded Secret Signs

*Co-Evolution
of Secrecy and
Revelation*

b) Simultaneous *esoteric and exoteric* secrecy arouses not only the curiosity and craving of the excluded, but also the temptation of a profitable betrayal. The dynamic co-evolution of secrecy and revelation, thus launched, has today produced several tamper-resistant *strategies of secrecy*:

- *Semantic double-coding*, in word and image, divides reality into a visible-and-real world and an invisible-and-virtual one (→ masks, whizzing-sticks, bread and wine in cults of life-renewal; allegories and the narration of parables in speech and writing).
- *Performative initiation and introduction* that make the individual a member of a closed chain (years-long rites of initiation in men's associations and brotherhoods; exclusive teacher-pupil and master-disciple relations; trials of courage).
- *Unexaminable vehicles of information*, such as ancestors, dreams, visions, divination, omens, oracles, miracles, and charms (→ Esotericism; Occultism).
- *Unverifiable histories* (narratives of → origin, ascensions to heaven, after-death reports and near-death experiences, eschatological histories and → apocalypses).
- *Magical secret rituals* that can be successful only when held without witnesses (→ Voodoo cults, spiritual alchemy, black → magic).
- *Secret cults* that render secrecy an immediate, ecstatic, and extraordinary experience of wholeness (ancient → mystery cults, Australian → Aborigines' corroborees).
- *Hierarchical structures*, in which the organization's secret can be known and used only by the invisible master-superior (certain Rosicrucian groups, the "Esoteric Section" of the → Theosophical Society, Opus Dei, → Scientology).
- *Transformation* of the—as yet—unknown or unknowable *to the status of the 'secret'* (mysteries of faith; promises of revelation; speculations on cosmology or on the theory of evolution; TV cult-series "The X-Files").
- *Self-reliance and independence*, which keep nothing secret except this fact (traffic in secrets; esoteric mania for betraying secrets; many secret societies after the abandonment of their original purpose of their organization, e.g., German Masonic Lodges in the nineteenth century).

These forms of secrecy are characteristic of all religions. They function on the principle that the whole is more than the sum of its parts. Only those in control of the whole are in charge of the secret. Individual participants in the secret, integrated but subordinate, cannot destroy the operational force of the secrecy. In the extreme case, the secret becomes a mystery of faith, and of self-bewitching imagination, impenetrable to all.

*Secret Knowledge by
Reflection*

c) On the other hand, *self-reflexive secrecy* knows and understands what it does. It successfully shifts the dynamics of concealment and revelation to the level of reflexive knowledge in the area of individual cognition. A self-aware, self-controlled, attentive ability to remain silent is characteristic here. In creative play, and secret, confidential experiment with the possibilities of representing sign and signal, limits and boundaries fall from around the respective axiomatic conceptions of world and self (→ shamanism, scholarly → Daoism, → mysticism, alchemy).

3. Of such elements, religious acts build up a world invisible and out of reach, a world of the spiritual and believed, an 'otherwise world,' a 'world behind,' behind the world of outward facts and conditions. Secrecy protects and immunizes this second world, which determines life here and hereafter,

together with the well-being of those who deal with the world of secrecy. The unequal chances for life and well-being, presented this way in gerontocracies, caste societies, patriarchates, or other forms of government has, as a rule, very stable credibility. It makes religions the connective tissue of human socialization. A self-reflexive piety of silence, and falling silent, can, on the contrary, become the catalyst and motor of cultural evolution, or make survival possible in an environment of deadly enemies (Jewish and Christian → gnosticism; Taquia and Sufi brotherhoods [→ Sufism]; 'Marranos').

4. The world's retransformation into an enchanted garden of occultism and esotericism, parliamentarily uncontrollable bank secrets, and new enchantment at the hands of the media, is at full speed. In this situation, secrecy still deserves the self-reflexive elucidation of who it is who produces which secrets, in what situation and against whom, for what reason and to what end, and how and by means of what procedure or operation.

Literature

ASSMANN, Aleida/ASSMANN, Jan (eds.), Schleier und Schwelle I: Geheimnis und Öffentlichkeit, Munich 1997; BOK, Sissela, Secrets: On the Ethics of Concealment and Revelation, New York 1982; BOLLE, Kees W. (ed.), Secrecy in Religions, Leiden etc. 1987; KEEN, Ian, Knowledge and Secrecy in an Aboriginal Religion, Oxford 1994; KIPPENBERG, Hans G./STROUMSA, Guy G., Secrecy and Concealment: Studies in the History of Mediterranean and Near Eastern Religions, Leiden 1995; MENSCHING, Gustav, Das heilige Schweigen. Eine religionsgeschichtliche Untersuchung, Gießen 1926; MEYER, Birgit/PELS, Peter (eds.), Magic and Modernity: Interfaces of Revelation and Concealment, Stanford 2003; SIMMEL, Georg, "The Sociology of Secrecy and of Secret Societies," in: American Journal of Sociology 1 (1905), 441ff.; URBAN, Hugh B., Tantra: Sex, Secrecy, Politics, and Power in the Study of Religion, Berkeley 2003; WOLFSON, Elliot R. (ed.), Rending the Veil: Concealment and Secrecy in the History of Religions, New York/London 1999.

→ *Apocalypse, Epiphany, Esotericism, Hermetism/Hermeticism, Kabbalah, Mysticism, Occultism, Perception, Symbol/Sign/Gesture, Trickster*

Hemma Boneberg

Sect

1. In antiquity, the concept 'sect' (from Lat., *sequi*, 'to follow'; free translation of Gk. *haíresis*, 'choice,' → Heresy) served to denote the followers of a philosopher; in republican Rome, it was also used for political followings. In Acts 24.5 (cf. 24:14), the concept appears in connection with the High Priest's indictment of Paul before the Roman governor as "a ringleader of the sect of the Nazarenes." Christianity adopted the concept 'sect' quite early. The term denoted the members of a community adhering to a faith orientation and teaching that had been declared deviant, but it could also be applied to an independent religion, such as Islam, which, in the Acts of the sixteenth-century Inquisition, was referred to the *secta de Mahoma* (Sp., 'sect of Muhammad').

The ecclesiastical application of the concept 'sect' to other groups is to be understood only from the relation between the → Church, regarded as rightly believing, and its self-concept (indeed as the one, universal, and

Concept

common Church), and 'deviation' from this orthodoxy. In religions in which a central instance and a hierarchical church do not exist, such as in Sunni Islam, the concept is not applicable. Both the conceptual application and the distinction between 'Church' and 'sects,' were subject to change.

Criteria in Christian Theology

2. Even in the primitive Christian Church, those who deviated from nascent orthodoxy in their views were excluded as heretics (→ Heresy) or schismatics. This judgment held as well for many dissenting and deviant groups of the Middle Ages, as, for example, the Cathars. In some cases, such groupings could be integrated into the Church by way of the founding of new orders. In the wake of the → Reformation, other definitions of 'sect' emerged: groups that were not included in the religious Peace of Augsburg and in the Peace of Westphalia, qualified as such; later, communities, as well, that introduced other scripture than the canonized texts of the Bible and held to them as vehicles of divine revelation. Finally, those who failed to acknowledge the apostolic succession and adopted other professions of faith were given the same label. In Protestantism today, Christian groups that have not joined the World Council of Churches, or ecumenical Christianity, or have not been received into them, are understood as sects. The same applies to those that, besides Christian traditions, use extra-biblical sources of revelation. Other criteria often cited are: (a) a split from a larger religious community, (b) cultic components in comparison with *Weltanschauung*, and (c) an unambiguous division from all other organizations in teaching and practice. Here it is often imputed to sects that, in disparate measure, they render their members psychically disturbed; make them dependent; destroy social connections; sketch an unhistorical image of history; see things in black and white; use all available means to prevent members from leaving the group; and not least of all, exploit their members financially. As representative of groups against whom these reproaches are made, we may here cite the Church of → Scientology (→ Anti-Cult Movements).

Sociological Criteria

3. Along with these theological distinctions, sociological criteria are also set up. Max → Weber and Ernst Troeltsch have established distinctions such as: One is born into a church; one joins a sect. Churches are institutions in which all can be members on an equal footing; in the sects only the true believers are promoted to such equality. In the sects, only one → *charisma* is acknowledged, while, in the churches, charisma is managed by professional → priests. In their relationship with the world, churches are said to be more available to compromise than are sects. Weber's classification had in view the effects of Calvinist and Pietistic religious motivation on economic activity; the extent to which his intent was sociological categorization is questionable. Furthermore, some characteristics of the sects do not apply to those of today; many of these evince a claim to universality, or readiness for compromise with the world.

R. Stark and W. S. Bainbridge offer another definition. They designate those groups as 'sects' that have split off from existing religious communities: groups that 'import' concepts, or that adhere to new images, are → 'cults.' According to this definition, Christianity would be a Jewish sect. B. Wilson and B. Johnson, on the other hand, have suggested that groups standing in social tension with their environment, and excluded on this account, or excluding themselves, be designated sects. But meanwhile, this criterion applies to many churches as well: in questions of sexuality and family planning, the Catholic Church, for example, might contradict the prevalent views of modern society. Another trait was seen in the number of members. On the other hand, many churches (as the Coptic Church or the Orthodox churches in Poland, Finland, and America), in spite of rather small membership numerically, are certainly not regarded as sects.

4. The colloquial use of the term, according to H. Hemminger, designates groups that "instead of freedom of development produce dependency, de-mean persons, and generate intolerance."[1] It is questionable whether new religious movements (→ New Religions) can be appropriately characterized with this usage, and whether religious studies ought to adopt this concept. Thus, H. Zinser points out that, with the application of this concept, "a dif-ference and an inequality [is] still held that [has] become essentially inap-propriate, through the dismantling of the state church, and the dissolution and transformation of the popular church into a community church."[2] Ap-plying the concept consequently neglects the altered position of religion and churches in modern Western societies.

Generation of Problems

The question arises whether the concept of sect is not invalidated by the privatization of religion issuing from religious freedom.[3] The concept of sect stems from religious traditions that it served for the purpose of self-defini-tion, and division from without. Although many (even Christian) scholars repeatedly indicate that the concept of sect is marked by undue bias, it is still used. But ultimately, it is nothing but a polemical concept and altogether unsuited for the formation of theory in religious studies.

1. HEMMINGER 1995, 65.
2. ZINSER 1997, 132.
3. Ibid.

Literature

BAINBRIDGE, William Sims, The Sociology of Religious Movements, New York/London 1997; HEMMINGER, Hansjörg, Was ist eine Sekte?, Mainz 1995; LEWIS, James R., The Encyclopedia of Cults, Sects, and New Religions, Amherst 1998; STARK, Rodney/BAIN-BRIDGE, William S., The Future of Religion: Secularization, Revival and Cult Formation, Berkeley 1985; TROELTSCH, Ernst, The Social Teaching of the Christian Churches (1911), trans. Olive WYON, Chicago 1981; WILSON, Bryan, Religious Sects: A Sociological Study, London 1970; Idem, The Social Dimensions of Sectarianism: Sects and New Religious Movements in Contemporary Society, Oxford 1990; ZINSER, Hartmut, Der Markt der Religionen, Munich 1997.

→ *Anti-Cult Movements, Church, Cult, Denomination, Group, Heresy, Minorities, New Religions, Polemics*

Babett Remus

Secularization

1. The term 'secularization' can represent either of two distinct concepts, as it denotes either of two distinct events. One of the latter is any process either of 'making worldly' or 'becoming worldly,' while the other refers to the state appropriation of church property. 'Secularization' has a somewhat different

Concept

meaning in the legal terminology of the Catholic Church, where it has its place in the distinction between 'order' priests and 'secular' priests or deacons, and denotes the juridical process of (at least a partial) dispensation of order priests from observance of the rules of their respective religious orders. Etymologically, it derives from the Latin *saeculum*, the meaning of which as '(world) age' was broadened in the Middle Ages to include 'world.'

'Secularization' as State Appropriation of Church Property

2. In the meaning of 'secularization' as the process of appropriating church property, the word itself can occur only in Christian religious history. But the process of an appropriation of religious property by state instances is by no means limited to that religion. Naturally, it is a prerequisite for secularizations in this sense that the special quality of property (as a rule, of property acquired by the Church in the bestowal of a foundation, or in the founding of a church institution) be previously formed as religious property that enjoys a different legal status than does the property of a private person. For the ancient pre-Christian religions, the temple comes especially to mind, reckoned, as it was, as the property of a deity conceived as present in it by virtue of the cultic image. In principle, all things belonging to the temple—including money deposited there—were regarded as sacrosanct. Nevertheless, in time of war temple treasuries were robbed again and again, and this act was frequently counted as sacrilege, even apart from cases in which an attempt was made to legitimize the destruction and plundering of a temple as 'punishment.' At bottom, the Christian Church adopted the ancient model of the formation and designation of religious property. Through gifts and other mechanisms, episcopal churches and monasteries inherited property that was extensively withdrawn from the disposition of their functionaries, and that, on account of the prohibition of alienation, had the tendency to grow. Similar procedures can be observed in Asia, in the societies that stood under Buddhist influence. Endowments fulfill the same function in Islamic lands, and in India. No extrinsic cause was needed for the property thus amassed to stir the greed of political institutions finding themselves in notorious financial need. Here it did not make much difference whether the political systems in question were friendly or hostile toward religion. In the Christian West, a number of secularizations can be observed: in the eighth century in Franconia through Charles Martel, in the sixteenth century in many countries of Europe with the introduction of the Reformation, in France in the wake of the Great Revolution of 1789, in the German Empire in 1803 by decree of the Imperial Deputation, in Russia after the October Revolution of 1917. Despite the different justifications attempted for these occurrences, the result was, in principle, always similar: the loss of treasure of the religious establishment was compensated only in rare instances. The secularizations of the Modern Age, especially, issued in the sale and privatization of the property of foundations that, at first, fell to the state, and thus joined the overall process of capitalist utilization. As one might expect, this privatization occurred also in Russia, and in still greater scope.

Secularization as Making or Becoming Worldly

3. Scarcely any other concept in history or sociology of religion is the object of such dispute as is secularization understood as making or becoming worldly. There are positions that adopt the concept of secularization as an irreversible development—of course with extremely diverse designations of the beginning of this process or event. For others, the point of departure is that there is no such thing as secularization at all, but only an alteration

of the social gestalt of religion. A third—and most recent—position argues that secularization has taken place in (Western) Europe only, thus making Europe the 'exceptional case,' while earlier on scholars saw Europe as the 'normal case' and the United States (→ North America) as the—religiously committed—exception.

This astonishing discrepancy is due first and foremost to the employment of different definitions of → religion. If the starting point is a functional definition of religion, then there can be no 'irreligion' in the strict sense. The indisputable deterioration of *ecclesial* influence on society and culture in the last two centuries is explained as the *religious* transformation of monopolistic religious organization into a → 'spirituality' whose orientation is to the individual. It is denied that rejection of church can be understood as secularization. On the other hand, if one's point of departure is a substantial definition of religion, that ultimately has a particular religious content (belief in God, conceptualizations of the hereafter, etc.,) as its subject, then a deterioration can indeed be verified, in traditional conceptualizations of faith and in religious acts (church attendance, baptism, etc.), that can be designated as secularization. Common to both positions is that their starting point is a transformation in the area of religion. But the very adoption of this point of departure entails problems, since it is only to a very limited extent that indisputable propositions can be made regarding the relation of religion to culture and society when it comes to a discourse upon the past. Even relatively simple phenomena, such as past participation in the operation of religious institutions, are known at all reliably for only approximately 150 years. The influence of religious notions on persons' activity is altogether beyond the range of our knowledge. The construct of secularization owes its survival to the assumption of a pre-modern condition in which religion—of whatever form and contour—is considered to be a major influence on daily life. That this influence was great on a certain circle of persons cannot be disputed. Of course, the same is applicable in the Modern Age, as well, including the present. To render the extremely imprecise concept of secularization operational, it might be helpful to define it in such a way that secularization will be an object when the participation of religious products in the overall quantity of goods and services deteriorates. This definition raises plenty of technical problems; but, under reference to a substantial concept of religion, it affords the opportunity of making empirically more fully charged propositions concerning religious changes. Here, in terms of an increase in production in society as well, it can be verified that, in certain circumstances, even with an increased production of religious goods in absolute quantities, a relative diminution is to be noted in the production of those goods. This very development is indicated in, say, the second half of the nineteenth century. An enormous expansion in productivity therefore favors primarily the proportionate balance of nonreligious goods and services. Whether this process should be called 'secularization' in an exacting sense depends once more on the observer's understanding of religion.

Literature

ASHFORD, Sheena/TIMMS, Noel, What Europe Thinks: A Study of Western European Values, Aldershot etc. 1992; BERGER, Peter L. (ed.), The Desecularization of the World: Resurgent Religion and World Politics, Washington 1999; BROWN, Callum G., The Death of Christian Britain, London 2001; Idem, "The Secularisation Decade: What the 1960s

Have Done to the Study of Religion," in: McLeod/Ustorf 2003, 29-46; Chadwick, Owen, The Secularization of the European Mind in the Nineteenth Century, Cambridge 1977; Davie, Grace, Religion in Britain since 1945: Believing without Belonging, Oxford 1994; Eadem, Europe: The Exceptional Case. Parameters of Faith in the Modern World, London 2002; Halman, Loek/Riis, Ole (eds.), Religion in Secularizing Society: The Europeans' Religion at the End of the 20th Century, Leiden 2003; Kehrer, Günter, Einführung in die Religionssoziologie, Darmstadt 1988; Lehmann, Hartmut (ed.), Säkularisierung, Dechristianisierung, Rechristianisierung im neuzeitlichen Europa, Göttingen 1997; Lübbe, Hermann, Säkularisierung. Geschichte eines ideenpolitischen Begriffs, Freiburg ³2003 (¹1965); Martin, David, A General Theory of Secularization, Oxford 1978; McLeod, Hugh, Religion and the People of Western Europe, 1789–1989, Oxford/New York 1997 (¹1981); Idem, Secularization in Western Europe, 1848–1914, Basingstoke 2000; McLeod, Hugh/Ustorf, Werner, The Decline of Christendom in Western Europe, 1750–2000, Cambridge 2003; Stark, Rodney/Finke, Roger, "Secularization, R.I.P.," In: Idem, Acts of Faith: Explaining the Human Side of Religion, Berkeley 2000, 57-79.

→ *Criticism of Religion, Disenchantment/Reenchantment, Economy, Endowment/Foundation, Enlightenment, Modernity/Modern Age, New Religions, Spirituality*

Günter Kehrer

Security

Needs for Security

1. From prehistoric times, security and shelter from the hardships of nature, from threats by hostile animals and human enemies, and from the risks of illness and death, have been among the key concerns of cultural practice. As civilizing and cultural achievements have multiplied, certain elements of security and expectations of safety, in various areas of that civilization and culture, have multiplied as well, and determinable risks have been reduced. Attire and housing, nutritional substances and stocks, social organization and cultural tradition, all set boundaries to times and zones of insecurity. Famine, drought, and cold, for example, are limited as far as possible, and danger zones are limited and bounded by building and fencing, by roads and bridges. Religious practices (rites, rituals) are involved, and expand, with collective resistance to possible enemies, with reaping, safe storage for harvest and fruits, and with the hope of success in certain undertakings. These religious practices legitimate, for one, the culture's achievement as such (e.g., sowing, foundation of a wall, gates and fences, walls and ditches, the defensive throw of a lance against the enemy); for another, they have the task of reducing the remaining uncertainties (contingency) connected with these activities, or of making them at least bearable. When prey are distant, when seed fails to grow, or a surprise drought supervenes, then hunting rituals or weather 'magic' have doubtless failed. They must be repeated, reinforced, and broadened. The emergence of complex → rituals is likewise the outcome of growing needs for security, and a consequence of reflection on possible uncertainties.

Explaining Failures

To the extent that cultural demands and needs for security grow and become a constitutive part of social organization, the religious patterns of interpretation shift as well—from a technical control of the rituals to the interpretation of possible failures (contingency control). Specific amplifications are bound up with the absorption of uncertainties and insecurities in religious and cultic systems, and with their forestallment thereby. Failures are no longer only failures of rituals, but consequences of an inimical, or even merely indeterminable, divine will. Discovering the will of the gods by way of divination and → oracle (→ Prophecy/Divination) means, at the same time, the fashioning of security for oneself concerning a future determined by the gods—or, in any case, the assurance of the agreement and consent of the highest god (as in Roman divination). Against the horizon of time that governed the outlook of the early city-states, the polytheistic pantheons, with their clashing, hating or loving, protecting or destroying gods, shifted security and insecurity onto a 'meta-level.' Under these conditions, it could ultimately offer more security to be 'loved by the gods' than rightly to fulfill all ritual obligations. With the transfer of security—and of reflection on insecurity—to the status of a privileged relationship with 'my' god (premised in the special case of the monotheistic religions), the structures or conceptualizations of security basically alter. Now, in given cases, security is guaranteed by a third person—becomes an element of a relationship of dependency. In circumstances of the 'professionalization' of religion (→ Experts [Religious]), it can be determined that a person has reverenced a 'false' god with 'false' rites. Security then becomes equivalent to professionalization, while insecurity must be a feature of 'dilettantism.' The problem of insecurity is then transferred, to an extent, to a meta-level. The security of a naively awaited connection between action and outcome is transformed, under certain conditions, to a paradoxical relationship of utter insecurity and utter certainty of → salvation. Election, redemption, and certitude then stand as key concepts of a Christian theology, at the end of the lengthy process here cited.

2. In parallel with a religious history of personal need for security, a religious history of the warranty or 'guarantee' of security was finally sketched out. Especially the great gods, the city and state gods, such as Babylonian Marduk, the Semitic forms of Baal, or the Artemis of Asia Minor, bestowed protection and security upon the city. Accordingly, their human representatives, the Hellenistic kings, were addressed as divine 'Redeemers' and 'Saviors' (*theoí sotêres*): in this position as guarantors, they are at once human beings *and* gods ('dyophysitism'). *Securitas*—being, along with 'peace' and 'freedom' (*pax* and *libertas*), an element of the idea of empire of the Imperium Romanum—finally overflowed into the protection of 'freedom and security' on the part of the Christian Emperors. Behind the latter then stood the Christian God, as "Defending Lord" (*protector*). With the Renaissance, *securitas publica* became an aim of political thinking, and, in the seventeenth and eighteenth centuries, issued in a definition of the goal of the state in terms of 'common well-being and security.' Absolutist rule saw its climax once more in the program of making the goal of state intervention an 'interior public security'—the 'general happiness,' the 'commonwealth.'

Warranty of Security

In parallel with this these processes of a state engineering of security, there develop, with the beginning of the modern age in Europe, concepts and institutions of an *individual* insurance. Both the state processes and those relating to the individual now occur in detachment from religious models or patterns. → Sacrifice to the gods of the sea, at the departure of a ship, in pre-Christian and Christian antiquity and beyond, has become life insurance or damage policy. The size and earnestness of the sacrifices corresponds to the dangers of the ocean voyage, just as, in modern insurance structures,

From Sacrifice to Insurance

premiums are balanced against risks. Similarly, entreaties and votives to Saint Florian disappear, to the extent that public fire protection and a system of fire insurance have reduced the dangers that threaten in case of a blaze. On the basis of a general securing of the public area, finally, reflections and considerations are entertained that have codetermined the conditions of modern rationality, joining theories of probability to risk management. "The revolutionary that divides the modern age from the historical past is the conception and the reflection that the future does not arise simply out of the caprices of the gods [...] The risk control that this produced has replaced a person's passion for game and hazard with economic growth, improved quality of life, and technological progress."[1]

God and Coincidence 3. In a tangled way, the emergence of the modern theory of probability is connected with a determination of the relationship between luck and God, and a wager on the existence of God. In the seventeenth century, Puritan clergyman Thomas Gataker noted that the outcome of a game of chance was determined not by divine law, but by the law of nature. Finally, Blaise Pascal employs the question, and the concepts, of hazard in the question of the existence of God: "God is, or God is not. For which alternative shall we decide? Reason can determine nothing here."[2] The central European question of the existence of God is clad in the schema of a wager (*le pari de Pascal*), and the risk of the two possible decisions is determined by the differing consequences of the outcome. Only the person who 'bets that God exists' is on the sure side, after the course of the ages, at the last judgment. If the other alternative—God does not exist—should turn out to be the correct one, then at least no insupportable disadvantages emerge. "Pascal's wager" has been dubbed the installation of the modern association between theory of probability and risk management: the inauguration of a life decision that leads to the passage of the inexorable incertitude of the future to a certitude actually resulting from calculation.

1. BERNSTEIN, Peter L., Wider die Götter, Cologne 1997, 9f. (See BERNSTEIN 1996.)
2. PASCAL, Blaise, Pensées. Über die Religion und über einige andere Gegenstände, Gerlingen 1994, 122f. (Engl. ed.: Pensées, trans. by A. J. KRAILSHEIMER, rev. ed., London 1995).

Literature

BECK, Ulrich, World Risk Society, Cambridge 1999; BERNSTEIN, Peter L., Against the Gods: The Remarkable Story of Risk, New York 1996; BERTOCCI, Peter A., Religion as Creative Insecurity, Greenwood 1976 ([1]1958); DOUGLAS, Mary/WILDAVSKY, Aaron, Risk and Culture: An Essay on the Selection of Technical and Environmental Dangers, Berkeley 1983; GLADIGOW, Burkhard, "Konkrete Angst und offene Furcht. Am Beispiel des Prodigienwesens in Rom," in: VON STIETENCRON, Heinrich (ed.), Angst und Gewalt, Düsseldorf 1979, 61-77; KAUFMANN, Franz-Xaver, Sicherheit als soziologisches und sozialpolitisches Problem, Stuttgart 1973; RESCHER, Nicholas, Pascal's Wager: A Study of Practical Reasoning in Philosophical Theology, Notre Dame 1985; VON GRAEVENITZ, Gerhard/MARQUARD, Odo (eds.), Kontingenz, Munich 1998; WILKINSON, Iain, Anxiety in a Risk Society, London 2001; WISSMANN, Hans (ed.), Zur Erschließung von Zukunft in den Religionen, Würzburg 1991.

→ *Fear/Dread, Meaning/Signification, Prophecy/Divination*

Burkhard Gladigow

Sermon

1. The word 'sermon' denotes that form of religious → communication fitted to the condition of public discourse. Sermon forms in this sense are found especially in the book religions Judaism, Christianity, and Islam. In the Christian tradition, the sermon is usually incorporated into the liturgical connection of a divine service, for the purpose of strengthening the certitude of faith entertained by the audience, as well as to provide an orientation in various life situations.

History of the Christian Sermon

2. In its historical origin, one of the orientations of the Christian sermon has been taken in the expounding of a citation from Scripture (in Heb., *dᵉrasha*) as presented in the synagogues of rabbinical Judaism. Another orientation is taken in the lecture on or presentation of philosophical teaching (in Gk., *diatríbe*), as practiced in the Hellenistic world for the purpose of offering counsel for persons' lives. Not a few texts of the New Testament are accounted oral proclamation in written form, and these have preserved certain testimonials of the earliest Christian preaching (Acts 2:14ff.; 17:16ff.). In the ancient Church, there followed a textual paraphrase (homily), extensively patterned on Origen's doctrine of the four-level sense of Scripture (literal, allegorical, moral, and that of salvation history). With → Augustine, the sermon underwent a modification, with an orientation to ancient rhetoric. In the mostly illiterate society of the Middle Ages, frescos, altar pictures, and sculptures were the preferred media of communication. The sermon, which it was long permitted to omit at Mass, then lost its importance, not to be reinstated as an 'essential part of the Mass' until Vatican Council II. In the monasteries, meanwhile, it has always retained its place, as also, since the thirteenth century, in universities, and now the lay movements have cultivated it. Wide propagation by agitators developed on the occasion of the Crusades (Bernard of Clairvaux), or in the struggle to oppose the 'heretics.' But the sermon was also at work in the heretical circles of the Cathars and the Waldenses, and with John Wyclif and Jan Hus; and it served in the mystical introduction to spiritual and ascetical 'composure' (→ Meister Eckhart, John Tauler). The penitential sermon of itinerant preachers and monks (Savonarola in Florence), denounced sinful behavior with its social criticism, and found strong echoes. In the cities of the up-and-coming middle class, a renewed culture of the sermon grew out of an increased need for education and formation.

Ancient Church and Middle Ages

With the Reformation, it was the word of the Gospel, in its literal and paraphrased communication (Augsburg Confession, Art. V), that won key importance for piety in Protestant Christianity. It was in terms of this communication that worship and the sacraments were understood. Religious assurance was expected then neither from conventionalized tradition, nor from the mere citation of Scripture, nor from inner impulse and inspiration alone. Instead, with Martin Luther, such assurance needed conveyance through example and experience, in a competent and responsible sharing of faith. → Conscience itself, as the confidant of the human heart before God, becomes the relevant instance for the sermon, both in its preparation and in its reception.

Reformation, Confessional Age, Modernity

A Muslim preacher (in Ar., *ḥaṭib*) at the Friday sermon. At noon prayer, in the mosque, a sermon (*ḥuṭba*) precedes the prayer. Supported by a staff, the preacher stands on the pulpit (*minbar*), usually to be found to the right of the *mihrab*, the prayer niche that faces Mecca. Minbars have been used only from the time of the Omayyad Dynasty, and exclusively in the mosque. Originally movable, today they are more often a stable component of the mosque. The sermon consists of two parts, between which the Hatib sits. The first part is rigidly formulaic, and includes praise of God and of the Prophet, as well as, traditionally, prayers for the faithful and their ruler. Together with the right of coinage, the mention of the ruler in the sermon was a traditional sign of the claim to sovereignty. The second part of the sermon gives the preacher room for his own thoughts. Although not originally of a didactic character, the genre of the sermon today is used in many places as an instrument for religious politics, for example by television preachers, who take a position on current problems. Traditionally, the sermon is preached in High Arabic rhyming prose, although, especially in Turkey, and at times in the diaspora, it is delivered in the national language. (Agnes Imhof)

It was to the lecture presentation that orthodox Lutheranism gave preference. That presentation was made repeatedly on Sundays, and it lasted, as a rule, up to an hour. With the Pietist sermon, on the other hand, it was a matter of awakening a practice of reverence that would embrace the hearer's entire life. But the pulpit was also a 'cathedra of the Enlightenment' (L. von Mosheim, J. J. Spalding, J. G. Herder). Court preachers worked under the regime of the determination of religious adherence according to the will of the respective regional sovereign. Abraham a Sancta Clara, in Vienna, stands at the highpoint of Catholic Baroque preaching. L. Bourdaloue, Court Preacher, along with J.-B. Bossuet, for Louis XIV, is said by Voltaire to have been celebrated as the "first to have permitted an ever eloquent (sense of) reason to speak," and Goethe has sung the praises of the "good and pure style of religion, and the moral doctrine so nearly akin to it," of H.-G. Zöllikofer, at work in Leipzig, as well as that of others. As pioneer of a sermon in the spiritual key of the modern age, we may cite its theoretical establishment by Friedrich Schleiermacher. This concept, foundational for the liberal → Protestantism of the nineteenth century, was contradicted, at the

In abrupt and provocative fashion, the Reformed Christians shape their identity through a distinction from the 'old believers' in their rituals and symbols. While Catholic divine service speaks to the eyes with the colors of the priestly vestments and the sweetness of grace-bestowing images, to the palate with the carefully prepared host and, occasionally, the taste of the wine, to the nose with incense, to the ears with a liturgy in song—the extremely jejune Reformed houses of prayer concentrate on 'the word' of God, in the intellectual language of the well-studied Pastor. Only Bible and lamp are on the smooth table, amidst bare walls. The baldachin over the pulpit functions as a sounding board, directing the minister's words to the congregation. The gold decoration actually looks a little Catholic, the empty cross has been added later. The laity are to listen from hard pews, and enter into themselves. In common song, however, the unison of their Confession of Faith, their articulation of the Our Father, and their enunciation of the words of the Bible, their means of community are evident. (Christoph Auffarth)

dawn of the twentieth, by dialectical theology, with its call to the 'essential sermon.' The latter style, with its pure exposition of Scripture, was regarded as adequately avoiding such 'figurative' subjects as 'people and fatherland,' which prevailed, for example, in the 'war sermon.'

3. In the culture of the mass media, today's sermon has met with many competitors. Replaceable functions, required in earlier times, include especially information, education and formation, and a ritualized interruption in everyday life. As shown by the television sermons of the TV church (→ Televangelism), the awakening sermon in → charismatic movements, or other forms of religious communication in the mass media, the pulpit is no longer the sermon's only place. As religious locution based on an ecclesial duty, the sermon today, even the laudatory one on special biographical occasions, must meet the requisites of a complex goal. An indispensable premise for doing justice to those requirements, a premise that is on an equal footing with that of a solid theological formation, is the perception of a differentiated society, and of the thrusts to modernization that alter that society.

Literature

A New History of the Sermon, 3 vols., Leiden 1998–2002 (vol. 1: CORRAN, M. C./ALLEN, P. [eds.], Preacher and His Audience: Studies in Early Christian and Byzantine Homiletics; vol. 2: MUESSIG, C. [ed.], Preacher, Sermon and Audience in the Middle Ages; vol. 3: TAYLOR, L. [ed.], Preachers and People in the Reformation and Early Modern Period); MÜLLER, H. M., Homiletik. Eine evangelische Predigtlehre, Berlin 1996; NIEBERGALL, A., "Die Geschichte der christlichen Predigt," in: Leiturgia 2 (1955), 181-354; SCHNEYER, J. B., Geschichte der katholischen Predigt, Freiburg 1969.

→ *Charismatic Movement, Communication, Language, Mission, Oral Tradition, Televangelism, Theology*

Hans Martin Dober

Sexuality

An Approximation: Sexuality in Myth

1. The relationships between sexuality and religion appear on many levels, and are reciprocal. On the one side, religions have a powerful effect on the meaning of sexuality and gender roles in a society (→ Gender Stereotypes), and on the other, sexuality is a key theme in religious systems of interpretation. Especially, the myths of the various religions illustrate the complex meaning of sexuality as a frontier between 'nature' and 'culture,' and their close connection with border regions of human experience, such as the appearance of life and creativity, the transient, and death, but also areas such as power and governance, dependency and love. A creation myth from Japan can illustrate these complex associations.

The mythological first couple, Izanagi and his sister and bride Izanami, carry out a commission attached to their duty to mold the earth by inventing a wedding ritual and the first sexual act. A 'leech child' results from this act however, who is consigned to death in the sea. According to an oracle of the gods, Izanami is responsible for this failure, since it is she who first spoke at the ritual. A second attempt—now the husband is the first to speak—results in the birth of the shimmering world of the Japanese isles, and the emergence of other gods. At the birth of the God of Fire, Izanami dies, and from the excrement, vomit, and tears of her husband, new deities emerge. An encounter with the underworld follows, with death and corruption, and a series of sexual encounters, which, in their true identity as struggles for power over divine and human governance, actually lead to the emergence of culture, and to the first race of Emperors.

Levels of the Relation between Sexuality and Religion

Sexuality as Concept and as Pattern of Explanation

2. a) Sexuality is not a 'phenomenon on its own,' or 'object in itself.' Rather, its meaning and importance emerge only in the co-efficiency of physiological 'conditioning,' individual experience and practice, societal institutions, and cultural and religious conceptualizations. Even the concept of *sexuality*, and its current meaning, first appeared only in the Western culture of the nineteenth century. Religions are concerned in this process somewhat as models of interpretation and bestowal of meaning, as they apply sexuality as a pattern of explanation. At the same time, of course, they integrate the meaning of sexuality into these models. Thus, many myths describe the emergence of the world in sexual metaphors, or as sexual relations among

gods (→ Cosmology/Cosmogony). 'Duality,' and the destruction of a 'para-disiacal oneness,' is often explained by a sexual transgression on the part of the human being (→ Dualism).

b) By way of exemplars ('idealization'), or dreadful presentations ('demoni-zation'), religion possesses a great deal of influence on imaginary images of gender and role-orderings. Insofar, for example, as abstract dualisms such as → 'body' and 'spirit' are transferred to real men and women, or certain behaviors are attributed to them as essential features, pictures of gender roles, gender relations, and gender differences firmly inscribe themselves, and become elements of stereotyped world-images. Often it is mythical fe-male images, such as Pandora (→ Prometheus) or Eve, who bring death and unhappiness into the world. Such images—such as that of Izanami, in the case above cited—often become bases for attempted religious justifications of woman's subordinate position in society, and thereby deeply affect the construction of rule, government, and social differences.

The Category 'Gender' between Myth and Science

In European culture, one of the agents of the undermining of the concept of a 'God-willed' or 'natural' polarity of the sexes was the new sexual science arising about 1900 (Richard Kraff-Ebing, *Psychopathia sexualis*, 1886; Mag-nus Hirschfeld's battle against the criminalization of homosexual practice). It began to distinguish biological gender from individual gender-identity. Then came the feminism of the 1970s, and today many research disciplines include the category of gender in their thinking. Since the 1980s, a distinc-tion has been invoked between (biological) sex and (social) gender. As the relation between sex and gender becomes defined, it is becoming the object of discussion, and is variously adjudged (Butler 1990; Irigaray 1993).

c) Sexuality can be an element of the molding of → cults, and key for the distinction between the 'sacred' and the 'profane.' Through a ritualiza-tion of the sexual, norms are observed in society, and rendered subject to control, whether sexual acts are 'sanctified' ('Holy Matrimony,' Gk. *hieros gamos*, ritual sexual intercourse, sacred → prostitution), and sex symbols are venerated (e.g., *yoni/linga* cult in Hinduism, veneration of symbolical sexual parts), or, just the other way around, sexuality is excluded from cultic acts (e.g. prescription of virginity or celibacy for religious specialists such as priestesses and priests). In the orgiastic experience of 'enjoying life to the full' at Carnival, and in a religious festival culture, sexuality, and other drives potentially dangerous for society (aggression, lust; → Emotions/Feel-ings), receive, as it were, a legitimate place.

Cultic rules, sanctions, and taboos are closely connected with the idea of → body and sexuality, conveyed as the former are by conceptualizations of → purity. Who may take part in a given function, and who may not, as well as who is invested with capacity and competency for cult, is often depen-dent on bodily condition or gender. Taboos are often related to body fluids (blood, semen), and to bodily indications of sexuality such as pregnancy, → birth, menstruation, or defilement by semen; in certain cases they may occasion (temporary) exclusion from cult or from gender-specific rituals.

The extent to which competency for cult becomes dependent on gen-der, depends on the gender roles that have validity at a given moment. Cult can be the place for crossing the boundaries of the gender role (shamanic transvestitism; → Gender Stereotypes). Men and women alike may be the principal characters in cultic celebration (e.g. priestesses, prophetesses, healers), take on certain tasks, or can be regarded as the only person capable

Founded in 1991, the large Christian organization 'Promise Keepers' has won hundreds of thousands of members in the United States. With their motto, "I can do all things in Him who strengthens me" (Phil 4:13), the 'task to change the world' challenges men to take over the leadership role in family and society, and as "followers of hero Jesus Christ" to battle against the collapse of modern society. Among their basic premises are: "spiritual, moral, and sexual integrity," "dedication to marriage and family," "obedience to the commandment of love, and the missionary commandment." In their emotion-laden ideal of friendship, and their display of maleness in the style of Hell's Angels (which helps to differentiate them from homoerotic elements) the historical tradition of the Crusades and the 'Holy Warriors' marches on.

of taking the leading role in a cult. Gender-specific presidencies in religious cult—one thinks of the office of bishop or pope in the Catholic Church—by way of esteem, public authority, and monopoly of interpretation, have a powerful effect on the hierarchization of genders.

d) Religions exert direct influence on the social role of sexuality by way of concrete directives, injunctions, and prohibitions. Especially religions that have developed a religious juridical system, as has → Islam, offer clear guidelines regarding permitted and forbidden relations, marriage, divorce, and family law, legitimate and illegitimate offspring, hygiene, the relation between the sexes, initiation and frequency of sexual intercourse, pregnancy and birth, and sexual behavior in various respective stages of the life-cycle. Initiation and puberty rites, such as the Jewish Bar Mitsva, mark sexual and religious maturity alike (→ Initiation; Puberty). Such determinations are far-reaching in the political and economic molding of a society, if, for example, property rights are connected with matrimonial law, or if women may not move in the public arena. Religions, too, that possess no express regulatory structure for daily life (e.g., many forms of Christianity), avail themselves of ethical and moral conceptions in order to exercise direct influence on the practice or sexuality, for example, by their position on birth-control (→ Abortion/Contraception), or their denunciation of homosexual practice (→ Homosexuality/Homoeroticism). Seeing that religion scarcely seems to exert an influence on sexual norms today, the 'secular' meaning of the sexual often takes its orientation (confirming or rejecting such norms) in religious traditions.

The religious interpretation of sexuality, however, is not limited to the production of social order. Its border-crossing and anarchic potential as well, the eradication of civilizing controls over the drives of the human being, plays a great role. Sexuality forms, as it were, a boundary line between 'consciousness' and 'the unconscious,' between 'sensuality' and 'supra-sensuality,' closely connected with the 'mystery of life,' with birth and creativity, death and aggression. It is not without basis that sexuality and 'potency' form a projection screen for (fantasized) power and violence—as well as for yearnings for salvation, happiness, and redemption—directed toward a state that stands beyond rational visualization. Hence its meaning in religion is closely connected with border-crossing conceptualizations of an existence after death, of a → hereafter and → transcendence, but also with the transitory and → nature. Thus, for example, Western religious culture, which has referred to the corporeal as 'devil' (Ger., the *Leibhaftige*) can be interpreted as a defense mechanism against the uncontrollable, destructive aspects of nature—in a revolt against human mortality (Paglia 1990).

In particular, the sex act and orgasm, as human boundary-experiences ('little deaths'), have been variously regarded in the religions. As a component of fertility cults, coitus represents, in many ways, veneration of nature in its cyclical return (→ Regeneration/Fertility). In some religions, the sexual act is regarded as an opportunity for spiritual experience, that can climax in the dissolution of the individual consciousness and an 'experience of cosmic oneness' (→ Tantra). Sexual unification as a metaphor for the conquest of duality, as *coincidentia oppositorum* (Lat., 'falling together' or 'coinciding of opposites'), is a very widespread religious motif. Even the Christian mystics of the Middle Ages applied the sexual language of 'union,' of 'fusion' and 'merging,' in order to describe the ecstatic deletion of the boundaries between the human being and God in the *unio mystica*.

On the other hand, the defeat or 'transcending' of sexuality is said to offer assistance on a salvific journey. It occurs in many religions as a notion of → asceticism. In Hinduism, for instance, no moral boundary is drawn between sexuality and spirituality. Instead, both areas are connected, in terms of an 'energy model': sexual self-denial represents an opportunity to amass *tapas* (Hindi, 'fire')—to transform sexual energy into spiritual. It would be interesting to know to what extent these religious interpretations of sexuality as an idealization affect the concrete practice of believers.

3. For religious studies, from the perspectives just sketched—the developing gender-interpretation of the discipline—emerges a cluster of new lines of questioning. What role does religion play in the formation of female and male identity, which stereotypes and expectations does it propose, and how does it legitimate them? How is the relation between the genders determined by religion? What opportunities are afforded men and women to participate in religion? What are the consequences of the conception of gender differences and sexuality for the human image, and for the social function of a religion? A critical consideration of the following material would be in order.

Sexuality in Terms of Questions Posed in Religious Studies

- Pronouncements by the religions *on* sexuality are not identical with the everyday practice of believers. Indeed, laws and prohibitions can even reinforce, or bring about, contradictory forms of sexual life. Thus, pornography flourishes precisely in the presence of a repressive morality. The object of investigation, therefore, ought to be, for one thing, the everyday religious consideration of theological norms and religious laws. For example, the object should include the interiorization and mythologization of a religious interpretation of sexuality in the early Modern Age, as persons were accused of sexual contact with the devil, or as impotence was ascribed to witchcraft (→ Witch/Persecution of Witches). On the other hand, and the other way around, the religious discourse on sexuality can be understood as a copy and thematization of human conceptualizations, and become useful for research into gender.

- The authors of religious sources have usually been males, of determinate functions and determinate interests, so that religious sources have neglected the reality of broad parts of society. Although the meager religious history of relations between the sexes, and of women, contains shocking data, the pattern of 'repression' as a one-sided perspective displaces a view of the active role of women in the emergence of the religious interpretation of sexuality. Furthermore, a theory of sexual repression must always submit to an investigation of the counter-concept of 'sexual freedom', which is just as culturally determined, and does not occur 'naturally'.

- It is precisely pronouncements on sexuality that are so frequently a part of the positive presentation of one's own religion, and the disparagement of that of others (→ Polemics). Thus, these pronouncements are not to be appraised as a description of reality. Neither theological nor scientific literature can be separated from a respective contemporary production of fantasies. This production will be specific to each society, and easily lets its own ideas of value and wish in the area of sexuality become the criterion not only of a perception of other religions, but also of their appraisal or condemnation. Answers to the question, how 'modern' or 'backward' Islam is, often refer, expressly or implicitly, to sexuality, not to mention being determined by the gender of the persons providing the answers to the questions. It was once the same with the outlook of Christian missionaries, or European literati, regarding the cults of a 'nature people'. Observers were shocked by → nudity, and by seemingly indecent fertility rites. Their sexual standards were why they so frequently adjudged these peoples' attitudes as either 'unholy' or 'paradisiacal'.

Feminist Criticism

4. a) The relationship between religion and sexuality in Western culture has become an object of self-criticism. Especially in recent, and feminist, theology, the 'Judeo-Christian tradition' is frequently made responsible for the expulsion of the feminine from religion, and for the hostility of Western culture to the body and the senses. This way of seeing things is problematic. First, it relates to conceptualizations of a feminine presence in the religions that are difficult to demonstrate and interpret (→ Matriarchy/Patriarchy), and that are not infrequently connected with the religious idea of a 'Golden Age'. What is certain is that there have been powerful female figures, and differently structured relations between the genders, in mythical notions and religious functions. Their operation on social relationships, however, is difficult to appraise. Second, the thesis in question ignores the fact that it has been from non-Jewish traditions of thought that biblical authors have adopted feminine/masculine polarizations between body and soul (Plato), matter and form (Aristotle), and (in a Manichean and 'gnostic' dualism) 'sinful flesh' and 'divine spirit'. Third, it is precisely with reference to sensuality, corporality, and sexuality, that the differences between Jewish and Christian doctrine are passed over. Conceptualizations of salvation in Judaism are in no way connected with a disparagement of the sexual; nor has the distinction of body and soul there the same motif as it has in Christianity. Indeed an enjoyable sexuality in marriage is of particularly high value, as it guarantees the preservation of the people of Israel (→ Kabbalah). What

connects Judaism and Christianity—and Islam as well—is, of course, the conception of one God (→ Monotheism), without a 'sexual biography,' such as have, for instance, the Indian or Greek gods. In both Judaism and in Islam there stands an androcentric morality, rigidly ordered by religious laws, along with a positive appraisal of the sexual, all of which is evident from the Jewish rejection of celibacy, or the glorification of male sexual fantasies in Islamic notions of Paradise. Ancient Christianity, especially through Paul and → Augustine, developed, in its doctrine, an essential devaluation of the sexual. The Fall is first and foremost a sexual transgression, that has been transferred to the whole of humanity. The original sexual lapse (→ Sin), and the idea of a defeat of the body (resurrection), bind 'the material,' along with its representatives, 'sexuality,' and 'woman,' to prevailing and conquering 'evil.' Thus, sexuality receives a theologically justifying place in soteriology, as an obstacle, and the sexual transgression becomes heresy. Just the contrary, in Greek and Roman antiquity, sexual morality had taken its orientation in the consequences of sexuality for a society apportioned by masculinity and militarism. It was not so much religious restrictions on enjoyable sexual relations, but a social 'code of honor,' that prevailed. Thus, it was the free middle-class male who had the active role to play where the act of sexuality was concerned, whether with free women, slaves, or men, and the gender of his partner was—at least for the moment—of secondary consideration. Asceticism and celibacy, in Christian contexts, are to be traced to the radical division of sexuality from the godly, and, comparably with gnostic groups and today's 'eschatological sects,' to be seen in connection with an imminent expectation of the End. Apart from the ascetical ideal, the exercise of sexuality was permitted, but only for purposes of procreation without sensation of pleasure, or of a necessary satisfaction of the sex drive, in marriage alone. Under this premise, special religio-sexual phenomena developed: a hostility to the body that stamped the mentality, the highly erotic presentation of an experience of God in medieval mysticism, with its spiritualization of a craving for → love, and a superabundance of sadistic sexual violence motivated by religion in the early modern persecution of witches.

b) In the Modern Age, the relation between religion and sexuality—along with inter-religious battles—was determined by the project of the → Enlightenment. The human being's self-concept as an individual was to be grounded, and—partially with a reference to Greco-Roman antiquity—a humanistic ethics was to be sketched out. First, Luther's concession of clerical marriage and sexuality was an element of the confessional rift. The Enlightenment requirement of personal responsibility and autonomy, two of whose preludes were the interiorization of piety and the ethic of Protestantism, was more fundamental, however: it changed existing morality. The development that led to the modern age was a movement of innovations and their counter-movements (Counter-Reformation, Counter-Enlightenment), even in the area of sexual morality and practice. One of the last attested witch-murders (1782) was practically contemporaneous with the high point of the Enlightenment—the declaration on human rights during the French → Revolution (1789). Sexuality and sexual morality became a component of the radical Enlightenment → criticism of religion. The Marquis de Sade, for example, conveyed his sharp criticism of the Christian categories of good and evil by way of sexual provocation. Rousseau's powerful picture of the human being, and of an ideal education and upbringing, again, idealized a 'natural'

Modernity: The Project of the Enlightenment

morality ultimately based on Christian norms, and indicated problematic areas of sexuality of 'culture,' an argumentation repeated as a pattern of religious cultural criticism down to the present.

For daily life in the eighteenth and nineteenth centuries, there was no progressive movement of 'sexual freedom.' The morality of the strengthening middle class, not least of all on account of church influence on pedagogy and legislation, was extremely 'normed' and narrow in the area of the sexual, and was tied to socioeconomic conditions of rising → capitalism. Counter-sketches of workers' and women's rights, as well, usually took a conservative stance in the area of sexual morality. An ambivalent role for the modern understanding of sexuality is played by the sciences. For one, they replace the Church in its function of authority, and produce 'dogmas' themselves: theological argumentations turn into scientific ones, moral verdicts are replaced by the concept of disease, as in the case of homosexuality or onanism. For another, the → theory of evolution, and critical sexual science, fundamentally challenge theology and sexual politics. Especially Sigmund Freud's psychoanalytical theory of drive and religion remains today, often against critical resistance, the focal point for the confrontation over religion and sexuality. Freud takes the 'libido' as a key human 'driving' power (even for the emergence of religion!), and coins the concepts of 'compensation,' 'sublimation,' and 'repression.' Thus he transfers human sexuality from the moral area to that of a value-free unconscious, open to analysis.

Sexuality Today

5. In the late 1960s and the 1970s, there appeared the 'sexual revolution,' which developed into a drastic social phenomenon. With the development of the contraceptive pill, a sexuality emphasizing lust and enjoyment, and severed from procreation, became the medium of anarchic social and political criticism, and central for the new myth of the person who now had been delivered from taboos and was engaged in self-development. The feminist → women's movement used the growing sexual knowledge of quantitative sexual research (Kinsey Reports, 1948 and 1953) in a radical critique of the erstwhile 'privately' handled sexual relationship of marriage and family, and insisted on its political meaning. As for the quest for a female identity not defined by structures of male dominance, most Western states saw the beginning of a revision of prevailing, extensively Christian-oriented norms, and this was reflected in an alteration of the law (right to divorce, position of female labor, immunity of homosexual acts from punishment). Through these alterations, Christian churches came under a growing pressure to revise their sexual norms in the direction of a 'modern' understanding. The Catholic Church in particular was fundamentally challenged by a waning acceptance of clerical celibacy, and a demand that women be accepted into the priesthood. A religiosity that was traditionally Christian was in crisis, and many persons sought alternative models in pre- or extra-Christian religions, in order to incorporate sexuality and corporality in a way that seemed positive (→ Esalen Institute; New Age; Paganism/Neopaganism). From the women's movement, there emerged—in part, neo-mythical—religious interpretations of a 'new femaleness,' and sketches of a 'feminist spirituality.' In new religious movements (→ New Religions), as well, sexuality plays an important role as a moment of attraction. Apart from organized religion, the relationship between religion and sexuality in the literature and music of the pop-culture (beat generation, flower-power movement, pop icon Madonna) grew into a key theme. It remains to be explored to what extent, through these develop-

ments, needs and expectations formerly directed to religion have today been transferred to sexuality.

Judgment upon the consequences of the sexual revolution has become an object of controversy. First, it is alleged that liberation from religious morality has been exhausted in the mere commercialization and medial presence of sexuality. The 'demystification' of sexuality is seen in opposition to the— even religiously coded—'allurement of the forbidden and concealed.' The spread of the HIV virus since the 1980s has stirred a counter-movement, which goes as far as to embrace conservative values (marriage, fidelity), and finds itself provided with new, fertile soil, so that even the new religious movements are revising their perception of 'free sexuality.' Thus, the Neo-Sannyas movement, on the occasion of the spread of AIDS, is radically altering its practice and interpretation of sexuality (→ Osho Movement). Again, increasing knowledge and acceptance of 'sexual variance' (homo-, bi-, trans-sexuality, S/M practices) has led to a 'neo-sexual revolution,' in which the meaning of sexuality, gender identity, and gender roles is open as never before. The tension among individual needs, traditional morality, religious orientation, the ideal of a positive, problem-free sexuality, and of independence from procreation and 'natural' ascriptions of role, has been problematized. The question of the meaning of sexuality, the relation of sex and mind or spirit, and bodiliness and sexuality is posed anew in our era.

Literature

Ariès, Ph. et al. (eds.), Western Sexuality: Practice and Precept in Past and Present Times, Oxford 1985 (French ¹1982); Biale, D., Eros and the Jews: From Biblical Israel to Contemporary America, New York 1992; Butler, J., Gender Trouble: Feminism and the Subversion of Identity, London/New York 1990; Foucault, M., The History of Sexuality, 3 vols., New York 1978–1986 (French ¹1976–1984); Garber, M., Vested Interests: Cross-Dressing and Cultural Anxiety, New York 1991; Giddens, A., the Transformation of Intimacy: Sexuality, Love and Eroticism in Modern Societies, Cambridge 1992; Irigaray, L., An Ethics of Sexual Difference, Ithaca 1993 (French ¹1984); Keuls, E., The Reign of the Phallus: Sexual Politics in Ancient Athens, Berkeley ²1993 (¹1985); King, U. (ed.), Religion and Gender, Oxford 1995; Pagels, E., Adam, Eve and the Serpent, London 1990; Paglia, C., Sexual Personae, London 1990; Parrinder, G., Sex in the World's Religions, London 1980; Idem, Sexual Morality in the World's Religions, Oxford 1995; Sigusch, V., "Lean Sexuality: On Cultural Transformations of Sexuality and Gender in Recent Decades," in: Sexuality & Culture 5 (2001), 23-56; Talvacchia, Bette, Taking Positions: On the Erotic in Renaissance Culture, Princeton 1999; Westheimer, R./Mark, J., Heavenly Sex: Sexuality in the Jewish Tradition, New York 1995.

For further literature see → Eroticism, → Gender Stereotypes, and → Love.

→ *Asceticism, Body, Celibacy, Communication, Criticism of Religion, Enthusiasm, Eroticism, Family/Kinship/Genealogy, Gender Stereotypes, Homosexuality/Homoeroticism, Initiation, Life Cycle, Love, Matriarchy/Patriarchy, Nudity, Puberty, Purity, Sin, Utopia*

Alexandra Grieser

Shamanism

1. Shamanism, originally and exclusively a theme for anthropologists, religious scholars, medical professionals, colonizers, and Christian missionaries,

On the day immediately preceding, or following, the night of the year's first full moon, in villages and city quarters of the island of Cheju (Republic of Korea)—at the point in time, then, traditionally celebrated as the beginning of spring—a shaman performs extended rituals such as those here illustrated. They are performed to the honor

has won more and more attention in Western industrial societies since the 1960s. Here it plays quite an important role in the quest for spirituality, in efforts to preserve the environment ('nature-based spirituality'; → Environmentalism), in projects for fortifying women's rights, and even in alternative medicine. Neither scientific nor political in its basic nature, shamanism nevertheless persists as an object of interest, including the more popular interest. Shamanism tenaciously captures perceptions and attitudes that surfaced in the older discussions, but that must now be considered deficient. New views and concepts have come in, as well, although they are often illusionary. Behind the multiplicity of interests, expectations, and attitudes that meanwhile play a role in discussions, there are facts that threaten to fade from view, thus blurring the limits of shamanism.

Older Types of Perceptions and Evaluations of Shamanism

2. The answer to the question of the nature of shamanism and the answer to the question of its geographic extent are mutually conditioned. Any definition of shamanism broadens or limits the number and size of the areas that come under examination in an investigation of 'shamanism.' Conversely, extensions or limitations of the space that one must bring into consideration, also lead directly to extensions or limitations of the concept of shamanism.

As a particular religious practice, shamanism was first observed and described in the seventeenth century, in communities of Northern Eurasia, especially Siberia (→ Northern Eurasia/Circumpolar Region). The term 'shamanism' derives from a designation first used among the Tungus, and applied to those who officiate in this religious practice; but the term itself

is probably not a Tungus word. The designation then found entry into Europe's intellectual world, and into its languages, through Russian and German. Like the term, the concept of shamanism was also first determined in relation to Siberian and Tungus contexts.

Then, over the course of time, religious practices and conceptualizations that had been met outside North Eurasian culture came to be designated by the term. In the meanwhile, there is scarcely any longer a part of the world lacking religious practices some would classify as shamanic. The extension of the perception and concept of shamanism has had two kinds of results. First, shamanism began to be seen as endowed with at least the potential of a worldwide, and therefore universally human, if not indeed primeval, religious manifestation. Secondly, in attempts to specify the nature of shamanism, external conditions were gradually renounced as the touchstone by which shamanism could be recognized. Thus, for example, specific ritual practices, or a shaman's attire, were less utilized for this purpose, and more and more attention was paid to → ecstasy and → trance, usually designated 'extraordinary states of consciousness,' or the like. Not only ecstasy and trance were gathered under these sorts of terms, but some researchers and authors even subsumed possession under them.

This development of the concept of shamanism occurred first in the academic disciplines concerned with shamanism. The older, evolutionistic religious history saw primarily an 'earliest beginning' in shamanism, but a phenomenon whose remnants had survived into the modern age. This view may have been based on the circumstance that religious scholars of a

of the local patronal deities, anthropomorphic beings one or two of whom guide and guard every locality. Marking the temporary presence of such deities among the people, these rituals afford the latter the opportunity of celebrating amusing and entertaining presentations that will ensure the benevolence of the deities for the year about to begin. The photographs show the climax of the annual ritual of the patron deities of Wahul. Amidst great excitement, and attention, Shaman Kang Chonggyu—seventy-seven years of age at the time the pictures were taken, on May 5, 1993—honors the deity before whom stands such a copious table of welcome.

former time had been concerned to work on the basis of written sources. But as shamanism is a cultic practice extensively performed in the absence of written associations, it was easy to assume, under the conditions just named, that it was an a-historical religion that had always existed. This assumption, in turn, readily led to the view, particularly outside of academic circles, that, unlike the writing religions, shamanism opened an access to elementary religious experiences. In this connection, then, it typically occurs that the designation of 'shamanism' is often applied to those religious conceptualizations and practices whose historical origins, in the absence of written sources, were lost in a 'dark prehistory.' The designation of 'shamanism' therefore also finds application to what would be more appositely designated 'local religion.' Hence, adopted without the benefit of much scientific reflection, Korean shamanism, for instance, can be ascribed the rank of a national religion in the Republic of Korea.

3. a) In this delineation, which many see as succeeding in its intent to do justice to shamanism as the all but worldwide phenomenon that it is, the following elements could apply. At the midpoint of shamanism stand *healing*, → *prophecy*, and the *escort of the dead*. The attainment of any of these rests on the notion that the world of human beings is circled by spirits (including, potentially, the dead), among which the maleficent must be barred from the human world, and the good must be invoked for assistance. Shamans are marked vis-à-vis other persons by the fact that they are able to control and overpower the spirits. The activity of a shaman, then, presupposes that shamans are open to the world of the spirits. They must undertake soul-journeys regarded as onerous, or even dangerous, into a beyond ('ecstasy'), or, as it were, allow spirits to enter them ('possession'). They demonstrate their suitability for shamanism by first subduing some life-crisis of their own, marked by sickness or physical disturbances. But only those persons are accounted shamans, who, having endured some life crisis of this kind ('shaman's sickness'), are acknowledged as such by their social environment. To this acknowledgment attaches the expectation that they will exercise their capacities for the good of their milieu. Shamans wear special apparel during their activity, and make use of particular musical instruments, especially drums and bells.

b) It is not possible, out of the complex of characteristics above described, to emphasize a few traits, or even some single earmark, and declare it the basic or indispensable one, without placing the range and span of the concept at risk, or without a blurring of the boundaries between shamanism and other religious practices. One or the other occurs when ecstasy, and only this 'extraordinary state of consciousness,' is specified as the indispensable element of shamanism. By taking this step, the observer excludes, on the one hand, from the area of shamanism, practices that otherwise would surely be designated as shamanic, such as, for example, certain rituals of Korea. On the other hand, shamanism is shifted into an adjacency to practices—for example, Christian mysticism—that indeed know ecstasy, but that usually no one would designate as shamanic.

Instead, it would be possible, as well as meaningful, to exclude the above-described complex from attention to the extent that the only capacity that would remain as characteristic of shamanism would be that of reaching and surviving the extraordinary states of consciousness named above, but then of bringing out this ability as an individual disposition of the shaman, as J. A. MacCulloch has already done. Then the determinative element of the

Elements of Shamanism

concept of shamanism would be the ability 'contained' in the individual to assume contact with a reality grasped as the world of spirits, and likewise the obligation to exercise this ability. Thus, a person would not be a shaman who would take up healing or another shamanic activity only because or when he or she had learned them from someone else. Just so, a person would not be a shaman who practiced a 'shamanic activity' because shamanism was hereditary in her or his family—when, then, someone would attempt to act as a shaman without having undergone a personal crisis and come in touch with the world of the spirits.

An emphasis on the shaman's individual disposition would assist in the abandonment of a circumscription of shamanism, such as the one described above, which is unsatisfactory because it lacks some necessary intrinsic connection. For it is not reasonable to see the shamanic as depending on social acknowledgment of any shamanic abilities, nor is it apparent in what sense the latter would necessarily have anything to do with a particular dress. Emphasis on the individual disposition would also allow a whole series of identifying notes to be seen correctly as utterly insignificant—notes that, in earlier scholarship had often been introduced as shamanism's typical conditions, and that even today are still occasionally cited, although the view of shamanism as a worldwide phenomenon has long since rendered them obsolete: shamanism is an early stage in the religious development of humanity; shamanism as the 'arctic hysteria' resulting as a physiological consequence of a certain slender nutritional base, and of a lack of daylight; shamanism as the religion ordered to certain economic and social contours.

Above all, an appeal to the individual disposition to shamanism would endow a certain quality of shamanism with the rank that it doubtless deserves, but which, in many determinations of the concept, is cited only peripherally: the *intimacy* of the shamanic. This intimacy is evinced, for one thing, as an image element in ritual; shamans maintain, with a particular spirit, or with several particular spirits, a closer relationship than with others. As a rule, the nearer spirits are those that have 'stood by' a shaman during the 'shaman sickness,' or those that he has rendered docile during this crisis. Thus, they have become his helping spirits, or personal patrons. Intimacy is evinced, for another thing, in the social; shamans must have comprehensive, and at the same time precise, knowledge of the life conditions of every member of their clientele, in order to be able to be successful in their occupation. Hence, the clientele must always be relatively small.

Familiar Commerce with the Spirits

4. Inasmuch as shamanism is currently surrounded by a series of different views, of which many are apposite only in a limited way, a critical commentary on such views may contribute to an understanding of shamanism on a deeper level.

Current Views on Shamanism

a) Shamanism is an independent religious teaching, and from this point of view, on an equal level with other religious doctrines. Shamans definitely preserve conceptions of the *essence of the world*. In no shaman, however, have such conceptualizations been reduced to any kind of comprehensive, somewhat closed, image, as is the case with other religions. Additionally, shamanic notions are not spread worldwide—as the name 'shaman' itself is familiar worldwide—or binding to the extent that they are in other religions.

Instead, shamanic conceptualizations are frequently recognizable only as something standing in close connection with surrounding religions. As

Essence of the World

such, worldwide, it is first and foremost Christian confessions, along with forms of Buddhism, that are at issue. Further, certain conceptualizations are found in shamanism, which play a role in a multiplicity of religions, and not only in those that immediately surround the shamanism of one region or another.

Soul

The *concepts of the soul* in the shamanism of a large number of Siberian populations are unambiguously influenced by Christian notions of the → soul, which must be ascribed to the activity of Christian missionaries. This sort of concept intersects, again, with other traditions. For shamans, it is not only human beings who have souls, but → animals, plants, mountains, rocks, rivers, and, finally, everything that, in the context of Judeo-Christian piety, is regarded as being inanimate, as many of these things are even ascribed consciousness (→ Animism). This platform supports the thought, so important for shamanism, that all of these things can also be the temporary domicile of the soul of another person. Naturally, this animistic concept of the soul also has to do with the notion that human beings have no triumphal position vis-à-vis other beings and things.

Concerning the notion of a comprehensive animation, shamanism participates in traditions that reach far beyond individual religions. This ubiquity holds even for the shamanic ideas concerning the causes of disease. Diseases erupt either because maleficent spirits penetrate the body, or because the soul has left the body and wanders about, or because it has been abducted from the body.

Cosmology

Not simply to bring other religions in connection with shamanism, we must note that the latter comports an apparently widespread rudimentary → cosmology. Along with the human world, there is often another world, usually thought of lying spatially beneath it, that, among other things, is a stopping place for the souls of the dead (→ Death and Dying), and a world above, as home of the souls ready for their return to the human world. There are, besides, more or less clear ideas about places of the exit or entrance, and the ways in which those souls, including the shamans, find their passage between worlds (→ Orientation).

Sources

Our picture of shamanism is almost completely limited to a shamanism connected with other religious traditions, which is an outcome of the limitation of *sources*. The reason why shamanism is accessible to us exclusively in its relations to other religions is that 'pure' shamanism—surely conceivable—is not provided by any sources that would permit what is shown or said there to be interpreted unambiguously as shamanic. Neither, then, does discourse upon a shamanism submitted to these connections encourage us to attempt the reconstruction of an original one, so that we might deduce conceptualizations and practices that would apply only to shamanism. Inasmuch as relationships between shamanism and other, more widespread, traditions cannot be explained by migration, the assumption would in any case be plausible that shamanism shares an elementary, primitive religiosity (without thereby qualifying to be ranked as such a religion itself).

Broadening One's Awareness

b) Shamanism broadens our consciousness. This view is typically to be met and implemented in circles of industrial societies ('Neo-Shamanism').

An exclusive, or nearly exclusive, attachment to the notion of conscious-ness-broadening, of course, will likely occasion a bypass of the fact that shamans perform no individual 'consciousness raising' themselves: instead, one possibility is that they take their position in the course of the 'shamanic illness's' extraordinary states of awareness, without the persons of the cli-entele endeavoring to attain them. These persons, then, are not visited by extraordinary perceptions, and they experience this transitus as anything from a threat to a torture. The other possibility is that this manner of percep-tion is indeed the aim of shamans, by reason of their professional practice, and that shamans expose themselves to it (only) because it is necessary for the preservation of their shamanic abilities, and thus for winning their own sustenance. Shamans who follow a calling, and earnestly pursue their profes-sion, are not getting themselves on a 'trip.'

c) Shamanism is called a female thing—a regard that often comports the notion that there is, as it were, a natural connection between shamanism and femaleness, so that shamanism has come to enjoy a certain attention and sympathy in feminist circles. Indeed, it is actually the case in many societies—such as, for example, in those of Eastern Asia—that a shamanic clientele, as well as the overwhelming proportion of the shamans them-selves, have, in recent times, been of the female gender. Accordingly, female concerns also play an outstanding role in the rituals, and female shamans are then, so to speak, the natural allies of women in their everyday needs (→ Gender Stereotypes; Women's Movement/Spiritual Feminism). *Female Capacity*

In many societies, shamanic rituals, performed by women or men, occa-sionally express an affinity for the opposite sex. In critical points in a ritual, female shamans at times embody deified military leaders—the eminently male figure. The embodiment may serve as a demonstration that, in their true strength, women do not stand behind men, and bring to expression a 'counter image,' as it were, to the repression of women as found in daily life. Or, vice-versa, male shamans may behave as women, as they do merely in wearing women's apparel. For some authors, ritual sex change is the rem-nant of an ancient, matriarchal shamanism (→ Matriarchy/Patriarchy). *Sex Change*

The latter interpretation appears rather questionable, if we recall that we cannot really know anything about ancient shamanism, nor therefore, anything about a 'primordial matriarchal shamanism.' Only the general assumption may be reasonable that female shamanism itself is only, once more, a historical phenomenon. It might also be a valid conclusion that, in certain societies, at a certain point in time, a discrimination against women is introduced, and that this then goes hand in hand with a diminishment in the phenomenon of shamanism. At all events, one encounters female sha-manism only in societies in which both forms of diminishment (marginal-ization) are indeed at hand.

d) Shamans are characterized as *psychically unstable persons*, if not out and out mentally ill (→ Psychopathology). This feature is part of the intrinsic character of shamanism: shamans, before they become such, undergo a phase of psychic and even physical instability, the 'shaman's illness.' The acknowledgment of shamans as such depends precisely on the persons in question defeating their diseases and disturbances. Only persons, who are able to mobilize the patron spirits and, with their help, regain their health, are trusted, precisely in virtue of this, to become active for others. Psychic *Psychic Instability?*

instability is often accompanied by physical and intellectual debility. But activity as a shaman, which often can continue for days without interruption, calls for the opposite, namely, an extraordinarily high measure of physical and psychic endurance, with intellectual strength as well. Finally, a shaman must be in control of a repertory of ritual acts, songs, and formulae that may well be one of the most comprehensive and exacting demanded in any religion. The pretensions of the repertory lie not only in its sheer extent, but also in the demand that it be memorizable—not to mention the requirement of a constant, lightning-like adaptation to unforeseeable situations, and consequently, the ability to improvise a suitable choice of elements from such a great repertory. All told, over and above their capabilities as ritual celebrants, shamans are often, as well, teachers, counselors, and confidants, and this with good reason. As a result they are personalities held in high regard.

Material Advantage

e) Shamans are said to be interested only in their *material advantage*, so they exploit the gullibility of their fellow human beings. This is the 'argument' so often encountered in the declarations of politicians, administrators, and intellectuals, whose ambition, in their societies, is to foster 'the modern.' Shamans do, of course, have this in common with other professionals, that there are among them the less competent, who are therefore inclined to awaken unfounded hopes in their clientele, as also to avail themselves of dishonorable means.

Clientele

It is to be observed, however that shamans have but few opportunities to abandon their nearly always spare clientele and find another. A high measure of risk therefore attaches to shamanic activity, that its practitioners may lose the basis of their life support. Prudence, therefore, enjoins shamans to awaken in their clientele no expectations that they may not be able to satisfy in some measure. It would likewise be imprudent of them to exaggerate their material demands. Shamans generally stand in competition with other religions. In addition, it is difficult for them to calculate the amount of their income in advance, if only because opportunities to practice shamanism are only conditionally foreseeable in a given space of time.

Gathered into one, all of these circumstances entail the fact that only a few shamans can live exclusively on their shamanic activity. But they must be available, whenever an opportunity for shamanic activity presents itself; thus, it is almost never possible regularly to pursue another activity, by which they could save some of their income. Consequently, by and large, there exist no prosperous or, especially, wealthy shamans. An exception in this regard occurs when an altogether special opportunity presents itself (such as in contemporary Korea; → China/Japan/Korea): in the wake of an establishment of a 'national identity,' shamans may see their activity and status increase in value—or even, in special cases, have themselves placed on the market as media stars.

Literature

Diószegi, Vilmos/Hoppál, Mihály (eds.), Shamanism in Siberia, Budapest 1978; Eliade, Mircea, Shamanism: Archaic Techniques of Ecstasy, London 1964 (French original 1951); Flaherty, Gloria, Shamanism and the Eighteenth Century, Princeton 1992 (shamanism in European intellectual discourse); Francfort, Henri-Paul/Hamayon, Roberte N. (eds.), The Concept of Shamanism: Uses and Abuses, Budapest 2001 (on the applicability of 'traditional' shamanism to modern phenomena and Stone-age art); Hoppál, Mihály (ed.), Shamanism in Eurasia, 2 parts, Göttingen 1984; HOPPÁL, Mihály/HOWARD, Keith D. (eds.), Shamans and Cultures, Budapest/Los Angeles 1993; HUTTON, Ronald, Shamans: Siberian Spirituality and the Western Imagination, London/New York 2001 (critical assessment of research into shamanism); KENDALL, Laurel, Shamans, Housewives, and Other Restless Spirits: Women in Korean Ritual Life, Honolulu 1985 (report and analysis of 'female shamanism'); LINDQUIST, Galina, Shamanic Performances on the Urban Scene: Neo-Shamanism in Contemporary Sweden, Stockholm 1997 (on modern Western shamanism in 'New Age' contexts); MACCULLOCH, J. A.: "Shamanism," in: Encyclopedia of Religion and Ethics 1 (1920), repr. 1974, 441-446; NOEL, Daniel C.: The Soul of Shamanism: Western Fantasies, Imaginal Realities, New York 1997 (on Eliade's influence in particular); VON STUCKRAD, Kocku, Schamanismus und Esoterik. Kultur- und wissenschaftsgeschichtliche Betrachtungen, Leuven 2003 (neo-shamanism and Western intellectual history); ZNAMENSKI, Andrei A. (ed.), Shamanism (Critical Concepts in Sociology), 3 vols., London/New York 2004 (the most extensive anthology available today).

→ *Ancestors, Animism, Body, China/Japan/Korea, Ecstasy, Enthusiasm, Illness/Health, New Age, North America (Traditional Religions), Northern Eurasia/Circumpolar Region, Possession, Psyche, Psychopathology, Soul*

Dieter Eikemeier

Shintô

1. The word-sign *Shintô* (Jap., 'Way of the Divinities') consists of the signs for 'divinity/ies' (Sino-Jap., *shin*; Jap., *kami*) and 'way' (Sino-Jap., *tô/dô*; Chin., *tao/dao*; Jap., *michi*; → Daoism; Road/Path/Journey; Martial Arts), and designates the native religion of Japan, which, however, must not be regarded as a unitary religious system (→ China/Japan/Korea). Originally, only local cults existed, independent from one another. After the introduction of Buddhism in the sixth century, the designation Shintô was conceived as a counter-concept to *butsudô*, 'Way of the Buddha.' Shintô embraces religious practices and functions that are very different from one another, and which can be ordered in four large groups: (1) state Shintô (the Shintô of the Imperial House), (2) sect Shintô, (3) shrine Shintô, and (4) folk Shintô. Shintô has no founder, no official sacred scriptures, no monolithic instructional system, no established system of instruction, and no religious profession in the Christian sense of a confession of belief. At the center of religious practice stands the *kami* veneration. *Kami* stands for female and male divine beings, for ancestors, spirits (e.g., house, forest, and water spirits), forces of nature (force of life, fertility), and extraordinary nature phenomena (sun, moon, volcanoes, rock formations, aged trees). Belief in the animation (ensoulment) of nature is central to Shintô (→ Animism). Very diverse usages, festivals, and legends exist locally. By contact with continental traditions (cult of ancestors, Chinese mythology, → Daoism, → Buddhism), Shintô altered its shape and self-image.

2. Along with shamanic practices (→ Shamanism), which were performed by women in antiquity, the most ancient religious expressions of Japan took the form of local and tribal cults, whose historical basis was the clan (*uji*) system. At the focus of religious veneration stood the ancestor-divinity of the clan. The superior of the clan was at once the political leader and the high priest of the cult. In the fourth century, the Tennô clan attained supremacy,

Mythology

Schoolgirls rinse their hands and mouths at a stone basin in the entrance area of a Shintô shrine. → Purity and cleanliness are key concerns of Shintô. The basin is earmarked as sacred space by its enclosure with consecrated straw ropes (*shimenawa*), to which white strips of paper (*shide*), cut out in zigzag shapes, have been attached. *Shide* are symbolic sacrificial offerings. Straw ropes with white paper strips often adorn the shrine structure itself, as well as annexed cult and offering spaces, and sacred trees and stones in the temple area. In the background of the stone basin are large vessels for rice wine, bestowed by firms and private contributors, and set out in a roofed wooden structure. The script on the vessels declares the name

and its mythology of Sun Goddess Amaterasu Omikami gained in influence. The main notion of these myths is the divine descent of the Tennô clan. On this ideological basis, the oldest written documents of Japan appeared: *Kojiki* ("Record of Ancient Happenings," 712 CE) and *Nihongi* ("Annals of Japan," 720). Together with mythic texts, they contain prayers and ritual texts that are applied in ceremonies even today. The myths begin with reports of the emergence of the Japanese islands, and plot the cosmological image of a three-dimensional universe: high fields of the sky, world of phenomena, and tomblike underworld. The primal pair, Izanagi and Izanami, stand on the bridge of the sky, and dip a spear into the brine. Drops of water flow to form an island. In the midst thereof, the couple erect a pillar reaching to the sky. Here they conceive and bear all of the things of the world. The most important offspring are Sun Goddess Amateresu, Moon God Tsukiyomi, and Storm God Susanoo. They divide the power of the universe among themselves. At the birth of the God of Fire, Izanami dies, and becomes Goddess of the Dead, in the 'Realm of Darkness' (*yomi no kumi*). Amaterasu installs her great-grandson, Ninigi, as first Regent of Yamato (designating ancient Japan), and confers on him the insignia of the crown: mirror, sword, and 'bowed jewels.'

3. Ninigi's grandson is the first legendary emperor, Jimmu. The third regent, Suinin (first century), has a permanent shrine built for the Sun Goddess, in Ise (principal island of Honshu, Prefecture of Mie), which is still today the central Shintô sanctuary. From ancient Shintô to the Shintô of today, a long road lies, along which, by way of external influences, the shape and contour of this tradition have been powerfully transformed. Even imperial decrees of the seventh century emphasized the function of Shintô as

national cult. In state-organized Shintô, cultic acts were institutionalized, piety lost its spontaneity, and woman her significant position in the cultic action. Under the influence of the Chinese juridical system, the "Office for the Shrine System" arose, which controlled state ceremonies and local shrines. Buddhist influences brought about the emergence of syncretistic forms (e.g., *Ryôbu Shintô*, from the thirteenth to the fourteenth century), according to whose teaching the *kami* are local manifestations of buddhas and bodhisattvas.

4. a) The influence of Neo-Confucianism, and the revival of Shintô by the 'National School' (*Kokujako*), led to new developments in the eighteenth and nineteenth centuries. The National School called for an orientation to antiquity, and to its writings, in the context of a clear ideological political target: veneration of the Shintô deities, acknowledgment of the Tennô as descendant of the Sun Goddess, and thereby the political and religious leader of Japan. Since mid-nineteenth century, the Tenno institution had deliberately produced a mythic aura that characterized the Emperor as a godlike being. The leaders of the Meiji restoration wanted a centralized state, after the pattern of a 'family ideology.' The Emperor, as the father-figure of this state (according to the Constitution of 1889), who had been proclaimed divine, officially held the entire power of the state in his hands and strove for the legitimization of the claim to the absolute power of a thoroughly authoritarian system. State Shintô, defined as a supra- or civil-religious cult of state ethics and patriotism (→ Civil Religion), obliged the members of all religions to observe the cult of the Emperor. By its means, the Meiji government (1868–1912) sought to provide the sense of a national and cultural identity with dense roots. After the military defeat of 1945, and the bankruptcy of the authoritarian national military regime, the then Emperor Hirohito, under pressure on the part of the American occupation, publicly and formally renounced his claim to supreme power, as well as the godlike position of the imperial office. According to the Constitution of 1947, the Tennô today ranks only as a "symbol of Japan, and of the unity of the Japanese people." He is no longer actively involved in politics. His appearances in public are limited to representative functions. Only his sacred functions as superior of Shintô, and the rites celebrated for the veneration of the Imperial Ancestors, remain his direct responsibility. For years, national and international criticism has opposed the unconstitutional, solemn visit of the Japanese Minister President, as well as of high-ranking political leaders, to the Yasukuni Shrine in Tokyo, where the Japanese war victims are honored; in particular, because since 1978 the names of the seven war criminals executed after 1945 have been included on the shrine's sacred roster. Before the war, the Yasukuni Shrine was the focal point of Japan's nationalistic movement. In 1945, on the heels of the sharp separation of politics and religion, it surrendered its position as Sanctuary of the Japanese State, and was privatized. Since as early as the 1950s, however, Japanese with nationalistic inclinations have fought for the reinstatement of the shrine under state jurisdiction.

b) *Sect Shintô* emerged against the background of state Shintô. The designation served officially to divide state Shintô from the newly arisen messianic movements in popular religion, which frequently absorb elements of various religions or spiritual traditions, and are considered a consequence of the 'culture shock' that Japan underwent after opening to the West. Between

of the donor. Rice wine (*sake*), rice kernels and plants are the most important sacred offerings in Shintô. Sake is used in many religious ceremonies (e.g., at the marriage ritual) as an offering of food, and distributed, for sacred draughts, as a gift to the community or the priests.

According to the classic Shintô understanding, behind 'impurity' (*kegare*) or 'guilt' (*tsumi*) lurks a blemish of an external kind, in blood (e.g., at the birth of a child, in menstruation), disease, death, or cultic impurity incurred in disobedience to a commandment or in the violation of a taboo (incest, sodomy). Impurity provokes the gods' displeasure, and results in the ostracism or temporary exclusion of an individual from the social community. There is no moral concept of impurity, nor is there one of sin, whose cause will have to be sought in the inner recesses of each human being. Thus, guilt, or 'evil,' can be eliminated through purification ceremonies. A distinction is made between a rite of purification by washing with water (*omisogi*), and the rite of *ôharai*, in which the Shintô priest pronounces prayers and waves a sacred ceremonial staff, hung with strips of paper and cloth, over the believer, or object, in order to sweep away its blemish, and to bless the person or thing. In the illustration, this is being done by a Shintô priest in traditional attire on the occasion of the blessing of an automobile in the entrance area of a Shintô shrine. His purpose is to ban the new car from evil influences (spirits), to purify it, and to bless it. On the right, in a meditative posture, is the car's owner. Similar ceremonies of purification and blessing take place on various occasions: at the purchase of a piece of land or the building of a house, in agrarian contexts, with illnesses. Twice a year,

1882 and 1908, the government recognized thirteen Shintô sects (e.g., Shinrikyô, Tenrikyô), and their number constantly rose. They are forerunners of Japan's → 'new religions.'

c) At the focus of *shrine Shintô* stand both cultic acts at shrines of the gods, and faith content conveyed by the shrines' priesthood. The Shintô community takes part in traditional rites and festivals of the year and the life cycle, such as the New Year's Festival (*shôgatsu*), semi-annual rites of purification (*harai*), wedding ceremonies, and ceremonies of maturity and socialization.

d) *Popular Shintô*, finally, is a designation for the multiplicity of the forms of popular religion, local rites, practices, and tales outside of organized forms of Shintô, the art of the oracle, use of → amulets, agrarian rites of the rural population, beliefs in spirits and demons.

5. The deities of the Shintô myths produce the Japanese islands, natural powers, elements, and plants; however, they are not understood as pre-existent, almighty gods, or as creators in the Christian sense. They themselves have emerged from the heart of the world, and are seen as the powers through which life in the world is generated, and grows. Thus, their veneration often stands in the context of fertility ceremonies (→ Regeneration/Fertility). The Japanese *kami* exist and function in this world. For Shintôists, then, the quest for a transcendent world is obviated. The present world is affirmed, and human participation in the preservation and promotion of life corresponds to the will of the deities. The beyond is conceived as a dark, tomblike sphere, freighted with filth and corruption. Shintô has not developed clear concepts of the beyond, or a cult of the dead. Nor have doctrines of redemption, or basic concepts of an ethics, materialized. Buddhism filled this vacuum. The key concepts of → purity (*sei*) and guilt (*tsumi*), in Shintô, should not be interpreted against a background of ethical or moral conceptualizations. Impurity arises through contact with blood, death, or corruption, and can be eliminated by rites of purification (*harai, misogi*). There is no concept of guilt or sin in the moral sense. Acts are not good or evil in themselves: their appraisal depends on circumstances. Evil, then, is not to

be found within us, but rests on outside influences. It can be dissolved by means of ceremonies of purification.

6. The ancient Shintô of the agrarian societies knew no institutionalized forms. Cultic acts were performed in the forest, on the fields, or along the coast. The cultic space was a quadrangular, consecrated surface on the soil, with the branch of a sacred tree in the center (*himorogi*). It was separated from unconsecrated ground by a straw rope (*shimenawa*). Gradually, temporary structures were added, and finally, permanent buildings—lasting dwellings of the deities, to facilitate veneration. The cultic places of today betray conditions of the ancient agrarian society in an astonishing way. Even in postmodern Japan, cultic areas are separated from unconsecrated places by straw ropes. Attached to the sanctuary, with the symbol of the divinity (*shintai*), are a prayer hall, an area for sacrificial gifts, a stage for sacred dance (*kagura*), and various administrative buildings. In Shintô, there are no weekly ceremonies or cultic actions. Believers themselves decide the frequency and duration of their visits to shrines. Frequently, they turn to the deities with personal requests—for children, for passing an exam, for protection from illness.

Religious practice in the community is marked by participation in annual, traditional usages, in rites and festivals (*matsuri*), in the framework of a local shrine. As a rule, a *matsuri* consists of a ritual, and a part with free celebration. The cultic act proper, conducted by the priesthood, includes the invocation of the divinities, recitation of prayers (*norito*), presentation of sacrificial gifts (e.g., rice, *sake*, salt, dried seafood, sakaki branches), and consumption of the offerings. The collective component, which actively includes the community, frequently features a → procession, at which the *kami* are brought forth in portable shrines (*mikoshi*) by celebrants in historical array, with traditional presentations of theater and dance, contests, kiosks at which items of devotion (fortune lots, amulets) are sold, and common eating and drinking. All of this, of course, underscores the folk character of the festivals. In Japanese popular belief, the *kami* have a function similar to that of patron saints in Catholicism. They are venerated in cult, borne in processions, and appealed to for counsel and aid in daily needs. In traditional families, along with the Buddhist home altar, there is a Shintô home shrine or wall shelf for the veneration of ancestors (*kamidana*), with framed pictures of deceased family members.

7. One cannot become a Shintoist. In Japan, one is a Shintoist by birth. Most Japanese are at the same time Shintoists and Buddhists. Today the two religions exist side by side, in an amicable manner; they demand no exclusive confession, and complement one another. One is born as a Shintoist. As a rule, the rites of the → life cycle (e.g., birth, maturity, marriage) are Shintoist; funeral ceremonies, nevertheless, are Buddhist. In the West, some people speak of Japanese 'cafeteria religion' with annoyance. Behind the manner in which the Japanese deal with religious traditions, however, another understanding of religion is at work than prevails in Christianized Western culture. Religion is not first and foremost profession of faith. Religions and their practices are paths of living, paths of comprehension, but not truth in itself. The believer makes use of these paths, without absolutizing and without exclusion. The Eastern watchword is "This, and also that." And this approach may impart pragmatic inspiration.

at the end of the sixth and twelfth months, at many shrines, elaborate, collective purification ceremonies (*ôharai*) for the people are held.

Literature

Breen, John/Teeuwen, Mark (eds.), Shinto in History: Ways of the Kami, Richmond 2000; Creemers, Wilhelmus H., Shrine Shintô after World War II, Leiden 1968; Kato, Genichi, A Historical Study of the Religious Development of Shintô, Tokyo 1973; Littleton, C. Scott, Shinto: Origins, Rituals, Festivals, Spirits, Sacred Places, Oxford 2002; Nelson, John K., A Year in the Life of a Shintô Shrine, Seattle 1996; Idem, Enduring Identities: The Guise of Shinto in Contemporary Japan, Honolulu 2000; Nobutaka, Inoue (ed.), Shinto: A Short History, London 2003; Picken, Stuart D. B., Historical Dictionary of Shinto, Lanham 2002; Plutschow, Herbert, Matsuri: The Festivals of Japan, Richmond 1996; Schwade, Arcadio, Shintô-Bibliography in Western Languages, Leiden 1986.

→ *Agrarian Religion/Agrarian Magic, Ancestors, China/Japan/Korea, Hereafter, Kyôto, Local Devotion, Marriage/Divorce, Nativism, Shamanism, Soul, Theocracy, Zen Buddhism*

Sabine Beyreuther

Shoah

1. Ever since the 1940s, the Hebrew word *shoah* ('catastrophe'), which is of biblical origin (Isa 10:3), has designated the persecution and murder of some six million European Jews carried out by German National Socialism. Connected to the article *ha-* (*ha-shoah*), it has come to epitomize the catastrophe of Jewish history. The choice of the term 'Shoah' implies a distancing from the expression prevailing since the end of the 1970s, 'Holocaust'.[1] Nevertheless, 'Shoah' and 'Holocaust' are becoming once more synonymous, the former predominating in the Hebraic linguistic areas, the latter in the anglophone ones.

In dealing with the historical experience of the Shoah, one seeks a connection with traditional religion. The modes of reflection on the Shoah therefore frequently contain elements of a religious dimension, these being differentiated in terms of the respective 'subjects' of the same, whether victims, perpetrators, or onlookers.

2. a) Jewish theological reflection on the Shoah begins in the 1960s, with its center of gravity in the United States.[2] In connection with the commemorative character of Judaism, which bears on the relation between faith and history, the various approaches seek an answer to the question of theodicy posed by Auschwitz. Extremely orthodox voices range the Shoah in the long Jewish history of martyrdom, as divine punitive judgment for sins committed (as Joel Titelbaum). Others see, in the Shoah, a time of the absence of God, followed, once more—with the founding of the State of Israel in 1948—by a time of God's benevolent presence (Eliezer Berkowicz). A more radical interpretation of the Shoah has been offered by Richard Rubenstein, who grasps it as proof of the death of God, and therewith as the destruction of traditional Jewish belief. Emil Fackenheim, on the other hand, sees, in a similar self-sacrifice on the part of Judaism, the posthumous victory of Hitler, and concludes to the imperative to hold fast, precisely now, to Jewish belief. Other positions interpret the experience of the Shoah in the light of a motif of a (co-)suffering God, either in congruency with Jewish tradition (Abraham Heschel), or in conscious departure from the biblical, almighty God (Hans Jonas). Doubt of the possibility of interpreting the Shoah in tra-

ditional theological patterns is especially strong in Arthur A. Cohen, for whom the 'Tremendum' of the death camps poses primarily the question of human responsibility.

b) In the State of Israel, the Shoah is dealt with primarily on the levels of politics and → civil religion.[3] The Israeli Declaration of Independence of 1948 asserts, in the founding of the State of Israel, and thereby in the purposes of Zionism, a liberating response to the Shoah. Still, in the years after the founding of the State, the Shoah was generally avoided as an object of observation: the image of the suffering and the passivity of the victims of the Nazis contradicted the ideal of the Israeli pioneer and hero in battle. With the laws for the establishment of the annual memorial day (*Yom ha-Shoah*), of 1951 or 1959, as well as of the memorial site (*Yad va-Shem*, "Monument and Name"; cf. Isa 56:5) of 1953, an attempt was made to achieve a balance: the national Memorial of the Shoah was charged with the motif of courage and valor, as Jews had shown in a battle of resistance. Correspondingly, for Yom ha-Shoah, the 27th of Nissan was selected, between Passover and Independence Day, since it had been in the month of Nissan, 1943, that the Warsaw → Ghetto uprising had taken place. In this fashion, commemoration of the Shoah was not bound to an already existing religious memorial day, such as, for example, the 9th of Av, which integrates into the Jewish faith the commemoration of various assaults of fate in Jewish history, such as the destruction of the Temple, in 70 CE. With the Eichmann trial of 1961, Israeli society made a transition to a phase dominated by enlightenment and information concerning the Shoah. The theme of National Socialist persecution now found entry into the curricula of the educational system. After the wars of 1967 and 1973, and the coming to power of the Likud in 1977—as well as after the switch of generations among the survivors of the Shoah—the Israeli attitude toward the Shoah got into a "phase of mythologization," in which the Shoah emerged "more and more as the raison d'être of Zionism and the State of Israel."[4] The state visit of high-ranking foreign guests at Yad va-Shem was established as a national ritual. Since 1980, the Shoah has been an obligatory subject for all pupils, and democratic, patriotic, and moral teachings are drawn from it. True, critics see an instrumentalization here, as well as an immunization. In the 1990s, it is observable that the Shoah is generally increasing in a capacity to bestow identity. This precipitates in its developments in literature, film, and historiography, as well as an incipient reception of theological reflection on the Shoah in the United States.

In Israel

3. Christian reflection on the Shoah was originally sparked by recognition of the guilty involvement of church and theology in National Socialist anti-Semitism. This reaction can be comprised under the general heading of Jewish-Christian dialogue, which has been taking place in the United States and, since about the 1960s, in Germany, as well. It is earmarked first of all by its goal of attaining an attitude among Christians that would evaluate Judaism as an independent theological quantity, in order to foster an unprejudiced encounter of both theologies and faith traditions. The imperative defeat of theological anti-Judaism here—such as of the prejudice against Judaism to the effect that the latter is legalistic, or the teaching that, since Jesus Christ, divine salvation is no longer to be found in the synagogue, but now solely in the Church—ought be reached through a self-critical review of Christian dogmatics and biblical interpretation, as well as through a more

Jewish-Christian Dialogue

On September 19, 1941, Viktor Klemperer, discharged Dresden Professor of Romanistics, notes in his journal: "The wearing of the Jewish Star, black on yellow material, containing, in roman face designed to resemble Hebrew letters, *Jude* [Ger., 'Jew'], on the left breast, the size of the palm of the hand, 10 penny, prescribed for us yesterday, beginning tomorrow, 9/19." The introduction of the Jewish Star, by order of the police of September 1, 1941, which came into force simultaneously with other harassing decisions—such as the order for Jews in streetcars to use only the front platforms—was part of a perfidious strategy of exclusion and harassment on the part of National Socialist Germany. Citizens determined by the State to be Jewish were simultaneously discriminated against by constantly new means, excluded from societal life as stigmatized, marked as 'a different kind,' and, for instance, isolated in 'Jew houses'—social death preceded murder in the Shoah. "Yesterday, as Eva [his wife] sewed on the Jewish Star, a frenzy of desperation shot through me" (Klemperer on September 20, 1941). The brand of the Jewish minority had a tradition in Christian Europe: At the Fourth Council of the Lateran (1215), in the 68th constitution, Pope

profound knowledge of Judaism founded partly on the basis of a Jewish self-testimonial. Judaism is gaining in meaning and importance not only as the root of Christianity, but also as current equal partner with the Church in the belief in a common, one God. Mindfulness of the Shoah, then, is shown principally in the theological review of Christian positions of judgment and prejudice. The steps in this process since 1945 can be read in various church declarations.[5]

In Germany

4. To deal with the Shoah in Germany is for Germans to recognize that they, or their ancestors, are the persons responsible for the commission of Nazi crimes. At the same time, there is a question of remembering the victims. This ever more dynamic set of problems touches the most varied areas, such as historiography, literature, film, art, religion, and theology. The memory of

the burden of the German past is extremely difficult, as it is a function of the enormity and complexity of the crimes that now stand, in a mode of self-criticism, before the eyes of the nation. Beginning in 1996, the anniversary of the liberation of the concentration camp at Auschwitz by Soviet troops (January 27) has been a national "memorial day of the victims of National Socialism." Programs are also presented in commemoration of the nocturnal pogrom of November 9, 1938. None of these commemorative rituals is universally accepted, however. Their function—definitely to be regarded as religious—is to indicate to society the meaning and importance of the Shoah for the present. But attitudes here swing between the 'case closed' mentality, which would like to forget the Shoah, or regards it as irrelevant for the present, and the effort to preserve a suitable recall of the Shoah and its victims in the cultural memory. German postwar history here is to be described rather as the consequence of a public dispute, rather coincidentally provoked. As stages in the discourse, the following might be cited as examples. R. Hochhuth's drama *Der Stellvertreter* (Ger., "The Deputy"), 1963; the book by A. and M. Mitscherlich, *Die Unfähigkeit zu trauern*, 1967 (Engl. as "The Inability to Mourn: Principles of Collective Behavior"; 1978); the American film series "Holocaust" (1979); Claude Lanzmann's documentary film "Shoah," 1985, and Steven Spielberg's feature film, "Schindler's List," 1994; the "historians' dispute," 1986–1988; the debate over Daniel J. Goldhagen's "Hitlers' Willing Executioners" (1996); and the Walser-Bubis debate (1998). Doubtless the lengthiest, and perhaps the most important, confrontation is the one being waged since 1989 over the 'Holocaust Memorial' in Berlin, right in front of the *Reichstag* (Parliament). On June 25, 1999, the German *Bundestag* (lower house of parliament) decided in favor of architect Peter Eisenman's design: a field of memorial pillars. Here it is clear that the → memory (historically without analogy) of the Shoah in Germany is faced with the challenge to maintain "a memory that undermines [Germany's] very identity" (A. Assmann). German identity here need not be disavowed by a 'shame memorial,' but ought, in its brokenness, maintain itself in a constant awareness, by a memorial to the victims of the Shoah, that will be at the same time a place of respect and reverence for them (→ Monument/Memorial Places).

Innocent III decreed the external marking of Jews and 'Saracens' (Muslims). With Charles V's Imperial Police Order, a yellow ring, indicating that the wearer was a Jew, was obligatory until the end of the eighteenth century. At the end of the sixteenth century, the 'Star of David' (correctly, 'Shield of David'; in Heb., *Magen David*) came into use as an emblem of Jewish identity, and was adopted by Zionism, until it was forcibly imposed, for the first time, in Poland, in October 1939 by order of the National Socialists, as a stigma. 'Macabre' is the word used by the Catholic Press Agency about this picture that shows the sale of the erstwhile sign of stigmatization. But ought the verdict not rather be against those who put such signs in the world, and force it upon their fellow citizens? (Hubert Mohr)

1. Münz 1995, 100-110.
2. Brocke/Jochum 1993; Münz 1995.
3. Liebmann/Don-Yehiya 1983.
4. Zimmermann, Moshe, "Die Folgen des Holocaust für die israelische Gesellschaft," in: Aus Politik und Zeitgeschichte 1-2 (1992), 33-43, p. 34.
5. Rendtorff/Henrix 1989.

Literature

Arad, Yitzhak et al. (eds.), Documents on the Holocaust: Selected Sources on the Destruction of the Jews for Germany and Austria, Poland, and the Soviet Union, Jerusalem 1981; Brocke, Michael/Jochum, Herbert (eds.), Wolkensäule und Feuerschein. Jüdische Theologie des Holocaust, Gütersloh 1993 (¹1982); Gutman, Yisrael (ed.), Encyclopedia of the Holocaust, 4 vols., New York 1990; Jonas, Hans, Mortality and Morality: A Search for the Good after Auschwitz, Evanston 1996; Laqueur, Walter (ed.), The Holocaust Encyclopedia, New Haven 2001; Liebman, Charles S./Don-Yehiya, Eliezer, Civil Religion in Israel: Traditional Judaism and Political Culture in the Jewish State, Berkeley 1983; Michman, Dan (ed.), Remembering the Holocaust in Germany, 1945–2000: German Strategies and Jewish Responses, New York 2002; Morgan, Michael L., Beyond Auschwitz:

Post-Holocaust Jewish Thought in America, New York 2001; Münz, Christoph, Der Welt ein Gedächnis geben. Geschichtstheologisches Denken im Judentum nach Auschwitz, Gütersloh 1995; Novick, Peter, The Holocaust and Collective Memory: The American Experience, London 2000; Rendtorff, Rolf/Henrix, Hans Hermann (eds.), Die Kirchen und das Judentum. Dokumente von 1945–1985, Paderborn ²1989; Wiedmer, Caroline A., The Claims of Memory: Representations of the Holocaust in Contemporary Germany and France, Ithaca 1999; Young, James E., The Texture of Memory: Holocaust Memorials and Meaning, New Haven 1993.

→ *Anti-Semitism, Conflict/Violence, Memory, National Socialism*

Evelina Volkmann

Silk Road

The Region

1. The silk Road was a network of trade routes, reaching from → China, through Turkistan and → Iran, to the Eastern Mediterranean Sea, and first peaked in the first century CE. Chinese silk-ware and ironware, as well as Indian ivory, were merchandise much sought after in Rome. The silk route served not only as a trade connection, but also as a cultural bridge. Although in the easterly direction woolen goods, Alexandrian glass, coral, silver, and gold were transported, more important was the cultural influence of the great world religions that reached Central Asia and China along this route. The merchants who traveled the various parts of the route functioned as missionaries and spread → Buddhism, → Manichaeism, Nestorian Christianity, and → Islam. With the discovery of the sea route to Asia, in the late fifteenth century, the importance of the land routes gradually dwindled, and in the following centuries, Central Asia grew politically and culturally isolated. In the nineteenth century, the region fell into the area of Chinese and Russian power interests. In 1884, East Turkistan (the basin of the Tarim) became a Chinese province, under the name Xinjiang, 'New Frontier,' and since 1949 has been part of the People's Republic of China. The West Turkistani protectorate of Buchara and Chiva was incorporated into the Soviet Union as part of the Socialist Republic of Uzbekistan. Since the disintegration of the Soviet Union in December 1991, the opportunity once more exists for the Muslim population of newly independent Republics of Uzbekistan, Tajikistan, Kyrgyzstan, Kazakhstan, and Turkmenistan, to enter into regular trade with other parts of the Islamic world.

A large part of the silk route ran through desert areas. The Tarim basin, through which ran all trade routes from China to the West, is enclosed by a ring formed by the Tien-Shan, Pamir, Karakorum, and Kun-Lun ranges, and receives extremely little rainfall. Further west, the landscape is characterized by the Iranian-Turanic wasteland. Between inhospitable wastelands and high mountains, the cultural life of the region took place in the oasis cities along the trade routes. The existence of Turfan (Turpan), the most important archaeological finding in East Turkistan, demonstrates the centuries-long coexistence of the Buddhist, Manichean, and Nestorian religions.

Development in Religious History

2. In West Turkistan, Bukhara and Samarkand developed into important urban centers. As in East Turkistan, here as well, art and culture were first decisively marked by Buddhism, which was favored by the Kushan dynasty,

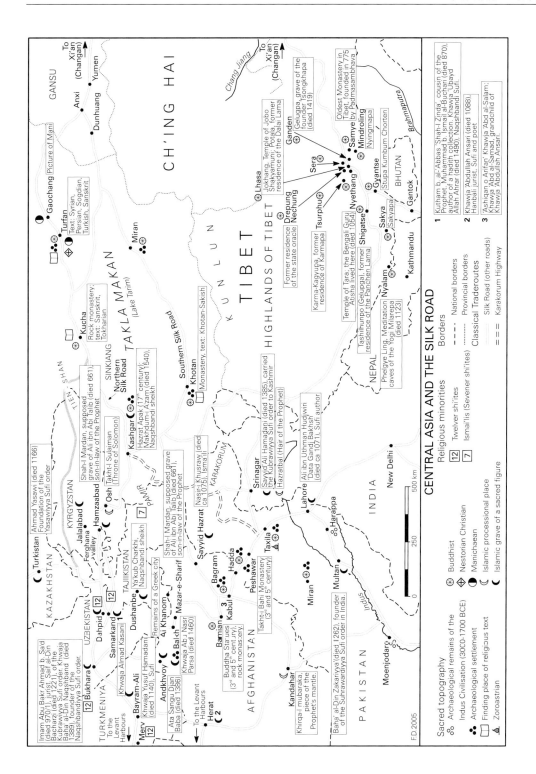

CENTRAL ASIA AND THE SILK ROAD

Religious minorities

[12] Twelver shi'ites

[7] Ismai'lis (Sevener shi'ites)

Borders

National borders

Provincial borders

Classical Traderoutes

Silk Road (other roads)

Karakorum Highway

Sacred topography

Archaeological remains of the
Indus Civilisation (3000-1700 BCE)

Archaeological settlement

Finding place of religious text

Nestorian Christian

Manichaean

Islamic processional place

Islamic grave of a sacred figure

Buddhist

Zoroastrian

F.D. 2005

1 Kutham b. al-'Abbas 'Shah-i Zinda', cousin of the
Prophet. Muhammad b Ismail al-Buchari (died 870),
author of a hadith collection. Khwaja 'Ubayd
Allah Ahrar (died 1490), Naqshbandi Sufi.

2 Khawaja 'Abdullah Ansari (died 1088),
Hanbali jurist, Sufi and poet

3 'Ashiqan o Arifan' Khawja 'Abd al-Salam;
Khawja 'Abd al-Samad, grandchild of
Khawja 'Abdullah Ansari.

and which spread, from the first century CE onward, from Northwest India, through today's Afghanistan, to Central Asia. Thus, it is assumed that the name of today's city of Bukhara derives from *vihara* (*vahara*), 'Buddhist monastery.' This institution is said also to have influenced the installation of the Islamic *madrasa*, the 'theological school.' In addition, the existence of Manichean, Nestorian, and Zoroastrian communities in Bukhara and Samarkand is documented. After the death (276 BCE) of their founder, Mani, the Manicheans were persecuted in Sassanid Iran; thus, in the third century, they removed their activities to Central Asia. Nestorian Christianity, which appealed to Patriarch Nestorius of Constantinople (c. 381–451)—who had strictly separated the divine and human nature of Jesus, and was therefore condemned as heretic (431)—reached Merv and Herat in the early fifth century. Shortly thereafter, an episcopal see appeared in Samarkand, becoming a metropolitan see in the eighth century. In the seventh century, → Zoroastrianism began to compete with Buddhism in this region.

Islamization

The Arabic capture of Bukhara and Samarkand, between 709 and 712, signaled the beginning of the Islamization of West Turkistan. In 751, the Arabs defeated the Chinese in the Battle of Talas, and thereby became undisputed rulers of the region, with Arabic campaigns resulting in the destruction of Buddhist sanctuaries. Subsequently, however, the new religion prevailed more pacifically, and relatively slowly.

Brotherhoods and Foundations

Islam established new opportunities for merchants and traders especially. The consolidation of the Mediterranean and Asian economic regions in Arab hands caused a growth in the rate of trade, lasting until the eleventh century. Besides traders, the mystical → Sufi brotherhoods were important vehicles of religion. The Qādirīyyah orders, founded in the twelfth century in Baghdad, played a significant role in Central Asia as well. At the end of the same century, the Kubrawīyyah order appeared in Chiwa. The Naqšbandīyyah order had its beginning in Bukhara, and was closely bound to commerce. Its founder, Bahā' al-Dīn Naqšband (1318–1389) is venerated as the patron saint of Bukhara even today.

   Of great significance for religious life were → endowments or foundations, by which mosques, theological schools, and benevolent institutions were maintained. Up until the eighteenth century, Bukhara was a renowned seat of scholarship, and its numerous madrasas attracted well-nigh 30,000 students, from Russia to India.

Under Russian and Soviet Supremacy

3. Russian colonization began in the nineteenth century. First, Tashkent (1865) and Samarkand (1868) were conquered. Bukhara became a Russian protectorate. Shortly thereafter, Chiwa (1873), Choqand (1876), and Merv (1884) fell. Muslim resistance against Russia took shape in the fertile Ferghana Valley, today divided among Tajikistan, Uzbekistan, and Kyrgyzstan. In 1869, 1885, and 1898, rebellions erupted in the city of Andishan (see map), inspired by the mystical brotherhoods and brutally crushed by Russian troops. The conservative religious Basmačī uprisings by the Bolsheviks, between 1918 and 1922, likewise found their beginnings in the Ferghana Valley. Other Muslims joined the Pan-Turkish reform movement (Panturanism), which was willing to cooperate with the new regime. Inspired by the Krimtatar Ismail Bei Gasprinski (1851–1914), the Jadīdists (from Ar., *jadīd*, 'new'), beginning in the nineteenth century, strove for a reform of the school

system, as well as for the development of a common literary language for all Turkic peoples. While the Jadīdists from Samarkand had rebelled against Russian domination as late as 1916, in 1920 a large part of this movement joined the Communist Party; nevertheless, these persons and their movement fell victim to the Stalinist mass cleansings of 1930.

The opposition of the Basmačī at first led the new Soviet power to a switch in policy. The foundation lands taken in 1919 were returned in 1922/23. Madrasas and Islamic courts of justice were reopened. Shortly thereafter, however, a frontal assault was mounted on Islam's institutions and culture. In 1927, the Islamic courts definitively lost their capacity to function. In the same year, in the name of the equality of women, the veil was done away with, a measure that even local communists opposed. There followed a systematic persecution of the Muslim clergy, as well as of the Naqšbandī Brotherhood. In 1930, Stalin nationalized all foundation land. Thousands of mosques and madrasas were closed. Between 1959 and 1964, other mosques fell victim to Khrushchev's anti-Islamic offensive. Of 33,000 mosques in the Russian Empire and the Protectorates of Buchara and Chiva in 1912, in 1958 only 1,500 were left. By 1968, their number had shrunk to fewer than 500.

The Soviet regime took pains to control all areas of religious practice. To this end, Muslim 'directorates' were established, the most important of these being the Directorate for Central Asia and Kazakhstan, with its headquarters in Tashkent. The only two madrasas in the Soviet Union were subjected to them, and thereby the formation of the clergy as well. Here the only Islamic publications—a newspaper, limited editions of the Qur'an, and religious calendars—were published. Religious life was placed within narrow limits. The pilgrimage to Mecca was reserved to a handful of chosen delegates. Fasting during the Islamic month of Ramadan was suppressed, for fear of a decline in productivity. Although the ritual slaughter of animals was forbidden, celebration of the sacrificial festivals of 'Īd al-Fiṭr and 'Īd al-Aḍhā was not entirely prohibited. Besides, the formation of the Muslim identity of the population continued to be determined by Islam. Women played an especially important role in the preservation of religious traditions, such as fasting and visiting local shrines. Just so, the rites accompanying birth, circumcision, marriage, and death continued to be governed according to traditional, and therefore religious, patterns.

4. Even before the collapse of the Soviet Union, a revival of Islam manifested itself in the erection of unofficial houses of prayer, and study circles that passed their knowledge on to the new generation. The numerous tombs of saints as well, that had always been a magnet for the believing population, and on which the activities of the mystical brotherhoods were concentrated, took on the function of substitutes for the mosques that had been shut up. In certain parts of Central Asia, the collapse of the Soviet Union led to a reinforcement of political Islam, which governments had classified as fundamentalism and suppressed. The Ferghana Valley is today the center of the Uzbek branch of the Islamic Revival Party, which has been banned since 1991. Even the building of mosques or other architecture, or the paying of stipends, on the basis of Saudi Arabian sources, was not regarded with a benevolent eye. Instead, the Uzbek government precisely took pains to present itself as the depository of official Islam, and to bind the clergy more tightly into the apparatus of state.

Situation Today

Religious life is determined by Sufi tendencies (→ Sufism). The Naqšbandīyyah and Qādirīyyah orders enjoy the greatest influence throughout Central Asia and Afghanistan. The Kubrawīyyah order is popular among the Turkmen and Karakalpak of Uzbekistan. The center of the Yasawīyyah order lies in Southern Kazakhstan and Northern Uzbekistan. A hundred thousand Twelfer Shiites are to be found among the urban population. A hundred thousand Ismaelites live on Mount Badakshan, in Southeastern Tadzhikistan. In 1992, Tajikistan became the scene of a civil war between members of the old order and an opposition mounted by Islamists and democrats, supported by Iran. Turkey's attempt, in the name of Panturanism, to gain influence in Central Asia, failed, for reason of, among other things, the length of the trade routes. For Turkmenistan and Southern Uzbekistan, the most direct access to the sea leads through Iran. The other states would be served by the dismantling of trade relations with Pakistan; this route, however, is blocked by the persistent war in Afghanistan.

Literature

BENNIGSEN, Alexandre/WIMBUSH, S. Enders, Muslims of the Soviet Empire, London 1985; ELISSEEFF, Vadime (ed.), The Silk Roads: Highways of Culture and Commerce, New York 2000; FRANCK, Irene M./BROWNSTONE, David M., The Silk Road: A History, New York 1986; LINDUFF, Katheryn (ed.), Silk Road Exchange in China, Philadelphia 2004; RASHID, Ahmed, The Resurgence of Central Asia: Islam Or Nationalism?, London 1995; ROBINSON, Francis, Atlas of the Islamic World Since 1500, New York 1982; WHITFIELD, Susan, Life along the Silk Road, London 1999; Eadem (ed.), The Silk Road: Trade, Travel, War and Faith, Chicago 2004.

→ *Buddhism, China/Japan/Korea, Islam, Manichaeism, Order/Brotherhoods, Sufism, Zoroastrianism*

Christine Nölle

Sin

The Concept-Symbol

1. From the religious viewpoint, sin designates the manifold forms of deviation from juridical, social, moral, and intra-religious norms. Connected with the conceptual address of sin, then, is the religious discourse upon the normative, the ritual, juridical, moral, and social construction of order and disorder. Interpretational work on the concept-symbol sin is bound up with ritual practices and procedures for the re-production of the *social order* and the *religious salvific order*, in the form of sanction and punishment, sacrifice and gift, confession, repentance and penance, judgment and re-socialization, remorse, pardon, grace, and therapy.

The discourse upon order and disorder belongs to the thematic spectrum of all religions. The specific concept 'sin' (in Lat., *peccatum*), of course, emerges only in the historical field of emanation of the biblical writings, and of the development of concepts in ancient Christianity and the construction of its dogmatics. A special form is the teaching of primordial or Original Sin.

2. In the writings and theological concepts of the Hebrew Bible, the story of the lost paradise in Gen 3 plays no particularly significant role for the question of sin and its origin. Only in the period of time between the first century BCE and the first century CE does a religious literature form concerning the first human being—who, in the figure of Adam, becomes the theme of the origin and consequence of sin in its meaning for the conceptualization of the whole of humanity as corrupted by sin. *Original Sin*

In this context, and in that of the emanations of the religious speculation of his time where Adam is concerned, stands *Paul*. Paul fixes Adam's role within the innermost core of Christian teaching on sin and salvation. Paul seeks to expound, for young Christianity, the meaning of Christ through an analogy, and antithesis, between the old Adam, and the second, new Adam, Christ. With the interpretational pattern conceived by Paul of the Adam-Christ typology, as in Rom 5, the role and meaning of Adam for the development and future elaboration of the Christian dogmatic mythology of sin is inscribed for history.

→ *Augustine* toughens the Pauline image of Adam, the first human being, in his self-assured exegesis of Paul on the concept, and fashions the concept of Original Sin. Adam is at once an individual person and a collective one, inasmuch as the whole of humanity, on the basis of Adam's disobedience, is gathered up in one single 'mass of sin' (*massa perditionis*), and stands before God in guilt. Now Adam's fall, caused by the combination of pride (*superbia*) and self-love (*amor sui*), is connected with the condition of subsequent humanity, produced by the construction of a sexual biological mechanism of transmission. The effect of the first sin consists in the awakening of the sexual appetite (*concupiscentia*), and the revolt of the flesh against the order of God. It is the body then, conceived in the lust of the flesh, which becomes the vehicle of sin for Augustine. Sin engenders sin. From the moment that the Augustinian doctrine of Original Sin shifts into the center of Western Christian dogmatics, sexuality becomes the medium of sin par excellence. If one wishes to know what sin is, one must observe sexuality. According to Augustine, *superbia* and *concupiscentia* are the central sins of every human being, without exception. Lust and original sin are manifested and reflected in each other indissolubly (→ Sexuality). For the inner religious dimension of Christianity's cultural history, it is crucial that 'the forgiveness of sins' be realized in the sacramental rites (especially those of baptism and confession) and/or in the responsiveness of faith (*sola fide*).

3. Throughout modernity, Western discourse upon freedom and evil, guilt and fate, power and helplessness, the craving and subjectivity of the self, transgression, perversion and corruption, sickness and health, or salvation, has been programmed by way of the Christian dogmatic concept of sin. These discourses, networked through the doctrine of sin, like the phenomenology of (mortal) sin that takes its orientation in the psychology of morality, enjoy cultural success and dominant influence.

In the trivial moralisms of the Western world, the patterns of interpretation of the concept-symbol of sin, previously grasped in religious fashion, live on in their own fashion (→ Secularization).

Literature

Gross, J., Geschichte des Erbsündendogmas, 4 vols., Munich 1960–1972; Reid, J. S., "Sin," in: Encyclopaedia of Religion and Ethics 11 (1920), 528-570; Rigby, Paul, Original Sin in Augustine's Confessions, Ottawa 1987; THOMSON, Oliver, A History of Sin, Edinburgh 1993; WILEY, Tatha, Original Sin: Origins, Developments, Contemporary Meanings, New York 2002.

→ *Body, Conscience, Devil, Eroticism, Ethics/Morals, Guilt, Sexuality, Will (Free)*

Joachim von Soosten

Singing / Song

Concept

1. Singing is a form of → communication belonging to many highly developed species, including the human being. Extending the concept somewhat, and thus including melodic articulations such as crying out, cheering, a soothing murmur, and the like, it seems altogether plausible that the more abstractly codifying communication of → language has arisen precisely from these 'song' forms. While language must be passed on culturally, the voice ranks as the immediate—non-arbitrary if possible—expression of a person's physical and psychic disposition. It is a multidimensional, differentiated instrument, conveying information and feelings through pitch, color (overtones, undertones), volume, and so on. Its timbre is channeled in singing, in which its aesthetics and meaning are culturally conditioned and learned.

2. Singing is an important phenomenon in all cultures. Many persons judge that singing can produce a communication in intimate areas, scarcely comprehensible through language, in sensory fashion. (After all, the content of language is more frankly cognitive and intellectual.) Included in these areas are religious moods and dispositions. By means of religious powers or elements, singing serves communication, and the 'information' of the members of a religious community. Singing is summons, prayer, blessing, veneration, and offering or sacrifice. In addition, singing is sometimes ascribed the meaningful and important capacity to articulate parts of a given religious reality, to share it with others, to bring oneself in harmony or connection with that reality, indeed, to create or generate it in a magical sense. The power of singing or sound (and this especially in many oral cultures, with their appraisal of the value of the word or the name) stands at the center of many processes of such creation or transformation when reported in myths, or ritually produced. It can embody knowledge, spirit, power, life, order, beauty, and cosmic harmony. It can offer protection, and can heal. With the Pygmies of the Central African rainforest, for example, singing stands at the center of their practice of religion. In singing, they stand in permanent contact with the personified rainforest and its powers. The forest is awakened, summoned, lured—and opened when it closes by reason of evil conduct. Many North American Indians regard the medicine songs, received from their protective spirits in visions, as their most precious possession (→ North America [Traditional Religions]). Many religions ascribe certain meanings even to vibrations, as also to vocally interesting overtones and undertones in their singing, as practiced, for instance, in Central Asia (→ Shamanism), or in modern → New Age music.

3. Religions that do not posit a crisp dichotomy between the spheres of the sacred and the profane, frequently ascribe an intrinsic effect to music,

Qawwali is a popular musical style in Islamic Sufi-currents on the Indian subcontinent. A standard ensemble consists of one or more soloists, a line of choral singers (who also clap), tambourines, and concertina-like instruments. The rousing antiphonal songs, with virtuosic improvisations, can rise all the way to ecstasy, but are outwardly almost expressionlessly presented and heard. They are a service to inward surrender, the personal quest for God, and group communication. Texts from the classic Sufi poets are sung (→ Sufism), as well as spontaneous portrayals of a personal experience of God. These (like the sometimes excessive lifestyle of the musicians) can take on forms rejected by orthodoxy as heretical. In Pakistan, great Qawwali singers are superstars, who are reverenced by their followers as saints. Nusrat Fateh Ali Khan even made the leap to international cult-star, and made Qawwali known in the West. The picture shows the regular Thursday Qawwali session in the shrine of the Sufi saint from Farid, Ganj-i Shakar, in Pakpattan, Pakistan.

as if it were altogether obvious that they should do so. Furthermore, hymns connect singing with → language. Their texts are part of oral or written tradition, and can convey an explicit message. Many world religions, which are less interested in music as an art form, than as a medium for a linguistic, cognitive, 'spiritual' message, take a rather ambivalent position vis-à-vis its sensory or aesthetic qualities.

The Christian churches demonize singing far less often than they do → dance or musical instruments. Singing also connects well with intellectualization and mission. Its potential for proclaiming the faith was used by Luther, for example. The Reformation, and hymns in the form of intellectualizing, didactic and confessional song, promoted each other. Singing lends ideal content and value conceptualizations a sensible presence, renders present the unseizable transcendent, guides → feelings and expresses them, effects the materialization of community, and mobilizes masses. It enjoys the advantage over instrumental music that all of the faithful, without training or educational background, can have an active share in it. In 1524, Luther's first hymnal appeared: the *Achtliederbuch* (Ger., "Book of Eight Songs"), followed over the course of the century by various regional

At the services of an Afro-American congregation in Savannah, Georgia (here photographed in 1996), gospel music stands front and center. One by one, Father Green invites members to step up front and present their songs and dances, in this thoroughly musical service. Gospel, as one of the most important forms of Afro-American music, has its roots in the 'spirituals'—sacred songs of European Americans that were adopted and transformed by the black slaves in the wake of their Christianization. The 'spirituals' retained formal and harmonic structures of the European popular and church music: to this was added Afro-American elements in melodic ductus ('blue notes,' the neutral playing or singing of the third and the seventh) and rhythm ('off-beat,'

hymnals. Subsequently, the confrontation over the 'correct' hymnal all but made the battleground for the struggle over Christian views of faith.

In many oral cultures, singing is understood only as a different, more elevated type of speech. The singing voice, however, purposes more dynamics, tone embrace, capacity for modulation, and range, than does the speaking voice, whose physiology is basically different. The mixed mode—'recitative,' speech with the singing voice, and in singing form—connects the opportunities for a good textual understanding with those of the range and aesthetics of singing. In Hindu and Buddhist rituals, such recitations acquire key importance. In the European Middle Ages, recitative was generally used in Gregorian chorales and the mystery plays, although, to be sure, it was then understood as a particular kind of speech, while we today perceive it as singing.

4. Only with the Renaissance was music discovered as an emotional language for subjective expression, and spiritual art-music developed, which with Palestrina was still mainly choral music, and the hymn sung by the congregation. Next, theological schemata presented song as a symbol of the transcendent, and as human reflex. In the practical exercise of religion, however, the functional incorporation of song into the framework of the liturgy, as an enhanced form of common adoration, takes precedence. Singing in the congregation, the church choir, the Gospel group, or even new religious movements, founds community, guides feelings, and conveys messages. But it is precisely in esoteric and → New Age milieus that singing can also become an art form, or theology-in-sound in itself, as, for example, J.-E. Berendt's popular *Nada Brahma* make evident.

5. In many ways, pop culture plays with religious forms and feelings. Singers especially take up religious elements as cultic thematizers of the

stage- or media event, and shape from them, consciously or ironically, a kind of musical → civil religion.

Literature

BERENDT, Joachim-Ernst, The World Is Sound: Nada Brahma. Music and the Landscape of Consciousness, Rochester 1991; BOX, Reginald, Make Music to Our God: How We Sing the Psalms, London 1996; CALAME, Claude, Choruses of Young Women in Ancient Greece: Their Morphology, Religious Role, and Social Functions, rev. ed., Lanham 2001; GROSSMAN, Maxine L., "Jesus, Mama, and the Constraints of Salvific Love in Contemporary Country Music," in: Journal of the American Academy of Religion 70,1 (2002), 83-115; JONCAS, Jan Michael, From Sacred Song to Ritual Music: Twentieth-Century Understandings of Roman Catholic Worship Music, Collegeville 1997; PINN, Anthony B. (ed.), Noise and Spirit: The Religious and Spiritual Sensibilities of Rap Music, New York 2003; REAGON, Bernice Johnson, If You Don't Go, Don't Hinder Me: The African American Sacred Song Tradition, Lincoln 2001; RECK, David, Music of the Whole Earth, New York 1977; SULLIVAN, Lawrence E. (ed.), Enchanting Powers: Music in the World's Religions, Cambridge 1997; TURNER, Steve, Amazing Grace: The Story of America's Most Beloved Song, New York 2002.

→ *Communication, Dance, Language, Music, Oral Tradition, Perception, Ritual*

Dietmar Neitzke

along with clapping for rhythmic accentuation). The exchange between soloist and choir is tense, rich, and typical of Afro-American folk music. A question-and-answer pattern occurs in the preaching, as well, when the congregation, with responding cries, confirms and extends what the preacher says. In the musical history of the twentieth century, Afro-American church music (gospel) and 'secular music' (jazz and blues) have exercised a mutual influence. (Kirsten Holzapfel)

Sinti / Roma

1. The Sinti and Roma were originally part of the population of India. In the time following the Sassanid conquests, they emigrated to the West from the region of the upper valley of the Indus. Some migrated to the northern coast of Africa, and to Europe, as far as Spain and Portugal. Others crossed the Black Sea region, and settled, for a considerable time, in Greece. From there, around 1300, they moved in family bands to Central Europe, and as far as Russia and Scandinavia. Byzantines and Europeans, ignorant of the immigrants' Indian origin, inserted them into their Christian image of the world as pilgrims, or penitents. Pope Martin V (1417–1431) issued them appropriate letters of protection and safe conduct. The land of their origin was thought to be Egypt, or Little Egypt (a region in Greece); so they were called 'kings from Egypt' (cf. 'gypsies'). The etymology of their designation 'Athinganoi,' (in Lat., *Adsingani*), from which later evolved the word *Zigeuner* (Ger., Dutch; in French, *tsigan*), usually translated 'gypsy,' refers to the fact that, in Greece, on account of their complicated, Indian-like prescriptions of purity (see below, § 3), they were called 'untouchables,' and were connected in the European mind with the gnostic sect of the Simonians. Sinti and Roma brought new cultural elements to Europe: Flamenco, Tarot, and storytelling contests. The original 'gypsy tarot' still betrays an Indian iconography.

Christian respect died away. The history of the Sinti and Roma in Europe is one of persecution. At the Imperial Diet of 1489, on grounds of suspicion of espionage for the Turks, the Sinti and Roma were expelled from the German Empire. Under Enlightenment absolutism, the policy of compelled assimilation began: Frederick the Great and Empress Maria Theresia issued decrees under which the Roma could be compelled to settle, children could be taken from their parents and placed in foster families. An attempt was made to prohibit marriage among Roma, a practice that remained partly in force in Switzerland until 1973.

The National Socialist Persecution

This undertaking, launched for reason of the concerns of an absolutist state, did not, however, reach the proportions of the German National Socialist persecution of 1933–1945. In France, Poland, Italy, Romania, Russia, and Germany, Sinti and Roma were interned in concentration camps, by authority of the racist legislation dictated by the 'Nuremberg laws,'[1] by men of the SS and SD, supported by the work of academic 'race scholars.' From the concentration camps, Sinti and Roma were transported to the death camps of Auschwitz-Birkenau (where the Germans had built a separate 'Gypsy family-camp') and subsequently murdered. The so-called 'extermination through work' was an objective of the persecution, as well. During the National Socialist rule approximately 500,000 Sinti and Roma were killed.

2. In Europe today there are some eight million Sinti and Roma, in Germany 100,000.[2] Organized in national unions, they strive for recognition as an ethnic minority, and as citizens with equal rights under reference to the UN Charter. Most Sinti and Roma today have a stable residence. The common language is Rómanes, which is most closely akin to Hindi, and can be traced back to the ancient Indian Sanskrit: the name 'Sinti,' for example, has been traced etymologically to the Sanskrit *Sindhu*, 'Indus' (or *Saindhava*, 'Dweller on the Indus'). *Roma*, the plural of *u rom* ('Rómanes,' 'person belonging to the people of the Roma [pl.]'), is a designation possibly connected with the adjective *Romaka*, in the Mahabharata. Its more exact meaning, however, is unknown. The Sinti and Roma no longer officially accept the foreign designation 'gypsy,' on account of its derogatory connotation. But there are a large number of designations for individual ethnic groups, distinct regionally, as in their traditions, language groups, and ethnic bonds: Sinti live preponderantly in German-speaking countries, the Benelux states, and Northern Italy; Manush in France; Roma in Eastern Europe and in the Balkans; Kale in Southern France and in Spain; Ciganos in Portugal; Romanischals in Great Britain. An especially frequently described sub-group of the Roma are the Romanian *Kalderash* (Romanian, *caldare*, 'copper kettle').

The Religion of the Sinti and Roma

3. Just as in the societal area, the Sinti and Roma have a 'multi-class identity' (K. Reemtsma) in that of the religious as well. They usually belong to the religion of the majority, but with indigenous religious conceptions and beliefs. Most Sinti, for example, belong to the Roman Catholic Church. The next most important confession is the Evangelical Church, especially the Pentecostal movement, an Evangelical faith-orientation. In Muslim regions, the Roma belong to Islam.

Faith Practice

Social life, in function of each ethnic group, centers on the (extended) family or the kinship group (clan). Faith practice is therefore determined by its common value-oriented behavior, as well as by the festivals and rituals of the → life cycle, and (especially among Catholics) by collective pilgrimages.

Among the norms of the Sinti and Roma are a series of prescriptions and restrictions with regard to purity (→ Taboo; Purity), which control a great number of social relations. These differ from 'tribe' to 'tribe' (e.g., especially among the Romanian Kalderash), but can possibly be traced all the way back to concepts from Indian religion. With regard to the content of the question, who or what is 'pure' or 'unclean,' as well as with regard to other commands and prohibitions, the counsel of the oldest men is determinative. Transgression against the rules effects 'impurity.' Woman's intimate sphere is especially protected. To be sure, the destruction of a large number of social structures in the National Socialist persecution, as well as adaptation to today's fashion, have caused some things to change, for example clothing conventions.

Prescriptions of Purity

Birth, marriage, and burial are great festivals for the Sinti. Social life in common is seen as an important component of culture. Thus, they prefer to keep the elderly within the circle of the family, rather than place them in nursing homes. Funerals (*pampanas*) last several days. Women and men loudly wail at the death of their loved ones. After the funeral, a banquet is held.

Rites of the Life Cycle

Many Christian usages maintained in Sinti villages were lost, however, because of the National Socialist persecution. The Marian piety of the Sinti is remarkable (→ Mary; see illus.). Pilgrimages are traditional, undertaken or led by the Sinti, with flower-adorned crosses and statues of Mary. A pilgrimage destination especially dear to the Sinti is Lourdes. Since the nineteenth century, the custom has been cultivated of meeting once a year, May 23–26, at Sainte Marie de la Mer, in Provençe, to honor Saint Sara, Egyptian servant of Mary Salome, and other legendary Marian figures.

Pilgrimages and Marian Piety

Conceptualizations of faith are not committed to writing, but are transmitted orally in myths and folk tales. Images and narratives may serve as documentation of the content of belief. Parents and the elderly recount stories to the children, as parables of particular principles of human life. In many groups, belief in spirits of the dead (*mulo*) is of importance.

Content of Belief

The attitude of the great Christian churches toward Sinti and Roma is ambivalent even today, and often powerfully influenced by social prejudices. On the Catholic side, a 'gypsy and nomad ministry' to the Sinti is performed in Cologne. Of course, there are constant tensions, owing to discriminatory pronouncements. At the German Evangelical Church Convention, the Central Council of the Sinti and Roma was represented from 1979 to 1991. Even at divine service, the status of 'exotics' has not yet been revised to 'normal.' The behavior of clergy and parishioners often deters Sinti from attendance at Mass. Polls revealed that Sinti were stared at 'as if they had escaped from the zoo,' and that their exclusion was effected in the most varied of manners.[3]

Between Attempts at Integration and Social Exclusion

4. Where observers of Sinti and Roma have known nothing of their culture, they have often sought to fill these gaps with the construction of stereotypes, and hostile images, that have not corresponded with reality. The image alternates between romanticizing desires that look for license, autonomy, and female eroticism, and social derogation as thieves and beggars. Until very recently, (quasi-) religious perceptions on the part of conventional religion were limited to those of 'gypsy fortune-tellers,' with crystal balls, tarot cards,

Reception and Stereotypes

Hostile Images vs. Information

A Sintiza places a lamp before a statue of Mary. Various locations in which Mary is venerated, especially Lourdes, are favorite pilgrimage places of the Sinti and Roma. The relation of these people to the Catholic Church, however, has been criticized, and they have been discriminated against by the 'nomad ministry' particularly for their Marian devotion.

and palmistry. By way of a *circulus vitiosus*, the piety of the Sinti was criticized, while a lack of interest in religion was also alleged. These accusations can only be described as attempts to upwardly evaluate the accuser's own identity at other persons' cost, a phenomenon repeatedly encountered in history: the 'scapegoat motif.' Here a collection of traditional stereotypes is appealed to, rather similar to those applied vis-à-vis the Jews. On the basis of Christian legends like one of the refusal to lodge the Holy Family in Egypt, or of the production of the manufacture of the nails of the crucifixion—a pseudo-biblical scenario in which a kind of legendary 'original guilt' notion occurred—the incriminations began to allege a collective sinfulness. It also began to be a matter of pre-modern, inquisitorial varieties of the battle against superstition (according to Himmler's decree of November 20, 1939, women under 'suspicion of fortune-telling' were deported to concentration camps); or of the hostile images of social myths, as that of 'restiveness,' and abduction of children. Finally, the 'scientific findings' of modern racial ideologies ensued ('racially conditioned' criminality, categorization as 'pathologically asocial'). Here the frequently interwoven → hostile images of → anti-Semitism and 'anti-gypsy-ism' reinforced each other. Even today, scientific investigation of the religion of the Sinti and Roma, which ought to be able to provide an objective picture, is yet to be developed: it is still burdened with the bigotries of the past, nor is it yet free of ethno-romanticism.

Still, through the attempt to be accepted as fellow human beings and citizens, without having to be utterly adapted to the majority, the Sinti have supported Western society in a learning process. It is ever more vigorously accepted that equality need not be accompanied by identity, and that what remains strange to the observer need not at once be classified as negative or dangerous. Granted, another backlash like that of the post-1990 discrimination against the Roma cannot be ruled out.

1. Cf. Circular Decree of the "Reichs- und Preußischer Minister des Innern, über das Verbot von Rassenmischehen" (Ger., Decree of the "Reich and Prussian Minister of the Interior on the Prohibition of Interracial Marriages") of November 26, 1935.
2. Sources: Declarations of Delegates to the Convention of European Council / OSCE / Office for Democratic Institutions, 1994, held at Rome; LEGEOIS, Jean Pierre, Gypsies and Travellers, Paris 1994, 16.
3. Cf. SEIDLER, Gerhard, Die christliche Gemeinde und die Angst vor Fremden. Aufgewiesen am Beispiel der Sinti und Roma, Frankfurt/M. 1989.

Literature

ACHIM, Viorel, The Roma in Romanian History, Budapest 2004 (Rom. [1]1998); BARANY, Zoltan, The East European Gypsies: Regime Change, Marginality, and Ethnopolitics, Cambridge 2002; BELTON, Brian A., Gypsy and Traveller Ethnicity: The Social Generation of an Ethnic Phenomenon, London 2005; CHARNON-DEUTSCH, Lou, The Spanish Gypsy: The History of a European Obsession, University Park 2004; GUY, Will (ed.), Between Past and Future: The Roma of Central and Eastern Europe, Hatfield 2001; KENRICK, Donald, Gypsies: From the Ganges to the Thames, Hatfield 2004 ([1]1993); KENRICK, Donald/CLARK, Colin, Moving On: The Gypsies and Travellers of Britain, Hatfield 1999; MALVINNI, David, The Gypsy Caravan: From Real Roma to Imaginary Gypsies in Western Music and Film, New York 2004; MARGALIT, Gilad, Germany and Its Gypsies: A Post-Auschwitz Ordeal, Madison 2002; MAYALL, David, Gypsy Identities, 1500–2000: From Egypcyans and Moon-Men to the Ethnic Romany, London 2004; STATE MUSEUM OF AUSCHWITZ-BIRKENAU (ed.), Memorial Book: The Gypsies at Auschwitz-Birkenau, 2 vols., Munich 1993; TEBBUTT, Susan (ed.), Sinti and Roma: Gypsies in German-Speaking Society and Literature, New York 1998; VAN DER STOEL, Max, Report on the Situation of Roma and Sinti in the OSCE Area, The Hague 2000; WILLIAMS, Patrick, Gypsy World: The Silence of the Living and the Voices of the Dead, Chicago 2003.
    Journal: Journal of Gypsy Lore (founded 1988, gathers fairytales and oral traditions in Rómanes, with English translations).

→ *Collective Representations, Family/Kinship/Genealogy, Hinduism, Indian Subcontinent, Minorities, Prejudices/Stereotypes, Purity*

Esther Kraus

Social Myths and Fantasy Images

1. On May 10, 1969, in the lovely French city of Orleans, a shop for women's clothing opened. Its name was provocative: *Aux Oubliettes*—Fr., "In the Dungeons." The management had thought up something quite special that was certainly expected to stimulate attention: the changing cubicles were outfitted after the fashion of a medieval dungeon. This idea did not remain without consequence. A scant month later, a number of shops and city-centers began to display the motto: "Don't buy from Jews. They traffic in girls." What had happened? Beginning in Catholic girls' schools, the rumor had spread, first among companions, then with parents and teachers as well, that in the changing booths young women were stunned with injections, abducted, and, at night, by means of, for example, submarines, shipped

The Rumor of Orleans

to oriental bordellos. It took two weeks for civil authorities and the local bishop to bring the situation under control.

The occurrence is so instructive because it unveils the unconscious and pre-conscious dynamics of social acts, and like a lightening bolt—the steering these dynamics by a repertory of collective models and violent images, and their interweaving and establishment by way of narrative. The point of departure for the scenario is a violent historical image that—not only for teenagers—conjures up the torture chambers of the Inquisitors and the witch-hunters. Thereafter, the thought is observable in its manufacture: in 'compelling' conclusion, the horrible medieval panorama is coupled, associatively, with two other tales: first, that of the oriental harem (→ Orientalism/Exotism), and second, anti-Jewish myths of child-abduction and ritual murder—as well as that of the 'Jewish businessmen' (→ Anti-Semitism). The medium is everyday conversation, gossip, and chatter, on the sidewalk, in the school, in the office, with negative facets. The collective 'spirit of the people,' mixed with residual stories of all kinds, 'mini-yarns' or anecdotes (H.-J. Neubauer), stereotypes, hostile images, bigotries, stirs up a scenario, a 'wild rumor,' whose 'fable-spinning poesie' (Morin: *poésie fabuleuse*) 'mythically doubles' (Neubauer) the reality and its protagonists. Now the process culminates in a fictive role-stereotype of one's neighbors or acquaintances: 'the Jew,' or 'the → witches' (→ Prejudices/Stereotypes).

Social Myths

2. If one considers the → collective representations, the thought processes, and the feelings of a community, these divide primarily into three forms of phenomena: stereotypes, fantasies and models, as well as narratives (collective and socio-mythic). Stereotypes, as the smallest units, are found in both other forms.

Imaginaires—Models and Fantasy-Images

a) Collective conceptual images, as to how society, world, sky, and earth, look, or could have looked, are found since antiquity: the 'Golden Age,' or, in the Middle Ages, the image of a class state divided into warriors, farmers, and priests. In both examples, the scintillating quality of this sort of picture can be easily shown. It is a matter of collectively obligatory and effective discoveries of images—of social fantasies, therefore—that have taken on ideological functions for the legitimization of government, and in societal sketches prevailing into the modern age. At the same time, they possess a fantasy-generating potential that has found its reflection in art and literature, and popular printed graphics, as well as in sermons and in philosophical treatises. It is especially in the French research into social history conducted by the *École des Annales* (Fr., "School of *Annales*"), that the first approaches of a 'social history of the *imaginaires* [fantasy images]' has been worked out, to include dreams as well as literary production, iconography, and emblematics (→ Emblem)—the 'symbolic structures' (G. Duby) of society across the board.

The 'Great Stories'

b) Every society has its 'great stories.' For the ancient Greeks, these were the Trojan War and Odysseus's wanderings, in the version of Homer. The ancient Israelites, and the Jews of today, enjoy the stories of Abraham, Joseph, and Esther. The life and death of Jesus is the original Christian story; the late Middle Ages, and modernity, attached Dante's journey to hell and heaven, the tragic inventiveness of Don Quixote, researcher Faust, or the narrative of the Happy Isles (→ Utopia). Stories of a thousand-year reign of peace have been influential (→ Millenarianism/Chiliasm). There are stories that nearly everyone in a given religion or culture knows 'somehow,' 'from somewhere,' that circulate in fragments, variations, and quotations, and are re-told, in ever new versions, without losing their arrangement and contours; that are read between the cover of a book, just as they are seen and heard in the theater or in films. They are distinguished from the 'normal' stories and myths by their social spectrum, and *longue durée* (Fr., 'long duration') through the centuries. They can be designated as 'macro-myths,' or 'grand narratives,' then. Religious myths (narratives of the gods, etc.), accordingly, are frequently special cases of social myths.

To what extent are collective myths and *imaginaires* components of the social unconscious?

Structures of the Unconscious

   a) They possess structures of *longue durée*, distinguish themselves by their durability, and continue to find communicative confirmation.

   b) They function as mythic metaphors in historical reality, as powerful historical images, and stories *à clée* (with a hint buried relatively early within them for the solution of a mystery being presented), that busy the collective fantasy and direct it to 'targets.'

   c) They convey life sketches, exemplars, and life goals, but also idologemes, and fragments of a → civil religion whose theology is political.

   d) As with many → fairytales, they identify the 'polyphony of process': even government needs the endorsement of the public, and thus needs the extension of the myth or other commanding image through further narrative or sketching. There arises a mesh of myths and anti-myths, of narrative fragments ('splinters'; Neubauer 1998) and mini-yarns, from which group members can withdraw only with difficulty.

   e) Social myths and *imaginaires* carry 'implicit knowledge' (Michael Polanyi), antecedent understandings, that, as long as they are stored in the cultural memory, are always latently at hand, and are thus ever open to summons ('latency of collective knowledge': Neubauer).

In correlating religion to the material of these considerations, a good part of the religious dynamism of such 'concealed' rules of interpretation could appear: explanation of the world (→ Myth/Mythology), the engendering of 'mythical doubles' (Neubauer), witches, and stigmatizing runs not only openly by way of laws and dogmas, but also covertly, by way of the 'informal stock of signs,' narratives, and images. These hidden signifiers lead out into the broad field of religious mentalities.

The Hidden Dynamics of Religion

Literature

Cohn, Norman, The Pursuit of the Millennium: Revolutionary Millenarians and Mystical Anarchists of the Middle Ages, London ²1970 (¹1957); Duby, Georges, The Three Orders: Feudal Society Imagined, Chicago 1980 (French ¹1978); Le Goff, Jacques, The Medieval Imagination, Chicago 1988 (French ¹1985); Neubauer, Hans-Joachim, The Rumour: A Cultural History, London/New York 1999 (Ger. ¹1998); Patlagean, Evelyne, "L'histoire de l'imaginaire," in: Le Goff, Jacques et al. (eds.), La nouvelle histoire, Paris 1978, 249-269.

→ *Collective Representations, Prejudices/Stereotypes, Witch/Persecution of Witches*

Hubert Mohr

Socialism I: Christian

1. Socialism, as a social and political movement, and as it developed in the nineteenth century, was nurtured by diverse sources, religious one among them. In the first half of the nineteenth century, social critics emerged who connected religious consciousness with the demand for a renewal of society. Claude Henri de Saint-Simon (1760–1825) represented (*Le Nouveau Christianisme*, Fr., "The New Christianity"; 1825) a humanization of entrepreneur-led industrialism. Wilhelm Weitling (1808–1871) aimed at a social equality, on the basis of Jesus's teaching, that would climax in the abolition of private ownership, inheritance, money, and punishment (*Das Evangelium eines armen Sünders*, Ger.; "The Gospel of a Poor Sinner"; 1845). Among the diverse conceptions of socialism, the Marxist variant (Karl Marx, 1818–1883) emerged as the apparently dominant one in Germany (→ Marxism). Middle-class propaganda began with the cliché of 'social democrats against religion.'

With Christoph Blumhardt (1842–1919), a prophetic personality, a member of the Württemberg awakening-Christianity, oppressed workers had a socialist option; Blumhardt entered the Württemberg Land Chamber as a deputy of the Socialist Democratic Party (SPD). In his widely noticed *Sie müssen!* (Ger., "They/You Must!"), Zurich Pastor Hermann Kutter (1863–1931) announced that the Social Democrats had actually appeared in the environment as an instrument of God, for the 'shaking and waking' of a failing Christian society. The religio-social movement that spread in Switzerland had its leading figure in Leonhard Ragaz (1865–1945), whose abiding friendship bound him to Jewish Martin Buber (1878–1963). For Ragaz, 'religious socialism' found its leading model in an idealized Israel. In such a perspective, the Israeli *kibbutzim* could stand as an exemplary realization of religious socialism (→ Zionism).

2. After 1918, Germany saw a multiplicity of group formations, whose ideological variegation can nevertheless be categorized, rather vaguely, under the concept of 'religious socialism.' A belligerent nature such as that of Mannheim Pastor Erwin Eckert (1893–1972) was needed to create, in the Union of Religious Socialists of Germany, a politically effective 'battle organization.' The ecclesio-political intent to wrest the Church from the middle class, so that it could serve the interests of the proletariat, was achieved only to a modest point (if at all). Marburg social ethicist Georg Wünsch (1887–1964) may be regarded as the movement's normative theoretician.

In the intellectual milieu of the time of the Weimar republic, the Berlin circle around Paul Tillich (1886–1965), Carl Mennicke (1887–1959), and Eduard Heimann (1889–1967), had Tillich for its 'head,' and Mennicke (an important social psychologist and social pedagogue) as the 'heart' of the circle. Heimann developed an important 'social theory of capitalism,' that contains concrete approaches to a social policy and politics of reform.

The spectrum of religious socialism may be reduced to the three positions of Wünsch, Paul Tillich, and—at the end of the twentieth century—Dorothee Sölle. Wünsch, in his *Evangelische Wirtschaftsethik* (Ger., "Evangelical Economic Ethics"; 1927) derives a political decision for socialism from factual necessities, but at the same time sees in socialism a "re-producing of the meaning of God's creation, whose meaning is love." Tillich develops a theory of time, understood as an existential situation of alienation. In the proletarian revolution, there dawns, instead, a 'theonomy' ('rule of the divine law')—an event that Tillich linked with the Greek concept of *kairós*, in the sense of 'fulfilled time.' Sölle writes her *Mystik und Widerstand* (Ger., "Mysticism and Resistance"; 1997) after the collapse of real socialism in the Eastern bloc and in Nicaragua. Like Erich Fromm (who expounds Marx humanistically), she opposes to capitalistic 'Hab-sucht' ('lust/addiction to "have"') the mystical ideal of 'Ledigwerden' ('becoming unencumbered'), in which the question, already arisen in the religio-socialist "Heppenheimer Conference" of 1928, of a 'socialistic shaping of one's life' in the renunciation of the 'have-mentality,' shifted front and center.

3. A new eruption occurred (for many, partly spurred on by the Vietnam War being waged by the United States) in solidarism with the poor in the 'Third World.' Base communities in Latin America had developed a → 'liberation theology' that adopted Marxist tenets. The revolutionary meaning of the Bible's prophetical proclamation was rediscovered—partly in conscious linkage with Blumhardt and Ragaz—by Christians for Socialism, as well as by a new generation in the old "Union of Religious Socialists."

4. The sum-total of the religio-socialist heritage can be contoured in four 'socialisms': a prophetical one (Blumhardt, Kutter), a doctrinaire (Eckart, and, to an extent, Ragaz), a rigoristic (the "Brotherly Courts" around Eberhard Arnold, 1883–1935; Eckert in the transition to the German Communist Party), and a biophilic. The biophilic type is represented by E. Fromm and D. Sölle, and has influenced parts of the ecology movement (→ Environmentalism). In its global comprehension and extension, biophilia, whose impetus is in the direction of new social shapes and forms, runs against every kind of situation of oppression: especially, the economic exploitation of the 'Third' and the 'Fourth' Worlds, woman's oppression, and the desecration of nature. It is not to be doubted that the battle against social injustice, as the legacy of the prophets of Israel and the 'church of the poor' will retain its currency and urgency.

Literature

Barnes, Kenneth C., Nazism, Liberalism, and Christianity: Protestant Social Thought in Germany and Great Britain, 1925–1937, Lexington 1991; Cort, John C., Christian Socialism: An Informal History, Maryknoll 1988; Deresch, Wolfgang (ed.), Der Glaube der religiösen Sozialisten, Hamburg 1972; Heimann, Siegfried/Walter, Franz, Religiöse Sozialisten und Freidenker in der Weimarer Republik, Bonn 1993; Norman, Edward, The Victorian Christian Socialists, Cambridge 1987; Pfeifer, Arnold (ed.), Religiöse Sozialisten, Olten 1976.

→ *Capitalism, Charitable Organizations, Industrial Society, Liberation Theology, Marxism, Socialism II*

Arnold Pfeiffer

Socialism II: Islamic

1. Intellectuals of the Islamic Middle East came in contact with socialist thought at the close of the nineteenth century, while studying in France and England. Beginning in 1908, and influenced by French models and

History

anti-imperialist convictions, socialist notions stamped the Turkish National Movement under Ziya Gökalp. The first socialist party in Turkey was founded in 1910, shortly after the Young Turks' Revolution of 1908, but dissolved three months later. In 1912 it formed anew, for one year. The term *ishtirāk-e emwāl* ('redistribution of wealth') at a time when neologisms reflected the new socio-cultural, economic, and political ideas adopted from Western Europe, became the basis of the term *ishtirākči* ('[a] socialist') and *ishtirāki* ('socialistic'). Soon, however, the terms *sosyalist* ('[a] socialist') and *sosyalism* ('socialism') came into use in Turkish and Persian.

Arabic Countries and Socialistic Movements

In 1912, Copt Salama Musa published the first book in Arabic with the title *al-Ishtirākiyya* ("The Socialism"). It gave information about Fabian socialism, of British coinage. Egyptian reformer Shiblī Shumayyil, of Syrian Christian origin, and Ismāʿīl Maẓhar carried on debates in their writings in the 1920s, on socialist ideas with an eye to reforms that would effect more social justice and state welfare. In Alexandria, surely in consequence of the Russian October Revolution of 1917, a socialist party was founded in 1920, and a communist party in 1921. Influences of → National Socialism, as well as of Fascism of German and Italian coinage, appeared in Egypt, as well as in Iraq (Rashīd ʿAlī al-Kīlānī) in 1941, partly conditioned by opposition to British colonial policy. After national independence, in the 1950s, regimes came to power in several Arab countries propagating socialist theory, usually depending on a unity party, and retaining Islam as the state religion. This occurred in Egypt under Nasser, in Syria and Iraq with the support of the *Baath* parties (*baʿt*, 'national reawakening')—which, however, would soon fall victim to internal strife—in Tunisia under Bourguiba, and in Libya in 1969 under Ghaddafi.

Fundamental Ideas

2. In contrast with socialism of a Marxist stamp, which strives for internationalism and rigorous atheism, Islamic socialism carries nationalistic traits, and appeals to the → Qurʾan, and to the commandments there formulated for right action (e.g., sura 5:8). It appeals especially to the 'poor tax' (*zakāt*) as one of the five 'pillars of Islam'— as the responsibility of every Muslim. These emphases did lead to agrarian and industrial reforms, for example in Egypt in the 1950s, that were bound up with the privatization of large landholdings and large industry, but did not, principally—unlike → Marxism—demand the dismantling of private ownership of means of production. Rather, representatives of Islamic socialism have always appealed to the social conscience premised by Islam, and the social responsibility of the well-to-do. They frequently cite the Ḥadīth, the second-most important source of Islamic law and the Muslim's conduct: the Prophet Muhammad has enjoined solidarity of community on every Muslim. "Every one of you is a guardian (defender), and each of you is responsible": that is, especially, the well-off are responsible for the poor.

Effectiveness in Social and Political Reality

3. Taking one's point of departure in the economic situation of a less developed industry—therefore, of a numerically weak industrial proletariat—representatives of an Islamic socialism see their social basis as stronger among the rural proletariat than in the working class. They generally seek a class harmony, as God-given human kinship, and not class struggle (as Marxism). The leaders of Islamic socialism, in their various molds, have always been intellectuals. In the Eastern-bloc countries, as well as among Near Eastern

Communists, their independence vis-à-vis Marxism occasioned their reputation as inconsistent, 'petit bourgeois' socialists. This indictment did not, however, prevent good foreign and economic relations between Eastern-bloc countries and countries, even parties, of the Middle East, that have striven for an Islamic socialism. For diplomatic reasons, Eastern-bloc governments silently tolerated a persecution of Communists, for example in Nasser's Egypt, or Baathist Iraq, or Baathist Syria. In Eastern-bloc countries, communist immigrants received asylum, but had to postpone their party activities. For example, Iraqi Communists in the German Democratic Republic held their party conferences in West Berlin.

Since the collapse of the Eastern bloc, Middle Eastern socialists of a more frankly secular orientation have begun to rethink their positions. These reflections have taken various directions. Even the representatives of different currents of Islamic → fundamentalism—beginning with the Muslim Brotherhood in Egypt after 1928, and Syria since 1935, then with Lebanon and Palestine, later, and into the present, with Afghanistan, today the FIS (Front Islamique du Salut, Fr. "Islamic Salvation Front") in Algeria, and the fundamentalist Shia clergy in Iran since 1979—all of these are turning mainly to the economically and socially frustrated urban and rural middle and lower class. In confrontation with Christianity, on the one hand, and Communism on the other, they interpret and propagate Islam first and foremost as *the* pragmatic religion—of comprehensive social justice, social responsibility, and the equality of all persons, in all of the values of these—a religion of freedom (including that of conscience) and human dignity from the outset. This had been reality already, in an (idealized) early Islam. According to Sayyid Quṭb (normative ideologue of the Muslim Brotherhood), it must now be the reality of political power once more. After all, Islam must seek to be—as it already is, according to the will of God—the comprehensive and determinative religion (that is, as political ideology) of nature, as well as of human life across the board. Practice in actually existing Islamic states does deviate from theory. By way of an important example: in → Iran (ruled since 1979 by Shia fundamentalist clergy), erstwhile pragmatic clergy (often as large landholders), along with the "Guardian Council," successfully opposed the demand of a counter-wing of the Mullahs for 'socialist' economic reforms, including a land reform and the nationalization of foreign trade.

Current Developments

Literature

DELANQUE, G., "al-Ikhwān al-muslimīn," in: Encyclopedia of Islam², vol. III, (1986), 1068-1071; HARRIS, G. S./VATIKIOTIS, P. J., Ishtirākiyya," in: Encyclopedia of Islam², vol. IV (1990), 123-126; KUTB, Syed, Social Justice in Islam, Washington 1958; LIA, Brynjar, The Society of the Muslim Brothers, London 1998; SAID, Abdel Moghny, Arab Socialism, London 1972.

→ *Fundamentalism, Industrial Society, Islam, Marxism, Socialism I*

Wiebke Walther

Socialization / Upbringing

Even if one's point of departure is the premise that the human being is by nature predisposed to religion (cf., Lat.: *homo naturaliter religiosus; homo religiosus*)—to a certain extent recent cognitive approaches to the study of religion present a resurgence of that view—it still remains to be explained how, ideally, a helpless nursling becomes a competent member or competent client of a given religion. From generation to generation, religions must be creatively reproduced. 'Socialization,' and 'upbringing,' 'education,' or 'rearing,' denote attempts to bring to the concept a simultaneous (1) continuity, that spans the generations, and (2) emergence of a religious competency and religious individuality on the part of the members of a religion. Furthermore, questions of socio-religious control and power are at stake. Socialization here describes a more comprehensive event than does 'upbringing.' As a rule, what is understood by socialization is a manifold interplay of individual persons with various dimensions of their respective environment, while 'upbringing' refers to an intended influence on the ones being brought up (as a rule, persons developing and growing) by the educator (as a rule, adults). 'Upbringing,' then, is a subset of incidents of socialization.

Multidimensionality of Incidents of Socialization

Older theoretical approaches understood socialization as a kind of '*making* social.' Newer approaches see socialization as the '*becoming* social' of an individual, whose own active attainments are more strongly emphasized. In recent scholarship, the insight has been increasingly acknowledged that processes of socialization last from birth until death. In other words: socialization is far from being completed with attendance at school or the university. Ecological approaches, furthermore, indicate that every individual is involved in several contexts of socialization at once. Here the spectrum spans from 'closer' environmental regions, interlocked and intermingled in various ways (family, friends, neighborhood, association, groups of workers), to 'more remote' environmental regions (transportation system, mass media, politics), to comprehensive environmental areas that provide a frame of reference for several regions of socialization (fundamental cultural value-systems).

'Religion,' in this context, should not be understood simply as a separate, partial area of the respective society or culture, but to a greater or lesser extent permeates all of these dimensions of socialization. 'Religious socialization,' then, is, on the one hand, an implicit component of a 'normal socialization' in the corresponding culture; but, on the other hand, it can be explicitly furthered or hindered through particular techniques and institutions. Religions contribute to the development of cultural systems, without being completely absorbed in them. Hence, various cultures dominated by the same religion can exhibit considerable differences; and religions, in various forms, or historical or cultural contexts, can legitimize different values.

Learning

Socialization and upbringing are instances of learning. 'Learning' generally denotes permanent changes in the behavior or capabilities of a person that are instigated by specific exercises and experiences. Religious socialization contains a whole series of learning processes. Learning from or in religions can occur continuously or discontinuously, for example through daily re-

ligious acts, or through intensive religious experiences ('illuminations'; →
Light/Enlightenment). The learning events can run according to plan, or
not, e.g., through purposive memorizing of religious texts (→ Oral Tradition), or through the unexpected appearance of missionaries or preachers.
Learning bears not only on cognitive events: besides religious knowledge,
for example, one must learn how and when to apply the texts that have been
committed to memory, or when and how to move at the proper moments
(for instance, the attitude of the hands, gross positions of the body as one
kneels or stands, direction of the eyes upward or downward, etc.). Learning
particular positions of the body, gestures, movements, and bodily functions,
is a key component not only of meditation techniques, as in Zen or Yoga,
but of most ritualized acts (→ Prayer/Curse). Feelings and emotions need
to be learned as well: cultures and religions (as segments of cultures) offer
determinate 'emotional stereotypes,' which pre-structure the experience.
For example, emotional expectations are frequently attached to religious
festivals. Further, one must learn how and in what social contexts to lend
expression to one's feelings (for instance, the presentation of mourning)
and how emotions are named. 'Meanings,' as soon as they are regarded as
relevant, can be learned and remembered in no time, while skills (e.g. the
performance of a ritual) are usually inculcated over a long period. Learning
can occur in institutions especially provided for it (schools), or simply 'in
passing' (as in the family). Some religious authorities insist that, rather than
ritual skills or the intellectual absorption of theological teachings, what is
actually important is their practical translation, their 'inner,' 'spiritual,' or
'mystical' content. One does not necessarily learn a religious doctrine, but
one learns to act in specific contexts. Thus, by participation in cult, one does
not necessarily learn (about) the teachings of the respective religion, but one
learns to be a part of the community. Learning is not first and foremost the
result of purposive instruction, but occurs preponderantly as imitation and
identification ('learning by model'). These models can arise out of altogether
distinct contexts, and are medially transmitted in different ways. There are
various motives for imitation. Frequently, a person is chosen who is chosen
or assigned as a representative model by reason of their behavior. In recent
times, the mass media (television, but also literature) are acquiring more
importance in constructing such models.

Cognitive Processes and Stages

Since Jean Piaget (1896–1980), researchers have accepted the insight that
cognitive processes are connected with certain stages of structural mental
development. Piaget distinguishes four stages. At each stage, reality is constructed corresponding to the mental potential of the respective stage: the
environment is 'assimilated' to the mental apparatus. If the attainment of
these assimilations fails over a long period of time, the respective cognitive structures can be basically altered and of adapted to the new demands
('assimilating'), in order to attain a condition of balance ('equilibrating').
The sequence of the developmental stages, which Piaget traces from the
'sensorimotor' stage to the stage of 'formal operations,' is irreversible. Each
stage integrates the preceding, and none can be 'hurdled.' Piaget's model of
cognitive development was later transferred to other areas, such as the development of gender socialization, social understanding, or the ability to make
moral judgments. Efforts in the development of the last cited were applied
by some American and German theologians to religious development. The

sequence of the steps is unalterable in this case as well, but not every person necessarily traverses all stages (e.g., one can 'hold' at stage two).

The 'structural genetic' model of religious development (Oser and Gmünder) sketches five stages: (1) an orientation to absolute heteronomy (rules are determined from without), wherein the instance of what is ultimately valid (for example, God) actively intervenes in the world, while the human being merely reacts; (2) an orientation to the principle of reciprocity (*do ut des*, Lat., "I give that you may give"), whereby the ultimate instance is presented as open to influence; (3) an orientation to absolute autonomy ('deism'), wherein the human being is seen as self-responsible, while the instance of the ultimately valid no longer intervenes in worldly events; (4) a recognition and acknowledgment of the limits of the subject's autonomy, wherein the instance of the ultimate stipulates a kind of 'salvation plan'; and (5) a direct relationship of the human being to the instance of the ultimately valid, for instance in mysticism. Another model (Fowler) is laid out more in multiple layers, and at the same time more fuzzy. Here it is a matter of the development of 'faith' in six steps (1) Intuitive-Projective faith; (2) Mythic-Literal faith; (3) Synthetic-Conventional faith; (4) Individuative-Reflective faith; (5) Conjunctive faith; (6) Universalizing faith (exceedingly rare).

Unquestionably, developmental stages of religious biography can be found in all cultures and religions. But the theories proposed up until now are valid principally for Western and Christian cultures, and they are clearly informed by a normative (albeit liberal) Christian understanding of religion. Comparative studies of religious development of religious development processes are still lacking. Here, 'indigenous' models of religious development, specific to each religion, must be taken into account.

Roles

Religions present a network of various roles. On the one side, there are specifically religious roles (priest, guru, shaman, monk, saint); on the other, non-specifically religious roles can be 'religiously fraught' or charged (as with the partners to a 'Christian marriage'). Connected with the respective roles are different rights, duties, and expectations, the fulfillment of which, as a rule, is connected with recognition and reward, while their disregard is met with disapproval and sanctions. The transmission and assimilation of certain role-complexes are important aspects of religious socialization and upbringing. These processes occur during the entire lifetime. The learning and assimilation of roles is connected with the acquisition of certain value-orientations, and progresses in several stages. Roles, for one thing, are structured, and, for another, are 'negotiated' among the respective participants, and are individually modified. The fundamental 'mastering' of roles implies the capacity to endure even unsatisfactory role-implementations, to gain control of ambiguous situations, and, if need be, to take a calculated distance from role stipulations. While certain roles occupy all of one's person ('total roles,' e.g., monks or nuns), the normal case will be that a number of roles, or diverse roles, are called for, in different situations and in varying degrees of intensity. This scenario can occasion conflicts between various role requirements. In certain ritual contexts, roles can be reversed (→ Carnival). The roles never involve only the respective 'players', but also their partners in interaction. The guru presents himself in terms of the guru role, and his pupils present themselves vis-à-vis the guru otherwise than they do toward their other fellow human beings. Roles change in different historical and geographical contexts. Some roles lose their attractiveness, or even vanish entirely, while others are created anew. The creation of new roles is an important aspect of innovations in religious history, and frequently accompanies fundamental conceptual and ideological changes. Examples have been the emergence of the roles of the prophet and the philosopher in Israelite or Greek religious history, respectively.

The role repertoire of the religions, of course, relates not only to the area of relations among human beings. In rituals, persons 'play' or 'perform' the role of gods, spirits, or religious founders, 'imitate' religious exemplars (e.g., Christ, Francis, Ali, Hussein, the Buddha), and even the extra-human communications partners (demons, angels, spirits, gods), generally act in a framework of calculable role patterns, which must be learned by those who 'use' religious systems. Employing the pre-structured repertoire of roles makes religious communication possible.

An instance of religious socialization that is presumably primary in all cultures is the family. By observation and imitation of the religious practices of family members, children familiarize themselves with religious realities. Children imitate the posture of family members while praying, and accompany them to the celebration of rituals. At home, they hear myths and legends. The concrete reality of families is culturally and historically variable, of course. Accordingly, the religious socialization ensured by families will vary, as well. Some examples: owing to a growing fulltime employment of women, membership and collaboration of women in religious organizations (e.g., parishes) in the United States has markedly declined in recent decades, and fathers play a more important role in children's religious upbringing.[2] A recent study from The Netherlands[3] draws attention to the concurrence of episodes of socialization within families and outside: the success of religious upbringing achieved by schools, or the mass media, seems to depend not least of all on the religious atmosphere in the family. Church membership, or a positive attitude-in principle of parents, of course, does not guarantee any 'successful' Christian socialization. More important for children, evidently, are the practical results that parents derive from their Christian profession.

Religious Socialization in the Family

Families are 'religious centers,' associated in various ways with their religious environments. In ancient Mesopotamia and Syria, for example, a rather unproblematic relationship prevailed between 'family' and 'state' forms of religion. But in Israel, a situation of competition developed, and a change in 'family religion.' On the one hand, the cult of the ancestors and the veneration of local deities were extensively suppressed: at the same time, certain feasts of the 'national religion' such as Passover were celebrated as family affairs.[4]

Religious upbringing often runs its course in individual relationships. Here, religious authorities are, e.g., the master, guru, dervish, hermit, tutor, best friend, master of initiation, father confessor, baptismal sponsor, religious educator, or spiritual companion. Another, non-school type of pedagogy is effected in → groups: e.g., clubs, ritual communities, orders, guilds, associations, school-age groups, youth groups.

Individual and Group Relationships

In various historical and cultural contexts, various forms of religious education in schools have developed. The history of the Indian 'forest schools' extends from the Vedic time into the twentieth century. Buddhism replaced this system with monastic training centers, including the famous 'university'

Schools

of Nalanda. In China private schools were often integrated into families instead. In Greco-Roman antiquity, there was no formal religious education. The same is true for the Christian schools of the time of the Roman Empire. In the Middle Ages, Judaism, Christianity, and Islam developed structurally similar theological schools of higher education. The characteristics of a school that we take for granted—a government controlled, public, obligatory school system, a curriculum, a separate faculty, classes, subjects, periods— are earmarks of the modern school, which, since the nineteenth century, has spread throughout the world. The initiation and form of religious education varies from country to country.

Even modern schools aim not only at transmitting knowledge, but also at the comprehensive 'disciplining' of the pupil. Many traditions value emotive and affective learning more highly than cognitive learning (as in → Sufism, → yoga, or → Zen Buddhism). Accordingly, corporeal affective processes play a stronger pedagogical role.

Conversion as Re-Socialization

The need to learn religions is key in the transition to other religions. This process may require an individual to make conscious connections with earlier socialization experiences, or to emphatically rescind them. The Talmud explicitly likens a convert to a newborn child (bYevamot 22a, bBekharot 47a). As an example from the present, we may adduce a study of Swiss women, who, one or two years after their marriage with Muslims from Arab countries, have adopted Islam.[4] They are confronted with a code of behavior that is at first foreign to them, which they assimilate more or less slowly, not without difficulties, whereby they may discover, in their new religion, familiar, 'Swiss' values such as punctuality, precision, and cleanliness. In the process of learning their new religion, already-converted Muslims may function as exemplars. The new socialization may proceed with a change of given name: Christina becomes Zainab. Prayers are learned in a foreign language (Arabic). The corresponding postures and times must be assiduously interiorized. Fasting, as well, is new territory, and can occasion irritation in the workplace, just as can prayer made at particular times. Food taboos lead to a relearning of habits of shopping, cooking, and eating (without pork and alcohol). The most serious changes have to do with gender roles: Muslim women must learn the observance of Islamic prescriptions concerning menstruation, and to behave reservedly toward the other sex (e.g., avoid eye-contact). The latter corresponds to the adoption of a new, anti-erotic style of dress, including the wearing of the headscarf, with which they also publicly display the role of believing Muslim women in the sight of others. This display can occasion depreciative and derisive reactions. To be sure, many basic components of previous experiences of socialization remain untouched, of course, and flow into their new religious identity: the Islam of Swiss Muslim women is more democratic and 'feminist' than that of many 'Islamic' countries.

The association of conversion and socialization is often stressed, with critical intent, by the religious establishment. Thus, one repeatedly hears that membership in new religious movements or communities (→ New Religions) is the result of a disturbed 'normal socialization'. Of course, this can be empirically established only in exceptional cases. Rigid patterns of religious socialization and learning in some groups are at times stigmatized as 'brain-washing'.

One of the key media of religious upbringing is storytelling. Religious experts even consciously adopt this strategy: Zen and Sufi masters, Buddhist monks, Hindu → sadhus and → gurus, Hassidic rabbis (→ Hasidism), Afro-American preachers, and African prophets assimilate the technique of using stories to 'latch on' to everyday experience and at the same time to transcend it. Nor is the importance of → singing to be underestimated. Furthermore, → myths can discharge a special role in religious socialization processes: they can be seen as differing from → fairytales, sagas, or legends in their pragmatic relevance for the creation of worlds, or an orientation in worlds already created. In its reference to exemplary patterns, the application of myths releases spaces of experience and agency. Thus, the handing on of myths gives the members of 'myth communities' the advantage of patterns (and roles!), with the help of which they gain access to new worlds. Socialization through myths, then, is not simply a reproduction, but, likewise, a construction of worlds of experience and actions.

Stories, Myths, and Rituals

The same holds true for → rituals, which contribute to religious socialization and upbringing on a number of levels. This function comes to its most striking expression in rituals containing verbal instructions, such as sermons (for example in Buddhism, Christianity, or Islam). Rituals of transition frequently contain entire learning programs, which, in a kind of compact seminar, transmit to the candidates both basic and secret cultural knowledge. Even simple rituals must be learned. The regular celebration of simple rituals, such as that of the Buddhist flower-gift (placing flowers before a statue of the Buddha), the most basic of all Buddhist rituals, can—for example in conformity with a given stage of religious development—be provided with a rich repertory of meanings. For example, the ritual may embody the relationship of the Buddha to those who honor him, it may express dedication to, or trust in, the Buddha, it may be held to emphasize the purification of the senses as a meditative exercise, or it may be seen to contain the ritual actor's profession of the insight into the transience of all life (that eventually will lead to redemption).[6] Ritual centers are often centers of doctrine, as well, such as monasteries, mosques, or temples. The design and layout, the construction, and the adornment of cult sites often unfold many-layered programs of formation. Such is the case with the medieval cathedral, the Hindu temple, or the Buddhist stupa. The celebration of certain rituals is reserved to certain functionaries, who must qualify for this duty by submitting to a specific training. By contributing to the socialization of the body and the feelings rituals are moreover bound up with episodes of 'ordinary' socialization.

A number of studies[7] have tried to establish a connection between forms of interaction with children in a culture, and systems of religious symbols there. Some studies reinforce the assumption that severe comportment with children encourages faith in a strict, even aggressive, spiritual world. Another study reports that societies for which leniency with children is the order of the day, less frequently fear the apparition of spirits at funerals. According to another study, however, forbearing deportment vis-à-vis children leads to the assumption that the gods can be influenced through rituals. Still other research attests that where children are treated somewhat cruelly, gods are to an extent also presented as cruel. This sort of seemingly empirically corroborated analysis is, of course, problematic in several respects. It sees

Behavior with Children– Conception of the Hereafter

biography as the purely passive product of parental influence, and rests on a questionable theory of religion. The naivety of this kind of study demonstrates the complicated connection among religion, culture, and socialization/upbringing. For example, is faith in severe or indulgent gods necessarily the consequence of a severe or lenient interaction with children, rather than its premise?

The connection between religions and cultures cannot be reduced to an unambiguous causal relationship. In various cultural and religious contexts, one encounters different goals of upbringing, theories of upbringing, and apprehensions of the nature of the child and of the meaning of life. Some recent studies distinguish between individualistic cultures and those whose orientation is social. In the former, then, such as those of Germany or Switzerland, a more aggressive attitude is said to prevail among the children than in the latter, such as those of Japan or Bali. However, the importance of religious orientation in the fundamental value system and its application is hard to determine here.

Pluralism and Socialization

The ideal type of the classic theory of socialization takes its implicit point of departure in the notion that the individual is socialized into a homogeneous world. This picture corresponds to fundamentalist fancy, but not to the reality of differentiated religions and pluralistic societies, in which individuals must assert their identities vis-à-vis contradictory requirements of socialization and different contexts of socialization (→ Pluralism; Secularization). The transmission of cultural competencies in dealing with religions and religious orientations is, therefore, a demand of modern socialization and education.

Socialization of the Religious Scholars

For religious studies, socialization, upbringing, and related areas of life are not only objects of study, for students of religion themselves pass through socialization processes specific to their culture, religion, class, and gender. These specificities, in turn, have an impact on the academic work of the scholars. An intensive religious socialization in childhood can either favor or impair an understanding of certain phenomena. An academic socialization as theologian, sociologist, physician, lawyer, or anthropologist will affect the subject's sensibility with respect to the questions to be addressed and the manner in which they ought to be addressed. Most scholars of religion, furthermore, have matured with an understanding of reality specific to a particular culture and religion, and this understanding occasions the emergence of 'religion' as an independent category and informs certain basic rules to scholarship. It is to be hoped, then, that in future more scholars with different backgrounds in their own history of socialization may enrich the scholarly discourse about religion.

1. MÜLLER-ROHR, Brigitta, "Das Paradies liegt unter den Füssen der Frau. Eine qualitative Studie über Schweizerinnen, die zum Islam übergetreten sind, dissertation, Zurich 1966.
2. HERTEL, Bradley R., "Work, Family, and Faith: Recent Trends," in: AMMERMANN, Nancy T./ROOF, Wade C., Work, Family, and Religion in Contemporary Society, New York 1995, 81-121.
3. DE HART, Joep, "Impact of Religious Socialization in the Family," in: Journal of Empirical Theology 3 (1990), 59-78.
4. Cf. VAN DER TOORN, Karel, Family Religion in Babylonia, Syria and Israel: Continuity and Change in the Forms of Religious Life, Leiden 1996.

6. Cf. Schalk, Peter, "Hur barn lär sig att uföra den buddhistiska riten 'blomstergåvan,'" in: Årsbok Föreningen lärare i religionskunskap 27 (1995), 85-108.
7. Cf., e.g., Kornadt, in: Trommsdorff 1989, 82-83.

Literature

Drijvers, Jan W./MacDonald, Alasdair A. (eds.), Centres of Learning: Learning and Location in Pre-Modern Europe and the Near East, Leiden 1995; Fowler, James W., Stages of Faith: The Psychology of Human Development and the Quest for Meaning, San Francisco 1981; Holm, Nils G. (ed.), The Familiar and the Unfamiliar in the World Religions: Challenges for Religious Education Today, Åbo 1997; Hurrelmann, Klaus/Ulrich, Dieter, Handbuch der Sozialisationsforschung, Weinheim ⁵1998 (¹1991); Lang, Bernhard, "Rolle," in: Handbuch religionswissenschaftlicher Grundbegriffe 4 (1998), 460-476; Sherkat, Darren E., "Religious Socialization," in: Dillon, Michele (ed.), Handbook of the Sociology of Religion, Cambridge 2003, 151-163; Thomas, R. M., "Religious Education," in: The International Encyclopedia of Education 9 (²1994), 4995-5008; Trommsdorff, Gisela (ed.), Sozialisation im Kulturvergleich, Stuttgart 1989.

→ *Child/Childhood, Emotions/Feelings, Family, Initiation, Life Cycle, Master/Pupil, Rites of Passage, Sexuality*

Michael Stausberg

Society

1. 'Society' denotes a comprehensive social connection, a holistic system of human life in common, signed by extensive autarchy. As a concept, society is never independent of the concrete historical framework-conditions in which it is being developed. Historically, it is a new concept that became possible only as the unity of state and society—and their close connection with religion—lost its self-evidence: a development that begins to materialize in Europe only with the beginning of the modern age. Today's understanding of society is marked by the conception of the 'middle-class society' arising in the eighteenth century.

Definition and Overview

According to Max → Weber, society is distinguished from community on the basis of its cohesion being not of an emotive nature, but of a rational goal-directedness. This distinction means that a society 'functions' independently of whether persons are emotionally close to one another or not: as a rule, societies are too large to make personal relations among all of its members possible, but they nevertheless live 'together,' in a certain sense, since this facilitates the organization of daily life, and of the circumstances of life.

As a further development, American sociologist Talcott Parsons (1902–1979) defined society as a social system that combines in itself all the functions needed for its continuation. Parsons takes his point of departure in four key functions that every society must realize: adaptation, goal attainment, integration, and pattern-maintenance. His functionalistic approach could be summarized as follows:

- 'Adaptation' means an accommodation to the physical environment. That is, every society must deal in a rational way with the resources standing at its disposition (raw materials, environmental conditions, labor power, etc.), and thereby regulate its economic requirements.

Even the great churches seek to broaden their appeal: highway churches, 'rave' services, or, as in this photograph, a 'biker' service. At a memorial service, motorcyclists pray for their comrades who have been killed in traffic accidents.

- 'Goal attainment' designates the task of realizing important goals of a society. Thus, in the broadest sense, what is at issue is the development and adjustment of political tasks.
- Even in societies characterized by little differentiation, it can frequently be discerned which roles a person must implement. The more complex a society, the more important it becomes to integrate individual roles into a comprehensive system. Without role 'integration,' a society eventually collapses.
- Lest behavior in concrete inter-human relations be governed solely by the immediate personal advantage or disadvantage, societies must develop cultural norms ('pattern maintenance').

The following material will be concerned with a brief historical survey of models for the description of society.

Unless explicitly stated otherwise, the material of the present entry will pertain to the societies of Western Europe. Taken basically, 'society' as a whole is necessarily a diffuse concept. Only by way of concentration on individual aspects (politics, → economy, degree of institutionalization, etc.) does it become intelligible and empirically manageable. Nevertheless, we shall here make the attempt to follow certain approaches being used in the current discussion in the social sciences—approaches to the task of rendering conceptually manageable the fundamental characteristics of modern society across the board.

2. Societies can be distinguished in terms of the degree of their inner differentiation, in terms of the number and quality of the societal sub-groups (status, classes, ranks), in terms of the degree of a society's openness to without, as well as that of individual groups reciprocally, and—closely bound up with the latter—in terms of the opportunities for mobility on the part of individuals (among and within the various generations).

Societal Forms and Structures: Historical Survey

a) *From the society of status to modern industrial society:* In Europe, to simplify greatly, four systems or structures of social order can be distinguished in the course of history from the Middle Ages until today, as follows: (1) pre-industrial society of status, (2) early industrial society's class structure, (3) the system of stratification in later industrial society, and (4) advanced industrial society. Each of these societal forms identifies itself by way of a particular form of inner hierarchical differentiation.

Status—Class—Rank

Up until the beginning of industrialization, society was divided into social states or conditions, clearly distinguishable from one another, and closed in upon themselves. The order of the conditions was legitimized through religious value concepts, membership in a status or condition was determined by birth, and mobility from one status to another was possible only in the rarest of cases.

Industrialization replaced the rigid order of status with the somewhat less rigid class society. The position of an individual in the social structure was then normally determined by ownership or deprivation of the goods of production. Mobility from one class to the next was indeed possible in principle, but, owing to economic barriers, was seldom the case.

In the course of the twentieth century, a hierarchy of profession or occupation developed, in which, by way of example, the situation of a supervisor and that of a cleaning woman would be far apart. For ever more persons, it was now no longer ownership, nor even origin, but the position of one's profession that was the most important determinant of one's living condition. The social system continued to be open to description only inadequately, through reciprocally antagonistic classes now designated by the more neutral term *status.* The systems based on social status overlay the systems of class and condition, without, it is true, either of the latter being fully superseded. Despite societal and social barriers as present as ever, individual status became pervious to social mobility. In the framework of this more and more sharply differentiated society, the notion of a society of achievement began to prevail. This development was reinforced by an explosion of prosperity, felt at all levels (the 1950s and 1960s), which provided large parts of the population with consumer and luxury goods to an extent previously unknown. In a situation of a collective economic climb, the idea was infectious that all, in proportion to their individual efforts, have the opportunity for success (measurable in economic dimensions).

This societal formation, experienced as new, was designated with various catchwords, like 'class society in a melting pot,' or 'leveled-out middle class.' Entrenched as ever, structures of inequality died away in persons' consciousness—as a rule, not only in broad parts of the population, but also among leading social scientists. In the presence of this euphoria of progress, religion (at least in central Europe) seemed to have been deprived of its power to function as a force for social integration and the maintenance of norms.

What now began to prevail could perhaps best be called a unitary petty bourgeois lifestyle. As for the Church, it made a certain minimal appeal to a sense of duty, but the real character of obligation was missing. People attended services now only on special feast days and contacted the Church only as a 'service undertaking,' one of setting up certain procedures in matters of life cycle (baptism, marriage, funeral). By and large, interest in religious topics had very much faded into the background.

Having, Being, Enjoying

b) *In the progressive industrial society of the close of the twentieth century:* The development described up to this point can be denoted a process of increasing modernization. The degree of modernization can be read in the degree of distribution of labor, bureaucratization, social differentiation, and growing technologization and 'rationalization.' What for a certain time appeared as progress that could not be halted, was, at the close of the 1960s and the beginning of the 1970s, at the latest, called into question not only by historical development, but on the theoretical and political level, as well. Western industrial societies collided with the 'frontiers of growth' (*Report to the Club of Rome*, 1972). The cruelty of the Vietnam War raised doubts in an entire generation as to the correctness of prevailing political and social discourse. Now the modern age was followed by the apparently vague concept of → postmodernity.

The analytical division of classes in terms of an objective social situation (overwhelmingly economically determined) seemed less and less reliable as a means for the adequate description of society. Thus, in the 1980s, especially for investigation of the market, youth, and the electorate, the Sinus Institute developed the concept of 'social milieu.' Milieus were defined in terms of subjective criteria. These combine persons whose concept and manner of life is similar, and who therefore form a cultural unit in society.

Milieus were determined whose members are distinct in value orientation and life goals, in their attitude toward work, free time, and consumption, toward family and partnership. Furthermore, they differ in their perspectives on the future, in basic political convictions, and in lifestyles. But not even this model escapes vertical differentiation, into lower, middle, and upper class: and here, by way of a second (horizontal) set of coordinates, a distinction of milieus was introduced according to their orientation along the spectrum between conservative/traditional values and value transformation. In the milieu models of the 1980s, the pole of 'value transformation' still seems still clear as monolithically post-materialistic—'being,' in contradistinction from a (petty) bourgeois 'having,' an ascription that for the 1990s, at the latest, is no longer valid.

Each of the idealized, typical, milieus has its typical age structure. Persons of the 'petty bourgeois milieu,' on the average, are noticeably older than in the 'hedonistic milieu,' and have their typical free-time habits and cultural preferences. To be sure, these elements are secondary for the concept of milieu, and variable. The decisive factors for legitimate ascription to a milieu are fundamental value-orientations (education and upbringing, money, social relations, etc.) and life goals (e.g., success, or self-realization). Based on these fundamental attitudes toward life, on a lower level of abstraction, a whole series of temporary and sub-cultural units are to be found, formed along new axes, such as sports, music, cult films, or certain vacation forms. Various immigrant cultures (Turkish, Italian, etc.) possess and enduring character; unfortunately, the concept of milieus does not sufficiently take these cultures into account.

With regard to religion, religiosity, and spirituality, in most Western European countries 'ecclesiality' as an indicator is more strongly marked only in the area of the conservative and lower-middle-class milieu. But if we adduce the broader indicator 'religiosity / interest in religious themes,' then this is a dimension describable in nearly all milieus (exception: a traditional and tradition-less worker milieu), although in varying quality. Thus, in the hedonistic milieu, the number of regular churchgoers is scarcely worth citing: on the other hand, 'alternative' offers on the part of the religious market (→ New Age) are definitely taken into account with interest. Close connections to religious groups are seldom the result. Rather, in the framework of a structure of opportunity, individual offers are chosen. An exact analysis, in terms of social science, of the religious orientations and 'consumer habits' in the individual milieus is still pending, but this analysis could probably yield instructive results vis-à-vis the structure of religiosity in today's society. And, to stay with the picture of the religious 'market': even the agents of the offers of religion (including the established churches) take account of the varying 'consumer habits' of their clients. The offer grows broader, seeks sub-cultural niches, and adapts to modish trends ('rave' service; see ill.).

3. It has already been mentioned above that postmodernity is a vague concept. On this account, recent scientific efforts seek to develop the characteristics that reflect Western service-societies or industrial societies. What follows, then, is a compendious description of some of the most current concepts of society that have prevailed in recent decades.

Modern Concepts of Society

a) Ulrich Beck caused a furor in 1986 with his postulate of a 'risk society' (→ Security). Without attempting to deny the inequalities that have so stubbornly prevailed, he emphasizes that the risks of a highly technologized society know no class boundaries: in other words, a threatened environment (→ Environmentalism), a nuclear menace, or even mass unemployment, have a tendency to be able to find and affect everyone. In Beck's appraisal, these risks characterize living conditions more prominently than do differences in material sustenance. Simultaneously, traditional associations dissolve (family traditions) and give each individual the freedom to decide what forms and arrangements her or his own life will have, thus taking on the risk of having to answer for the consequences of his or her own activity. One result of this trend to individualization is that it is now no longer automatically fixed whether and how persons may arrange their religious life: they may switch religious communities, choose one or more of the offers of various groups and institutions, or simply ignore all offers. For Peter Berger, this priority of personal decision constitutes 'the heretical imperative.'

b) Society grows ever more complex and specialized. Nearly every area of life is bureaucratized and technologized. Thus, it becomes important for individuals to gain access to the corresponding knowledge, and have it available; and this produces important social changes. And so, American sociologist Daniel Bell can speak, with some justice, of a 'knowledge society.' The conveyance of knowledge by the media is no longer worldwide; the media spread it to divide it. Modern → media provide access to information in colossal density and assortment. This novel quality and quantity has prompted scientists to speak in generalizing terms of an 'information' and 'media society.' No attention is given here to the fact that interpretation and manner of utilization are never independent of a society's social and political conditions. It is always important, for example, to know whether the quality and plurality of mass media are regulated by conditions of a juridical framework, and what the particular nature and identity of that framework is. For all religious communities, the conditions of the framework have fundamentally changed, owing to the sources of information available to nearly all. These communities must themselves be present in the media. Those who are not, find it difficult even to be noticed as existing. On this account, it is no longer unusual, to cite one example, for the Catholic Church to offer financial support for films in which clergy emerge as *sympathiques*. Of even more importance, however, is the constant situation of competition among the religious communities, arising from the fact that, in principle, all users of the media have information available concerning many different religions. For most persons, → television plays a vital role: it is present everywhere, and simple to receive. Televised presentations confer certain advantages on religions: their content is altogether open to visualization, and their cult creates strong visible impressions.

c) For most persons in progressive industrial societies, the working week and life is so shaped that a great deal of time remains for—more or less arranged—free time. Here, many persons have frankly more opportunities to select how to distribute their time than in the framework of their breadwinning activities. Thus, it is obvious that the form and arrangement of free time becomes an important means to the opening out of one's personality, and therefore to self-realization, and the development of one's own self-image. The catchy phrase, 'leisure society,' has been coined to do justice to the meaning of the field of free time in one's life. Gerhard Schulz's 'event society' is a specific elaboration of this concept. Schulz emphasizes the fact that many persons (as long as they have economic means) not only mold their lives according to the standard of their elementary needs, but also pursue the goal of making an 'event' out of almost every act. Whether this need is a natural one, or one induced by 'advertisement,' is open to question. The need to arrange one's own life corresponding to the desired event-intensity is of course far from being an equally strong facet of all of the milieus cited above. It is not only in the classic area of consumership that the need for an event-intensive arrangement of free time represents an important market; persons who offer propositions along the entire spectrum of the shaping of religion and life find an important clientele here. Courses of meditation in Santorin, or trance-dancing weeks on Lanzarote, have just as much a business cycle as do introductions to Zen Buddhism in adult evening classes. Whole → tourism enterprises live on the 'folkloristic' presentation of native piety. Visits to the Aborigines in Australia, or to the Indian reservations of North America, not only enjoy great popularity, but actually change the consumed 'reality.' There are Indian Sun Dances now performed only for tourists. Whole festal calendars are rearranged to conform to typical tourist seasons and expectations.

d) Most modern societies are, de jure or de facto, pluralistic (→ Pluralism). In the Federal Republic of Germany, for instance, religious and cultural pluralism are guaranteed in the Fundamental Law by the Right to Liberty of Action (art. 2) and the Mandate of Equality (art. 3). The extent to which this is implemented, and whether one may speak of a generally accepted multicultural society, is not readily determinable. The political discussion is governed by a fatal identification of ethnic origin or extraction with religion and culture. It is easily overlooked that, in Germany, even without immigration, membership in one of the two great Christian churches is no longer self-evident. Some one-third of the population does not belong to them, and nearly twenty million belong to no religious community. In political discourse, however, it is customary to treat 'German' and 'Christian' synonymously, since those who are not themselves Christian have nevertheless 'at least' been 'Christianly socialized,' which is regarded as sufficient for a verbal consensus. Conversely, anyone not of German extraction, and especially anyone not a Christian, is said to be a 'part of the problem' (→ Ethnicity; Migration).

Globalization

All but a very few progressive industrial societies have to do battle with the 'dissolving' of their unity in terms of a national state identity. Markets, currents of merchandise and finances, migration of labor power, and even cultural 'products' such as religion, have long since ceased to be restricted to particular countries. We have a world economy, and, in the cultural area, a strong American/Western dominance is perceptible worldwide. A centuries-long colonization enabled the Catholic and Protestant churches to create a presence in nearly all of the regions of the earth, meeting a counter-balance only in countries of a strong Islamic domination. On the international level, for instance with the discussion, in a framework of the United Nations, of how human rights are to be defined, Christian conceptualizations have overwhelmingly prevailed.

None of this has as yet occasioned the generation of a 'global society.' The social (!) connection among world citizens is only rudimentary. Most persons do not feel themselves to be 'citizens of the world.' What happens in Africa, for example, is meaningless for the majority in Europe. In view of the extreme inequality of world distribution of goods and culture, it is not surprising that few things can operate as a force for integration. Ideologically, the poorest countries have little to oppose to the defensive strategies of the wealthy countries (superiority of Western/Christian democratic culture, the 'principle of achievement'). Only on the level of the 'threshold countries' have counter-movements formed in the last decades (liberation theology, political Islamism). Following Samuel Huntington in this connection, a 'clash of civilizations' is readily invoked, without any consideration of what integrative potential is at hand (for an emerging world society?).

Résumé

4. Up until a few years ago, theses on the development of the social structure were characterized by optimistic fundamental appraisals. The point of departure was an increasing unification/standardization of living conditions, an ever more differentiated set of social conditions, and the hope that purely material differences would lose in importance in favor of 'horizontal'

inequalities. The individualizing of living milieus, lifestyles, and life situations is leading to the dissolution of class-typical subcultures, indeed to a 'destratification' of the world of living across the board. Class membership is no longer the object of conscious identification. Instead, what arises is a pluralization of lines of conflict. Everyone, of either gender, can choose amongst an endless multiplicity of opportunities, whether in the arrangement of the parlor, in the choice of school, of life-partner, of occupation, of religious community, of friends, and so on. In practice, however, decisions are never actually free: as a rule, we make 'typical' decisions. We seek our partners in a typical social environment, we often decide in favor of the religious community in which we were socialized, and in the selection of living-room furniture, something of our biography can be read. Thus, 'alternative' modes of living (such as living-communities, unmarried partnerships), are factually limited to a biographical 'experimental phase' (mostly between the ages of twenty and thirty), are also accepted as such socially, and are most often in statistical conformity with established forms (marriage and family). Nevertheless, it is 'normal' to try out shamanic trance rituals or Buddhist meditation, and then marry in the village church.

In other words, from a theoretical liberty of selection, no endless multiplicity can be deduced of decisions actually faced. Norms, expectations, and traditions have become more multiple and flexible; but they still exist, as they always have.

Literature

ADAM, Barbara et al. (eds.), The Risk Society and Beyond: Critical Issues for Social Theory, London 2000; ALDRIDGE, Alan, Religion in the Contemporary World: A Sociological Introduction, Cambridge 2000; BECK, Ulrich, World Risk Society, Cambridge 1999; BELL, Daniel, The Coming of Post-Industrial Society: A Venture in Social Forecasting, New York [2]1976; BERGER, Peter L., The Heretical Imperative: Contemporary Possibilities of Religious Affirmation, Garden City 1979; BORGOTTA, Edgar F. (ed.), Encyclopedia of Sociology, 5 vols., New York [2]2000; CIPRIANI, Roberto, Sociology of Religion: An Historical Introduction, New York 2000; McGUIRE, Meredith, Religion: The Social Context, Belmont 1997; PARSONS, Talcott, Essays in Sociological Theory, rev. ed., Glencoe 1949; RITZER, George (ed.), Encyclopedia of Social Theory, 2 vols., Thousand Oaks 2005; SCHULZE, Gerhard, Die Erlebnisgesellschaft. Kultursoziologie der Gegenwart, Frankfurt/M. 1992; SWATOS, Jr., William H. (ed.), Encyclopedia of Religion and Society, Walnut Creek 1998.

→ *Charitable Organizations, Civil Religion, Economy, Everyday Life, Minorities, Political Religion, Popular Culture, Publicity, Religion, Utopia, Weber*

Claudia Haydt

Son / Daughter

A Piece of Me

1. Unlike that of 'child', the concepts 'son' and 'daughter' have a special value in terms of parents' feelings. They are a piece of the parent that receives the opportunity to live life over again, and better—to continue life and work 'a step ahead' of the parent. When the corporeal daughter and son shake off these bonds to seek their own life, the parent's projection of self can transfer to other young persons: the junior partner in the business, the daughter-in-

law. And then the concepts are applied metaphorically. However, the Western, Christian-formed limitation of the extension of the concept of family, and the compulsions of the 'flexible person' of the so-called third industrialization, generate altogether different associations from those of a culture in which kinship determines the key social position. Both the emotional and the juridical association can be intended in these metaphors. Indeed, many cultures apply them without knowing the concept of 'metaphor' itself.

2. a) In the Semitic languages, the word *ben* means 'son', denoting a membership in, or a belonging to, a family, slaves included; appurtenance to an office, whose designated successor is called 'son'; membership in a people, with a fictitious tribal father, like 'the children of Israel'; a belonging to a class or type. The Arabic expression *bin adam* ('son of Adam'), for instance, means 'human being'. This fictitious and mythological manner of speaking has an orientation to the real relation of kinship.

Heir and Successor

   b) In Mesopotamia, kings called themselves 'sons of gods and goddesses', to legitimate the claim to power made by their dynasty. In this case, what is stressed is the juridical relation between son and elders: the 'parents' have transferred power to their 'son', and the king is the legitimate heir of the monarchy. The 'parents', being gods, are obligated to afford their 'son' succor and assistance. In the Hebrew Bible, as well, steeped in the ancient Eastern conceptual world, the relationship between the king and YHWH is described as that between a son and father (Ps 2:89).

   c) 'Son' has a special significance in the expression, 'son of man.' Here, 'man' (in the sense of 'human being', not 'male human being'), while singular in number, represents a collectivity. The most ancient locus is Dan 7:13, where (in either of the likely readings of the text—'man' or 'son of man') the expression denotes the people of Israel in the End Time, and is clearly applied metaphorically. In the apocalyptic literature after Daniel, the meaning has changed to that of the title for the Messiah. This word was taken over by early Christian communities as a title for Jesus; possibly Jesus had already spoken of himself in this way. This word indicates both Jesus's high position as Messiah, and his lowliness, and position as slave, vis-à-vis the human being. However, the expression 'son of man' was still not understood literally. It is otherwise with the concept 'Son of God' in Christianity. The concept is found in the apocryphal literature of the Hebrew Bible, but there it denotes Israel, or the human being, in general. The Christians referred this expression to Jesus, without understanding it in the biological sense. In the Roman Empire, Christ came into cultic competition with the emperors, among whom Augustus was to have been miraculously conceived by the god Apollo. The Semitic chosen delegate of God became the biological divine son. In the ancient councils, embittered battles were waged over the correct understanding of this phrase.

'Son of Man' / 'Son of God'

   d) In a patriarchal society, the figurative application of 'daughter' far less accentuated as that of the 'son.' In Hebrew, we encounter the expression, 'daughter [of] Zion' (as in Isa 1:8; Lam 1:6; 2:1) for the city of Jerusalem. That use of 'daughter' in this instance is grounded on the fact that the grammatical gender of the place name is feminine. 'Daughter', in the Bible, unlike 'Son', actually has no theological meaning of its own.

Daughter

3. The concepts 'son' and 'daughter' are known in the religious sense apart from Judaism and Christianity, as well. Thus, in Buddhism, monks and nuns are called sons and daughters of the Buddha. Granted, the Buddha is never called 'Father.' After all, the metaphor can also be so understood that—at least 'ideologically'—monks and nuns stand equally placed vis-à-vis each other, like sons and daughters respectively, and in the teaching of the Buddha have a common goal. However, the Buddha's daughters were subordinated to his sons, just as daughters were subordinated in the actual relation of brother and sister in India and East Asia.

In Christianity, the concept of 'son' has a special position, founded in the notion that Jesus is the Son of God. Christianity is unique in this respect; and it is of course also due to the central theological meaning of Christology that 'son' and 'daughter' are by no means applied metaphorically. But neither in the goddess movement is 'daughter' ever applied to denote the relation of a follower to any of the goddesses. Rather, an identification is made with the goddess. For us modern persons, the metaphors of 'son' and 'daughter' probably connote a dependency that is not pleasing to us.

Literature

BURKETT, Delbert, The Son of Man Debate: A History and Evaluation, Cambridge 1999; HAHN, Ferdinand, Christologische Hoheitstitel, Göttingen ⁵1994; HENGEL, Martin, Der Sohn Gottes. Die Entstehung der Christologie und die jüdisch-hellenistische Religionsgeschichte, Tübingen 1975; SCHLISSKE, Werner, Gottessöhne und Gottessohn im Alten Testament, Stuttgart 1974; SENNETT, Richard, The Corrosion of Character: The Personal Consequences of Work in the New Capitalism, New York 1998.

→ *Child/Childhood, Family/Kinship/Genealogy, Gender Stereotypes, Matriarchy/Patriarchy, Socialization/Upbringing*

Leo Tepper

Soul

Multiplicity of Souls

1. After the idea of God, the idea that a human person has one or more souls became a widespread driving force of religious orientation and cultic instruction books. By way of extremely different conceptualizations, the soul is bound up with, especially, the whole history of religion, but without being exhausted in the area of religion. In view of the broad spectrum of cultural constructions, different demands and needs present themselves by way of notions of the soul. Conceptions of bone souls, breath souls, organ- and body-souls have their point of departure in concrete physiological experiences, and transfer this aspect of life into concepts of an afterlife, or at least of a continued existence. After death, persons might continue to exist 'in' their last breath, as a 'breath soul,' or through their bones, which "will be again clothed in flesh" (cf. Ezek 37). Other aspects place the division of the soul from the body in the foreground—during its life as a free spirit, a soul of fate, or a special instance of the *alter ego*, after its death as a shadow-soul, or as a breath- or picture-soul. All of these religious patterns transform reflections into concrete conceptualizations, whose orientation is to questions such as "What is left over, when someone dies?"; "How do ancestors

and rulers continue to operate after death?"; "What temporarily disappears, when a person falls into a faint, a trance, or an ecstasy?"

2. In view of the various cultures and different eras, it can be maintained that in an earlier period a multiplicity of souls existed side-by-side in persons' conceptions. Ancient Egypt and Homeric Greece may serve as examples of the Mediterranean course of European history of religion.

    The notion that a person possesses 'only' *one* soul, and that this soul represents the person in her or his totality, is first found in European tradition with Heraclitus. There is more here than a simple combination of life-principle with a spirit of the dead. It is the decisive 'psychological turning point' in European history of religion. Heraclitus is one of the Pre-Socratic philosophers, who, from Anaximenes onward, equated 'soul substance' with the 'fundamental material' of the world (*arché*), thus guaranteeing the soul a special rank in their cosmologies. On still another count Heraclitus introduces a turning point: with him, the soul is characterized above all by its capacity for cognition. According to the archaic cognitive principle that like can be cognized or known only by like, the fiery soul (→ *psyché*) is the component of the person that is predestined to know the world represented in fire.

The One Soul

3. The notion that the soul can be released from the body, a common component of the notion of a soul, opens up certain new possibilities. The soul comes to spaces that have been inaccessible to the body (journey to the sky, journey in the beyond), retains its knowledge after death, also improves its form of existence after death—or, indeed, precisely by death. As a professionalized practice of commerce with the soul (according to M. → Eliade, the shaman is the great 'specialist' of the human soul; only shamans 'see' it, for they know its 'shape' or formation, and its destiny; → Shamanism.) Without a doubt, shamanism has essential elements to contribute to the tradition of the soul, and to its integration into complex societies. The 'autonomy of the soul' and a professional interaction with it become constitutive elements of religious groups (Pythagoras) and mystery cults (→ Mysteries).

    In this historical and cultural framework, in the seventh and sixth centuries before the common era, conditions developed in Greece that turned the notion of soul into the religious concept that—together with the notion of God—determined European history of religion in the transition between ancient and Christian history. It is in the Socratic 'concern for the soul' (*epiméleia tes psychés*) that the cathartic anticipation of the Mysteries culminates: the soul of the human being that has come from the gods and that has accompanied a person throughout life, and outlasts death as his and her own *self*, must be constantly preserved from 'blemishes.' The limited cathartic of the general practice of cult is thus transformed into a constant claim on a 'pure life.' Under pressure of a "Puritanical psychology" (E. R. Dodds), the methodology developed of a lifestyle that presented a basically new pattern of religious orientation. With the 'latent historicization of the soul'—the idea that the soul has a history of its own, and a history of guilt, ordered to it—the religious premises of psychiatry are given.

Independence of Soul from Body

4. With concepts of a soul independent of the body, and against the various cultural horizons, 'soul' became the preferred medium of an integration into

Stranger in the World

various contexts: as soul of the ancestors, it comes among them, and guarantees collective norms; as 'soul divine,' it returns to the region of the gods; as soul charged with fire, it climbs to the sphere of the ether; as soul redeemed, it is with God. Finally, with the conclusion that it is not in its proper place, → gnosticism shaped it into a 'twin alienation': thus, anthropologies and soteriologies, with their pedagogical and political drafts, at the same time are shot through with the concept of soul. With his three parts of the soul (the *logistikón*, the *thymoeidés*, the *epithymetikón*), not only has Plato sketched out a fundamental pattern for Western psychology to live by, but has pointed to the pregnant connection between psychology and politics (→ Platonism). For Plato, structure of the soul and structure of the state, parts of the soul and social ranks, must be brought into a harmonious correlation determined by justice, if the state is to endure. In Platonism, the state's claim on the human soul has found a theoretical foundation, one of whose consequences is the state's 'maintaining imperative' with respect to the 'salvation of the soul' of the citizen. Only human rights and freedom of religion have sundered this nexus from 'uniformity.'

An Endless History?

3. However the linguistic equivalents for the concept of 'soul' (e.g., Fr. *âme*, Ger. *Seele*) may be determined in non-European languages, they belong to those religious conception-complexes that are characterized by a *longue durée* (Fr., 'long duration'), over epochs and cultural boundaries. For the European tradition, this durability means that the Platonic and Neo-Pythagorean concepts of the soul, developed in a Mediterranean polytheistic context, has survived in (or against) a monotheistic, industrial, and post-industrial environment. The foundations of this long-term plausibility for a concept of the soul can be seen in its postulation that a part of the person potentially withdraws from the "pressure of reality" (S. Freud), from even that of a hereafter or a later incarnation. Closely connected, here, are the conceptions that posit the destiny of the soul as independent of that of the individual incarnation, so that the soul has its own history of culpability and ascent. In this fashion, under certain conditions, the soul becomes the preferred object of 'self-help,' of control and discipline (leading or guiding the soul). It can also replace or redefine the older techniques to be applied to the → body (catharsis, disciplining, asceticism). The other foundation for the trans-cultural plausibility of a concept of the soul probably lies in the fact that the soul is capable not only of achieving an integration of the person into the society of persons, but also of connecting him or her to the environment, from plants to the world as a whole. To ascribe plants, animals, and human beings a soul (or a common soul-part) is to order the 'animate' environment, the beings having life, to an 'anthropological' schema. To ascribe the whole world a world-soul, integrates the individual human soul into a cosmic scenario.

Literature

BAUMGARTEN, A. I. et al. (eds.), Self, Soul and Body in Religious Experience, Leiden 1998; Bos, Jacques, Reading the Soul: The Transformation of the Classical Discourse on Character, 1550–1750, dissertation Leiden 2003; BREMMER, Jan, The Early Greek Concept of the Soul, Princeton 1983; Idem, The Rise and Fall of the Afterlife, London/New York 2002; DODDS, Eric Robertson, The Greeks and the Irrational, Berkeley 1951; GEHLEN, Arnold, Man in the Age of Technology, New York 1980 (Ger. ¹1957); GLADIGOW, Burkhard, "'Tiefe der Seele' und '*inner space*'. Zur Geschichte eines Topos von Heraklit bis zur

Science Fiction," in: ASSMANN, Jan (ed.), Die Erfindung des inneren Menschen, Gütersloh 1993, 114-132; JÜTTEMANN, Gerd et al. (eds.), Die Seele. Ihre Geschichte im Abendland, Weinheim 1991; KIRSCHNER, Susanne R., The Religious and Romantic Origins of Psychoanalysis, Cambridge 1996; MacDONALD, Paul S., History of the Concept of Mind: Speculations about Soul, Mind and Spirit from Homer to Hume, Aldershot 2003; OTTO, Walter F., Die Manen oder von den Urformen des Totenglaubens, Darmstadt 1963 (¹1923); SPRANGER, Eduard, Magie der Seele, Tübingen 1947.

→ *Animism, Aristotelianism, Gnosticism, Immortality, Platonism, Psyche, Psychoanalysis, Shamanism*

Burkhard Gladigow

South America

1. Some few years ago, in Colombia, the Zenú undertook their traditional Easter pilgrimage to a cave on Mt. Sierrachiquita, abode of the mythical Kazike, Mohana. The white proprietor of the mountain paralyzed the 'pagan' cultic system by having the cave filled. As his punishment—so the Zenú believe—Mohana blinded him. At the same time, a firm from Barranquilla consolidated the mountain, the nature sanctuary, the reservoir for medicinal herbs, and the place for shamanic rituals, with the purpose of mining street-gravel. But since the mountain, as a Caiman, supports the earth, the Indians now fear the end of the world, through the flooding of their area by the sea beneath the world.

The Holy Mountain of the Zenú

2. For Indio-American cultures and religions such as those of the Zenú, 'Latin American identity' is: adjacency of Christian usage and the ancient gods and myths; Western economic imperialism and unlawful settlement of the land and territory; an urban slum-existence and exploitation of raw materials, in these regions, the remotest of the world. Basically, the Indio-American cultures are considered to be those that embrace the indigenous peoples of South and → Central America, as far as Honduras (to a line drawn between San Pedro Sulla and the Gulf of de Fonseca). The first Indians emigrated to America 14,000 years ago, hunters and gatherers from Northeast Asia, and settled the subcontinent all the way to Tierra del Fuego. Today they inhabit the three major anthropo-geographical regions 'Caribbean—Pacific—Andes' (they are the descendants of, among others, the Aymará and the Inca) and dwell in the tropical rainforest (Amazon, East Brazil), as well as in the Gran Chaco, all the way to Patagonia and Tierra del Fuego. Owing to the sometimes early mix with European immigrants ('mestization'), as well as to a vague assignment of land and water to fishing and farming populations (Caboclos of the Amazon, peasants), with their indigenous high-cultural inheritance, and owing to newly awakened Indian consciousness, statistical data on the Indians now living are unreliable. At present, demographers suppose populations totaling over 15 million (among others, eleven million Andeans and one million Amazons) for South American Indians. Aside from Peru and Bolivia, where Indians make up the lion's share of the population, and 'white' Argentina, the numerically largest group in South America is comprised of mestizos. South America displays an extraordinary cultural, ethnic, and linguistic diversity. More than one hundred and

Indio-American Identity

The feasts of the saints, as here in San Andrés de Sotavento, on the Colombian coast of the Caribbean, exhibit the motif called the 'world upside-down.' Carnivalesque celebrations are ritualized rebellions, mounted by the socially and economically repressed Indians and Indo-Mestizos: even the 'whites' lionize Indian San Simón, who, as a mythical Cazike, defended the Indians against the whites, and they offer him contributions of maize beer (*chichi*) or money. In the orgiastic, powerful acts of the feasts, 'heated' society periodically 'cools off.'

twenty indigenous peoples live in Brazil alone: there are hunters (the Aché, Paraguay), planters (the Shuar, Ecuador), the Quaechua-speaking rural population of Peru (descendants of the Inca), Indians in remote areas (Kogi, Colombia), and 'acculturated' Indian farmers (Zenú, Colombia), besides the broad spectrum of the mestizo cultures. Despite numerous local types and divisions, religious world-images and cultic practices are bound by similar concepts, and these govern the thinking and acting of indigenous or Indio-Mestizo groups of South America. Hence it is possible to speak of a unitary 'Indio-American religion.'[1]

Today, millions of Indians are nominally *Christians*. Shortly after the 'discovery' of America (1492), European colonization and missionary activity began. The political and economic interests of the conquerors (read, greed for gold) received the religious stamp of approval as a 'Crusade' through papal bulls, especially since the Indians were said to be practicing → cannibalism, unbridled sexual activity, and devil worship. For the native inhabitants, 'discovery' meant physical annihilation, enslavement, forced Christianization, and the prohibition of their 'demoniacal' religious practice. The missionaries' cunning, with which they built churches on ravaged sites of indigenous worship, supplied the Indians with the opportunity to practice their 'heathenism' in thenceforth 'syncretist garb.' In this fashion, many Indian Christians continued to practice their respective Indian religions, as they always had.

Indio-American Worldview

3. The Indio-American cosmos consists of several layers, held together by a 'world axis': regions of the sky, then the earth, then the ocean of the lower world, upon which the earth rests. The 'life force' (in Span., *espíritu*) of sun or moon, of the wild, or of a lower world of 'living waters' (in Andean thought, source of the cyclical course of water), nourishes the cosmos. The vertical distinction is the outcome of destructions of the world having occurred in primeval time, through world flood and conflagration. The lower world is the domain of mighty water beasts (anaconda, caiman), heaven is the powerful realm of the robber birds (king vulture, harpy eagle), and the

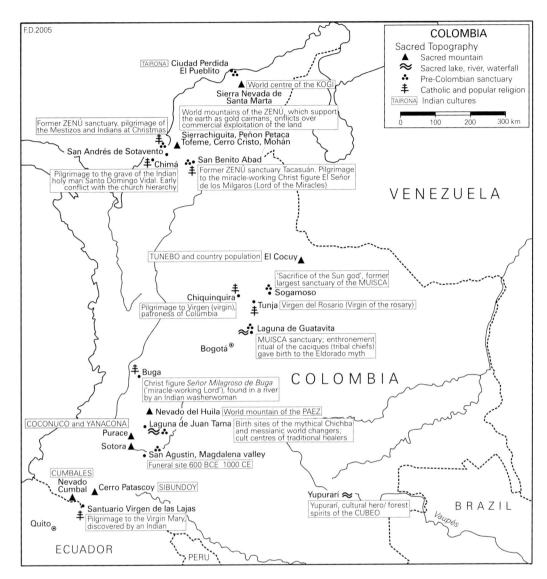

F.D.2005

COLOMBIA
Sacred Topography
▲ Sacred mountain
≈ Sacred lake, river, waterfall
⁝ Pre-Colombian sanctuary
‡ Catholic and popular religion
TAIRONA Indian cultures

0   100   200   300 km

TAIRONA Ciudad Perdida
El Pueblito
▲ World centre of the KOGI
Sierra Nevada de
Santa Marta

World mountains of the ZENÚ, which support
the earth as gold caimans; onflicts over
commercial exploitation of the land

Former ZENÚ sanctuary, pilgrimage of
the Mestizos and Indians at Christmas
Sierrachiguita, Peñon Petaca
▲ Tofeme, Cerro Cristo, Mohán

San Andrés de Sotavento
‡ Chimá
San Benito Abad
Former ZENÚ sanctuary Tacasuán. Pilgrimage
to the miracle-working Christ figure El Señor
de los Milgaros (Lord of the Miracles)

Pilgrimage to the grave of the Indian
holy man Santo Domingo Vidal. Early
conflict with the church hierarchy

VENEZUELA

TUNEBO and country population El Cocuy ▲

'Sacrifice of the Sun god', former
largest sanctuary of the MUISCA
⁝ Sogamoso

Chiquinquira
Pilgrimage to Virgen (virgin),
patroness of Colúmbia
‡ Tunja Virgen del Rosario (Virgin of the rosary)

≈⁝ Laguna de Guatavita
MUISCA sanctuary; enthronement
ritual of the caciques (tribal chiefs)
gave birth to the Eldorado myth

Bogotá ◉

COLOMBIA

‡ Buga
Christ figure *Señor Milagroso de Buga*
('miracle-working Lord'), found in a river
by an Indian washerwoman

▲ Nevado del Huila World mountain of the PAEZ

COCONUCO and YANACONA
Purace ▲
≈⁝ Laguna de Juan Tama
Birth sites of the mythical Chichba
and messianic world changers;
cult centres of traditional healers

Sotora ▲
⁝ San Agustín, Magdalena valley
Funeral site 600 BCE 1000 CE

CUMBALES
Nevado
Cumbal ▲ Cerro Patascoy SIBUNDOY

Yupurarí ≈
Yupurarí, cultural hero/ forest
spirits of the CUBEO

BRAZIL
Vaupés

‡ Santuario Virgen de las Lajas
Pilgrimage to the Virgin Mary,
discovered by an Indian

Quito ◉

ECUADOR

PERU

South America is strewn and studded with places of mythic qualities. Every waterhole, every mountain, every lake, every site along a river, may have the potential meaning and importance of a sacred place. Every people, then, every village, has its sacred places—the places of its mythical origin—as the symbolic cultural basis of its relations. The cartographical survey here shows that an Indio-American pilgrimage, as a collective mass-presentation, is fittingly regarded as the phenomenon of a 'high culture.' There is a mingling, on Colombian territory, of Incan and Aymarán tradition, and in Colombian territory, of pre-Spanish elements with Christendom. In the case of these cultures, even pre-Spanish pilgrimages are attested. Thus, these maps include only important cultic centers and meaningful pre-Colombian sites.

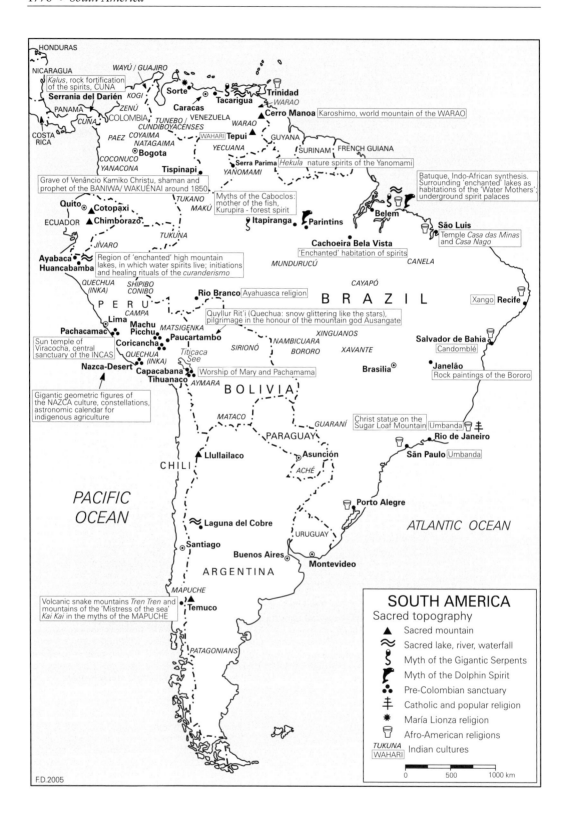

HONDURAS

NICARAGUA

WAYÚ / GUAJIRO

Kalus, rock fortification of the spirits, CUNA

Serrania del Darién KOGI

Sorte

PANAMA ZENÚ

CUNA COLOMBIA

COSTA RICA

PAEZ COYAIMA NATAGAIMA

COCONUCO YANACONA

⊗**Bogota**

Tispinapi

TUNEBO / CUNDIBOYACENSES

YECUANA

Caracas

Tacarigua ● **Trinidad**
WARAO

VENEZUELA

WARAO

WAHARI **Tepui**

▲ **Cerro Manoa** Karoshimo, world mountain of the WARAO

GUYANA

SURINAM FRENCH GUIANA

Serra Parima *Hekula* nature spirits of the Yanomami

YAÑOMAMI

Batuque, Indo-African synthesis. Surrounding 'enchanted' lakes as habitations of the 'Water Mothers'; underground spirit palaces

Quito ⊗

JÍVARO

ECUADOR

Cotopaxi ▲ **Chimborazo**

TUKANO

MAKÚ

Grave of Venâncio Kamiko Christu, shaman and prophet of the BANIWA/ WAKUÉNAI around 1850

TUKUNA

Myths of the Caboclos: mother of the fish, Kurupira - forest spirit

● **Itapiranga** ● ▲ **Parintins**

Belem ⊌

⊌ **São Luis**

Temple Casa das Minas and Casa Nago

Cachoeira Bela Vista
'Enchanted' habitation of spirits

Ayabaca ● ≈
Huancabamba ●

Region of 'enchanted' high mountain lakes, in which water spirits live; initiations and healing rituals of the *curanderismo*

QUECHUA (INKA)

SHIPIBO CONIBO

MUNDURUCÚ

CANELA

CAYAPÓ

Rio Branco Ayahuasca religion

B R A Z I L

Xango **Recife** ⊌

P E R U

CAMPA

Lima ⊗

Machu Picchu ●

Pachacamac ● ●

Sun temple of Viracocha, central sanctuary of the INCAS

Coricancha ● ● **Paucartambo**

MATSIGENKA

QUECHUA (INKA)

Quyllur Rit'i (Quechua: snow glittering like the stars), pilgrimage in the honour of the mountain god Ausangate

XINGUANOS

NAMBICUARA

SIRIONÓ

BORORO

XAVANTE

Salvador de Bahia ⊌
Candomblé

Nazca-Desert

Capacabana ● ●
Tihuanaco ●

Titicaca See

AYMARA

Worship of Mary and Pachamama

Brasilia ⊗

● **Janelão**
Rock paintings of the Bororo

Gigantic geometric figures of the NAZCA culture, constellations, astronomic calendar for indigenous agriculture

B O L I V I A

MATACO

GUARANÍ

Christ statue on the Sugar Loaf Mountain

Umbanda ⊌ ‡

CHILI

Llullaillaco ▲

PARAGUAY

Asunción ⊗

ACHÉ

● **Rio de Janeiro**

São Paulo Umbanda

⊌ **Porto Alegre**

PACIFIC OCEAN

≈ **Laguna del Cobre**

Santiago ⊗

URUGUAY

ATLANTIC OCEAN

Buenos Aires ⊗

Montevideo

A R G E N T I N A

MAPUCHE

Volcanic snake mountains *Tren Tren* and mountains of the 'Mistress of the sea' *Kai Kai* in the myths of the MAPUCHE

▲ ● **Temuco**

PATAGONIANS

SOUTH AMERICA
Sacred topography

▲ Sacred mountain

≈ Sacred lake, river, waterfall

Myth of the Gigantic Serpents

Myth of the Dolphin Spirit

●●● Pre-Colombian sanctuary

‡ Catholic and popular religion

✳ María Lionza religion

⊌ Afro-American religions

TUKUNA
WAHARI Indian cultures

0   500   1000 km

F.D.2005

The village of Charazani celebrates the Feast of *Todos Santos* (Sp., 'All Saints'). Here, the Christian feasts of All Saints and All Souls, November 1 and 2, are connected with pre-Christian conceptualizations of the return of the dead (cf. → Death and Dying). In this region, loved ones return after their deaths as *almas nuevas* (Sp., 'new souls') for three feasts of All Saints, and visit the cabins in which they have lived. On November 2, the villagers go out to the cemetery, accompanied by music groups, whose flutes and drums have played uninterruptedly since the day before. Families with a 'new soul' bring gifts along. Days before, sugar-cane poles have been constructed, in their cabin, hung with breads and fruits, and standing on a richly draped table. Nor must bottles of whiskey be lacking. Many of the celebrants are already tipsy, since, after Mass on November 1, they have entered the homes in which the 'new souls' have paid a visit, spoken prayers, and conversed all night long, drinking alcohol. At the cemetery, the gifts are supposed to be placed at the graves. In what one might call the Quechua catechism, the position taken by the Catholic Church with regard to the usages of *Todos Santos* becomes ambivalent. Nevertheless, in the everyday ritual of the Bolivian Andes in the area of the usages pertaining to the dead, a contiguity of Christian and non-Christian religious elements is feasible. (Kirsten Holzapfel, following Ina Rösing)

forest supports the jaguar. In some instances, these sorts of animals are also supernatural beings, even with their human traits—after all, an incarnation or 'ensocietization' of the universe will generate a 'mythic familiarity' with it, preserving, naturally, its often menacing ambivalence. Regions of the sky and underworld harbor mythical primitive beings, and souls of the dead. The horizontal perspective is ethnocentric: the region of one's own we-group, human culture, is ensconced in the center of space, and separated from the 'without': from the wild, with its spirits, and other unfamiliar beings.

The Wild

A sacred geography marks the inhabited areas of indigenous peoples, makes territorial claims visible in battles over land, forms places of pilgrimage, and constitutes an identity in the ethnicity of cultures. The key orientation pattern is the uncontrollable wild, with its life and power, so different from the zone of culture. The wild (watering places, caves) is the gate to the lower world, and as cultic 'border region,' the place of shamanic initiation. Water, medicinal plants, and wild beasts are tentative gifts of the universe; they have spiritual masters and mothers (Lord of the Animals, plant spirits, Water Mother). With the utilization of these nature-resources (mythically: 'life force,' *espíritu*), the human being must observe a complicated network of rules of reciprocal relations ('principle of reciprocity'). He must kill only the number of animals that he receives as 'gifts,' granted by the guardian spirits in exchange for souls of the dead or sacrificial offerings (tobacco, coca). Uncontrolled contact with the wild entails the risk of losing one's own life power. The spirits punish greedy persons, like the Colombian mountain-owner mentioned above, with bad hunting or illness. In a context of the indigenous "philosophy of dynamic equilibrium" (G. Reichel-Dolmatoff), the prohibitions connected with the use ('taming') of the wilderness or with hunting are mechanisms of ecological control that are frequently misunderstood as the wisdom of Indian 'Eco-saints' in a Western, mystifying interpretation (→ Orientalism/Exotism; Environmentalism).

The Two Worlds

"There are two ways of seeing things." When the Kogi proclaim their thought, they speak of *aluna*—'spirit,' 'thought,' 'essence of things,' 'concealed true reality.' 'Everyday reality' is illusion. The polarity between the visible and the invisible world explains the importance and meaning of ritual drug-consumption (e.g., of *Yagé*, or Quechua *ayahuasca*, 'soul liana'—a brew of jungle liana, *Banisteriopsis sp.*; → Trance), the importance and meaning of shamanic ecstasy and vision. The two worlds entirely interpenetrate; the invisible world can turn on human beings; shamans are the defenders of their own community, since they have at their disposition mighty spirits of defense and assistance (e.g., the jaguar); through these spirits, they are able to regulate relations between human beings and spirit beings. The power of the shamans rests not least of all on their knowledge (legitimized in ecstasy), on their seeing 'true' reality in visions, and on their deliberately seeking out this reality, in which they are then able to act. Their tasks, then, are: healing, weather control, interpretation of presages and dreams, provision of hunting animals, handling (socialization) of fare, escort of the souls of the dead to the region of their cosmic destination, and execution of the rituals.

Hot and Cold—a
Dynamic Equilibrium

Dialectically complementary polarities (not → dualisms!) are characteristic of Indio-American thought. The principle that everything in the world possesses a certain measure of *espíritu* or *calor* ('heat'), determines the 'religious everyday.' Objects or events in the *espíritu* world are 'hot,' *espíritu*-poor ones are 'cold,' the human being attains wellness and serenity only when s/he maintains a dynamic equilibrium among factors separately containing a 'too much' or a 'too little' of *espíritu*. By periodic 'coolings,' festivals prevent too great a 'heating' of society and cosmos. Violent activity, and wild drinking bouts, are the expression of the creator's craving for destruction, and serve for the maintenance or renewal of the world order.[2] Thus, at Andean festivals, the male (*ira*) and female (*arka*) principles crash into each other, in a bloody, frequently deadly, ritual battle, and are dialectically reconciled in the *tinku*, the dynamic equilibrium of complementary opposites.

Healing from culturally specific, spiritual illness is the affair of the shaman (*curandero*, Sp., 'healer'), in situations such as when, in ecstasy, he seeks out the cosmic regions and brings back the sufferer's soul. A diagnosis is possible only through the shaman's clairvoyance, for instance, through the recognition of infectious spirits in the patient's urine. The Indian medico-religious complex testifies to uninterrupted vitality: the Sibundoy Indians (Southwestern Colombia) practice their trade in remedial plants as far as Costa Rica, and shamans are active in the big cities of Latin American 'whites.' The spirituality of the shamans, mediators of the conflictive relationships among the classes, cultures, and ethnic groups, becomes a coveted commodity: one buys spirit for money. The socioeconomic impetus to acculturation, sharpened by international technology and globalization, is balanced out by indigenous 'magic,' and charms meant to harm (sometimes as a weapon in the battle of the classes!).

Illness and Healing— the Curandero

6. Even five hundred years after Columbus, massive Christian attempts to missionize and repress Indio-Americans achieve only partial outcomes. In 'syncretistic piety,' usually the result of 'quiet' cultural resistance on the part of the defeated, not infrequently the Indian underlay shines through a Christian veneer. Thus, Catholic saints have been incorporated as a 'foreign word' into the indigenous 'religious grammar.' For a successful harvest, the descendants of the Incas in Peru and Bolivia make offerings to the Blessed Virgin Mary, who has fused with the earth mother Pachamama. *Curanderos* work with saints and angels, their 'shamanic' succoring spirits. For Indio-mestizos, Jesus is the Sun, traversing the sky with his medicine bag, resting at noon and chewing coca. Indio-Americans make pilgrimages to the ancestors' sacred mountains, in whose caves the mythical gold caiman and Catholic saints peacefully coexist.

The Indio-American Religions Today

However, the picture of peaceful coexistence can be deceiving. On the heels of a newly awakened Indian awareness and movements of revitalization, Indian saints—charismatically gifted Indians, reverenced as saints after their death—and miraculous sacred images discovered by Indians in the wild are set up over against the 'dead' saints of the whites. The operations of fundamentalist, evangelical sects from the United States, such as the Pentecostalists, or the Summer Institute of Linguistics in Northwestern Amazonia, were frequently the prelude of later economic exploitation of resources (mineral oil, etc.) in Indian regions, and hence had more of a destructive than an enhancing effect on Indian cultures. To be sure, a mixture of indigenous religion and Anglican Protestantism are leading to syncretistic revival

Charismatic Movements and Messianic Hopes

movements ('Hallelujah religion'): shamanic prophets among the Akawaio Guayanas announced the falsification of the salvific message by white missionaries who sought to dissuade the Indians from entertaining any hope of material riches (→ Charismatic Movement).[3] In the future-vision of the descendants of the Incas, the rule of the Christian God is at an end when Inkarrí, the mythic personification of the Inca ruler murdered by Spaniards, and leader of rebellions, rises up once more from his dismembered body: 'blood flow,' and 'blood sun,' then mark the 'world turner' (*pachacuti*), the end of the 'white' world, and the beginning of a new, Indian world-age. The sources of Inca mythology nourished the early-colonial, religio-political possession cult of the *taqui oncoy* ("Song/Dance of the Pleiades"; c. 1560), just as did, finally, the 'liberation ideology' of the Peruvian guerrilla movement "Shining Path" (*Sendero Luminoso*). Eschatological hopes also nourished Andean popular theater, which presented the colonial trauma—the Spanish invasion—experienced as a cosmic catastrophe, from the 'standpoint of the defeated,' and thereby overcame it. Messianic movements are attested even in pre-Spanish Indio-America—phenomena intensified, it is true, by a social situation of contact with the 'whites'—as with the religious migrations of the Tupí-Guarani (Brazil, Paraguay) in quest of the 'land without evil.'

In the modern metropolises of Latin America as well, Indian life is by no means characterized by adaptation alone. Guajiro women (Venezuela/Colombia) react to the 'Wilderness' Macaraibos with "their longing to shamanize,"[4] the Andean rural population who have migrated to the cities contribute their earnings (from taxis and shops) to Pachamama, along with their traditional drink offerings (*ch'alla*). City cults of healing, based on the Indian drug Yagé, transcend all classes and ethnic groups: in Brazil, Peru, and Bolivia, there has appeared the *Ayahuasca* religion that propagates the drinking of the 'sacramental drug' (especially for salvific purposes), under the direction of a shaman or spiritist.[5] In the common life of the cultures, forms are mixed together, such as the Indio-African Batuque religion (Northern Brazil), or the Indio-African-European synthesis of Venezuela's Maria Lionza religion. The region of the dead of Cuna (Panama), overflowing with Western consumer goods, the rocky places of the spirits with the golden skyscrapers, parades, and telephones, all testify to the ability of Indian culture to rework influences of modern times without surrendering their own culture.

1. Hofer, Florian, Der "heiße" Strom des "kalten" Wassers, Munich 1995; Faust, Franz, Totgeschwiegene indianische Welten. Eine Reise in die Philosophie der Nordanden, Gehren 1998.
2. Cf. Sullivan 1988, 195ff.
3. Münzel, Mark, Die Indianer, vol. 2: Mittel- und Südamerika, Munich 1985, 234f.
4. Perrin, in: Langdon/Baer 1992, 117ff.
5. Taussig 1987; Ramirez/Pinzón, in: Langdon/Baer 1992, 287ff. (Colombia); Luna, Luis Eduardo, Vegetalismo. Shamanism among the Mestizo Population of the Peruvian Amazon, Stockholm 1986; Fichte, Hubert, Lazarus und die Waschmaschine, Frankfurt/M. 1985 (pp. 187-203; "Blue Castle," in Rio Branco, Brazil).

Literature

Gossen, Gary H. (ed.), South and Meso-American Native Spirituality: From the Cult of the Feathered Serpent to the Theology of Liberation, New York 1993; Griffiths,

Nicholas, The Cross and the Serpent: Religious Repression and Resurgence in Colonial Peru, Norman 1996; LANGDON, Jean/BAER, Gerhard (eds.), Portals of Power: Shamanism in South America, Albuquerque 1992; MACCORMACK, Sabine, Religion in the Andes: Vision and Imagination in Early Colonial Peru, Princeton 1991; MCDOWELL, John Holmes, Sayings of the Ancestors: The Spiritual Life of the Sibundoy Indians, Lexington 1989; PERRIN, Michel, The Way of the Dead Indians: Guajir Myths and Symbols, Austin 1987; REICHEL-DOLMATOFF, Gerardo, The People of Aritama, London 1961; Idem, The Forest Within: The World-View of the Tukano Amazonian Indians, Totnes 1996; SULLIVAN, Lawrence, Icanchu's Drum: An Orientation to Meaning in South American Religions, New York 1985; TAUSSIG, Michael, Shamanism, Colonialism and the Wild Man: A Study in Terror and Healing, Chicago 1987; Idem, Mimesis and Alterity: A Particular History of the Senses, New York 1993.

→ *Afro-American Religions, Animal, Central America, Colonialism, Cosmology/Cosmogony, Liberation Theology, Mission, North America (Traditional Religions), Shamanism*

Josef Drexler

Southeast Asia

1. a) Southeast Asia comprises (Islamic) Malaysia and the (primarily Buddhist) states of Burma (Myanmar), Thailand, Laos, Kampuchea, and Vietnam.

The Region

b) Imperialism, first that of the British and French, then of the United States in the Vietnam War, inflicted deep wounds. The Khmer Rouge reign of terror shocked and stunned the entire region. Even after the withdrawal of soldiers, however, cultures collided once more. Armies were succeeded by economy and tourism, both sometimes viewed as another kind of imperialism. Millions of persons work for subsistence wages, many earn their money in the dangerous sex market for years, and then pay dearly with their misery. Alarming modernizations in the cities, and retardation on the countryside, plunge the region into crisis after crisis. The West perceives China and Communism as heavily tinting the region's independence, but (especially Theravada) Buddhism from India shapes an older class identity affecting these countries. Buddhist monks, in their own way, repeatedly struggled with the foreign conquerors.

Wars and Crises without End?

c) In the second century BCE, North Vietnam fell under a roughly one-thousand-year Chinese hegemony. With the occupation, there arrived in the region not only the teachings of Chinese → Daoism and → Confucianism, but later various schools of Mahayana Buddhism as well, that had developed in China. In the course of time, these currents were mixed with an indigenous veneration of → ancestors, and there arose a variegated popular religion.

Beginning in the third century, Indian traders brought philosophical and religious ideas from their homeland into today's Burma (Myanmar), and in post-Christian times, all the way to Vietnam by sea. In Middle Vietnam and Kampuchea, the Hindu-influenced realms of Champa and Angkor materialized. Rather at the same time, Buddhist-influenced dominions formed in Burma and Thailand. In the twelfth century, in Burma, Theravada Buddhism was elevated to the status of state religion. The contemporary rulers

On a street in the inner city of Rangoon, Burma (Myanmar), in the afternoon of the November full moon, a *kathina* festival is held. The Buddha himself was the originator of the direction that fully ordained members of orders should stop at one place during the four-month rainy season (*vassa*), between the months of *savanna* (July/August) and *kattika* (October/November). The obligation of residence lasts three months. *Vassa* is an opportunity for the lay members to express their veneration, and to gain merit by supplying the orders with necessities. When the rainy season is at an end, the *kathina* period begins, lasting until the next full moon. The *kathina* period extends the gift-giving time to the month of *phagunna* (February/March). The most important event

of Thailand, Laos, and Kampuchea followed this example. Beginning in the fifteenth century, the kings of the lands of Southeast Asia reinforced their positions of power vis-à-vis Buddhist order-communities (*sangha*). The clergy of these countries is even today controlled by the state.

With the exception of Vietnam and Malaysia, the writing systems of the countries of Southeast Asia developed from the writing systems of India. The cultic language of the lands of Theravada Buddhism is Pali.

2. The *practice of religion* is possible even in the Socialist states of Laos and Vietnam, and the number of monks and novices—in Vietnam also nuns—is great. In Theravada countries, women are fully ordained only in exceptional cases, and, as a rule, do not enjoy the great respect accorded by believers to the monks.

In popular conceptualizations, it is important for the laity to acquire merit in order to achieve a favorable rebirth. Monks provide them with the opportunity to do so, by accepting meals from them, for example. Merit can also be acquired through contributions of money or goods to monasteries. On all important occasions in the life of a person (birth, marriage, death), monks are invited into the houses of the laity to conduct ceremonies. In many difficulties, those in search of counsel turn to the clergy. The monasteries also offer the laity instruction in Buddhist teaching.

a) As a rule, believers do not visit temples on a daily basis, but only on religious or personal festival days, or on pilgrimage. Early in the morning, a ritual takes place before the home altar. Before personal meditation, one offers flowers, incense sticks, vegetables, or the like, to the statue of the Buddha.

b) In Southeast Asia, various 'religious levels' are superimposed that have existed there even before Buddhism, and that play a role alongside Buddhism even today. It is particularly in Theravada Buddhism that the

Buddha stands for a path of salvation without a divine function attaching to him. Persons turn to the gods of → Hinduism for the fulfillment of their desires, or avail themselves of → amulets for protection against all manner of iniquity and insult. Before weighty decisions in life, before a marriage, for example, or a long journey, men and women are summoned to consult as astrologers or prophets, or advice is sought from oracles. Monks are not actually supposed to turn to these practices, but they tolerate them, and are usually present at them when popular religious rites are performed that are regarded as subordinate to Buddhism.

Belief in spirits long preceded the arrival of Buddhism in Southeast Asia. Only certain persons could enter into contact with this special world: the mediums or the shamans. Even in Southeast Asia's modern cities, little spirit-houses in front of homes testify to belief in this old tradition. In order to placate the potential hostility of the spirit upon whose territory human persons have come, a Brahmin or an astrologer must perform a ceremony of consecration. The house spirit is thenceforward to be nourished with daily sacrifices of food and drink. Even the spirits of trees, mountains, and waters must be dealt with, as well as with that of an unnatural death. Magical powers are visibly attributed, especially to high, old trees, through the many variegated wish-ribbons around their trunks. Notions of the spirits have kept pace with changes: repeatedly, one sees on the rear-view mirror of an automobile, or on the bow of a boat, fresh garlands—for the spirits who are to watch over one's journeying. Among the important family celebrations (naming of a child, marriage, important journeys, the New Year, but not a funeral), the *Baci* ceremony is included, presided over by a respected member of the family or neighborhood. Here as well, monks may be present, but do not take part in the ritual. The reconciliation of human beings with one another, and of the world of human beings and spirits, takes place here, around the Baci Tree. Reciprocal good wishes are wrapped around the wrist in the form of a cotton ribbon, an act intended at the same time to ward off evil spirits.

c) According to Buddhist notions, death is but a way station along the route to a new rebirth. Still, in many countries of Southeast Asia, families commemorate their dead on the anniversary of the day of their death. Especially in Vietnam, but also among Thais of Chinese extraction, the veneration of ancestors takes place according to the Chinese model.

The countries of Southeast Asia are home to a multiplicity of ethnic minorities, partly immigrants of recent centuries, partly the early rulers of the region, such as the minority of the Cham in Vietnam and Kampuchea, who today belong to Islam. Most ethnic groups have heir own (tribal) religions and cults, influenced little, if at all, by Buddhism.

The Buddhism of Southeast Asia has repeatedly had to adapt to new circumstances in the course of its history.

With entry into a monastery, monks renounce secular life, and therewith politics as well. However, it has repeatedly occurred that, in times of crisis, the clergy has surrendered its neutral position, and monks have always, to a greater or lesser extent, been active in political actions. We can see this clearly in Burma (Myanmar) during the colonial period, and still today. The West has observed the resistance emerging from the monasteries in the fiery self-immolation of Buddhist monks during the Vietnam War.

Subjects discussed today in the countries of Southeast Asia are, among

is the bestowal of the *kathina* garments to the community of the order. The robes are further distributed among the individual monks who have spent the rainy season in the monastery in question. The donations may consist simply of material for sewing, or of finished robes—the latter being more customary in Rangoon. At the bestowal, the veneration of the Buddha, and the triple 'flight' formula is recited ("I flee to the Buddha …"). Then a lay member, holding a pile of robes in both hands, says: "Revered ones, modestly bring we forth these *kathina* robes, and other gifts of the community." The monks respond, "Sadhu" ("Good"), and recite verses, such as "Merit is the flight of all beings in the next world." There is also a custom of holding weaving contests in large pagodas during the November full moon. Young women vie with one another to weave a robe that, subsequently, is usually draped over a figure of the Buddha. Usually, families (including those of the neighborhood) invite the monks to come before their houses. Electric amplification assures that, at least acoustically, the whole street participates in the festival.
(T. Fessel and M. Petrich)

Religion and Politics

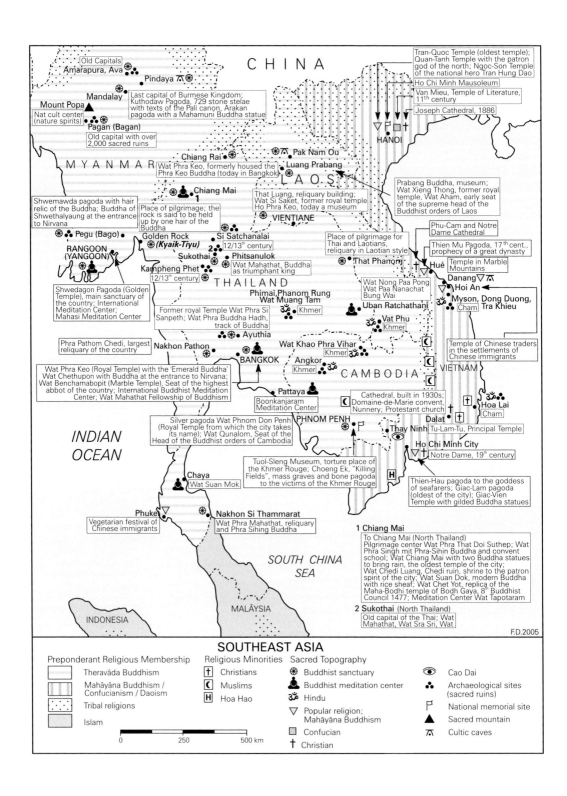

others, a democratization of the hierarchy of the order, engagement for peace, dialogue with other religions, and the introduction of women's ordination. Opportunities for meditation, which attract more travelers from the West each year, have been developed recently in various monasteries of the region.

In Vietnam in the twentieth century, two very syncretistic religious movements have developed: the Hoa Hao, which emphasizes the simplicity of a cult of a Buddhist hue, and the community of the Cao Dai, so striking, among other reasons, for the colorful attractiveness of their sacred installations and their cult.

Tourism The countries of Southeast Asia are favorite destinations for travelers. The negative effects on those whose lands the tourists visit are often emphasized. However, → tourism has positive aspects, as well. Among them belong, for instance, restorations of historical and religious sites, and the study of their own culture and religion by indigenous groups who work in tourism, often attracted by dialogue with travelers from other cultural circles. Travelers gain insight into religious traditions, standing in parallel or merged, and into another style of everyday life, in which religion obviously belongs. And they learn tolerance toward foreigners, not only in the religious area, but in personal contact, as well—experiences that can contribute to a better understanding of foreign cultures.

Literature

BOYES, Jonathan, Tiger-Men and Tofu Dolls: Tribal Spirits in Northern Thailand, Chiang Mai 1997; BUNNAG, Jane, Buddhist Monk, Buddhist Layman, Cambridge 1973; MENDELSON, E. Michael, Sangha and State in Burma, Ithaca 1975; TERWIEL, Barend Jan, Monks and Magic: An Analysis of Religious Ceremonies in Central Thailand, Bangkok ³1994; VIETNAM BUDDHIST RESEARCH INSTITUTE, Vietnam Buddhism and Its Activities for Peace, Ho Chi Minh City 1990.

→ *Amulet, Ancestors, Buddhism, China/Japan/Korea, Confucianism, Daoism, Hinduism, Islam, Shamanism, Tourism*

Brigitte Heusel

Southeast Asia: Time Chart

Era 1: Migratory movements

| from 3000 BCE | Immigration from North to South | Peoples unwilling to subject themselves to a China now expanding southward, emigrate to Southeast Asia, partially dislodging the original population. They dispose of better tools and farming |

		methods than do the natives there.
c. 300 BCE	Dong Son culture	Sacred bronze drums have been found throughout Southeast Asia. Their decorations break open notions of the other world, and to shamanic rituals of the time in question.
208 BCE	The first empire in Southeast Asia	Nam Viet (today's South China and North Vietnam) is established in the tangles and disorders of the end of the first Empire of China as an independent state—the first realm that can be historically indicated in Southeast Asia.
2nd cent. BCE	Expansion of China	The trade route from China westward leads through today's Myanmar (Burma). The realm of Nam Viet will be a colony of China for a thousand years (111 BCE to 938 CE).

Era 2: Influences from India and China

first centuries CE	Indian and Chinese traders in Southeast Asia	With the rise of maritime commerce, the mainland and the islands of China constitute an important objective for Indian merchant ships. It is not only wares, but ideas as well, that reach Southeast Asia with the ships.

	First "Indisized" Empires: Funan (today's Kampuchea), Langkasuka and Tambralinga (today's Malaysia). Oc Eo an important harbor city	The empires will organize on Indian models. Hinduism marks the elite of Funan. In both realms of Malaysia, it is especially Buddhism that spreads. The written language is adopted from India. Tribute to China is required.
4th–8th cent.	Broader extent of Hinduism and Buddhism	Indian influences reach from Arakan (today's Myanmar) to the island world. Further "Indisized" realms are founded, whose rulers are oriented toward Buddhism (Mon realms) or Hinduism (Champa). Flourishing cultures arise, with a tendency toward the architecture and art of India. Maritime commerce with farm products, precious metals and stones, precious cloth and spices, flourishes between the Mediterranean region and the Far East. Prosperity finds its expression in the construction of sacred installations, e.g., Borobodur.
9th–13th cent.	God-kings: The Realm of Angkor	'Revolution' in rice farming. A network of irrigation canals spreads through the Kambodjan plain, supporting three harvests annually. The superabundance of rice is the foundation of the Khmer Realm.

		It becomes possible to support many types of labor and craft. Kings are seen as the progeny of Indian gods (especially of Shiva), and have absolute power. An expression of this power is constituted by the sacred installations created by hordes of workers at once, as, e.g., Angkor Vat (mid-twelfth century).
11th cent.	Buddhist realm of Bagan (Pagan)	With the assistance of monks from Sri Lanka, the King of Bagan introduces pure Theravada into his country, as the high religion of the country, while the veneration of Nat (spirits) continues. Close contacts with Sri Lanka.
12th–15th cent.	Flowering and end of the Hindu kingdoms of Southeast Asia: Theravada Buddhism on the march	Wars between the two Hindu Realms, Champa and Angkor, weaken the power of both. In the thirteenth century, there is more immigration to deal with, at the advance of the Mongols. In mid-thirteenth century, realms of the Thai materialize: c. 1250 Sukothai, Ayutthaya in 1350, and Lan Chang (1354).

Era 3: The influence of Islam

from the 7th cent.	New Order in maritime trading	With maritime mercantile supremacy in Arab hands, Islam

		arrives in Southeast Asia by the sea trade. Missionaries do not enter with fire and sword, but little by little the natives adopt the new faith, as had been the case with India.
13th–15th cent.	First Islamic realms in Southeast Asia: Sumatra, Malacca	Dynasties of Islamic coloring and tone replace the Indian system of government. Followers of Islamic mysticism are often teachers of a native elite.

Era 4: Christianity comes

1511	Portuguese conquer Malacca	With the capture of Malacca, and the continued Portu-guese advance, the old mercantile order in Southeast Asia is destroyed. In 1493, the Pope divides the (then known) world into Spanish and Portuguese spheres of authority for mission and trade.
16th–19th cent.	Beginning of the colo-nization of Southeast Asia	Unlike that of the sailors from India and Near Asia, the appear-ance of the Europeans is no example for the population (i.e., Chris-tianity is not voluntar-ily adopted).
19th cent.	Division of Southeast Asia among Holland, Great Britain, and France	A reconsideration of the individual cul-tures and religions. In Thailand, King Rama IV introduces a re-forming structure into

		Theravada Buddhism (Thammayut). In Burma, the fifth Buddhist Council (1871).
Era 5: Independence		
early 20th cent.	Reconsideration and New Order	A reconsideration of the native religions, and, where necessary, their reform, reinforces a resistance to the colonial lords.
from 1945	Colonies become independent states	To an extent, independence is followed by civil wars, and renewed assaults from the West (Vietnam). Sixth Buddhist Council (1956), in Rangoon (Yangoon, Burma/ Myanmar). The attempt at a Buddhist socialism fails.
1966–1973	Vietnam War	Buddhist monks and nuns burn themselves alive, in protest against the role of the United States and the South Vietnamese government.
from 1975	In quest of the paradises	The religions of Southeast Asia, especially Buddhism, awaken the interest of searchers for meaning from Western countries.
2001	New conflicts	After bloody battles, East Timor (Christian) becomes an independent state. Reforms in the socialist states of Southeast Asia (Laos, Vietnam) proceed in the same

direction, and enable a freer religious practice. In the South Philippines and Indonesia, further tensions between Islamic minorities and the (Catholic) majority.

Brigitte Heusel

South Sea / Australia

'South Sea' is an old name for the Pacific Ocean. Today it means the part of the Pacific comprising the Islands of Oceania. This is an area of ca. 70 million square kilometers, all surrounding 7,500 Pacific islands between America, the Philippines, and Australia. Oceania can be divided into Melanesia, Micronesia, and Polynesia. New Zealand in the South, and Papua-New Guinea in the West, are also numbered among the states of the South Sea, while Australia, as a continent by itself, no longer belongs to it geographically. The islands of Hawaii and Easter Island, lying along the northern and eastern perimeter, do indeed spread into the region of Oceania, but are territories either of the United States (Hawaii) or of Chile (Easter Island). Considering their extensive political and economic dependency on, and the transformation of the values of their social culture by the states possessing them, they will need no further mention in the following consideration.

The Area

The South Sea has always been a fascinating destination for travelers of every bent and purpose. Soldiers, researchers, painters, and missionaries have traversed the islands, atolls, and coral reefs of the Pacific Ocean ever since their discovery. The native population were seldom taken into consideration. A recent example was the French atom-bomb experiments in the Moruroa Atoll (French Polynesia), in 1995. Just as earlier, with the Americans on the atolls of Bikini and Eniwetok (Marshall Islands), or the British on Christmas Island (Kiribati), so neither does the French colonial power exercise any consideration for inhabitants and environment, but, just as always before, asserts its right to make any determination whatsoever over the native population's life and goods. This disregard has always had multiple societal effects, not least of all upon the religion of the South Sea Islanders. What missionaries have not managed to finish, soldiers and politicians have finished by force. Thus, Polynesians in Tahiti (French Polynesia), persons ruled by French and economically controlled by Chinese, feel like tolerated foreigners in their own country. Although Oceania was divided up into an extensively postcolonial society by independent states, the old economic and political dependencies remain.

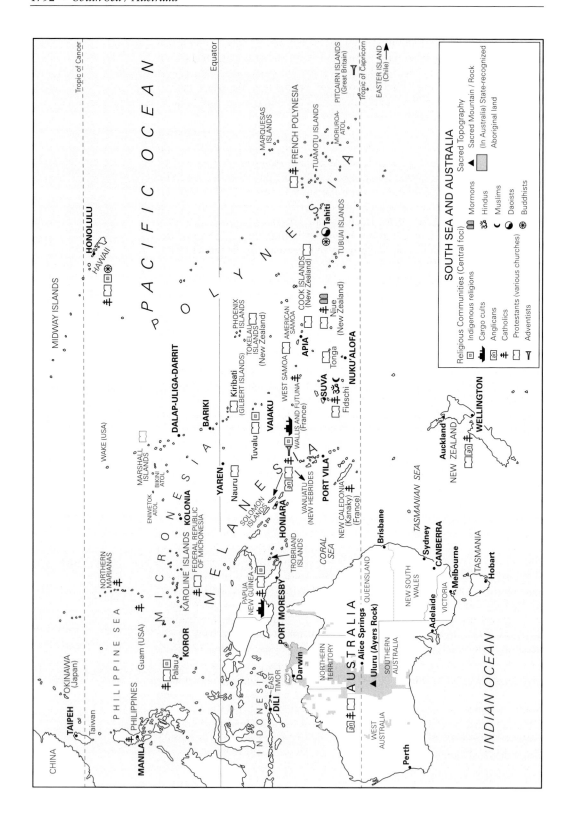

2. Considering the religious landscape of Oceania today, it is first notable that the current religions of Oceania are determined by their colonial Christian legacy. The original, indigenous religions, cults, magic, and myths of the islands of Oceania either were overwhelmed culturally, or perished in social upheavals and in the annihilation of traditional forms of subsistence (fishing, → Exchange/Gift).

a) To the Polynesian group of islands, over a surface of about 50 million square kilometers, belong the independent states of Tuvalu (former Ellice Islands, population c. 10,000 inhabitants), Tonga (c. 110,000), West Samoa (c. 215,000), and New Zealand (c. 3.5 million). In addition, there are regions figuring as dependent colonies, including, under New Zealander administration, the Cook Islands (c. 20,000 inhabitants), American Samoa (c. 60,000), and French Polynesia (c. 220,000). Polynesia is thus the region most dependent on the erstwhile colonial powers in Oceania. This dependency has effects in all areas of life, and, after two hundred years of Western influence, traditional culture in Polynesia has dissolved. Societies and religions of Polynesia have very extensively conformed to Western culture.

Polynesia

The systematic missionizing of the South Sea began at the end of the eighteenth century. In the wake of the discoveries by Englishman James Cook (1729–1779), missionary ships, especially from Great Britain and America at first, began to cross the South Sea. In particular, the London Mission Society, Methodists and Presbyterians, were at work in the South Sea from this time on, which explains the extensive spread of Protestantism. By the end of the nineteenth century, the missionizing of Polynesia was already complete, and independent churches had arisen. The reason for the surprisingly rapid Christianizing of Polynesia, and the almost total extinction of the ancient religions (which anthropologist of religion Nevermann once described as "the most mature and best reasoned thing […] that nature peoples have produced")[1] may have lain not least of all in these religions themselves. For one thing, there already was, in the polytheistic pantheon, a supreme God, who, as creator, had created heaven and earth. For another thing, the aristocratically organized traditional societies of Polynesia had developed specialized priestly classes that were responsible for cult. Thus, there were two essential preconditions for a rapid adoption of Christianity. Strict cultic restrictions ('→ taboo rules,' from the Polynesian *tápu*) were imposed on priests and chieftains, which, far from being understood as prohibitions, were counted on for the protection of their fellow human beings. An extraordinary 'power of activity' (in Polynesian, *mana*) resided in political and religious leaders, as in the gods. It could vary in strength, but for ordinary persons, it was accounted very dangerous. Accordingly, dealings with vehicles or vessels of *mana* needed to be regulated by prescriptions of *tápu*. It is true that the *tápu* system was reinforced and became a kind of ritual system of compulsion, so that even the accidental touching of a single hair of a bearer of *mana* could be a capital transgression. This circumstance may have likewise contributed to Polynesians' ready acceptance of Christianity, which brought them a substantial reduction in the weight of ritual procedure: as a result of the plenitude of the taboo prescriptions, no one had any longer been able to be sure that she or he had not unwittingly violated one of them.[2] Finally—and this factor contributing to the rapid spread of Christianity as

Christian Mission and the Fall of the Ancient Religions

Tápu and Mana

well—missionaries had recognized the importance of native assistants, and soon found eager Polynesian collaborators, who moved the missionizing of Oceania forward.

Today, in Polynesia (without New Zealand), the Protestants, with all of their subgroups (Lutherans, Baptists, Presbyterians, Methodists, Congregationalists), and almost 70% of the population as members, constitute the largest confessional group. Catholics come second, with 24.2%. Catholicism is represented especially in the regions governed by France. The high proportion of the Chinese population in French Polynesia (12%) corresponds with the high proportion of other religions. On the little island of Niue, Mormons are 10%. On Tuvalu—Christianized by the London Mission Society since the mid-nineteenth century, and a British protectorate since 1892—nearly the whole population are Congregationalists, of the Church of Tuvalu. In addition, under the ever-powerful societal influence of that community, traditional usages, along with belief in the presence of spirits, still thrive. With their Cook Islands Christian Church, virtually all inhabitants of those islands are Protestant. Here again, missioners of the London Mission Society were active. These latter, along with Methodist missionaries, were active early on Samoa as well (from the beginning of the nineteenth century), and have left behind the largest Congregationalist Church in Oceania, with 50% of the inhabitants. The Adventists, a particularly 'mission-minded' sect, with their faith entirely concentrated on hopes in the eschaton, are represented in a higher proportion than in their ratio world-wide, and have convinced all fifty-six of the inhabitants of Pitcairn, descendants of the Bounty mutineers.

Micronesia

Micronesia includes, especially, the Federal Republic of Micronesia, Kribati (formerly Gilbert Islands), the Marshall Islands, Northern Mariana, Guam, and Palau. In this gigantic region, with more than 3,000 islands, on c. 8 million square kilometers, approximately one-half million people live. In the time of the Japanese occupation, between the two World Wars, Japanese missionaries failed in their attempt to convert the Micronesians to Buddhism or to Shintô, and the Christian mission was fundamental. Nearly 65% of the Micronesians (on Guam, 98%) are Catholic today, which goes back to the early discovery of the Marianas by the Spaniards. Discovered in 1565, occupied and missionized since 1668, the Marianas were the first Islands in the Pacific to be expressly Christianized. The societal systems of Micronesia, with their hierarchically partitioned classes and an inherited status of chieftain, as well as of cultic systems orientated to the veneration of ancestors, were soon things of the past. Surviving in Western museums, there are occasional material witnesses of these cultures, such as the architectonically spectacular men's clubhouses from Palau, with their picture stories on gable ends and beams telling of mythical or historical events. The islands of Micronesia were relatively uninteresting for the colonial powers, but had great importance geo-strategically. During and after the Second World War, on the basis of the financial and material wealth of American troops, the 'Americanization' of Micronesia's island world proceeded apace (the atolls of the Marshall Islands suffered under American testing of atomic bombs), and, for want of goods and services, government moneys flowed there from the islands purely for the intent of 'welfare.' The dependency of the islanders that was produced in this fashion accelerated the cultural, religious, and

social breakdown of many Micronesian societies, whose orientation today
is entirely to Western values and concepts.

c) Up to borders of the French Transoceanic Territory of New Caledonia   *Melanesia*
(c. 190,000 inhabitants), Melanesia is independent. Papua New Guinea
(c. 4,400,000), Fiji (c. 78,000), Solomon Islands (c. 410,000), and Vanatu
(formerly New Hebrides, c. 180,000), comprise the four distinct states of
Melanesia. As in the remainder of South Sea, missionaries naturally have
worked in Melanesia, and regarded superficially, were successful here as well.
Protestantism accounts for 38% of all Melanesians, and 21.1% are Catholics.
In French New Caledonia, Catholics number 60%, to be explained by the fact
that here nearly 40% of the population are Europeans, especially French. The
original inhabitants (Kanakes), likewise with 40%, have become a minority
in their own country. Six-and-one-half percent of Melanesians belong to
the Anglican Church (in the Solomon Islands, with 34%, they are the largest
confessional group). While Anglicans in Micronesia and Polynesia are simply nonexistent, in Melanesia the geographical proximity to the large regions
of the Anglican Religion of Australia (26.1%) and New Zealand (34%) becomes visible. In Vanatu (6%), and in the Solomon Islands (10%), Adventists
are stronger than anywhere else in South Sea. Fiji, the most populous island
state of Oceania, became 46% Indian, this population having been recruited
during the British colonial time. There is a correspondingly high proportion
of Hindus among the Fiji Islanders (38%). Eight percent of the total population of Fiji are Muslim; the majority (51%) are Christian, of whom 43% are
Protestant. It is striking that Melanesia has a high proportion of members of
indigenous religions, a datum otherwise scarcely to be verified in Oceania.
Besides Vanatu (7.6%) and Solomon Islands (4%), this holds especially true
on the—still scarcely accessible—Papua New Guinea (34%). Almost no
Europeans live in these three states, so that the proportion of Melanesians
here is well over 90%.

Upon a more precise consideration of the religious orientation of the Mela-   *Papua New Guinea*
nesians of Papua New Guinea, it becomes clear that, while many of them
have indeed converted to Christian confessions, this has frequently been
a mere formality. Christianity and traditional belief lie adjacent to one
another. In the Church, the Christian religion is practiced, but in daily life,
indigenous rites, magic, and myths play the determining religious role as
much as they ever did. The reason is that the missionaries, who had settled
primarily in the coastal regions, did not visit Papua New Guinea's huge
backcountry, with its wild, all but impenetrable nature. Furthermore, the
population density there is very slight, and the over seven hundred different
languages and dialects of the individual, widely separated tribal groups make
it difficult to gather information of any kind. This dispersion is the cause of
great cultural and religious diversity. Usually only a few hundred persons live
in the small, separated, traditional settlement entities, without a hierarchical,
social structure ('segmentary social form'). There is no inherited chieftain or
priestly office (such as in Polynesia and Micronesia), or, therefore, central
structures that could multiply the effects of the missionaries' efforts. On the
other hand, the Melanesian 'big men' have since become stereotyped figures
in anthropology.[3] It is their → prestige, which rests on economic and military success, and not their extraction or provenance, that establishes their
reputation. They possess special *mana*: they have many adherents and great

From Cult to Artistic Cultivation

ceremonial influence. The most important foundation of traditional belief was the veneration of → ancestors. In secret male organizations, connections were struck with the ancestors. Like the totem forebears of the Australian → Aborigines, the Melanesian ancestors were the antecedents and creators of the world, and both mystical primordial beings, and souls existing in the present. Men's houses, along with → masks, are the renowned material outcropping of this religion. In particular, Melanesian cult-masks are today snatched from their ritual and mythic connection, to become 'art without context,' and are classified in the Western museum culture in their particular form as 'aesthetic objects.' They stand as examples of the social and religious paradigm-swap of the Oceanic cultures: the de-consecration of religious tradition to art, to theater, to a spectacle for tourists.

Cargo Cults

A reaction to the pressure of modernity is demonstrated by the *cargo cults*. In Vanatu and the Solomons, and especially in Papua New Guinea, the mighty shattering of religious and social life, launched by the confrontation with the 'whites,' constitutes a special form of the acceptance and rejection of the new and the foreign. At first held to be ancestors, the whites were soon recognized as persons who, of course, possessed unimaginable riches. Confrontation with the unexplainable goods of the whites, their 'cargo' that had landed, whose production the Melanesians could not understand or duplicate, led only to the conclusion that these goods originated in the land of the ancestors, and had been stolen by the whites. But the ancestors would wreak vengeance, would return, would expel the whites, would restore social order, and would hand over firearms, automobiles, and aircraft to the Melanesians. In expectation of this event, not only were moorings, wharfs, and high masts set up for divine radio signals, but plantings were destroyed, animals slain, and houses burned. A sense of the end of the world, and hope in the future, culminated in this pre-modern catastrophe. Up until the present, the existence of more than two hundred individual cargo cults, separated in time and space—in the meantime acknowledged and understood as precursors of nationalistic movements—has been demonstrated. There are early reports of the cargo movement in 1893, on Milne Bay, in British New Guinea. This movement reached a first climax in the 1920s and 1930s, in Melanesia, especially in New Hebrides and the Solomons. The years between 1946 and 1954 witnessed a second cargo-cult spurt in Melanesia, although some of these instances were transformed into social movements.

Australia and New Zealand

3. In Australia, about 90% of the some 18,000,000 inhabitants are of British descent. The original inhabitants of Australia, the → Aborigines, today make up only one percent of the population. The statistical proportion of traditional religions is correspondingly slender, inasmuch as either the immigrants and their churches have absorbed the natives, or the latter no longer appreciably tilt the balance. Ancient hunting rituals can no longer play a role in the big-city context. White Australians, descendants of European immigrants (Irish, English, Italian), belong, in rather equal proportion, to the Anglican (26.1%), the Catholic (26%), or the Protestant (24.3%) churches.

The situation is similar in New Zealand. Europeans of British extraction make up the majority (88%) of the population. New Zealanders are 28% Protestant, 24% Anglican, and 15% Catholic. It is true that the indigenous Maori, with nearly 9% of the population, still comprise a noteworthy share of the population of 3.5 million. However, they have been absorbed more and more into the urban population, and their traditional religious forms have not survived the modern age.

3. Erotic wishes, and images of free sexuality and nature-connected primitivity on lonely beaches, a Robinsonade on variegated coral reefs in turquoise water, an existence under palms swaying in the wind and casting cool shadows, are imprinted in the South Sea dreams of the modern city-dweller to the present day—the South Sea as the Paradise afar—projected to its apex in the American film, Randal Kleiser's "The Blue Lagoon" (1980) with the scantily clad yet ever chaste, unthreatening Brooke Shields. However, Gauguin's wild romanticism of a paradise in the South Sea at the turn of the twentieth century, had soon to be exchanged for the sobering reality of a colonial deformation of Polynesian society. Today, as well, little has survived—aside from an inspiring landscape—of the enticing dream of the South Sea paradise ($\rightarrow$ Garden/Paradise). Traditional cultures of the South Sea have extensively given way to the powerful cultural pressure of Western civilization, and are now mostly marketed as mere tourist spectacles.

South Sea as Paradise—the Exotic Fantasy

1. NEVERMANN 1968, 62.
2. Ibid., 17.
3. SCHULTZ, Hermann, Stammesreligionen. Zur Kreativität des kulturellen Bewußtseins, Stuttgart 1993, 93.

Literature

Classic Anthropological Studies: FIRTH, Raymond W., We, the Tikopia: A Sociological Study of Kinship in Primitive Polynesia, London 1957; MALINOWSKI, Bronislaw, Coral Gardens and Their Magic: A Study of the Methods of Tilling the Soil and of Agricultural Rites in the Trobriand Islands, 2 vols., London 1935; MEAD, Margaret, Sex and Temperament in Three Primitive Societies, New York 1950 ([1]1935).

General Literature: GOLDMAN, Irving, Ancient Polynesian Society, Chicago 1970; KRAMER, Fritz, Verkehrte Welten. Zur imaginären Ethnographie des 19. Jahrhunderts, Frankfurt/M. 1981; NEVERMANN, Hans, "Die Religionen der Südsee," in: NEVERMANN, Hans et al. (eds.), Die Religionen der Südsee und Australiens, Stuttgart 1968, 1-123; PARMENTIER, Richard J., The Sacred Remains: Myth, History, and Polity in Belau, Chicago 1987; SAHLINS, Marshall D., Social Stratification in Polynesia, Seattle 1958.

Cargo Cults: LAWRENCE, Peter, Road belong Cargo: A Study of the Cargo Movement in the Southern Madang District, New Guinea 1964; WORSLEY, Peter, The Trumpet Shall Sound: A Study of "Cargo" Cults in Melanesia, New York [2]1968.

$\rightarrow$ *Aborigines, Colonialism*

Gerhard Schlatter

Specialists, Religious

1. a) The concept of religious specialist can denote the results of a permanent division of labor within a religion. The individual members of a religious $\rightarrow$ group possess distinct competencies when it comes to practicing religion and its acts. In many religions, those who lead religious acts are those who occupy a leading position of honor and power, such as the

Young female rabbis, in prayer shawls, and wearing kippas, during a service on the occasion of the First European Convention of female rabbis, cantors, and Jews (of both genders) with training or interest in rabbinical matters, in Berlin, May 1999. Some 120 female specialists in matters of Judaism, including seven active rabbis, met in the New Synagogue, in Berlin, to join together in the battle for the acceptance of female cultic personnel in the worldwide Jewish community. Up until now, it has only been Reform Judaism that has admitted female rabbis: in Germany, at present, there is only one. The Berlin center for studies *Bet Debora*, "House of Debora," named for the biblical judge and military leader against the Canaanites, and deliberately connected with the liberal tradition of Berlin, was where Regina Jonas (born in Berlin in 1902, murdered at Auschwitz in 1944) was the first woman to be ordained to the rabbinate (December 27, 1935). Although there were several women in America who had completed a rabbinical course of studies at the same time, it was only in 1972, with Sally Priesand, that the first American female rabbi took office. Just as in the area of the Christian churches with the acceptance of women as clerical ministers, the admittance of women to the rabbinate has led to tensions with conservative and orthodox groups in the Jewish community. With the help of historical research, then, an attempt is being made to find legitimizing exemplars in the past. (R. Deines)

chiefs of an enterprise, or of the state. But religious specialists can be spoken of meaningfully only where a specific competency in religious acts and knowledge must be actually acquired. The sociological concept affords the possibility of a description. Concepts like 'priest,' 'prophet,' or 'shaman' originate in particular religious traditions, and are frequently understood polemically. Should we seek to apply, for example, 'priest' trans-culturally, it will obscure differences in cultic activity, personal holiness, lengthy formation, and full professional dedication. Even a seemingly general determination such as 'intermediary (of salvation)' becomes highly problematic: this designation is a product of the Protestant polemic that no intermediary can be employed between human beings and their God.

b) The division of labor in question can be described under two aspects. (1) The relationship between specialists and non-specialists is a connection of varying degrees of proximity (social density). Thus, this relationship more or less determines how often believers seek out a specialist. As

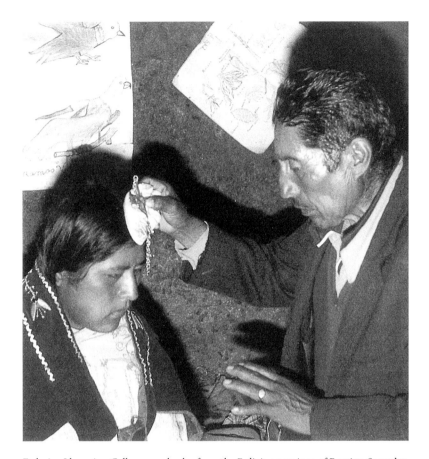

Federico Llaves is a Callawaya, a healer from the Bolivian province of Bautista Saavedra, in the Department of La Paz. In the villages of the Apolobama, and of Muneca Cordillere, in the Andes, live traveling medicine men, who also work their farms. They function in the area of herbal medicine, as well as in that of symbolical healing. For eighteen-year-old Irene Ramos Vila, who has lost her first child, he here performs a night ritual, the "Banishment of Grief." After all, as he says, "grief is still in the house" after a death. "And so a purification is always performed, lest the unwholesome continue to pursue us." In the course of the night, he prepares one white and one mourning *mesa* (Span., 'sacrificial gift', lit. 'table'), for the 'white healing' and for the repulse of evil and harm. All have removed their hats, as the ritual gets under way. In its course, a moment occurs when—as pictured here—the healer places an embroidered stole, from the sacristy of the church, around Irene's shoulders, and blesses her with a white *q'into* of sacrificial offerings (wool, coca leaves, lama suet, and alcohol, in a white towel), and his iron cross, in the name of the Trinity. Mountain peaks, Mother Earth (Pachamama), and the wind, are summoned as well. Between parts of the ceremony, there is sometimes time for talking, eating, smoking, chewing coca, and drinking alcohol. Federico Llaves practices in the Callawaya tradition, integrating Catholic elements into the ceremony, and lending the event his own personal style. His participation, his ritual capacities, and his competency in interpreting death and grief, help survivors in this difficult time of transition. (Kirsten Holzapfel, after Ina Rösing)

for the degrees existing in the relationship of authority—discipleship (→ Disciples), or → master-pupil relations—this measure may be grounded in personal → charisma. (2) It may also be a matter of a stable relation between a spiritual 'official' and a community, or the services of a specialist may be sought only in 'critical' situations, such as prophecy or fortune-telling (astrology, card-reading), or rituals of the → life cycle (such as funeral preachers, marriage priests). Stores of knowledge (of ritual, of theology) have to be preserved and elaborated through monopolization, or at least close control, and corresponding specialists have to be relieved of other activities. Staffs of administrators, then (cashiers, recording secretaries, registrars), and assisting personnel (slaughterer for sacrificial rituals, musicians, attendants), can be distinguished into cultic specialists and theologians. The formation or 'training' of religious specialists has been of special meaning and importance for European history of religion, and for Christianity. These specialists would be persons whose tasks were to attend exclusively to reflection on, and systematization of, stores of knowledge, assume responsibility for doctrines, and interpret and apply the generalizations thus achieved (→ Theology) to new situations (and texts). Special training, proper rules of lifestyle, and hierarchical control, were necessary in order to assure the inner coherency of such an organization. Certain instances of specialization form religious 'virtuosi'—as, for example, ascetics, who live religion especially intensively, and, for that purpose, organize into closed groups, in → monasticism—or else they build systems of two-degree membership, of general members and of the 'perfected,' as did the medieval Cathari.

2. a) It was characteristic of the ancient urban religions of the Greco-Roman world to display minimal organization. They usually consisted of priesthoods that recruited their membership among the (usually male) members of the upper class, or even only among certain families. Here it

Antiquity

was a matter of 'leisure-time priests,' who had often delegated their routine cult to slaves or personal assistants, and who were 'professional priests' only in particular cases, then living on the income of their temple installations (except in Egypt). 'Full-time priests' (such as the Roman Vestal Virgins) were rare. Of course, there were purveyors of religious services, in healing-cults and oracles, who seemed to live on their activity, as well as itinerant experts who seemed to do the same. In the Judaism of the Diaspora, we see a high percentage of members of synagogues in honorary offices, while professional scholars were rare. The very early Christian system of cultic, social, or theological specialists comes as a surprise, then, and it soon led to efforts to finance an independent 'clergy,' as well as to array it with privileges, as political leaders gradually promoted the new religion. Along with the ever more closely intertwined offices that, in Christianity, as well, developed into careers, independently operating specialists (such as teachers, exorcists), still had importance and meaning at first.

b) For further European history of religion, the institutionalization of the Christian Church, and especially that of Rome, with its functionaries, played an important role. On the one hand, ever-higher formation was

Christianity

demanded of priests, and greater personal holiness, which fostered the 'sacralization' of the organization (such as with Gregory VII's reform in the High Middle Ages). At the same time, however, such measures encouraged criticism. The sense and meaning of the prevailing religious division of labor came more and more into question—after all, salvation is to be available to all persons equally. Thus, in the Reformation, the doctrine emerged of a 'universal priesthood of all of the faithful.' The organizational power of even the medieval Church, and the lack of competition on the part of state organizations, resulted in tasks of formation devolving upon the competency of religious specialists in Latin schools and universities, throughout broad expanses of European history.

3. The organizational and differentiating patterns just described are observable in extra-European cultures as well. Outside of urban societies, the village priest, with his far-reaching and little differentiated religious authority, and the various, and often crisply differentiated, ranks of temple priests—became the most important forms of religious specialization. The extreme case of regulated priestly states (theocracies) is to be observed alike in the monastic republic of the Greek Athos, and in Buddhist Tibet before the Chinese occupation. Special types of religious authority, such as that of the → guru or healer, are exported to Europe even today.

Extra-European Cultures

4. Current discussions on religious specialization are—at least in the West—strikingly restricted to the problems of the status of Christian priests. On the one hand, the role represents a fully transmitted professional activity, possessing all of the indications of a 'profession' in the most cogent sense. On the other hand, the loss of public respect, and the increase of role diversification in the area of the common priesthood of all Christian confessions, has led to insecurity with regard to status, and tendencies to de-professionalization. Or, in the public area, in connection with the confrontation concerning Islamic religious education in public schools, there is discussion of how religious specialists are legitimated, and how representative they are for such religions with looser organization.

Current Discussions

Literature

BEARD, Mary/NORTH, John (eds.), Pagan Priests: Religion and Power in the Ancient World, London 1990; DYKEMA, Peter A./OBERMAN, Heiko A. (eds.), Anticlericalism in Late Medieval and Early Modern Europe, Leiden 1993; FULLER, C. J., Servants of the Goddess: The Priests of a South Indian Temple, Cambridge 1984; GRABBE, Lester L., Priests, Prophets, Diviners, Sages: A Socio-Historical Study of Religious Specialists in Ancient Israel, Valley Forge 1995; Idem (ed.), The Priests in the Prophets: The Portrayal of Priests, Prophets and Other Religious Specialists in the Latter Prophets, London 2004; GUYOT, Jean (ed.), Études sur le sacrement de l'ordre, Paris 1961; JAMES, E. O., The Nature and Function of Priesthood, London 1955; KIECKHEFER, Richard/BOND, George D. (eds.), Sainthood: Its Manifestations in World Religions, Berkeley 1988; McEWAN, Gilbert J. P., Priest and Temple in Hellenistic Babylonia, Wiesbaden 1981; McGUIRE, Meredith B., Ritual Healing in Suburban America, New Brunswick 1988; RANSON, Stewart et al., Clergy, Ministers and Priests, London 1977; RÜPKE, Jörg, Fasti Sacerdotum, 3 vols., Stuttgart 2005; SABOURIN, Leopold: Priesthood: A Comparative Study, Leiden 1973; STRAUBE, Helmut, Die Stellung des Regenmachers und verwandter Funktionäre in akephalen Gesellschaften des Süd-Sudans, Munich 1984; Voss, Klaus Peter, Der Gedanke des allgemeinen Priester- und Prophetentums: Seine gemeindetheologische Aktualisierung in der Reformationszeit, Wuppertal 1990.

→ *European History of Religion, Group, Guru, Monasticism, Priest/Priestess, Weber*

Jörg Rüpke

Sphinx

1. The (male!) sphinx, in Egypt, consists of a recumbent lion with the head of a Pharaoh (androsphinx). The lion has been the royal beast since time immemorial, so that, in the sphinx, the brute strength of the mighty predator is linked with the wisdom of the human governor, as a phenomenal image of royalty, and beyond this, as a divine → composite being. In the sphinxes watching at the entrances of temples or necropolises, the power of the Pharaoh is mightily displayed as guardian and defender of his sanctuary. Granted, in Egypt the sphinx is usually male, but female potentates, as well, used that symbol of majestic power, so that, even in Egypt, if only rarely, the female sphinx does occur.

It is the Great Sphinx of Giza (Fourth Dynasty) that is world-renowned. With its length of some 73.5m, and its height of 20m, it may be the most powerful construction of a mythical beast in existence. Its monumental figure symbolizes the sacred royalty of the Old Kingdom at the height of its power. It lies along the path to the Pyramid of Chefren, and it was believed that it pictured the Pharaoh of that name. New material, however, indicates his father Cheops (c. 2604/2554–2581/2531 BCE) as its builder. Through the connection of aspects of the sun cult and the royal cult, the Sphinx of Giza was venerated in the New Kingdom as 'Horus on the Horizon' (in Greek, *Harmachis*), and thereby regarded as a form of the apparition of the Sun God, Re. Thus, Amun-Re also became a new King of the Gods, as well as the Sun God, and the figure of the sphinx featured Amun's typical ram's head ("Kriosphinx").

2. In Greek mythology, the unambiguously female sphinx was depicted as the Demon of Death, a winged lion with the head of a woman. The sphinx became the synonym for the enigmatic, a development owed to the famous myth of the Theban Sphinx, who slew all who failed to solve her riddle. → Oedipus, however, found the correct solution, whereupon the sphinx plunged into the depths. Despite the gender alternation, the sphinx was probably adopted in Greece from the ancient East.

3. In Europe, beginning in the Renaissance, the figure of the sphinx experienced a 'rebirth,' in architecture, sculpture, painting, and literature, and this in both its Egyptian and its Greek phenomenal forms. In the sometimes monumental sculptures of sphinxes in park and palace installations, from the Baroque until the twentieth century, these guardian figures served the representational needs of state and nobility or upper class. In art, the sphinx was increasingly eroticized. In the Symbolism and *Décadence* of the close of the nineteenth century, in Felicien Rops and Fernand Khnopff, in the lyricism of Oscar Wilde (*The Sphinx*, 1894), she became a male fantasy of the *femme fatale*, the timeless cipher of the enigmatic, perilous eros of woman.

Literature

DEMISCH, Heinz, Die Sphinx. Geschichte ihrer Darstellung von den Anfängen bis zur Gegenwart, Stuttgart 1977; EDMUNDS, Lowell, The Sphinx in the Oedipus Legend, Königstein 1981; LEHNER, Marc, "Reconstructing the Sphinx," in: Cambridge Archaeological Journal 2 (1992), 1-26; MODE, Heinz, Fabeltiere und Dämonen in der Kunst, Stuttgart

1974 (illustrations); ZIVIE-COCHE, Christiane, Sphinx: History of a Monument, Ithaca 2002 (French ¹1997).

→ *Composite Beings, Egypt, Gender Stereotypes, Monarchy/Royalty, Oedipus, Reception*

Edmund Hermsen

Spiritism

1. Spiritism or Spiritualism (from Lat. *spiritus*, 'soul', 'spirit') is to be understood here not simply as belief in spirits, but as belief in the continued life of the soul in a beyond, and the possibility of communicating with the spirits of the departed. Often in the spiritistic literature, the designation 'spiritualism' is used instead. Spiritism is one of the important international new religions of the nineteenth century. It came from the United States and seized Europe in the latter half of the nineteenth century. After the First World War, original spiritism quickly lost its importance in the Old World. But in Brazil, for example, its significance grew, and there, for instance in the Umbanda religion, even adopted Afro-American cultic elements.

2. Although the lay religion of spiritism appeared only in the middle of the nineteenth century, there are many movements that could be cited by way of precedent. Besides centuries-old popular traditions still appearing in 'popular spiritism', like belief in ghosts and spirits, necromancy (conjuring the dead), and fortune telling, there were also spiritistic currents that were attacked by Enlightenment authors. The latter included especially the teachings of Emanuel Swedenborg (1688–1772), which sought to open the view of a higher world of spirits, and even more, Mesmerism, the 'animal magnetism' of Franz Anton Mesmer (1734–1815), a kind of hypnotic technique ('magnetic sleep'), which Mesmer and his pupils preferred to apply by occasioning 'somnambulism', (from Lat. 'sleepwalker'), in order to interrogate things from the world of the supernatural as well (→ Power; Occultism; Electricity; Energy).

The Forerunners: Mesmerism and Swedenborgians

3. The actual starting point of spiritistic mass religion may be taken to be the 'tappings' detected or, more precisely, generated by children of the Fox family in the United States, and their interpretation as means of communication used by the deceased. These perceptions may or may not have been a direct religious reaction to the installation of the first Morse telegraph line, between Washington and Baltimore, in 1883/84, and to its 'democratic' character (being publicly accessible and privately owned). There was then talk, in the United States, about a 'spiritual telegraphy' between the living and the dead. Within a few years, 'table tipping' had become a fashionable game, as well as a means employed by a cult of piety on both sides of the Atlantic. Contact with spirits took place during private *séances* (Fr., 'sessions'). Under the direction of an accomplished 'medium', in the framework of a 'circle', a few persons would assemble, usually around a table (see illus.). The trance 'mediums', the → specialists in this telecommunication with the beyond, played the traditional role of the Christian prophetesses and prophets, just as that of the → witches and healers, but in addition showed some of the traits of

History and Varieties

This photograph of an experimental levitation shows the famous medium, Eusapia Paladino (1854–1920), at a table-raising. The course of the *séance*, according to the eyewitness account (slightly blurred by male fantasies) of a celebrated Italian criminologist, was as follows. "The persons sitting around the table lay their hands on it, forming a chain. Each of the medium's hands is held by the nearest hand of each of her two nearest neighbors, and each of the medium's feet is lying beneath that of her neighbor, who also presses his knee against that of the medium." Then the table "usually rises ten to twenty centimeters. [. . .] At times, it remains in the air several seconds, making irregular motions. [. . .] In these attempts, the medium's face becomes distorted, her fists clench, she moans, and seems to be suffering" (LOMBROSO, Cesare, Hypnotische und spiritistische Forschungen, Stuttgart, no date [1909], 68f.).

modern entertainment stars. Soon certain (especially female) mediums attained an international reputation. The entertainment value of their religious 'shows' came from the *levitations* (objects wafting freely in the air, in seeming contravention of the laws of gravity), *apports* (mustering of objects without human hands), and *materializations* ('embodiments' of, especially, the dead) that they were able to produce. The production of voices, tones, apparitions, and disturbances in the air accompanying the presentations appealed to the senses in a certain synaesthetic manner, and together with the half-light of the scene and the tingling proximity of the other gender, contributed to the appeal of these cultic presentations. Supported in particular by messages from the beyond that the mediums could impart (by speaking in trances, through 'automatic' notation of reports, by 'talking tables,' etc.), a spiritistic world image was promptly produced.

Further organization appeared as well, among middle-class 'scientific' spiritists in associations, as among 'religious' spiritists in 'churches.' Educated spiritists rejected religious spiritism as 'revelation spiritism,' and the Christian churches rejected spiritism in its entirety, on account of its concepts of self-redemption. Spiritists' attitude toward authorities and government varied. Besides an affirmative spiritism maintained by the respectable citizenry and nobility, there even emerged, in England and France, with its origin in America, a liberal social-reform direction (Andrew Jackson Davis,

1826–1910). This phenomenon led the heritage of a utopian socialism (Fourier, Saint-Simon, Owen; → Commune) even further. The politically failed notions of equality and liberty were then projected into the world beyond of a paradisaic 'summerland.' These ideas included equal rights for women and 'free love.'

Spiritism in Europe took on entirely national characteristics, not least of all on grounds of the countries' respective religious colorations. In France, it was determined more in a Catholic hue (Allan Kardec, 1804–1869), in Germany more in a Protestant tone. In Germany, unlike France and England, the *petit bourgeois*, authoritarian 'popular' (*Volk-*) spiritism of Josef Weissenberg (1855–1941) carried the day, with a membership in the tens of thousands ("Evangelical-Joannine Church") after the First World War. Davis's "harmonial philosophy," paired with a Christian spiritist piety, found German support only during the era of Bismarck, especially among textile workers and miners in Saxony.[1]

Taken as a whole, the spiritism of the nineteenth century can be understood as an attempt to afford a scientific guarantee of components of traditional Christian religion regarded as indispensable. This effort would oppose the age of materialism and science. Included among these components were, especially, belief in the immortality of the soul, and a continued life in the beyond, after death ('everlasting life'). The methods employed to offer this guarantee would be empirically verifiable. Then the guarantee would be reconciled with the secular *Zeitgeist*, the 'spirit' signed by individualism and a belief in progress. By way of the 'spiritist method,' those who took part in the séances and circles could defeat death, by extending the existence of their intimate community of devoted 'siblings' and friends in a 'revolt against mourning.'

4. The 'outside effects' of spiritism are meaningful and important. The mediums and their 'spirit-' manifestations became a favorite field of studies in the 1880s, for new "societies for psychical research"—research entities interested in 'experimental psychology.' This early research in → 'parapsychology' contributed decisively to a popularization of the concept and doctrine of the unconscious. True, the sketches created by German spiritists of an experimental-'transcendental' doctrine of the soul regarded that doctrine as a mere transitional phenomenon. The ultimate goal was an experimental psychology of the sub-/unconscious that would be delivered from metaphysics. At the same time, spiritism was a great attraction for the arts. Authors such as Victor Hugo were fascinated by the recently opened look at mental border regions. Modern sculpture, in particular, received powerful impulses from the spiritist unlocking of the unconscious and the supra-sensory, for example with Wassily Kandinsky. Further, with its preponderantly female mediums, spiritism played a role in the historical movement for women's liberation (→ Women's Movement/Spiritual Feminism).

External Effects and Reception

5. In Europe and North America, spiritism as a mass phenomenon, as well as in its quality as a world-view has 'closed down' since the First World War—by contrast with Brazil especially, where it has been transformed, and integrated into the Umbanda cult. Here, spiritism has become a national religion. Its spirit-healing fascinates Europeans as well, in their quest for new forms of therapy (→ Afro-American Religions). In Europe and North America, spiritism lives on solely its techniques for receiving 'messages

Spiritism Today

from beyond.' It persists as a 'secularized' form of social interplay, as well as a spiritual practice of listening to audiotapes and voices on the radio, or of glass-moving (in 'youth occultism'). Transmitted in part by theosophy, spiritism has continued to have its effects, in the → New Age movement and in modern → esotericism, by way of concern with death and dying (thanatology), or through reception of mediated messages (→ Channeling).

1. Linse, Ulrich, "Das Buch der Wunder und Geheimwissenschaften. Der spiritistische Verlag Oswald Mutze in Leipzig im Rahmen der spiritistischen Bewegung Sachsens," in: Lehmstedt, Mark/Herzog, Andreas, Das Bewegte Buch, Wiesbaden 1999, 219-244.

Literature

Source: Kardec, Allan (ps. Hippolyte Léon Denizard Rivail), Le livre des esprits, Paris 1857 (many translations in various languages).
  Secondary Literature: Barrow, Logie, Independent Spirits: Spiritualism and English Plebeians, 1850–1910, London 1986; Brandon, Ruth, The Spiritualists: The Passion for the Occult in the Nineteenth and Twentieth Centuries, New York 1983; Braude, Ann, "News from the Spirit World: A Checklist of American Spiritualist Periodicals," in: Proceedings of the American Antiquarian Society 99 (1989), 399-462; Eadem, Radical Spirits: Spiritualism and Women's Rights in Nineteenth-Century America, Boston 1989; Goldsmith, Barbara, Other Powers, New York 1998; Hazelgrove, Jenny, Spiritualism and British Society between the Wars, Manchester/New York 2000; Hess, David J., Samba in the Night: Spiritism in Brazil, New York 1994; Linse, Ulrich, Geisterseher und Wunderwirker, Frankfurt/M. 1996; Moore, R. Laurence, In Search of White Crows: Spiritualism, Parapsychology, and American Culture, New York 1977; Nelson, Geoffrey K., Spiritualism and Society, London 1969; Oppenheim, Janet, The Other World: Spiritualism and Psychical Research in England, 1850–1914, Cambridge 1985; Owen, Alex, The Darkened Room: Women, Power and Spiritualism in Late Victorian England, Philadelphia 1990; Podmore, Frank, Mediums of the Nineteenth Century, 2 vols., New Hyde Park 1963; Sawicki, Diethard, Leben mit den Toten. Geisterglauben und die Entstehung des Spiritismus in Deutschland 1770–1900, Paderborn 2002.

→ *Afro-American Religions, Channeling, Communication, Death and Dying, Esotericism, Occultism, Parapsychology, Psyche, Soul, Specialists (Religious), Spirits/Ghosts/Revenants, Theosophical/Anthroposophical Society*

Ulrich Linse

Spirits / Ghosts / Revenants

1. Spirits are supernatural beings of neither unambiguously human nor divine origin. It is difficult to distinguish spirits, ghosts, and → demons, and their concepts are usually employed synonymously. The concept of spirit has a broad spectrum of meaning. Under the concept of 'spirits,' for instance, fall super-sensory beings and departed persons who tarry yet in the world of the living. A related notion is that of the 'revenant' (Fr., 'coming back'), which names a person who has died an unjust, wicked death, and is now attempting to return (→ Soul). The word 'ghost' (from Old English, orig. 'spirit' or 'demon') is a synonym for spirit, but with a more 'threatening' connotation.

2. The development of the European conceptualizations of the 'spirit' demonstrates how apparitions of spirits are variously deduced and explained.
Classical Greeks expressed fear of the souls of the dead, especially when a
death had been early or unnatural. Reports have been handed down of spirits
that imparted counsel to the living, or reproached them. As in other ancient
reports of spirits, they were concerned for their memorial, and begged for
appropriate rituals of transition.

   Christian Europe adopted many of the ancient conceptions of spirits that
inform, instruct, and persecute, appearing in aspect fearful or terrible, or
else in a form similar to that of their life on earth. Christian teachers cite
them, in order to afford the saints an opportunity to demonstrate their supernatural capacities vis-à-vis the malevolent spirits of the dead. Accounts
of wandering spirits, who complain that they have not been buried according to Christian funeral rites, reinforce the reality of purgatory, and the
value of prayers and offerings for the dead. Thus, the reports that give us
information on the notions of spirits are not simply the expression of a 'folk
mentality' but come from the pens of educated clerics, who are seeking to
instruct persons, and to convince them of the truth of Christian teaching.
Spirits of the dead appear in many types: veiled in white garments, as an
animal, or as an orb of light. Frequently they draw attention to themselves
by knocking, shuffling, or scratching ('poltergeists'). Often, their wounds
and mutilations offer testimonial of their sojourn in purgatory. Especially
the spirits of those who have been executed or have fallen in battle, or of
women dying in childbirth, awaken the sympathies of the living, in part because the resurrection of those dying in such ways is placed in question, in
part because their terrible, cruel death both frightens and fascinates. Spirits
are frequently encountered at cemeteries, gallows hills, and crossroads. Reports tell of spirits who beg forgiveness, or who seek justice. A story may
tell of a dying knight who asks a relative to give his mount and his other
possessions to the poor; but out of greed, the latter keeps the horse. On the
eighth day, the spirit of the knight appears, protesting that this transgression is postponing his deliverance from purgatory, and demanding that the
miscreant be punished. On the next day, the evil-doer dies in unnatural circumstances. This story illustrates the fact that conceptualizations of spirits
reinforce social norms of behavior.

   Since the Reformation, many Protestants have rejected the idea of wandering spirits of the dead, and hold the apparitions in question to be manifestations of the Devil. Despite theological confrontations over the nature of
apparitions, faith in spirits, phantoms, and ghosts remains active. In the seventeenth century, European spirits had a stronger orientation to the 'here'
than they did to the 'hereafter,' and behaved in a more human fashion. Thus,
they no longer came through the wall, but politely knocked. In the eighteenth century, skepticism grew concerning the idea of spirits as the wandering dead. In the nineteenth century, spirits won new followers in 'black
Romanticism,' along the field of tension between reason and faith, especially
in → spiritism. With the help of mediums, or certain technological apparatus, the spiritist movement attempted to come in contact with the spirits.

*European
Conceptualizations of
the 'Spirit'*

3. Kindred notions of spirits, in our sense, are found in all cultures. In
Asian traditions, the spirit of the fox appears in popular lore. Japanese
sources speak of the departed who have had no offspring, and thus no one
to perform the correct obsequies for them, so that they wander unredeemed

Spirits in Asia

through the world of the living and inflict injury on them. Unredeemed spirits of the dead are held to be capable of taking → possession of living persons; in the contrary direction, religious → specialists conduct rituals of expulsion (→ Exorcism). Ideas concerning apparitions of the dead have produced images of succoring, protective spirits, as well as of spirits that play practical jokes.

Psychological Interpretations

4. → Parapsychology often holds spirit apparitions to be real, and researches them with scientific methods. On the contrary, → Freud deems the creation of spirits to be human beings' first theoretical achievement. Freud explains them as projections of the living upon the dead, in which contradictory feelings like dread and awe come to expression. Aside from the question of the reality of spirits, the latter do express something about the feelings and fantasies of the person to whom they appear. Thus, fear of spirits can be interpreted as a bad conscience, and their appearance as the expression of a powerful wish.

The merry 'creepiness' of a ghost train, the materialization of spirits in films like "Ghostbusters" or "Poltergeist," serves for more than entertainment. In the present, spirits come into play, once more, in → occultism and → channeling, working as assistant decision-makers and guides through life. In a modern society of information and media, from which all good spirits are expelled, the quest for spirits seems endless.

Literature

FINUCANE, Ronald C., Appearances of the Dead: A Cultural History of Ghosts, London 1982; FOWKES, Katherine A., Giving Up the Ghost: Spirits, Ghosts, and Angels in Mainstream Comedy Films, Detroit 1998; FREED, Ruth S./FREED, Stanley A., Ghosts: Life and Death in North India, Seattle 1993; GUILEY, Rosemary Ellen, The Encyclopedia of Ghosts and Spirits, New York 1992; IWASAKA, Michiko/TOELKEN, Barre, Ghosts and the Japanese: Cultural Experience in Japanese Death Legends, Logan 1994; JOYNES, Andrew (ed.), Medieval Ghost Stories: An Anthology of Miracles, Marvels and Prodigies, Woodbridge 2001; MACGREGOR, Alasdair Alpin, The Ghost Book: Strange Hauntings in Britain, London 1955; NICKELL, Joe, Entities: Angels, Spirits, Demons, and Other Alien Beings, Amherst 1995; ROSE, Carol, Spirits, Fairies, Gnomes, and Goblins: An Encyclopedia of the Little People, Santa Barbara 1996; SCHMITT, Jean-Claude, Ghosts in the Middle Ages: The Living and the Dead in Medieval Society, Chicago 1998.

→ Ancestors, Channeling, Death and Dying, Fantasy, Funeral/Burial, Hereafter, Magic, Occultism, Possession, Shamanism, Spiritism, Veneration of the Saints, Voodoo

Inken Prohl

Spirituality

'Spirituality' is a fashionable word, used in contemporary religious discourse for a spiritual attitude toward life, a style of piety. It occurs in the Christian and the non-Christian areas alike. This diffuse application is connected with a twin history. From the French (*spiritualité*), the word has been taken over into other languages, especially so since the 1960s, by Catholic theologians, who wished to describe certain forms of piety actively lived: from a contemplative monastic life (for laity, as well, who occasionally share this life, and integrate it into their daily lives), to a political and social engagement from Christian motives, for example in the 'spirituality of liberation' (G. Gutiérrez; → Liberation Theology). Behind all of this stands the Latin adjective *spiritualis*, which in the Middle Ages meant 'pertaining to monasticism.' In this sense, then, spirituality is a modern form of active Christian piety that applies itself in the direction contrary to that by which religion withdraws from the world, and/or holds contemplative elements to be important. Similarly, the category has been adopted in the Evangelical area as well.

From Anglo-Saxon linguistic space comes a second, independent line of tradition. As early as the close of the nineteenth century, 'spirituality' began to denote a free-spirited attitude that appealed to inner experience in religious things, by contrast with Christian tradition's 'blind belief in dogma.' Unitarians and other free religious movements molded the word in this sense. Others transferred it to non-Christian religions, as for example, at the World Parliament of Religions in Chicago in 1893, Swami Vivekananda applied it to Hinduism. In this application, it denotes a 'mystical' nucleus of potentially any religion, which—unlike its theological or dogmatic formations—is experienced preponderantly, or only, in the individual, private religious practice of the 'God-seeker.' In the West, the → New Age movement has been among the agents propagating this meaning, adopting it as a self-description of 'unchurched religiosity,' 'nature-based spirituality,' etc.

Literature

BOCHINGER, Christoph, "New Age" und moderne Religion, Gütersloh ²1995, 377-398; FULLER, Robert C., Spiritual, But Not Religious: Understanding Unchurched America, Oxford 2001.

→ *Emotions/Feelings, Esalen Institute, Mysticism, New Age, Private Religion*

Christoph Bochinger

Sports

1. Since the nineteenth century, the term 'sports' (from 'disport'; 'to amuse oneself,' 'to frolic')—to busy the body by play, and in pleasure, but, at the same time, in fair competition, and according to strict rules—has become an umbrella concept for all kinds of corporeal motion and playing (with or without the character of a competition). In the connection of the two components, a normative meaning resonates, influencing the ordering and acknowledgment of sports in modern society.

The origin of all sports activity on the part of the human being is the natural impulse to movement. 'Bodily exercises' have served for the configuration of physical potentials such as speed, strength, agility, or endurance, of which that body stands in need in order to dominate the original conditions of life: running made hunting easier. The intentional training of these abilities awakened joy in the control of the body, independently of the original purpose. A new pleasure came to expression in physical comparison

Sports as Pleasure and Contest

How difficult it is, especially in the modern age, to distinguish religious characteristics from profane, entertainment from bestowal of meaning! This similarity is seen in many examples from today's team sports. The rituals of the opening and closing ceremonies of great presentations such as the → Olympic Games, or world championships, provide productive material. At the kickoff celebration of the world soccer championships in France, on June 9, 1998, four twenty-meter-tall "ethnofuturistic giants" (German Press Association dpa) float in a star march to Place de la Concorde in Paris, intended to symbolize the (soccer) cultures of Asia, Africa, Latin America, and Europe. The figures were escorted to their destination by balloon figures of (in order) musicians, dancers, in-line skaters, and speaking soccer-players. Hundreds of thousands of attendees lined the processional route. The closing ceremonies, to be seen here, remind those reared as Christians, of the 'dance around the golden calf' (the stylized soccer-ball goblet in the middle). A less critical sort can identify the spectacle with the motto *Seid umschlungen, Millionen!* (Ger., "Embrace, ye millions!"—Schiller, in the "Ode to Joy" of Beethoven's Ninth Symphony). That the scene is not simply to be divided into 'sacred' and 'profane,' but that it presents a multi-layered *civic ritual*, is suggested by a glance at the giants: they stand in the tradition of Baroque continent-allegories, as well as in the folkloristic magical festive custom of over-sized dolls, the *mannequins* (for example, in the Tarascon in Southern France). Third and finally, they can be ascribed among the figures of a modern hero-cult—after all, the ritual exaltation of sports stars into superhuman demigods is known from Greek antiquity. But does this now make them 'soccer gods'— → idols of a 'religion of the masses'? (Hubert Mohr)

with others. The physical competition to be observed in nature peoples is a sportiveness that behavioral scientists interpret as the expression of a natural drive to play. Bodily and sportive playing was integrated into the respective traditions of cultic rituals among the various peoples (especially nature and seasonal festivals, celebrations of the dead, fertility cults).

2. a) European antiquity, which, from the perspective of sporting history, reaches from the first → Olympic Games (presumably in 776 BCE) to their prohibition in 394, is characterized by two continuous sporting motifs. For one, sports served for the training of the body in its military abilities. We may take Sparta as an example. Here, sportive upbringing was a collective military upbringing. With the consolidation of the ancient community, education aimed less at the military function than at complex moral and behavioral upbringing. Over and above positive corporeal experience, sportive upbringing (gymnasium) was necessarily completed by a spiritual education aiming at individual perfection. A concept of competition was added (*agón*). Now the 'Olympic Games' had become a sporting event. Independently of any ideal functional ascription, such events made sports popular with audiences.

Sports in Antiquity

b) This situation remained in the European Middle Ages, a period marked, vis-à-vis the sportive, both by a Christian skepticism and by a (pagan) openness to enjoyment of the body and sensory activity. Human desire for play scarcely contested the latter. Thus, for example, entire villages took part in ball play, which was subject to no temporal or ordinal limitations, and became out-and-out 'fun,' hosting a drive almost in the spirit of a public festival. In their ritualized form, the chivalric tourneys of medieval society were more theater, or even cult, than they were sport. In form (costuming, ornament, and scenery), and course of events, the actual tourney was part of a drama of latent eros, in whose course the 'sportive' knight adopted a ritualized role in a rapturous chivalric drama of romantic love (J. Huizinga).

Middle Ages

As early as the sixteenth century, England had horse racing, foot racing, wrestling, and boxing, for the leisure-time occupation of 'sportsmen' (the nobility). Part of the ideal of this 'disport' was that the contests be held according to rules of fairness, and in that spirit. This understanding of sports harmonized with the norms of the industrial society forming from the beginning of the eighteenth century onward. Formally equal chances, competition, achievement, and comparison were tested in sports. Sports became a messenger of modern industrial society. As 'schools of Christian character,' typically English sporting games were transplanted to the colonies. Here, indeed, they attained unanticipated 'success': the new 'sports' became veritably identifying 'national sports' (e.g., hockey in India).

English Sporting Movement

As soon as these collective effects entered the scene—if not, indeed, before—they made sports available for appropriation in the interest of socio-political goals (ideologization). In Germany, this led to a doughty struggle between the middle-class tourneys and the workers' sporting movement. Beginning with Guthsmuth's 1793 *Gymnastik für die Jugend* (Ger., "Gymnastics for Youth"), German gymnastics, called to life by Ludwig Jahn (*Turnvater Jahn*—"Gymnastics-Father Jahn"), bodily training was understood as

Tourney Movement and Workers' Sporting Movement

improvement of the *Volkskörper* ("people's/nation's body"). This regimen meant purely and simply a universal pre-military training under nationalistic auspices. By contrast, the workers' sporting movement formulated the task of sports and games as part of a discovery of identity in the class struggle. Both movements kept their distance from the spirit of the individualistic contests of the English sporting movement.

Cult of the Body in
National Socialism

c) The anthropological aspect, as well as the cultural side, indicates the original universality of sports. A European or Hellenocentric view, however, shaped an idealized, goal-free understanding of competition, after the Greek model ('agonal attitude'—Jacob Burckhardt), from which the modern Olympic movement was able to extract and further a new universality of sports. But Hellenocentrism actually belittled foreign sporting traditions as 'unagonal.' This pattern of limitation configured bigotries that, in the Nazis' anti-Semitic propaganda, ultimately occasioned the cliché of the nonsportive, 'physically debilitated' Jew. Conversely, it installed the ideal of a sportive striving for success, achievement, and bodily presence: the powerful (naked) → hero.

Differentiation—
Sports as 'Event'

4. Under such auspices, and still in high tones, the connection between sports and personality development (ethical, or moral, and social) is easy to emphasize. But actually, structures that dominated societies, and whose effects are lasting, such as, for example, male groups, then become marginalized. In sports, 'successful' virtues, such as strength, endurance, speed, achievement, and competition are first and foremost masculine virtues, the gaining of which becomes a modern initiation rite into maleness.

To be sure, acknowledgments of this kind remain vague, as long as their point of reference is still a comprehensive, unitary understanding of sports. Actually, sports today are more and more differentiated according to motive and use. Everyone defines her and his 'own' sport. While, for some, it is a kind of identifying 'substitute religion,' which they, for instance, practice as fans of a soccer team, for others it is spare-time 'fun'—something 'on the side.' If sports for school and health oblige one to pursue educational or therapeutic purposes, in high-achievement sports the motive that dominates is that of promoting and enhancing the commercial value of products for the market (e.g., Basketball Kids). If on the one hand, by way of differentiation, sports participation withdraws one from appropriation by ideologies, on the other hand this 'gain in autonomy' has a tendency to ground respective particular normative systems, which occasionally are frankly corrupt (performance-enhancing drugs).

Referred to itself, for individual self-perfection, sport does offer its own promises of happiness. Physical fitness is elevated to the norm. But a new external appropriation threatens sports. A world fixated on media and advertising already dominates the symbols accounted as hallmarks of self-perfection. There is no jogging without the right outfit. In the uniformity of the 'body cult,' the erstwhile sports practitioner becomes a lonely figure.

Literature

BLANCHARD, Kendall/CHESKA, Alyce Taylor, The Anthropology of Sport: An Introduction, Westport 1995; BRAILSFORD, Dennis, Sport, Time, and Society: The British at Play,

London 1991; Chidester, David, "The Church of Baseball, the Fetish of Coca-Cola, and the Potlatch of Rock 'n' Roll," in: Forbes, Bruce David/Mahan, Jeffrey H. (eds.), Religion and Popular Culture in America, Berkeley etc. 2000, 219-238; Craig, Steve, Sports and Games of the Ancients, Westport 2002; Evans, Christopher H./Herzog II, William R. (eds.), The Faith of Fifty Million: Baseball, Religion, and American Culture, Louisville 2002; Fleming, Scott/Tomlinson, Alan, Ethics, Sport and Leisure: Crises and Critiques, Aachen 1997; Guttmann, Allen, From Ritual to Record: The Nature of Modern Sports, New York 1978; Guttmann, Allen et al. (eds.), Essays on Sport History and Sport Mythology, College Station 1990; Huizinga, Johan, Homo Ludens: A Study of the Play Element in Culture, London 1970; MacClancy, Jeremy, Sport, Identity and Ethnicity, Oxford 1996; Prebish, Charles S., Religion and Sport: The Meeting of Sacred and Profane, Westport 1993; Price, Joseph L. (ed.), From Season to Season: Sports as American Religion, Macon 2001; Putney, Clifford, Muscular Christianity: Manhood and Sports in Protestant America, 1880–1920, Cambridge/London 2001; Riordan, James/Krüger, Arnd, The International Politics of Sport in the 20th Century, London/New York 1999; Wilkins, Sally, Sports and Games of Medieval Cultures, Westport 2002.

→ *Body, Hero/Heroism, Luck/Happiness, Olympic Games, Popular Culture, Publicity*

H. Georg Lützenkirchen

Stigmata / Stigmatics

'Stigma' (Gk., 'brand,' 'tattoo'), generally denotes a mark artificially made on the body as ornament, proprietary sign (slaves, animals), or mark of criminality. In antiquity, slaves who attempted escape or theft were 'branded,' usually with a mark on the forehead.

The phenomenon of stigmatization became important as a corporeal concomitant of Christian → mysticism. What is meant is the spontaneous, usually periodic, emergence of the bleeding wounds of Jesus crucified—on the palms of the hands, on the feet, and on the breast ('wound of his heart,' or of his 'side')—on the bodies of living persons without organic cause. In connection with stigmatization, other corporeal phenomena usually appear as well, such as a bloody sweat, tears of blood, living without nourishment, blindness, and → ecstasy. The first and most famous stigmatic is → Francis of Assisi (1181/82–1226). In his succession, we have descriptions of the wounds of some hundreds of persons. Remarkably, despite the male identification figures of Jesus and Francis, stigmatization appears preponderantly with women. The cause, here, is ordinarily of a psychopathological nature, often attributable to a dissociative disturbance. An extreme intensity in the veneration of the Passion of Christ, as practiced in the Christian mystique of suffering, can, by way of auto- or external suggestion, lead to the psychosomatic emergence of the wounds. Self-wounding and simulation have also been evidenced in many cases. An example that concerned the public for decades may be cited in Therese Neumann of Konnersreuth (1898–1962; see illus.). After various illnesses, and supposed cures, it was in 1926 that the wounds first appeared on her body. From this time forward, she is supposed to have lived—in the tradition of medieval female mystics—entirely without food or drink. Her stigmatization appeared regularly on Fridays, the day of Christ's death on the cross, and entailed ecstasies, during which she re-lived that salvific event. A number of medical testimonials refer to her 'severe hysteria.' Therese Neumann was the object of extensive veneration

Therese Neumann is shown during one of her so-called 'passion ecstasies,' around 1950. Her body bears the Five Wounds of Christ, and she weeps blood. This phenomenon, occurring mainly on Fridays, and in the Passion Weeks, regularly drew hundreds of the faithful and the curious to Konnersreuth. Despite the large number of visitors, no one ever observed the onset of the stigmatization. Neumann always declined an examination. A sober observation must come to the conclusion that Therese Neumann maneuvered herself into a situation in which her piety, combined with expectations from without, were the components permitting her intentional simulation.

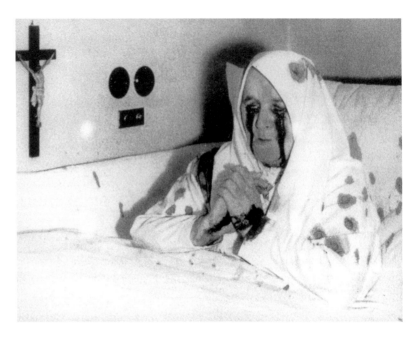

in her very lifetime, on the part of a great multitude of devotees, whose expectations she declined to disappoint, so that, alongside the documented psychosomatic reactions, simulation (especially with her 'no food or drink' regimen) has also been cited.

Clear parallels to Konnersreuth are to be observed in the case of the most celebrated male stigmatic since Francis, Padre Pio, of Pietralcina in Apulia (1887–1968). The Capuchin father had surrendered to the mysticism of suffering, and, beginning in 1918, bore the wounds of Christ, which, in a wondrous manner, disappeared after his death in 1968. Church authorities most energetically collected 'evidence' of a deceitful behavior on Pio's part. Only Pope John Paul II disallowed the doubts of his predecessors, and in May 1999, in the presence of 300,000 of his devotees, pronounced the beatification of the Padre.

Literature

BATACANDOLO, Dennis L., The Stigmatine Spirituality for the New Millennium: A Philippine Perspective, dissertation Rome 2001; BOUFLET, Joachim, Les stigmatisés, Paris 1996; GRAEF, Hilda C., The Case of Therese Neumann, Cork 1950; LHERMITTE, Jean, Mystiques et faux mystiques, Paris 1952; THURSTON, Herbert, The Physical Phenomena of Mysticism, London 1952; YAROM, Nitza, Body, Blood, and Sexuality: A Psychological Study of St. Francis' Stigmata and Their Historical Context, New York 1992.

→ *Body, Ecstasy, Mysticism, Pain, Psychopathology, Suffering, Tattoo*

Guido Schmid

Suffering

1. a) Suffering can be defined as the experience of situations interpreted and felt psychically, physically, and/or socially (e.g., poverty) as painful. Frequently, these longer or shorter periods are accompanied by the conscious and/or unconscious perception of loss, frustration, fear, sadness, and vulnerability. As with pain, suffering as well has both a physical and a psychic dimension. Only the entity of suffering, however, broadens the preponderantly individual character of pain, and binds individuals with their fellows, in a more or less highly developed capacity for empathy.
   b) Grief represents a universally present phenomenon, even apart from the human species. Suffering, however, ranks as a typically human experience. Thus, suffering is a key theme in the religions, although not necessarily the central theme, as it is, for example, in Buddhism. Suffering is primarily a personal experience, but is also a social phenomenon: sharing suffering unburdens the individual, and can strengthen the community. The religions offer rituals to channel the 'working through' of personal experiences and community crises.
   On the level of the understanding and interpretation of suffering, which is experienced as negative, the representatives of religion, philosophy, politics, as well as the sciences, have two complexes of questions to confront: Why is there suffering, what causes suffering, does suffering make sense— have meaning (cf. § 2)? And: can individuals and/or the community avert suffering? If so, then how (cf. § 3)?

Basic Human Experience

2. *Why is there suffering, what causes suffering, does suffering make sense?* a) Suffering is a fact. It is experienced every day, although not at every time by everyone. *Monotheistic religions* have the problem of theodicy: why does God allow this (injustice)? That suffering is a punishment for personal transgressions or violation of norms obviously does not always hold true. For an explanation of the suffering of the 'innocent,' a sense must be attributed to suffering, for example suffering as purification, suffering as asceticism, suffering as desire, suffering as imitation of the passion of Christ, suffering as a consequence of the Fall. The classic image is in the biblical character of the pious Job, to whom the devil had God's leave to send the heaviest suffering, in order to test whether he would remain loyal to God. Or else the question of meaning is given up, and suffering is interpreted and accepted as the opaque will of a higher power. It is precisely the question of theodicy that challenges criticism of religion, especially of the monotheistic religions.

Sense of Suffering?

b) Buddha the reformer elevated the question of the causes of suffering to the status of a major theme, attempting thus to transcend the Brahmanism of his time. The Four Noble Truths have always constituted the foundations of Buddhism, from its origin until this very day. To express them in abbreviated fashion: (1) there is no life without suffering (in Pali: *dukkha*); (2) the cause of suffering is avidity and desire (literally: 'thirst'); (3) suffering is removed through the annihilation of avidity; (4) the annihilation of avidity is reached by traversing the noble eightfold path. Suffering, in Buddhism, counts as a natural part of life, conditioned by transgressions committed in previous incarnations: the idea of karma. By following determinate rules, it is possible, usually through several rebirths, to release oneself from the

Deliverance from Suffering

At the focus of the Christian religion stands the death of a human being: the execution of Jesus of Nazareth on the → cross. The grief that it has aroused occasions an ecstatic mystique of suffering, and has led to the creation of crucifixes and the Pietà. The body hanging on the cross, and the man on his mother's lap for whom that mother weeps, are profound 'pathos formulae' (Aby Warburg) of religious mentality. The liturgical occasions of such emphatic presentation of suffering include the processions of Holy Week in the Roman Catholic Mediterranean region, as here in Ruvo di Puglia in Apulia, Italy. This procession is held on Holy Saturday, and is organized by a special fraternity, the *Confraternità di S. Maria del Suffragio*; it is an honor for the bearers to carry the heavy burden of the "Image of Suffering" (*Mistero*), an honor often handed down from generation to generation. The images themselves are from the seventeenth century, and were created by sculptor Giuseppe Manzo, of Lecce. The 'compassion' (in Ital., *pietà*) of a mother for her dead son belongs to those basic human moments that are valid even beyond the purview of the religious; but it is in the religious framework that it has its mighty social place. (Hubert Mohr)

cycle of living and dying (*samsara*)—and thereby release oneself from suffering—and effect nirvana.

c) Although the basic orientation of Christianity and Buddhism vis-à-vis life could not be more opposed (the name here: everlasting life; there: extinction), the capacity for compassion ('empathy') is of great importance in both. Doubtless the expressions of this compassion can be different: compassion, 'co-suffering,' is looked upon as a Christian virtue, and thereby as pleasing to God—and so, not altogether selfless; Buddhist teaching counsels the cultivation of benevolence and sympathy, but not 'co-suffering.' Because suffering is a most profound, universal human experience, monotheistic

and non-theistic 'religions' like Christianity and Buddhism invoke the succor of beings placed at one's side, who, as capable of pity, can bring alleviation to earthly suffering: in Christianity, the angels and saints, in (especially
Mahayana) Buddhism the Bodhisattvas. However, in both religions, human
beings are invoked for assistance, summoned to the active practice of mercy.
In this context, Christian pastoral activity can be interpreted as a spiritual
(sacred) assistance, to be bestowed upon living human beings—human beings such as, through this concrete experiencing of suffering, now respond
to their previous understanding of God with increasing skepticism, or turn
away from belief or faith in the good.

Consequently, we have numerous examples in Christianity of suffering
actually being sought, whether by martyrs or ascetics or flagellants. Altogether plausibly, a 'craving for suffering' can be explained neuro-physiologi-
cally as a 'craving for pain' that, in certain circumstances, can be addictive.
In Buddhism, the meaning of suffering is generally limited to the development of the consciousness that what is life is also suffering.

d) Meaning attaches to suffering in an atheistic system of meanings, as
well, although here it is the social cause of suffering that is seen, and, in
Marxism its defeat is the goal of the system. In his *Capital*, Marx discusses
the cause of the suffering of the working class, which, first and foremost, is
'alienation.' But ultimately it is a craving (for profit) on the part of individuals. Thus, suffering can even be defined mathematically, in a comparison:
the amount of 'surplus value' is proportional to the degree of the exploitation that correlates directly with the suffering (and pressure of suffering) of
the exploited.

e) Since Descartes, and certainly since Darwin, discussion on the concept *Coping with Suffering*
of 'suffering' in the sciences has been dominated by a (genetic) pragmatism.
Suffering is 'pain as the phenomenon of a conscious or unconscious perception,' and constitutes a natural part of life. Anything beyond the perception
of pain is deemed subjective interpretation—influenced by environment
and genetics—of neurological processes. Various psychoanalytic and psychotherapeutic approaches ascribe a necessary function to the experience
known as suffering. At present, suffering is gradually shifting into focus in
the field of medical ethics, as demonstrated by intensified interdisciplinary
dialogue. (Headings of this dialogue: intensive therapy, active/passive →
euthanasia, → genetic engineering, → abortion.)

3. For the purpose of resistance to suffering, of the individual as of the com- *Soul/Body*
munity, Christianity and Buddhism each have their 'ways.' 'Right activity'
can afford redemption (heaven or nirvana). Differences in the way to that
redemption can be identified. The Christian is the object of the grace and the
will of God; the Buddhist, instead, is subject to his or her own capacity for
knowledge. In Christianity, pastoral activity is ascribed an important function in the alleviation of suffering; indeed, together with medicine and psychology, pastoral work can show routes to a better handling of suffering.

Marx insisted that the suffering human being should recognize the
fact of her or his suffering, analyze its causes, and actively alter the status
quo. It is not only in the hereafter that everything should take a turn for
the better. Joining the battle (revolution) is a 'preliminary,' not only to the
diminution, but—depending on the phase of the battle—also to the increase
of suffering.

In the sciences—and here in a special way in contemporary medicine, which is certainly more than merely scientific—the prevention and reduction of suffering assumes one of the major roles (if indeed not *the* major role): the lessening of, especially, physical (psychological, as well, however) pain that can be attained through various procedures, ranging from drugs to behavioral therapy. Also, living 'healthily' is sure to minimize suffering. Particularly with terminal or life-threatening diseases, a rapprochement of medicine and religion can be attained.

Literature

Christianity and Judaism: GLUCKLICH, Ariel, Sacred Pain: Hurting the Body for the Sake of the Soul, Oxford 2001; MAZZONI, Cristina, Saint Hysteria: Neurosis, Mysticism, and Gender in European Culture, Ithaca 1996; PERKINS, Judith, The Suffering Self: Pain and Narrative Representation in the Early Christian Era, London 1995; BRAND, Paul/YANCEY, Philip, Pain: the Gift Nobody Wants, New York 1993; SPAEMANN, Robert, Happiness and Benevolence, Edinburgh 2000.—*Buddhism:* TIN LIEN, T. N./BHIKKHUNI, T. N., Concepts of Dhamma in Dhammapada, Columbia 1996; VERDU, Alfonso, Early Buddhist Philosophy in the Light of the Four Noble Times, Delhi 1985.—*Marxism:* BOWKER, John, Problems of Suffering in Religions of the World, Cambridge 1970.—*Medicine and Ethology:* EIBL-EIBESFELDT, Irenäus, Ethology, the Biology of Behavior, New York 1970; MORRIS, David B., The Culture of Pain, Berkeley 1991; GOOD, Mary-Jo D. et al. (eds.), Pain as Human Experience: An Anthropological Perspective, Berkeley 1992.

→ *Atheism, Charitable Organizations, Criticism of Religion, Feelings/Emotions, Flagellants, Illness/Health, God/Gods/The Sacred, Mysticism, Pain, Stigmata/Stigmatics*

Peter Kaiser

Sufism

Sufism and 'Mysticism'

In traditional scholarship as well as in conventional usage, Sufism is commonly referred to as the 'mystical tradition of Islam' (→ Mysticism). This ascription is problematic for three reasons. First, it divides → Islam artificially into two traditions presumably separable from each other; secondly, not all manifestations of Sufism are 'mystical';[1] and thirdly, the idea of a universally valid category of Mysticism manifesting itself in particular interpretations of different 'world religions' is itself increasingly disputed.[2]

Orientalist scholarship coined the term 'Sufism' in the late eighteenth century within the context of European → colonialism. Particular to the early European conceptualizations of Sufism was the attempt to describe it as a phenomenon distinct or only superficially attached to Islam. In this view, the deep personal spirituality discovered among the 'Sufis' was incompatible with the prevalent stereotypes of a legalist and spiritually superficial Islam. Rather, it fit into the romantic category of Mysticism that was understood—and still is—as essentially transgressing the boundaries of religion.[3]

The Concept

The Arabic epithet *as-Sūfī* appears already in the eighth century. It is most likely a derivative of *sūf*, 'wool,' a reference to the woolen garb these early Sufis used to wear. They were pious ascetics, like Hasan al-Basrī (d. 728), and Ibrāhīm Ibn Adham (d. 770?), fiercely criticizing immersion in the false splendors of 'the world' (*dunya*). The first Sufis were vigorous reformers, urging a return to the pure faith of the Qur'an, which they perceived as having been lost in the context of the territorial and material gains of the Umayyad Caliphate (661–750).

The Muslim term for Sufism is *tasawwuf*, literally meaning 'becoming a Sufi.' Soon it became a common name for the practice and philosophy of the Sufi movement. Abstinence of worldly pleasures was the remedy they prescribed, and it was achieved through practices of prayer, meditation, fasting, seclusion, and sleep deprivation. Sufis themselves sometimes prefer to derive *tasawwuf* from *safā*, 'purity.' This etymology would render *tasawwuf* 'the process of becoming pure,' and the Sufi would accordingly be the one embarked on this process—an interpretation very much in line with the initial character of the Sufi movement and Sufi self-understanding.

While otherworldly orientation and asceticism remained important features of Sufism until today, they were tempered and sometimes countered with more positive attitudes towards the creation and especially the creator. Still in the tradition of the ascetic movement that regarded the world as mere illusion, Rābia al-Adawīya (d. 801) is the woman credited for introducing the theme of mystical love into Sufism. For her, absolute devotion to the Beloved (a Sufi metaphor for God) was the means to achieve a state of mystical union with God. In fact, the poems ascribed to Rābia make for some of the earliest examples of 'mystical' themes within the Sufi movement. For the first two Muslim centuries it is, however, very difficult to limit mystical interpretations of Islam—which can be found from early on, arguably already in the Qur'an—to a distinguishable social group within the Muslim community.[4]

Early History of Sufism

A gradual institutionalization of Sufism occurred from the ninth century onwards. It found its expression in Dhū al-Nūn al-Misrī's (d. 859) attempt to systematize the nature of the Sufi path (*tarīqa*), conceptualized as a sequence of stages of mystical maturity (*maqām*, pl. *maqāmāt*) to which particular psychological states (*hāl*, pl. *ahwāl*) were attributed. This basic categorization became a cornerstone of Sufi discourse, subsequently refined by later Sufi authors, who developed sophisticated roadmaps of the mystical path—mostly divided into the four *maqāmāt sharīa, tarīqa, marīfa* ('esoteric knowledge'; → Esotericism), and *haqīqa* ('truth'). Advancing from stage to stage, the seeker (*murīd*) has to confront and gradually overcome his lower soul, or ego-self (*nafs*) that binds him to the world, in order to eventually achieve its annihilation (*fanā*). The ultimate goal of the path is to achieve unity with the Divine in the realization of absolute truth (*haqīqa*), sometimes also referred to as *baqā*, i.e. 'abiding' (in union with God).

The systematization of Sufi thought and practice went along with Sufism's growth as a social movement, a first expression of which was the development of master-disciple relationships. Early examples of small circles around eminent Sufi teachers can be dated back to the eighth century. These informal circles used to dissolve with the master's passing. The earliest examples of Sufi manuals, small guidebooks designed for the core exercise of conscience examination for Sufi novices, date from the ninth century. From the twelfth century onwards, Sufi circles began to transform into traditions; revolving around the personalities and teachings of venerated past Sufi masters, distinct Sufi orders (*tarīqa*, pl. *turuq*) emerged, led by Sheikhs (Ar., *shaykh*; Pers., *pīr*) believed to carry the spiritual knowledge and authority of

Systematization and Growth

a unbroken chain of holy men reaching back to the prophet → Muhammad himself. This sacred chain (*silsila*) embodies the legitimacy of a Sufi master (→ Master/Pupil). The Sufi orders spread quickly, and established their branches virtually everywhere Muslims lived.

In its earlier stages, Sufism had been the domain of a religious elite, i.e. ascetic, poetic, and philosophical virtuosi. Some of the greatest masters of Sufi poetry such as Farīduddīn Attār (d. 1131?) and Mawlānā Jalāluddīn Rūmī (d. 1273), and major theoreticians of Sufism such as Ibn Arabī (d. 1240) were not initiated into Sufi orders.[5] The emergence and rapid development of the Sufi order as a new Muslim institution, and the Sufi lodges and convents (Ar., *zawīya*; Pers., *khānqā*, *dergāh*; Turk., *tekke*) as new Muslim spaces, contributed to a popularization of Sufism, which then became accessible to a much broader audience. Different degrees of → initiation and different levels of sophistication in the study of the Sufi path allowed for more or less commitment. Organized hierarchically—ideally in accordance with the individual stages of spiritual maturity—Sufi orders became efficient socio-religious networks with often considerable political influence. They distinguish themselves from each other mainly through their lineages, the religious rules they subscribe to, and the practices they follow.

Dhikr *and the "Whirling Dervishes"*

The practice most characteristic of Sufism is the *dhikr*, literally 'remembrance' (of God). *Dhikr* is a meditation on the names of God and selected Qur'anic sequences, often inducing ecstatic states (*wajd*). It can be done individually or in community, silently or aloud; which formulas are used for the invocation, as well as the outer form a *dhikr*, differs from order to order. Audible *dhikr* often involves particular breathing techniques, and rhythmic body movements. Some Sufi orders have their *dhikr* accompanied by music and/or dance ceremonies such as e.g. the Turkish Mevlevis, widely known as the order of the 'Whirling Dervishes.'

Sufism and Modernity

Until the nineteenth century, the Sufi orders were in almost all Muslim societies well accredited institutions with often considerable social, political, and economic powers.[6] Since then, however, Sufism became increasingly marginalized within Muslim discourse, and sometimes even declared un-Islamic. In the last two centuries, secular nationalists and Westernist modernizers (such as e.g. Kemal Ataturk from Turkey) have targeted Sufism as a major obstacle for modernization and rationalization. They regarded Sufism as a seed of irrationality and superstition, and thus as an obstacle on the road to modernity; they mistrusted the networks and authority structures of the Sufi orders, which were based on close personal allegiances, as a potential threat to the centralizing measures a nation state required.[7] Today, anti-Sufi sentiments are mostly fed by revivalist movements (such as the Wahhābiyya and the Salafiyya), which aim to restore an idealized pure form of Islam by cleansing it from all traditions and customs not sanctioned by → Qur'an and *hadīth* (authorized collections of the sayings and deeds of Muhammad).

Both secular and religious propaganda have contributed to the declining significance of Sufism as a major form of social organization in Muslim societies, even if there are still some orders with considerable social and political influence (e.g. the Muridiyya in Senegal). Artistic manifestations of Sufism, however, especially the amazing beauty and diversity of Sufi poetry and → music, are still an integral part of Muslim culture. With capitalism's discovery of → 'new age' and 'well-being,' Sufi commodities also entered the West European and North American markets, where Sufi poetry, music, and practices are advertised and sold under the labels of esoteric globalization such as 'Eastern spirituality,' 'world music,' 'world literature,' and 'Islamic Mysticism.' This market sometimes overlaps, but mostly contrasts, with the presence of Sufi Muslims in Western countries, where branches of many orders were established in the second half of the twentieth century.[8] As in most Muslim majority lands, these Sufi communities in the West lead a marginal existence at the edge of Muslim communities and are hardly noticed by the non-Muslim public. Nevertheless, they have proved to be in many instances very successful in the adaptation to new environments, often attracting considerable numbers of converts.

Sufism is today in a defensive position, often having to justify its very location within Muslim discourse. Nevertheless, the Sufi tradition within Islam is still very much alive, responding to needs for charismatic guidance and close personal relationships in small-sized communities, as well as strong religious experiences.

1. See CHITTICK, W. C., Faith and Practice of Islam: Three Thirteenth Century Sufi Texts, Albany 1992, 168-173.
2. Cf. KING, R, Orientalism and Religion: Postcolonial Theory, India and 'The Mystic East,' London 1999, 7-34; SCHMIDT, L. E., "The Making of Modern 'Mysticism,'" in: Journal of the American Academy of Religion 71 (2003), 273-302.
3. The Orientalist interpretation of Sufism as a movement of freethinking ecstatic mystics had—and has—little to do with the average outlook and behavior of the Sufis, also called 'dervishes' (lit. 'poor ones'), who for the most part subscribe to the practical and legal prescriptions of Islam (*sharīa*). Libertarian and antinomian strands in Sufism certainly exist, but have always been in the minority. Cf. ERNST, C. W., The Shambhala Guide to Sufism, Boston 1997, 8-16.
4. In fact, the gradual objectification of both 'Sufism' and 'Islam' as signifying categories was not completed before the nineteenth century; ibid., XIVf.
5. For examples of their work see CHITTICK, W. C., The Sufi Path of Love: The Spiritual Teachings of Rumi, Albany 1983; FARĪD AL-DĪN ATTĀR, The Conference of the Birds, trans. D. Davis et al., Harmondsworth et al. 1984; CHITTICK, W. C., The Self-Disclosure of God: Principles of Ibn al-'Arabī's Cosmology, Albany 1998.
6. For a closer look at some selected Sufi orders see GABORIEAU, M. et al., Naqshbandis: cheminements et situation actuelle d'un ordre mystique musulman. Actes de la Table ronde de Sèvres (Varia Turcica 18), Istanbul et al. 1990; POPOVIC, A./VEINSTEIN, G., Bektachiyya. Études sur l'ordre mystique des Bektachis et les groupes relevant de Hadji Bektach, Istanbul 1995; POPOVIC, A./VEINSTEIN, G., Les voies d'Allah. Les ordres mystiques dans l'Islam des origines á aujourd'hui, [Paris] 1996.
7. A good example for a Sufi order becoming the organizational platform for a resistance movement against the secular nation state is the Sheykh Said uprising in Turkey (1925); see v BRUINESSEN, M., Agha, Shaikh and State: The Social and Political Structures of Kurdistan, London et al. 1992, esp. chapters 4-5.
8. See e.g. HERMANSEN, M., "Hybrid Identity Formations in Muslim America. The Case of American Sufi Movements," in: Muslim World 90 (2000), 158-197; SCHLESSMANN, L., Sufismus in Deutschland. Deutsche auf dem Weg des mystischen Islam, Cologne etc. 2003.
9. For anthropological accounts of contemporary Sufism see e.g. FREMBGEN, J., Derwische. Gelebter Sufismus, wandernde Mystiker und Asketen im islamischen Orient, Cologne 1993; GILSENAN, M., Saint and Sufi in Modern Egypt: An Essay in the Sociology of Religion, Oxford 1973; LINGS, M. A., Sufi Saint of the Twentieth Century: Shaikh Ahmad al-'Alawī. His Spiritual Heritage and Legacy, Cambridge 1993; WERBNER, P./BASU, H. (eds.), Embodying Charisma: Modernity, Locality, and Performance of Emotion in Sufi Cults, London et al. 1998; WERBNER, P., Pilgrims of Love: The Anthropology of a Global Sufi Cult, Bloomington 2003.

Literature

Awn, P. J., "Sufism," in: The Encyclopedia of Religion, ed. M. Eliade, New York, vol. 14, 1986, 104-123; Chittick, W. C., Sufism: A Short Introduction, Oxford 2000; Ernst, C. W., The Shambhala Guide to Sufism, Boston 1997; Farīd al-Dīn 'Attār, Muslim Saints and Mystics: Episodes from the Tadhkirat al-Auliya' ('Memorial of the Saints'), trans. A. J. Arberry, London etc. 1990; Gramlich, R., Die schiitischen Derwischorden Persiens, vol. II: Glaube und Lehre, Wiesbaden 1976; Karamustafa, A. T., God's Unruly Friends: Dervish Groups in the Islamic Later Middle Period 1200–1550, Salt Lake City 1994; Knysh, A. D., Islamic Mysticism: A Short History, Leiden etc. 2000; Lewisohn, L. (ed.), The Heritage of Sufism, 3 vols., Oxford etc. 1999; Massignon, L., The Passion of al-Hallāj: Mystic and Martyr of Islam (Bollingen series 98), 4 vols., Princeton 1982; Radtke, B./De Jong, F. (eds.), Islamic Mysticism Contested: Thirteen Centuries of Controversies and Polemics, Leiden etc. 1999; Schimmel, A., Mystical Dimensions of Islam, Chapel Hill 1992; Sells, M. A., Early Islamic Mysticism: Sufi, Qur'an, Mi'raj, Poetic and Theological Writings, New York 1996; Trimingham, J. S., The Sufi Orders in Islam, New York 1998.

→ *Dance, Esotericism, Islam, Kabbalah, Monasticism, Music, Mysticism, Order/Brotherhoods, Orientalism/Exotism, Qur'an, Rhythm, Trance*

Markus Dressler

Suicide

Concept

1. a) For the intentional termination of one's own life, there are a number of synonymous expressions in English: suicide, self-destruction, free death. Some of these expressions have been coined by religion, philosophy, and law, so that they are powerfully suggestive of moral value, often with the connotation of 'murder of oneself' (as in German *Selbstmord*, Dutch *zelfmoord*, etc.). Condemned by both religion and law, Latin *sui cidium* or *sui caedere* means 'killing of oneself'; 'suicide' was used for the first time in 1177.

Shrouding of Suicide

b) The problems to be associated with the statistics of suicide are of basic importance in all countries in which religion and law attach a strong moral (ethical) value to, and strong sanctions against, this act. With respect to the statistical data, it must be kept in mind that the killing of oneself—even with official data—is strongly influenced by the country's religious confession, and the penalization of the act of suicide. Thus, in Catholic countries (e.g., Italy, Spain, Brazil), the cause of death by suicide is frequently disguised, which conceals its actual numbers. On the other hand, in Protestant countries, such as in Sweden, Denmark, and Finland, the statistical estimate is likely to be more precise. Likewise questionable are the statistical findings in places with a conservative religious attitude, as in some states of the United States, in Northern Ireland, and in Scotland. However, in general, Protestants manifest a stronger tendency to suicide than do Catholics.

Theories

c) Among the theories of suicide most often cited are the following. (a) The *sociological* that was proposed by Émile Durkheim (1858–1917) in the year 1897, in his *Le Suicide* (Fr., "Suicide"), sees suicide rates as connected with the degree of the integration of individuals into society. Here, the condition that can be called rootlessness, and that involves the absence of norm or rule, plays an important role. (b) The *psychoanalytic* view is based on Sigmund → Freud's theory of aggression, according to which the aggressive drive takes an unconscious turn against the subject. (c) The *psychiatric* theories handle suicide in terms of a psychic illness (e.g., depression, or psychoses; → psychopathology).

2. Of all human acts, suicide is the object of the most divergent assessments. *Religious Perspectives*
For some, suicide is a transgression of the fifth commandment, a sacrilege or sin that is never forgiven, as it surely goes unrepented. For others, it means greatness of soul, contempt for death, or an act of human autonomy. Each varying position is the result of a particular culture, as seen in the mirror of its various standpoints on religion, ethics, *Weltanschauung*, and social relationships. Suicide is not a phenomenon of modern civilization only. It occurs—if less frequently—in other cultures and eras, as, for example, with the 'nature peoples,'[1] or with the Aztecs and Mayas, who actually had gods of suicide.

From the religious perspective, it can be said that most theistic religions take an expressly negative attitude toward suicide. This valuation could also be the reason for the complete refusal to handle the subject in relevant Christian theological dictionaries.

In ancient Christianity, many believers sought to provoke their own martyr- *Christianity*
dom, as they saw it as a guarantee of their entry into Paradise. In the Bible itself, no explicit prohibition of suicide is to be found. Only with the Church Fathers, and in the conciliar decisions (Arles, 452; Orleans, 533; Prague, 563; Auxerre, 613; Toledo, 693; Nimes, 1184), and papal encyclicals (e.g., that of Pope Nicholas I, c. 860, in which suicide was declared mortally sinful), was suicide, or its attempt, negatively evaluated, and more and more severely punished. Writings that defend suicide went on the Index.

The medieval Christian Church battled suicide determinedly, especially under the terms of its denuncication by Thomas Aquinas (1225/6–1274), who, in his *Summa Theologiae* (II-II, q. 64, art. 5), sees it as a sin against the Creator, nature, and society. Thus, persons who commit suicide are con-demned to eternal damnation as a spiritual punishment; the legal conse-quence is the confiscation of property (in England until 1873; and there, the unlawful quality of an attempt at suicide held until 1961). Suicidal persons were categorized as transgressors, and punishment was carried out on the corpse. Until the end of the nineteenth century, the Church refused sui-cidal persons church burial and determined that the place of burial must lie outside the cemetery, and that the burial times must be early morning, late evening, or night (and with the exclusion of the public).

Protestants very largely adopted the Catholic notions. But Martin → Lu-ther modified the main focus: he condemned the act of suicide, but not the persons committing it, regarding suicide as a work of the devil (*furor diabolicus*—Lat., 'diabolical frenzy').

Basing itself on the Talmud, Judaism takes an unambiguous position against *Judaism*
suicide. In the case of one's own intentionally provoked death (and not the product of a confused spirit), there were no mourning prescriptions, until into the twentieth century. It is, however, for Jewish believers, a moral obliga-tion to commit suicide as the only alternative to the commission of murder,

incest, or idolatry (conceptualized as *qiddush ha-shem*, Heb. 'sanctification of the (divine) Name' vis-à-vis the medieval crusades).

At present, the Christian churches, as well as Judaism, interpret suicide as the act of a pathological state of mind on the part of the person committing it. Here they accept the medical interpretation of suicide as the product of an 'illness compelling one to choose death,' such as a profound depression. This explanation attenuates a negative moral evaluation, without prejudice to the churches' basic positions: suicides may now receive a religious burial, and survivors may be offered support. Nevertheless, to this very day, there is no immunity from punishment for attempted suicide in canonical Christian law.

Islam

Islam, too, rejects suicide. Some Muslims support this rejection with an appeal to the Qur'an (sura 4.29), although the pronouncement here is not unambiguous, and can be understood in the reciprocal sense. However, the prohibition of suicide in the oral tradition of the Prophet → Muhammad's messages (Hadith) is unambiguous. Here, we read: "Who kills himself, will suffer in the fires of hell [. . .] Everlastingly will he be shut out of heaven."[2] Muslims' worldview is scored with the premise that the course of life, as well as the manner and moment of death, is predetermined by God, and suicide in Islamic countries is rare. The special case of suicide bombers is a very recent phenomenon, and against the background of Islamic traditions it needs a network of spiritual authorities to legitimate this suicidal act—to turn the 'sin' of committing suicide into an act of 'martyrdom' (→ Martyr).

Hinduism and Buddhism

India has many forms of institutionalized suicide: they are recommended in the holy scriptures, and in the epics are presented as exemplary. Buddhism, like Hinduism, regards suicide as ethically neutral, although in Hinduism a divided attitude frequently prevails: according to the teaching of karma, the annihilation of the body does not mean the annihilation of one's karma. Accordingly, one cannot escape one's destiny through suicide. In Buddhism and Hinduism, suicide is accounted a negative influence on the prospects of one's next rebirth, since, through it, a living being is killed. Suicide, then, means an extension of the soul's wandering.

Special Social Forms

3. In addition to the self-sacrifice (martyrdom), special social forms of suicide include ritualized forms, such as those in sympathy with the dead, hara-kiri, suicide as a protest, or collective suicide.

Institutional religious suicide of women as a form of accompaniment of, or loyalty to, deceased men was practiced in, for example, the tradition of the Indian burning of widows (*Sati*) until well into the twentieth century. Here, the voluntary character of such acts of killing was usually only conditionally present, as religious and societal sanctions allowed women little room for other action.

The *hara-kiri* of the Japanese (that of men being called *seppuku*, that of women *jigai*) was historically celebrated, and intensely suffused with aesthetic and other motives. It was a prerogative of the Samurai—thus, originating with the military ethic—and had a profound religious meaning.[3]

Political and socially motivated suicide, which seeks to have its act and attitude accepted, and/or elucidated, is a form of social → protest. As an example, we may cite the suicide of Catholic Bishop John Joseph, who shot himself to death in a courtroom in Pakistan, in May 1998, to protest the capital sentence of a young Catholic.[4]

The tragic collective suicide in Guayana of members of the People's Temple, who had moved from the United States, in which 914 members of the community obeyed the command of their religious leader Jim Jones to kill themselves, as well as the suicide of members of the Solar Temple, in Canada, France, and Switzerland (74 cases in three years), seem to suggest that the level of the capacity for violence to be committed upon one's own person in the 'new religious movements' (→ New Religions) is sharply higher. Apocalyptic prophecies, longings for a blissful hereafter, aggression against an enemy before whom one believes oneself impotent, and the panic of a threat 'from without,' lead religious groups to commit violent deeds against their own members and themselves.

4. Currently, suicide is no longer to be found as a culturally obligatory institution, and even ritual suicide has become an infrequent individual case. But other occasions are developing, on the basis of new circumstances: the loneliness of, in particular, older persons favors the increase of 'suicide of the elderly,' while the growth of intolerable burdens even in early years, causes more and more children and youth to seek a 'final escape.' Religious persons often undertake corresponding preventive measures (even in the framework of the rite of confession) or institutions (telephone counseling, pastoral psychology, attention to and care for persons wearied of life). But the greatest obstacle to an efficient prophylaxis remains the taboo of and denial of the existence of the threat.

1. Stubbe, Hannes, "Suizidforschung im Kulturvergleich," in: Kölner Beiträge zur Ethno-psychologie & Transkulturellen Psychologie 1 (1995), 57-77; Rost, Hans, Bibliographie des Selbstmords (1927), Regensburg 1992; Pfeiffer, Wolfgang, Transkulturelle Psychiatrie, Stuttgart 1994.
2. Cf. Khoury, Adel Theodor, Der Koran, Gütersloh 1988, 297.
3. Cf. Pinguet 1993.
4. O Público, May 14, 1998, p. 11.

Literature

Anderson, Olive, Suicide in Victorian and Edwardian England, Oxford 1987; Crepet, P. et al. (eds.), Suicidal Behaviour in Europe—Recent Research Findings, Rome etc. 1992; Droge, Arthur J./Tabor, James D., A Noble Death: Suicide and Martyrdom among Christians and Jews in Antiquity, San Francisco 1992; Durkheim, E., Suicide: A Study in Sociology, New York 1951 (French [1]1897); Headley, Lee A. (ed.), Suicide in Asia and the Near East, Berkeley/London 1983; MacIntosh, John L., Research on Suicide: A Bibliography, Westport 1985; Minois, Georges, History of Suicide: Voluntary Death in Western Culture, Baltimore 1999 (French [1]1995); Perlin, Seymour (ed.), A Handbook for the Study of Suicide, New York 1975; Pinguet, Maurice, Voluntary Death in Japan, Cambridge 1993 (French [1]1984); Tseng, W.-S., Handbook of Cultural Psychiatry, San Diego 2001; van Hooff, A. I. L., From Autothanasia to Suicide: Self-Killing in Classical Antiquity, London 1990.

→ *Ars Moriendi, Death and Dying, Ethics/Morals, Euthanasia/Assisted Suicide, Martyr, Psychopathology*

Chirly dos Santos-Stubbe

Sunday / Sabbath

1. a) In most Western societies where Christianity has been the dominant religion for a long time, Sunday has a special place as a 'day off.' As a day of rest and pause from labor, however, Sunday is not very old. In societies defined by the sowing, cultivating, and reaping of nutrients, season and weather govern the rhythm of work and rest. Animals must always be cared for: feeding, milking, and carrying out the dung must be seen to. The farm family cannot take a 'day off.' The dyers had their 'blue Monday,' when they dried and oxidized the wool that had been steeped in dye on Sunday.

The Sabbath, a Day without Work

b) It was altogether unusual, then, to specify a day of God, which, with the Third Commandment (Exod 20:8-11) in Judaism became a basic rule. The mythological foundation was that God himself had made the world in six days, but rested (*shabat*) on the seventh (*shebi'i*), as in Gen 2:2, the day on which, later (Exod 40), the temple was used for the Sabbath divine service. In the Commandment, there is nothing about a divine service, but only about rest. Not only the people of God, but non-Jewish neighbors, or foreign slaves, even oxen were to rest. With the loss of political self-determination, and of a homeland, the observance of the Sabbath became especially important. Strictly speaking, nothing might be done that was not unconditionally necessary for the maintenance of God's creation, and therefore, for saving life. A literal interpretation, for example, of the proposition that no fire was to be lighted—lighted for cooking—means that, in today's Israel, air traffic is prohibited, since neither may a motor be 'lighted.'

c) The Jewish Shabbat begins on Friday evening—'as soon as three stars are to be seen'—with a supper in the family, often with guests. Candlelight, a blessing of the children, and the solemn drinking of wine makes it a holiday meal. In the morning, the family goes to synagogue, and eats cold cuts from what has been prepared the day before, or a soufflé. Sabbath ends when darkness falls. Beginning a holiday the evening of the previous day is also the usage in the Christian calendar, when Christmas begins with the Christmas Eve or Easter with the 'New Fire.' The reason for this practice is simply that the Genesis story says that "it became evening and morning—the second/third etc. day."

Sunday

2. a) *The religious quality of the day of rest:* In order to distinguish itself from the Jewish communities, Christians celebrated their 'Sabbath' on the following day, the first of the 'working' week. It became the Lord's Day (in Gk., *Kyriaké*; in Lat., [*Dies*] *Dominica*), since, according to the Gospels, it was the day on which Christ rose from the dead. Only when Christianity became the Roman religion did the Christian day of rest become exclusive—the *Dies Solis*, 'sun's day,' adopting the name of the Roman Sun God. Like the other days of the week, Sunday too bore the name of a planetary god—such as *Lunae Dies*, 'Moon's Day,' and *Veneris Dies*, 'Venus' Day,' (later 'Freya Day')—but the rising sun came to be explained as a symbol of the risen Christ. The Sabbath, on the other hand, can be explained as the anti-Christ day, the day on which, for example, the witches gather to celebrate their diabolical sacred service.

b) The Christian Sunday is the day of the common divine service, originally in the early morning, if not actually on the eve. Before or after, work was permitted. In the medieval Church, assistance at Mass in church, and not recreation, became the Sunday duty. The frequent reiteration of the rule shows the difficulty of imposing its regular observation. Only in the city could it be assured that Sunday, and as a rule only the morning thereof, was actually without work—particularly, without work being done by one's avaricious neighbors—and as well as just the evening of the holiday, or the time during which shops were closed. A work-free day is an economic disadvantage that one is happy to share with others.

c) In Germany for instance, only from 1878 onward was Sunday a general day of rest. Industry was loath to surrender the (half) workday, but workers became ever more rebellious, and sermons on obedience, suffering, and the order willed by God, kept recommending suggested improvement. This intent of the holiday bore no fruit, of course, and Emperor Wilhelm would have been glad to rescind it. Citizens were using Sunday-morning Mass time more and more for profane gatherings, or cultural meetings, instead of religious ones. Unions called meetings at which workers could be educated, and could come to know their political rights, right while the church bells were pealing.

3. The Sundays in the calendar each have their own names and character (their *proprium*), grouped around Christmas, then around Easter. The names come from the particular psalms, gospels, or epistles read at Mass on these days, or are merely counted: *Septuagesima* Sunday means seventy days until Easter; *Quasimodogeniti* means 'As-just-born [infants']' Sunday (the first reading on the First Sunday after Easter, 1 Pet 2:2), when children are admitted to the Eucharist (to Confirmation on the following Sunday, *Dominica in Albis*, White-Vestment Sunday); Palm Sunday celebrates Jesus's triumphal entry into Jerusalem, as the citizens of that city strewed palm branches before him; *Cantate* (i.e., *Domino*, Lat., "Sing to the Lord"; Ps 98:1) Sunday is the 'choir's Sunday.'

Names

Literature

CARSON, Donald A. (ed.), From Sabbath to Lord's Day: A Biblical, Historical, and Theological Investigation, Grand Rapids 1982; DUBY, Georges, The Legend of Bouvines: War, Religion and Culture in the Middle Ages, Cambridge 1990 (Fr. ¹1973); ESKENAZI, Tamara C. et al. (eds.), The Sabbath in Jewish and Christian Traditions, New York 1991; LABAND, David N./HEINBUCH, Deborah Hendry, Blue Laws: The History, Economics, and Politics of Sunday Closing Laws, Lexington 1987; MacCROSSEN, Alexis, Holy Day, Holiday: The American Sunday, Ithaca 2000; ODOM, Robert L., Sabbath and Sunday in Early Christianity, Washington 1977; SOLBERG, Winton U., Redeem the Time: The Puritan Sabbath in Early America, Cambridge/London 1977; WEBSTER, Hutton, Rest Days, New York 1916; WEILER, Rudolf (ed.), Der Tag des Herrn. Kulturgeschichte des Sonntags, Vienna 1998; WEISS, Herold, A Day of Gladness: The Sabbath among Jews and Christians in Antiquity, Columbia 2003.

→ *Calendar, Feasts and Celebrations, Time*

Christoph Auffarth

Superstition

The designation is a polemical one, connoting a distance taken from the acts of persons, other than oneself, which must be called religious, but which either seem exaggerated (*super*stition), or are forbidden by official religion. Pastors, especially, and (other) intellectuals use it to disparage the piety of the 'uneducated folk.' From an atheistic viewpoint, any religion can be called superstition.

→ *Atheism, Polemics, Religion*

Christoph Auffarth

Symbol / Sign / Gesture

Introduction

1. a) Religions are complex and culturally conditioned systems of interpretation, symbol, and communication, with varying stores of signs. Through signs, in their respective ways and manners, these systems interpret ('code') perceived reality. Here the potential repertory, and broad spectrum, of religious signs or symbols includes, besides 'audible' sounds, words, and propositions of → language, also all other forms of sensory → perception. These forms are, variously, spatially orienting, smell-(olfactory) or taste-specific, and visual signs, as well as 'haptic' or tactile 'signs of touch.' Thus, for example, the spatially ordering principles of breadth, height, and depth, as well as of proximity and distance, define the simplest coordinates of human environments, as well as more or less elaborate cosmographies and cosmologies. Examples of highly differentiated and unambiguously shaped forms of olfactory signing are found in antiquity, among other venues, where every sacrificial act was attended with a sequence of different odors. The particularly expansive palette of the visual elements of religious communication extends from objects, pictures, statues, and edifices, on to the most varied forms of conventionalized courses of bodily movement, among which, besides gestures, ritualized movements, too, and dances, are to be numbered. Religious acts, in this connection, can be defined as symbolical acting in a sign-determined field, by which individual signs or symbols, always occurring and interconnecting in chains, take their reference—and extract their foundation and existence—from their respective systems of meaning, interpretation, and belief.

b) The special accomplishment of systems of religious signs lies, above all, in the fact that they generate, steer and guide, and place in mutual relationship, the entire array of cognitive, emotional, normative, social, and cultural processes. Thus, for instance, → art can be assigned a function within

Communication

religious communication, according to which, as in medieval Christianity, it is constrained to make the contents of belief and doctrine visible in symbolism. The differentiation of an independent sign-system of 'art,' already present in antiquity, came back to life within Europe in the → Renaissance, and can easily be followed by pursuing, among other choices, developments in the medium of the pictorial image. Unlike those who employ other systems of signs, users of a religious one never fail to refer the validity of their

A priestess in Bodhanilkanta, north of Katmandu, in Nepal, gives a pilgrim the *tika* after the Ceremony of Veneration. A mark is made on the forehead with sandalwood resin or cinnabar, to signal believers' participation in the divine service. The priest/priestess is remunerated with a contribution of money. For a woman to give the *tika* is unusual: the gesture of blessing indicates the high ritual rank and social status of the one bestowing it. Thus, a layperson receives the *tika* from a priest, a junior person from an elder, and, conventionally, a woman from a man. Believers who are clients of a lower-ranking priest impose the forehead marking themselves. In the case illustrated, the pilgrim receives the *tika* after he has offered his veneration to the statue of Vishnu of Bodhanilkanta. Here, Vishnu reposes on the serpent Ananta, in a pool symbolizing the primeval ocean. The King of Nepal need not visit Bodhanilkanta, as he is himself regarded as an incarnation of Vishnu. The King, in an annual celebration, receives the *tika* from a girl residing in the Kumari Bahai Temple in Katmandu as the living Virgin Goddess, and thus has his authority certified. (Benita von Behr / Kirsten Holzapfel)

system of interpretation to certain structures of rule and principle. The rules and principles in question are indubitable, obligatory for the community, and authoritatively present. Structures of rules can, as in Christianity and Islam, be established by founding personalities, or be established by age and tradition. Foundational principles can be supported by narrative sign-codes, such as myths or symbolical acts (→ Sacrifice). In all of these cases, a supreme principle (God, Fate, the All-One) can serve as a communicative anchor. Just so can an all-embracing plenitude of signification of world and nature ("pansemiotic metaphysics"—Umberto Eco) get in solid communicative 'touch.' Again, a universal accord with a cosmic order can be a similar anchor, as can a 'world law,' or simply a proclaimed connection between doing and prospering, between conformity and success. In monotheistic religions, in this regard, the character of obligation attaching to the system of signs in question is usually fastened to another obligation—that of its content, as well as to the programmatic exclusion of other interpretational systems. Polytheistic religions, on the other hand, show that a systematic pluralism can be admitted, and can belong to the repertory of signs, and that a division of labor in terms of the cults is possible, at least as long as no fundamental social and political consensus seems to have gotten under way. Then, of course, a danger to 'sign identity' within the community may threaten. Then as well, as in the times of Plato, in the Greek city-states, it will be regarded as a crime to introduce new gods, and it will seem in order to prohibit private cults.

c) Another possibility for control over a religious sign-system consists in religious → specialists receiving a monopoly over interpretation. The establishment of religious signs as omen, or as signs or judgments of the gods (whether they rest on phenomena in nature, → dreams, → visions, monsters, or miraculous actions), then lies in the hands of priests, shamans, prophets, monks, nuns, preachers, singers, or storytellers. Control over correct interpretation likewise rests with these specialists. In their hands lie exposition, transmission of interpretation, and normative evaluation, and they separate 'coincidental' events or psychic experiences from 'messages' containing signs (presages and portents). As a rule, these specialists are elevated above the rest of the community even outwardly, by → clothing, → hair style, or → tattooing. In scriptural religions, such as Christianity or Judaism, collections of signs and their interpretations are stored, and the principles of their exposition fixed, in the medium of → writing (→ Text/ Textual Criticism; Exegesis; Hermeneutics). Thus, the question of how the sign (in Lat., *signum*) is connected with the 'signed' (*signatum*) was especially important in the Jewish and Christian tradition of belief—whether by participation (partial identity), by similarity (*similitudo*), or by analogy (substitution or representation, reflection). What is the relationship between God (the Emperor) and his statue (his → image)? Are they identical, does God only dwell in it, or is God's likeness a sensible sign of God's invisible power? What is the relationship between God the Father and his Son, the Redeemer? How ought one to conceive the relationship between bread, and the body of Christ? An explanation and classification of these matters, in terms of meaning and pattern of interpretation, is part of the (self-) interpretation undertaken by religious specialists, in the systematizing inner perspective of a religious system of meaning. Together with the forms of 'simple,' everyday ritual acts, and their logic, the theologies (→ Theology), canonical texts (→ Canon), and theological dogmatics (→ Dogma) arising in consequence of their discourse, constitute important elements, members, and building blocks of religious symbolic systems. Further, they must be ascribed a controlling function that will exclude other gods and patterns of interpretation (→ Polemics).

Emblems and Symbolics: The Emergence of the Christian Repertory of Signs

2. During its emergence, Christianity's religious system of meaning and interpretation found itself in a direct relation of competition with a series of other, already established, religious systems of sign and interpretation. There were the Greek and Roman cults, the Eastern religions, and not least of all, Judaism. Christian theologians like → Augustine assumed and absorbed numerous principles of order, and complexes of signs, especially after Christianity had entered a symbiosis with the political structures of domination after the 'Constantinian turn' of the fourth century, and had established itself as the dominant system of meaning (→ Late Antiquity). It was above all the imperial representations of supremacy, the court ceremonial, the Mysteries, and the system of norms for intercourse with clients, that were available to Christianity as primary systems of reference. They helped the young religious communities to produce and mold a sign-system of cultic actions, together with an independent repertory of group symbols, mythic images (Dionysian symbolism of the Bacchus sarcophagus), and theological representations. In the sequel, existing presentation *modi* were taken and applied: both of transcendence (Christus Pantocrator; → Epiphany), and of the religious specialists, the clergy, and the arsenal of representations of the Roman Emperor. In the Middle Ages, ritual adoption by the body of specialists, or by the ordained priestly class, once more imitated entry into the status of vassal. The universal revaluation of existing negative signs to group emblems representing bestowal of identity, such as the fish or the → cross, is a noteworthy process. Thus, for instance, the crucifixion of Jesus of Nazareth was reinterpreted by religious specialists, at high semantic expense, from stigma to sign of redemption, readiness for suffering, and capacity for the same. In the further course of things, there came an increasing accumulation, multiplication, and inflationary presence of Christian symbols: miracles, relics, sacramental signs, and cultic actions. In contrariety with

this process stands an increasing tendency to the reduction of signs, and to the theological construction of dogma, as, for example, the reduction of the number of the sacraments to the number of seven, and its fixation there (see under § 4).

3. a) The theological hierarchization of meanings—effected in the framework of a Christian establishment of signs, which framework is also that of the exegetical politics of sign—subordinates both the sign of gesture, and the material sign that is a component of cultic activity, to the primacy of the verbal sign. This sign finds its loftiest correspondence in the incarnation of the Logos, Christ, the Word Incarnate. In Christian faith then, in the field of tension between acoustical and visual media, the spoken word enjoys a privileged status vis-à-vis the gesture. That is also the reason why, with the help of sign language, the members of certain monastic orders that maintain a vow of silence (Trappists, Carthusians), can understand one another without violating the monastic rule of silence. During church history, the physical sign was repeatedly exposed to internal ecclesial criticism: it was said to go counter to the 'hierarchy' of meaning, and to 'switch,' or otherwise distort, the duties of the several parts of the body. The control of this theologically suspect sensory expression of the body was now undertaken by way of a process of assignment of meaning ('semantization'). The latter now divided temperate, chaste, and virtuous 'gesturing' (in Lat., *gestus*) from prolix, exaggerated, and wicked 'gesticulation' (*gesticulatio*). Bound to the ideal of a rigid, stationary, and curtailed spirit of celebration, 'gesturing' was positively evaluated. The theological ascription of meaning here was that of an ordering, healing effect on the soul. By contrast, 'wild, unbridled, and monstrous' gesticulating is ascribed a negative, harmful meaning. Here we see a 'puritanical' tendency in Christianity to place limits on corporeal gesture in cult, or in everyday religious practice. Convulsive, ecstatic motions or expressions of the body are interpreted either as demoniacal possession, calling for exorcism, or as a condition of mystical enthusiasm and excitement (in Lat., *raptus*; → Mysticism). In theological discourse,

The Amish Brethren in the United States and Canada posit a sign with their clothing. Simple and old-fashioned, it is the expression of a collective delineation from the world, decisiveness, and the subordination of individual preferences to the group code. Uniform clothing, as the expression of a common duty, signifies the Amish twenty-four-hours-a-day service of God. With so many communalities, there are nevertheless fine differences, through which the individual denominations are distinguished. Each possesses its own forms of hat, shirt, stockings, and not least of all, suspenders. When suspenders came into style at the close of the seventeenth century, they were at first rejected by the Amish. Later, however, having become a symbol of awareness of rural traditions, they found their way into the catalogue of Amish clothing. Thus, in Pennsylvania, men of Lancaster County wear two suspenders, crossed in the back (in the form of an "X"), while members of the Renno Group in Mifflin County prefer to go without suspenders. The question, too, of whether the suspenders may be buttoned, is variously answered from group to group—and in any case, many Amish taboo belts as a sportive vanity. (Benita von Behr)

these are referred to as two distinct forms of 'border-crossing' (one to be prohibited and the other permitted). 'Tamed' gestures—the hand for blessing and prayer, kneeling, the carrying of cultic objects—of course, belong to the basic stock of Christian ritualism, and determined especially the cult of post-Reformation → Catholicism.

Cultic Dance Gesture
I: Hawaii

b) Thus, Christianity, and its rules for signs, tamed, and precisely de-eroticized, the body as its 'sign-bearer.' In many religions, on the other hand, expressive bodily techniques enjoyed reception as means of expression in cult and ritual. The Christian procedure—until recent times, in scattered efforts—altogether excludes dance as a mode of religious communication, while Native American (East and West) or Circum-Pacific religions exhibit an extremely elaborate code for the same. In the religious symbolic system of the original Polynesian inhabitants of Hawaii, for example, the rhythmic types of bodily expression held an important place. One significant ritual expression of divine veneration was the Hula dance, in whose flowing movements myths and powers of nature were visibly presented, communicated, preserved, and transmitted adown the generations. In our own day, in Hawaii, dances expressing the mythical histories of the world's creation—cosmogonies—have been given an important place as a consciously perceived, intentionally introduced means to the raising of Hawaiians' awareness of their own identity. Simultaneously, the Hula also represents one of the most important tourist attractions of the region, a late example of the adaptation of the (secular) exotic, and of the exploitation of non-European religions (→ Orientalism/Exotism; South Sea/Australia; Tourism).

c) Along with expressive gestures, many religions use sophisticated linguistic signs, as we have already mentioned in reference to certain Christian monastic orders. With the help of such signs, entire narratives, particularly myths, can be presented nonverbally. As an example of systems of religious interpretation that have produced an especially broad palette of symbolical gestures—hand and finger positions, as well as bodily postures—we may cite Hindu religions, likewise by contrast with Christian reticence with regard to signs. The Sanskrit word *mudra* ('seal,' 'mark') refers to a multiplicity of meaningful hand and finger positions—to which, among others, belong the gesture for teaching (*dharmacakra mudra*), the gesture for greeting and for compassion (*varada mudra*), the gesture for meditation (*samadhi mudra*), the gesture for fearlessness and renunciation (*abbaya mudra*), and the gesture for argumentation (*vitarka mudra*). The *mudras* are complemented by a wide variety of positions of the body, each having its own particular meaning.

Cultic Dance Gesture II: India

4. a) The current situation with regard to religious systems of symbol or sign is well illustrated by the situation of the Roman Catholic Church. In the course of the twentieth century, the Catholic system of belief was characterized by an increasing loss of the connection between its own interpretation, and the understanding of its signs throughout broad parts of the Church. In other words, knowledge concerning the approach to and correct interpretation of religious signs—especially, interpretation of the Latin language—has become limited in increasing measure to specialists or members of the clergy. It was a matter of a development that harbored within itself the danger of a gradual routinization, petrification, and general endangerment of the individual symbols and their superordinate connections of meaning. The liturgical reform of the Second Council of the Vatican (1962–1965) therefore brought a long-awaited deliverance from the abundant Baroque and post-Baroque overgrowth of the old cultic store of the Roman Catholic confession. Many groups welcomed the Vatican II reforms with open arms. Fifteen years later, the periodical *Concilium*[1] observed a remarkable void and penury within modern Catholicism in its store of sensible appeals and attractions. Catholic development was said to stand in crass contradiction to the stormy advance of the audiovisual media in society. Cultural anthropologists corroborated this finding. In her study of the Irish Catholic community in London, and with respect to the 1967 dismantling of obligatory Friday abstinence from meat, Mary Douglas[2] saw in the Catholic episcopate a blindness to the meaning-content of nonverbal symbols. Thus, modern Western culture of information constantly creates new opportunities for modern rituals of interaction, and for 'sign worlds.' But, in the framework of religious communication and theological signing, what occurs is an intensifying curtailment, restriction, and "destruction of the sensory" (A. Lorenzer).

Religious Signs in the Modern Age

Using hindsight, this finding can be listed in the ever more firmly established tendency of European history of religion, in a 'process of civilization' (N. Elias), to regulate, and as far as possible to exclude, bodily excesses, extravagances, or any dismantling of boundaries. Only in the 'tumultuous plebeian forms' of corporeal expression, such as those of → carnival, do we still find any 'sensual anarchy' (disciplined, to be sure, in the spirit of the middle class). The 'de-sensualization' of religious communication at the present time, as we have briefly shown by the example of the

Roman Catholic Church, marches on. Meanwhile, the task of the extreme appeal of the sensory organs, including that of an 'overload of attraction', has been assumed by a multiplicity of other cultural institutions, and partial systems of society, such as the media and modern art (e.g., in performances of Hermann Nitsch's "Theater of Orgies and Mysteries"; → Blasphemy, with ill.).

Polyvalence

b) The marketing situation, plurality, and variety of choice constantly available in past and present, is especially great and well-defined in the modern 'society of information'. This appraisal is verified not only among various religious sign-systems (imprinted with meaning and culture) and their cults, but with individual ones, as well. Conflicts and competitions are fixed and delivered by way of individual religious symbols or signs, that, in the discourse of the media, are charged with still more meaning, and with numerous emotions. To cite two regional examples of such a 'battle over the symbols', reference can be made to the display of the cross in Bavarian class-rooms (→ Cross/Crucifixion), or the prohibition of Muslim girls' wearing headscarves in French schools (→ Laicism; Veil).

At the same time, the new, and secularized, meaning-systems of the post-modern present shape our perception and signs in the same manner and mode as did the 'old', and religious, patterns of interpretation. What enters the scene here, in the theory of signs, is the characteristic of *polyvalence*. Signs, whether gestures, images, or words, possess several 'reference indicators' (indices): they can refer to several areas of meaning or object at once. Thus, for example, in the framework of an attribution of meaning whose orientation is ecological, any dying tree of the tropical rainforest, a hole in the ozone layer, or whaling, can be a symbol of a universal (apocalyptic) end time (→ Environmentalism). But these signs can indicate not only the ecological movement, but religious myths, as well (world-tree, animal peace, destruction of the world), and can be part of a political position, or of a system of interpretation in the sense of the destruction of the world. It is this polyvalence, in the sense of value, and thus ambivalence, of signs, that makes communication in today's societies so rich, but also so complex, and often ambiguous: religion is often but one more 'sign index' among so many others, multiplied and concealed in the snowstorm of images of the world and patterns of orientation.

1. POWER, D., "Symbol and Art in Worship," in: Concilium, February 1980, 19-27.
2. DOUGLAS 1973.

Literature

ALDRETE, Gregory S., Gestures and Acclamations in Ancient Rome, Baltimore 1999; BOURDIEU, Pierre, Language and Symbolic Power, Cambridge 1991 (Fr. [1]1982); BREMMER, Jan/ROODENBURG, Herman (eds.), A Cultural History of Gesture, Ithaca 1992; CASSIRER, Ernst, The Philosophy of Symbolic Forms, 3 vols., New Haven 1953 ([1]1923–1929); COR-BEILL, Anthony, Nature Embodied: Gesture in Ancient Rome, Princeton 2004; DAVIDSON, Clifford (ed.), Gesture in Medieval Drama and Art, Kalamazoo 2001; DÖBERT, Rainer, Systemtheorie und die Entwicklung religiöser Deutungssysteme, Frankfurt/M. 1973; DOUGLAS, Mary, Natural Symbols: Explorations in Cosmology, London [2]1973 ([1]1970); ECO, Umberto/MARMO, Costantino (eds.), On the Medieval Theory of Signs, Amsterdam 1989; ELIAS, Norbert, The Symbol Theory, London 1991; EMMOREY, Karen/REILLY, Judy S.

(eds.), Language, Gesture, and Space, Hillsdale 1995; FEHLER, Michael (ed.), Fragments for a History of the Human Body, New York 1989/1990; GEERTZ, Clifford, "Religion as a Cultural System," in: BANTON, Michael (ed.), Anthropological Approaches to the Study of Religion, London 1966, 1-46; GOFFMAN, Erving, Interaction Ritual: Essays on Face-to-Face Behavior, New York 1976; HALL, James, Illustrated Dictionary of Symbols in Eastern and Western Art, New York 1995; KENDON, Adam, Gesture: Visible Action as Utterance, Cambridge 2004; LEACH, Edmund, Culture and Communication: The Logic by which Symbols Are Connected. An Introduction to the Use of Structuralist Analysis in Social Anthropology, Cambridge/New York 1976; LIUNGMAN, Carl G., Dictionary of Symbols, Santa Barbara 1991 (Swedish ¹1974); LUHMANN, Niklas, Funktion der Religion, Frankfurt/M. ³1992 (¹1983); MESSING, Lynn S./CAMPBELL, Ruth (eds.), Gesture, Speech, and Sign, Oxford 1999; SAUNDERS, E. Dale, Mudrā: A Study of Symbolic Gestures in Japanese Buddhist Sculpture, Princeton 1960; SCHMITT, Jean-Claude, La raison des gestes dans l'occident medieval, Paris 1990; Idem (ed.), Gestures, Chur 1984; SKORUPSKI, John, Symbol and Theory: A Philosophical Study of Theories of Religion in Social Anthropology, Cambridge 1976.

→ *Body, Communication, Dance, Exegesis, Materiality, Media, Miracles, Oral Tradition, Perception, Polytheism, Proskynesis, Specialists (Religious), Veneration of Relics, Veneration of the Saints*

Andrea Kaserer

Taboo

1. The word 'taboo' comes from the Polynesian *tápu* and denotes, on one hand, a prohibition by which an object is withdrawn from everyday use, and on the other, the object itself.

A taboo can pertain to gods, human beings, bodily parts, objects, types of relationship, words, areas or regions, or, for example, a tribe. Depending on who prescribes it—for example a chief or a transcendent power—the nature of the obligation, and in case of transgression the severity of the punishment, can oscillate. A taboo can also be removed.

2. At first, conceptions of the taboo were researched regionally in Polynesian cultures, as, for example, with the Maori. Then, by way of expansion and abstraction, a history developed that was particularly rich in its effects on the scientific study of religion. In the anthropological evolutionary theories of the nineteenth and early twentieth centuries, 'taboo,' alongside totemism and magic, became an embodiment of the 'primitive thought' of 'uncivilized peoples' (Frazer). Freud stands in this tradition, seeing taboo as a regulation of the drive-satisfaction. In terms of religious science, marriage regulations, the 'incest taboo,' and dietary prescriptions were investigated in particular.

In a very general sense today, 'taboo' designates anything which has its thematization in society suppressed by unwritten rules; thus, one can speak of a taboo on sexuality, death, or sometimes even religion.

Literature

DOUGLAS, Mary, Natural Symbols: Explorations in Cosmology, London ²1973 (¹1970); HOLDEN, Lynn, Encyclopedia of Taboos, Oxford 2000; MILLS, Alice et al. (eds.), Utter Silence: Voicing the Unspeakable, New York 2001.

→ *Religion, Holy, South Sea/Australia*

Ansgar Jödicke

Talmud

The Talmud as a Compendium of Jewish Life and Teaching

1. "The Talmud and all of its expansions form the backbone of Jewish tradition."[1] The Talmud (Heb., *talmud*, 'study,' 'instruction,' 'doctrine') is appropriately described as *the* compendium of the life and teaching of Judaism since the end of ancient times. More narrowly, this is true only of the *Babylonian* Talmud, so called from the place of its emergence in the Jewish academies of Sura and Pumbedita in Babylonia, from the fifth to the early eighth century. This text is what "*the* Talmud" usually indicates. The Jerusalem, or Palestinian, Talmud (the *Yerushalmi*, as it is often called), received its final configuration from Jewish scholars in Tiberias, and has a much smaller popular function in the history of piety than the *Babli*, or Babylonian Talmud. Only the Jewish resettlement of Palestine, and the agriculture of the country of Israel, generated inquiries into religious law, for which only the Yerushalmi supplied the traditional historical material. This circumstance occasioned an upward religious evaluation in parts of Israeli Judaism.

Common to both *Talmudim* (the Hebrew plural form) is their character as commentaries on the *Mishna*, or 63-tractate compendium of religious law (or 'halachic' compendium)—more specifically, of the written and oral Torah in the form in which the latter was available at the beginning of the third century CE. The Yerushalmi includes thirty-nine tractates handed down as the *Gemara*, while the Babli has thirty-seven. The tractates of the *Mishna* are divided, according to content, into six 'Orders' (in Heb., *seder*; pl., *sedarim*), upon which the *Talmudim*, as well, are based. The Orders can be described in brief as follows.

The First Order (*Zerʿaim*, "Seeds") consists of eleven tractates, in which especially the laws pertaining to agriculture are collected. The first tractate, the *Berakhot* ("Blessings"), which are *hors série*, contains the specifications for regular daily prayers, and has the laudations to be prayed for the consumption of particular foods, or in certain situations. Every single one of the remaining ten tractates bears on the religious taxes (the 'tithes') or on field specifications (Sabbath year). The harvest taxes are levied exhaustively only on harvests reaped in the country of Israel.

The Second Order (*Moʿed*, "Festive Times"), in twelve tractates, deals with the feast days of Israel bidden in the Hebrew Bible. Somewhat *hors série* stand the *Sheqalim* ("Shekel") and *Taanit* tractates, concerned with the Temple taxes, or with the special fast days and their prayers.

The Third Order (*Nashim*, "Women"), in seven tractates, is devoted primarily to engagement, marriage contracts, marriages of duty, adultery, divorce, and remarriage. Two additional tractates are concerned with 'vows' (*nedarim*) in general, or (the *Nazir* tractate) with special 'Nazir' vows (cf. Num 6:1-21).

עין משפט נר מצוה | כה | הקורא עומד פרק שלישי מגילה | מסורת הש"ס

מתני' יברכוך טובים הר"ז דרך מינות · שאינו כולל רשעים בשבחו של מקום וחכמים למדו (כריתות דף ו:) מחלבנה שריחה רע ומנאה הכתוב בין סממני הקטורת שצריכין הכתוב בהרלאתן להיותן באגודה אחת: על קן צפור יגיעו רחמיך · (ד) כלשון הזה רחמיך מגיעין על קן צפור כך רחם עלינו: ועל טוב יזכר שמך · על טובותיך נודה לך או שאמר שני פעמים מודים כשהוא כורע מודים אותו ובגמרא מפרש לה: המכנה בעריות · בגמרא מפרש שדורש פרשת עריות בכינוי ואומר לא ערוה ממש דיבר הכתוב אלא כינה הכתוב בלשונו וקרא אותה ערוה המגלה קלון אביו וקלון אמו ברבים כינוי הוא לשון היפך שמהפך דיבורו לשבח או לגנאי והרבה יש בלשון חכמים בספרי אספה לי שבעים איש (במדבר יא) ולא אראה ברעתי (שם) ברעתם היה לו לומר אלא שכינה הכתוב כיוצא בדבר וימירו את כבודם בתבנית שור אוכל עשב (תהלים קו) כבודי היה לו לומר אלא שכינה הכתוב: האומר ומזרעך לא תתן להעביר למולך · לא תבא על הכותית ותוליד בן לע"ז: משתקין אותו בנזיפה · שעוקר הכתוב ממשמעו שהוא עבודה חוק לאמוריים להעביר בניהן לאש ונותן כרת לבא על הכותיות ומחייב מיתה על הבנה ומיתת המזיד בהתראה: **גמ'** כשתי רשויות · ומקבל ומודה אלוה אחר: על הרעה · ברוך דיין האמת: על הטובה · ברוך הטוב והמטיב: מטיל קנאה · לומר על העופות חס ועל הבהמות וחיות אינו חס: ואינן אלא גזירות מלך להטיל עליהן עול להודיע שאנחנו עבדיו ושומרי מצותיו: דכתבינהו משה בתורה · האל הגדול הגבור והנורא אשר לא ישא פנים (דברים י): אנשי כנסת הגדולה · בספר עזרא (נחמיה ט) ועתה אלהינו האל הגדול הגבור והנורא שומר הברית והחסד: חוץ מיראת שמים · אותה מסורה בידי אדם שיהא הוא עצמו מכין לבו לכך אע"ג שהיכולת בידו להכין לבבו אליו דכתיב הנה כחומר ביד היוצר כן אתם בידי בית ישראל (ירמיה יח) והסירותי את לב האבן מבשרכם (יחזקאל לו): אמר מילתא מילתא ותני לה · כל תיבה אומר ושונה אין כאן משמעות שתי רשויות אלא מגונה וסכל הוא: חברותא כלפי שמיא · וכי כמנהג חבירו נוהג בהקב"ה לדבר לפניו שלא במתכוין וחוזר ומרצה לו בכופלו: בארזפתא · מרזפתא: מרטי"ל בלע"ז ותפס את המקבת מתרגמינן מרזפתא (שופטים ד): תני רב יוסף · לפרושי מכנה דמתני' כדמתרגם ערות אביך וערות אמך קלנא דאבוך וקלנא דאמך ולא תגלה שום דבר קלון שבהן: תנא דבי רבי ישמעאל · לפרש מתני' בישראל הבא על הכותית הכתוב מדבר:

יברכוך טובים · פי' שמוציא את הפושעים מן הכלל או נמי משום דמחזי כשתי רשויות כלומר אלהים טובים: **מפני** שעושה מדותיו של הקב"ה רחמים ואינן אלא גזירות · וק"ק לתנן על מה *שיסד הקליר בקדושת שאנו אומרים ביום ב' של פסח לדקו אותו ואת בנו (ו) לא תשחטו ביום אחד דמשמע שר"ל שהקב"ה חס על אותו ואת בנו והוא אינו אלא גזירה: **הכל** בידי שמים חוץ מיראת שמים · קשה דהא בפרק אלו נערות (כתובות דף ל. ושם) אמרינן הכל בידי שמים חוץ מצנים ופחים ונראה דהכא מיירי בתולדות האדם אם יהיה חכם או טפש עני או עשיר גבור או חלש שהכל נגזר עליו חוץ מן היראה כדכתיב אל יתהלל (ז) עשיר בעשרו והגבור בגבורתו כי אם בזאת יתהלל המתהלל השכל וידוע אותי (ירמיה ט) והתם מיירי במאורעות האדם שהן באין עליו אחר שנולד שהכל בידי שמים חוץ מצנים ופחים שהוא פירוש הקור והחום ולא קשה מהא דכתיב לפני קרתו מי יעמוד (תהלים קמז) דה"פ אם ישלחנה בפעם אחת כדכתיב ברישא דהפסוק משליך קרחו כפתים וגם לא קשה מהא דכתיב ולא נסתר מחמתו (שם יט) דהסיה בעוברי דרכים הוא דקאמר אבל כל זמן שהוא בביתו ודאי יכול הוא ליגלל ממנו: **אין** מפטירין במרכבה ורבי יהודה מתיר · וקיימא לן כר' יהודה: מה

*יברכוך טובים הרי זו דרך *המינות *על קן צפור יגיעו רחמיך ועל טוב יזכר שמך *מודים מודים משתקין אותו המכנה בעריות משתקין אותו האומר ומזרעך לא תתן להעביר למולך לא תתן לעברא בארמיותא משתקין אותו בנזיפה: **גמ'** *בשלמא מודים מודים משום דמיחזי כשתי רשויות ועל טוב יזכר שמך נמי דמשמע על טוב אין ועל רע לא ותנן *חייב אדם לברך על הרעה כשם שהוא מברך על הטובה אלא על קן צפור יגיעו רחמיך מ"ט (א) פליגי בה תרי אמוראי במערבא ר' יוסי בר אבין ור' יוסי בר זבידא חד אמר מפני שמטיל קנאה במעשה בראשית וחד אמר מפני שעושה מדותיו של הקב"ה רחמים ואינן אלא גזירות ההוא דנחית קמיה דרבה אמר אתה חסת על קן צפור אתה חוס ורחם עלינו (*אתה חסת על אותו ואת בנו אתה חוס ורחם עלינו) אמר רבה כמה ידע האי מרבנן לרצויי למריה א"ל אביי והא משתקין אותו תנן *ורבה לחדודי לאביי הוא דבעא ההוא דנחית קמיה דרבי חנינא *אמר האל הגדול הגבור והנורא האדיר והחזק והאמיץ אמר ליה סיימתינהו לשבחיה דמרך השתא הני תלתא אי לאו דכתבינהו משה באורייתא ואתו (ג) אנשי כנסת הגדולה ותקנינהו אנן לא אמרינן להו ואת אמרת כולי האי משל לאדם שהיו לו אלף אלפים דינרי זהב והיו מקלסין אותו (באלף) דינרי כסף לא *גנאי הוא לו אמר רבי חנינא *הכל בידי שמים חוץ מיראת שמים שנאמר ועתה ישראל מה ה' אלהיך שואל מעמך כי אם ליראה מכלל דיראה מילתא זוטרתי היא אין לגבי משה רבינו מילתא זוטרתי היא משל לאדם שמבקשין הימנו כלי גדול ויש לו דומה עליו ככלי קטן קטן ואין לו דומה עליו ככלי גדול *אמר רבי זירא האומר שמע שמע כאומר מודים מודים דמי מיתיבי הקורא את שמע וכופלה הרי זה מגונה מגונה הוא דהוי שתוקי לא משתקינן ליה לא קשיא הא דאמר מילתא מילתא ותני לה הא דאמר פסוקא פסוקא ותני לה א"ל רב פפא לרבא ודלמא מעיקרא לא כיון דעתיה והשתא כיון דעתיה א"ל *חברותא כלפי שמיא אי לא מכוין דעתיה מחינא ליה בארזפתא דנפחא עד דמכוין דעתיה: המכנה בעריות משתקין אותו: תנא רב יוסף קלון אביו וקלון אמו: האומר ומזרעך לא תתן להעביר וכו': תנא דבי רבי ישמעאל בישראל הבא על הכותית והוליד ממנה בן לע"ז הכתוב מדבר: **מתני'** *מעשה ראובן נקרא ולא מתרגם מעשה תמר נקרא ומתרגם מעשה עגל הראשון נקרא ומתרגם והשני נקרא ולא מתרגם ברכת כהנים מעשה דוד ואמנון (ג) נקראין ולא מתרגמין אין מפטירין במרכבה ורבי יהודה מתיר ר' אליעזר אומר אין מפטירין בהודע את ירושלם: **גמ'** תנו רבנן *יש נקרין ומתרגמין ויש נקרין ולא מתרגמין ויש לא נקרין ולא מתרגמין אלו נקרין ומתרגמין [א] בל"ת עק"ן נשפ"ה סימן: מעשה בראשית נקרא ומתרגם פשיטא מהו דתימא אתו לשיולי מה למעלה מה למטה ומה

מתני' מעשה ראובן · וישכב את בלהה פילגש אביו (בראשית לה): נקרא · בבית הכנסת: ולא מתרגם · חיישינן לגנותו: מעשה תמר · ויהודה: ומעשה עגל הראשון · כל פרשת העגל עד ואשליכהו באש (שמות לב) ומה שחזר אהרן וספר המעשה הוא קרוי מעשה עגל השני הוא שכתוב בו ויצא העגל הזה (שם) ולא יתרגם פן יטעו עמי הארץ ויאמרו ממש היה בו שלא מאליו יצא אבל המקרא אין מבינין: הודע את ירושלם · את תועבותיה פרשה היא ביחזקאל: **גמ'** ויש לא נקרין ולא מתרגמין · מפרש בסיפא מעשה דוד ואמנון לא נקרין בהפטרה: מעשה בראשית כו' · ואמרינן במסכת חגיגה (דף יא:) המסתכל בארבעה דברים ראוי לו כאילו לא בא לעולם והתם *מפרש טעמא אין רצונו של מלך שיזכירו שמו על אשפה כו': קמ"ל

עין משפט נר מצוה: עה א מיי' פ"ט מהל' תפלה הלכה ז: [עי' תוי"ט פ"ה דברכות מ"ג] [ע' רמב"ם דרך הצדיקים] עו ב מיי' פ"ט הלכה ד טוש"ע א"ח סימן קכא סעיף ג: פ ג מיי' פ"י מהלכות ברכות הל' ג סמג עשין כז טוש"ע שם סימן רכב סעיף ג: פא ד מיי' פ"ט מהל' תפלה הלכה ז: פב ה מיי' פ"ה מהל' תשובה הלכה ג: [נדה טז: ע"ש כתוב'] פג ו מיי' פ"ב מהלכות ק"ש הלכה יא סמג עשין יח טוש"ע א"ח סימן סא סעיף ט: פד ז מיי' פי"ב מהל' תפלה הלכה יב סמג עשין יט:

רבינו חננאל

מסורת הש"ס: ברכות לג: ע"ש; שם נג:; שם נד.; [מגילה]; ברכות לג: וע"ש; ברכות לג: ע"ש נדה טז:; ברכות לג: [סוכה נג:]; [ברכות לד.]; [פי' תוי"ש]; [תוספתא פ"ג]

הגהות הגר"א: [א] גמ' ויש לא נקרין ולא מתרגמין תא"מ

הגהות הב"ח

גליון הש"ס

This layout of a traditional page of the Talmud is that of a page of the Bomberg edition, printed in Venice in 1520–1523. The format and pagination were adopted by nearly all later editions. The additions of a basic overview of the text and further commentaries and apparatus followed, between 1880 and 1886, in the edition of the Widow and Brothers Romm, in Vilnius. The commonly appearing editions are photomechanical reprints of this edition. The citation of the Talmud by tractate name and page (recto/verso = a/b), is made accordingly: the page represented would be cited as bMegilla 25a (b = Babylonian Talmud). A vocalized (pointed) edition—in which the traditional Rashi script (see below) is replaced by the conventional Hebrew 'square script,' and in which only a part of the usual commentaries (including Rashi) and apparatus are supplied—has been published by Adin Steinsaltz, beginning in 1967 (as the "Steinsaltz Edition," now a standard text; an English translation and a corresponding edition of the Jerusalem Talmud are also in preparation).

A. Aids to Orientation ('Paratext')

(1) Page number: Always in the upper left-hand corner of the recto of a leaf; in Hebrew letters (which are also numerals). On the verso, in the upper right, is the pagination in Roman numerals. The Hebrew letter indicates the leaf with recto (a) and verso (b), although the Roman numeral is always twice as tall as the Hebrew. Citations, however, are according to the Hebrew numeral.

(2) The page superscript/title consists of three parts: *Right:* chapter name, usually the first or first two words of the chapter (here: *Ha-Qoreh omed*, "The Reader stands"); *Center:* chapter number (here: *Pereq shlishi*, "Third chapter"); *Left:* name of the Mishna tractate presented (here: *Megillah*, "Scroll"; the scroll that is meant is the scroll of Esther, which is read on the festival of Purim); according to the usual numeration, it is a matter, in the text reproduced here, of the Mishna tractate Megillah, chapter 4, section 1, abbreviated as mMeg 4,1. Before printed editions, the citation was usually by chapter name.

B. (Main) Text: Mishna and Gemara (= the Talmud itself)

The actual text of the Talmud consists of the *Mishna* (3) as the text to be laid out (printed in its entirety) and the *Gemara* (4), which, to be sure, is far more than a simple layout. Associatively, or by aligning captions, *Gemara* incorporates traditional material that can adopt the form of anything from short excursuses to lengthier treatments.

(3) On the first 5½ lines of this page (side), the Mishna to be laid out is cited. The text reads, in translation: "If anyone says: 'Let the good praise you,' this is the way of heresy. [If anyone says:] 'Over the birds' nests your mercy stretches' [or] 'For good, praised be your name' [or] 'Thanks! Thanks!' let him be silenced [i.e., he may read [aloud] no further from the text of the Bible]. If anyone paraphrases the incest [prohibitions], let him be silenced. If anyone translates [the following verse of the Bible:] 'And of your progeny, you shall not accede [to their being] given over to the Moloch' [for example, in this fashion:] 'And of your progeny you shall not accede [to their being] given over to paganism,' let him be silenced with a rebuke."

In the seventh-to-last line below, the next Mishna citation begins.

(4) The Gemara (as a commentary of the first rank) supplies the explanation why the manners of expression cited in the Mishna are prohibited. They are in danger of being misinterpreted dualistically: "It is presumed [with the prohibition of] 'Thanks! Thanks!' that [the reader has] two powers in view, [and thereby a dualistic conceptualization of God]; and correspondingly, 'For good, praised be your name,' because it implies, 'For good, yes, [but] for evil, no.' But we have learned [= introductory formula for the transmittal of an older tradition]: a person is obligated to praise [God] concerning evil just as he praises him for good. But what is the basis for which 'Over the birds' nests your mercy stretches'? There is a difference of opinion concerning this with two Explainers in the West [in Palestine], [namely, between] Rabbi Jose ben Abin and Rabbi Jose ben Zebira. One says[, . . .]and the other says[, . . .]"

The Gemara for the second section of the Mishna on this page begins at the end of the fourth-last line, indicated by the two enlarged letters (see 5).

(5) Indicators in large type, referring to the Mishna or the Gemara: the abbreviation *MTNJ* stands for *Matnitin*, "Our Mishna," and introduces a citation from the Mishna; the abbreviation *GM* stands for *Gemara*.

(6) Indications for sections and sentences: A colon divides meaning-sections; while within a section, units are divided by a point. With the translation into English, further subdivisions are frequently necessary.

(7) Textual conjectures or variants: Parentheses enclose doubtful readings, and in the opinion or the editor, are to be omitted, or replaced by another reading, which often follows in brackets. Brackets indicate additions to the text according to other manuscripts or sources. They indicate a comparison, not of scholarly textual readings and criticism, but of different traditional readings.

C. Marginal Commentaries (commentaries of the Second and Third Order)

(8) The Commentary of Rashi is always in the inside margin, the margin at the gutter. According to A. J. Heschel (see Lit. for §3), the ascent of the Babli to the status of Jewish popular book can be ascribed to the short commentary on it, which R. Shlomo ben Jizhaki (1040–1105), called Rashi, had composed. It is printed in its own, semi-cursive, script, called the Rashi script.

This makes the distinction between commentary and layout a visual one, as well. The division of the commentary is by citation: the expression of the Mishna or Gemara to be explained is cited (the end of which is indicated as in the text; see above, 6); then follows the explanation. A raised point marks the division between the two parts. The explanations are not thorough, but are limited to the necessary, and to explanations of difficult elements. A colon indicates the end of each explanation. In the case of a few tractates, the text attributed to Rashi is not by himself, but by a pupil, or his son-in-law and grandchild.

On the page reproduced here, Rashi begins on the upper right, with the commentary on the Mishna: "'May the good praise you,' this is the manner of heresy" (is a citation of the text; then, by way of explanation:) "For the evil are not included there, that they should praise God, while the wise (i.e., rabbinical scholars), instead, taught [. . .]." (This typical introduction to a citation is followed, in parentheses, by the location of the citation that now follows: *Keritot* [another Talmud tractate], page 6): "The odor of galbanum [a plant] is unpleasant, and yet is it prescribed among the roots for the smoke offering, and its use is prescribed in order to indicate being in a community" [meaning: Even the wicked should praise God, for their wickedness is as little as the slight odor of the galbanum that the divine service excludes; the colon ends this explanation).

(9) The Tosafot ("Complements") to Rashi's commentary: thus, commentaries of the Third Order vis-à-vis the Mishna, usually by Rashi's pupils and successors (often designated Tosafists, 'complementers'). The Tosafot are set in the Rashi script, as is this one, and are always on the outside of the page (in the outside margin). They represent the Talmudic discussion in France (and, in part, in Germany) in the twelfth and thirteenth centuries. The separation of the text and commentary is likewise presented visually: the word printed in larger, square type is the first word of the Mishna or the Gemara that is laid out in what follows. A point and a colon are used as described under no. 8, above.

On the page before us, the commentary is limited to four short loci. The first explanation goes with: "'Let the good praise you': an explanation that extracts the workers of wickedness [as Rashi understood it] or [alternatively] because it looks as though there were two powers, that is, a God [only] for the good (the Gemara, then)."

(10) Commentary of the Rabbenu Hananel (990–1055). The author lived in North Africa, and is nearer than Rashi to the traditional Babylonian elucidation. Its indications are usually concerned with whole sections, and concentrate on the principal content. Its commentary here bears on a later passage in the text.

D. System of References (to biblical, intra-Talmudic, and other rabbinical parallel loci)
(11) Parenthetical observations in the text of Rashi and in the Tosafot: Reference to the parallel or supporting loci; not originally a part of the commentaries, but inserted by later redactors.

(12) *Ayn Mishpat* ("Source of Law"): a reference system, instituted in Italy by Rabbi Yehoshua Boaz, to the three classic compendia of religious law: Maimonides (1135–1204), *Mishne Torah*; Moshe von Coucy (13th cent.), *Sefer Mizvot Gadol*; and Yosef Karo (1488–1575), *Shulkhan Arukh*. In the actual text of the Talmud, superscript in square script serves to indicate this marginal commentary.

(13) *Torah Or* ("Light-Torah"): Reference system (as marginalia, on the right, next to the core text) to the biblical loci cited or mentioned in the text of the Talmud. Likewise begun by Jehoshua Boaz (see 12), and completed by later writers. A superscript circle (°) in the text indicates that the reference is to be found at the same height in the break between the text and Rashi. The locus cited in the Mishna is Leviticus 18 (verse 21; only chapter numbers are indicated).

(14) *Masoret Ha-Schas* (i.e. "Transmission [or Tradition] of the Six Orders" [meaning of the Mishna or Talmud]): Reference system, in the main text, to Talmudic parallels. Begun, as with 12 and 13, by Yehoshua Boaz, and repeatedly supplemented (supplements indicated with brackets). In the text of the Talmud, references are made to these propositions, which are to be found at the same line-height, at the innermost marginal split. The first reference is to the tractate *Berakhot*, leaf 34a. The abbreviation following means "See in that place," and indicates that further parallels are listed at the locus cited.

(15) *Gilyon Ha-Shas* ("Column of the Six Orders"): Reference system (outside left) to intra-Talmudic or other rabbinical parallels not given in 14; frequently, indications to material thematically akin are given, as well. The author is Aqiba Eger (1761–1837), celebrated as Rabbi of Posen. A superscript circle with a slash follows the indication.

E. Critical Apparatus (to Text): Critical indications and emendations (= Haggahot)
(16) *Haggahot Ha-Bakh* ("Emendations of Ha-Bakh" [acronym for Joel Sirqes]): Critical commentary (outside left) to the Gemara, Rashi, and the Tosafists, composed by Joel Sirqes, a Polish rabbi of the seventeenth century. In the text of the Talmud, a Hebrew letter in Rashi script (in parentheses) reads as a numeral. As to the first locus, it notes as a variant a reading that dissolves and does 'not' complete the abbreviation, i.e., it reads: "*No* difference of opinion [. . .]."

(17) Haggahot Ha-Gra (*"Emendations of Ha-Gra"* [acronym for the Vilnius Gaon]). The indication follows in the main text by way of a superscript Hebrew letter in square script, set in a single left-hand bracket, to make a distinction from 12.

Other than these standard commentaries and apparatus, further commentaries are found in individual tractates in the Vilnius edition, either in the margin, or as an appendix. They also span the time from the tenth to the nineteenth century.

Roland Deines

The Fourth Order, the *Neziqin* ("Injuries"): Of the ten tractates here, the first six are devoted to the laws of punishment, jurisdiction, and punitive decrees, as well as to oaths. The remaining four tractates are of a varying character: *Eduyot* ("Testimonies") is a collection of one hundred instructional declarations on halachic pronunciations of earlier rabbis. In *Aboda Zara* ("Idolatry"), it is a matter, especially, of daily contact and commerce with non-Jews, as well as with dealing with pagan cults. *Abot* ("Fathers") is doubtless the best-known tractate of the Mishna, a kind of spiritual vade mecum of ethics, which has also become part of the Prayer Book. It is the sole 'haggadic' ('recounting') tractate of the Mishna. The last tractate of the fourth order, *Horayot* ("Teachings/Decisions") handles halachic decisions erroneously pronounced.

The Fifth Order, *Qodashim* ("Holy," "Sacred"), in eleven tractates, takes up the various kinds of sacrifices. It also contains the order of further tractates connected with Temple worship and taxes. The tractate *Keritot* (the "Extirpating Punishment") is a special case; with this notion, the rabbis described the transgressor's premature death, decreed by God himself.

The Sixth Order (*Toharot*, "Purifications"), the most comprehensive Order of the Mishna, is divided into twelve tractates. It is concerned with the contamination of things and persons, and the various possibilities for the reconstitution of purity. Especially important are the tractates on the uncleanness of the dead, and on the impurity of women pursuant to menstruation, birthgiving, or diseases of the underbody (*nidda*, 'uncleanness').

The explanatory *Gemara* has always been far more ample than the text of the religious prescriptions (Mishna) itself. Approximately one-third of it consists of haggadic traditions, and it is of an encyclopedic character. Everything taught in the rabbinical schools and deemed worthy of preservation was included. Numerous Jewish legends, folklore, and narratives are transmitted here, besides scientific material from medicine, biology, mathematics, astronomy, and so on. The other two-thirds presents halachic discussions. There the positions of approximately 2,500 instructors are presented, and confronted with one another, without always concluding to a conformity of opinions. In the Middle Ages, the immensity of this material led to systematic presentations of religious law.

The Talmud in Christian Perception

2. Since the thirteenth century, there has been a Christian perception of and confrontation with the Talmud expressing itself in two contrasting manners of relationship: (a) opposition and extermination, or (b) use of the Talmud as a testimonial tool of Christian truth, and thereby as a means to mission. A late effect of the first approach is (c) the Talmud-baiting of racist anti-Semitism since the nineteenth century. Anti-Jewish stereotypes acquired their specious verisimilitude by way of the fact that, unlike the Bible, Talmud

had not been translated into European languages until the modern age. Such translations would have been all the more desiderated by reason of the fact that the great composition was written in a difficult Middle Hebrew, or Babylonian Aramaic—expressed in a peculiar, frequently abbreviated diction, and obviously extending far beyond the scope of the Bible—whose linguistics therefore kindled defensive attitudes, calculated to stir up alarm and calumniation.

(a) From 1242 on, in Paris, at the instigation of the Church (usually in local form), Talmud burnings were held, on the basis of the notion that the Talmud was responsible for Jews' contempt of Christ and Christian teaching, and their refusal to acknowledge the truth of Christianity. Instigators were often Jewish converts, wishing to demonstrate their new faith by calling the attention of the church to the alleged threat posed by the Talmud. The designation 'Talmud' repeatedly stood, *pars pro toto*, for Judaism's entire rabbinical (and Kabbalistic) tradition, as it had taken form in various collections since the third century CE. At the beginning of the sixteenth century, Moravian convert Johannes Pfefferkorn (1469–c. 1524) sought to mount a burning of the Talmud and the rabbinical writings in the German Empire, but he was foiled by the opposition of humanist Johannes Reuchlin (1455–1522). A consequence of this controversy was Pope Leo X's imprimatur for the Babylonian (1520) and Palestinian (1523) Talmud (which, however, was withdrawn by his successor, Julius III) The printings by Daniel Bomberg at that time in Venice are the first complete editions of the Talmud, and stand to present as the exemplar for the printing of the Talmud. Only two decades later, even Luther, in his late composition *The Jews and Their Lies*, in which the entire arsenal of popular-culture late-medieval anti-Jewish polemics was permeated with earnest theological ratiocination, recommended that the Jewish schools be burned, the rabbis be prohibited from teaching, and these latter be deprived of their prayer books and the Talmud. While the ruling princes did not convert Luther's suggestions into law in his time, there were Talmud burnings at papal behest, for example in 1553 in Rome, and in the cities of the ecclesiastical state. The last burning motivated by religious considerations took place in Poland in 1757. Likewise, in connection with the destruction of Jewish culture in broad parts of Europe by the Nazi government, on the basis of a racist ideology, in 1938–1945 numerous Jewish libraries were destroyed or misused as objects of spectacle and research in the National Socialist institutes for their fight against Judaism.

Opposition and Extermination

(b) Together with the battle against the Talmud, beginning in the thirteenth century there were also attempts to 'prove' the Christian truth to the Jews through appeal to the Talmud, and thus to gain them for the faith without the application of violence. A basic source for many authors into the eighteenth century was Dominican Raimundus Martini's *Pugio Fidei* (Lat., "Dagger of the Faith"), appearing in the second half of the thirteenth century (first printing in Paris, 1651). Protestant theologians' positions oscillated between hard polemics (Johann Benedikt Carpzov II, 1629–1699) and serious research (Johann Buxtorf the Elder and the Younger: *Lexikon Chaldaicum, Talmudicum et Rabbinicum*, Basel 1639). Here as well, two purposes predominated: the explanation of the New Testament on grounds of the Jewish, and that meant, especially, Talmudic sources; and a demonstration that the Christian messianic teaching is contained in the Jewish sources

Instrumentalization

(e.g., Christian Schöttgen, *Horae Hebraicae et Talmudicae in Theologiam Judaeorum Dogmaticam Antiquam et Orthodoxam de Messia;* Lat., "Hebrew and Talmudic Instances against the Jews' Ancient and Orthodox Dogmatic Theology of the Messiah"; 1742).

These studies were taken up once more in the second half of the nineteenth century in a context of the missionary work among the Jews. Here lie the beginnings of Christian Judaic studies, as it was established in the twentieth century, first in a framework of the *Instituta Judaica*, at individual Evangelical theology faculties in the German universities. Since the end of the nineteenth century, translations of the Talmud and related texts have appeared in the most important European languages. These have replaced the frequently very faulty and, to a certain extent, tendentious, partial translations of individual sections or tractates of the Talmud into Latin and numerous other languages—translations that, in consequence of the burnings of the Talmud at Paris, had appeared since the thirteenth century.

'Talmudism': The Anti-Semitic Polemics against the Talmud

(c) The extensive Christian ignorance with regard to the content of the Talmud, and to Jewish approaches to it ('Jewish learning'), was fertile soil, in times of hostility toward Jews, for the most absurd suspicions (legends of ritual murder, profanation of the Host, exemption from law in contact with non-Jews, etc.; → Anti-Semitism). The same ignorance explains the phenomenon of 'Talmud,' 'Talmudism,' and 'Talmudic Jew' becoming anti-Jewish and anti-Semitic expressions since the nineteenth century. In the Talmud, non-Jews, and enemies of the Jews, saw (and see today, in extremist circles of the right) the source, as it were, of everything strange and foreign, everything offensive, and everything perilous about Judaism. *Der Talmudjude. Zur Beherzigung für Juden und Christen aller Stände* (Ger., "The Talmudic Jew: For Reflection on the Part of Jews and Christians of All Classes"), by Catholic Old Testament scholar August Rohling (1839–1931), a book first appearing in Münster in 1871, became an important source of the anti-Semitic reception of the Talmud. It came out in twenty-two editions in all, and was translated into several other languages. Rohling sought to offer a scholarly demonstration of the thesis that, by virtue of their religion, Jews have the capacity to corrupt, physically and morally, secretly or openly, those of other beliefs. This view was refuted in a number of juridical proceedings, and in numerous books and decrees by Jewish and Christian scholars,[2] but such refutations proved to be no hindrance to the wide popularity of the Rohling work. A source appealed to by Rohling (and by many of his imitators) was the older work of Heidelberg orientalist Johann Andreas Eisenmenger (1654–1704), *Entdecktes Judentum* (Ger., "Judaism Discovered"), 2 vols., 1st ed. 1700, 2nd ed. 1711. Also, in *Handbuch der Judenfrage. Die wichtigsten Tatsachen zur Beurteilung des jüdischen Volkes* (Ger., "Manual of the Jewish Question: Most Important Facts for an Assessment of the Jewish People"), which emerged from Theodor Fritsch's (1852–1933) *Antisemiten-Catechismus* (Ger., "Catechism for Anti-Semites"; originally appearing in 1887); an extensive section was included containing relevant known citations of the Talmud, with calumniations. In the "Department for Research on the Jewish Question," founded in Munich in 1936, the National Socialist regime attempted to supply these populist distortions with a scholarly legitimization. Here, the Talmud served, first and foremost, not as a source of religious history, but as an expression of the racist, distorted image of the essence of the Jew. Favorite loci were those that handle relationships with non-Jews in the area of business and commerce, or else the occasionally detailed descriptions of sexual episodes in the Talmud in a context of purity or of marriage law. Here the traditional clichés, and pictures of Jews as usurers or swindlers, or sexual perverts, were speciously 'evidenced' from their own sources. The results page for "Talmudism" in an Internet search engine is instructive with respect to how extreme rightist circles paint anew the specter of a Talmudic 'secret teaching.' One of the efforts of books like *Talmud ohne Maske* (Ger., "The Talmud without Disguise"), by Jürgen Graf, is the denial of the Shoah, and an explanation of why there can be no peace in the Middle East: the 'Talmud as the Zionist law book.'

3. Jewish religious philosopher Abraham Joshua Heschel (1907–1972), who came from Eastern European Judaism, called 'the democratization of Talmudic study' the most important achievement of the Judaism of that area.[3] The precondition had been the dissemination of the Talmud and related writings through the newly invented printing press, which Judaism pressed into the service of learning from the very beginning. Famous rabbis taught in numerous Talmudic schools in Poland, composing commentaries that, even today, as marginal commentaries, are a lasting component of traditional editions of the Talmud. This caused the appearance of different traditions in its presentation, depending on whether it was the Talmud itself, or the biblical tradition underlying it, that made for the point of departure.

The Talmud in Eastern Europe, and Jewish Dealing with the Talmud

By the dawn of the eighteenth century, the traditional Talmudic piety of rabbinical orthodox Jews had become a religiosity of the elite. Now it gained a contrary vector: a nonintellectual, interiorized faith practice gave Talmudic studies new impetus. At the center stood Lithuanian rabbi Elijahu ben Solomon Salman Kremer, better known under his honorific title, the Vilnius Gaon (1720–1797). His commentary is the most recent to have found a place as a marginal commentary. → Hasidism today has an important place in the United States and in Israel, having succeeded in joining traditional Talmudic scholarship with personal piety.

Hasidism

Beginning in the eighteenth century, a common intra-Judaic adversary flourished in both currents: the Jewish Enlightenment (Heb., *Haskala*), which itself waged a bitter battle against the Talmud. The *maskalim* ('Enlightenment persons') saw the 'ghetto walls' as the element preventing the Jews from becoming citizens, with equal rights, of the nations in which they lived. But the roots of the Enlightenment criticism of the Talmud reach further back. After the Careans' medieval criticism of Judaic tradition (→ Judaism), the Netherlands in the seventeenth century had been the scene of confrontations over the divine origin (and, thus, over the validity) of the rabbinical traditions, as these latter now found their reflection in the Talmud. Protagonists of this criticism had been Uriel da Costa (1585–1640) and Baruch Spinoza (1632–1677). These altercations still define Judaism today. In terms of organization, we see this in the fact, among others, that since the nineteenth century in all Jewish centers foundations have incorporated higher education—as alternatives to the classic Talmudic schools (*Yeshivot*)—including instructional institutions, seminaries, and universities in which the rabbinical documents are researched on fundamental principles of historical criticism. The contrast between Yeshiva and university abides. The

Talmudic Criticism at the Hands of Jewish Enlightenment

confrontation in Israel is especially sharp, where orthodox and secular Judaism, especially, stand in opposition, without liberal or conservative Judaism functioning as a link between the extremes, as they do in the United States (and as they did in Germany before 1933). How important the Talmud is for Jewish self-understanding even in the universities, however, is illustrated by the fact that a course in the Talmud is obligatory for all Israelis studying for the degree of Bachelor of Arts at the Faculty for Sciences of Judaism. Popular, inexpensive editions of the Talmud (even, in some cases, in translation), with simple explanation, often based on Rashi, make up an important component of religious publishing in Israel even today. There is, besides, an entire series of editions on CD-Rom, intended to appeal to children and youth as well. In the public discussion, a particularly virulent question is how far the prescriptions of the Talmud, which so deeply concern private and public life, may be rendered binding for secular Jews, indeed for the state, by the rabbinate.

1. Thus KROCHMALNIK in his entry on → Judaism.
2. WIESE 1999, 88-99 and 112-123.
3. HESCHEL, Abraham Joshua, Die Erde ist des Herrn. Die innere Welt des Juden in Osteuropa, Neukirchen 1985, 33 (see HESCHEL 1978).

Literature

Sources: The first complete English edition of the Babylonian Talmud was edited by Isidore EPSTEIN: The Babylonian Talmud. Translated into English with notes, glosses and indices, 35 vols., London 1935–1952; the translation is further part of the bilingual Soncino-Edition: Hebrew-English Edition of the Babylonian Talmud, London 1989 (30 vols., 1984–1990); a new translation was edited and mainly made by Jacob NEUSNER: The Talmud of Babylonia: An American Translation (appeared since 1984 in Brown Judaic Series, starting with vol. 72, continued in: South Florida Studies in the History of Judaism). A helpful edition with the commentary of Rashi and other explanations is currently being published under the leadership of Adin STEINSALTZ: The Talmud: The Steinsaltz Edition (since 1989). An English translation of the Jerusalem Talmud was also organized by Jacob NEUSNER: The Talmud of the Land of Israel, 35 vols., Chicago Studies in the History of Judaism, 1982–1994. A new bilingual edition edited by Heinrich W. GUGGENHEIMER appeared since the year 2000: The Jerusalem Talmud: Edition, Translation and Commentary (Studia Judaica), Berlin/New York.

Secondary Literature to §§ 1 and 4: MACCOBY, Hyam, Early Rabbinic Writings, Cambridge 1988; PARRY, Aaron, The Complete Idiot's Guide to The Talmud, Indianapolis 2004; STEINSALTZ, Adin, The Talmud: The Steinsaltz Edition. A Reference Guide, New York 1989; Idem, The Essential Talmud, New York 1976 (many reprints); STRACK, Hermann L./ STEMBERGER, Günther, Introduction to the Talmud and Midrash, Edinburgh 1991.

To § 2: MOORE, George Foot, "Christian Writers on Judaism," in: Harvard Theological Review 14 (1921), 197-254; OBERMAN, Heiko A., The Roots of Antisemitism in the Age of Renaissance and Reformation, Philadelphia 1984; RUMMEL, Erika, The Case against Johann Reuchlin: Religious and Social Controversy in Sixteenth-Century Germany, Toronto 2002; WIESE, Christian, Wissenschaft des Judentums und protestantische Theologie im wilhelminischen Deutschland, Tübingen 1999.

To § 3: HESCHEL, Abraham Joshua, The Earth is the Lord's: The Inner World of the Jew in East Europe, New York 1978.

→ *Bible, Book, Hermeneutics, Kabbalah, Judaism, Hasidism*

Roland Deines

Tantra I: Hindu

1. *Tantra* (Skt., 'woven chain,' 'web,' 'instruction book') denotes, in general, a pathway of practices along which ritual, corporeal, and mental techniques are applied, in order to obtain, in one's lifetime, extraordinary capacities (*siddhi*) or deliverance from all worldly conditions (*mukti*). Elements of the Tantra are found in various religions, as in the Hindu systems of Shivaism, Vishnuism, and Shaktism, as well as in → Buddhism (→ Tantra II). The Tantra, then, is not an independent religion, but an articulation, usually sectarian, of various religious symbolic systems. The origins of the Tantra lie in the Indian cultural sphere. There, Tantra means, first, a literary genre, which includes, along with instructional texts in religious philosophy, a literature of revelation. The revelation in question is that of particular instructional traditions. In the ritual context, the adjective 'Tantric' (*tāntrika*) serves, on the other hand, to establish a demarcation and distinction from 'Vedic' (*vaidika*) ritual schools (for 'Veda,' → Hinduism). However, there is no unitary metaphysics or philosophy of the Tantra. One of the things evincing this diversity is that Tantric systems have developed both within the Hindu tradition and in the Buddhist: in both varieties, elements of the classic philosophical systems are adopted, reinterpreted, and further developed in terms of each of these religious environments, each in reciprocal effect with ritual practice. But the relationships between Buddhist and Hindu Tantras have thus far been little researched.[1] The doctrines of the Hindu Tantras formed between approximately the sixth and eleventh centuries CE. The first Buddhist Tantras appeared around 400 CE. The heyday of Tantric Buddhism in Northern India was followed by its spread in Tibet and Mongolia (eighth, eleventh centuries, respectively). The current application of the designation 'Tantrism' has plainly been withdrawn from the original context. The horizon of meaning today was impacted by the Western reception of the Tantra in the nineteenth and twentieth centuries.

Concept

2. Tantric teachings and rituals, in their Hindu and Buddhist configurations alike, are esoteric. The special traditions of each are the object of → secrecy. An essential mark of the Tantra is the ritual adoption and initiation (*dīkṣā*) into the respective religious tradition by a Tantric master (→ Guru), who incorporates a specific doctrinal succession. The ritual initiation is usually connected with the surrender of one's worldly name, a communication of specific Tantric mantras, and introduction into the secret teachings and ritual practices of the Tantric community in question. This → initiation is determinative of the religious identity of the competing Tantric groups. Depending on the context, the Tantric initiation can be performed as an appendix to initiation as a monk or nun, as admittance into a community of ascetics, or as a reception of lay followers into a religious community. Frequently, the esoteric character of the doctrines transmitted is emphasized by the use of a secret language, accessible only to the initiated. The particular way of salvation (*sādhana*), and ritual practice, are imprinted, among other things, by the application of ritual diagrams (*yantra*, → Mandala), finger gestures (*mudrā*, → Symbol/Sign/Gesture), and by the recitation of Tantric → mantras. The inscribing of mantras on the body (*nyāsa*), and the latter's cleansing and transformation, is often regarded as a prerequisite for the cultic veneration of a given deity.

Ritual Adoption and Esoteric Practice

A Shivaite ascetic, and member of the group of the Aghorīs, uses a human skull as a drinking bowl. This practice is part of the antinomian behavior of Tantric ascetics. Daubed with the unclean ashes of a crematorium, berating people in a mixture of unintelligible, insulting, and obscene language, with a preference for impure substances like alcohol, meat, and allegedly human flesh as well, the Aghorīs intentionally expose themselves to societal condemnation. But the heterodox Tantric practice is not exclusively, or even preferably, shaped by the individual. Rather, it is the product of a vow (*vrata*), and marks a stage on the ascetic's salvific path. Ascetics gain religious merit precisely on grounds of their rejection by the social order.

Anthropology and Speculative Psychophysiology

A feature of Tantric teaching is a sophisticated anthropology, especially speculations on the psychophysiology, and macrocosmic correspondences, of the body. The channels (*nādī*) peculiar to the body, the centers (*cakra*), energy currents (*kuṇḍalini*), and breathing and recitation techniques, all known from the Tantric → yoga, are important for the esoteric levels of Tantric ritual and yogic practice. The value attributed to the pleasure (*bhukti*) of the extraordinary capacities thus acquired, on the one side, and the effort for ultimate liberation during one's lifetime, on the other, differs greatly from tradition to tradition.

Feminine and Masculine Principles

In the Tantra, especially in Shaktism, the goddess, or female power and energy (*shakti*), has an important place. The reciprocity between the masculine, static principle and the feminine, dynamic one is reflected in Tantric traditions in many ways, through their psycho-physiological practices, visualizations, and iconography. The presentation of the sexual union of god and goddess is the sensory image of the cosmic act of creation. Heterodox practices, which, unlike the orthodox traditions, deny the duality of clean and unclean substances (*advaitācāra*), include ritual sexual intercourse. To be sure, Tantra teaches the equality of man and woman, but any textual perspective is almost exclusively masculine, so that there is no radical differentiation of woman in the Tantric milieu in which we might take our point of departure for an analysis of the principles of the feminine and the masculine.[2]

In sectarian Tantric traditions, there are antinomian attitudes and behavior, with which, in the framework of a vow (*vrata*), norms of attitude and behavior are deliberately spurned. This dismissal materializes precisely through attitudes of rejection of the environment, and of any acquisition of religious merit (Aghorī type, see illus.). Heterodox practices and veneration of the goddess are important aspects of the Tantra. But they are often overvalued in reception: there are Tantric currents, attested in India even before the year 1000, that—perhaps under social pressure—renounced all heterodox practice, and celebrated a liturgy to a male god.

Antinomian Attitudes and Behavior

3. Two media have decisively influenced reception of the Tantra in the West, and have established distinct chains of reception: textual translations, as well as popular volumes of pictures and images. In the first half of the twentieth century, a British judge on the Supreme Court in Calcutta, Sir John Woodroffe (1865–1936), published numerous textual editions and translations of Hindu Tantras, as well as essays concerned with them. Part of his work was done under the pseudonym of Arthur Avalon, and in close collaboration with an Indian assistant Atal Behari Ghosh.[3] Woodroffe's important pioneering labor made Tantric works accessible to a wide public for the first time, and definitively shaped the reception and understanding of 'Tantrism' in the West. Because of his choice of sources, however, his fundamentally apologetical approach, and his sometimes erroneous ordering of the texts, Woodroffe's work must today be regarded as extensively outdated, despite the relatively recent vintage of some of his publications.

Tantra in the West: On the History of Its Reception

The image—and exploitation—of the Tantra as an 'exotic form of pornography,'[4] has, in turn, been influenced by the publication of numerous volumes of pictures and images of erotic Indian art, which give the impression of a coherent religious system of sex, indeed, somewhat, as a 'religion of sex' (B. Soulié). Thus, the Tantra is received in parts of the esoteric movement as an Oriental, holistic sexual therapy (→ New Age; Esalen Institute). The → Osho movement and its environment keenly shaped this phenomenon. The combination of Tantric elements with modern psychotherapeutic methods leaves the context of a Tantric practice of religious ritual almost entirely out of the picture.

1. Guenther, "Foreword" to Dasgupta, Shashi Bhushan, An Introduction to Tantric Buddhism, Berkeley ²1974 (¹1958), ix-xi; Bharati, Agehananda, Die Tantra-Tradition, Freiburg 1993, 319-330.
2. Kakar, Sudhir, Shamans, Mystics, and Doctors: A Psychological Inquiry into India and Its Healing Traditions, Delhi 1982.
3. Taylor, Kathleen: "Arthur Avalon: The Creation of a Legendary Orientalist," in: Leslie, Julia (ed.), Myth and Mythmaking, Surrey 1996, 144-164.
4. Hardy, Friedhelm, The Religious Culture of India: Power, Love, and Wisdom, Cambridge 1994, 165.

Literature

Sources: BRUNNER, Hélène, Somaśambhupaddhati: Rituels dans la tradition śivaite selon Somaśambhu, vols. 1-4, Pondicherry 1963–1998 (Shivaite ritual handbook with text, French trans., and annotation; probably the best introduction to Hintu tantra ritual).

Pictures: SOULIÉ, Bernard, Tantra: Erotic Figures in Indian Art, Fribourg 1982.

Secondary Literature: AVALON, Arthur (alias John WOODROFFE), Principles of Tantra, Madras ⁶1986 (¹1914); ELIADE, Mircea, Yoga: Immortality and Freedom, New York ²1969 (French ¹1954); GUPTA, Sanjukta et al., Hindu Tantrism, Leiden 1979; KRIPAL, Jeffrey J., Kālī's Child: The Mystical and the Erotic in the Life and Teachings of Ramakrishna, Chicago/London ²1998 (¹1995); SANDERSON, Alexis, "Shaivism and the Tantric Traditions," in: HARDY, Friedhelm (ed.), The World's Religions: Religions of Asia, London 1990, 128-172.

→ *Buddhism, Esalen Institute, Guru, Hinduism, Lamaism, Mandala, Mantra, New Age, Orientalism/Exotism, Osho Movement, Sexuality, Tantra II, Yoga*

Jörg Gengnagel

Tantra II: Buddhist

1. As it does in Hinduism, 'Tantra' in Buddhism denotes a system of texts that appeared in India in the second half of the first millennium, and that represent the groundwork of 'esoteric Buddhism.' The oldest texts date from around the fifth century CE. According to Buddhist Tantric tradition, the Tantras date back to the historical → Buddha or his pupils. Not all Buddhist schools acknowledge the Tantras, however. The texts are based on the foundation of the Mahayana philosophy (esp. *Mādhyamika*), and integrate an elaborate ritualistics, magical practices, and elements of → yoga. In addition, they contain a cosmology, the key proposition of which is the correspondence between microcosm and macrocosm. The Tantras make use of a language and symbolism of their own, which renders them accessible only to initiates. Initiation is indispensable for an understanding and application of the texts, and requires a teacher (in Skt., *guru*; in Tibetan, *lama*). In Buddhist art, the pictorial presentation of a complex didactic content depicts an elaborate Tibetan Buddhist pantheon. In a multi-faceted sexual symbolism, what comes to expression is the concept of the defeat of polarities.

Tantric Classes

In the twelfth and thirteenth centuries, the texts were systematized in four hierarchically ordered Tantric classes.

(1) *Kriyā Tantra* ("Action"): On this level, the ritual actions and sacrifices predominate. What is important here is the legacy of karmic merit and demerit, but especially the purification of one's individual actions, the emotions connected with them, and their translation to a means of enlightenment.

(2) *Charyā Tantra* ("Exercise and Implementation"): Ritual actions and interior concentration or composure are of equal value. These first two classes emphasize the exterior aspects of Buddhist practice.

(3) *Yoga Tantra* ("Yoga"): With the help of a purposeful visualization of certain mandalas, one's own spirit is identified with its Buddha aspect.

(4) *Anuttarayoga Tantra* ("Supreme Yoga") represents the highest step of spiritualization. Spiritual (mental) capacities and effectiveness increase at each stage; at the same time, physical actions recede (gradually) into the background. On the way to the highest knowledge, not all of the steps need necessarily be taken in order.

2. Tantra, within Buddhism, is a system of ritual techniques and meditation practices, in combination with magical abilities. The Tantra belongs to the *Vajrayāna* ('Diamond Vehicle') school. Its purpose is the defeat of the three fundamental evils: greed, hatred, and delusion. The Buddhist concept of redemption—deliverance from the cycle of existence—is attainable on an accelerated path, by means of 'dexterous means' (Skt., *upāya*): the Tantric methods of yoga, meditation, and exercises in visualization. In common with the *Mahāyāna* ('Greater Vehicle') school, Tantric Buddhism begins with a potential enlightenment (the Buddha nature) interior to all living beings, and sees its realization in the ('existential,' as it were) understanding or knowledge of emptiness (Skt., *śūnyatā*). In order to attain this goal, an active confrontation with the content of Buddhist doctrine is given precedence over purely textual study. A spiritual teacher is essential for the celebration of the complex rituals, and for an understanding of the text, especially since Tantric practice on a basis of the introduction and application of psychogenic methods is not regarded as entirely without risk. The inaccessibility of the texts leads to the observance of a hierarchy between clergy and lay members that is not explicit in the doctrines of Tantric Buddhism.

Goal of Tantric Practice

The religious dimension of Tantric Buddhism contains practices and conceptualizations of popular religion. Tantric ritual indicates parallels to the death process, analogies between the unconscious developmental and maturational processes of human life, and the consciously traversed stages of meditation. The emphasis is on the transformation of body and consciousness, in a process of understanding through quasi-physical sensation and experience. An example would be the transitions detailed in the *Tibetan Book of the Dead*. These transitions are called 'bardo,' of which six are distinguished. Here it is not only the condition between death and rebirth that is comprehended as a transition/bardo. Tantric Buddhism is characterized by the interlocking of transcendent Buddhas, with elements, celestial directions, colors, sounds/syllables, and aspects or wisdom, all of which exhibit a web of micro- and macro-cosmic levels. Occasionally, a distinction is posited between a right-handed and a left-handed Tantra. The right-handed Tantra stresses the sublimation of human cravings, and the conquest of the dualities, on a visualized level. The left-handed Tantra stresses the feminine principle, and the experience of the unification of the polarities on a corporeal level.

3. Secret, or esoteric, Buddhism (in Jap., *Mikkyō*), with roots in Indian Tantrism, came to Japan at the beginning of the ninth century, where it was introduced by Saichō (767–822 CE), a monk of the 'Tendai' school (a Chinese Buddhist school on Mount T'ien-t'ai), and by Kūkai (774–835), the monk from whom the 'Shingon' school descends (after the Chinese translation of the Sanskrit mantra *chen-yen*, 'true word'). Both had studied in China, where, in the eighth century, Tantric Buddhism had appeared under the T'ang dynasty. Meditative practices and visualizations, as well as magical

Esoteric Tantric Buddhism in Japan

procedures (especially the summoning of rain and rites for the lengthening of life) helped the two teachers to great success among the nobility, and later with the uneducated populace. Their religiosity was characterized by the elaborate ritual system that stands in connection with the art of *mikkyō*. In this art, constructions of images were understood both as the temporary seat of spiritual energies and as an illustration of specific qualities like, for example, wisdom and compassion—the acquisition of which is regarded as indispensable along the way to Buddhahood. After initiation by a teacher, practitioners aim, by means of meditation and ritual actions, at the goal of unification with the Buddha, or with another figure of the broad Buddhist pantheon, in their present existence (*zokushin jōbutsu*). This attainment occurs through the translation or application of the three secrets or mysteries (*sammitsu*): (1) bodily acts, especially the execution of symbolical positions of the hands (Skt., *mudrā* → Symbol/Sign/Gesture), (2) the recitation of magical formulas (Skt., *mantra*, application in language and aloud), and (3) meditative visualization (mental and spiritual application), through which cultic practice (*jisō*), in complement, forms a unity with speculative doctrine (*kyōsō*).

Literature

Astley, Ian (ed.), Esoteric Buddhism in Japan, Copenhagen 1994; Dasgupta, Shashi Bhushan, An Introduction to Tantric Buddhism, Berkeley ²1974 (¹1958); Hopkins, Jeffrey, The Tantric Distinction: A Buddhist's Reflections on Compassion and Emptiness, Boston ²1999 (¹1984); Hopkins, Jeffrey (ed.), Tantra in Tibet: The Great Exposition of Secret Mantra. With an introduction by the 14th Dalai Lama, London 1977; Mishra, T. N., Impact of Tantra on Religion and Art, New Delhi 1997; Shaw, Miranda, Passionate Enlightenment: Women in Tantric Buddhism, Princeton 1994; Thubten Yeshe (Lama), Introduction to Tantra: The Transformation of Desire, Boston ²2001 (¹1987); Wayman, Alex, The Buddhist Tantras: Light on Indo-Tibetan Esotericism, New York 1973; White, David Gordon (ed.), Tantra in Practice, Princeton 2000.

→ *Buddhism, Mandala, Mantra, Mysticism, Sexuality, Tantra I*

Stephanie Lovász (§§1, 2) and Ursula Hüge

Tattoo

1. 'Tattoo,' from the East Polynesian *tatau*, to 'strike correctly,' denotes a pattern, image, or ornament, scratched, pricked, or struck through the human epidermis. With *scar tattooing*, used especially with darker skin, the skin is seared or scratched with an instrument (fragment of stone, bamboo or bone knife, razor-blade). Healing is delayed (rubbing in of ashes, clay), in order that a pattern of swelling may emerge. With *color or pricking tattooing* (used especially with fair skin), dyed material is brought in contact with, and introduced under, the epidermis through the use of toothed wooden hammers (today usually an electric tattooing needle). Unlike body-painting, tattooing leaves an enduring mark on the body, changing it in a lasting way. The word *tatau* was imported to Europe from Tahiti by English seafarer James Cook. The connection between nudity and ornament on the body among the inhabitants of the South Sea told Europeans of 'wildness,'

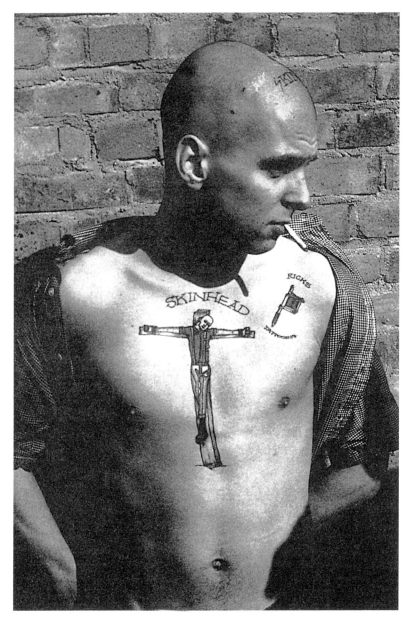

Even in Western industrial societies, tattoos can be for more than just aesthetic and decorative purposes. In youth subcultures, tattooing confers identity (in the sense of a demarcation), and denotes initiation into a 'tribal alliance.' The blood that flows during the imposition of the tattoo emphasizes the transmutation. Thus, the body image of Jesus's Crucifixion attached by skinheads to their bodies is fraught with religious conceptions of Christian sacrificial ideology—the skinhead as misunderstood 'sacrifice,' as 'scapegoat' of a society against whose values he rebels—and he wears his tattoo in protest.

and awakened a certain longing (erotic, to some extent), but also provoked a revulsion before the naked cannibal. Meanwhile, the tattoo has spread worldwide since the Paleolithic Age.

2. The occasions in life for the tattoo are as varied as the signs themselves. In the South Sea, persons have their tongues tattooed out of grief and pain over the departed. Then there is the 'revenge tattoo,' which threatens repayment after the murder of a relative. The facial tattoos of the Maori (New Zealand), again, document the bearer's social rank, origin, and descendancy, so that they constitute a 'visible visiting card.' Further, the tattoo can serve

Occasions and Functions

for protection against misfortune and disease. Unlike the art of tattooing in the West, frequently performed for the purpose of aesthetic decoration alone, tattooing in traditional societies interweaves this purpose with socio-religious connections. Western tattoos express individuality, or → protest against prevailing social norms. In tribal societies, by way of an aesthetic code of skin ornamentation, tattooing expresses a society's central values, and conceptualizations of belief.

Tribal Religions

3. In a mythic and cultic connection, tattooing is used primarily with → initiation. Thus, the searing of pubertal men by the Iatmul of New Guinea, is referred to the story of creation. The scar sign, sensible image of reception into the society of adult men, produces an equivalency with the mythical crocodile of primordial times, from which the tribe draws its descendancy. In a framework of culturally specific conceptualizations concerning death and rebirth, scar patterns can be interpreted as wounds received from the bites and blows of the mythical 'greedy one' (Straube 1964). A further purpose of scar tattooing among the Iatmul consists in the spilling of the impure blood of his mother by the male initiand: novices' bodies are transformed from that of a child to that of an adult male. Ritual tattooing can permanently etch cosmological conceptualizations and powers in the body: thus, at the climax of their sun ritual, the Omaha (North America) tattoo marriageable girls with a dish (sensible image of the cosmic deity of the sun) and a star (feminine cosmic power of the night). The signs instill the girl with fertility and life energy. Initiands bear the pain in silence—a test not only of their courage, endurance, and physical strength, but also of their silent agreement to their society's social charter, that brooks no dialogue, nor any contradiction. Thus the individual body becomes the social body—the 'cultural linen' on which this society enduringly inscribes its social and religious concepts: the "body is memorial" (P. Clastres). The tattoo has a memory-bolstering function: it 'inscribes' the individual with the laws and privileges of society.

In private rituals as well, tattoos can refer to religious conceptualizations. Thus, in the view of the Sarawak Kaya (Borneo), disease appears through loss of the soul. After the ritual expert has recalled the soul into the patient's body, he tattoos it with signs, to prevent the soul from being lost in perspiration once more.

Book Religions

4. The three book religions, Judaism (Lev 19:28; Deut 14:1), Christianity (2 Nicaea 787 CE), and Islam (e.g., according to a Hadith of the Prophet's companion Abd Allah ibn Umar)[1] forbid tattooing. Concepts of the integrity of the human body as the 'image of God,' or the intent to distinguish one's own cultic practice from that of pagans, may have been the basis for this prohibition. Still, Christians and Muslims alike wore tattoos as visible documents, for example, of their participation in pilgrimages (crusades, pilgrimages to Mecca). In other societies with an aversion to tattoo, it was sometimes performed with marginal groups and outsiders, such as criminals (Japanese, *yakuza*), or homosexual persons, for identification and retribution. Only in

Subcultural Tattooing

recent years has tattoo become the fashion in the West: subcultures have adopted it across broad classes of the population, usually in a secular context. (In the countercultures, tattoos with a religious reference are common;

Revitalization of Indigenous Traditions

see illus.). Indeed the Western trend has occasioned the revival of forgotten traditions of the South Sea. Consequently upon the Western mission, South Sea Islanders had frequently given up the tattoo. Now, however, it has been revived, partly as a symbol of a distance taken from Western modernity. It also, of course, emphasizes cultural independence and ethnic membership.

1. Transmitted in the *Sahib* collection of the Buhari.

Literature

CLASTRES, Pierre, Society Against the State: Essays in Political Anthropology, New York 1989; DEMELLO, Margo, Bodies of Inscription: A Cultural History of the Modern Tattoo Community, Durham 2000; JAGUER, Jeff, The Tattoo: A Pictorial History, Horndean 1990; MILLER, Jean-Chris, The Body Art Book: A Complete, Illustrated Guide to Tattoos, Piercings, and Other Body Modifications, New York 2004; SANDERS, Clinton R., Customizing the Body: The Art and Culture of Tattooing, Philadelphia 1989; STRAUBE, Helmut, "Beiträge zur Sinndeutung der wichtigsten künstlichen Körperverstümmelungen in Afrika," in: Festschrift Jensen, vol. II, Munich 1964, 671-722; THOMAS, Nicholas et al. (eds.), Tattoo: Bodies, Art, and Exchange in the Pacific and Europe, London 2004; TURNER, Victor, "Bodily Marks," in: Encyclopedia of Religion 2 (1987), 269-275.

→ *Body, Initiation, Symbol/Sign/Gesture*

Josef Drexler

Teleology

The word 'teleology,' formed from the Greek *télos* ('end,' 'goal,' 'purpose,' 'completion') and *lógos* ('word,' 'reason,' 'teaching'), was originally a coinage by philosopher Christian Wolff (1679–1754). His neologism was based on the thought of the 'purpose,' or 'final cause' of a thing, which Aristotle had conceptualized in a framework of his doctrine of the four causes. Accordingly, the point of departure of teleological thought is the goal-directedness, or purposefulness, of changes or processes. As early as Homer's *Iliad*, a similar motif is to be found in the form of belief in an overall order of the world, connected with the thought of divine providence (in Gk., *prónoia*). By contrast, Democritus and Leucippus developed an atomistic conception of reality, governed by causal laws other than, and without, purpose or teleology.

Areas of the application of teleological thought are, especially, the field of behavioral theory or ethics, the philosophy of history, and cosmology or nature theory. In the field of → ethics, teleological thought is, as a rule, presupposed, since responsibility for acts can only be posited from a starting point in the notion that agents pursue a freely chosen intent in their activity. Thus, it is in the other two areas cited above that teleology is more frequently exposed to criticism. In particular, in terms of the 'end' of really existing socialism, it has become the norm to refer to concepts of a *Philosophy of History* philosophy of history grounded in a scientifically predictable, goal-directed historical process (→ Utopia). Even earlier, Karl Löwith and Karl Popper, from different perspectives, made important contributions to the construction of a genealogy, or epistemology, of thought in the area of a philosophy of history.

In the astrophysics or cosmology of the present, a renaissance of teleological *Cosmology* thought is to be observed with the 'strong anthropic principle.' Simplified, this principle states that the universe is 'the way it is' in order that there be human life. Beginning in the 1980s or so, especially in → New Age thinking, references have reappeared to the model of the succession of ages, building on classical Greek models, the doctrine of yugas in Hindu thought, and astrological circular thinking. An indirect influence may perhaps also be ascribed to the ideas of mystic Joachim of Fiore (1145–1202).

Literature

LÖWITH, Karl, Meaning in History, Chicago 1949; POPPER, Karl R., The Poverty of Historicism, New York 1964; SPAEMANN, Robert/Löw, Reiner, Die Frage Wozu? Geschichte und Wiederentdeckung des teleologischen Denkens, Munich 1981.

→ *End/Eschaton, Evolutionism, History, Millenarianism/Chiliasm, Origin, Salvation/ Redemption*

Georg Hartmann

Televangelism

Elements of Televangelism

1. 'Tele-church,' or 'electronic church,' designates a North American phenomenon, and denotes the evangelization of believers, with the assistance of the medium of television, by preachers who are usually from the conservative Protestant camp. This programming is the basis of another term, 'televangelism.'

Various elements are presupposed for this special form of interior missionizing, or, better, 'awakening.' The principal elements in question are:

- A special *religious tradition* is supported by a particular conceptualization of salvation history (America as 'God's own country'; a special sense of mission)—a tradition that has traversed several phases of the awakening movements of the nineteenth and twentieth centuries. The religious tradition in question is sometimes characterized by a radical individualization of 'religion,' which, in turn, frequently goes hand in hand with patriotism, anti-Semitism, anti-modernism, and anti-state tendencies. Nevertheless, televangelism can be regarded only with reservations as a tendency to the privatization of religion (→ Private Religion).
- A *new form of the mediation of religion* is introduced, through the use of mass media, such as → television or radio. Despite televangelism's conservative stance and basis, it surrenders its reservations vis-à-vis modern technology, which is so useful in preparing for the 'Second Coming of Christ.' According to B. Bretthauer, conservative Protestants in the United States have a well-nigh unlimited monopoly on religious television, and control three-fourths of all religious radio programming.[1] This dominance explains why evangelical movements of awakening have been so successful in the last twenty-five years.
- A *more limited institutionalization and 'doctrinalization' of religion* is posited as a presupposition for personal religious experience—for the 'grace of a personal rebirth,' shifts to the center of religious life. Such an experience of grace is supposed to be reached through the special form of 'religious experience in the divine service.' This service is offered in the form of a well-presented television show, with gospel choir, entry of

the preacher, healing of the sick, and spontaneous conversion. Here the community of believers gradually becomes an 'audience cult' or even 'fan club,' supporting their special preacher with financial contributions, and intermeshed with other such audiences worldwide, by way of 'mega-' or 'para-churches.' This involvement does not necessarily mean the abandonment of local church communities: often, support of a tele-church and an active community life apart from it go hand in hand.

2. Billy Graham (born 1918) is an internationally famous awakening preacher. *The Television* Graham recognized the enormous potential of the new mass medium of *Preacher as a Star* television for the spread of his message as early as 1950. Just as prompt to seize on televised communication was Jerry Falwell, founder of the 'new Christian right' and the 'Moral Majority' (→ Fundamentalism). The medium often contributes to the popularity of the messenger, as in the case of Pat Robertson, founder of the Christian Coalition, who campaigned for the Republican presidential nomination in 1988. Currently his organization numbers more than one million committed members.

Today it is calculated that the audience of these religious programs comprises between 13 and 60 million viewers, mostly white Protestants. Moral questions constitute the main themes, such as that of → abortion, or of pre- or extra-marital sexual intercourse (in the 2004 presidential election, the issue of homosexuality played an important role as well, and helped the Bush campaign to win the race). But the conviction is propagated also that devout prayer, along with financial contributions, guarantees happiness, wealth, and professional success—the whole often coupled with a simplification of the facts at issue, and a populist anti-intellectualism. One premise for success—besides the topics of the preaching—is the professional planning and organization of the programming. Religious presentations are prepared as professional entertainment, with technical perfection, sensational showmanship, and frequently a powerful emotional charge (→ Charismatic Movement). The television preacher becomes a television star, who presents his audience with other stars as well.

The appeal for contributions is an important element. It is this mechanism that primarily sustains the tele-churches. More than ten percent of program time is spent on such appeals. Further sources of income are 'gifts' sold to the audiences, in the form of videos, books, cassettes, stickers, and so on. The format persists, despite the fact that a multi-religious research group in England took a poll in 1994, concluding that an amount of time devoted to self-advertising was undesirable (→ Television). The moneys serve mostly for the construction of churches, social institutions such as hospitals or kindergartens, as well as schools and universities, which form a further point of attraction for members and their relatives and friends.

Over and against the propaganda and announced intention of the TV *The 'Fan Club'* preachers, whose goal is the conversion of unbelievers and the awakening of those fallen from the faith, the audience of these broadcasts possesses a special affinity for the themes presented, and is highly selective. Viewers often already belong to the fundamentalist, charismatic, or evangelical spectrum, are usually associated with a particular religious group, or even are already members of the 'born again' (polls reveal that in 2004 thirty percent of the American people described themselves as 'Born Again Christians'). These observations support the assumption that, from the side of believers, what is sought from these broadcasts is a confirmation of their already confirmed faith position. This motive would also explain why the TV church cannot, or does not wish to, offer any replacement for an active community life, but rather must be interpreted as an additional variety of religious experience.

1. BRETTHAUER 1998, 232.

Literature

ALEXANDER, Bobby C., Televangelism Reconsidered: Ritual in the Search for Human Community, Atlanta 1994; BRETTHAUER, Berit, "Geschäftsmänner Gottes auf Erden: Fundamentalismus und Medien in den USA," in: BIELEFELDT, Heiner/HEITMEYER, Wilhelm (eds.), Politisierte Religion, Frankfurt/M. 1998, 232-255; KINTZ, Linda/LESAGE, Julia (eds.), Media, Culture, and the Religious Right, Minneapolis 1998; PACKARD, William, Evangelism in America: From Tents to TV, New York 1988; PECK, Janice, The Gods of Televangelism, Cresskill 1993; SCHULTZE, Quentin J., Televangelism and American Culture: The Business of Popular Religion, Grand Rapids 1995.

→ *Charismatic Movement, Civil Religion, Endowment/Foundation, Fundamentalism, Media, Mission, Private Religion, Sermon, Television*

Jutta Bernard

Television

Religion and Television

1. *Between appropriation and criticism*: The Christian churches have always made use of the various means available to them for the extension of their concerns, in every phase of the development of cultural techniques. They have not failed to participate in the emergence of television as the principal transmitter of social and cultural identity, and vehicle of everyday culture. In Germany, it was only six months after the first experimental radio broadcast of a popular concert on October 29, 1929 that the first church proclamations were received in the new medium. And in the wake of the development of television after the Second World War, the first church service was broadcast on December 4, 1952 during experimental television in West-Germany (1950–1953).

Parallel to the employment of the media, an intra-church discussion was held on the use of television as an 'instrument of proclamation.' The most problematic area seemed to be the new medium's focus on images. What was presented on television—so went the criticism—constructed an independent reality. From this point of view, the visually constructed television generates new frameworks of meaning that, for the viewers, on grounds of their seeming authenticity, are unimpeachably valid. If at all, then, the medium of film and television could only be an aid to the proclamation of the message, and might only possess a supporting character in the 'search for truth' and 'communication of truth.' This view had two results: (1) the postulate, emerging from their task of proclamation, that the churches possessed a genuine right to share in the use of the new medium; (2) the duty of the churches to set up fundamental propositions for the correct application of the new medium.[1] After 1945, these results practically meant a co-construction of, and co-responsibility for, public and legally controlled

A monument erected 1996 by the Afghani Taliban in their former capital Kandahar serves as a gallows. Here, bound to a steel scaffolding, old televisions and videos are pilloried. For the Taliban, a Pashtun militia of 'students of the Qur'an,' supported in the Afghan civil war by the United States and Pakistan (before they were attacked by the same allies), television and videos are 'idolaters,' that contravene the Islamic proscription of images by showing representations of living beings. The rigid measure can be explained only in terms of the general introduction and imposition of basic fundamentalist elements of Islam, such as that of the Sharia here being enforced by the Taliban.

television in West Germany. In order to avoid problems and minimize conflict, a distinction has always been made between 'proclamatory programs,' for whose content the churches have sole responsibility (in the Netherlands, Germany, etc.), and 'editorial programs,' for which the TV station's professional editorial staffs are co-responsible. The purposes pursued here are: (a) to report news in the areas of church, theology, and religion, (b) to promote the exchange of ideas and information concerning the church community, and (c) to promote a dialogue between church and world, and thereby to counteract societal splintering and polarization. The so-called 'third broadcast right' (the production of programs lying in the sole responsibility of the churches) is an exception in West Germany to which, otherwise, only governmental bodies or the parties are still entitled.

Criticism

An attitude toward the new medium of television, ranging from critical to altogether negative is observable in Islamic countries as well, especially in Iran and in Afghanistan. Here the most vociferous reproach is that of a 'cultural invasion by the West,' and this notion is part of the motivation for rigid prohibitions, ranging from the use of television for domestic programs, to the use of satellite antennae, with which 'un-Islamic broadcasts' from Hong Kong, Bombay, or the Arab Emirates could be received. To a certain extent, this process promotes an anticlerical attitude in the population, which feels increasingly threatened by the strict imposition of Islamic behavioral norms even in their private sphere.

3. a) *Religious Television and its audience*: It has become evident since the 1970s that not even the churches have succeeded in adapting the presentation of their content to the public taste. New approaches and contents are indicators here. Thus, an analytical type of religious program, along the

Audiences

lines of TV documentaries, replaces transmission of church services, and aesthetic, non-theological criteria prevail in films. The problem of a heterogeneous, and, especially, anonymous target audience actually compels an openness to a thematic multiplicity that sets frankly ethical, or generally socially relevant problems in the foreground. With contributions to subjects like abortion, genetic engineering, old age, and violence against women, it is guidance that takes center stage, rather than proclamation in the proper sense—unlike the topics and approaches of television's early days. This is also consistent with the observations of an English study from the year 1994.[4]

The expectations of viewers of the multi-religious target group (Christians, Muslims, Jews, Hindus, Pentecostalists), with varying degrees of personal engagement, was not limited, vis-à-vis the theme of religion on television, to the presentation of television preachers or religious programming. An overwhelming proportion of those polled spoke in favor of having religion presented in other program forms, such as news, discussions, films, and 'soap operas' or talk shows. Of interest here would be not only information on, and insight into, other faiths and values, but also positions taken on ethical questions. According to the respondents, religious groups should use television less for advertising themselves, or as sales institutions (videos), than primarily for news about themselves, and, besides edification, also for guidance and problem-solving in the area of ethical or religious conflicts. Most of those polled were in agreement that, in any case, religion should be one of the topics of television, and assigned television an educational function here. The content would be: (a) material on religious minorities, or on one's own religion; (b) material presented in the role of an intermediary among religious groups.

b) *Competitors in the 'market of opportunities'*: Public and commercial television are beginning to move closer together, and to shape one another, both in respect of topics addressed, and in the manners of the presenta-

'Entertainment'

tion of those topics. Here the magic word is 'entertainment,' inasmuch as adequate market shares must be guaranteed, along with viewer rates. Entertaining forms of presentation, such as discussions, or hybrid forms like features, mingle documentary elements with sequences from feature films, and have long since conquered their audiences on all channels. But it is likewise evident that particular religious subjects—frequently innovative, to stay abreast of commercial approaches—are tumbling out like an avalanche, since they can count on a particular reaction among the viewers.

4. *Television and Reality—or Reality of Television*: Television is not limited to the classic tasks of news, education, and entertainment. Today, as a medium of social communication, it plays a key role in the construction and profiling of 'reality' and public thought. As 'storyteller,' on the most diversified levels, it creates new meaning-connections and myths, and thereby captures areas traditionally occupied by other institutions, such as the religions. In the form of an experience of immediacy ("I was there!"), it increasingly transports world 'views' and images of the world into the living rooms. These images also help to shape public awareness concerning religion and religions. Important here are special structures of production, on the one hand—along with the content presented by way of the medium—and then, on the other hand, the function of the medium as 'cultural form.' Television shows what is current and can be sold, which therefore is subject to journalistic principles. Simultaneously, it mounts a claim to present an image of 'reality,' to 'document' reality. This 'authenticity of the shown'—up to and including the fiction of the unstructured documentary film of the 1960s and 1970s, with its spare, and aloof, or missing, commentary—keeps silent about the fact that film has a reality of its own, an inherent and constructed one, and that, therefore, film does not simply reflect reality as it was before any filming. Only by revising and touching up that which has been 'registered,' for example by forming it into the montage, can the purely photographical image convey to viewers authenticity and sense. Nor, correspondingly, is there any difference on the level of production between documentation and fiction. Both convert 'pre-filmic' reality into 'filmic.'

    Under these aspects—the journalistic as well as those pertaining to production technology—the question arises: to what extent can religion be conveyed over television? Or: how 'telegenic' is religion? On first impression, at least, the 'presentability' of the religious is mainly limited to the area of cult and ritual. Here the 'illustration drive' genuinely inherent in the medium has its escape valve. The presentation of subjects that promise exotic, mysterious, bizarre, or outlandish images can be concessions to the prevailing public taste, and reinforce trends, prejudices, or stereotypes. This dynamic holds especially when, in addition, the filmic means of metaphor or picture-distancing (by coloring, perspective-switch, 'worm's-eye view') is applied. Under these premises, films express more about our selves and our habits of seeing than they do about the object that they intend to picture. A further aspect of the medial transmission of strange cultures and religions is that the original meaning of religious signs loses its 'sense.' Loosed from the cultural context, the accent shifts from the religious experience of the 'believer' to pure information for the viewer. The presence of the camera, and the conditions of the 'shooting,' are not without influence on a cultic act, which in a given case becomes a pure presentation in terms of the premises of medial technique.

5. *Television as Storyteller*: On an entirely immediate level, television is first of all a teller of tales, taking up familiar myths or setting them in new meaning-connections. The topics of television productions, or of feature → films shown on television, include stories from the Judeo-Christian context (e.g., 'Bible films'; or stories from the life of Jesus), as well as from regions of Greco-Roman mythology (so that even a specific genre, the 'sandal film,' has developed). But television also goes back to forms of mythic thought and narrative in a more indirect way. Television stories are usually simple and

Conditions of Production

Content and Presentation

easy to understand, as well as socially acceptable. They are stories that contribute to the interpretation of life as it is lived, in a 'good and evil' schema (→ Dualism), combining the foreign with the familiar, and most often with a happy ending. At the same time, the complexity of life as it is actually lived is reduced to a minimum, and emotionally strengthened. Thus, on the one side, television is part of the familiar world of every day, taking up its relevant subjects, while, on the other, permitting 'side trips' into another, but, again, familiar, world, or 'reality', in which the expectation of deliverance, of victory of good over evil, is usually met. The subjects of love and violence, life and death, success and failure, are recounted, over and over again, as existential bases of human life, in ever new 'garments'—whether in the form of → science fiction, or in the regular noon talk show.

Television Rituals　　6. *The ritual dimension of television*: There has never been a pause in the discussion of whether television has taken over religious functions themselves, or is merely being used by religion(s) medially. Television seems to be possessed of quasi-divine qualities merely by the attributes attributed to it: omnipresence, ubiquity (global extension), as well as its seeming omniscience, that allows it to be assigned the import of a kind of 'last instance' (N. Schneider). To formulate it radically, 'reality' wins its existence ultimately by way of its presence on television: what is not conveyed here, has but a slight chance of being perceived at all. Further: television itself gains a ritual dimension, by (a) creating 'television rituals,' by (b) structuring and ritualizing the everyday, through the cyclic character of the presentation of its products, and by way of its use, and (c) 'transcending' the everyday, and—as with traditional religious rituals—creating a 'we-consciousness' (G. Thomas). Major events, such as sports presentations (e.g., the World Soccer Championship in France in 1998, which celebrated its 'soccer gods' altogether as such; → Sports), or the funeral of the British 'Queen of Hearts,' Lady Di, who died in 1997 in an automobile accident, are not only televised globally, but are first formed, or even first made possible by television. Television, then, on one hand, can be regarded as an inseparable part of the ritual event (the sports program corresponds to the sports presentation), and on the other, the 'TV ritual' in question can be also a ritual event on television itself. A further aspect is normative here: repeatability, which creates rites of memory. This dimension was shown, for example in the first days after the death of the British princess: on German national television twenty-five programs were aired on twelve channels between August 29 to September 1, not counting those showing the ceremony of mourning or stories from the life of the Princess of Wales. Then, in relatively short order, the first TV-films were produced, retelling, in modern terms, the ascent of Cinderella to 'High Society Queen.'

Furthermore, intrinsic to television itself, and to its use, are ritual moments directed, in principle, to periodic return. These moments structure the experience of time. Continuity results from the expectation of regular returning occurrences, such as the news, at a particular hour of the day, or the broadcast of a weekly installment of a series. Television thus offers fixed points, and order, in daily reality. Here, content is frequently secondary, and reception or choice of program comes by reason of particular viewing times (e.g. Saturday or Sunday evening), or the offer made by the individual channels. Once more the question arises, as to what function may television have for the individual. As part of a pluralistic society, television has taken over the task of providing us with reflection on our culture. In reports, TV-films, plays, or talk shows, reality is not only transmitted, but newly constituted. The materials of the new constitution are conveyed in the media, and in daily reality. Sentiments like "I am there, and I feel that way too," are bounded by time but are surely globally 'networked.' I am part of a community of viewers, and this participation, for the moment, can determine my identity. Transitory communities are formed, along with the ritual structuring of everyday life, the satisfaction of the need for order, and the simplification of complex, immense connections. Aside from this, the question whether television can be an equal compensation for gratifying religious requirements of its audience is still unanswered.

1. Conciliar Decree on Social Communications Media *Inter Mirifica*, art. 3, issued December 4, 1963.
2. GUNTER/VINEY 1994.

Literature

DAVIS, Douglas, The Five Myths of Television Power or Why the Medium Is Not the Message, London 1993; GUNTER, Barrie/VINEY, Rachel, Seeing Is Believing: Religion and Television in the 1990s, London 1994; LINDERMAN, Alf, The Reception of Religious Television: Social Semeiology Applied to an Empirical Case Study, Stockholm 1996; NEWMAN, Jay, Religion vs. Television: Competitors in Cultural Context, Westport/London 1996; PECK, Janice, The Gods of Televangelism, Cresskill 1993; SCHNEIDER, Norbert, "Das Fernsehen: ein Mythenproduzent?," in: HICKETHIER, Knut (ed.), Fernsehen. Wahrnehmungswelt, Programminstitution und Marktkonkurrenz, Frankfurt/M. 1992, 109-127; SCHULTZE, Quentin J., Televangelism and American Culture: The Business of Popular Religion, Grand Rapids 1995; THOMAS, Günter, Medien—Ritual—Religion: Zur religiösen Funktion des Fernsehens, Frankfurt/M. 1998.

→ *Communication, Film, Media, Publicity, Televangelism*

Jutta Bernard

Terrorism

1. The word 'terror' (Lat., *terror*) designates fear and horror, whether or not intended. *Terrorism*, on the other hand, is a label for strategies that consciously introduce terror in order to reach goals extrinsic to it. It is a matter of a kind of 'symbolical violence' or 'force' (→ Conflict/Violence). The actual intended objects of terrorism are less the persons directly affected, or their pain, than those in whom the pain or fear of terror inspires its own terror; this result is an ulterior intent in the minds of the terrorists. Whether, in what measure, and in whom a given deed of violence will inspire fear and horror, depends on the collective fears, norms, and opportunities for communication that prevail in the cultures in which they are perceived. Nearly all known cultures accept certain forms of violence as legitimate, or at least as de facto normal. Thus, fear and paralyzing shock are to be expected only when and where violent deeds transcend the expected borders of inter-human violence. In ancient Eastern mythologies, the capacity and willingness for in- and super-human violence was especially ascribed to deities and

On November 4, 1995, Israeli Prime Minister Yitzhak Rabin was murdered in Tel Aviv. In recognition of his work in negotiations between Israel and the Palestinians, he had received the Nobel Peace Prize in 1994, together with Yassir Arafat and Shimon Perez. During the weeks after the act of terror, persons, mainly youth, assembled at the square where he had been murdered, and they held protest vigils, carrying storm lanterns, flowers, and letters. The wall at the place of the crime was spontaneously filled with images and graffiti. The government offered its contribution only later, with a memorial plate in the soil and by officially naming the square "Rabin Place." The graffiti, of which the picture shows a section, were varnished, and kept as a historical memorial. In this time of terror, the graffiti writers adopted the Hebrew biblical expression, *Yakum Damo*—"His Blood Be Avenged!" Whether these words represent a petition to God or a challenge to human beings, remains ambiguous. The references to the Song of Moses (Deut 32:43), as well as that to Ps 79:10, indicate that the murder calls for the wrath of God, as it brought down a person who acted according to God's will, Yitzhak Rabin. The expression used at parting, *Shalom, Haver*—"Goodbye, Friend" (on the left, under the portrait)—originally an expression of sympathy, grief, and shock, has long since become a widespread saying. It was the last sentence in President Bill Clinton's address (otherwise in English) at the funeral ceremony. Meanwhile T-shirts and bumper stickers recall the deceased. Members of the Socialist Party use it to greet Rabin as a comrade. Partisans of the peace movement appeal to him as a person of like mind. And a fragment in the picture suggests the frequently applied verse *Ata Haser* ("We Miss You"). The greeting of peace has become a slogan, with which inhabitants of Israel express their support for the peace process. (A. Kleefeld and Kirsten Holzapfel)

divinities: the Hebrew Bible includes the Great Flood, the destruction of Sodom and Gomorrah, punitive droughts. However, in societies with unstable hierarchies, conscious and unilateral contravention of social moral bounds has also repeatedly served as a means to the establishment or maintenance of everyday relations of power. The demonstrative transgression of the 'normal' horizon of expectancy of inter-human power relationships underscored the agents' pretensions, beyond or above the conventions of existing society. It could also serve to surround them with the halo of categorical, almighty power (→ Government/Rule/Politics/State). Frequently, there was also an 'emphatically public' presentation of symbolical acts of violence (public executions, murder of highly placed personalities in public places, destruction of public places of cult).

2. In the political vocabulary of the modern age, the designation 'terror' has been linked principally to conceptualizations of tactics of terror and intimidation mounted by the state. Here the prime exemplar is the *Terreur* of the Jacobin revolutionary government in France (1792–1794), where the purpose was to intimidate the royalist opposition and establish a realm of 'virtue' (→ Revolution [French]). Just as, later, with the 'Red Terror' of the Bolshevist revolutionary government in Russia, the concept of 'terror' was utilized here by the agents themselves, namely, in the (positive) sense of a particularly reckless application of violence for the purpose of creating a perfect society in this world. Assaults of terrorism by anarchists on leading officials in the nineteenth century were frequently justified as 'creative' acts, for the construction of an ideal society, one without state or God.

From the Terreur *to* Terrorism

In the twentieth century, the concept was transferred more and more to the work of *non-state* agents. In this connection, it sank to the status of an—often polemical—collective category for forms of illegitimate political violence that were to be spurned. The viewpoints as to what was to be regarded as illegitimate violence, of course, and what was not, diverge widely, as dictated by the position of the respective speaker. Hence the consecrated bon mot, "One man's terrorist is another's freedom fighter." Western mass media and governments today are overwhelmingly inclined to label politically motivated deeds of violence as 'terrorism' when they (seemingly) are perpetrated by non-state agents, and are directed against civilian, non-military targets.

3. Many religions endorse terrorism to a limited degree. For example, it has often been sanctioned as applied to lawbreakers or the heterodox. Nonetheless, mono-causal connections between religion and terrorism seem almost nonexistent. Organized religious terrorism generally presupposes a social environment that supports, or tolerates, the agents of terrorism. Here, the borderline between organized terrorism and the 'spontaneous' terror of individual agents is fleeting. Radical religious milieus and doctrines that justify violence promote militancy among their followers. The willingness of agents to risk their own lives in public assaults (as, for example, with 'suicide attacks' by Shia and Sunni extremists in Lebanon and Palestine) need not always be based only on religious considerations, of course. Agents' psychological and material problems as well, coercion, and coincidence can play a role. But, interpreted as a testimonial to the power of one's own belief, such assaults can produce a martyrial cult, or, in case a religious disposition to a martyrial cult already exists, can be stylized as models that inspire imitation (→ Martyr).

Religion and Terrorism

State Terrorism, Religious

(a) Massive terrorist violence has emerged in history especially where the means for it have been abundantly present, namely, with the state. Accordingly, religious state-terrorism has prevailed where particular religions have ranked as beneficial to state or community. Even the biblical Book of Deuteronomy provides for horrible deterrents against polytheistic cults in Israel. Prominent examples from recent times have been, in medieval Europe, the persecutions of the Albigenses and the pogroms against the Jews, or elsewhere, the violent Shiitization of → Iran in the sixteenth century under the Safawids, or Saint Bartholomew's Night (1572) in France. If Communism and Fascism can be conceptualized as secularized → 'political religions', then the Anti-Semitic terror of the National Socialists, or of the Stalinist mass liquidation of 'class enemies' can be labeled as religious state-terrorism in the broadest sense.

Assassination and Tyrannicide

(b) As the principle of divine right in government was superseded by the evident supremacy of material might, the notion gained prominence that 'unrighteous' rulers might be violently removed, for purposes of the reestablishment of the divine order. In ancient Athens, the regicides Harmodios and Aristogeiton were honored with the first statues dedicated to humans rather than gods. Breaches of the unity of throne and altar in medieval Europe repeatedly led to the 'excommunication' of disobedient rulers by parts of the clergy, and, in case of conflict, could occasion a demonstrative justification of 'tyrannicide' by Catholic scholars. Standing as examples are the murders of Henry III (1589) and Henry IV (1610) of France. In the twentieth century, religiously motivated assassinations of politicians of one's own religious community reflected the pairing of religious fanaticism with nationalistic ambitions, as with the murder of Mahatma → Gandhi by a Hindu (1948), Anwar al-Sadat by Islamists (1981), or Yitzhak Rabin by a Jewish extremist in 1995.

Non-State Terror Groups

c) With non-state groups, the organized transition to terrorism has nearly always depended on the concurrence of certain conditions of society, politics, and historical attitude:
   (1) A perception of prevailing society as basically unjust.
   (2) An activist, world-altering ethic.
   (3) A consciousness of one's own military weakness.
   (4) The reasonable expectation that, through spectacular deeds of violence, publicly effective signs can be posited.
   (5) The availability of adequate logistics.
Thus, in the first century, an especially militant group of Jewish zealots, called by the Romans *sicarii* (from Lat., *sica*, 'dagger'), would publicly stab to death Romans in Palestine, or prominent Jews who cooperated with them, in order to set off an eschatological conflict between Romans and Jews. The Shia sect of Nizari Ismaelites that became famous in Europe under the name of 'assassins' (from Ar., 'hashish-eaters'; → Intoxication/Drugs/Hallucinogens) compensated for their political and military weakness by spectacular murders of highly placed personalities. In neither case was it only the killing of political adversaries that kindled fear and horror, but the impression of confronting a hidden power that attacked from out of the dark.

In the nineteenth and twentieth centuries, a good many nationalistic movements took up terrorism. It is true that, until into the 1970s, religion was
often an important component of the formation of a national tradition,
for example in the case of Algerian, Armenian, Chechnian, Cypriot Greek,
Hindu, Irish, Palestinian, Serbian, Tamil, or Zionist nationalism. But the
transition to terrorism was accomplished predominantly by organizations in
which secularists provided the tone—for instance, by the Zionist *Irgun Zeva'i
le-Umi* ("National Military Organization"), the Algerian *Front de Libération
Nationale* (FLN), the Irish Republican Army (IRA), the People's Front for
the Liberation of Palestine (PFLP), or the Liberation Tigers of Tamil Eelam
(LTTE) in Sri Lanka.

*Nationalistic and
National Religious
Terror Groups*

Only since the 1980s has the attention of the international mass media
been much more attracted to acts of terrorism with religious or national
religious background. Of high symbolical meaning was the success of the
Iranian Revolution (1978–1979; → Iran), which, with the four hundred
forty-four day 'Teheran Scourge Affair' (1979–1981), humiliated a world
power, the United States of America, and was able to challenge the consensus of the Western world, with the → Fatwa of Ayatollah → Khomeini
against British writer Salman Rushdie (1989), which was tantamount to a
death sentence. Then, further, the suicide attacks of Shia activists on American and Israeli troops in Lebanon (1983–1985) propagated the conviction
that religious enthusiasm sparked less fear of death than readiness for sacrifice, and thereby superior power in battle. Relatively successful groups like
the Lebanese Hizbulla, in the wake of their military consolidation, distinguished ever more clearly between attacks on military and civilian targets,
while weaker religious militant groups, in quest of unprotected targets in
the 1990s, have multiplied blood baths among civilians, front and foremost
among these organizations being the Algerian *Groupe Islamique Armée*
(GIA), the Egyptian *Jamaa Islamiyya,* and the Zionist *Kach* Party.

Apocalyptic groups, awaiting a prompt end of the world (→ End/Eschaton),
are especially inclined to activities of terrorism in terms of the world crises
that they foresee. When they announce the crisis that, in many traditions
(such as that of the Christian → Apocalypse of John) is to proclaim the approaching final struggle between good and evil, they not only long for it to
come, but (a) try to hasten it by acts of violence that effect polarization (poi-
son-gas attack in the Tokyo subway, March 1995; plans of Jewish extremists
to destroy the Dome of the Rock in Jerusalem), or (b) stockpile weapons in
an attempt at least to prepare for it (Branch Davidian commune in Waco,
Texas, 1993). At the opposite pole on the scale of violence stand introverted
attempts to reach a new and better world by collective suicide (doubtless
not always voluntary), for example the mass suicides of the members of the
People's Temple under Jim Jones in Guyana (1978), of the Solar Temple in
Switzerland and Canada (1995, 1997), or of Heaven's Gate in the United
States (1997).

Apocalyptic Groups

Purposive terror against civilians emerges from movements with a religious
coloring, as well, which struggle with social developments or particular state
institutions, laws, or measures. These traditions early included the terror
campaigns of the American → Ku Klux Klan against Afro-Americans after
emancipation, as well as, in more recent times, lethal assaults on → abortion clinics by American 'defenders of life,' or, again, the bomb attack on

*Social Religious
Groups*

the United States Government office building in Oklahoma by a Christian 'patriotic militia' (1995), with which the government in Washington was supposed to have been struck a blow as a conspiratorial mythical symbol for foreign domination.

It is questionable whether the high numbers of victims registered in the 1990s, especially with attacks by religious groups, are to be referred mainly to the religious motivation of the agents. Equally important elements could be an ever more intense competition for the attention of the mass media, and improved defensive measures for military and state objects.

Literature

DEMANDT, Alexander (ed.), Das Attentat in der Geschichte, Cologne 1996; FORD, Franklin L., Political Murder: From Tyrannicide to Terrorism, Cambridge 1985; HALL, John R., Apocalypse Observed: Religious Movements and Violence in North America, Europe, and Japan, London/New York 2000; JUERGENSMEYER, Mark, Terror in the Mind of God: The Global Rise of Religious Violence, Berkeley 2000; LAQUEUR, Walter, A History of Terrorism, New Brunswick 2001; LINCOLN, Bruce, Holy Terrors: Thinking about Religion after 9/11, Chicago 2002; RAPOPORT, David C., "1984: Fear and Trembling. Terrorism in Three Religious Traditions," in: American Political Science Review 78 (1984), 658-677; REICH, Walter (ed.), Origins of Terrorism: Psychologies, Ideologies, Theologies, States of Mind, Cambridge 1990.

→ *Anarchism, Conflict/Violence, End/Eschaton, Fanaticism, Fundamentalism, Political Religion, Revolution (French), Violence*

Thomas Scheffler

Teutons

Discovery of the Teutons in Romanticism

1. a) The early nineteenth century's emphasis on appreciating one's own people and history resulted in a rediscovery not only of the Middle Ages, but also Teutonic prehistory. Research into the folktale, popular sagas, and folk usages began during this time. Jacob Grimm (1785–1863) attempted to expose ancient, concealed folk material, and thereby, presumably, to meet with a plethora of pagan relics of pre-Christian times. This work, however, has been surpassed by today's scholarship. In the popularization of ancient Teutonic myths (*Walhall, Götterdämmerung* [Ger., 'Twilight of the Gods']), a special contribution has been Richard Wagner's musical dramatic cycle, *Der Ring der Nibelungen* (Ger., "The Ring of the Nibelungs"), an 'art myth' referring to the thirteenth-century epic, *Nibelungenlied* ("Song of the Nibelungs"). Wagner's work applies a variety of Nordic Teutonic poems. Religious elements, orbiting the questions of guilt and redemption, do arise here, but they exclude the philosophical, educating and educated, religion of the nineteenth century.

Ariosophy

After the founding of the Reich (Empire) in 1871, the political right appropriated the symbol of Teutonic spirituality (*Völkische* Religion), and shaped it, in varying fashion, into a Romantic popular, and anti-Semitic, 'art faith.' 'Ariosophy' preached redemption by a strict separation of races, and the subordination of presumably inferior races to the superior ones. This interest in the Teutonic, which served certain currents in → National Socialism (Himmler's foundation *Ahnenerbe*, Ger., 'Ancestral Legacy'; Alfred Rosenberg), largely collapsed after 1945. Nevertheless, some groups of this circle (on the political and cultural right wing of postwar society) are still found today as continuations or revivals of their earlier forms.

b) Currently, on the one side, there are organized communities, resembling orders. They mount appeals to the organizational forms and content of the popular neo-paganism of the first half of the century (Armanic Order, *Godi, Germanische Glaubensgemeinschaft* ['Teutonic Faith Community'], *Treuekreis Artglaube Irminsul* ['Faithful *Irminsul* Circle of Race Belief']). On the other side, there appears a universalistic 'neo-Teutonism,' more consistent with the new nature piety of American origin, British neo-Celtism, and other Western and Eastern 'spiritual paths.' While the older neo-paganism evinced a racist piety (→ Race/Racism), the later 'esoteric' neo-paganism, under the application of the same myths, represents a variety of today's feminist ecological piety. This distinction says nothing as yet about reciprocal influencing and possible future developments.

'Neo-Teutonism'

Teutons, today, serve not only as the subject of their myths, but also as an object of the new myths of a racist or ecological spirituality, which in turn serves to proffer an alternative vis-à-vis Christian conceptualizations of God. Odin, then, according to a widespread interpretation, represents the shamanic archetype, and the Eddaic narratives serve to describe the spiritual effects of corresponding archetypes. There are no myths of old-Teutonic religion, but only narratives calculated to establish a cosmic-ecological and feministic-psychological spirituality of the close of the twentieth century.

2. The history of the research shows how little we actually know about the life of the Teutons. Under 'Teutonic religions' are understood tribal religions of Northern, Central, and Eastern European peoples of related language and culture (→ Celts; Europe I), from their first mention by ancient writers (first century BCE) to the Christianization of Scandinavia, which had been accomplished by the eleventh century. Like all of Europe's pre-modern cultures, these peoples were agrarian societies (→ Agrarian Religion/Agrarian Magic). The subjects of their myths and cults are fertility, life and death, and defense from outside enemies. Along with vegetation festivals, we have reports of rites of transition for the life cycle. The custom of leaving burial gifts at gravesites, of building mounds or rune stones on the graves of princes, indicates that a life after death was held to differ from earthly life only in incidentals.

Teutonic Religions

a) *Cult* was practiced at determinate places. There were also, among the Teutonic peoples, sacred functionaries, whose tasks included the celebration of public cult as well as the supervision of sacred law. Holy women served as seers, who could also bestow great power among peoples with whom oracle and omen were of high importance. A matriarchal societal structure, however, cannot be concluded from these facts. Religion focused on the existence of associations of kinship ('tribes'): thus, it was a public concern, which could also have a juridical character. Extremities such as famine or disease, and events of war, were accompanied by sacred acts. Among them were the war sacrifices in sacred glades, attested by literature and archaeology. Human beings were also sacrificed.

b) The *gods and goddesses* of the Teutons were figures of an agricultural world, who had to protect fertility and ward off evil. The three supreme gods, whom Roman historian Tacitus enumerates in his *Germania*, are colorless, and unspecific, and must by no means be identified with otherwise known gods Tivaz, Wodan/Odin, and Donar. Tacitus or his informant translates their function in Roman terms, giving their names as Jupiter, Mercury, and Hercules, responsible respectively for power, act/mobility, and strength. We have little concrete information about the veneration of these deities. But they were neither nature gods nor ethical ideals, but, as tribal divinities, are comparable to the original state gods of Rome.

The appeal of neo-Teutonic circles to medieval Nordic sources is problematic. Not only Icelandic sagas and Skalden songs, but also the two collections of myths under the name of *Edda* ("Songs of Edda," and the "Edda of Snorri Sturleson," both of the thirteenth century) have appeared only against a Christian background, and are therefore not unreservedly or unconditionally applicable as sources for pre-Christian religious history.

Literature

Sources: CHURCH, Alfred J. et al. (trans.), The Germania of Tacitus, London 1924; DRONKE, Ursula (ed./trans.), The Poetic Edda, Oxford 1969; Eadem (ed./trans.), The Poetic Edda, vol. II: Mythological Poems, Oxford 1997; RYDER, Frank G. (trans.), The Song of the Nibelungs: A Verse Translation from the Middle High German "Nibelungenlied," Detroit 1962.

Secondary Literature: ACKER, Paul/LARRINGTON, Carolyne (eds.), The Poetic Edda: Essays on Old Norse Mythology, New York 2002; BECK, Heinrich et al., Germanische Religionsgeschichte, Quellen und Quellenprobleme, Berlin 1992; CUSACK, Carole M., Conversion among the Germanic Peoples, London 1998; DAVIDSON, H. R. Ellis, Gods and Myths of Northern Europe, Harmondsworth 1964; Eadem, The Lost Beliefs of Northern Europe, London 1993; DE VRIES, Jan, Altgermanische Religionsgeschichte, 2 vols., Berlin ²1959 (still an important work, despite its uncritical use of mythological and historical sources); GOODRICK-CLARKE, Nicholas, Black Sun: Aryan Cults, Esoteric Nazism and the Politics of Identity, New York 2002; Idem, The Occult Roots of Nazism: Secret Aryan Cults and Their Influence on Nazi Ideology, rev. ed., London 2004; LINDOW, John, Handbook of Norse Mythology, Santa Barbara 2001; RUSSELL, James C., The Germanization of Early Medieval Christianity: A Sociohistorical Approach to Religious Transformation, New York 1994; SIMEK, Rudolf, Dictionary of Northern Mythology, Cambridge 1993; STANLEY, Eric Gerald, Imagining the Anglo-Saxon Past, Cambridge 2000; WOLF, Jürgen, Neopaganismus und Stammesreligionen, Münster 1997.

→ *Celts, Europe I, National Socialism, Paganism/Neopaganism, Reception*

Jürgen Wolf

Text / Textual Criticism

1. The word 'text' derives from the Latin *textus*, 'tissue,' and then acquires the meaning, still familiar today, of a supply of linguistic signs written down and gathered in a 'work' or textual corpus—a manuscript, a novel, a sermon, a sacred writing such as the → Bible or the → Qur'an. The rhetorical concept of 'text' was coined by Roman orator Quintilian, first in the sense of

an 'address connection' (9, 4, 13), in his influential work *Institutio Oratoria* (c. 95 CE). Humanistic philology adopted this concept, and applied it to the object of its work: a 'text' became that to which a relation was articulated in the form of a commentary. The concept established itself only against the background of a philologically oriented culture of explication (→ Hermeneutics; Exegesis)—thus, in dealing with written statements whose direct understanding became problematic, due to their great age, or on other cultural grounds. Since humanism and the → Renaissance, an examination of the texts of ancient cultures has formed the field of activity where philological textual criticism has established the central importance of the concept of 'text' as 'work with texts.' In recent scholarship in the area of literature and linguistics, the concept of 'text' is preferably applied as a communicatively founded basic concept, vis-à-vis concepts of genre (Fr., *genera*) like 'poetry' and → 'literature.' It seems impossible to give a clear definition of a word whose denotation is as general as 'text,' which has entered everyday language. Still, one must keep in mind the fact that its application is not restricted to written fixations of linguist communication, but that, in today's semiotics compositions, there is a more generalized concept of text. The latter also includes other communicative statements based on systems of signs that are responsive to repetition and to the adoption of relationships, such as image-signs ('icons'), or ritual gestures (→ Symbol/Sign/Gesture).

2. Production of religious texts can occur orally or in writing. Religious communities may acknowledge a more or less broadly apprehended → canon as the set of binding religious statements. These then receive a specially legitimized rank and value vis-à-vis other religious texts. As a rule, canonized texts manifest an extremely narrow spectrum of variation, in the oral as in the written traditions. Thus, in the discoveries at → Qumran, an additional textual constancy for individual books of the Bible is evident over a millennium. In this connection, the concept 'book religion' is relevant. It denotes the peculiarity of a religious community in centering its identity on a sacred writing. Judaism, Christianity, and Islam were constantly aware of it, although, for example, it is also to be found in the religion of the Sikhs. It is striking, however, that, unless they are produced in special forms for sacred use (Torah scroll), canonized texts are not linked to a determinate medium of conveyance: the Bible, New Testament, or Qur'an are found today digitalized on CD-ROMs or on internet servers.

Textual Media, Textual Constancy, and Canonization

3. Texts consist of a core text, and a descriptive or disclosing 'paratext,' such as title, preface, notations, marginal material, subtitles, dividing signs (see diagrams at → Talmud). Even as 'sacred scripture,' they are artificial and artful linguistic images. These signs are artificial because, despite their frequent claim to divine inspiration and authorship (verbal inspiration, 'word of God' or 'message from the beyond'), scriptures are the result of an often complicated process of textual production and redaction, representing a multiplicity of textual 'genres' (genera), in which, as in the Gospels of the New Testament, similitudes (parables), sayings (in Gk., *logia*), prayers, hymns ("Magnificat"), miracle accounts, and so forth are gathered together. These same signs are artistic because they contain, or can be read as, literary texts, because they are composed by way of rhetorical ornament, and because they are rendered aesthetic by poetical, dramatic, or narrative means. Texts

Form of the Text: Textual Loci (Genres) and Poetic/Rhetorical Quality

in the Hebrew Bible that employ lyric art-forms, include, for instance, the Psalms, and the Song of Songs. The form of the short story is employed as in the arrangement of the material on Joseph. In the Bible, very heterogeneous material is presented literally, and, to an extent, is elaborated in multiple ways. In the Qur'an, instead, one observes that stylistic gestalt takes effect even in a religious textual corpus that essentially owes its existence to one person, and that this need by no means stand in contradiction with the subjective honesty of the presumed author. To an extent, the fact of a conscious conformity to the exemplar of other religious assertions can go hand in hand with spontaneous religious emotion. The all but constant employment of rhyming prose certainly stands under the influence of ancient Arab *Kahin* sayings, but is first of all an adequate medium of expression or proclamation especially of eschatological content. Later, as the regulation of the Muslim community system by way of juridical elements moved into the foreground for Muhammad, rhyming prose became an outward stylistic trait.

Authorship

The special → authority of religious texts, the claim to be indeed the word of God, offers various strategies of legitimatization that lay special claim to the concept of authorship. This authority is especially evident with the concrete authorship of a particular person, if, for example, the religious founder steps forward as personal author (Mani as author of the *Kephalaia*, Muhammad as author of the Qur'an, Hubbard as author of *Dianetics*). Anonymity, as in the case of the Bible, or with Vedic hymns, is often to be observable bearing high authority with religious writings. But false ascriptions (intentional or in good faith), as well, to persons of great authority, but frequently of doubtful historicity, are also often encountered ('pseudepigraphy,' e.g., Denis the Areopagite, or Hermes Trismegistus).

Intertextuality

Even with religious texts, as with fictional literary texts, various textual relations can be established. Of course, account must be taken of the fact that religious texts normally act outside purely literary validity, even in the area of religious practice. Intertextuality—the more or less broadly defined reciprocal relation among texts—is a very important phenomenon with religious texts. New texts emerge against the background of (and often in competition with) established religious structures and their texts. The meaning context of religious assertions is textual content, fixed in writing in the same degree as the social environment is fixed.

Dealing with the Text

4. The historical process of the forming of canonized sacred texts, when these are fixed 'to the last jot and tittle,' necessitates their exposition and commentary. The longer they have been fixed, the stronger this necessity will prove. In many religious organizations, in parallel with the canonization of the text corpus, there emerges a monopoly of interpretation on the part of religious → 'specialists,' who specify rules of exposition and establish dogmatic interpretations. This theological 'exegesis' enfolds the sacred text in an aura of commentaries, marginal glosses, or collections of excerpts ('catenae'), thereby producing further text. To its corpus corresponds everyday, practical propagation, then exposition and interpretive adaptation of the text in the life of religious communities.

5. In the course of historical development, the strict establishment of the sacred text has led to the ever-growing challenge of the maintenance of the text—that is, of the perfectly accurate conveyance of the text, even in an oral form. A typical example of a religious culture at whose center stands a sacred text, is → Islam. The → Qur'an is the first book to appear in Arab literature. As the Prophet died, he did not leave the Qur'an as a book completely composed; rather, the individual parts of the revelatory text lay before its redactors, and they set to work on it some twenty years after → Muhammad's death. From the very beginning until today, with the conveyance of its exact text, an oral communication of the Qur'an, along with its written form, has played an important role. The textual accuracy of versions of the Qur'an had wide-reaching cultural consequences. A concern for the fixing of the sacred text, and for its propagation—concretely, for the copying of its manuscripts—promoted the development of Arab script (→ Writing), in whose connection a lexicography and grammar developed, as well. In parallel, out of the collections and critical judgments of the oral reports of the words and deeds of the Prophet and his contemporaries, a scholarship and historiography of the Qur'anic tradition appeared. The foundations of legal scholarship lay here, as well: the Qur'an, and the reports of the words and deeds of the Prophet were soon established as the most important sources for Islamic law. Beginning in the ninth century, translations of especially scientific texts from the Greek welded two cultures of textual tending and exposition: the Arabic exposition of the Qur'an, and the ancient tradition of—profane—textual commentary. This historical fact shows—over against fundamentalistic positions—that historical developments owing to foreign influences have an essential share in the whole culture, and thus in the interpretation regarded by a culture as valid for its sacred scripture.

Maintenance, Conveyance, Tradition of the Text—Example of the Qur'an

6. Christianity established a special approach to dealing with the canonical text. There emerged a commitment to philological confrontation with original texts, in their original language, and this in the sense of the humanistic watchword, "Back to the sources" (*Ad fontes*), and of the Reformation slogan, *Sola Scriptura*, "by Scripture alone." The text of the Bible was then approached with the same philological toolbox with which, for example, the ancient pagan texts were examined, and an entirely new relation developed to traditional exegesis, which was now measured more and more by the touchstone of textual criticism. Pursued with consistency, this route led to an approach to the text of the Bible as one literary testimonial among others, and today the text of the Hebrew Bible is considered in close connection with other texts of the Ancient Near Eastern environment. The recognitions gained by such a procedure place the claims of the religious proclamation before a difficult challenge to their exclusivity. Thus, for example, Ugaritic research showed that psalms heretofore understood as referring to the one God of Israel—so that plural forms of the name of God have traditionally been interpreted as the 'majestic plural' of that name—exhibit close parallels with Ugaritic hymns that are addressed to several gods. A philological approach to the biblical text in terms of textual criticism first found acceptance in → Protestantism. At the roots of this acceptance stood Luther's efforts to make the text of the Bible accessible to every believer, by way of his translation of the Bible. A correct understanding of the biblical text was then seen as a duty, for whose performance concrete efforts must be undertaken, and in which it was perfectly possible to fail. In the course of the nineteenth

Textual Analysis through Historical Criticism

century, along with a traditional theological exegesis, there arose—against opposition that was sometimes robust—a textual scholarship and culture of interpretation in terms of scientific historical criticism. This approach, now used with the Christian Scriptures themselves, gradually succeeded in establishing itself in the institutional context of theological teaching.

Thus the situation was created that has split today's Christian theologies between a pretension to scholarship—hegemonic, rational, and secular—and the actual handing on and expounding of the faith. This development repeatedly leads to tensions, some of them powerful, even within the confessions, as, for example, in the case of the clash over modernism in the Catholic Church, or in the confrontations over → fundamentalism and the Evangelical movement.

Literature

Battersby, James L., Reason and the Nature of Texts, Philadelphia 1996; Black, David A. (ed.), Rethinking New Testament Textual Criticism, Grand Rapids 2002; Dane, Joseph A., The Myth of Print Culture: Essays on Evidence, Textuality, and Bibliographical Method, Toronto 2003; Greetham, David C., Textual Scholarship: An Introduction, New York ²1994; McGann, Jerome J., A Critique of Modern Textual Criticism, Chicago 1983; Thorpe, James, Principles of Textual Criticism, San Marino 1972; Tov, Emanuel, Textual Criticism of the Hebrew Bible, Minneapolis/Assen 1992.

For further literature, see the entries "Bible," "Qur'an," "Writing."

→ *Bible, Book, Language, Literature, Qur'an, Symbol/Sign/Gesture, Oral Tradition, Qur'an, Talmud, Tradition, Translation, Writing*

Heidrun Eichner

Theater

1. Originally, 'theater' denotes a 'space for viewing' (in Gk., *théatron*, from *theásthai*, 'consider,' 'contemplate,' 'observe'). In this space, human beings and their acting (in Gk., *dráma*), are brought before an audience as a scene, whether in free, improvised performance, or on the basis of (poetical) narrative. To theater as an art form, then, belong players (actors), audience, and theater as a place where acting occurs. Depending on whether the presentation—or performance—prioritizes verbal or nonverbal means of communication, the term 'speaking theater' or 'body theater' is used. In sacred theater, expressive means of presentation are often preferred that emphasize the body: → masks, → dance, gestures of the body (→ Symbol/Sign/Gesture).

In sacred → drama, means or media are introduced as part of complex rituals. But in many cultural traditions, secular forms of theater have developed, from or together with, sacred forms. In turn, and in manifold wise, these are enriched with religious content and means of expression. Secular theater can be a place for the revitalization, aestheticization, and production of myths, as in the Western theater of modernity, where ancient myths have come to be presented out of 'pagan,' Greco-Roman tradition. As a 'moral arrangement,' it can reinforce, or call into question, the ethical demands of a religion; or it can itself seek to undertake ritual tasks that are equivalent to those of religion.

This Buddhist demon theater from Ambalangoda, in Sri Lanka, is to be found today in the puppet theater museum of the Alois A. K. Raab foundation, Kaufbeuren. It is a mechanical theater, with two-dimensional wooden figures on a three-level stage. The lower and upper levels are cut off by swathes of flame. The figures' parts are movable, to an extent, with ropes and pulleys. The theater originated in mid-twentieth century, and was set up for temple festivals. According to the museum founder, T. Wilson de Silva, the theater had a curtain in front, but was accessible to pilgrims. Buddhism has extensive and detailed depictions of hell, with long, cruel, and ingenious scourgings. The devil theater threatens pilgrims with other, similar punishments in the afterlife, to be executed by demons (branding, sawing to pieces, skewering) as sanctions for deviant behavior. In the background, on a throne on the upper level, is a 'chief demon.' The scene is flanked by a cluster of corpses, which can be moved by ropes like a jumping jack. (M. Herzog)

2. *Ancient theater* can be regarded as the actual cradle of Western drama. First came choral dances and songs, which, in connection with the sacred celebrations of Dionysus, developed forms that were ever more fixed. With the formation of the *polis*, around 500 BCE, these forms underwent a further differentiation. Tragedy, on one side, became the human being's tension in mythical dependency, between free will and an enthrallment by fate (in Gk., *moíra*; → Destiny/Fate). The hero's catastrophe was verification of the existence and activity of a superordinate power. On the other side, it attracted interest in real conflict among human beings. Aristotle described theater as *mimesis*—as the 'imitation' of reality. He designated the effect of tragedy as a → *catharsis*, a 'purging,' that delivered one from *hybris*, sacrilegious pride, and rendered one capable of sympathy, and of bearing one's fate. *Comedy*, by contrast, had developed from the sacred Dionysus tradition of merry, mocking songs (satyr plays), and delivered up the heroes of myth and politics to public hilarity.

Roman theater served at first to reflect the virtues of the state ideology. Burlesque comedies that attributed to the gods the passions of human beings, such as Plautus's (250–184 BCE) intricate "Amphitruo," brought pleasure to a wide audience. With the incipient imperial era came the age of state-financed spectacles, a sign of the power of rule: chariot races, gladiatorial combats, and rough popular improvisations, to serve the entertainment of a broad public. *Panis et circences*—'bread and circuses'—became the slogan for the employment of theater as social technology.

With the beginning of the Christian age, mimded burlesques of Christians and their rites were favorite presentations. The Church prohibited the frequenting of theaters. With their myths of the gods, or even their vulgar burlesque, theaters stood in the pagan tradition, and spectators were threatened with excommunication. In the fourth century, the renunciation of such *spectacula* actually became an article of the Christian baptismal creed. At the same time, the Church itself utilized the experiential sensory worlds of theatrical forms. In the area of symbolical actions, these forms frequently supplemented liturgical celebrations ($\rightarrow$ Liturgy/Dramaturgy), and in the Middle Ages, via the 'mystery plays,' developed into an independent Christian genre of sacred $\rightarrow$ drama.

3. During the *Counter-Reformation,* the spiritual play and the didactic piece presented for moral edification flourished for the last time in the Catholic Baroque theater. Calderon de la Barca's "Life Is a Dream" (premiering in 1635), exemplifies and explicates the proposition that the transitory quality of worldly values prevents anyone from finding life unless united with God and guided by faith. With the Enlightenment, however, and the triumphal campaign of the middle class, *modern theater* definitively established itself as a confessionally independent platform, from which to take up the conflictive existence of emancipated citizens responsible for themselves. The price of this new worldly affiliation is doubt and confusion. The secular person finds redemption by divine grace (Schiller, "Maria Stuart," 1801; Goethe, "Faust": part 1, 1806; part 2, 1832). The myth of the 'Faustian man,' with his double soul, who finds redemption only through 'love from on high,' has been a theme of currency for many a landmark presentation of "Faust," from Max Reinhardt (1909) to Christoph Marthaler (1993).

Twentieth Century

4. a) At about the turn of the twentieth century, in distinction from the naturalistic theater of illusion, an *avant-garde movement* developed that demanded a new intercourse with stage space, stage image, light, and even the actor's art. Representatives such as Adolphe Appia (1862–1928) and Edward Gordon Craig (*Toward a New Theater*, 1913) sought to free theater from the shackles of literature. Under the provocative slogan, "Theater of Cruelty," Antonin Artaud called for a theater of 'bodiliness,' a consciousness of the language of the body. He worked with indigenous traditions, such as that of Balinesian and Tibetan ritual theater (*Le théâtre de la cruauté—premier manifeste*, 1932; *second manifeste*, 1933 [Fr. "The Theater of Cruelty—First Manifesto ... Second Manifesto"]). Erwin Piscator's and Bertolt Brecht's 'epic theater' used *Verfremdungseffekte* ('effects of alienation') in order to generate an emotional distance in the audience, and stimulate it to reflect on a reality in need of change. It was not the relationship of the human being to herself, nor her relationship to God, but the meaning of her societal function that ought to stand at midpoint in the performance.

Theater of the Absurd

b) *The theater of the absurd* distinguished itself as theater presenting the quest of the human being who has lost himself in a world devoid of meaning. It is intimately coupled with the existentialist ideas of Jean-Paul Sartre and Albert Camus, who described the world as a metaphysical 'no man's land,' in which the human being is condemned to freedom, and, in permanent struggle against absurdity, must himself give meaning to his existence. The protagonists in Samuel Beckett's "Waiting for Godot" (premiering in 1953), or Harold Pinter's "The Caretaker" (1960), manifest their condition as 'lost,' and their existential 'fear,' by way of their 'automated' speech ($\rightarrow$ Existentialism).

Theater of Experience

c) In the *theater of experience*, artists such as Jerzy Grotowsky, Peter Brook, Eugenio Barba, Adrienne Mnouchkine, and Richard Schechner adopt elements of the ritual theater of the Far East (Japanese *noh* theater, Beijing opera), and other traditions with a religious anchoring. These playwrights include the usages of ritual ceremony, such as gestures, movements, and

masks, as well as elements of the trance and mystery play. By contrast with the psychologism of speech-centered European theater, it is the actor's body that becomes the tool of self-revelation. Even more than the presentation itself, it is now a process of 'testing' that becomes the locus of an existential self-knowledge on the part of the actors, the self-knowledge that bestows on them their meaning. Here, classic texts are dismantled, linked with elements of bodily ritual, and, by means of personal experiences, joined together in a new system (Peter Brook—Shakespeare, "The Tempest," 1990). The ensemble becomes the 'ritual group,' blending the boundaries between theater and ritual drama (Richard Schechner, "Bacchae," 1969; Robert Wilson, "KA MOUNTAIN and GUARDenia Terrace—A Story about a Family and Some People Changing," 1972). Typically enough, the presentations programmatically overstep the place and time of customary presentation: they take place from sunset to sunrise in a quarry (Peter Brooks, "Mahabharata" in Aix-en-Provence, 1985), or even, as for Wilson, take spectators and players, for seven days, on seven mountains around Shiraz, in Iran. American avant-gardist and theoretician Richard Schechner's collaboration with anthropologist Victor Turner, for example, attests the route 'from ritual to theater,' and shows the sacred drama of India and Africa as a source of inspiration for the contemporary Western stage.

d) Theater in the age of the mass media is still a place where myths and existential themes are recalled and displayed. Wilson's theater of apocalyptic images develops its effect by way of a 'teamwork' of rhythmic movements by the players in slow motion, light, music, individual words, and bizarre costumes ("Death, Destruction & Detroit," 1979, 1987, 1999); meanwhile, theater directors such as Peter Stein (Ibsen, "Peer Gynt," 1971; Aischylos, "Orestia," 1980), or authors such as Botho Strauss (*Trilogie des Wiedersehens*, Ger., "Trilogy of Return," 1976), Hans Neuenfels ("Medea," 1976), Frank-Patrick Steckel ("Penthesilea," 1978), reach back to classical texts of the

In December, 1972, with his troop of eleven international players, director Peter Brook spent a hundred days traveling in North and West Africa, to help discover the extent to which understanding and agreement is possible among people from various parts of the world. With improvisations based on the ancient Persian legend, "The Conference of the Birds," in which many birds gather in order to deliberate as to how God can best be found, Brook was trying out a 'universal theater.' Was a meeting site possible for the sharing of human experience, independently of language and culture? In this scene, poles lead the players, and help them to lose their egos on the stage. The players' bodies become vehicles of the rhythms of the gods, so that "God may pass before our eyes" (J. Heilpern). Brook names this theater the "Theater of Naiveté or Innocence." Its symbol is the circle.

collective European memory. These performances lead (universal) theater back, once more, to its origin: the space for illustration and visualization of human existence in being and acting.

Literature

Ashby, Clifford, Classical Greek Theatre: New Views of an Old Subject, Iowa City 1999; Brauneck, Manfred, Die Welt als Bühne. Geschichte des europäischen Theaters, 4 vols., Stuttgart 1993ff.; Idem, Theater im 20. Jahrhundert. Programmschriften – Stilperioden – Reformmodelle, Reinbek 1982; Brockett, Oscar G./Hildy, Franklin J., History of the Theatre, Boston 2002; Brook, Peter, The Empty Space, London 1968; Croyden, Margaret, Conversations with Peter Brook, 1970–2000, New York 2003; Flashar, Hellmut, Inszenierung der Antike: Das griechische Drama auf der Bühne der Neuzeit, Munich 1991; Schechner, Richard, Between Theater and Anthropology, Philadelphia 1985; Schnusenberg, Christine, The Relationship between the Church and the Theatre: Exemplified by Selected Writings of the Church Fathers and by Liturgical Texts until Amalarius of Metz, 775–852 A.D., Lanham 1988; Sennett, Herbert, Religion and Dramatics: The Relationship between Christianity and the Theater Arts, Lanham 1995; Turner, Victor, From Ritual to Theatre: The Human Seriousness of Play, New York 1982.
    Journal: The Drama Review, ed. by Richard Schechner.

→ *Drama (Sacred), Liturgy/Dramaturgy, Mysteries*

Elke Sofie Frohn

Theocracy

1. What has occurred in → Iran and in Algeria in the last two decades of the twentieth century, in terms of deadly violence, deprivation of individual rights, and coercion to live according to the rules of religious laws, is perceived in the West with horror and revulsion, and labeled 'theocracy.' 'Theocracy' (Gk., 'God's government') contradicts 'democracy' (Gk., 'people's government'). The former designation fuses a criticism of the religious grounding of political crimes with a criticism of religion across the board. Both of the countries above cited were subjected to a rapid modernization, and the West had shown its ugly face: human rights were valid on paper alone. In Algeria, in addition, democratic elections were halted, as a siege of the Islamists seemed imminent. "Backslide to the Middle Ages!" was one formula with which the West rejected the model. "How could you bear [a] theocracy?" was another.[1] But the West has only preached the value of the Enlightenment in colonialism, not realized it. It is to this reality that the ideal of an Islamic theocracy is opposed.

Sketch of a Constitution for the New Beginning

2. *Theocracy as a utopia*: a) The cry for a 'government of God' first emerged in a determinate historical situation. In Israel/Judaea, in 586 BCE, the royal palace and the Temple in Jerusalem were destroyed, and the people lost their independence. The upper classes were carried off into exile in Babylon. Along with those who clung to the old model—insisting on insurrection, and a king of their own—and along with those who established themselves in Babylon, others managed a return to Israel, drafting an entirely different constitution (Ezek 40-48, Deuteronomy). The equality of all was guaranteed.

Land apportionment in equal areas for each family continued its effect for a while: exploitation and debtors' slavery were impossible, since, every seven years, in the Sabbath year, debts were cancelled, and every forty-nine years, in the Year of Jubilee, the original land apportionment was restored. There would be no more kings, since it was this institution that was regarded as being at the root of the accumulation of power, and as having inevitably introduced inequality. Instead of kingship, a 'contract', a 'covenant between God and man', was to be obligatory. The Commandments bound all equally, irrespective of social position. God needed no representative: the 'covenant' of the law, struck of old 'with (under) Moses', represented God in any current government and under any particular laws.

b) The word 'theocracy' was introduced by Josephus (c. 94 CE) in order to describe the particular character of Jewish society for a Greco-Roman audience.[2] Scion of a priestly family of Jerusalem, Josephus advocated the theocracy, which assigned the priests an important function. The theocracy is distinguishable from a variety of community organizations constrained to the religious area, as was necessary in rabbinical Judaism after the loss of sovereignty under Roman rule. But it is also to be distinguished from the model of the Messiah King. Even the latter, however, was seen more as laying the groundwork of a divine government than as presage of a return to the monarchy. Thus, out of the monarchy of the royal family emerged the rule of the priestly nobility.

Josephus: Rule of the Priestly Nobility

c) This model base shapes the foundation of Jesus's message of the *Basileía Theoû*, "when God comes into His Kingdom." Planned not as a 'reign of heaven' in the beyond but as the constitution of an earthly society, its effectuation promptly falls under the Christian reservation that it can only be realized outside history, outside earthly reality. Thus, under the condition of 'antecedence', secular rule is made over no longer to the covenant of the law but to the future, while life in the state is 'still' under the customary order.

Reign (Kingdom) of God?

   d) Unlike the Lutherans, the Reformed (Zwingli, Calvin) take the viewpoint that the 'royal rule of God' must be measured by reality. Their city-republics may be taken as the model of democracy and civil society. However, here as well, 'religious constitutions' frequently stand under the compulsion of having to right all things, above and beyond the humanly possible. Religion becomes terror, theocratic rule turns into police state. Calvin's Geneva is as just as much an example of → terrorism as is → Khomeini's Iran.

3. *Who is the sovereign?* The deciding question for a theocratic constitution concerns the government—the institution, therefore, which is to represent God, and which, on the human, social level realizes the everyday 'translation of the law into laws'. A subordination advertised as identical with that required by Jesus of his disciples[3] can disguise violence with religion. The Pope as *Servus Servorum Dei* can at the same time, as *Vicarius Christi*, require utter obedience. In a theocracy, the 'Servant of the Servants of God', because he is 'Vicar of Christ', can claim for himself the absolute rights of a monarch. Thus, theocracy makes for a power uncontrollably unleashed. But the Jewish model aims at a sacred limitation of the rule of persons by persons: the government of God in the form of the law makes the current government just as surely controllable as the currently valid laws. → Democracy, with its

Control of the Executive

distribution of power, is every bit as genuine a consequence of theocracy as is religious tyranny.

1. COLPE, Carsten, Problem Islam, Frankfurt/M. 1989, 142; 61-88.
2. JOSEPHUS, *Contra Apionem* 2, 16; trans. in TAUBES 1987, 65, 79.
3. Matt 22:21; that loyalty to the state here is identical with that of Paul's Rom 13 is disputed by Pinchas LAPIDE; see LAPIDE, P., Er predigte in ihren Synagogen: Jüdische Evangelienauslegung, Gütersloh 1980, 34-55.

Literature

ASSMANN, Jan, Moses the Egyptian: The Memory of Egypt in Western Monotheism, Cambridge 1997; BOHATEC, Josef, Calvins Lehre von Staat und Kirche, Breslau 1937; BABER, Johansen, Contingency in a Sacred Law, Leiden 1999, 263-348; KEPEL, Gilles, La revanche de Dieu: Chrétiens, juifs et musulmans à la reconquête du monde, Paris ²2003 (¹1991); REVENTLOW, Henning et al. (eds.), Politics and Theopolitics in the Bible and Postbiblical Literature, Sheffield 1994; RUNCIMAN, Steven, The Byzantine Theocracy, Cambridge 1977; TAUBES, Jacob (ed.), Religionstheorie und Politische Theologie 3: Theokratie, Munich 1987; WALTON, Robert C., Zwingli's Theocracy, Toronto 1967; WEILER, Gershon, Jewish Theocracy, Leiden 1988.

→ *Democracy, Government/Rule/Politics/State, Iran, Law, Papacy*

Christoph Auffarth

Theodicy

The question of the meaning of this world's → evil—of natural evil (natural catastrophes), of moral evil, in the sense of war and crime, and of personal suffering (hunger, disease, death)—is encountered by every human being. It seems to have become fundamental for personal meaning. Thus, for some religions, the fact that there is such a thing as 'bad' poses problems of no little significance. How is a good and caring God to be reconciled with blind fate, and evil? The believer feels frequently exposed to these forces. A 'justification of God' is called for, for the evil that God permits: 'theodicy' (from Gk., *Theós*, 'God'; *díke*, 'right,' 'righteousness'). German philosopher Gottfried Wilhelm Leibniz (1646–1716) first coined the term. In Leibniz's *Essais de théodicées sur la bonté de Dieu, la liberté de l'homme, et l'origine du mal* ("Essays in Theodicy: The Goodness of God, the Freedom of the Human Being, and the Origin of Evil"; 1710), he sought to reconcile the fact of evil in the world with the idea of God's justice and perfection. The question of the moral justification of God appears in its full import especially in the monotheistic religions (Judaism, Christianity, Islam), whose point of departure is in the existence of an almighty and omniscient, personal God, ultimately responsible for the divine creation. Other concepts, especially polytheistic, dualistic, or gnostic, emphasize either the ambivalence of God/the gods, assume a concrete cause of evil, for example a demiurge—in an attenuated sense, this function is fulfilled by the Christian → Devil—or explain suffering through reference to a guilt personally incurred by the human being in a previous life (concept of karma in → Buddhism).

With the intent to establish a theological foundation for evil and suffering in the world, the discussions of theodicy have adopted the following assumptions: (1) the free will of the human being who can decide for or against the good; (2) the accompanying sinfulness of the human being (indeed, in Christianity, an original fault or → sin), that incurs a 'punishment from God'; (3) the believer's testing and instruction, as it comes to expression in the biblical story of Job, the 'undeserving sufferer.' A solution to the problem emerges from the assumption that there is a justice that 'evens things out' in the next world, for example in the form of a final judgment. In all of the monotheistic religions, however, there is also the tendency to accept that a judgment upon God and upon the divine creation is beyond the capacity of the human being to manage; this position is explicit in Calvinism, for example.

Attempts at Theological Solutions

Two events in European modernity raised the question of the 'justice of God' in a special degree of keenness. The earthquake in Lisbon, in 1755, which killed tens of thousands of persons, shook the assumption of modern → rationalism that the goodness and existence of God could be justified in terms of the laws of nature of an ordered world, a world as the Enlightenment had come to see it. In the twentieth century, the problem of theodicy flared up anew, under new omens, on the occasion of the existence and function of the National Socialist extermination camps. The question of the moral legitimization of God is found mirrored in the question of 'anthropodicy'—the 'justification of the human being': How can persons permit this suffering? Does that moral failure mean a *reductio ad absurdum* for the concept of 'further ethical development'? Today, a tendency prevails to interpret catastrophes and suffering as artifacts, engendered by persons in many ways, for example by means of technological and civilizing incursions into nature.

Crisis of Theodicy

Literature

BEAL, Timothy K., Religion and Its Monsters, New York/London 2002; KREINER, Armin, Gott im Leid. Zur Stichhaltigkeit der Theodizee-Argumente, Freiburg 1997; PETRIK, James M., Evil Beyond Belief, Armonk 2000.

→ *Devil, Ethics/Morals, Evil/Evil One, God/Gods/The Sacred, Hereafter, Meaning/ Signification, Progress, Sin, Suffering, Will (Free)*

Jutta Bernard and Stefan Hartmann

Theology

1. The word 'theology' (from Gk., *theología*) denotes "reflective discourse concerning the being and acting of God or gods." The function of theology is to solve (1) the individual's problems of meaning, and (2) society's problems of interpretation of the world, as well as those of order or structure—in reference to the bases and foundations of a given religious system (which not infrequently means: in terms of a transcendent point of reference).

Reflected Speech

Theology—Not Only in Christianity

2. Until the mid-twentieth century, theology was a concept referred primarily to Christianity. It designated especially any teaching resting on biblical revelation, and in itself rationally grounded, concerning the being and works of the triune God of the Christians and that God's relationship to the human being and the world. It included Mariology, any teaching concerning the human being in need of salvation, salvation history, and the opportunities for the attainment of salvation and for communication with God. It likewise included the doctrine of the mediating role of the Church and the saints, including church law. But the increasing scrutiny, since the middle of the nineteenth century, of other religions, in language and content, demonstrated the fact that they, too, possess theology. This observation applies to → Judaism, → Islam, and the monotheistic religions of → Hinduism, as well as many polytheisms. Obliquely, it holds even for religions in which no 'God' (*theós*) stands at the focus, but in which, indeed, there is a transcendent point of reference, as, e.g., in → Buddhism, or in the Vedanta of the Hindus.

As long as the concept of theology seemed to denote a primarily Christian phenomenon, it was adequately defined as authoritative Christian doctrine, legitimated by the instances of ecclesiastical control. Since the Second Vatican Council (1962–1965), however, the extension of the concept 'theology' to other religions—a concept widely accepted by the other Christian churches, even those without comparable institutions of ecclesiastical control—implies that it can be defined today neither by specific content of belief, nor by doctrine conformed to the church. Rather, reference must be made to a more general characteristic, one that is the property of all theology. Thus, one may conclude: "Theology is the product of a rational reflection, accompanied by premises of belief, on the content of a given religious tradition, and on the instructions concerning salvific activity that are to be deduced from that content, when the latter is legitimized by previous initiation and by consent of leading supporters of a community of belief." It is its perspective determined by belief that distinguishes theology from the → academic study of religion. The latter regards the religions, including their theologies—likewise rational—from an outer perspective, one that includes a neutral attitude toward belief. Initiation into an authoritative tradition distinguishes theology from the philosophy of religion.

Theology as Religious Tradition's Rational Self-Reflection

Meaning and Order

3. The function of responding to questions of meaning, and problems of structure, falls to myths as well, or texts of revelation. That is, it falls to the reports concerning the will and activity of God or the gods, which, in the self-concept of a given religion, stem from a divine source. The religious level on which theology is settled distinguishes it from these forms of bestowal of religious meaning. Theology is not the word of God, but human reflection on, and interpretation of, the word of God. It is not the visionary sight of divine acting, or a mythic report concerning the creation event and other deeds of God or the gods. Instead, it is an attempt to arrange in structures of meaning the activity of God as known from such sources. That is, theology is an attempt to understand and base the volitional impulses of suprahuman powers—those impulses that can be deduced from religious tradition and from nature—and to set them in a connection with the activities of human beings.

Doctrine of Obligation

4. It is characteristic of theology, then, to attempt to generate a meaningful system of thought that will bind deities, world, nature, human beings,

and society into a consistent model of interpretation. Theology gathers, searches, orders, and evaluates the traditional discrete, disparate utterances of religious experience. It canonizes them, explains them, and connects them into an intellectual system. The character of its interpretation as a system permits it to draw conclusions concerning the being of God or the gods, concerning the meaning and order of the world, and concerning the duties and obligations of human beings. Theology also clarifies and shapes religious acts, in → sacrifice and → prayer, sacraments and → liturgy, which produce an immediate relation to the religious life of the community. Oriented to the structure of the society that is its vehicle, it develops ideals of cosmic order (→ Cosmology/Cosmogony), and of a paradisiacal world free from suffering, disease, and death, attainable in the hereafter or realizable in the present world (→ Garden/Paradise; Heaven/Sky; Luck/Happiness; Utopia). Oriented to conceptualizations of ideals like these, it can occasion social changes. It lays down, legitimizes, and alters norms of social behavior. It orders and weighs 'sins,' on a scale that can extend from light transgressions to mortal sin, it establishes penances and punishments. It reflects on → guilt and repentance, on beatitude and suffering, on merit and grace. Its responses relate to questions on the purpose of being, on the meaning of → suffering, and on death and victory over death, as well as on questions touching on the role assignment of the individual in society—on the human being's rights, duties, and goals. At the same time, it sketches and represents general ideals to which individual and societal life can be oriented, e.g., peace, truth, order, eternal life; or love of neighbor, compassion for living beings, responsibility for creation and the environment.

5. However, the development of relations of meaning is not theology's only task. Theology also constantly adapts the interpretation of religious experience and tradition to the evolving conditions of life, and to the social and cultural context. It alters, complements, or thrusts aside earlier understanding and misunderstanding, then integrates new knowledge, but also defends important traditional values. Only when theology petrifies, and no longer performs these functions, is a religion seriously threatened from within. However, this dynamic also signifies that theology frequently stands amidst the tension between orthodox conservation, and a renewal or renovation of → tradition in keeping with the times. Both renewal and the judgment as to what may be regarded as orthodox need legitimization. This condition holds for all religions. It does not presuppose organization, but does require acknowledged types of entry into religious specialization, and the construction of consent. As a rule, legitimization is consequent upon → initiation, which is ordinarily performed by the already initiated, through examination or testing and consecration after the candidate has spent time as a student. Examples include various phenomena such as priestly ordination, or initiation by a → guru after a time of studies. But initiation can also be directly conferred by a divinity, which selects, or takes possession of, a person, and then expresses itself through a knowledge 'self-acquired' by (revealed to) the person, together with a personal → charisma, by inspiration, prophetical power, or supernatural abilities and miracles. In such cases of the manifestation of divine powers, subsequent formal initiation is not necessary. But recognition by other religious → specialists is indeed required; these latter must accept the person thus selected as an authentic representative of their religious tradition. Without that acceptance, the crucial legitimization of the

*Norm and
Development*

religious tradition will be missing, and along with it, the possibility of altering a prevailing theology from the inside, under normative auspices. (There
have been numerous exceptions, however, one of which was the refusal of
Jesus of Nazareth to seek legitimization at the hands of those influential
contemporaries whose knowledge of scripture could have been expected
to be determinative.) Theologians' purposed reforms thus have their limits,
defined by foundations of belief emerging from their own religion's character
as a system. They may indeed alter forms of reverence or worship, and content of belief, or adopt them from other religions, so long as these alterations
fit into their own system without friction. When, however, new intellectual
approaches, or syncretistic adoption of foreign content of belief, change basic
structures of their own system, then theological renewal transforms into
→ heresy, and is rejected.

History of the Concept   6. a) The word 'theology' appears for the first time with Plato (Politeia
379a), and denotes myths, which, to be sure, ought not to falsify the basic
traits of the being of the gods. Here, the call for a rational, critical appraisal of
myths is articulated, which was shortly to lead to a division between → myth
and theology. Aristotle lists theology as a subdivision of metaphysics (*sophía*,
philosophia prima [Gk., Lat., resp., 'wisdom,' and 'first philosophy'])[1] that is
ordered to all reflection on the last things, including the being of the gods. In
Hellenism and the time of the Roman Empire, 'theology' included not only
the interpretation of the myths (*ratio quae de diis explicatur*—Lat., "reasonable element explained concerning the gods"), but also the teaching of the
intercourse with the gods in *ritus* (Lat., 'rite') and cult. In ancient Christianity, the word was adopted by Origen (d. c. 254), but it was soon restricted:
with Eusebius of Caesarea (d. c. 339), it again denoted only knowledge concerning the being of Christ, and the God of the Christians, and excluded all
statements concerning pagan gods. This constraint also confined the concept
of *theología* even more: now there was a distinction between the attempt
to understand God himself, and the last principles, and on the other hand,
oikonomía (Gk., 'economy'), which concerned itself with God's activity, especially his salvific activity, and his coming to human beings as human being
and redeemer. Both were aspects of *sacra scriptura* and *sacra doctrina*. Only
in the Middle Ages, through Abelard (1079–1142), were these two parts of
divine doctrine once more joined in the concept of theology.

Theology and   Other problems appeared in the relationship of theology and philosophy.
Philosophy   From Boethius (480–525) to the heyday of scholasticism (eleventh to thirteenth centuries; → Aristotelianism), Aristotelian logic became an essential
aid in theological intercourse with the content of faith. Granted, philosophy
was still the 'handmaid of theology' (in Lat., *ancilla theologiae*), and thus
subordinate both to God's revelation, and to the concept of unconditional
faith. 'Pagan' philosophy, and with it, the claim of human reason (*ratio*)
on autonomous knowledge, was not admitted, as shown by the Justinian's
closing of the Platonic Academy and other places of learning of the ancient
philosophy (525 CE).
    b) A similar distinction between theology and philosophy, arisen from
a situation of competition between the two, does not appear in other reli-
Islamic Philosophy   gions, such as in Buddhism, in the Hindu religions, and in the East Asian re-

ligions. Even in Islamic theology, *Ilm al-kalan* ('scholarship of disputation'), to an extent, it was overcome through an incorporation of basic disciplines of philosophy (epistemology, logic, etc.), and natural science (elements of nature, theory of motion, etc.). Islamic theology's research and investigations were directed to the 'foundations of religion' (*usul ad-din*).

Its formative period, the norm for modern Islamic theology, ended at the beginning of the twelfth century—shortly before the time of the climax of Christian scholasticism. The fruitful influence of Islamic sciences and scholarship on Christian scholastic theology, and the discovery by the West of other works of Aristotle, began with Avicenna (Ibn Sina, 980–1037) and Averroes (Ibn Rushd, 1126–1198). Finally, with the growing importance of theological university faculties, the concept of 'theology' expanded to embrace all subjects taught there and having a bearing on life, religious or social.

1. Aristotle, Metaphysics VI, 1 1026a19; XI, 8, 1064b3.

Literature

Di Berardino, Angelo et al. (eds.), History of Theology, Collegeville 1997ff.; Ford, David F. (ed.), The Modern Theologians: An Introduction to Christian Theology in the Twentieth Century, 2 vols., Oxford 1989; Hanson, Bradley C., Introduction to Christian Theology, Minneapolis 1997; Meyendorff, John, Byzantine Theology: Historical Trends and Doctrinal Themes, New York ²1979; Roberts, J. Deotis, A Philosophical Introduction to Theology, London/Philadelphia 1991; Smith, William Cantwell, Towards a World Theology: Faith and the Comparative History of Religion, Philadelphia 1981; von Stietencron, Heinrich, Theologen und Theologien in verschiedenen Kulturkreisen, Düsseldorf 1986.

→ *Academic Study of Religion, God/Gods/The Sacred, Liberation Theology, Meaning/ Signification, Metaphysics, Myth/Mythology, Religion, Scholasticism, Spirituality*

Heinrich von Stietencron

Theory of Evolution

The theory of evolution (from Lat., *evolvere*, 'turn out,' 'develop'), in the strict sense, means a series of biological concepts that gives a scientific explanation for the arrival of life and the development of species. It is common to these interpretations that they do not regard life as a divine and inalterable creation, but hold life forms to be the product of a progressive development (theory of derivation, origin of species). By the beginning of the nineteenth century, Jean-Baptiste de Lamarck (1744–1849) had already proposed, as an explanatory model, the notion that differentiated organs develop for the preservation and protection of their elementary needs, and that these purposeful self-adaptations to an environment could be inherited. Charles Darwin (1809–1882) ascribed evolution to a 'natural selection' of varying biological materials ('mutations') by coincidental, chance mutations. Current theories, on the other hand, such as represented by Manfred Eigen (b. 1927), shift evolution to the area of molecular biology.

The Christian side raised opposition to the theories of evolution, re-proaching the scientific explanations with contradicting the biblical myth of creation. To this day, specific circles of Protestant fundamentalists in the United States assert the word-for-word validity of the myth of Genesis in the first Book of Moses, according to which God created the earth and living things in seven days, with the human being enjoying a unique position in creation. Thus, in the 1920s, some Southern states succeeded in legislating a prohibition of the teaching of the Darwinian theory in public schools (leading to a spectacular "Monkey Trial" of a teacher in Tennessee). The Catholic Church, in recent times, has given up this opposition. Evolution—according to an enunciation of John Paul II—may be interpreted of the expression of a *creatio continua* (Lat., 'continuous creation').

Literature

DARWIN, Charles R., On the Origin of Species by Means of Natural Selection, or The Preservation of Favoured Races in the Struggle of Life, London 1859; DI GREGORIO, Mario A., From Here to Eternity: Ernst Haeckel and Scientific Faith, Göttingen 2005; RIEDL, Rupert, Order in Living Organisms: A Systems Analysis of Evolution, London 1979; WILSON, David Sloan, Darwin's Cathedral: Evolution, Religion, and the Nature of Society, Chicago/London 2002.

→ *Evolutionism, Fundamentalism, Natural Science, Origin, Progress, Science*

Stefan Hartmann

Theosophical / Anthroposophical Society

1. The object of the following considerations will be not the older, Christian theosophy (Gr., *theosophía*, 'divine wisdom') of Jacob Böhme and others,[1] but that of Helena Petrovna Blavatsky (1831–1891). This, the most important neo-religious creation of the nineteenth century, ostensibly gathered Europe's various 'occult' traditions (Neoplatonism, → Gnosticism, → Kabbalah, → Hermeticism, the Rosicrucian teaching, → Freemasonry; → Esotericism) into an assembly also containing elements of extra-European religions (Coptic Christianity, → Sufism, → Zoroastrianism, → Hinduism, → Buddhism). The result was a supra-confessional, universalistic, 'primitive' and 'world' religion, intended as a contrast with the orthodoxies of Judaism and the Christian churches, along with 'materialistic' Darwinism. This formulation is what gained institutional housing in the Theosophical Society. Blavatsky presented a neo-gnostic conceptualization of the divine descendancy of the human being, its ever more significant submersion in matter and corporality, and its already accomplished introduction to new spiritualization and divinization (→ Gnosticism). Blavatsky also taught 'magical' practices, then, for the division of the astral body from the physical. The new inter-religious and intercultural Theosophy was of great importance as a transporter of syncretistic content like monism, holism (→ Wholeness/Holism), → reincarnation, and the notion of karma. Among

Helena Petrovna Blavatsky, surrounded by the three 'Masters,' Koot Hoomi, Morya, and Prince Ragoczy. As 'spiritual supermen,' said to live on the 'roof of the world,' in Shigatse, in Tibet, they authoritatively legitimated Theosophy. The 'letters of the Masters' were its sacred scripture. The myth of the 'Masters' profited from the fact that the realm of the Dalai Lama had long since been closed, and thus surrounded with mystery—for instance, as late as Heinrich Harrer's *Seven Years in Tibet*! England and Russia sought to gain political influence over the country (British expedition of 1904), and Blavatsky was suspected of being an agent of Russia sometimes, of England at others.

the recipients of this content is the → New Age movement (the concept of a 'New Age' gained great popularity through Blavatsky's disciple Alice Ann Bailey, 1880–1949). As early as the death of the founder, and still more keenly afterwards, the Theosophical Society split into fractions, sometimes with a national stamp. One of them was the Anthroposophical Society, inspired by Rudolf Steiner (1832–1907) (see §3).

2. After an adventurous life of spiritual quest, German Russian Noble Blavatsky, together with Henry Steel Olcott (1832–1907), founded the Theosophical Society, a 'universal brotherhood of man' in New York in 1875. With her *Isis Unveiled* (1877), she moved away from an original foundation in → spiritism, and, as she traveled with Olcott to Bombay a year later, the turn eastward was intensified. She then filled out the Theosophical doctrine with concepts of Hinduism and Buddhism (cosmic cycles, reincarnation, karma). In India, she also connected with members of the indigenous elite (cf. her

Madame Blavatsky and the Theosophical Society

emphasis on a common 'Aryan' origin), for purposes of cultural and political renewal. In 1882, the Theosophical Society's headquarters were moved to Adyar near Madras. But in India the movement found its keenest crisis, with the publication of the Hodgson Report of the Society for Psychical Research in England: Blavatsky was accused of charlatanry.[2] In particular, her legitimating appeal to the secret 'Great White Brotherhood' of the 'Masters,' 'Adepts,' or 'Mahatmas,' enlightened 'world teachers' allegedly hiding in Tibet, and their "Mahatma Letters," were interpreted as Blavatsky's counterfeits. Only in recent times has K. Paul Johnson sought to offer evidence that, behind the 'Masters' were concealed real and sometimes politically influential persons—including well-known Hindu and Sikh leaders—who were important for Blavatsky's spiritual development and political strivings. Blavatsky's most productive literary period began with her final return to Europe in 1885, as she published in London her multi-volume *Secret Doctrine: The Syntheses of Science, Religion, and Philosophy* (vols. 1, 2 in 1888; vol. 3 posthumously, in 1897). In this work she created a new mythical, poetical 'genesis,' (cosmogony and anthropogony), entwining Eastern thought with Western concepts typical of her time—especially with evolution, progress, and racial doctrine—and connected them with her claim to a scientifically based religion.

Crisis and Division

After Blavatsky's demise, not only did the unity of the Theosophical Society break apart once and for all, but the First World War occasioned the collapse of its international order: the Adyar organization, with its many members in Australia and New Zealand, openly took sides with the Western powers against Germany, and appealed to the British Empire as the model for the coming 'world commonwealth.' Another conflict was sparked by the announcement, shortly after the turn of the century, of the return of a 'World Teacher': Lord Maitreya and Christ in the person of Jiddu Krishnamurti (1895–1986). The proclamation of this global savior was propagated by the Adyar Society, under Annie Besant (1847–1933) and Charles Webster Leadbeater (1847–1934), by way of the Order of the Star in the East.

Independence for Anthroposophy

3. These conflicts within the Theosophical Society led to institutional independence for Theosophy in Germany. The split began with Franz Hartmann (1838–1912), reaching its climax when Rudolf Steiner (1861–1925) stepped down as Secretary General of the German Section of the Theosophical Society, an office which he had held since 1902, and created (1912/13) an independent Anthroposophical Society. Steiner's motivation, besides personal competition, was his anti-Eastern position. Steiner rejected the notion of Krishnamurti's election, strengthening instead his appeal to Rosicrucianism and esoteric 'Christosophy,' with a central event in the 'mystery of Golgotha.' Steiner's cosmic message of salvation, his *Geisteswissenschaft*, on the other hand, stems from Theosophy, just as does his vision of a future spiritual superman bound up with racial notions ("From Homo sapiens to Homo divinus"), or his doctrine of karma and reincarnation.

At first, the world center of Anthroposophy's strivings was to be Munich's artistic and cultural quarter Schwabing, with parallels, in its intended religious practice, to Richard Wagner's *Bühnenweihefestspiele* (Ger., 'stage dedication plays') held in Bayreuth. The offer of a tract of land in Dornach, near Basle, definitively determined on the construction, beginning in 1913, of the new sacred place on the 'hill'—a 'karmic selection,' as well, since it turned out to be a politically and economically advantageous location through two World Wars.

4. Common to both Theosophy and Anthroposophy is the eventual forma- *Religious Praxis and*
tion of 'Churches' orientated to worship and liturgy (*Liberal-katholische* *Membership*
Kirche, 'Liberal Catholic Church,' 1916), or *Christengemeinschaft* ('Community of Christians,' 1922), as well as the success among the nobility of their
anti-egalitarian, hierarchical image of the world and persons, and among
the upper-middle class of a message of self-redemption through self-rearing
and self-education. Now Steiner attempted a social 'tripartition,' which he
developed, from 1917 on, under the influence of a presumably lost war, and
through which he wished to draw the working class into the societal model
of a class state. He found, however, no response from these addressees. With
Steiner, Blavatsky's anti-Darwinism (aimed, among others, at Ernst Haeckel), *Goetheanism*
issued in a 'Goetheanism'—a variant of the cult of Goethe that appealed to,
in particular, Goethe's scientific writings, concluding to the epistemological path of an intuitive 'gaze,' as well as to a spiritual formulation of nature.
Steiner's sacred edifice, the *Goetheanum* in Dornach, was dedicated to the
concept of the 'metamorphosis.'

By contrast with Theosophy, Anthroposophy developed a decided trait of
the reform of life. Steiner's *Geisteswissenschaft* not only sought to point to
a goal of interiority, but strove for the transformation of the world through
practical work on that world. An implementation of (conducted by, and
on the principles of) Anthroposophy preserves not only the heritage of
the reform movements of c. 1900 (→ Ascona/Monte Verità), but config-
ures a considerable part of Anthroposophy's attraction the world over: sacred architecture ('temple building'; cf. first and second "Goetheana") and
'mystery dramas,' reform schools ("Waldorf Pedagogy"), and 'biologically
dynamic' agriculture (Demeter Reform products), holistic medicine, health
and body-care means (Weleda products), as well as the translation of the
expressive dance of the turn of the century into a pedagogical and therapeutic means ('eurhythmia') all embody this kind of successful project. On
the other hand, certain projects failed after the First World War: the alternative economic projects *Der Kommende Tag* (Ger., "The Coming Day"),
and *Futurum A.G.* From the Protestant youth movement, finally, emerged
the inspiration for the founding of the Christ Community (1922), with the
aim, fostered by Steiner's Catholic heritage, of a Christian renewal through
worship and sacrament.

5. The political contents of Theosophy and Anthroposophy have attracted *Content in Terms of*
particular interest, and are likewise devalued as 'undemocratic' and 'rac- *Political Ideology*
ist,' like the impulse expressed in *völkisch* nativism, especially the Celtic
and Neo-Teutonism.[3] It is true that Blavatsky and her followers (including Steiner) had proclaimed an unequivocally racial concept, in the sense
of a 'cosmological evolution,' nor were anti-Semitic tones lacking. However, Theosophy possessed a strong liberal, internationalistic, and thus

'Enlightenment', counterbalance, and only the particular Austrian/German development of the 'Ariosophy' of a Jörg Lanz von Liebenfels (1874–1954) could absolutize the 'occult', 'karmic', racial doctrine of Theosophy/Anthroposophy in the sense of a racial biologism.

External Effects

Just as with their predecessor, the spiritistic movement (→ Spiritism), one of the most important external effects of Theosophy and Anthroposophy has always lain in their fertilizing influence effect on *modern art*, to which, with its 'fantastic science', it opened new 'invisible worlds'. Stimulated by Richard Wagner's project of a 'holistic work of art' (*Gesamtkunstwerk*), Steiner promoted the bonding of elements of architecture, sculpture, painting, dancing, and vocal presentation in a liturgical and sacred framework. Not only did the Theosophical and Anthrosophical revelation of the 'supra-sensory' inspire important artists of classical modernity, such as Wassily Kandinsky (*Über das Geistige in der Kunst*—Ger., "The Spiritual Element in Art"; 1912), or Piet Mondrian; its effect ranges all the way to Anthroposophically-based concepts of the 'social plastic' in Joseph Beuys. More recently, new fields of influence have opened to Anthroposophy, for instance in the area of ecological construction, or state-free schooling, which have found new addressees in the alternative/ecological movement since the 1970s.

Theosophy and Anthroposophy Today

6. The various Theosophical Societies today, as well as the Anthroposophical Societies, are active worldwide, even on the Internet. Their geographical distribution is historically conditioned. Theosophy has its center of gravity in the Anglo-American world (especially in the United States and Australia), and in the lands that it has particularly influenced. Anthroposophy flourishes especially in German-speaking countries. The Adyar Theosophical Society, for example, stresses the ecological, and socio-political dimension of its message (combat against war, overpopulation, exploitation). Anthroposophy, meanwhile, offers not only its theoretical responses to the spiritual crisis of the present, and to the many questions of our contemporaries that are concerned with living, but also, and especially, to its practical proposals, which range from recreational activities to care of the mentally and physically challenged.

1. Cf. the title of the 1730 edition of the complete works of Jacob Böhme, *Theosophia Revelata* (Lat., "Theosophy Revealed").
2. Report of the Committee Appointed to Investigate Phenomena Connected with the Theosophical Society (Proceedings of the Society for Psychical Research, vol. 3), London 1885.
3. Antroposofie en het vraagstuk van de rassen: Eindrapport van de commissie Antroposofie en het vraagstuk van de rassen, Zeist 2000. Cf. Zander, Helmut, "Sozialdarwinistische Rassentheorien aus dem okkultem Untergrund des Kaiserreiches," in Puschner, Uwe et al., Handbuch zur "Völkischen Bewegung" 1871–1918, Munich 1996, 224-251.

Literature

1. Theosophical Society
Sources: Blavatsky, Helena Petrovna, Collected Writings, 14 vols., Wheaton 1966–1985; Gomes, Michael, Theosophy in the Nineteenth Century: An Annotated Bibliography, New York 1994.

Secondary Literature: CALDWELL, Daniel (ed.), The Esoteric World of Madame Blavatsky, Wheaton 2000; CAMPBELL, Bruce F., Ancient Wisdom Revived: A History of the Theosophical Movement, Berkeley 1980; CRANSTON, Sylvia, The Extraordinary Life & Influence of Helena Blavatsky, Founder of the Modern Theosophical Movement, New York 1993; GODWIN, Joscelyn, The Theosophical Enlightenment, New York 1994; GOMES, Michael, The Dawning of the Theosophical Movement, Wheaton 1987; JOHNSON, Paul K., The Masters Revealed: Madame Blavatsky and the Myth of the Great White Lodge, Albany 1994; Idem, Initiates of the Theosophical Masters, Albany 1995; MEADE, Marion, Madame Blavatsky: The Woman behind the Myth, New York 1980; MÖLLER, Helmut/HOWE, Ellic, Merlin Peregrinus. Vom Untergrund des Abendlandes, Würzburg 1986; TAYLOR, Anne, Annie Besant: A Biography, Oxford 1992.

2. Anthroposophical Society
Sources: DEIMANN, Götz et al. (eds.), Die anthroposophischen Zeitschriften von 1903 bis 1985. Bibliographie und Lebensbilder, Heidelberg 1987; STEINER, Rudolf, Gesamtausgabe, Dornach 1955/56ff.; WAGNER, Arfst, Dokumente und Briefe zur Geschichte der anthroposophischen Bewegung und Gesellschaft in der Zeit des Nationalsozialismus, 5 vols., Rendsburg 1991–1993.
Secondary Literature: AHERN, Geoffrey, Sun at Midnight: The Rudolf Steiner Movement and the Western Esoteric Tradition, Wellingborough 1984; KLATT, Norbert, Theosophie und Anthroposophie. Neue Aspekte zu ihrer Geschichte, Göttingen 1993; LAMPRECHT, Harald, Neue Rosenkreuzer. Ein Handbuch, Göttingen 2004, 191-205; LEIJENHORST, Cees, "Anthroposophy," in: HANEGRAAFF, Wouter J. et al. (eds.), Dictionary of Gnosis and Western Esotericism, Leiden 2005, 82-89; LINDENBERG, Christoph, Rudolf Steiner. Eine Biographie, Stuttgart 1997.

→ *Esotericism, Gnosticism, New Age, Occultism, Orientalism/Exoticsm, Paganism/ Neopaganism, Spiritism*

Ulrich Linse

Tibet

1. With its extreme climatic conditions, the highland of Tibet is only sparsely populated. Few live here other than cattle-raising nomads. Soil is farmed until an altitude of 4,000 m. The center of gravity of settlement and agricultural geography lies in the Tsangpo Valley. Politically, today, what exists is the 'Autonomous Region of Tibet,' established in 1965 in the People's Republic of China. Parts of the region that had stood under the regime in Lhasa were annexed to Chinese provinces after the incursion of Chinese troops.

2. In Tibetan popular religion, the objects of worship are regional and local supernatural beings, who dwell, for example, in mountains and stones, trees, rivers, lakes, soil, and the air. For the assurance of material well-being, and in order to ward off dangers, Tibetans ascertain the spirits' influence by → prophecy, and render them benevolent in rituals and sacrifices. *Popular Religion*

Buddhism was brought to Tibet in two phases—in the seventh to the ninth centuries, and again from the end of the tenth century—and made its way on a broader basis. On the basis of the teachings of Mahayana and the *Buddhism*

→ Tantras, schools of an independent Tibetan Buddhism developed, each with its respective particular doctrinal traditions, philosophical systems, practices of meditation, and monasteries. As a result of cultural exchange, the southern regions of the Himalayas, broad parts of Central Asia, and the regions of the Mongols, all exhibit noteworthy Mongolian qualities. Tibet's form of government after the second unfolding of Buddhism can be called theocratic, inasmuch as, along with the landed proprietors, it was monastic hierarchies that exercised political power (→ Lamaism; Theocracy). Beginning in the seventeenth century, the monk who held the highest position of the *Gelugpa*, the → Dalai Lama, was also regarded as the country's political sovereign (although with varying actual political authority).

Bön

Islam and the Bön religion are important minority religions in today's Tibet. Followers of the latter are called Bönpo. In pre-Buddhist times, Bönpo were religious specialists entrusted with caring for the dead in the world to come, through sacrifices, as well as with the state cult. Today, Bönpo designates the followers of a religion that, in parallel with Buddhism, has developed its own philosophy and monastic system. With regard to the central teachings of karma, rebirth, and redemption, the Bönpo are in agreement with the Buddhists. Their sacred texts are partially identical with those of the Buddhists, but apply their own terminology, and are considered to be the teaching of their (not historically identifiable) founding personage, Dönpa Shenrap.

Religious Practice

Both Tibetan Buddhism and Bön have adopted or accepted practices of folk religion. Thus, partially reinterpreted figures of popular religion have been incorporated into the Buddhist pantheon. The divine worlds of the Tibetan Buddhists and the Bönpo are nominally and iconographically distinct, however. Members of religious orders in either religion can be active as ritual specialists, devote themselves to intellectual schooling and the art of debate, and practice exercises of meditation (→ Monasticism). Characteristic of the religious practice of Tibetan laity is the recitation of salvific syllables and expressions (→ Mantra), which they also activate by way of prayer wheels and banners (→ Prayer/Curse). Pilgrimages and the ritual circling of stupas—clockwise by Buddhists clockwise, and counterclockwise by Bönpos—are regarded as meritorious.

Fantasies and Projections

Until well into the twentieth century, Europeans visited this 'land on the roof of the world' only extremely rarely, due to its geographical and political inaccessibility, and the Tibetan government reacted with great disapproval to a colonizing European presence in Asia. In the service of religious and ideological controversies in Europe and North America, Tibet became the place of fantasies both positive and negative. It was then a timeless, concealed garden of wisdom and spirituality, or an example of dark despotism and prison of superstition, or a 'degeneration' of Buddhism. The perception of ancient Tibet was occasionally overlaid with the Tibetan myth of that realm of paradise and peace, *Shambhala*, visualized as an accessible utopia, and premise of clarity of consciousness, to be attained along the path of the spirit. Even the fictitious, hidden valley of Shangri-La, on which James Hilton's fantasy novel *Lost Horizon* (1933) was founded, now became a long-lived premise for mystifying images of Tibet. The tendency to posit Tibet as an idealized counter-image of one's own experiential world all too often distracts one's view from the real concerns of Tibet and Tibetan religion, even today.

Tibet today is also home to a sizeable number of Chinese immigrants, invited by Beijing in its resettlement policy. The devastation in the wake of the invasion and the Cultural Revolution, created a wave of refugees beginning in 1959, that carried along with it many representatives of the clergy, abandoning their country, whose situation with regard to religion was bleak indeed. Numerous monks and nuns found themselves in political imprisonment, as they had played an important role in the resistance against the Chinese government. Some religious were able to return to the monastery, but access to religious training in Tibet is all but nonexistent. In exile, Tibetan Buddhists, and, to a lesser extent, Bönpo, have built a network of institutions, in order further to hand on the religious culture of Tibet to Tibetans and non-Tibetans alike.

Present Situation

Literature

BAUMER, Christoph, Tibet's Ancient Religion Bön, Trumbull/Bangkok 2002; BECHERT, Heinz/GOMBRICH, Richard (eds.), The World of Buddhism: Buddhist Monks and Nuns in Society and Culture, London 1984; HOFFMANN, Helmut, The Religions of Tibet, Westport 1979 (Ger. ¹1956); KVAERNE, Per, The Bon Religion of Tibet: The Iconography of a Living Tradition, London 1995; LOPEZ, Donald S., Prisoners of Shangri-La: Tibetan Buddhism and the West, Chicago 1998; POWERS, John, Introduction to Tibetan Buddhism, Ithaca 1995; Idem, History as Propaganda: Tibetan Exiles Versus the People's Republic of China, New York 2004.

→ *Buddhism, China/Japan/Korea, Dalai Lama, Lamaism, Reception, Reincarnation, Silk Route, Tantra II, Theocracy*

Kirsten Holzapfel

Lines of Tradition in Tibetan Buddhism

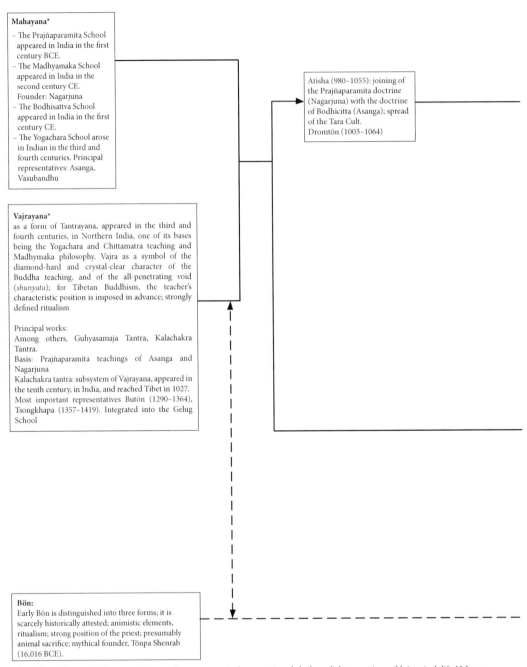

Mahayana*
- The Prajñaparamita School appeared in India in the first century BCE.
- The Madhyamaka School appeared in India in the second century CE. Founder: Nagarjuna
- The Bodhisattva School appeared in India in the first century CE.
- The Yogachara School arose in Indian in the third and fourth centuries. Principal representatives: Asanga, Vasubandhu

Vajrayana*
as a form of Tantrayana, appeared in the third and fourth centuries, in Northern India, one of its bases being the Yogachara and Chittamatra teaching and Madhymaka philosophy. Vajra as a symbol of the diamond-hard and crystal-clear character of the Buddha teaching, and of the all-penetrating void (*shunyata*); for Tibetan Buddhism, the teacher's characteristic position is imposed in advance; strongly defined ritualism

Principal works:
Among others, Guhyasamaja Tantra, Kalachakra Tantra.
Basis: Prajñaparamita teachings of Asanga and Nagarjuna
Kalachakra tantra: subsystem of Vajrayana, appeared in the tenth century, in India, and reached Tibet in 1027.
Most important representatives Butön (1290–1364), Tsongkhapa (1357–1419). Integrated into the Gelug School

Atisha (980–1055): joining of the Prajñaparamita doctrine (Nagarjuna) with the doctrine of Bodhicitta (Asanga); spread of the Tara Cult.
Dromtön (1003–1064)

Bön:
Early Bön is distinguished into three forms; it is scarcely historically attested; animistic elements, ritualism; strong position of the priest; presumably animal sacrifice; mythical founder, Tönpa Shenrab (16,016 BCE).

* The difference between Mahayana and Vajrayana lies to an extent in the conception of whether enlightenment is possible in a single life. Mahayana accepts this premise, Vajrayana holds it as possible only under certain conditions and extreme discipline with an appropriate teacher. But the shorter the path to enlightenment, that is, to the end of the rebirths, the more complex the doctrine. This practically leads to restrictions, since very few are in a position to arrive at this understanding. Interestingly, Western Buddhists feel especially attracted to precisely this form of Buddhism—in spite of the fact that it adopts an extreme attitude toward the overcoming of the ego, in contradiction to individualistic concepts of the West.

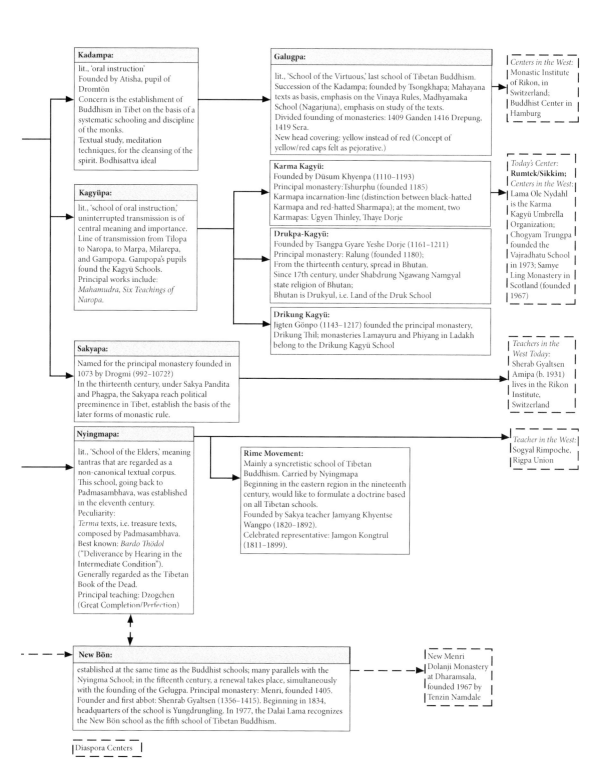

Kadampa:

lit., 'oral instruction'
Founded by Atisha, pupil of Dromtön
Concern is the establishment of Buddhism in Tibet on the basis of a systematic schooling and discipline of the monks.
Textual study, meditation techniques, for the cleansing of the spirit. Bodhisattva ideal

Kagyüpa:

lit., 'school of oral instruction,' uninterrupted transmission is of central meaning and importance. Line of transmission from Tilopa to Naropa, to Marpa, Milarepa, and Gampopa. Gampopa's pupils found the Kagyü Schools. Principal works include: *Mahamudra, Six Teachings of Naropa.*

Sakyapa:

Named for the principal monastery founded in 1073 by Drogmi (992–1072?)
In the thirteenth century, under Sakya Pandita and Phagpa, the Sakyapa reach political preeminence in Tibet, establish the basis of the later forms of monastic rule.

Nyingmapa:

lit., 'School of the Elders,' meaning tantras that are regarded as a non-canonical textual corpus.
This school, going back to Padmasambhava, was established in the eleventh century.
Peculiarity:
Terma texts, i.e. treasure texts, composed by Padmasambhava.
Best known: *Bardo Thödol* ("Deliverance by Hearing in the Intermediate Condition").
Generally regarded as the Tibetan Book of the Dead.
Principal teaching: Dzogchen (Great Completion/Perfection)

Galugpa:

lit., 'School of the Virtuous,' last school of Tibetan Buddhism.
Succession of the Kadampa; founded by Tsongkhapa; Mahayana texts as basis, emphasis on the Vinaya Rules, Madhyamaka School (Nagarjuna), emphasis on study of the texts.
Divided founding of monasteries: 1409 Ganden 1416 Drepung, 1419 Sera.
New head covering: yellow instead of red (Concept of yellow/red caps felt as pejorative.)

Karma Kagyü:
Founded by Düsum Khyenpa (1110–1193)
Principal monastery:Tshurphu (founded 1185)
Karmapa incarnation-line (distinction between black-hatted Karmapa and red-hatted Sharmapa); at the moment, two Karmapas: Ugyen Thinley, Thaye Dorje

Drukpa-Kagyü:
Founded by Tsangpa Gyare Yeshe Dorje (1161–1211)
Principal monastery: Ralung (founded 1180);
From the thirteenth century, spread in Bhutan.
Since 17th century, under Shabdrung Ngawang Namgyal state religion of Bhutan;
Bhutan is Drukyul, i.e. Land of the Druk School

Drikung Kagyü:
Jigten Gönpo (1143–1217) founded the principal monastery, Drikung Thil; monasteries Lamayuru and Phiyang in Ladakh belong to the Drikung Kagyü School

Rime Movement:
Mainly a syncretistic school of Tibetan Buddhism. Carried by Nyingmapa
Beginning in the eastern region in the nineteenth century, would like to formulate a doctrine based on all Tibetan schools.
Founded by Sakya teacher Jamyang Khyentse Wangpo (1820–1892).
Celebrated representative: Jamgon Kongtrul (1811–1899).

New Bön:

established at the same time as the Buddhist schools; many parallels with the Nyingma School; in the fifteenth century, a renewal takes place, simultaneously with the founding of the Gelugpa. Principal monastery: Menri, founded 1405.
Founder and first abbot: Shenrab Gyaltsen (1356–1415). Beginning in 1834, headquarters of the school is Yungdrungling. In 1977, the Dalai Lama recognizes the New Bön school as the fifth school of Tibetan Buddhism.

Centers in the West:
Monastic Institute of Rikon, in Switzerland;
Buddhist Center in Hamburg

Today's Center:
Rumtek/Sikkim;
Centers in the West:
Lama Ole Nydahl is the Karma Kagyü Umbrella Organization;
Chogyam Trungpa founded the Vajradhatu School in 1973; Samye Ling Monastery in Scotland (founded 1967)

Teachers in the West Today:
Sherab Gyaltsen Amipa (b. 1931) lives in the Rikon Institute, Switzerland

Teacher in the West:
Sogyal Rimpoche, Rigpa Union

New Menri Dolanji Monastery at Dharamsala, founded 1967 by Tenzin Namdale

Diaspora Centers

Tibetan Buddhist Lines of Tradition: Explanation of the Schema

Between the eleventh and the fourteenth centuries, Buddhism was definitively established in Tibet. This involved the formation of the Buddhist traditions of the *Kadam-pa, Kaglyü-pa, Sakya-pa, Nyingma-pa,* and *Gelug-pa,* all of which retain some relevance today.

a) The founding of the Kadam-pa, the 'school of oral instruction,' is ascribed to Atisha and his disciple Dromtön (1003–1064). This school was reformed, in the fourteenth century, by Tsongkhapa, and was absorbed by the Gelug school, founded by him. Atisha, in Tibet, introduced the veneration of bodhisattva Avalokiteshvara (Chenrezig), as well as the Tara cult, and established the Bodhisattva Way as a method for the realization of enlightenment. The altruistic virtues of compassion, and all-embracing love, are central for this Way. Also of great importance and meaning is observance of the Rules of the Order. Monks live in celibacy. Study and meditation count a great deal.

b) The founding of Kagyü-pa, 'School of the Transmitted Commandments,' goes back to tantra master Milarepa (1052–1135), doubtless the most famous saint of Tibet and a disciple of Marpa. Characteristic of the Kagyü tradition is the doctrine of the *mahamudra,* the 'Great Seal.' The most important exercise is the meditation called the 'restful lingering,' that is to lead to the knowledge of *shunyata,* the all-penetrating 'emptiness.' The interiorization of the 'four noble truths' and the spiritual cleansing of body and soul prepare the practitioner for the knowledge of the absolute vacuity of all phenomena. The Kagüpa have their ancestral seat in the monastery of Tshurphu, founded in 1189.

c) The Sakya school of Tibetan Buddhism is named for its principal monastery, Sakya, founded in 1073. The monks of this tradition are subject neither to celibacy nor to an obligation of residence in a monastery. Meditations, especially on transiency, the realization of all-penetrating compassion, as well as indifference and the knowledge of *shunyata,* belong to the core points of this school. In the thirteenth century, the Sakyapa reached the high point of their political power, after the Mongol ruler Godan had installed the abbot Sakya Pandita (1182–1251) as regent of Tibet. Investiture with economic and legal privileges formed the basis of the monastery's political power. Until the overthrow of the Mongol rulers in China in 1368, the political unification of Tibet prevailed under the rule of the Sakyapa.

d) In their doctrinal structure, the Nyingma-pa, the 'School of the Elders,' are descended from Padmasambhava, and represent the first expansion of Buddhism in Tibet. But they formed as an independent and closed tradition within Tibetan Buddhism only in the wake of the formation of the other schools. In Padmasambhava, its followers see an incarnation of Avalokiteshvara, the bodhisattva of infinite compassion. The Nyingma-pa stress that the relationship between teacher and disciple is of key importance for the upholding of the chain of tradition, and for the guarantee of the authenticity of teaching. In this connection, the *Terma* texts play an important role—religious texts hidden in secret places, to be discovered at a given time by suitable persons and made accessible. A famous example of these treasure-texts is the "Tibetan Book of the Dead," the *Bardo-Thödol.*

e) Tsongkhapa (1357–1419), the great restorer of Tibet's clerical structure, belonged at first to the Kadam line of tradition, but then founded the School of the Gelug-pa, the 'virtuous,' by renewing the discipline of the order. He integrated the teaching of Indian scholars Nagarjuna and

Asanga into his Way: that of the 'steps to enlightenment' (*lamrim*). The point of departure for this doctrine is that human existence is the favorable form of being for the attainment of enlightenment. The exercises of the Way of the Steps include both corporeal and meditative schooling, and join body, speech, and mind to the process of redemption. For this school, as well, the proper goal is the redemption not of the individual, but of all living beings.

Tsongkhapa introduced the Monlam Chenmo, the great prayer festival, in the first month of the Tibetan calendar. Symbolically, this feast represents Tibet's symbolic surrender to Buddhism. Tsongkhapa initiated numerous monastic foundations, including Ganden (1409), Drepung (1416), and Sera (1418). With his disciple Gendün Drub, superior of the Gelug-pa and founder of the monastery of Tashilhunpo, began the chain of reincarnations at whose end, for the time being, stands the fourteenth Dalai Lama. In the fifteenth and sixteenth centuries, with the support of the Mongol khan, the Gelug-pa established not only their spiritual, but also their political predominance in Tibet. Altan Khan, converted to Buddhism by Sonam Gyatso, emerged as patronal lord of the Gelug-pa, and in 1578, conferred on its superior the title of *Dalai Lama* ('Ocean of Wisdom'). The fifth Dalai Lama, Ngawang Lobsang Gyatso, extended the political power of the Gelug-pa throughout Tibet. At the same time, he ended the power of the other schools of Tibetan Buddhism, but not without extensive integration of their teachings into the doctrinal structure of the Gelug-pa.

f) Today, a distinction is made between the older forms of the Bön religion and the tradition of the New Bön, which was established, in the eleventh century, in parallel with the founding of the Buddhist Order. To this day, little is known of the origin or content of the archaic Bön. The reputed founder of the Bön religion is called Tönpa Shenrab, whose birth is dated in the mythic year of 16016 BCE. The school of the New Bön evinces many parallels to the Nyingma tradition of Tibetan Buddhism. In the fifteenth century CE, the New Bön executed a kind of restructuring of the organization of the Order. The founder and first abbot of the Menri monastery (founded 1405) was Shenrab Gyaltsen, Tsongkhapa's contemporary. In 1834, the center of the Bön School moved to the newly founded monastery of Yungdrungling. The abbot there is the elected superior of the Bön-pa.

g) After the flight (1959) of the fourteenth Dalai Lama, many Tibetans left their homeland, including many high 'clergy,' to settle in exile in India, Europe, or the United States. By way of their new centers, founded there, Tibetan Buddhism is becoming known in the West. With the wave of support for Tibetans' political concerns, interest in the Tibetan form of Buddhism has increased as well. Recognized teachers such as Chögyam Trungpa (Karma-Kagyü; 1939–1987), Sogyal Rimpoche (Nyingma; founder of the syncretistic Rigpa Union), Dudjom Rimpoche (Nyingma; 1904–1987), or Namkhai Norbu (Nyingma; *Rime* movement; born 1938), have founded Buddhist schools, and created learning traditions, that seek to develop a form of Vajrayana Buddhism tailored to Western conditions. Western teachers also follow the Tibetan tradition, and themselves found centers (in which doctrinal authenticity is not always preserved, however). The Hamburg Buddhist Center, under the leadership of Geshe Thubten Ngawang (b. 1931), as well as the Monastic Tibet Institute, under Geshe Ugyen Phulotshang (b. 1914), in Rikon, near Zurich (founded 1968), are two of the important Gelug monasteries in Europe.

Stephanie Lováse

Time

A Primary Category

1. Like space, time belongs to the primary categories of human perception and human construction of the world. There is no priority between the two. Time is repeatedly described in metaphors of space (length of time, axis of time), concrete space, at the same time by movements, and therefore by time (three-day trip, or three light-years away). Time appears as a fixed property of the world—unchangeable, encompassing, and subjecting everything to temporalization. Acts and events can be described as occurring 'before' or 'after,' and thus ascribe → meaning to fortuitous co-incidences; *post hoc, ergo propter hoc* (Lat. "After this, therefore because of this"). Particular experiences and the social construction of time emerge in truly manifold guise: duration is experienced differently from the succession of a series, and concentration on the present is distinct from the fixation of a point in time, which slips out of the future, through the present, into the past. The same unit of time can be perceived as different periods, the same rhythms as distinct tempi. Although theoretical approaches exist that assume different forms of time, it seems more sensible to start from a unitary concept of time, and precisely thus to attempt to describe the different time forms as individual, area-specific, or cultural differences.

The Social Character of Time

2. Time is fundamentally *socially structured* time. Even where it is experienced as abstract physical (chronographs), or concrete natural (phases of the moon, 'day' from sunrise to sunset) time, the latter is always a matter of historically emerging symbolic structures of meaning. This contingency is concealed by the metaphors of 'measurement': one proceeds from the fiction that what is (ever more precisely) determined is only that which is naturally given. The successive refinements of the measurement of time make possible a precise determination of the internal concatenation of the acts of all persons and things involved, but make the 'time-screen' that much less available to individuals or groups.

The assumption of a social construction of time does not militate against the existence of certain constants in the human, or even animal, perception of time, as indicated by psychological or chrono-biological investigation: the minimal duration of perceptible stimuli ('absolute time-threshold'), as well as the minimal interval of stimuli whose sequence is correctly determined ('judgment of succession'), both in the range of milliseconds; the period still perceived precisely as a unitary moment ('present time'), in the range of a few seconds; finally, physiological phases repeated, for example, every twenty-four hours ('circadian'). An absolute 'biological clock' that uses the counting-off of regular neuronal occurrences as absolute standard of the sensation of duration (and of the control of biorhythms), has not been identified. On the other hand, 'free-running' rhythms are characteristic, as, for example, the average twenty-five-hour (with a large margin of variability) human rhythm of waking and sleeping. (By way of signals natural and social—sun, alarm clock—this rhythm is then coordinated with social time, ultimately to reveal its periodicity only in sleep-experimentation.) Social time may succeed in supplying life with a rhythm, however imperfect that success: the night manager is an individual deviant, yet even different groups may use different social time-rhythms in the same world of living. For example, Jews in the Roman Empire had to be allowed special rules when donations of wheat fell on Sabbath. The orienting capacity of societal constructions of time is not to be underestimated, however. Linguistic metaphors make time into a grammatical subject ("It's time," "The time is coming," "Time heals all wounds"). They also ascribe 'dominion' over time to high gods—indeed, identify time with the divine—which indicates the perceived dominion of time itself. Indeed, time flows so inexorably that, precisely because it does, it can appear as a severe God. Only highest gods can, by way of exception, interrupt the normal course of time or promise it as time 'devoutly to be wished,' outside (before, after, beyond) our world of experience, as a state of salvation (→ Eternity; Immortality).

3. *World time*: The multiplicity of the constructions of time, of such varying breadths, can be ordered to two poles. The first deals with constructions of time that embrace 'the whole' of → history, and seek the boundaries of time. The second concerns time-constructions that serve the coordination of activity in the social setting.

    a) *Cosmological time* maintains the possibility of fundamental changes. The world was not as it is, nor as it is will it be. The questions arising with time-models of this particular breadth reach to a beginning (cosmogony) and end (eschatology, → End/Eschaton). Accordingly, these questions also regard whether time exists beyond these temporal limits, what meaning the time in between has, such as → progress, → teleology, or decadence, and whether, within this horizon, time runs continuously or leaps. Under the scholarly cloak of complicated calculations and epochs of inconceivable length, the → specialists in cosmological time practice a critique of the present and a prognosis of the future: for example, "The 'Golden Age' lies behind us and before. Knowledge thereof is secret, and a mystery." Thus the unproductive 'work' of the knowing is legitimated.

The Time of the World: Cosmos and History

b) From the viewpoint of the history of religion, an interesting observation is to be made in this discourse, and in its systematization of cultural history. Images of 'foreign' conceptualizations of time, generated by a nimble selection of sources, themselves serve polemical goals. An opposition has been posited between (1) the *linear* conception of time, of the Judeo-Christian tradition, with its direction toward progress and thereby, ultimately modernity, and (2) a *cyclical* conception of a time ever and again returning to its 'origin,' and thereby ultimately emptying history and the effort of historical act of all value. The latter conception of development can be seen to be one hostile to history, and shaped by antiquity (and present also in the European Renaissance), such as by the culture of India. Nietzsche sketched out this opposition polemically, against a bourgeois Christian notion of progress. Thus, in this sketch, he appeals to antiquity. The opposition becomes a commonplace of anthropology and cultural comparison, praising the primitive and the original, and reviling the modern, as in the work of scholar of religion Mircea → Eliade. Now the antinomy is the prisoner of asymmetrical description. There are recurring routines and rhythms, from time-constructions of recent social history, which are under obligation to attempt to reproduce any current society. These routines and rhythms return even in the 'leveled-out' societies of the cosmological time-models, in the long-term perspectives entertained by these latter. Here as well, they are invested with the constraint to reproduce their respective societies. On the other hand, periodical elements of cosmological sketches are frequently

Linear/Cyclical

plucked from complex contexts: the ancient Stoic notion that the world 'burns up' at regular intervals (*ekpyrosis*) and emerges anew, does not rule out the possibility that, within a world age, progress appears (the world can grow better and older). Neither does it mean the return of the same, if time is seen as repetition of worsening world ages. If time continues 'running' as the world repeatedly ends, then a mere position in time guarantees an adequate difference between world ages.

God's Timelessness and Human Time

c) A question repeatedly arising in cosmological sketches of time is the problem of the beginning of time, or: Before the beginning, was there nothing ('creation out of nothing')? If God is continuously timeless, and releases human beings into materially determined time, then creation turns out to be a state of deficiency, which is possibly transitory, and can be defeated by leaps between the levels. The possibility of divine prescience arises, just as does the coordination of individual (over the course of history) and collective eschatological time. The latter then includes the 'before' of the departed as well. Contrariwise, Hindu and Buddhist concepts, which lay stress on individual suffering in temporality, usually reject the notion of a ('secondary') beginning of time.

d) For the development of the conceptualization of time in Europe, the relatively brief chronology of world history became important. The latter was developed in ancient Christian historiography, from the third century onward, and adopted the six (thousand-year) days of the world—that rest on Jewish speculations on the chronology of world history—before God and his people can celebrate the world Sabbath. Competing chronologies and doctrines of the world ages (such as the *saecula* of the Etruscans and the Romans), likewise produce a brief chronology—perhaps typical of city-states' limited universalistic need for legitimization. Here is a picture altogether opposite from that of the tremendous numbers of the Indian cycles that leave room for highly complicated sequences of rebirths (→ Reincarnation). This sort of short projection screen managed to deliver simpler stopping places for movements of a millenarian character. It must be emphasized, however: → Millenarianism does not stop at an even thousand, and still less for a hundredth anniversary, but, instead, designates the present as the immediate prelude to the eschaton ("It's five to twelve"). The radical New Time can produce the New Person. Cosmological time, then, no longer offers a (remote) horizon of the justification of everyday constructions of time, but legitimizes their radical critique. Thus it is not so much a question of consolidating trans-cultural differences in the identification of fundamentally diverse models of time. Instead, it is a matter of the 'historicizing' question of the presence and function of determinate cosmological conceptualizations of time, in their respective 'presents.'

Conceptualizations of Time in the Social Environment

4. *Current time and calendar*: Time is doubtless the most important *tool of coordination* in the social environment. Pocket calendars, watches, travel plans, office plans, and time plans determine the daily life of industrialized societies. Clocks are visible everywhere, and even children have to know how to read them. The coordinating service of these tools is a double one, then: they concentrate persons in the same place, or at least in the same activity, or else they divide them up, in order to avoid lumping and queuing. Again, 'time slips' allow work time to be calculated, unless it is not the same for everyone in a group. Independently of societal distribution and technical

precision, clocks and → calendars are instruments for drawing up records and schedules. Thereby they offer orientation for activities. Even if the year is marked by an abundance of annual (or even more frequent) events, it thereby offers few points of reference that are unambiguous and foreseeable. Only societal convention creates a sufficient number of this sort of points of relation for the structuring of the activity of the entire society, or of individual segments.

a) *The week and the month* are among the most effective constructions of time. Weeks usually run from four to ten days, and are structured by boundary days. Regionally: the local border days are preferably scheduled on different days, and thereby coordinated. Weeks themselves permit a comparatively high frequency of common activity outside the family. The importance that the weekly assembly of religious communities has gained, in post-classical Judaism, in Christianity, and then in Islam, is altogether atypical, and a theoretical norm rather than a social reality even for the religions cited (→ Sunday/Sabbath). Nevertheless, alternatives were unsuccessful, such as Stalin's short-lived five-day week in the 1930s—offering, as it did, no common weekly holiday, and merely retaining individual days of rest. By way of complement, a monthly rhythm enters the scene, especially where weeks run unevenly, and thus need to be coordinated with the month. The latter was the case in ancient Greece, as in the French Revolutionary calendar, with their ten-day weeks. Even in more complex societies, many economic, judicial, political, and societal, as well as religious routines, can develop in monthly periods (tax due dates, judicial and session days, organizational meetings, full-moon and/or new-moon celebrations). The discrepancy of mensual lengths in the Julian and Gregorian calendars, as such, were no problem, since they were predictable. Only the growing calculability of economic time-units, in the absence of a commensurability of the lengths of the month (and of the quarter), ushered in problems (e.g., coordination of the thirty-day tax month with the actual calendar month), and these repeatedly sparked projects of calendar reform. True, in the popular understanding (weather forecasting, rules for marriage), and graphic illustration, individual months acquire individuality. Nevertheless, the religious qualification of entire months is rather rare (the Islamic fasting month of → Ramadan, the—liturgically sparsely marked—Marian month of May).

Week and Month

b) *The year* gathers larger social units into → feasts or festivals, these being celebrated either at one central location or simultaneously in all places. The year is simply calculated by the rhythm of weeks or months, or else is promptly 'evoked' after the appearance of the first blossoms. More or less complicated festival calendars are a typical form of temporal organization in the religions. In their function of conferral of identity, they are much adopted by the national states, and re-shaped. The style and expenditure of coordination, here, is clearly higher than in the more important weekly rhythms. Easter letters, festal proclamations, printed calendars, and lists of feast days are necessary for the coming year. For periodicities of more than one year, the ancient Olympiads, revived in 1896, constitute the most familiar example (→ Olympic Games). The Holy Years of the Roman Catholic Church are celebrated in counted years (in periods meanwhile shortened to twenty five years); there is, however, a growing tendency, with this sort of infrequently celebrated grand event, to supplement or replace fixed rhythms

Year

by setting dates according to social need (a new government, for example).

c) The establishment of the societal time-premises rests on their attractiveness as generally familiar for planning activities, but, in individual cases, also for the maintenance of sanctions and police supervision. The establishment of time-constructions is also a question of power. Political and economic powers compel timely behavior even against the particular interests of the individual. It is typical of the highly differentiated modern → industrial societies that the partial systems gradually develop their own calendars, established in respective organizations. The task of coordination falls to the individual. The clear marks placed on the days of the (religious) week that characterize early and high European industrialization seem to represent rather a transitory phase: now the religious ethics of time that defines Sunday as a day of rest from labor is being successfully reversed—six full workdays—and utilized for economic purposes. But there is longer-lasting interest in abstract conceptions of time, whose units of time stand open to qualification in terms of the system (opening day, delivery date), and demonstrate no progressive qualifications (festival day, rest period, bad-luck day).

Hours

d) A high density of interaction in organizations calls for a temporal precision that the calendar no longer provides. *Clocks* have been familiar since ancient times, but frequently could reveal only short periods (hourglasses), or lead to dissimilar units (sundials). The driving force behind the massive spread of mechanical miniaturized clocks, even of clocks that can be held in the hand, is economic need for measurable work time. In late antiquity, the powerful introduction of rhythm in a total organization like the Christian monastery was able to do without such devices. Nevertheless, the multiplication of the clock shows how the prestige value of technology can outrun massive economic need. Neither the precision of the late-medieval tower clocks, nor of today's pocket chronometer, was 'necessary.'

Life Cycle and 'Crises'

5. Time and religion: The orientation of religious systems is typically played out primarily on the level of cosmological time. For individuals, the concrete link with this super-ordinated level comes by way of rituals of the → life cycle. These acquire their permanent characteristics by temporal placement or analogy-formation. Besides, for individual problematic situations, techniques of → divination are available, often concentrated on the problem of timing: when do I make the trip, marry, or lay the foundation? (Geomancy, the question of whether the location is appropriate, on the other hand, is less common.)

Usage of Time

Faced with competing systems, the individual must come to grips with the problem of the brevity of time, and of an ethics of usage of time. In a rigoristic phase of industrial capitalism, this demand led to a dominant position of the area of economics, legitimized by religion. Activity without profit was a waste of time. This core element of the Weberian thesis of the connection between Protestantism and Western modernity is extended in individual micro-economic theories (→ Economy; Money): "Time is money." The 'leisure time,' as well, is calculated as lost profits. But this rigoristic economic option (just as a rigoristic religious concentration of all time on religious activities) is not actually available for many: Work for profit is not unlimited, or freely available. Further, consumption is replaceable by consumer goods only to a very limited extent: Prosperity in terms of time also becomes an important concept in new economic outlines.

On the other hand, substituting time with time is more plausible. Delaying the payment of a loan by way of an indefinite post-mortem grace period is a common religious approach. By way of a limited life (death), the brevity of time conditioned by 'responsibilities' (in turn conditioned by the brevity) is compensated by an open-ended promise. True, 'time off,' and 'extra time' of old age, broaden the opportunities for the activities of this life, so that this form of compensation loses its attraction. This schedule, however, raises the problem of contingency again—death immediately before retirement—and thus a specific area of religious competence. Characteristically, religions provide claims of orientation beyond their own partial systems and consequently focus more on the temporal structures of their members than on the time budget allotted to the religions themselves. From an organizational point of view, this problem can be compensated only through full-time religious specialists, i.e. through a division of labor.

Literature

BALSLEV, Anindita Niyogi/MOHANTY, J. N. (eds.), Religion and Time, Leiden 1993; BIERVERT, Bernd/HELD, Martin (eds.), Zeit in der Ökonomik. Perspektiven für die Theoriebildung, Frankfurt/M. 1995; CHAPIN, F. Stuart, Human Activity Patterns in the City: Things People Do in Time and in Space, New York 1974; DAVIES, Paul, The Mind of God: Science and the Search for Ultimate Meaning, London 1992; DOHRN-VAN ROSSUM, Gerhard, Die Geschichte der Stunde. Uhren und moderne Zeitordnungen, Munich 1992; ELIAS, Norbert, Time: An Essay, Oxford 1992 (Ger. [1]1984); FRAZER, Julius et al. (eds.), Time, Science, and Society in China and the West, Amherst 1986; GELL, Alfred, The Anthropology of Time: Cultural Constructions of Temporal Maps and Images, Oxford 1992; HARNONCOURT, Philipp/AUF DER MAUER, Hans Jörg, Feiern im Rhythmus der Zeit II/1, Regensburg 1994; HELFRICH, Hede (ed.), Time and Mind, Seattle 1996; NOWOTNY, Helga, Eigenzeit. Entstehung und Strukturierung eines Zeitgefühls, Frankfurt/M. 1989; SOROKIN, Pitrim Alexandrowitsch, Sociocultural Causality, Space, Time: A Study of Referential Principles of Sociology and Social Science, Durham 1943; WENDORFF, Rudolf, Zeit und Kultur. Geschichte des Zeitbewußtseins in Europa, Opladen 1980.

→ *Astrology, Economy, Feasts and Celebrations, History, Calendar, Sunday/Sabbath*

Jörg Rüpke

Tolerance

1. Tolerance means the 'enduring,' 'bearing,' or (colloquially) 'standing' or 'putting up with' the views, lifestyles, goals, interests, and so forth, of others, which do not conform to one's own positions, or that, indeed, contradict them. Socially, or societally, an obligatory organization, like a political state, which possesses the corresponding (or necessary) means of power to impose its position, can accord 'tolerance' to deviant groups, minorities and individuals. However, material and ideal grounds may advise a majority to tolerate deviating notions. The principle of tolerance is also suggested by the insight that persons can err, and that therefore other ideas are to be tolerated. There has been, and still is, intolerance in all areas of human life. The idea of tolerance has developed in Europe particularly in religious questions

A Commandment of Peace

since the wars of religion of the sixteenth and seventeenth centuries. Christian revelation could be made obligatory only for its believers, while faith can be "no object of compulsory laws" (Religious Edict of Wöllner, 1788). Thus, in the modern age, the attempt has been undertaken to make obligatory for all only the conceptualizations established by scientific means, that in principle can be accepted by every qualified agent of the corresponding domain. This standard is based on the presumption that the human being is an insightful being, endowed with reason. Discoveries by modern psychology, especially by → psychoanalysis, that views a human being as essentially determined by drives, admit of considerable doubt with respect to this premise. However, particularly the social sciences, which are responsible for questions of social and individual relations, do not agree in these issues. The result is that they cannot rise to the measure of the hopes reposed in them, so that they could have made their findings the basis of decisions binding for all. In the modern age, what cannot be scientifically proved is declared a private matter. Other views, then, must be tolerated. Only the essentials that underlie these sciences are excepted, while their findings pertaining to value, for example in the constitutions, are withdrawn from alteration even by majority decision. As a rule, these essentials are legitimized by the fact that, without them, even a peaceful coexistence is impossible. Of course, here a distinction must be made between external actions and internal judgments. As a rule, deviant views on these fundamentals are tolerated, provided that they do not lead to concrete actions. Since the → Enlightenment, the fostering and maintenance of tolerance has been regarded as a duty of the state. The foundations of tolerance were the ideas of → human rights. These ideas go back to Christian and Western culture and tradition, and have for some time been regarded as unique. Hence the demand for tolerating such positions, which themselves remove the foundation of tolerance. This conundrum became clear in the discussion on the justification of violence, in which freedom from violence as a presupposition of tolerance finds itself implicitly canceled, and to tolerate force, under the name of revolution, is justified. Here the question of the limits of tolerance is posed. Can a position that is itself intolerant be tolerated in the public sector—and if so, to what degree? Today, no voluntary community (such as a religious, a political, or a sports community) must be based on tolerance, since a resignation from that community is possible at any time.

Subject of Tolerance   2. Religious tolerance is allowed by a state, or by a dominant religion allied in some way with the state, to other religions, or to deviant views in the main religion. It must be clearly distinguished from → freedom of religion, which is a fundamental right of all human beings. Religious freedom presupposes that at least two religions, or two different concepts of one religion standing in mutual contradiction, exist in one society at the same time, and that this divergence leads to conflict. Thus, the question of a religious tolerance arises in societies that host a variety of religious notions, cultural contact, missionary activity, and so on, with each of these factors developing in its own way. These societies will then be confronted with mutually incompatible, and conflicting, convictions of faith and belief, along with mutually irreconcilable sacred acts. In tribal societies, as a rule, culture and religion are very closely connected. Thus, the problem of religious tolerance is rarely posed there. Furthermore, as also in segmented societies, these conflicts can be circumvented by separating them (Sigrist 1967). Deviating doctrines and behaviors become a problem only in despotic societies, when the solidarity of the community, order, or government is called into question. When a number of such cultural communities come together, and create a unitary product, or are brought together by a military defeat, the problem arises as to whether, and to what extent, the different parts can be brought together. Accordingly, tolerance can also be regarded as a compromise among conflicting positions. Furthermore, all religions give different answers to the questions: How should I live, what may I do and what not, in order to partake in a promised salvation? On the basis of different religious views, therefore, history displays a plethora of wars and militant confrontations. Contrary to the commonly expressed opinion, religions *per se* are neither pacific nor tolerant. Rather, tolerance has had to be wrested from them. The only exceptions are communities that withdraw from society and renounce a societal structure. It is observable, of course, that the foundation of tolerance has emerged from confrontations within religions. With the privatization of religion, religion today could become an instance of the proclamation of tolerance.

2. Different forms of tolerance have developed in the history of religions. In the ancient *Roman Empire*, with some exceptions, deviant religious notions and cults were tolerated—as long as the cult of the Emperor, the symbol of Roman rule, was recognized. *Christianity*, from the time of its installation as state religion at least until the Reformation, inclined rather to religious intolerance. ("Error has no rights.") Apart from certain intolerant phases, *Islam* granted the members of the scriptural religions, as a rule, tolerance. Ever since the experiences of the division of India and Pakistan and the subsequent militant conflicts between Hindus and Muslims (destruction of the mosque in Ayodhya, December 6, 1992; see Hacker 1957), the tolerance formerly attributed to the *Indian religions* is evidently a misunderstanding. Only those religious concepts were indulged that could be integrated into the Dharma and the Karma system. Hacker, then, speaks of 'inclusivism.' *Buddhism*, as well, which explicitly teaches tolerance, has been unable to prevent intolerant phases in its history, as one sees currently in the civil wars in Sri Lanka and the reaction to them by numerous Buddhists.

Historical Forms

Literature

ABU-NIMER, Mohammed, Nonviolence and Peace Building in Islam: Theory and Practice, Gainesville 2003; FORST, Rainer, Toleranz im Konflikt. Geschichte, Gehalt und Gegenwart eines umstrittenen Begriffs, Frankfurt/M. 2003; GRELL, Ole Peter/PORTER, Roy (eds.), Toleration in Enlightenment Europe, Cambridge 2000; GUGGISBERG, Hans R., Religiöse Toleranz, Stuttgart 1984; HACKER, Paul, "Religiöse Toleranz und Intoleranz im Hinduismus," in: Saeculum 8 (1957), 167ff.; LAURSEN, John Christian (ed.), Religious Toleration: "The Variety of Rites" from Cyrus to Defoe, New York 1999; LAURSEN, John Christian/NEDERMAN, Cary J. (eds.), Beyond the Persecuting Society: Religious Toleration before the Enlightenment, Philadelphia 1999; LOCKE, John, A Letter Concerning Toleration (1689), ed. by J. HORTON and S. MENDUS, London/New York 1991; NEDERMAN, Cary J., Worlds of Difference: European Discourses of Toleration, c. 1100–c. 1550, University Park 2000; SIGRIST, Christian, Regulierte Anarchie, Olten 1967; STANTON, Graham N./STROUMSA, Guy G. (eds.), Tolerance and Intolerance in Early Judaism and Christianity, Cambridge 1998; ZAGORIN, Perez, How the Idea of Religious Toleration Came to the West, Princeton 2003.

→ *Conflict/Violence, Freedom of Religion, Heresy, Peace, Pluralism, Religion, Sect, Witch/ Persecution of Witches*

Hartmut Zinser

Tourism

"The Tourist Way of Knowledge"

1. "The Tourist Way of Knowledge" was a performance by David Byrne in the Public Theater in New York at the beginning of the 1980s. Taking the denotations of the title, we seem to see something like the hero of old, the seeker of knowledge and new impressions. These 'heroes,' however, carry their limited, limitable knowledge along with them, within their own limits, everywhere they go, all of it available on the inside of their own limitations. They are not requited with knowledge and wisdom, then, as the ancient proclamations teach (→ Daoism; Martial Arts; Zen Buddhism), but with their own projective corroboration of the exotic. Tourists are the 'ignorant abroad.' They journey through the imaginary geography of their own day-dreams (collectively or privately arisen), and their route to thinking, seeing, discovering, and feeling is walled in by their personal world, by the perceptual reality of their 'homeland'—to which, in their far-off adventures, they always take their ultimate orientation.

Rise of Tourism

2. Travel as an end in itself is attested in ancient times, this is true. We need only recall Pausanias and his Greek travel guide of the second century CE. In modern times, however, it was unknown until well into the eighteenth century. One traveled if it was necessary. Travelers were soldiers, statesmen, criminals, couriers, and merchants. In early Hebrew, the word for traveler and merchant is the same (Heb., *rokhel*). Mountain climbers must be accorded a key role in the history of tourism. In the forefront here are the English founders of Alpinism. In 1857, the Alpine Club was founded in London as the first association of mountain climbers. The Alpine movement defines what tourism is all about. Its trade names, still claimed by all tourists today, are 'Adventurous,' 'Elementary,' 'Untouched.' (Mountain) tourists seek, and yearn for, the blessing of freedom—but also the satisfaction of their curiosity. The two ends of the parable of experience mark (1) Petrarch's ascent of Mount Ventoux in 1336, with Augustine's *Confessions*, and their hymn of creation, in his pack (→ Landscape), and (2) today's extreme sportsman à la Reinhold Messner, the one who looks for borderline experiences, and shocks of self-discovery.

3. a) The rising tempo of tourism is caught and 'notched' by Hans Magnus Enzenberger, in three categories, of which each is indispensable for the development of an industry in the grand style: *Normung, Montage, Serienfertigung* (Ger., 'standardization, assemblage, series-manufacture'). With the concept of 'worth seeing'—a 'sight' in the touristic sense—an element of the journey becomes fundamental and 'normed,' like the trip-leader's 'course book.' The invention of the latter goes back to the year 1836, the year of the appearance of John Murray's *Red Book*, which makes a list of 'the things worth seeing,' or 'sights,' selecting them from Holland, Belgium, and Rhineland. "The sight is not only worthy of visitation; it demands it peremptorily."[1] Tourists perform their duty in order to give their journey a meaning.

The strange and foreign evokes our 'hunger for looking,' especially when its guise is as picturesque as the bathing and burning places of the banks of the Ganges (→ Benares), with their entries down to the water. The boat trip past the eighty-four *ghats*, part of the tourist's compulsory program, furnishes an ideal glimpse into the unfamiliar cultic practice. As far as the view from the Holy City is concerned, it is indeed permitted for Western travelers to enjoy the lovely view from one side of the city unhindered. The uncomfortable part begins when onlookers must 'stay outside' and not be integrated into the sacred cult. Especially in the case of an intimate act like the ritual bath in the River, they get into the position, willy-nilly, of voyeur-like 'peeking,' and of 'eying' believers as if they were fish in an aquarium. Still, with their tense attitude, tourists betray the fact that they have taken to heart the prohibition of photography. The perspective from the boat, by the way, is also adopted by pilgrims who abridge their lengthy routes to remote sites of religious reverence, in such a way as to be able to fulfill their ritual obligations from the water. (Hubert Mohr)

Touristic sightseeing, here, runs the risk of competing with the practice of religious cult, and with a sacred power of signification. Cultic construction such as Saint Peter's Basilica and the Sistine Chapel in Rome, Notre Dame in Paris, or the Cologne Cathedral become extensively invested with the tone of a museum, travel groups outweigh groups of pilgrims, the perspective of art history or even of art religion dares to tread on intimate sectors, or sacred, banned areas such as the sanctuary of the altar (→ Art Religion; Museum). Sights are still only buildings. Especially in bus tourism, competition prevails between stable and mobile architecture. The mobile architecture of modern tour buses is dedicated to the purpose, outfitted as it is with movie seating, air conditioning, a kitchen, with full-circle glass all around, to show and reach as many 'sights' as possible. By way of the *assemblage* of sights for the prepared trip, these 'sights' can be specifically marketed. Wholesale tourists obtain the 'sights' strung on a line, and they can uncoil them without any inconvenience. Like any consumer goods, the trip or journey must be set up in long series. In 1845, Thomas Cook organized the first 'club' trip. Mass tourism had been born.

b) Even modern individual tourism no longer changes this. The normative touristic destinations no longer need be equipped and set in a series. They are ubiquitous. The holy mount in the Himalayas and the Greek procession of the Saints, together with the 'hip' *Kaphenion* that still sent the 'dropout generation' of the 1960s and 1970s scurrying about after secret tips, are discovered today when the tourist finds them in illustrated travel guides, or newspaper travel-supplements, and all of the other tourists come running to peek. Enzensberger, in this connection, decries the 'denunciation of tourism.' Indeed, the detractors are frequently concerned with the maintenance of their privileged position, the retention of the exclusive trip, without the cheap 'tourist crowd'—tourists are still always 'the others.'

The touristic self-disavowal, however, is a self-deception. The attempt to preserve the 'untouched adventure of freedom' ends in the destruction of the object. The untouched elementary—the traditional feast, the 'hearty hospitality,' the once-in-a-lifetime experience of this landscape, the 'authentic' tribal rites—become present only through contact. Thereby the 'untouched

Authenticity Claims and Commodification

Shiva is the great god of Hindu ascetics. By way of the most strenuous practices, performed in the heights of the Himalayas, he inherits the power to destroy the universe—and the unknowing that blocks the route to salvation. Lord of the peaks, he is also accounted the guardian of a hotel proprietor and her establishment in Gandhruk, a resting place for wagon pullers in the mountains of central Nepal. Accordingly, she reverences him by way of a poster on the wall of her Shiva Hotel—a usage occurring in Hindu lands, to the honor of various deities, on the walls of houses, shops, and factories (Lakshmi, goddess of fortune and prosperity; Ganesha, remover of all obstacles). The lady also knows, however, that the colorful world of the gods will not fail to leave its impression on her principal clientele, Western mountain-climbers with spiritual inclinations. (S. Stapelfeldt)

elementary' is annihilated as well. "The disappearance of the uniqueness of places through their constant technological accessibility, can be interpreted by comparison with the loss of the aura of a work of art through technological reproduction."[2] Aspirants also reach a dead end when they go to distant lands for a discovery of self, or to the consumption of intoxicating drugs by the Kabul-Katmandu connection in the 1960s and 1970s, or as with the disciples of Maria Sabina or Carlos Castaneda in Mexico. Foreign cults and cultures all too often serve only as material for filling up the modern, individual emptiness of a society of superfluities. Marlboro has bought up the freedom of adventure, however. And even the hole in your shoe is no longer a lacuna in the market. In ever-new attempts, tourism, embittered, struggles to escape the cycles of freedom, and destruction of the same things, of foreign experience and self-projection, of pretension to authenticity and marketability, change of scenery, which are its law of life. And time and again, it fails.

Tourism in Numerical Figures

c) International tourism today is a billion-dollar business. In 1961, the outlay was 6.8 billion dollars; by 1985, it had risen to 10.5 billion. These figures can be concretized in the storm to the Alps. In 1871, the first cog-rail track was built, at Rigi, and transported 70,000 persons in its second year of operation. By 1816, only three hundred persons had climbed this mountain. In the 1980s, Switzerland had a good 1,700 cable and elevator installations, with a capacity of around some 1.1 million persons—per hour! The harm done to nature is immense. Ski slopes need 24,000 hectares of land. That is as much as taken up by the Canton's railroad. Every second, another square meter is built up in Switzerland. "The danger of tourism's self-destruction is not empty chatter, but an altogether real process—although one transpiring by steps and often unnoticeably."[3]

Pilgrim Tourism

4. Worldwide, some one-third of all tourists travel for religious or spiritual reasons. 'Spiritual tourists' usually go it alone, with a backpack, and into

remote areas of India, where they are already awaited by 'shamans,' or to places of power and cult like Stonehenge or → Machu Picchu. Rituals can be 'co-booked.' Pilgrims move in groups, as they always have. Twenty million Muslims alone start out for Mecca; Saint Peter's Basilica in → Rome sees six million tourists a year (in the Holy Year 2000, ten to twenty million pilgrims visited Rome); eleven million pilgrimage to Lourdes. All in all, around 300 million pilgrims are on the road in Europe each year. In order to channel these travel currents and skim off a yield most profitably, specialized travel agencies have been formed for pilgrim tourism. All important pilgrimage destinations are made accessible. The pilgrimage bureaus woo even those who go to Thailand, or India, to study world religions. The concept of the pilgrimage is promoted, along with exchange among those of like mind. With many trips, besides the technical tour leaders, priests are available. At the end of their journey, tourists on pilgrimage will surely return home interiorly enriched. Frequently, the sponsors of these undertakings are church institutions.

1. ENZENSBERGER 1987, 670.
2. GEHLEN, Rolf, Welt und Ordnung, Marburg 1995, 220.
3. MÄDER, Ueli, "Sturm auf die Alpen," in: Universitas 7 (1987), 692.

Literature

BURNS, Peter M., An Introduction to Tourism and Anthropology, London 1999; CHAMBERS, Erve (ed.), Tourism and Culture: An Applied Perspective, Albany 1997; ENZENSBERGER, Hans Magnus, "Eine Theorie des Tourismus," in: Universitas 7 (1987), 660-676 (¹1958); NASH, Dennison, Anthropology of Tourism, Oxford 1996; NASH, Dennison (ed.), Beginnings of an Anthropology of Tourism: A Study in Intellectual History, Oxford 2004; Ross, Glenn F., The Psychology of Tourism, Melbourne 1994; ROSSEL, Pierre (ed.), Tourism: Manufacturing the Exotic, Copenhagen 1988; SHIELDS, Rob, Places on the Margin, London 1991; SMITH, Mick/DUFFY, Rosaleen, The Ethics of Tourism Development, London 2003; SMITH, Valene L. (ed.), Hosts and Ghosts: The Anthropology of Tourism, Philadelphia ²1989 (¹1977); VUKONIC, Boris, Tourism and Religion, Oxford 1996; WOODSIDE, A. G. et al. (eds.), Consumer Psychology of Tourism, Hospitality and Leisure, 3 vols., Wallingford 2000–2004.

→ *Colonialism, Environmentalism, Landscape, Local Devotion, Mission, Orientalism/ Exotism, Pilgrimage, Place (Sacred), Religious Contact, Road/Path/Journey, Sports*

Gerhard Schlatter

Tradition

The concept of 'tradition' plays an important role in the study of religion. It invokes the continuity that justifies historical analysis and comparison. Were there no religious tradition(s), scholars would have nothing to study, no threads with which to card and spin their own academic traditions. The fact that 'tradition' can serve as a synonym for both → 'religion' and 'culture'—terms notoriously fraught with definitional and ideological tensions—hints at hidden depths. Tradition raises complex questions, as do all acts of transmission or → translation. Does that which is transferred remain the same or is it changed, as it passes between different generations, social groups, → languages, and cultures? To what extent is the continuity of tradition a 'natural' effect of social and institutional structures, and to what extent is it a strategic construct of human (or superhuman) agents? What epistemological and ideological issues are implicit in attempts to characterize traditions as authentic or inauthentic, genuine or invented? Is it possible to evaluate such judgments beyond simply choosing allegiances among potentially incommensurable perspectives, e.g., orthodoxy/heterodoxy, primary/secondary source, insider/outsider, and colonized/colonizer?

Etymology and Antonyms

Tradition is the act of handing over. Early meanings (many now archaic) emerge from religious (especially Christian) conceptions of → authority: beliefs passed down, above all orally (→ Oral Tradition), from generation to generation, including the Oral Torah (→ Bible); oral instruction, including teaching the Creed to catechumens; the apostolically-legitimized teachings of the Roman Catholic Church; and the *sunna* of the Prophet → Muhammad. In the sixteenth century, 'tradition' was generalized to include both transferring the possession of objects and custom, or normative usage more generally. Insofar as the content of tradition is seen as sacrosanct, questions of authenticity are shifted to the process of transmission. This shift is indicated by a third cluster of meanings, according to which tradition is also betrayal, including delivery of oneself or others over to Satan and the surrender of Christian scriptures to persecuting authorities.

Just as 'sacred' takes on determinate meaning in contrast to 'profane,' and 'culture' in contrast to 'nature,' 'tradition(al)' becomes clearer in relational tension with other concepts. Tradition is commonly held to be static, ancient, unitary, local, continuous, received, and repetitive in contrast to that which is dynamic, modern, plural, global, discontinuous, invented, and innovative. The basic metaphor of 'handing down unchanged that which is meaningful and valued' portrays 'tradition' as the other of various forms of semantic rupture. Tradition roots continuity of meaning in (a) externalities (e.g., creeds, → texts, → rituals, institutions) that (b) function as warrants of authenticity by virtue of their perceived contiguity to the past: e.g., the authority of the *Hadiths* is a function of their repetition of historical originals. Discontinuity can result from severing the link to externalities: e.g., the Radical → Reformation was radical due to its internalization of discipline, breaking the self-consciously historical and institutional relation between *restitutio* and *traditio*. It can also result from severing perceived links to the past: e.g., → colonialism, modernization (→ Modernity/Modern Age; Postmodernity), and globalization have created social, economic, and political ruptures, undermining the long-established → identities of cultural groups around the world.

Great and Little Traditions

Robert Redfield (1956), drawing on anthropological studies of Mayan culture(s), drew an influential distinction between 'great tradition' and 'little tradition.' The former tends to be elite, urban, universal, textual, 'religious,' orthodox, scholarly, refined, central, and, above all, "consciously cultivated and handed down" (p. 70); whereas the latter tends to be popular, peasant-based, local, oral, 'superstitious,' heterodox, folk, unrefined, peripheral, and unreflective. Redfield stressed the need to study mutual interactions between the two: "Great and little tradition can be thought of as two currents of thought and action, distinguishable, yet ever flowing into and out of each other" (p. 72). McKim Marriott (1955) suggested that processes of 'universalization' and 'parochialization' were responsible for the slow two-way movement between village and more global levels. Milton Singer (1972) emphasized the strategic use of public ritual to manage portrayals of India's great tradition, arguing, contra Redfield, that great/little does not correspond to modern/traditional, because much that is 'modern' is old and many 'traditions' are recent inventions. The great/little distinction has been criticized as over-generalized, under-theorized, colonialist or orientalist (reflecting biased outsider discourses; → Orientalism/Exotism), and elitist or fundamentalist (reflecting biased insider discourses; → Fundamentalism). Even granted its potential value, the distinction has suffered from two main problems: it hides normative assumptions behind a descriptive tool; and it has too often justified an exclusive focus on one or the other extreme (e.g., on village-level micro-analyses or global generalizations based on normative texts), ignoring the question of mutual influences and the ideological dimensions of the distinction itself.

Seeing tradition as 'the given' ignores agency, i.e., the strategic value of claiming the high ground of 'tradition' in struggles for power. Malinowski emphasized that myth is "a hard-working active force" (1992 [1926], 101); recent scholarship goes further in seeing tradition as a tool. Eric Hobsbawm distinguished genuine from invented traditions: "insofar as there is [. . .] reference to a historic past, the peculiarity of 'invented' traditions is that the continuity with it is largely fictitious. In short, they are responses to novel situations which take the form of reference to old situations, or which establish their own past by quasi-obligatory repetition [. . .]" (Hobsbawm/Ranger 1983, 1). Hobsbawm suggested that the invention of tradition (and the '(re)-invention' of 'extinct' traditions) has become more frequent in modernity, as 'the old ways' of genuine traditions have been threatened by rapid social transformation (pp. 4-8). Terence Ranger, in the same volume, argued that Western scholars and administrators invented African 'tradition' as the other of modernity: where African societies had, as a matter of historical fact, been characterized by "multiple identities" and "overlapping networks of association and exchange," this "pre-colonial movement of men and ideas was replaced by the colonial custom-bounded, microcosmic local society," whereas "there rarely existed in fact the closed corporate consensual system which came to be accepted as characteristic of 'traditional' Africa" (pp. 247-248; 254).

The agency of invention is not limited to the colonizers: (re)invention of tradition can be an important indigenous strategy in resisting or rejecting colonization, modernization, and globalization (see, e.g., → North America [Traditional Religions]). In this light, the authenticity of tradition can be framed in terms of autonomy—not historical truth—as characterized by a wider or narrower scope of agency: tradition is "volitional temporal action," with its contrary being "not change but oppression" (Glassie 1995, 409 and 396). Is the Melanesian re-invention of tradition through the discourse of *kastom* inauthentic because it self-consciously appropriates and inverts colonial discourse, or is it authentic because it is a product of indigenous agency (cf. Babadzan 1988)? The latter alternative is closed if we insist that post-colonial invented traditions are necessarily oppositional and counterhegemonic: i.e., that "the discourse of the dominant shapes and structures the discourse of the dominated" (Keesing 1994, 41; → Discourse). Less deterministically, "Just because what is done is culturally logical does not

The Invention of Tradition

mean the logic determined that it be done [. . .]. [T]raditions are invented in the specific terms of the people who construct them [. . .]" (Sahlins 1999, 409).

Academic Traditions   Western academic traditions on 'tradition' manifest the usual spectrum of views, from realist through constructionist to relativist. For example, the distinction between genuine and invented traditions—between historical facts and orientalist/colonialist constructions—presupposes the modernist distinction between real and represented (Friedman 1992, 849). This raises the possibility that any search for genuine religious tradition(s) reflects an invented aspect of Western political/academic traditions: "how do we defend the 'real past' [. . .] and 'genuine' traditions [. . .] if we accept that all cultural representations—even scholarly ones—are contingent and embedded in a particular social and political context?" (Linnekin 1992, 250). 'Tradition' quickly unfolds into issues of truth, authenticity, authority, autonomy, and power; and distinct academic traditions inform varying answers to questions such as the following: Can we make sense of the alleged unity of → 'Hinduism' as an ancient tradition founded on the Vedas without giving a central role to both (a) the Western academic tradition on this 'tradition' and (b) the traditions invented by nineteenth-century Hindu Reform movements as they reacted to colonial portrayals of Indian history (cf. Fitzgerald 2000, 134ff.; Sontheimer/Kulke 1989)? Richard King suggests that the secular and reductionistic tendencies of the academic study of religion are rooted in a post-Enlightenment valuation of modernity vs. tradition, a constructed rupture often linked to another: progressive West vs. timeless East (1999, 46; → Progress; History). Extending this view, religious studies can never escape the situated and limited perspective of its own invented tradition(s) re 'tradition(s).'

However, it may be possible to chart a less radically relativistic course—losing a few colleagues to Scylla rather than the whole boat to Charybdis—by analyzing 'tradition' in relational tension with other concepts. Likely the most significant analytical appeal to 'tradition' in the study of religion has been the Weberian distinction between traditional, charismatic and rational-legal forms of authority, especially as embodied in the tension between → priest and → prophet (1978; → Weber; Charisma). Here, 'tradition' is defined in terms of its conservative function, and it is analyzed from the point of view of specific social and institutional structures (Bourdieu 1987 [1971]). As such, tradition—whether it is believed to be invented from whole cloth or guaranteed authentic by divine authority—is both 'traditional' and radical, depending on one's analytical frame.

Literature

BABADZAN, Alain, "*Kastom* and Nation-Building in the South Pacific," in: GUIDIERI, Remo et al. (eds.), Ethnicities and Nations, Austin 1988, 199-228; BOURDIEU, Pierre, "Legitimation and Structured Interests in Weber's Sociology of Religion," trans. Chris TURNER, in: LASH, Scott/WHIMSTER, Sam (eds.), Max Weber, Rationality and Modernity, London 1987, 119-136; ENGLER, Steven/GRIEVE, Gregory (eds.), Historicizing 'Tradition' in the Study of Religion, Berlin/NewYork 2005; FITZGERALD, Timothy, The Ideology of Religious Studies, Oxford 2000; FRIEDMAN, Jonathan, "The Past in the Future: History and the Politics of Identity," in: American Anthropologist 94/4 (1992), 837-859; GLASSIE, Henry, "Tradition," in: Journal of American Folklore 108 (1995), 395-412; HOBSBAWM, Eric/RANGER, Terence (eds.), The Invention of Tradition, Cambridge 1983; KEESING,

Roger M., "Creating the Past: Custom and Identity in the Contemporary Pacific," in: Contemporary Pacific 1 (1989), 19-42; KING, Richard, Orientalism and Religion, London/New York 1999; LINNEKIN, Jocelyn, "On the Theory and Politics of Cultural Construction in the Pacific," in: Oceania 62 (1992), 249-263; MARRIOTT, McKim (ed.), Village India, Chicago 1955; MALINOWSKI, Bronislaw, Magic, Science and Religion, New York 1992; REDFIELD, Robert, Peasant Society and Culture, Chicago 1956; SAHLINS, Marshall, "Two or Three Things That I Know about Culture," in: Journal of the Royal Anthropological Institute 5 (1999), 399-421; SINGER, Milton, When a Great Tradition Modernizes, New York/London 1972; SONTHEIMER, Günther/KULKE, Hermann (eds.), Hinduism Reconsidered, New Delhi 1989; van HENTEN, J. W. /HOUTEPEN, A. (eds.), Religious Identity and the Invention of Tradition, Assen 2001; WEBER, Max, Economy and Society, Berkeley 1978.

→ *Academic Study of Religion, Colonialism, Demise of a Religion, Discourse, History, Memory, New Religions, Oral Tradition, Reception, Translation, Text/Textual Criticism, Writing*

Steven Engler

Trance

1. The word 'trance' derives from the Latin prefix *trans-* ('over,' 'beyond'), and occurs for the first time at the end of the eighteenth century, in connection with Mesmerism. It means a condition of consciousness 'beyond' normal waking consciousness. It denotes a sleep-like condition in which those involved seem no longer to be themselves. Anthropologists of the twentieth century have observed that trance plays an important role in the rites and cults of all cultures. Here it is described as a condition of dissolution, accompanied by a deficiency in controlled movements, as well as by hallucinations and visions, which are then often forgotten. Trance appears in two principal forms: *possession* and *ecstasy*. In the condition of possession, or → 'enthusiasm' (from Gk., *én-theos*, having a 'god within'—being god-enthused or in-spired), a god, a spirit, or a demon takes possession of the believer and penetrates the believer's body. With the trance-form of ecstasy, just the other way around, the psyche leaves the body, which—as frequently in → shamanism—may fall into a stupor-like rigidity.

2. Under usual circumstances, human perception takes place consciously. This condition is generally experienced as normal. There are, however, numerous other states of consciousness that are not perceived as normal, such as sleep and → dream, → intoxication and → ecstasy. These altered states of consciousness include trance, which occurs in a religious context as well as in a secular. Trance is a congenital behavioral pattern that can be activated through certain corporeal techniques (dancing, running, swaying with the upper body). Trance instills those affected with a feeling of dissociation: they feel themselves to consist of two observers, one part of their consciousness being directed within, while the other part has a sense of leaving the body, and observing itself and its surroundings from without.

The Psychology of the Condition of Trance

Trance allows subjects to be released from everything learned hitherto, and renders them capable of accomplishments of soul and body that they would not otherwise attempt. Considered from a psychological viewpoint, the trance stage makes possible a grasp of psychic processes that are hidden

An interesting form of the secularization of trance can currently be observed in Morocco. The cult actors of the Gnawa Brotherhood are disconnecting themselves from their old traditions, and broadening their opportunities. Selected by a Danish gallery director, some of them have even begun to paint pictures while in a trance, and thus to render visible their inner life. This process becomes extremely clear in a painting by Mohamed Tabal. Here Tabal expresses his own possession by the spirits of the water, and thereby alludes to the origin of Gnawa on the Niger River. One can see fish, but also camels, which represent the voyage from Nigeria to Morocco. The expression on his face is that of a person all in ineffable rapture and referring to a frenetic presentation of the spirits, who incite self-mutilation. (F. Welte)

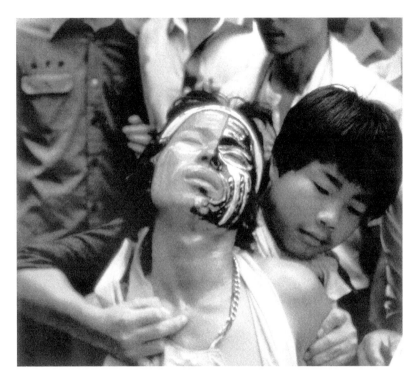

A medium, the human representative of a divine being, incarnates a divine 'General,' at the Festival of Beigang in Taiwan. He is in a deep trance and belongs to a group of eight 'generals' who must precede the divine litters, in order to restrain the spirits. After his emergence, he collapses, falling into the arms of the members of the cult. The finger pressure on the tip of his breastbone is intended to extract him from the trance condition. The medium has shifted his consciousness completely inward, and is insensitive to normal external stimuli. The pressure on his breastbone represents a conditioned stimulus ('trigger release'), which makes it possible to resume contact with him. Exactly the same pressure can be used to place him in a deep trance. The same mechanism is employed by the Moroccan Gnawa cult (see other picture), where mediums are enfolded in a trance, and extracted again, through the use of incense. The trigger release varies with the particular cult; the conditioning is essential, and it is molded by cult and culture. The medium's face is altogether enraptured. Without his companions' attention, he would be completely helpless. Only the consciousness of being protected makes possible the extraordinary exploits of the trance medium, such as self-mutilation, or the receipt of visions and prophecies bestowed in the depths of a trance.

from waking consciousness. Normally, knowledge of these other forms of reality is available only through a recall of dreams, by the ingestion of drugs, and by reports of things not available to personal experience—→ visions by prophets and seers, clairvoyants and mediums.

The most important characteristic of the trance is the extensive exclusion of waking consciousness. The goal is to shift one's consciousness from without to within, so that the outer world is effaced. The results of research into consciousness suggest that it draws from a determinate palette of possible experiences. Segments of it can be activated by certain experiences, and thus become sensible to the subject. Familiar techniques include → fasting, flogging (→ Flagellants), hyperventilation, sleep deprivation, extreme athleticism, dancing, techno parties, under-stimulation, over-stimulation, and ingestion of intoxicating drugs and hallucinogens. Trance is often induced through the use of music, especially that of rhythmic instruments such as drums or rattles (→ Rhythm).

3. The experience of trance is extremely varied. A distinction is made between moving and unmoving, lighter and deeper trance. Trance can be either self-induced, or induced by other persons, with or without drugs.

a) *Everyday trance* is scarcely perceived. Driving a car through the rain, looking through the constant back-and-forth of the windshield wipers, one may find one's sense of time altered. One is lost in a daydream. Space and time are now deprived of any objects, as likewise occurs in sexual intercourse and orgasm, when one's perception is shifted away from its accustomed objects.

b) The most familiar example of the self-induced unmoving trance is *autogenous training*, a type of self-hypnosis. By way of the inner pronunciation of standardized autosuggestions, such as "I am becoming entirely

During the vegetarian festival, celebrated annually among Chinese immigrants on the island of Phuket in Thailand, scenes like this one can be observed. In a trance, this man has pierced his cheek with a television antenna, in order to be able to introduce positive energy into his body. This procedure is supposed to bring health to himself and to his family. The apples impaled on the antenna stand for the prosperity for which he hopes. Apples do not grow in Thailand, and must be imported; thus, they are among the country's costly fruits, and have a high prestige value. (B. Heusel)

peaceful," the consciousness is turned inward, and the outside world is to a large extent effaced. In this way, a light trance is attained, making it possible to affect the vegetative nervous system. It is a matter of a voluntary form of auto-manipulation—a manner of proceeding reminiscent of prayer, with which, by the recitation of set vocal formulas like the Lord's Prayer, the prayers of the Rosary, or the Hindu → mantras, an altogether determinate state of consciousness is intended.

Hypnosis

c) Purely externally, *other-induced unmoving trance* resembles the state of sleep, and is therefore named hypnosis, which derives from *hýpnos*, the Greek word for sleep. The two states, however, differ significantly. Clinical investigation by electroencephalogram (EEG) has established that, with hypnosis, so-called alpha waves emerge, corresponding to the normal waking state of someone who is excited. With autogenous training, or in prayer, as above, suggestions are pronounced interiorly; but with hypnosis, the subject takes careful note of the hypnotist's suggestions with 'free-floating attentiveness.' The hypnotist, by way of enunciation of the suggestions, also enters a light state of trance, with greater receptivity receptive to the condition of the subject than is available in the waking state.

Deep Trance

d) Especially gifted trance personalities, such as mediums, shamans, and spiritual healers, have the capacity to go into *deep trance*, and to direct their consciousness far deeper within than is possible for average people. The characteristic peculiarities of this kind of ecstatic trance are eyes staring aloft, slightly open mouth, and wild nodding and shaking of the head—to the point of catalepsy, an extreme state of corporal rigidity. Everyday awareness can be completely excluded, and messages, visions, or even prophecies can be received. Deep trance is accompanied by loss of memory, and so, for their journey to their interior, mediums need a guide, to attend to them, and to note down or interpret their messages.

e) The exclusion of waking consciousness is also used in *occult and spiritistic practices.* With glass and table shifting or moving, a focus of the eyes on the glass or table produces a *self-induced group hypnosis*, in which a harmony of unconscious muscular movements is achieved, which then leads to the seemingly improbable movements of glass and table (→ Spiritism, with ill.). Simultaneously, a group fantasy is formed, which is then referred to the intervention of invisible spirits.

Spiritism

f) Trance finds its most impressive form in the *trance play*, a dramatic presentation. Spirits are represented, most of whom are regarded as responsible for diseases, ancestors, gods, demons, totem animals, and even historical personalities such as rulers and saints (obviously Caucasian), and objects, such as satellites or an automobile, whose presence ought to be impossible. The presentations are of the highest intensity. Trance is reached by way of a superfluity of external stimuli. Roaring music is one of the means, as is the burning of incense, or a scenic presentation by members of the cult, frequently to the point of raging, screaming, and self-mutilation. This spectacle is followed by a calm on the part of the preponderantly female participants, who then allow themselves to fall into a trance, with a pronounced cathartic effect (→ Colonialism I, with illus.).

Trance Play

4. In Western society, trance, when evident, has until now been a monopoly of the churches. With the increase of secularization, however, this monopoly has been extensively lost. The need, afterwards, has remained, however, and is satisfied, e.g., by the utterly copious offers of the → New Age and the modern esoteric scene. Bhagwan Shree Rajnesh was a spiritual leader, who, in the 1960s, propagated Hindu trance practices among Westerners as group therapy, and had himself venerated by his disciples as a guru (*The Orange Book*, 1985; → Osho Movement). American anthropologist Felicitas D. Goodman has chosen an altogether different route to a satisfaction of the enduring need for trance. She concerned herself scientifically with psychological anthropology and linguistics, researching various forms of religious ecstasy. By way of experimental research with her students, she discovered that, with the adoption of certain bodily postures, linked with a drawn out, monotone auditory stimulus, the state of trance can be induced. From this practice she has developed her particular trance technique, which she calls 'ritual bodily postures.' She teaches worldwide.

Trance in Western Reception Today

Literature

BOURGUIGNON, Erika (ed.), Religion, Altered States of Consciousness, and Social Change, Columbus 1973; GOODMAN, Felicitas, Where the Spirits Ride the Wind: Trance Journeys and Other Ecstatic Experiences, Bloomington 1990; KRAMER, Fritz W., The Red Fez: Art and Spirit Possession in Africa, London 1993 (Ger. [1]1987); LAMBEK, Michael, Human Spirits: A Cultural Account of Trance in Mayotte, Cambridge 1981; MANA, Abdelkader (ed.), The Gnawa and Mohamed Tabal, Casablanca 1998; ROUGET, Gilbert, Music and Trance: A Theory of the Relations between Music and Possession, Chicago 1985 (Fr. [1]1980); SURYANI, Luh Ketut/JENSEN, Gordon D., Trance and Possession in Bali: A Window on Western Multiple Personality, Possession Disorder, and Suicide, Kuala Lumpur 1993; WELTE, Frank M., Der Gnawa-Kult. Trancespiele, Geisterbeschwörung und Besessenheit in Marokko, Frankfurt/M. 1990.

→ *Channeling, Dance, Dream, Ecstasy, Enthusiasm, Intoxication/Drugs/Hallucinogens, Music, Possession, Psyche, Rhythm, Shamanism, Vision/Auditory Experience*

Frank Maurice Welte

Transcendence

Transcendence is originally a philosophical concept that distinguishes the immediately accessible, differentiated world of reality from a foundational space that lies behind it. The theological theme of God's quality as a reality 'beyond' was open to a corresponding development, which has indeed been realized. Since antiquity, transcendence is essentially a space reached neither by sensory perception nor by speech. Thus, God remains in the realm of the ineffable. Approaches to the transcendent God belong to 'negative theology,' which generates its propositions by way of negations.

Boundaries Drawn
An application of this concept in terms of the study of religion can take as its point of departure the fact that all systems of religious symbols find a boundary between the approachable and the unapproachable, the controllable and the uncontrollable. But it is not to be assumed that the areas thus set in mutual relation lead to the same propositions in all religions, or even that they are used with constancy and consistency in the same religion. Instead, variable, and multifariously vague, boundaries present themselves, in some instances in a multiplicity of areas. Nor is it only a question of the being and quality of transcendence that is at issue. Also involved is the (ever asymmetrical) relation between the realm 'beyond' and the region 'here.'

Localization of Transcendence
Transcendence can be variously located, most obviously in outer space. Thus, for example, cultivated space can be bounded off from uncultivated space, with varying positive or negative qualities. For example, the forest or → water can be seen as a realm of menace, or of life-promoting powers. The development of this space varies. Areas of the sky, or of the underworld, can be considered thematically, either in detail, or sparsely. Even the inner world of the human being (→ Soul), the region of ecstatic and uncontrolled experiences (→ Trance), offers an occasion for the localization of transcendence. In the dimension of time, the area before the beginning or after the end comes into question. Finally, transcendence can be considered in a context of transitory processes (→ Time), as the uncontrollable coincidence.

→ *God/Gods/The Sacred, Hereafter, Metaphysics, Place (Sacred), Religion, Theology*

Fritz Stolz

Translation

Insofar as → religion is a cross-cultural phenomenon—and because its academic study is international—translation is integral to its history and study. Yet scholars of religion rarely critically examine the creativity, limitations, or biases of translation. This omission is surprising given that complex relations between → language, → meaning, culture, and ideology clearly undermine the ideal of a simple, transparent correspondence between statements in different languages. Several issues present themselves here: the place of texts and translation in religion(s) and in the study of religion(s); the 'non-transparency' of translation and the inevitability of semantic distortion; ideological issues raised by relations between source and target cultures; and theoretical issues raised by claims of a common cross-cultural core that allegedly justifies the use of a generic concept of 'religion.'

Texts are central to most religions, though entirely absent in others, and they are the primary religious materials for scholars of religion (→ Text/Textual Criticism; Writing). The study of 'religion' has consisted primarily of contextualized readings of selected texts from many cultures, above all 'sacred scriptures,' including revelation, theology, commentary, hagiography, creeds, legal codes, sectarian history, and devotional literature. Max Müller's translation of the *Upanishads* (1879), inaugurating the fifty-volume *Sacred Books of the East* series, was just one milestone marking the importance of translation to the development of the modern study of religion. Scholars have recently placed greater emphasis on non-scriptural phenomena, such as oral traditions, rituals, art, and architecture, but here too texts remain central, e.g., transcriptions of oral performances by the Haida story-teller Ghandl, instructions for ritual purification in the Zoroastrian *Avesta*, statements on iconoclasm by the ninth-century Christian Councils, or architectural norms in the medieval Hindu *Agamas*.

The Focus on Texts

The translation of religious texts has both insider and outsider dimensions. On the one hand, members of a given religion often belong to different linguistic and cultural groups, e.g., Muslims who read Indonesian or Turkish renderings of the *Qur'an*. On the other hand, scholars of religion work with and publish both primary and secondary sources in various languages. In all these cases, to translate is to transpose, transform, transfer or transplant: difference always intervenes between what can be said in any two languages, between educated and casual readers, and between the cultural, social, and political contexts of source and target languages. These same issues of translation are also raised by the transposition of texts within what is arguably a single language: from ancient to modern Greek, Chinese or Hebrew, or from Shakespeare's tongue into colloquial twenty-first-century English.

Insider and Outsider

Perhaps the most significant long-term translation project in history was the diffusion of Buddhist texts from Pali and Sanskrit into Tibetan and Chinese. Many of the translators, such as Kumarajiva, were widely esteemed for their genius. Three central issues in the translation of religious texts are illustrated by this centuries-long endeavor. First, the treatment of technical terms demanded the expression of ideas foreign to the intellectual traditions of the target languages. Early Chinese efforts used transliterations of Pali and Sanskrit terms or borrowed concepts from Daoism. There is a trade-off here beyond ease of comprehensibility and corruption of meaning. (Christians faced similar problems in translating 'Holy Spirit' into African languages, sometimes drawing on indigenous concepts for 'spirits' or 'wind' and sometimes importing Latin or other European loan words. The related decision to sometimes translate 'demons' using words for 'ancestors' underlines the role of ideology here.)

Technical Terms, Standardization, and Audience

Second, the variety of solutions to problems of translation resulted in disparate renderings of the same or similar texts. Chinese and Tibetan translation efforts were generally piecemeal, with only limited use of more standardized approaches—as in the work of the seventh-century pilgrim and translator, Xuanzang. (In a variant of this problem, conservative Christian views that the Holy Spirit guided the writing of the Bible generally fail to note the correlated need for a theory of inspired translation, especially given the proliferation of modern-language English versions [Allert 1999].)

Third, these Buddhist translations varied greatly according to their intended audience. In China, for example, educated lay readers preferred paraphrases that used classical stylistic devices, where scholars preferred more literal versions. (Similar tensions exist among twentieth-century English translations of the Jewish Talmud. The recently-completed seventy-three-volume Schottenstein edition is aimed at a popular audience largely unfamiliar with Talmudic nuances, but scholars prefer the more literal Soncino edition or the JTS *El 'Am* partial translation, with its lengthy critical commentary.)

Historicity and Colonialism

Scholars of Christian scriptures have also had a long fruitful engagement with issues of translation. Biblical scholars have paid admirable attention to developments in translation theory: e.g., formal vs. dynamic equivalence, implications of → discourse analysis, and cultural ideologies. This consideration is partly because the Christian Bible is always already in translation. (Most Christians believe that God became incarnate as a speaker of Aramaic. Yet the → Bible is in Hebrew and Greek.) Muslims and Orthodox Jews hold, respectively, that the → *Qur'an* and the *Torah* are God's literal revelation in Arabic and in Hebrew. In contrast, the historically determinate diffusion of God's Word through translation has always been essential to Christianity, with the Bible now translated, in whole or in part, into almost 2,000 languages. Lamin Sanneh argues that Christianity's emphasis on "mission by *translation*" has led to a "radical pluralism of culture" that aims "to make the recipient culture the true and final locus of the proclamation" (1989, 1, 29). As a result, Christianity has sometimes empowered the languages and cultures of the colonized by invoking them as worthy vessels for the Word. Post-colonial theology has also highlighted less optimistic relations between translation and ideology. R. S. Sugirtharajah, for example, holds that European translators imposed alien textual values in South Asia (e.g., an emphasis on fixed texts as scriptural archetypes). He argues for "a wider intertextuality which will link biblical texts with Asian scriptural texts" (1998, 90-92).

Cultural Context and Ideology

Although discussions of translation have traditionally tended to focus on the extent to which a given translation is 'faithful' to an 'original', recent theory of translation pays greater attention to issues of cultural context, ideology, and power relations between source and target cultures. The extent to which complex cultural issues intervene as texts are translated is illustrated by two cases involving gender. The Koiné Greek original of Rom 16:7, in the Christian *New Testament*, mentions 'Junia'—clearly a woman's name on the evidence of contemporary non-biblical texts—as 'prominent among the apostles.' Medieval translators and commentators frequently changed this name to the extremely unusual masculine form 'Junias.' The King James Version preferred the weaker 'of note,' rather than the more frequent 'prominent' or 'outstanding.' Some modern commentators suggest that *epísêmoi en tois apostólois* is best rendered as 'well known *to* the apostles.' Many feminist scholars see, in this history of translation, a patriarchal erasure of women's participation in the early Church. A contrasting change occurred in East Asia from the seventh to tenth centuries CE. The male bodhisattva of compassion, Avalokiteshvara in Indian Sanskrit texts, became the male Chenrezig in Tibet (incarnate in the Dalai Lamas) but was transformed into the female Guanyin in China (Kannon in Japan, Kwanŭm in Korea, Quan'Am in Vietnam, and Kanin in Bali). This shift was prominent in iconography as well as in texts. The reasons for this transformation remain unclear, but culturally specific attitudes toward gender roles are clearly part of the story. The complex trajectories of these Christian and Buddhist figures remind us that, in translation, the linguistic surface invokes complex historical, cultural, and ideological depths.

Another complex set of translational boundaries involves distinctions between insider and outsider, between data and theory, between religions and their study. The history of the → academic study of religion is replete with examples of terms from a specific cultural context that come to be used as generic concepts for describing religious phenomena across cultures, e.g., tabu (→ Taboo), mana (→ Power), shaman (→ Shamanism), → sacrifice, spirit, → sin, grace. This act of cross-cultural categorization begs questions regarding the nature of the phenomena under study: applying common labels can blind us to differences. In addition, as J. Z. Smith, Russell T. McCutcheon, and others emphasize, the use of emic terms as etic concepts threatens to import biased presuppositions into the basic categories of religious studies.

Critical Approaches in Religious Studies

The concept of → 'religion' itself is open to these critiques. Hans Penner, Nancy Frankenberry, and others have made theory of translation central to a semantic critique of essentialist views of religion. If all religions are characterized by participating in—or referring in some symbolic manner to—the sacred (→ Holy), and if the sacred is ineffable or wholly other, as phenomenologists often claim, then how does this trans-linguistic other come to be translated into the many languages of different religions? Translation is a relation, however complex, between spheres of determinate → meaning; but the generic, cross-cultural concept of 'religion' is hypostatized as beyond determinate meaning (unless it is defined in a reductive, functionalist, or purely descriptive manner). Translating between different religions is one thing; translating between religion and religions is something else entirely. Yet, unless we can make sense of the latter, how can we claim that all the things we call 'religions' truly fit under that one umbrella term? These sorts of critiques indicate that theory of translation has much to contribute to discussions of the nature and function of comparison as a method in the study of religion.

Literature

ALLERT, Craig D., "Is Translation Inspired? The Problems of Verbal Inspiration for Translation and a Proposed Solution," in PORTER/HESS 1999, 85-113; ENGLER, Steven et al., "Consider Translation: A Roundtable Discussion," in: Religious Studies Review 30/2 and 3 (2004), 107-120; MUNDAY, Jeremy, Introducing Translation Studies: Theories and Applications, London/New York 2001; FRANKENBERRY, Nancy K. (ed.), Radical Interpretation in Religion, Cambridge 2002; PORTER, Stanley E./HESS, Richard S. (eds.), Translating the

Bible: Problems and Prospects, Sheffield 1999; SANNEH, Lamin, Translating the Message: The Missionary Impact on Culture, Maryknoll 1989; SUGIRTHARAJAH, R. S. Asian Biblical Hermeneutics and Postcolonialism: Contesting the Interpretations, Maryknoll 1998.

→ *Bible, Book, Communication, Literature, Meaning/Signification, Qur'an, Text/Textual Criticism*

Steven Engler

Trickster

What Is a Trickster?

1. The concept of the 'trickster' is a concept of figure typology. In the anthropology of religion, cultural anthropology, and literary studies, it expresses the being and activity of (usually male) mythical, literary, or historical (but now inserted into literature) figures, now more precisely identified as in human or animal form. In the eighteenth century, in English, 'trickster' meant someone of dubious morality and principles, but appreciable intelligence. English philosopher Shaftesbury (1671–1713) characterized (1711) → Prometheus as such—that is, as a deceptive 'quack' or dangerous 'swindler.' Trickster figures emerge in the mythology, folklore, and literature of nearly all cultures. The trickster's body and soul are, or become, identified to a certain extent through his actions.

Tricksters play their tricks by way of unusual incorporeal powers, for example, techniques of cunning and deceit, secret knowledge, and the arts of transmutation (→ Mask). Nonetheless, tricksters are 'foolish,' and their actions often miscarry or work against them, so that they also represent ungodly, disorganized areas, such as those of laughter and humor (→ Fool, Upside-down World, → Carnival). But they are also tied up with the comical and laughable; their actions caricature or ridicule anything serious or important. Trickster figures look strange and striking, which marks them as outsiders: unnatural bodily development, altered appetites (enormous hunger or digestion/excretion, or sexuality), enlarged or diminutive, multiple or missing, bodily (e.g., sexual) parts. Thus, with Wakdjunkaga (lit. the 'roguish one'), a trickster of the North American Winnebago people, his over-long penis is either backwards or rolled up. A squirrel casually gnaws off his sexual part and plants it: out of it grow useful or vital crops like maize, turnips, or (sweet) potatoes.[1] In François Rabelais's satirical serial novel *Gargantua and Pantagruel* (1522–1564), a modern-age literary match for a Trickster story-cycle, the protagonists are remarkable for their body size and proportions, their extremes of gluttony and intemperance, and their frivolously scatological earthiness. Some literary → animal legends in European culture are based on elements and figures of a trickster sort, such as the crafty, sly Fox or the Raven with the droll blotches. As trickster figures fail to abide even by biological norms, then, surely, we must expect them to transgress, at will, other, 'sacred,' boundaries—law, ceremony, convention—most often spontaneously, less often working from a plan, but always out of a craving for novelty. In this manner, they broaden their own latitudes, as well as the frames of standardization of those with whom they come in contact. Hence they are (further) designated as 'liminal' beings (→ Marginality/Liminality). On the basis of cunning and ridiculous craftiness, the trickster often appears as a cultural → hero, the one who brings down fire and other two-edged techniques of culture, such as agriculture and labor, medicine and disease, and death (→ Prometheus, cf. above, Wadjunkaga). Often he is the dangerous counterfoil of the Supreme Creator, who 'brands' a mark on the trickster's spirit and body (→ Stigmata/Stigmatics) as the one who has dared to transform the ordained world order.

2. A famous trickster of the Mediterranean region, along with Prometheus, is Hermes, messenger of the Greek gods. Hermes roams everywhere with impunity, protects thieves and the underhanded, and is identified with Ibis-headed Egyptian Thoth, the master of secret knowledge (→ Hermetism/Hermeticism). In Teutonic mythology, the crucial trickster is Loki the troublemaker (→ Teutons). Wolf, Fox, and Raven frequently emerge as his cohorts. African trickster figures such as the Hare and the Hyena of the Kaguru people, the spinning Ananse (or Ture) of the Ashanti, or Eshu Elegba of the Yoruba, somewhat similar structurally to the Judeo-Christian Lucifer, all have multiple connections with everyday life. Rich in their variants, trickster tales and their protagonists can become metaphors for human conduct ('busy as Eshu'). North American trickster figures frequently appear in the guise of animals (→ North America [Traditional Religions]). Among peoples of the Northern Pacific coasts, the story is that Raven has stolen the sun that had been hidden by the Supreme Being, and thereby brought light into the world. The Coyote trickster, in the Indian picaresque cycle, often transforms itself into a dish, to gobble up food or provisions, or among Plains peoples, frequently acts as a demiurge. Navajo material sees in the Coyote the cultural hero who has stolen fire from the sky. In this he is similar to the Hare, the most important trickster in Southeastern North America. Hare and Rabbit, who live with Grandmother, and everlastingly nibble away her provisions, are also the clumsy ones, whose stupid-heroic pranks make the world such as it is. As trivialized, modern assimilations of these trickster figures, in the form of American 'slapstick' humor, popular films in trick photography and cartoons feature characters like Bugs Bunny (film hero since 1938, comics since 1941), Coyote, Duffy Duck, or 'sexually liberated' Fritz the Cat, in style since around 1970 (comics and film). From the Hollywood heroes of Harold Lloyd to Buster Keaton to Charlie Chaplin to the current films of a Woody Allen, the trickster traditions continue in film. Optional subjects like transformation (costuming) feature a reversal of relationships, and grotesque exaggerations of moral and religious norms. Thus they vary the trickster's comic-tragic figures of central relationships and present portraits of his everyday form in nearly all social contexts. Examples would be the 'idiot,' the court jester, the clown, the charlatan, the *Schlemiel*, the artist of life, the idealist, the scapegoat.[2] Tricksters of the native peoples of → Central and → South America are usually animal beings, who, strikingly, often work by manipulated openings-out of the body—turn their concealed 'insides' outward and render them visible. Thus, the Yanomami of Northern Brazil report of the bird-being Hasimo, who stole the fire caught in the jaws of a primitive crocodile by bombarding the crocodile with its excrement, and thus causing it to laugh.[3]

3. Trickster tales emerge, in considerable number and in a great wealth of variation, in non-writing societies (Anomami). In agricultural societies, they appear on the boundary between the religious and the secular everyday, in ceremonies of healing, carnival festivals, or rites of initiation, as a folkloristic legacy still in living memory (e.g., among Indian *brujos* in Central

Figures of the Trickster

America). As a part of the Western culture of entertainment, they come in written or film form. Trickster tales usually occur in considerable number, and with a great wealth of variation. Frequently, they come as serialized stories, to whose extension there is no limit. Examples would be the Tyl Eulenspiegel cycle, the Trickster Hare cycle of the Winnebago, the 'to be continued' structure of many comic strips and animated films. The great quantity and variability of the 'stories' told guarantee the strongly defined continuation of a tradition. With the freedom of variation at hand, trickster figures can be brought right up to date, and adapted to the times. Finally, the culture of their provenance cannot be determined with any degree of reliability, and is only to be met in the area of the disreputable, laughable, and comical; thus, trickster figures outlast the transformations of times and alterations of fashions. Of course, their image and appearance change, which is typical of their essence.

1. RADIN 1969, 39.
2. Cf. illustrations of Joseph Beuys's theatrical presentation, "I Like America and America Likes Me," under entry, "Art."
3. SULLIVAN et al. 1987, 15 and 52.

Literature

BIANCHI, Ugo, "Der demiurgische Trickster und die Religionsethnologie," in: Paideuma 7 (1961), 335-344; ERDOES, Richard/ORTIZ, Alfonso (ed.), American Indian Trickster Tales, New York 1999; HYNES, William J./DOTY, William G., Mythical Trickster Figures: Contours, Contexts, and Criticism, Tuscaloosa 1993; KÖPPING, Klaus-Peter, "Absurdity and Hidden Truth: Cunning Intelligence and Grotesque Body Images as Manifestations of the Trickster," in: History of Religions 24 (1985), 191-214; RADIN, Paul, The Trickster: A Study in American Indian Mythology, commentaries by K. KERÉNYI and C. G. JUNG, New York 1969 (¹1956); SULLIVAN, Lawrence E. et al., "Trickster," in: Encyclopedia of Religion 15 (1987), 45-53.

→ *Animal, Carnival, Hero/Heroism, Marginality/Liminality, Mask, North America (Traditional Religions), Prometheus*

Michael Weis

Truth / Dogma

Levels

1. The dimension of the religious problem of truth is determined according to the levels on which the question of truth is posed.

a) On the level of *historical facts* and *empirical perception*, truth is related to the correctness of enunciations. Religious propositions are true or false in this sense, to the extent that they are related to historical or empirical facts. The designation "the five books of Moses" is untrue on this level, because these writings do not come from one author, but from various sources.

b) Furthermore, the question of truth indicates a need for *compulsory knowledge of orientation*. In this connection, truth means reliability of attitudes, opinions, convictions, and manners of behavior. In this sense, all religions and systems of belief raise a comprehensive claim to truth. They differ, however in the degree to which that claim is systematically reflected and linguistically formulated. Here the function of *dogmas* enters the scene. These fix the basic condition of what is to be held as valid in a system of belief. Dogmas elucidate the ideological interrelation of inner and outer, by defining orthodoxy and repelling heresies.

c) Finally, the question of truth is posed in the context of *theoretical knowledge of the world*, with respect to the plausibility of an interpretation of reality. Inasmuch as a religion often claims to elucidate not only one sector of reality, but reality as a whole, it emerges as true, if its interpretation of the world (e.g. as a creation of God) is universally acknowledged.

Accordingly, truth attaches to a system of belief when it corresponds to empirical experience, practical orientation, and theoretical interpretation of the world as a whole. It comes into a crisis, on the other hand, when religious propositions on one or more of these levels are contested. The occasion of this sort of crisis is identifiable as the *historical* (§ 2) and *cultural* (§ 3) relativization of truth.

2. a) Both in the Greek city states and in the Roman Empire religion was a public affair. The gods were venerated as those of the community. The determination and establishment of truth was the obligation of the state. However, along with the official cults, a multiplicity of offers of religious meaning were present. Mystery religions, together with local and individual spirituality, satisfied the individual needs for certitude of salvation. In this religious landscape, Christianity arose as one belief system among others. In the wake of its expansion, it increasingly found itself with conflicting salvation doctrines (→ Gnosticism, cult of Mithra) and faced the philosophical consciousness of truth. Thus, with the establishment of Christianity as the state religion at the close of the fourth century, the process of the *canonization* of the Bible began, along with the *institutionalization* of church offices, and finally, the *dogmatization* of fundamental truths of faith. Henceforward, the imperial → Church established binding truth and battled its denial ever more stoutly over the course of the Middle Ages. Nor did it eschew the cooperation of state power.

Truth and Truths

b) Since the early modern age, the Church's claim to a monopoly over truth has seen itself exposed to growing criticism. As a consequence of the → Reformation, truth is no longer accepted simply upon authoritative presentation. It is now to be preserved in critical reference to the Bible. Instead of dogmas, *confessions* (→ Profession of Faith) are important, and their intent is less a universal validity than a personal adaptation in a 'confessing' (professing) community. Humanism and the universities founded in the Middle Ages occasion the rise of a 'scientific community,' in which truth is produced from a confrontation among varying positions. Furthermore, state order and questions of religious truth are now uncoupled. These approaches are first brought into service, for the peaceful coexistence of various faith convictions, in the Peace of Westphalia (1648).

c) An awakening historical consciousness and the discovery of foreign cultures, in the wake of the Enlightenment, led to further conflicts between ecclesial and general truth-consciousness. Subsequently, questions of religious truth were increasingly *privatized* and *subjectivized*. The state of Frederick II enjoined: "Each one becomes blessed [enjoys sacred happiness] in his own fashion." Schleiermacher understood dogmas as "conceptualizations of Christian pious frames of mind." Another tendency interpreted doctrinal tradition *ethically* (Lessing, Kant). Not doctrinal belief, but moral convictions and casts of mind would then decide the plausibility of pretensions to religious truth. On the other hand, any clinging to time-honored doctrinal propositions for their own sake is designated *dogmatism*. The course of this concept in Protestantism leads to the plea for an *undogmatic Christianity* (Harnack), emphasizing one's own decision of conscience, the personal assimilation of the content of faith, and the impossibility of closure in the discovery of truth. In Catholicism, the concern of dogmatic hermeneutics is a transmission of the historical genesis and current of dogmas.

d) On grounds of the progressing globalization, the current situation of the problem of religious truth is signalled by the coexistence of different cultures, with their differing religious elements, and varying systems of belief, all of which have developed differing procedures for approaching truth:

Source of Truth

(1) *Intuition*: In ancient cultures and non-writing societies, truth often culminates in feeling. Since truth is understood as a substance or sphere, it is reached by empathetic understanding and intuition. Cultures with a monistic image of the world share this conceptualization of truth as a feeling of unity. This route is extended in → mysticism: the oneness of everything is a truth that can only be felt intuitively, since it transcends the restrictions of the thinking faculty and sensible perception.

(2) *Communication*: Unlike intuition, this route takes its point of origin in the concept that truth is not immediately accessible, and can be attained only by transmission. The true is the outcome of communication, so that it takes its nourishment from authoritative sources: prophets, seers, stars, oracles, or sacred scripture. In particular, the transition to → writing and the canonization of sacred texts (→ Canon/Canonization) are fundamental for the further development of pretensions to religious truth, because they lead to the emergence of elites in exposition, and of teaching systems.

(3) *Reflection*: A relatively late concept finds the royal road to truth in the independent activity of reason. Where religious truth is sought in this manner, salvation transforms itself into knowing. The attraction of this route lies in its free accessibility to truth, without the transmission of the latter from elites and hierarchies. Nevertheless, when all is said and done, this model turns out to be limited, since it can only discover the rational aspect of religious truth.

(4) *Sensation*: For the most recent model in the history of thought, what is true is only what can be grasped by the senses (→ Perception). The process does have analogies in the sensory practices of religion. Nevertheless, sensory perception has turned out to be the greatest enemy of the claim to religious truth, since the sense and meaning of religious phenomena remain closed to it.

3. After the "end of the grand narratives" (Lyotard), religion is experiencing a renaissance. The loss of belief in both enlightened reason and a meaning of history leaves a vacuum that can be filled with the 'other's truth.' Accordingly, the question of its truth appears in how it brings to utterance what is referred to as the 'reality of the Holy.' Measured by a rationalistic concept of truth, this claim is not a small one. Still, in the case of Christianity, religion's genuine concern is not correctness, but existential truth—salvation.

Literature

Sources: HARNACK, Adolf, What is Christianity?, New York 1957 (Ger. ¹1900); KANT, Immanuel, Die Religion innerhalb der Grenzen der bloßen Vernunft (1794), in: Kants Werke, Akademie Textausgabe VI, Berlin 1968; LESSING, Gotthold Ephraim, Nathan der Weise, Berlin ²1983; SCHLEIERMACHER, Friedrich, Der christliche Glaube, Berlin 1960 (²1830/31).

Secondary Literature: BLONDEL, Maurice, The Letter on Apologetics and History and Dogma, Edinburgh 1995; FERNÁNDEZ-ARMESTO, Felipe, Truth: A History, London 1997; KIRKHAM, Richard L., Theories of Truth: A Critical Introduction, Cambridge 1992; LYOTARD, Jean-François, The Postmodern Condition: A Report on Knowledge, Minneapolis ¹²1999 (Fr. ¹1979); MACGRATH, Alister E., The Genesis of Doctrine: A Study in the Foundations of Doctrinal Criticism, Oxford 1990; SCHMITT, Frederick F. (ed.), Theories of Truth, Malden 2004.

→ *Authority, Canon, Christianity, Church, Fundamentalism, Knowledge, Pluralism, Profession of Faith, Revelation, Science, Theology, Tolerance*

Markus Buntfuß

UFO

1. The abbreviation 'UFO' (for 'Unidentified Flying Object') has long been an all but magical concept of everyday culture. But, as the 'U' expresses, it lies pretty much in the dark what the term properly relates to. Regarded phenomenologically, a UFO experience contains an encounter with an (at first, or altogether) unexplainable celestial apparition. It belongs in the area of → new myths and systems of belief of the twenty-first century, however, by reason of the fact that the apparition can be, and is, interpreted as a meeting with extra-terrestrial intelligent beings (aliens), where the eyewitness accounts range from simple sighting to out-and-out abduction (see § 3). It is disputed whether all sightings that at first seem unexplainable can actually be related to what is familiar. (German Astrophysicist Illobrand von Ludwiger calls them—all sightings—'UFOs in the broad sense.') In this case, what would be present in the UFO phenomenon would be either an ongoing process of mythologization, or, as other scientists maintain instead, indeed a problem of a small percentage of these sightings remaining mysterious even after analysis—'UFOs in the strict sense.'[1] The reality of an encounter with extraterrestrials is not excluded (but see § 6).

Characteristic of the UFO phenomenon, in any case, is precisely the fact that a massive psychological complex has formed out of speculation, disinformation, and mythic fascination. This complex embraces not only the 'UFO believers,' but also the military and political sector (for example, a UFO belief could conceal secret arms projects), the millions constituting the audience of the entertainment industry, as well as the scientific community.

2. There have been reports of remarkable disc-shaped or wheel-shaped flying objects for millennia (e.g. Ezek 1:4-28). The twentieth century received its UFOs on June 24, 1947. Amateur pilot Kenneth Arnold, flying over Washington state, saw nine semicircular discs "that moved like saucers flung over a wet surface"[2]—a momentous simile, which remained inseparably joined

On the History of the Phenomenon

At the Pyramid of Gizeh, white-clad believers in UFOs attempt to attract extraterrestrials to Earth. Cultic actions such as appear here are inseparably connected with the phenomenon of UFOs, but are to be ascribed directly only to the secondary mythic complex that has taken shape around the unexplained core phenomena (the 'unidentified flying objects'). It is an altogether open question what all of this is ultimately 'about': the 'extraterrestrials' hypothesis is only one possible explanation among many.

with the phenomenon. There followed the first 'flap' in the history of the UFO: by July 30, 1947, 850 sightings of UFOs in the broad sense had been reported. On July 4, United States Independence Day, there were 162 sightings in 37 states. Under the code name "Sign" (later "Grudge"), the U.S. Air Force began to collect the cases. On July 6, 1947, a farmer in Roswell, New Mexico, took Air Force officers to his ranch, where he had found the wreckage of a remarkable flying apparatus. The 'Roswell crash'—still unexplained today, according to some—attracted worldwide attention in 1995, when film shots appeared of the alleged autopsy of an alien allegedly killed at that time (→ New Myths/New Mythologies, with illus.).

In 1951, under the leadership of four Air Force officers and astronomer J. Allen Hynek, Project Blue Book was inaugurated, with the task of assembling the ongoing reports of UFO sightings. In 1956, a scientific institute evaluated some 4,000 reports of sightings between 1947 and 1952: the most reliable of these (from pilots, etc.) contained the highest number of genuine 'alien' sightings, those of 'unknown' objects. This analysis contradicted the thesis of the skeptics that it was mainly poor observers who 'saw' anything unknown.

In 1968, with some 12,000 sightings on file with the U.S. Air Force, a team from the University of Colorado issued the Condon Report under commission of the military. Fifty-nine cases had been investigated. Of these, 33 remained unidentified. Nonetheless, in his Foreword Edward Condon came to the conclusion that there was nothing to the UFO reports. The study therefore drew criticism. Obviously, the reality of the phenomenon cannot be concluded simply from the frequency of the sightings. The possibility of individual and mass suggestion must be taken into account, as with the witch persecutions (see § 6).

There were waves of sightings, among others, in France in 1954, in the United States in 1952, 1966, and 1973, and in the Soviet Union in 1960, 1967, and 1978. In 1989, in Belgium, for nearly a year, there were repeated sightings of giant triangular objects in the sky.[3]

3. Following Hynek, a distinction had been adopted between UFO sightings and 'close encounters.' In encounters of the *first* and *second kind*, the UFO is very close and affects things and persons physically (through light, electromagnetic waves, gravitation, etc.). Encounters of the *third kind* involve contact with apparently living alien beings. Since 1961—and recently, more intensively—encounters of the *fourth kind* have been reported: abductions by 'the aliens' on space ships, frequently with painful and humiliating physical manipulations. American artist Budd Hopkins collected and published such reports. The presentations by New York writer Whitley Strieber ("Communion," 1987; "Transformation: The Breakthrough," 1988) are probably the most detailed.

Typology of the Sightings

4. A common element in the reports of Hopkins and Strieber is that the statements and first-hand reports of the victims of the abductions had usually materialized only under conditions of hypnotic recall. This method, with all kinds of encounters, raises fundamental problems of source criticism. Interdisciplinary research teams can perform good work. But in order to address the primary controversy regarding the existence and nature of UFOs, there is a need for consensus regarding the reasonableness and scientific merit of such investigations. Investigators such as Jacques Vallée and Illobrand von Ludwiger have developed useful systems of classification for the quality of the sightings and the credibility of the witnesses. Only a common interdisciplinary understanding of the matter can shed light on whether the things described are what they seem to be phenomenologically, or, instead, in their profound ontological structure, are something altogether different.

The Problem of Sources

5. At the beginning of the 1950s, with the reports of a certain George Adamski (1891–1965), the UFO cult began. Adamski claimed to have had, after the landing of space ships from Venus, telepathic contact with their passengers. Since then, in numberless UFO groups, spiritistic revelations through channel-mediums (→ Channeling) and eschatological and redemptive expectations have fused into an (often sectarian) worldview. At the beginning of 1997 one of these groups in the United States, named Heaven's Gate, committed collective suicide, in order to get on board a hoped-for UFO in the train of the Hale-Bopp Comet, just then appearing in the sky. German and Swiss 'Light Siblings' constantly speak of an 'evacuation' by waves from an electronic-wave ship. Reports by persons claiming to have contacted UFOs are often exposed as falsifications, as in the case of the Swiss Billy Meier. Hollywood, too, has for decades strongly contributed to the UFO cult with → films like "The Day the Earth Stood Still" (1951, dir. Robert Wise), "Close Encounters of the Third Kind" (1977, dir. Steven Spielberg), and "Independence Day" (1998, dir. Ronald Emmerich), just as has television series "X Files" (USA 1993ff., writer Chris Carter), which reached non-English audiences as well in the 1990s.

UFO Cults

6. A scholar wishing to research the core phenomenon seriously still risks a loss of professional and social status today. The fact that the UFO cult is propagated precisely through ignorance of serious scholarship, however, is increasingly acknowledged, as in the words of para-psychologist Eberhard Bauer: "It is better to go into the subject seriously, than to leave it to the profiteers and charlatans."[4] What ought to be fostered would be an official

Science and the UFO Phenomenon

sighting office with a multidisciplinary team of researchers, in which both natural scientists and technologists, as well as psychologists, anthropologists, and scholars of religion, should take part. The greatest obstacle in UFO research, according to Jacques Vallée, is the hasty assumption (met largely in UFO cults) that UFO space ships would have to be from other planets. Accordingly, the state of the research is disparate and tangled. However, once the subject as such were accepted—just as with the equally exotic astronomical project, Search for Extraterrestrial Intelligence (SETI)—there would be a multiplicity of reasonable hypotheses: UFO phenomena could be connected with, for example, other dimensions of reality (including the future), or an archetypical middle realm, like the collective unconscious (Kenneth Ring, Jacques Vallée), or a realm of 'pre-personal' and 'transpersonal' energies (Stanislav Grof, Ken Wilber), or, finally, the impulses of an extraterrestrial intelligence. It would be highly advisable to take into account the → psychopathology of traumatized depths of the soul, where (from 'poltergeists' to C. G. Jung's 'psychoid projections') very important research problems lie hidden. Collective imaginations and traditional social myths play a role, like the (green!) water men and 'little people' of Celtic Mythology (U. Magin), or traditional stores of religious beliefs such as epiphanies of God and apparitions of Mary.

1. Von Ludwiger 1992, 17.
2. Ibid., 105.
3. Societé d'Études des Phénomènes Spatiaux (ed.), UFO-Welle über Belgien. Zivile, polizeiliche, militärische und wissenschaftliche Augenzeugen berichten. Eine Dokumentation der Massensichtigung, Frankfurt/M. 1993 (Fr. ¹1991).
4. Bauer, Eberhard, "Forschungsobjekt Ufo?", Interview in Süddeutsche Zeitung, 29 December 1994.

Literature

Desmond, Leslie/Adamski, George, Flying Saucers Have Landed, London 1953. Denzler, Brenda, The Lure of the Edge: Scientific Passions, Religious Beliefs, and the Pursuit of UFOs, Berkeley 2001; Hynek, J. Allen/Vallée, Jacques, The Edge of Reality: A Progress Report on Unidentified Flying Objects, Chicago 1975; Korff, Kal K., Spaceships of the Pleiades: The Billy Meier Story, Amherst 1995; Lewis, James R., The Gods Have Landed: New Religions from Other Worlds, Albany 1995; Magin, Ulrich, Von Ufos entführt. Unheimliche Begegnungen der vierten Art, Munich 1991; Matheson, Terry, Alien Abductions: Creating a Modern Phenomenon, Buffalo 1998; Pritchard, Andrea/Stein, Gordon, "Alien Discussions: Proceedings of MIT Abduction Conference," in: The Skeptical Inquirer: The Zetetic. Journal of the Committee for the Scientific Investigation of Claims of the Paranormal 19,5 (1995), 46 (see also pp. 43-45); Saler, Benson et al., UFO Crash at Roswell: The Genesis of a Modern Myth, Washington 1997; Shepard, Leslie A. (ed.), Encyclopedia of Occultism and Parapsychology, Detroit ²1984; Vallée, Jacques, Passport to Magonia: From Folklore to Flying Saucers, Chicago 1969; Idem, Anatomy of a Phenomenon, London 1974; von Ludwiger, Illobrand, Der Stand der UFO-Forschung, Frankfurt/M. 1992.

→ *Epiphany, New Myths/New Mythologies, Science Fiction*

Michael Schaefer

Unification Church

1. The Unification Church, popularly known under the designations 'Moon Sect,' or even 'Moon Movement,' stands among the new religious movements (→ New Religions). It emerged from elements of → Confucianism and Korean → Protestantism. Its founder is Sun Myung Mun (in English, 'Moon,' whence the coarse name for his followers, 'Moonies'), whose family stems from Chon-gin (North Korea). In 1930, the family converted to Presbyterianism, when Moon was just ten years old. As early as 1936, Moon is reported to have had his first visions, in which Christ appeared to him and enjoined him to complete the mission that had remained unfulfilled because of the crucifixion.

The Beginnings

Moon's religious course began in 1946, in North Korea, where he had returned from Japan after studies in electro-technology. Beginning in 1951, Moon—then in South Korea—preached a doctrine of his own, and three years later, in 1954, founded the Holy Spirit Association for the Unification of World Christianity, incorporating it under civil law. Quite soon afterward, the first missionary activity began, in Japan, the United States, and Europe. The Society for the Unification of World Christianity, founded in 1964, numbered only its seven founding co-members. Finally, the street mission turned out more successfully. The following years (1972–1981) were the most active for the Unification Church, and, especially after Moon's move to the United States in 1972, the principal activities began to be transferred to North America. With Moon's return to Korea, in the mid-1980s, the active missionary phase came to an end. At the end of the 1980s, the Church numbered an estimated 150,000-200,000 members (including Korea).

2. The Unification Church's organization is divided hierarchically, with Moon's authority undisputed. In addition, there are Moon's direct descendants, and his second wife. His sons gradually receive more and more leadership roles. Moon's wife, especially in recent years, entered the public consciousness as founder of a women's movement, the Women's Federation for World Peace. Every country involved has its own leadership, whose individual centers are each presided over by a center leader. In the inner circle, to be sure, that of the foundational superiors, a Korean dominance is unmistakable.

Organization

Connected with the Unification Church are a number of other organizations, partly with a religio-cultural character (e.g., Assembly of World Religions), at times of a religio-economic nature (e.g., Happy World, Inc., in Japan, with some 600 offices), or the publishers Aquarius and KANDO.

3. Moon's principal writing, *The Divine Principle*, appeared in 1957, and achieved the status in the community of a sacred book, along with the Bible. Ultimately more important for instruction and missionary activity, however, was Prof. Young Oon Kim's Study Guide (*Divine Principle and Its Application*, 1960). Kim came under the influence of the work of Swedish theosophist Emanuel Swedenborg (1688–1772), and is of great importance for the entire development of the philosophy of the Unification Church.

Teaching and Religious Life

In its basic characteristics, the Unification Church is apocalyptic (→ Apocalypse) and chiliastic (→ Millenarianism/Chiliasm), and rests on two elements in particular: (1) a peculiar exposition of the Bible, and of components of the Yin-Yang philosophy, and (2) the emphasis, originating in Confucianism, that matrimony, generational antecedence, and family stand at the focus of theology. Thus, God committed to man and woman the duty of becoming perfect spouses. The Fall is interpreted as a frustration of the divine plan, consisting in the premature sexual union of Adam and Eve. Moon interprets the whole of Jewish and Christian history as God's attempt to reconstitute his relationship to the human being, disrupted since the Fall. Moon's own commission, as 'Lord of the Second Coming,' is to continue the unfinished work of Jesus Christ, and, in a perfect marriage and → family, fulfill God's original plan of creation. Moon's second marriage, contracted in 1960 as the 'Wedding of the Lamb,' is therefore equivalent to the beginning of a new age. As 'true parents,' Moon and his wife can realize spiritual perfection even physically, and lead humanity to a condition of sinlessness, in order to erect God's ideal world on earth.

In Moon's theology of unification, good and evil confront each other in the form of a mitigated → dualism. In its view of the Korean War (1950–1953) and the Cold War, the Communist world was the incarnation of evil, and must then be dutifully overcome by democratic systems, first and foremost by the United States. Moon's anti-Communism is based on the personal experience of his internment in a Communist labor camp from 1948 to 1950. His mission, in his consciousness, is therefore the unification of Korea, and only then that of the world. In recent years, however, the agenda has taken more and more distance from the idea of a military confrontation, and the idea that has been propagated is that of a battle to be waged on a spiritual and political level.

Cult

Cult in the Unification Church is centered on the wedding, marriage itself, and the 'blessing' of couples in great numbers. Most followers lead a bourgeois life. Beginning in 1961, there have been 'mass weddings,' at which 'perfect marriage' and a sinless progeny are vowed. In 1982 in Seoul, 5,837 couples are supposed to have been 'blessed.' In 1995, the last mass wedding of couples was performed, simultaneously on three continents, by telecommunication. Today, non-members, or even persons already legally married, are permitted to participate in these ceremonies.

Membership

One becomes a new member of the Unification Church by participation in seminars, and through study of the *The Divine Principle*. The reception is finalized by an official vow, in which the candidate recognizes the *Principle*. Daily and weekly meditations are customary, at which Moon and his wife are present in pictorial image, as 'True Parents' (a title which does not betoken their deification). Mission in the West is no longer particularly worthy of note; the Church's earlier fundraising through collections, or the sale of flowers, pamphlets, etc., has ceased.

Situation Today

4. With the collapse of Communism, the year 1989 signaled, for the Unification Church, the beginning of the end of an active confrontation between the forces of good and those of evil. Today, dialogue is the watchword, and mission in the erstwhile Eastern bloc is long since under way. The Unification Church has always been reproached for too strong an interference, in existing family conditions, between members and their families. Increasingly, the Unification Church has had to fight the appearance of following destructive

and authoritarian structures. Today, then, the Unification Church prioritizes the cultivation of a positive image, a change in both its internal practices and its religious and political claims. To what extent its religious community, as a child of the East-West conflict, can also make its message plausible under the changed conditions of world politics, remains to be seen. The task of surviving its charismatic founder, and institutionalizing a mechanism of succession, is something that the Unification Church has yet to face.

Literature

Sources: SAN MYUNG MUN, The Divine Principle, trans. and comp. by YOUNG OON KIM, ed. by the Holy Spirit Association for the Unification of World Christianity, Yong San Ku/Seoul 1956; JONES, W. Farley (ed.), A Prophet Speaks Today: The Words of Sun Myung Moon, New York 1975; YOUNG OON KIM, Unification Theology, New York 1980.

Secondary Literature: BARKER, Eileen, The Making of a Moonie: Choice or Brainwashing?, Oxford 1984; CHRYSSIDES, George D., The Advent of Sun Myung Moon: The Origins, Beliefs and Practices of the Unification Church, Basingstoke 1991; DEAN, Roger A., Moonies: A Psychological Analysis of the Unification Church, New York 1992; KAROW, Yvonne, Bhagwan-Bewegung und Vereinigungskirche. Religions- und Selbstverständnis der Sannyasins und der Munies, Stuttgart 1990; KEHRER, Günter, Das Entstehen einer neuen Religion. Das Beispiel der Vereinigungskirche, Munich 1981; LOWNEY, Kathleen S., Passport to Heaven: Gender Roles in the Unification Church, New York 1992; MICKLER, Michael L. (ed.), The Unification Church, vol. 1: Views from the Outside; vol, 2: Inner Life; vol. 3: Outreach, New York 1990.

→ *Anti-Cult Movements, Mission, New Religions, Sect*

Jutta Bernard and Günter Kehrer

Utopia

1. Etymologically, the word 'utopia,' derived from the Greek, means the 'place [*tópos*] that is not [*ou*],' or 'no such place.' Ever since Thomas Moore's *De Optimo Rei Publicae Statu, deque Nova Insula Utopia* (Lat., "The Best State of the Republic, and the New Isle of Utopia"), 'Utopia' has been a luminous popular concept. As a generic concept, it denotes the (mostly literary) forms of utopian delineations ('utopian state novel'). Henceforth Utopia, the 'not-place,' is an imaginary place, a wish-picture, at a spatial and/or temporal distance. As an 'abstract Utopia,' this place emerges as the utterly Other, delivered from all historical and material conditionings. In a more modest sense, the 'concrete utopia' (Bloch) reflects the resulting situation (→ Marxism). In utopia, both abstract and concrete, what comes to expression is a yearning, immanent to human thought from time immemorial, for the better, the best. This 'utopian consciousness' is a prerequisite and impulse for every piece of societal progress that human beings are to produce. It may even be that the 'circensian element' (Ueding) that emerges, a counterpart of thinking in mere logic, lends utopia the quality of an instrument of criticism. It is in this sense that Ernst Bloch recalls → art, → fantasy, and → dreams as loci of the utopian, since what comes to expression here is what must be translated in function of the 'not yet realized' (objectively) and the 'not yet conscious' (subjectively).

Abstract and Concrete Utopia

2. The vision of the better, the perfect, in the consciousness of an autonomous power of action, is an exploit of the modern age. Consequently, the concept of utopia in the modern age is only conditionally transferable to other human ages and social vantages. Nevertheless, even with a ban upon myth, nature, and religion, utopian content is identifiable.

Temporal (Time) Utopias

The Genesis narrative—known also to other cultures, in various conjugations—'recalls' a harmony lying on the threshold of history, and lost through human misbehavior. The promises that come to expression, as well as the perspective of salvation history in everything that occurs, point to the option of reaching this harmony once again, 'after' history. In the Judeo-Christian tradition (in its apocalyptic traditions; → Apocalypse), this 'utopia content' appears to the human being in the shape of a concrete goal, attainable along a kind of railroad of time, and portrayed plastically, in powerful, effective language, and therefore credibly. By way of the prophetical impulse of those who believe that they can determine the exact point in time of a future happy age, on the basis of special knowledge (→ astrology, numerology, division into time-periods, discipleship of the Messiah/false messiah), this notion receives a dramatic concretization. As examples here, we may cite Joachim of Fiore (c. 1130–1202), with his 'Third Empire of the Spirit' dealt with in his *Liber Concordiae Veteris et Novi Testamenti* (Lat., "Book of the Concord of the Old and the New Testament"; first printing, 1519). Through integration into utopian content, chiliastic and eschatological materials enjoy a considerable potential for radical change and revolution. Further, the conceptions imply the (current) world's imperfection, and thereby the thought of divine imperfection. Here we have an assault on prevailing relationships.

Spatial Utopias

Beginning with the Renaissance, temporal (religious) utopias, which seemed 'attainable' along the path of time, were supplanted by (humanistic) spatial utopias. The utopian sketches that then emerged returned to an ancient model: Plato's *Politeia* and his Myth of → Atlantis. Common to these outlines was an origin in their respective temporal contexts. As they begin there, they reflect the optimal state. Moore's *Isle of Utopia* introduced a flood of literary utopian sketches. Here belong Tommaso Campanella's *City of the Sun* (1623), Johann Valentin Andreae's *Christianopolis* (1619, in the spirit and milieu of Lutheranism), and Francis Bacon's *Nova Atlantis* (1626). There appear at the same time a plethora of sketches of the ideal city; these complement the abstract utopias of space and state, since they obviously cannot be generally regarded as the architectonic materialization of the latter. As forms of a utopian effort, nevertheless, they aim at an independent 'utopian perfection' (Joergensen). On this point, they are also to be distinguished from monasteries, whose model translation of an ideal, one taken from the tradition of the 'evangelical counsels' (poverty, chastity, community of goods, obedience), posits less a utopia, than a concretization susceptible of composition. Such a plan is a rationally governable architectonic ideal, intended for the real world as a model, while at the same time being referred to that world in order to be able to survive.

In ever new and distinct ways, the successive utopias of the Baroque era reflect the worlds of experience ('exotic lands'), and philosophical discoveries (Enlightenment) of their time. The spatial utopia is rich in variants, and is applied to different contexts and popularized. Thus, for example, J. G. Schnabel's *Insel Felsenburg* (Ger., "Isle of Felsenburg," 1731–1743) binds the utopian social outline to 'Robinsonades' and to adventure literature critical of civilization.

From the Renaissance onward, another element complemented utopian consciousness. The former was not as compelling, in its quality as a utopian element, as were the state utopias. *En revanche*, however, as an aesthetic sign, it was subjectively clearer and plainer, in terms of its interior appreciation as a utopian sign. This new element was that of the 'Arcadia,' whose image Jacopo Sannazaros's novel, *Arcadia* (printed in 1504), coined definitively. Arcadia had been the object of yearning since antiquity (Vergil). But in the Middle Ages, Arcadia's landscape, despite its similarities with that of Paradise, had been forgotten. The pagan character of Arcadia was too obvious; its origin as a place of pleasure could unfortunately not be wiped away. Henceforward, however, the idyll of the shepherd indicated a Utopian (Arcadian) longing ever critical of the present, and gave Arcadian thought a 'concrete' fundament that could be felt subjectively: homeland (Bloch). | *Arcadia*

From the nineteenth century onward, the classic spatial utopia was itself eclipsed by new temporal utopias. The utopias of liberty and equality, of socialism and communism, as utopian constructs, evince cultural similarities to the (religious) temporal utopias. | *New Temporal Utopias*

In terms of Engels's demand, "From utopia to science!" out of 'utopian socialism' comes 'really existing socialism.' Over the course of the twentieth century, however, disillusionment with the Soviet system of government, on the one side, and the experience of totalitarian Fascism on the other, fashioned a variant of the original optimistic spatial utopia. The variant, at the same time, can be interpreted as the final chord of the utopian song as such: the negative utopia. It sketches the pessimistic picture of a future society in which, through psychological manipulation, totalitarian governmental systems enslave human beings in unfreedom (George Orwell, *1984*, 1948), and interdict them, once and for all, through artificially generated promises of happiness (Aldous Huxley, *Brave New World*, 1932). | *Negative Utopias*

While the utopian novel thus bears utopia to the grave, it solemnizes its trivial resurrection in the genre of → science fiction. In the 'endless spans of outer space,' in "Star Wars," and the land of the 'Jedi knights,' utopian longings find themselves squeezed into myths as fanciful as they are popular. | *Science Fiction and Utopia*

3. An attempt to defeat the troubling paradox of utopia—that antithesis of what is and what ought to be—places high demands on any engagement in utopia. Its defamation as utterly unrealistic fantasy, and the censure of ideologization, come readily to hand. 'Misunderstandings' such as these inevitably issue in attempts to fetter utopia in practical categories. Karl Mannheim differentiates utopia according to types: (1) the salvation doctrines (orgiastic chiliasm), (2) the liberal, humanitarian notion, (3) the conservative idea, and (4) the socialist/communist idea.[1] These approaches rightly reflect the ideological content of self-styled (temporal) utopias, whose practical realization in history often conditioned, or still conditions, totalitarian governmental structures. But, in their limitation to practice, these categories reduce the different potentials of the utopian consciousness to a | *The Principle of "Hope"*

programmatic determination of ends. The category 'hope,' introduced into philosophy by Ernst Bloch, takes the aspiration for the better, the perfect, in earnest, and places it in a new connection with societal practice. Hope can be disappointed, but never falsified! The 'utterly Other,' for human beings, is still both an orientation and a motive for action. In the gray monotony, Arcadia glistens …

1. MANNHEIM, Karl, Ideologie und Utopie, Bonn 1929.

Literature

Sources: BLOCH, Ernst, The Spirit of Utopia, Stanford 2000 (Ger. [1]1923); Idem, The Principle of Hope, 3 vols., Cambridge 1986 (Ger. [1]1959); BRUCE, Susan (ed.), Utopia / Thomas More. New Atlantis / Francis Bacon. The Isle of Pines / Henry Neville: Three Early Modern Utopias, Oxford 1999; MORE, Sir Thomas, Utopia: A Revised Translation, Backgrounds, Criticism, trans./ed. by Robert M. ADAMS, New York/London 1992.
  Secondary Literature: JOERGENSEN, Sven-Aage, "Utopisches Potential in der Bibel. Mythos, Eschatologie und Säkularisation," in: VOSSKAMP, Wilhelm (ed.), Utopieforschung. Interdisziplinäre Studien zur neuzeitlichen Utopie, 3 vols., Stuttgart 1982, vol. 1, 375-401; SAAGE, Richard, Utopieforschung. Eine Bilanz, Darmstadt 1997; MANUEL, Frank E./ MANUEL, Fritzie P., Utopian Thought in the Western World, Cambridge 1979; SCHAER, Roland et al. (eds.), Utopia: The Search for the Ideal Society in the Western World, New York/Oxford 2000; WEGNER, Phillip E., Imaginary Communities: Utopia, the Nation, and the Spatial Histories of Modernity, Berkeley 2002.

→ *Apocalypse, Atlantis, Dream, Fantasy, Garden/Paradise, History, Millenarianism/ Chiliasm, Science Fiction, Time*

H.-Georg Lützenkirchen

Values

1. Even in the colloquial sense, values and their imagined or actual change are exposed to a nearly inflationary usage. At the same time, varying understandings of values are cultivated by several scientific disciplines, especially philosophy, religious studies, economics, pedagogy, psychology, and sociology. Common to their efforts is an attempt to grasp human acts less as arbitrary, than as possessed of a tendency to calculability. Viewed from the standpoint of the social sciences, values are social rules or outlooks, of an emotive and/or rational kind, settled in individuals and supporting the activity of individuals or groups. Apart from professional argumentation, each more or less socially relevant expression or change of opinion can then be referred to values, such as when pregnancy counseling (→ Abortion/Contraception) or youth violence are discussed controversially.

Max Weber

2. Today's predominantly sociological reception of the theoretical socio-economic efforts of Max → Weber conveys an interpretation according to which "given reality is ordered according to categories that [. . .] present the *premise* of our knowledge, and are bound to the premise of *value* of that truth that alone can give us the knowledge of experience" (Weber 1904, 213). The objects of Weber's investigations, however, are not societies in the

sociological sense, but cultural circles of world religions, and the actions of the persons shaped by them. For Weber, "belief in the value of scientific truth" is the "product of determinate cultures, and not naturally given." At the same time, he ascertains a "belief in the supra-empirical validity of the last and highest value concepts" and an "unexposed alterability of concrete viewpoints." Therefore, "the concrete shape of the value relation is still [...] fleeting, subject to change" (ibid.). Today, in retrospect, Weber's warning seems to have been wasted, so that a "wild pursuit of new viewpoints and conceptual constructions" is indeed judged to be the "proper task of social science" (ibid., 214).

3. Scholarship poses questions of the meaning and possibility of freedom of values. In religions, it remains a matter of dispute whether, or to what extent, human concerns for self-definition, and for knowledge, are acknowledged merely as culturally relative, or as universally valid (e.g., human values and → human rights). Conflicts of value emerge daily, individually as well as inter-individually. Here it is a matter either of simple inclinations or of levels of knowledge in the sense defined by philosophically ambitious *Jean Piaget* child psychologist Jean Piaget (1898–1980). To explain values as social rules (philosophically: morality), as an expression of personal competency within a structurally transparent maturation process in Piaget's sense, is to broaden the theme of a dimension neglected in sociology and religious scholarship. How does consciousness arrive at the point of attending to rules? Setting heteronymous and autonomous decisions in mutual opposition, and analyzing the connection between the two as a maturation process, Piaget explains the process of socialization as the progressive development of individual competency, especially that of cognition (Piaget 1977). In the course of an increasing differentiation of personalities, the child develops a mental attitude that consists in a step-by-step dismantling of childish egocentrism. Relatively early, children notice that their parents, and other persons, are neither almighty nor omniscient (infallible), nor ubiquitous, so that they are not gods. In parallel, the childish worldview becomes extensively overcome as a whole, including that of belief in an animated nature, and so in sun, moon, wind etc., as seemingly outfitted with intentions (→ Animism). At the age of about eleven to thirteen years, children grasp that social rules cannot only be laid down by authorities (parents, gods), but also freely negotiated.

For the co-founder of sociology as an academic discipline, Émile Durkheim *Émile Durkheim* (1858–1917), the source of morality lies in the collective, and values 'are products of the general opinion.' Their objects possess no value of themselves, but only in relationship to certain states of consciousness. The totality of the ideas, convictions, and feelings are presented by society (see Durkheim 1954). For Durkheim, the liberty of the individual lies in the insight into social necessities. While Piaget would have the level of the individual, in the sense of a capacity for knowledge, decisive for social judgments, therefore for values as well, Durkheim finds the level of social environment determinative. This arrangement does not inhibit the individual as part of a pre-modern—that is, with little differentiation of labor—clan, nor as a member of a modern society. In the clan, moral rules are not valid universally, and so not, in principle, independently of culture and society, but with a relation to culture—here in a special measure vis-à-vis one's extended kinship. In the clan, conflicts of value are decided strictly hierarchically, and, in case of doubt (as currently to be observed), by force, while in modern societies with a division of labor, a growing trend is to be seen in the direction of self-development, which contributes to a pluralistic order of values (→ Pluralism). The latter's premise, it must be added, is a type of socialization, whose state of maturation and concept of society accepts a position different from—and, as the case may be, even opposed to—one's own, as enjoying equal rights.

4. One's own hierarchy of values does not always furnish desires or appraisals that are essential and relevant for action. Tenacious ambivalences—that is, orientations appropriated by feelings at once positive and negative—result in futility. Results appear that compare cultures, in → group conformity, in positions and attitudes taken vis-à-vis authorities and innovations, and finally, in feelings concerning achievement (Boesch 1971).

5. Different attitudes with regard to values can widen, and become images of the world, such as emerged in the Cold War between East and West, until approximately 1990. In both political systems, specific types of activity and patterns of interpretation developed, and the transitory risk of a military confrontation increased. Within the Western system of values, to be sure, capitalism and socialism converged in respect of ideas of self-devotion and self-control in connection with the process of the progressing industrialization of the moment (Gouldner 1970).

In a word, value represents a collective designation of mutually complementary or exclusive interpretations of motives, interests, and goals—in toto, of essential foundations of human acts. All evaluations are based on orientations in time, space, symbol, and rule (cf. Durkheim 1968). Religious content in terms of sense and meaning contains evaluations, and is transmitted symbolically.

Literature

Boesch, Ernst E., Zwischen zwei Wirklichkeiten. Prolegomena zu einer ökologischen Psychologie, Bern 1971; Durkheim, Émile, The Division of Labour in Society, London 1984 (Fr. ¹1893); Idem, Sociology and Philosophy, London 1954 (Fr. ¹1898); Idem, The Elementary Forms of the Religious Life, London 1968 (Fr. ¹1912); Gouldner, Alvin W., The Coming Crisis of Western Sociology, New York 1970; Helle, Jürgen, Soziologie und Symbol. Verstehende Theorie der Werte in Kultur und Gesellschaft, Berlin 1980; Idem, Verstehen and Pragmatism: Essays in Interpretative Sociology, Frankfurt/M. 1991; Joas, Hans, The Genesis of Values, Chicago 2000; Piaget, Jean, The Child's Perception of the World, London 1929 (Fr. ¹1926); Idem, The Moral Judgement of the Child, Harmondsworth 1977 (Fr. ¹1932); Weber, Max, Die "Objektivität" sozialwissenschaftlicher und sozialpolitischer Erkenntnis (1904); Idem, Der Sinn der "Wertfreiheit" der soziologischen und ökonomischen Wissenschaften (1918); Idem, Wissenschaft als Beruf (1919), in: Gesammelte Aufsätze zur Wissenschaftslehre, Tübingen ⁷1988 (¹1922).

→ *Abortion/Contraception, Authority, Economy, Ethics/Morals, Group, Meaning/Signification, Money, Prestige, Ritual, Science, Socialization/Upbringing, Symbol/Sign/Gesture, Weber*

Harmut Salzwedel

Vegetarianism

1. The term 'vegetarianism', defined by the founders of the British Vegetarian Society in 1842 as meatless nutrition, is derived from *vegetus* (Lat.,

'alive'). This means that vegetarian food excludes the products of a slaughtered animal (including fish). Within the groups of persons who live according to vegetarian principles, there are three forms of diet:[1]
- Ovo-lacto-vegetarians constitute the largest group. These do consume milk, milk-products, and eggs, besides vegetable products.
- Lactovegetarians avoid eggs, in addition to meat and fish.
- The most rigorous section among the devotees of a meatless diet is composed of the vegans, who restrict themselves to a vegetable diet. Vegans avoid animal products across the board (including leather, wool, silk, and honey).

Vegetarianism, nevertheless, is more than a manner of nutrition, and is understood and defined, today more than ever, as a *Weltanschauung*. The motives for a vegetarian lifestyle are manifold and extend from ethical (moral) and religious (spiritual) considerations, to health, hygiene, and aesthetics, then to ecological and social motives. Amidst this multiplicity, according to polls, motives of health and morals predominate (→ Ethics/Morals). The religiously signed rejection of the killing of living beings and the extension of the object of the Fifth Commandent ("You shall not kill") to all beings endowed with life, enter this discussion. So does the capacity of animals for suffering, and reflections on modern treatment of animals. Thus, vegetarianism stands in direct connection to movements for animal protection and animal rights (→ Animal).

2. The basis for meatless nutrition was laid in antiquity itself. Ethical motives *Antiquity* stood in the foreground, followed by considerations of health. The first impetus for the renunciation of meat consumption emerged from the religious sect of the Orpheans in the sixth century BCE. The dietary counsels of the followers of mythical Orpheus lent the Greek understanding of religion new insights. By comparison with received (sacred) dietary proscriptions, a total, and especially, a persevering abstinence represented an altogether new mindset vis-à-vis the sacred food prohibitions.

Until well into the nineteenth century, the vegetarian diet was designated the 'Pythagorean fare,' a designation coming down from philosopher and mathematician Pythagoras (592–493 BCE) and his school. Through belief in a → reincarnation of souls, abandonment of meat and the non-consumption of 'animate' (Lat., 'ensouled') beings became an essential, elementary component of Pythagoreanism.

Being essential to various traditions of → Hinduism and → Buddhism, the vegetarian tradition played a certain role in Christianity, as well.[2] The doctrine of reincarnation is crucial to Buddhist tradition; at the same time Buddhism considers non-violence and vegetarianism as belonging to the five fundamental steps to self-knowledge. The ultimate goal is the state of Nirvana, the ending of all suffering and the release from the circle of rebirth. Hinduism, for its part, is not only one of the oldest religions, but probably the religion with the highest esteem for animals; according to the Vedas and other Hindu texts the eating of meat and thus the acceptance of killing is inconsistent with the liberation from the circle of reincarnation.

In church history, nevertheless, throughout the centuries, the anthropocentricism of the biblical image of the world and the human being prevailed. In its resistance to → Gnosticism, and in order to set itself apart from Pythagoreanism, Christian doctrine now placed human beings, by virtue of their immortal souls, above the animals, which were corruptible beings.[3]

Modernity

Only in mid-nineteenth century did the transition to modern vegetarianism occur, from a point of departure in English vegetarianism. The *Vegetarian Society* in the UK, as the most important organization worldwide, today has more than 28,000 members. Now the traditional elements of a millenia-old dietary system were joined by the institutionalization of the vegetarian movement. Thus, in 1867, in Nordhausen in Northern Thuringia, the first vegetarian association in Germany was founded, the *Verein für natürliche Lebensweise* (Ger., 'Association for a Natural Lifestyle'), followed by several other organizations. On an international level, the *International Vegetarian Union (IVU)* was founded in 1908, and is still active today, with little change.

3. Vegetarianism can be a component of various systems. Obvious here first of all is an incorporation into the multiplicity of dietary systems ($\rightarrow$ Eating/Nourishment). The vegetarian diet is an alternative nutritional regime, standing in clear contrast to conventional dietary habits, especially in Western industrial countries. Not coincidentally, modern vegetarianism emerged in the nineteenth-century age of industrialization ($\rightarrow$ Industrial Society) and technologization, and in the nutritional changes involved with that period. Vegetarianism was a response to the changing nutritional habits and the diseases of a civilization dependent on nutrition, with its sufficiently well known and scientifically attested diseases emerging from dietary patterns. A first overview of the alternative nutritional tendencies (for example, macrobiotics, raw diet) demonstrates that a meatless (or at least greatly reduced meat content) nutritional recommendation represents the lowest common denominator of these alternative models, and that the vegetarian regime is thus a significant component in today's nutritional behavior.

The life-reform movement in general offers a further opportunity for integration. Naturism, with its 'Back to Nature' effort, as well as its active animal-protection and antivivisection movements, may be especially singled out in this connection. In 1975, Australian ethics professor Peter

Peter Singer

Singer wrote *Animal Liberation*, which was the first scholarly work to present ethical arguments for not eating animals or experimenting on them ($\rightarrow$ Bioethics; Genetic Engineering). This inspirational book was the perfect compliment to F. M. Lappé's *Diet for a Small Planet* (1971), which showed exactly how to go about eating things other than animals. What *Diet for a Small Planet* did for vegetarianism, *Animal Liberation* did for animal rights, virtually launching the animal rights movement in the U.S. overnight. Animal rights groups started popping up everywhere, including PETA (People for the Ethical Treatment of Animals) in the early 1980s and the ALF (Animal Liberation Front) in the 1990s ($\rightarrow$ Environmentalism).

The Situation Today

4. Various estimates and polls indicate that, in Europe at this time, some three to five million persons practice vegetarianism. In Great Britain, vegetarians make up about seven percent of the population. In the industrialized countries three to seven percent consider themselves vegetarians and 20-30 percent buy vegetarian products. The practice of vegetarianism today is not historically determined. But on the basis of the world situation, it is an invitation to individuals. Advocates of meatless nutrition see vegetarianism as the sole possible diet of the future. Citing the same efficiency concerns as environmentalists and economists, many vegetarians see natural resources as being freed up by vegetarianism. Many people believe that the production of meat and animal products at current and likely future levels is environmen-

tally unsustainable. They also argue that even if it does prove sustainable, still, modern industrial agriculture is changing ecosystems faster than they can adapt. While vegetarian agriculture produces some of the same problems as animal production, the environmental impact of animal production is significantly greater. It takes about 10 kg of good quality plant protein—such as wheat and soy—to produce 1 kg of meat protein.

The multiplicity of vegetarian cookbooks in bookstores and the great variety of recipes for vegetarian dishes in women's magazines show quite clearly that a meatless diet has become an element of Western eating culture and nutritional situation. At the same time, more and more persons reflect how a responsible interaction with nature, the environment, and our fellow creatures, can or must appear. The discussion in Christianity of the person/animal relationship (which includes the nutritional aspect) has been carried further in recent years, in talks, discussions, declarations, and the like. Thus, a responsible behavior with animate as well as inanimate nature is pursued as a goal. The extent to which a renunciation of meat is regarded as a logical consequence of this effort is a very individual judgment, even today. Today, acceptance of vegetarianism by medical authorities and the general public is at an all-time high.

1. In Germany, there are c. 250,000-460,000 vegans (and 5 million vegetarians); in the USA estimates give a number of c. 0.9% vegans (and 2.5% vegetarians), with a tendency toward increase. Unfortunately, confirmed estimates are lacking with regard to the number of vegans world-wide; it is reasonable, however, to assume that c. 1% of the global population follows a vegan diet.
2. The vegetarian elements in primitive Christianity have not yet been exhaustively addressed; cf. Rosen 1987.
3. Cf., especially, the work and contributions of Eugen Drewermann.

Literature

Barkas, Janet, The Vegetable Passion: A History of the Vegetarian State of Mind, London 1975; Berry, Rynn, Food for the Gods: Vegetarianism and the World's Religions, New York 1998; Dombrowski, Daniel A., The Philosophy of Vegetarianism, Amherst 1984; Dyer, Judith C., Vegetarianism: An Annotated Bibliography, Metuchen/London 1982; Lappé, Frances Moore, Diet for a Small Planet, New York 1971; Rosen, Steven, Food for the Spirit: Vegetarianism and the World Religions, New York 1987; Singer, Peter, Animal Liberation, New York 2002 (¹1975); Spencer, Colin, The Heretic's Feast: A History of Vegetarianism, Hanover 1995; Walters, Kerry S./Portmess, Lisa (eds.), Ethical Vegetarianism: From Pythagoras to Peter Singer, Albany 1999; Idem (eds.), Religious Vegetarianism: From Hesiod to the Dalai Lama, Albany 2001.

→ *Animal, Buddhism, Eating/Nourishment, Environmentalism, Ethics/Morals, Hinduism, Nature Piety, Reincarnation, Sacrifice*

Judith Baumgartner

Veil

1. In many societies, the covering of the head and → hair, from the simple headscarf to a complete cloak, has a long tradition. A person's head is literally of outstanding significance. It is not only the bearer of the brain, and

ZEIT-*Punkte*
Nr. 1/ 1993 - 5,00 DM
81 893

Der Islam –
Feind des Westens?

DIE ZEIT
ZEITmagazin

ISLAM
Die Begegnung am Mittelmeer

People have preconceptions and → prejudices regarding the veiling of Islamic women. These two title photos from the German-speaking press show the extent to which these ideas are dependent upon their presentation in the media. The woman masked in a tent-like black veil, from the magazine *ZEIT-Punkte*, vol. 1 (1993)—with the title "Islam: Enemy of the West?"—from whose face only the staring, black-framed eyes are to be seen, looks the observer straight in the face. Immediately, a subliminal impression of foreignness, of threat, arises, generated and reinforced by the caption under the picture, which the photograph associates with Islam. The question posed there is actually only a rhetorical one. The answer is given in the photo. Islam is indeed an 'enemy of the

thus the seat of thought and reason, but it is also the locus of all sensory organs. On it, as the highest area of the body, decoration and covering stand out most meaningfully.

The veiling of the body, or parts of the body, has always served two principal purposes. First, it is meant to protect the wearer from evil influences, be it from the → evil eye, or from → demons, who could penetrate the body at any of the several apertures of the head. By veiling the head, and outwardly altering the appearance, or even making oneself unrecognizable, one thinks to be able to deceive the demons. Because many cultures regard women as the weaker sex, among them the obligation of veiling themselves, or the wish to do so, occurs more frequently. Second, the veiling of the body or its parts is meant to defend wearers against their own evil powers, among which are those of sexual attraction, and therefore of seduction (→ Eroticism). Further: headgear, just like clothing, adornment, or coiffure, is a part of nonverbal communication, and signals to the environment that the wearer belongs to a particular cultural group, or even documents a particular condition (→ Mourning), social state (e.g., married/unmarried), or ideological posture (e.g. orthodox) within the group.

2. A fundamental assertion may be made, to the effect that a head covering possesses a double effect in terms of signal. It is equivalent to a social status, as well as to sexual unavailability. As early as 2000 BCE, it is reported that, among the Assyrians, widows and wives—thus, respectable women—wore veils, while slaves and whores were not permitted a veil, so that they were identified as unfree, unmarriageable, and sexually available. Urban, free, Byzantine women also wore it, in order to distance themselves

from poorer women, who went about without a veil because it would have hindered them while working. These influences then determined Islamic practice.

In Christianity as well, the veil was important. According to Paul (1 Cor 11:3-16), a woman is obliged to wear a veil at divine service (where she 'prays or prophesies'). As this commandment is grounded in the Hebrew Bible, it is understandable that it would inform the everyday practice of the Christian-Jewish environment, which prescribed the wearing of the veil. Modern theologians, as Max Küchler, see in the veil a 'crystallization': on the one side, it betokens the subordination of the woman, her position beneath the man, and on the other, it serves for a defense against → eroticism. In the time of the Carolingians (seventh to tenth centuries), it became the obligation of women to cover their heads, especially when attending church. Furthermore, uncovered hair stood for woman's inner sexual and magical power, which it was important to keep under control (→ Witch/Persecution of Witches).

The form of the head covering, however, was at once a modish element, and strongly dependent on worldly events. Thus, at the time of Charlemagne, there was a preference for Byzantine material, worn in the style of the oriental veil, leaving the face free, however. While in the fourteenth century the style was in bonnets, in the fifteenth, Spanish and French hats ruled.

As early as the Byzantine age, clothing, and especially the head covering, served the class society of the Middle Ages to demonstrate membership in a class. As late as the nineteenth century, no lady went out of the house without a head covering. This rule slowly changed with the emerging women's movement at the end of the nineteenth and the beginning of the twentieth century. It rejected the bonnet as a sign of woman's subordination to man, just as it battled against the corset and for leg hose and a free selection of hairdo. While this last goes without saying nowadays, the scarf that the farmer's wife still wore in Western countries until the 1950s, and that is still widespread in Italy (especially in Sicily and Sardinia), bears witness to the earlier importance of a head covering. Similar relics include the bridal veil and nuns' clothing ('brides of Christ').

3. Through its broad spread in the East, as well as through contact with Byzantine Christians, the veil found entry into Islam. In the → Qur'an itself, it is true, it is only recommended that orthodox women wear part of their scarves over the necklines of their garments (suras 24:31; 33:59). However, there is also a hadith—a declaration of the Prophet Muhammad—that women are to veil themselves when they leave the house: face, hands, and feet are excepted. This hadith forms the basis for the most varied manners of veiling in the Islamic world.

The latter are principally founded in sex. Women are to provoke no lust in men, and neither are they to expose themselves to their lustful gaze. The reason for this is the high value of virginity in Islamic families, which, indeed, also obtains in pre-modern societies generally. Virginity is supposed to guarantee the exact control of reproductive behavior (→ Regeneration/Fertility). Girls' virtuousness was of great importance for the honor of the whole family, and frequently still is today. In order to protect it, besides spatial division of the sexes, the optical neutralization of woman is an important factor.

However, the variety of the manners of, and prescriptions for, the wearing of the veil show that these are just as much determined by culture as by

West.' It is altogether otherwise in the picture on the right, on the cover of the Swiss cultural newspaper *Du* (Ger., "You," 7-8/1994), with the title reading "Islam: The Mediterranean Encounter." Here the dark headscarf scarcely has a negative effect: its wearer openly, and a little slyly, smiles at the reader, and thereby comes into contact with her or him. Oppositely from the depersonalized presentation on the left, here it is the person that counts, not the scarf. The cover picture is a friendly invitation to come into contact with the foreign culture and religion.

Qur'an

religion. From the simple scarf of the farmer's wife in Turkey or Egypt, to the black tshador of the Iranian woman, to the burqa in Pakistan, which permits women only a partial view through a fence-like opening in the whole-body garment, every nuance is present.

The attitude of Muslim women themselves to the veil, however, is a matter of oscillation. With the opening of the twentieth century, a powerful movement of emancipation emerged among Islamic women, in the course of which its members demonstratively ripped the veils from their heads as a sign of the conclusion of male dominance. In our own day, it is still especially the middle class, with its orientation to Europe and to Western values, that regards the unveiled head as a sign of freedom and progress.

The Veil and Political Discourse

Since the end of the 1970s, a robust return to the veil has occurred. It was first manifest among the women in black tshadors, who paraded them in the face of the West as a symbol of the revolution in → Iran. The linkage of religion and veil with political goals has made the veil a symbol of otherness between Islam and the Western world. The latter sees it as a sign of the rejection of civilization and progress, the former a symbol of their own cultural and religious identity. This symbolic charge explains why so many women have voluntarily donned the veil in recent years. Here a distinction must be made between urban, often well educated, women, who have consciously decided in favor of the veil on grounds of their religious conviction, as a symbol of their self-awareness as emancipated Muslim women—and women, chiefly of rural origin, for whom it is part of the maintenance of a farming tradition. Although most cases are those of this last, the scarf or veil in the Western world has become simply a symbol of the Muslim woman, or even simply of Islam, as the 'scarf debate' (→ Laicism) shows. The media, with their tendency to oversimplification, have also contributed to the emergence of 'veil' as a negative stereotype, so that the very word is now a buzzword arousing or denoting hostility or distaste towards foreigners in Western Europe.

Literature

BAILEY, David A./TAWADROS, Gilane (eds.), Veil: Veiling, Representation and Contemporary Art, Cambridge/London 2003 (exhibition catalogue); BIEBUYCK, Daniel P./VAN DEN ABBEELE, Nelly, The Power of Headdresses: A Cross-Cultural Study of Forms and Functions, Brussels 1984; BULLOCK, Katherine, Rethinking Muslim Women and the Veil: Challenging Historical and Modern Stereotypes, Herndon 2002; GÖLE, Nilüfer, The Forbidden Modern: Civilization and Veiling, Ann Arbor 1996; GUINDI, Fadwa El, Veil: Modesty, Privacy and Resistance, Oxford 1999; KNIEPS, Claudia, Geschichte der Verschleierung der Frau im Islam, Würzburg 1993; LLEWELLYN-JONES, Lloyd, Aphrodite's Tortoise: The Veiled Woman of Ancient Greece, Swansea 2003; MACLEOD, Arlene Elowe, Accomodating Protest: Working Women, the New Veiling, and Change in Cairo, New York 1991; ÖZDALGA, Elisabeth, The Veiling Issue, Official Secularism and Popular Islam in Modern Turkey, Richmond 1998; SCOTT, Georgia, Headwraps: A Global Journey, New York 2003; SHIRAZI, Faegheh, The Veil Unveiled: The Hijab in Modern Culture, Gainesville 2001; VOGELSANG-EASTWOOD, Gillian, Veiled Images, Rotterdam 1996 (photographs).

→ *Clothing, Eroticism, Evil Eye, Gender Stereotypes, Hair, Islam, Laicism*

Silvia Kuske

Veneration of Persons / Personality Cult

1. 'Veneration of persons,' or 'personality cult,' indicates reverence for a special personality. This reverence can go so far, in certain cultures, that the venerated persons are actually ascribed divinity. As a result, the designation, which has not yet established itself in religious studies, is often applied polemically, as a 'counter-concept' to reverence for God. Originally, 'veneration of persons' was a 'buzz phrase,' with a negative connotation. It was coined by Nikita Khrushchev in 1956 at the Twentieth Convention of the Communist Party of the Soviet Union, as a criticism of the Stalinist brand of leadership. In a system of collective leadership, veneration—or 'cult'—of persons denoted the amassing of power and authority in a single person, and his/her exaggerated veneration. The concept, with a background in political history which is mostly forgotten today, is nevertheless the earmark of a broader spectrum of religious phenomena. A basic distinction must be made as to whether it is living persons who are venerated in cult, or whether the veneration occurs posthumously.

2. In the Rome of imperial times, the ruler was accorded special veneration. The original reverence paid to the Roman divinity Genius—the deified power of male generation (cf. Lat., *gen-*, 'generate')—was transferred to the ruler's genius, or creative power (→ Genius). In the year 29 BCE , the Senate determined that, at all meals, public and private alike, a solemn gift was to be offered to the genius of Augustus. Two years later, Augustus had the Temple of 'Divine Julius' (*Aedes Divi Julii in Foro*), with its own priestly service, erected for Julius Caesar (murdered 44 BCE) on the Forum Romanum. After his own death, a corresponding *Templum Divi Augusti* was constructed to his own honor, on the Palatine. By 192, temples were built to seven more deceased Emperors by their successors. After Nero and Trajan, even the title of the reigning ruler (e.g., *Dominus et Deus*: Emperor Aurelian, reg. 270–275) bore the divine designation. The title of divinity survived even the end of the ancient veneration of persons under Constantine I, who in 324 prohibited the temple cult to the veneration of the ruler, and his interdict prevailed into the Byzantine Age.

Roman Emperor Worship

3. With Polycarp at the latest (second century CE), we meet the tradition of honoring Christian martyrs (and later, saints in general) in a memorial cult. Early indeed, it would seem, believers had begun to gather on the anniversary of the martyr's birth or death, at the place in which her or his bones were buried (Lat., *memoria*, 'memorial place'), to remember the person. Later, such places became the sites of churches, which, as a rule, bore the names of the martyrs. The background of this devotion—besides the community-building commemoration—was the concept that, thanks to their suffering and death for their faith, martyrs were especially possessed of sacred powers (→ Charisma; Power), so that miracles occurred at the location of their graves or → relics. A new type of saint to whom devotional veneration was accorded, appeared on the scene in late-third-century Egypt: the monk of the ascetic life, who had abandoned life in community, and settled in the wilderness, or in remote, uninviting places (→ Monasticism). From the late tenth century onward, however, only those who had been canonized by the

Christian Martyrs and Saints

The young Peronist who lights an altar candle in the meeting room of a local Peronist group of Buenos Aires, pays tribute to the founding couple of the Party, Juan Domingo Perón (1895–1974) and his wife, Eva ('Evita') Duarte (1919–1952). Perón led Argentina from 1946 to 1955 with an authoritarian presidential regime that had taken on the characteristics of a mass, social revolutionary, → political religion, such as that recognized in the European Fascism of the twentieth century. His wife 'Evita,' a singer and motion picture actress by profession, succeeded, in exultant scenes, in making herself and the regime advocates of the 'shirtless' poor (Span., *descaminados*) and women. Evita's early death from cancer, at the age of 33, contributed to her becoming the object of an enthusiastic cult of the dead, promoted by Perón's Labor Party (*Partido Laborista*). Her corpse was embalmed, and her mausoleum was preserved as a place of pilgrimage, while her office at union headquarters became a room for memorial and meditation. In modern political movements, the veneration of persons encourages an intentional eradication of the boundaries of nation, party, and salvation movement. The devotional shrine pictured here may serve as an example. It is at party headquarters, and features a Catholic altar furnished with missal, crucifix, and Madonna, but dominated by photographs of the 'holy couple,' Juan and Evita. The transition from commemorative picture to image for meditation (perhaps even divine idol) seems fleeting. Granted, charisma and veneration of persons cannot be planned, as was acrimoniously shown at the close of Perón's career. After his political comeback in 1973, Perón tried to 'clone' Evita, presenting his second wife, dancer María Estella Martínez (b. 1931), as 'Isabel,' the new popular leader. After Perón's death, Isabel did succeed him in the presidential chair, but did not possess the capacities for control of the masses that her predecessor had demonstrated, and in 1976 she was ingloriously overthrown by a military junta. (Hubert Mohr)

Pope in a formal process could be regarded as officially 'holy,' or 'saintly,' and thus as worthy of veneration and cult. The Reformers dismantled canonization in all of its forms, but the sacred elevation of men and women as 'blessed ones' or 'saints' survived in Catholicism. Since 1918, this process has taken on the form of a trial, with one attorney or advocate for, and one (colloquially, the 'Devil's Advocate') against the candidate. The process is regulated in the Codex Juris Canonici—the "Code of Canon Law" (canons 1999–2141; → Veneration of Saints).

4. A particular form of personality cult is found, for example, in Asia, in the manner of reverence or veneration of the religious teacher or 'master.' In some traditions, one's personal → guru is regarded as an embodiment or incarnation of the divinity (*sad-guru*) from whom a direct transfer of power and salvation to the pupil is expected, and to whom a special reverence is accorded. Gurus like Satya Sai Baba in India, who lays claim to being a divine incarnation (Skt., *avatara*), or Sri Chinmoy, in New York, whose photograph is used by his followers as an object of meditation, are not so much teachers for the few, as an object of veneration for the many.

Outside Europe

5. As examples of personality cults in modern times, we may consider phenomena within national states and → political religions. Here, politicians have been met with an enthusiastic veneration that can definitely have religious traits. In the Far East (Kim Il Sung in North Korea; Mao Cult in the People's Republic of China), in Europe (Benito Mussolini in Italy; 'Generalissimo' Franco in Spain), and in the USSR (V. I. Lenin, Joseph Stalin), the emergence of a dictator or *Führer* (Ger., 'Leader'; in It., *Duce*) in the twentieth century, with its effect on the masses, provided an occasion for the ritual presentation of politicians as 'saviors.' We may cite, for example, the ingenious Führer cult around Adolf Hitler (→ National Socialism). In some cases (Lenin, → Mao, Kim Il Sung), a political veneration of the dead has even made use of the magical presence of the mummified body in mausoleums (→ Mummification). Many dictatorial regimes of the 'Third World,' as well, cultivate a frank veneration of persons, although in most cases they do not survive their champions.

Modern Personality Cult, Political

Less well known today is the cult around the unifier of Germany, and founder of the German *Reich* (Ger., 'Empire') from 1871, Otto von Bismarck (1815–1898). Some five hundred monuments to Bismarck were erected, among them the characteristic Bismarck pillars and towers, for which monetary contributions were made amounting to well over 60 million dollars (in today's value and purchasing power). The symbolic content of these was amplified by the fact that they were intentionally built on remnants of prehistoric or medieval constructions, and that they exhibited 'altars,' 'fire altars,' and 'sacrificial stones,' on which could be held the 'circles of the Fatherland' on Bismarck's birthday, and the ritual of the 'Bismarck fires' at the solstices. "Thus, we set fire basins before him, half in his celebration, half smoking with sacrificial incense, beside his temple. And two sentries, who protect the devout pilgrim, repel malevolence, and shield the rising steps."[1] Here was the 'German Messiah,' who had once known how to join a severed Germany, and from whom one hoped for succor in an unsure time. "O Bismarck, stride down from heaven, grasp once more the tiller of the Empire," as the newspaper *Bismarck-Bund* ("Bismarck Federation") put it in 1904, making

The Cult of Bismarck

Bismarck the equivalent of a patron saint. After 1945, it is true, the Bismarck cult mostly fell into oblivion.

Pop Culture　　That prominent persons of pop culture and show business (→ Idol) can now, for all practical purposes, be saints, was proclaimed and demonstrated, in 1999, at the London Tate Gallery's exposition "Heaven" (shown in Düsseldorf and, subsequently, in London). There, for example, a life-sized figure of the Madonna with the face of princess Diana was exhibited—and vigorously criticized in England, where many believers took it as an insult to their religious feelings. The gallery defended the concept with the argument that people today adore supermodels and pop stars, and prefer to go on pilgrimage to princess Diana's grave than to venerate traditional religious figures.

1. Insert with a sketch of a national monument to Bismarck in Dingerbrück; cited according to HEIDINGER, Hans-Walter, "Der Bismarck-Kult. Ein Umriß," in: STEPHENSON, Gunther (ed.), Der Religionswandel unserer Zeit im Spiegel der Religionswissenschaft, Darmstadt 1976, 201-214, p. 212.

Literature

BROWN, Peter, Society and the Holy in Late Antiquity, London 1982; CONG DACHANG, When Heroes Pass Away: The Invention of a Chinese Communist Pantheon, Lanham 1997; GLEDHILL, Chr. (ed.), Stardom: Industry of Desire, London 1991; HUNTER, Helen-Louise, Kim Il-Song's North Korea, Westport 1999; JOURDAN, Annie, Napoléon: Héros, imperator, mécène, Paris 1998; LEVITTE HARTEN, Doreet (ed.), Heaven (exhibition catalogue Tate Gallery London/Kunsthalle Düsseldorf), Ostfildern-Ruit 1999; VELIKANOVA, Olga, Making of an Idol: On Uses of Lenin, Göttingen 1996; WALTER, Tony, The Mourning for Diana, Oxford 1999.

→ *Genius, Government/Rule/Politics/State, Guru, Hero, Idol, Mao (Cult of), Masses, National Socialism, New Myths/New Mythologies, Political Religion, Veneration of Saints*

Stephan Peter Bumbacher

Veneration of Saints

Saints and Divine　　1. Non-Christian and Christian saints are considered divine persons, in the
Persons　　sense of enjoying a special religious bestowal of grace, although, in their lifetime, in society, they have frequently occupied the position of an outsider. On the basis of the exemplary life ascribed to them, they become phenomena of the daily piety or devotion of believers and groups. → Charisma and the attribution of miracles can raise persons to the status of saints in their own lifetime, since it is not through their death—as it is with martyrs—that they reach religious perfection at last. Especially at a saint's grave or tomb, believers oftentimes erect a devotional center, at which a relic, a statue, or a lifelike fragment of the saint is venerated. The grave, church, and chapel are memorial places of the historical persons, their advents, and their miracles. They draw a boundary between the profane and the sacred worlds, serve as places of common liturgy, and demonstrate that the miraculous power of the saint is still at work.

2. Veneration of the saints is not bound up with ritually established frame-works, and is differently marked in different religions. Common elements, however, are pilgrimage, prayers, objects used in exercises of personal piety (e.g., images of the saints), and the application of devotional objects: prom-ised or spontaneous votive offerings, offered in thanksgiving, with a petition for help, or in fulfillment of a vow, such as candles, documents, votive im-ages, or monetary contributions. The relationship between the believer and a saint, which becomes visible in these actions, is not to be reduced to the sheer function of the *Do ut des* (Lat., "I give in order that you may give") 'contract,' but is frequently the expression of a profoundly religious act. In everyday life, saints serve as succor, protection, and patronage in situations of crisis and challenge. In Christian theology they are only the bearers of petitions to God. But over and above this intermediary function, they are at-tributed both good powers (the power of healing) and a power of retribution (causes of diseases or death in return for unfulfilled promises). *Devotional Practice*

The *statue*, in believers' religious practice, is the worldly, human side of the saint, and the symbol of an auspicious, miraculous power, reminding the believer of the exemplary function of the saint's life. It represents the confluence of the human need for the visible manifestation of divine power and its personification. In addition, statues appear at church feasts, or on saints' days and in processions, as theatrical and dramatic symbols. The legends, tales, songs, and hagiographies transmitted by the faithful, carry 'ideal' and edifying reports of the saint's life. In Catholic Christendom, a person is officially regarded as 'holy' after, first, a beatification (declaration as 'blessed,' following an official church veneration), and then only when she or he is declared holy, a 'saint,' in a second step, consequent upon a strictly regulated procedure. Pope John Paul II, in his more than twenty-year reign (until 2005), had pronounced more than 280 men and women saints, and more than 800 blessed—more than any of his predecessors. In particular, a relationship with the present is becoming ever more important: the Saints and Blessed not only need to belong to every age of life and to different nationalities. They must also, so far as possible, have lived and died in the twentieth century, as did Edith Stein, a German Jew converted to Catholi-cism, who was murdered by the Nazis in a concentration camp. Besides these 'canonized' persons, however—persons inscribed in the official church catalogue of saints—there are many other persons, not officially legitimized as saints, who are venerated by the faithful, such as → Hildegard of Bingen. Meanwhile, certain 'traditional saints'—for example, Saint Christopher, or Saint George—can be excluded from the church's official list.

3. *Christian veneration of the saints* developed from the reverence paid to the martyrs of the second century CE, which was succeeded by an intensi-fication of the ancient cult of the dead. Ever since the third century, venera-tion of the saints has borrowed elements of the Greek veneration of heroes. Veneration of the grave as a 'house of the dead' and the veneration of relics, based in antiquity, are still important today for the veneration of the saints. In modern times, by way of the Enlightenment and the sciences, the saints have been stripped of their miracles and myths. It is true that, for example in the wake of industrialization, devotion to the saints has received a new meaning, especially among the working class, with the veneration of Joseph, encouraged by the Church. *Historical Practice*

Saints in Other Religions

Phenomenologically, the *Islamic saint* stands nearest to the Christian. While lacking legitimization according to the Qur'an (Suras 9:31; 10:19), the Islamic saint is classed, in venerability, as the 'Friend of Allah,' and as mediator between the human being and God. For believers, it is Islamic saints' miraculous activity, or wondrous efficacy, that stands in the foreground. Then, further, they rank as instances of right and truth. In *Judaism*, saints' graves and tombs, and the pilgrimages involved, are essential for their veneration. In addition to the sacred acts of veneration performed at the pilgrimage destinations, the festivals celebrated on the anniversaries of their deaths are noteworthy. Saints in the *religions of India* are venerated as such in their very lifetime, and after their death. They are regarded as ideals of → asceticism, and thus vessels and vehicles of higher wisdom.

4. The orientation of veneration of the saints to the aspect of the piety of the 'simple folk' has, on the one hand, neglected the theatrical and dramatic potential of this religious practice. On the other hand, the individual fragments of usage or veneration often were not integrated into cultural and religious everyday life. But everyday religious life is part of the power relationship among religion, church, state, politics, and society. Thus, the veneration of the saints is not only a religious force, but also a societal one, that stands at the point of the complex intersection of the formation of individual, kinship, religious, territorial, and political identity. In Palermo, for instance, Saint Rosalia, a patron against the plague from the twelfth century, and patron saint of the city of Palermo, is at the same time a figure of the integration of various social groups in their revolt against Mafia structures in Sicilian society.

Literature

ABOU-EL-HAJ, Barbara, The Medieval Cult of Saints: Formations and Transformations, Cambridge 1994; BEN-AMI, Issachar, Saint Veneration among the Jews in Morocco, Detroit 1998 (Heb. [1]1984); BROWN, Peter, The Cult of the Saints: Its Rise and Function in Latin Christianity, Chicago 1981; CARTWRIGHT, Jane (ed.), Celtic Hagiography and Saints' Cults, Cardiff 2003; DINZELBACHER, Peter/BAUER, Dieter R. (eds.), Heiligenverehrung in Geschichte und Gegenwart, Ostfildern 1990; FARMER, David Hugh, The Oxford Dictionary of Saints, Oxford 1978; MERI, Josef W., The Cult of Saints among Muslims and Jews in Medieval Syria, Oxford 2002; SLUHOVSKY, Moshe, Patroness of Paris: Rituals of Devotion in Early Modern France, Leiden 1998; TAYLOR, Christopher S., In the Vicinity of the Righteous: Ziyāra and the Veneration of Muslim Saints in Late Medieval Egypt, Leiden 1999; THACKER, Alan/SHARPE, Richard (eds.), Local Saints and Local Churches in the Early Medieval West, Oxford 2002; VAUCHES, André, Sainthood in the Later Middle Ages, Cambridge 2005 (Fr. [1]1997); WILSON, Stephen (ed.), Saints and Their Cults: Studies in Religious Sociology, Folklore and History, Cambridge 1983.

→ *Charisma, Drama, Joan of Arc, Miracles, Relics (Veneration of), Pilgrimage, Veneration of Persons/Personality Cult*

Annemarie Gronover

Violence

Theologically, it can certainly be concluded that all religions have the goal of peace. But the opposite goal can just as easily be deduced. The rejection of violence among the historical conditions of a religion's emergence says nothing as yet about the possibility, in other situations, of justifying violence, and founding it in religion. The historical experience of Christians' crusades and Islamic tolerance occasions doubts as to whether the images of the 'sword of Islam' and that of the 'God of love,' have an objective basis at all. Religion is a feature of identity and differences among societies. In → conflict, it can just as well be put to use by warmongers and advocates of violence, as be appealed to by pacifists and opponents of violence.

→ *Conflict/Violence, Fundamentalism, Holy War, Peace, Tolerance, War/Armed Force*

Christoph Auffarth

Vision / Auditory Experience

1. On October 9, 1949, four ten and eleven-year-old girls went to the park of the Castle of Heroldsbach, in Franken (Germany), to gather fall foliage.[1] They had just participated in an evening meditation on Mary. Upon leaving the wood, first one of the girls, then the others, felt a sudden compulsion to pray. Immediately thereafter, they saw, first, a black figure between the trees, then the abbreviation 'JHS' (in the popular German reading, *Jesus—Heiland—Seligmacher*, 'Jesus—Savior—Beatifier'), in green script between two birch trees, and finally, a female figure in white, 'like Mary,' atop one of the trees. Out of this children's afternoon outing, there developed, unstoppably, one of the longest series of visions in modern history, lasting until October 31, 1952. On the third day of the visions, the Christ Child was seen as well; on the fifth day the children first heard the apparition speak, resulting in a somewhat extended interplay of questions and answers. Subsequently, on the eighth day of the visions 5,000-6,000 of the faithful were present; from October 19–21 the Archiepiscopal Investigation Commission were on the scene. On December 8, 1946, a 'miracle of the sun' occurred—as at Fatima, the visitors saw the solar disc turn. This was adjudged a 'sign' of the Madonna, who came ever nearer to the children. On February 3, 1950, the tactile threshold was crossed for the first time, and Gretel, one of the children, touched Mary's cloak, which felt 'like silk.' From Christmas Eve 1949 on, however, two ambiguous, dark figures were emerging: first a 'black man,' presenting himself as the apparition of the deceased lord of the castle, Baron von Sturmfeder-Horneck, and then, on February 7, 1950, the Devil in very person, who at once gave Gretel "three powerful blows on her chest." The horror reached its climax on May 16–17, 1950, with the 'Russian vision,' as the children saw themselves transported to a landscape of debris and martial combat on the Soviet Crimean Peninsula. The positive side came with the 'Garden of Heaven visions.' As in medieval visions of the afterlife, the children were transported into a celestial garden by rapture, with angels working fields of flowers (May 7–9, 1950). From the end of April onward, the children reported olfactory (scent of roses) and even gustatory (drinking honey-water from rose blossoms) impressions. Another climax was reached on June 8, 1950, as the young visionaries, with those escorting them, went walking on the 'hill of the apparitions' with the Child Jesus. Unfortunately, the Holy Office in Rome failed to share the visionaries' enthusiasm. On December 10, 1951, it had its definitive judgment read from the

Heroldsbach 1949–1952

pulpits: the "apparitions cited are not supernatural." One visionary and one male companion were excommunicated for disobedience. Still, the Diocese of Bamberg discerned 1971 the necessity of a new proscription of a 'Heroldsbach cult.'[2] But finally, in 1998, the enduring pilgrimage to Heroldsbach was officially tolerated by the Catholic Church and its Marian Pope John Paul II and the unauthorized prayer house was consecrated.

The extraordinary perceptions of Heroldsbach belong to a religious tradition of ancient deference: since earliest times, visionaries, prophets, nuns, mystics, and shepherd children have claimed to have received visions (from Lat., *videre*, 'to see'), apparitions (→ Epiphany), or heard voices ('auditions,' from Lat., *audire*, 'to hear'), containing unheard-of insights and messages from hidden worlds. How are these to be understood?

Different answers can be given, from the side of perceptual and cognitive theory, from social psychology, or from social and religious history. Here the clear-headed observer treads on thin ice. Almost more than in case of miracles, visionary reports differ enormously regarding to appraisals and judgments, broadening the gap between subjective experience and other persons' descriptions, even to sheer misunderstanding. No neutral denominative vocabulary exists. On one hand, the designation 'vision' comes from Christian theology and mysticism, and today is used in general speech to exalt the profane and the commercial, sentimentally or prophetically ('visionary enterprise,' 'technological vision'). At the same time, there are scientific descriptions, mostly in → psychopathological speech: let one speak of 'sensory delusions,' 'phantasms,' 'optical' or 'acoustical hallucinations' (P. Schallenberg), and 'illusionary' misconstructions of perception, and one is at once open to suspicion of criticism of religion, or even of plain rationalism.

Determination of the Concept

Should one attempt to walk a middle path in religious studies, and find a value-neutral application of the concepts, then visions (and correspondingly, auditions) in the strict sense will be defined as extraordinary experiences of consciousness bound up with optical (or acoustical, etc.) sensations. Under 'sensations' we shall understand not only hypothetical external objects and phenomena, but also those of the imagination or other subjective function—hallucinations, illusions and → projections, individually ('seer' or 'visionary,' → 'prophet,' 'medium' [→ Channeling]) or collectively generated and attested, and received as 'sight,' 'summons,' or 'call'—sensations which mostly are interpreted as religious → experience. Visions in the broad sense are complex psychosocial events, resting indeed on individual mental processes, but imbedded in a sometimes confusing network of a collective work of interpretation and of '(re)actions.' In brief, visions are to be approached as '*social syndromes*.' Among optical and acoustical experiences, the former are reported more frequently, and as a rule are allotted greater importance by those involved. Therefore, one often speaks of 'visions' even when, in the course of the experiences, other sensory hallucinations emerge as well. And here we shall do the same.

With respect to content, visionaries claim two special forms of experience of and knowledge of higher worlds. One is insight into hidden knowledge, including prophetical, 'pre-cognitive' (fore-'seeing'), or actually 'visionary' perception of future events. The other is the equivalently sensory, imaginative perception (especially, hallucinatory 'sight') of mythic or historical persons, animals, places, events—gods, guardian spirits, angels, saints, the departed, the landscapes of the afterworld with heaven, purgatory, and hell. The theological distinction between (passive) vision and (active) apparition or → epiphany of a transcendent individual, seems, of course, just as unsatisfying as a restriction to 'full visions' (see § 2), after the model of the medieval journeys to, or in, the beyond (P. Dinzelbacher). According to our present understanding, therefore, apparitions of gods or Mary, just like dreams, are special instances of visions, which, for their part, belong to a societal production of fantasies.

2. a) Visions and auditions are among the phenomena that constitute the borderline between → perception and → fantasy. They are imagined sensory impressions. More precisely, they represent inner perceptions that are themselves generated less, if at all, by the stimulus information of the sensory apparatus, than by the spontaneous action of the → psyche: by fantasy, by → memory, by representations residing in the memory, by associations, by learned thought-patterns, and/or by dispositive and cultural image-impressions. Such intra-psychical constructs of perception are not restricted to seeing or hearing impressions, but include also olfactory sensations ('phantosmy': 'odor of sanctity', scent of roses), stimulus of touch and feeling (touching the cloak of the Madonna or the wound in Jesus's side), or indeed gustatory sensations.

Psychodynamics: Between Sensory Hallucination and Imagination

Besides their sensory quality, visions can be distinguished according to the measure of their superimposition on observable inter-subjective 'normal reality.'
- With *'partial visions',* also called pseudo-hallucinations or illusions, sensory impressions or sensory constructs emerge within the subjective, environment-related field of perception—a dark figure at the edge of the wood (Marian apparition in Heroldsbach), a diaphanous specter (of a dead person) in the bedroom of the bereaved (→ Spirits/Ghosts/Revenants), a 'voice from heaven' (Matt 3:17), a → UFO on the horizon.
- With *'full visions',* on the other hand, the visionary feels transported to another world. He or she undertakes, for instance, a journey through the skies, where the fate of the good and the wicked is shown, as in moralizing near-death narratives recounted since antiquity, or finds himself or herself in a distant place ('Russian visions' in Heroldsbach; Muhammad's flight through the skies to Jerusalem, sura 17), or undertakes a perilous shamanic journey to overcome demons of disease (ecstatic 'trip' of Friuli Benandanti to a place 'out on the fields').
- At the other extreme we find *'intuitive,' aniconic understanding* (Augustine's *visio intellectualis*,[2] Zen Buddhism's *satori*), to be listed as an experience of enlightenment (Lat., *illuminatio*; → Light/Enlightenment) rather than as a vision.

b) Neurophysiologically, and in the psychology of perception, visions rest on the fact that the human brain is extensively disconnected from environmental stimuli. Sensory impressions are perceived as mental representations, or 'percepts', whereby a few (or, as in hallucinations, no) external stimuli suffice to (re-)construct known patterns out of the memory. "The memory is our most important sensory organ."[3] In the case of the religious vision, this observation means that the religious socialization of visionaries holds a decisive meaning. In the storage capacity of their brain, they have a pre-formed mythic store of signs, ever on call, a language of forms that endows them

Psychology of Perception: Mental Representations, Attitudes of Expectation, and Environment-Related Conditions

with a double capacity: to model the inner (and possibly the outer) process of perception according to the precedents of tradition, and to vary this process. Perceptual expectations, predisposed by religious upbringing or social milieu, assign themselves an important role here. Just as I suddenly think that I recognize on the street someone I am looking for, someone for whom I am on the 'lookout,' in many persons, so can a perception-dispositive 'Mary' be summoned and therefore 'found,' under certain circumstances, by way of a scenario of the environment. If the person's interaction with environment is cramped by hunger or weariness, by ascetic practices like → fasting or going without sleep, by the use of drugs, by → trance, hypnosis, or forms of psychic illness such as neuroses or psychoses, the process gains strength (→ Psychopathology). The 'censor system,' with its ability of reality-testing, recedes into the background, in favor of the 'emotion and fantasy system,' to which intensified sensory qualities are attributed (B. Grom). The case of apparitions under post-traumatic stress is familiar, when, early in a time of → mourning, survivors behold their loved ones bodily before them. The same thing occurs in the contrary case of the removal of sense stimuli ('sensory deprivation'), when the environment, screened by a special localization, is minimized, and the psyche is left alone with its percepts. Not by chance did Jesus meet the Devil after forty days in the wasteland, or the Angel Gabriel appear to Muhammad in or before a cave, or today's seekers venture after visions to one of bleakest of wildernesses in America, the edge of Death Valley, on a journey undertaken for the sake of 'self-experience.' Traditionally, it is precisely the 'blind seer'—Teiresias in the Greek myth (→ Oedipus), who sees with his inner, 'third' eye—and who gains special credibility. Spontaneous or neuropsychological processes are indicated by → light phenomena that stand at the beginning of many visionary syndromes, and that are at once filled with mythic shape—and mythic meaning, as with Ezekiel's "cloud with brightness [. . .] and fire" (Ezek 1:4), and the "four living creatures" of the chariot of the throne (v. 1:5). Experiences of brightness here span the arch to the light-tunnel visions, such as are attested in reports of near-death experiences. Especially remarkable are cases in which the vision is inscribed in the body of the visionaries, by way of a mechanism of psycho-somatic identification—for example, when stigmatics show the recorded wounds and stripes of Christ, in the imitation of his sufferings (→ Stigmata/Stigmatics; Francis of Assisi).

Dissociation of the Ego Consciousness

c) Whether arising spontaneously, or consciously initiated, the attested perceptual images or patterns move according to the respective psychic disposition and social situation between 'normal' production of fantasies and being pathologically overpowered by them. Psychologically, one may perhaps speak of a splitting ('dissociation') of the ego-consciousness (B. Grom): thoughts and feelings 'in the head' are projectively shifted to the outside, and there seen, heard, felt as percepts of the objective world—forms of wish-fulfillment, psychic compensation, or fear-repression. But there may also be the possibility of 'secret thoughts' being expressed, of the ambiguous being rendered unambiguous, as repressed or unconsciously wished psychic materials take on form and voice. The perception of hearing an 'inner voice,' that warns, incites, or commands, is widespread. As a psychic instance of the → conscience, this form of subjective perception has found its place in Europe's cultural history since the Socratic *daimónion*—although, of course, also in the criminal history of psychopathological agents. The transitions to mythic personalizing ("the voice of God is speaking to me") are fleeting.

d) Common to all visions and hallucinations is the fact that subjective perceptions of what is without are observable only conditionally, if at all, by bystanders (e.g., as shadow or light reflexes). This uncoupling of subjective and collective reality posits a key problem for evaluation (including evaluation within the religions). But it seems to be responsible for the enormous psycho- and socio-dynamics of visions. The paradoxical premise, "I see something that you do not see," provokes both the interpreting facility of the community and the seers' charismatic power of conviction. A great deal is at stake: the local group's self-image, the specialists' skill and power of appraisal, the religious distribution of roles, the unity of the world of perception, and, last but not least, the credibility of all of the persons involved. This crisis requires common efforts of interpretation, a 'work on the vision' by a social group, so as to be able to integrate individual 'experience' and social expectations in a collectively negotiated pattern of experience. This integration happens, for example, when that which is perceived becomes filled with the depths of a religious tradition of images and doctrines—whether in the form of figures ('Madonna,' 'The Angel Gabriel'), messages ("Pray three hours a day"—Medjugore, 28 July 1983), or scenarios ('gardens of heaven,' 'suffering of sinners')—, and thereby becomes identifiable as culturally comprehensible signs (→ Symbol/Sign/Gesture). Unless the subjective reality of the experience of the image is anchored in a solid religious framework, an 'epidemic of visions' looms. The collective will be swept away by the suggestive current of perceptions of the 'seers.' 'Waves of sightings,' as with the Marian apparitions in Basque Ezkioga (1931–1933), or the → UFOs over Belgium (1989–1990) offer abundant example. Or else those involved, by reason of failed communication, end up at the stake or under psychiatric treatment.

Subjective and Collective Reality

3. a) Thus, in each of these experiences, the question of the *Sitz im Leben* is just as important as is that of its individual genesis. "There will be visions as long as people believe in them. In order to understand visions, then, we must study those who believe in them."[4] Even when they are received in the desert, visions do not happen in empty social space. A typical constellation of involved persons determines the course of the visions, as well as the configuration of their content. In terms of a typology of roles, we can distinguish the following.

Socio-Dynamics: Visions and Hallucinations as Social Events

(1) The *mediums (the visionaries)*: As the center of the event, they are the triggering factor. With 'hot visions' (see § 3b), they can have a precipitous and seductive career from outsider to insider and religious 'guru': indeed, they can advance to the status of spiritual stars—a gratification that could be too much for children especially.

(2) One or more *co-visionaries*: Persons who supervise, confirm, and guide the visionaries—the religious → specialist or master (shaman, etc.), or spiritual director (in the medieval and Catholic area, frequently the father confessor), or, indeed, relatives and familiars. These regulate outside contact but also, at times, make the visionary their own creation and preform content and messages, by supervising, or themselves producing the (written, etc.) documentation of the event. They vouch for the authenticity of the spiritual experience (even in confrontation with other representatives

of their religious community), and can of course make use of their protégés for political or religio-political purposes.

(3) The *audience*: These people form the echo chamber, the sustaining instance, and, if they are in tune with one another, the audience can even replace the visionaries. Especially, the 'hot visions' of the modern age are → mass events, the expression of a 'religion from below', here blazing its spectacular trail. The core event constitutes the point of crystallization for forms of piety in popular religion, which are all too often sensationalistically and politically chopped up and sold by the media. Representatives of the hierarchy regard this kind of spontaneous religious counterculture or 'counter-public' with understandable mistrust.

Social Dynamics: 'Cold' and 'Hot' Visions

b) We are faced with a revealing paradox, at this point, in terms of social history. In many ethnic or traditional religions, visions have possessed, or still possess, their solid place, in initiations, in master-pupil relations, with prophetical role-playing, or with the regular arrival of the dead. In modern industrial society, however, visions seem to occur irregularly, 'chaotically.' One can almost speak of two fundamental forms of the visionary syndrome: one 'cold,' imbedded institutionally, and one 'hot' form, as part of 'ecstatic religion' (Ioan M. Lewis) and spirituality, settled at 'hot spots,' on the far edges of society and institutional control.

Institutionalized Visions

As an example of the *initiatory vision*, let us examine the 'vision quest' conducted by North American candidates for → shamanism. In 1890, anthropologist Franz Boas reported that young men of the tribe of the Shushwap in British Columbia go into the mountains at puberty, build a sweat lodge, and stay overnight there until an animal appears to them in a vision. They take this animal as their spirit helper or 'protective lord.'[5] *Doctrinal visions*, accompanying and guiding the master-pupil relation, are found in contemporary Egyptian → Sufism (as well as with the Christian Copts of the same vicinity; see V. J. Hoffman). *Prophetical visions* are familiar from ancient Israel—most far-reaching, in Ezekiel's 'chariot of the throne' (*merkabah*) vision, the vision of vocation out of which the mysticism of the → Kabbalah would eventually develop: "In the thirtieth year, in the fourth month, on the fifth day of the month, as I was among the exiles by the river Chebar [near Babylon], the heavens were opened, and I saw visions of God" (Ezek 1:1). Ezekiel's symbolism, which was joined on an equal footing by that of John's → Apocalypse, constitutes a transition to *fictional visions*: political or didactic allegories (→ Hildegard of Bingen; often as a vision by the ruler in a dream: Gen 41, Dan 2 and 4), as well as tendentious literature in visionary garb. Doubtless the most elaborate is Dante Alighieri's *Divina Comedia*. Thus, the wealth of the religious image-worlds rests not least of all on a visionary production of fantasies and the development of these.

'Hot Visions'

The visions of the ancient Israelite prophets—like the visions of the monks, nuns, and hermits of the Christian monastic culture, and those of → mysticism—occur on the boundary between institution and charismatic 'outsiderdom.' From the 'saint' to the 'witch,' from the divine vision to the diabolical is frequently but a little step.[6] Despite the unforeseeable nature of these spontaneously emerging, *hot visions*, they follow a typical protocol along their course.

(1) A *subjective perception* occurs (apparition of light, lightning/voice/touch).

(2) The perception is received with a *mythic interpretation* or orientation, through the visionary or a co-visionary, as epiphany (of gods, angels, demons), as the 'voice of God,' etc.: it becomes a vision or 'audition.'

(3) The 'reception' of the vision/audition is *routinized* and ritually solidified (even by way of → trance techniques), while the content is imaginatively decorated and systematized. 'Learning effects' accrue, with both actors and audience; group-dynamic processes of building up (P. Schallenberg) are often discernable, processes that can be promoted from the side of the visionaries by the proclamation of 'secrets' or messages (cf. Fatima).

(4) The *stage of decision* is reached. A juridical examination, from the side of the established → authority, decides whether the vision/audition is reconcilable with official doctrine, and thus is either integrated or prohibited.

(5) The event is *institutionalized:* a church is built at the place of the apparition, a new destination for pilgrimages emerges. In case the authenticity is rejected, a special group (→ Sect) can be constituted, as in Heroldsbach in Franken.

4. a) Extraordinary religious perceptual experiences such as visions and auditions also enter the picture in the choice of the sensory channel through which they manifest themselves to those concerned. The channels are not optional, but are tied to the respective mythic premises. Thus, the God of Israel is an invisible God; his glance slays (Gen 32:31; Ex 33:30)—hence, the modus of perception chosen by God as a mythic person is auditory. YHWH uses a human voice; speaks in a person's sleep (1 Sam 3); thunders from the storm (Job 37:2-5; Deut 4:12; 33); 'roars like a lion' (Hos 11:10; cf. Amos 1:2); at the divine apparition at Sinai, trumpet blasts resound from the mountain. That the people lose their sight and hearing is not coincidental. Perceptual extremes belong to the pathetic enormity of many pictures of God. The German word *Donner* ('thunder') is to be connected with the name or the ancient Teutonic god of the storm, and of fertility, Donar (Thor). Ancient Roman believers also perceived more or less audible 'sky voices' (Lat., *voces caelestes*), where they largely rang from temples or groves. The warning voice coming from the grove of Vesta, in 391 BCE, under the name Aius Locutius ('Divine Speaker'), was even personified as a god, and venerated in religious worship.[7] In ancient Greece, on the other hand, as in European modernity, with its sight-oriented societies, visions predominate: Odysseus sees Athena, the children of Lourdes and Fatima see → Mary before they have any other sensory experience of her.

b) Visions and auditions are dramatized, and subjectively experienced, myth. Figures of faith suddenly become sensibly perceptible: as if on an 'inner stage,' they unfold a fantastical, and phantasmatic, life of their own. But visions are also 'religion risky and risked.' Their 'dramatics' result from a seemingly immediate plunge into daily life on the part of the 'Utterly Other'—without reflection, without censorship, at times even without church and safe framework of interpretation. The risk is unveiled when the 'discernment of spirits' and therefore the examination of inner and outer reality is at stake. Here is shown how much revelation a religion endures. Or whether the seer can stand his or her sight.

Dynamics of Myth: Mythology and Perception

1. What follows is according to SCHALLENBERG 1990, 164-208, and the documentary appendix, 393-397. Schallenberg evaluates unpublished papers of one of those involved.
2. Augustine, *De Genesi ad Litteram*, 7,16. Cf. RUH, Kurt, Geschichte der abendländischen Mystik, 1 (1990), 103-113.
3. ROTH, Gerhard, Das Gehirn und seine Wirklichkeit, Frankfurt/M. ³1996 (¹1994).
4. CHRISTIAN 1996, 71.
5. BOAS, Franz, The Shushwap, Leeds 1890; cf. ELIADE, Mircea, Shamanism: Archaic Techniques of Ecstasy, Princeton 1964 (Fr. ¹1951).
6. DINZELBACHER, Peter, Heilige oder Hexen?, Zurich 1995.
7. Varro, *Antiquitates Rerum Divinarum*, frag. 107 (Cardauns).

Literature

Sources: DINZELBACHER, Peter (ed.), Mittelalterliche Visionsliteratur. Eine Anthologie, Darmstadt 1989; FOSTER, Steven/LITTLE, Meredith, The Book of the Vision Quest: Personal Transformation in the Wilderness, rev. ed. New York 1988 (¹1980).—*Cf. also* SCHALLENBERG 1990.

Secondary Literature:
Psychology: GROM, Bernhard, Religionspsychologie, Munich 1992; SCAGNETTI-FEURER, Tanja, Religiöse Visionen, Würzburg 2004; SCHALLENBERG, Gerd: Visionäre Erlebnisse. Visionen und Auditionen in der Gegenwart. Eine psychodynamische und psychopathologische Untersuchung, Augsburg ²1990 (¹1980); SIEGEL, Ronald K., Fire in the Brain: Clinical Tales of Hallucination, New York 1992.
   History of Religions: BENZ, Ernst, Die Vision, Stuttgart 1969; CHRISTIAN, William A., Visionaries: The Spanish Republic and the Reign of Christ, Berkeley 1996; CLARKE, David, The Angel of Mons: Phantom Soldiers and Ghostly Guardians, Chichester 2004; CLAUSBERG, Karl, Kosmische Visionen. Mystische Weltbilder von Hildegard von Bingen bis heute, Cologne 1980; GINZBURG, Carlo, The Night Battles: Witchcraft and Agrarian Cults in the Sixteenth and Seventeenth Centuries, London 1983 (It. ¹1966); GOODMAN, Felicitas D., "Visions," in: Encyclopedia of Religion 15 (1987), 282-288; HOFFMAN, Valerie J., "The Role of Visions in Contemporary Egyptian Religious Life," in: Religion 27 (1997), 45-64; KNOBLAUCH, Hubert: Berichte aus dem Jenseits. Mythos und Realität der Nahtod-Erfahrung, Freiburg 1999; MYERHOFF, Barbara, The Peyote Cult, Ithaca 1974; SAHLIN, Claire L., Birgitta of Sweden and the Voice of Prophecy, Woodbridge 2001; SMITH, Forrest S., Secular and Sacred Visionaries in the Late Middle Ages, New York 1986; SPEYER, Wolfgang, "Himmelsstimme," in: Reallexikon für Antike und Christentum 15 (1991), 286-303; VOADEN, Rosalynn, God's Words, Women's Voices: The Discernment of Spirits in the Writing of Late-Medieval Women Visionaries, Woodbridge/Rochester 1999; WIEBE, Phillip H., Visions of Jesus: Direct Encounters from the New Testament to Today, New York/Oxford 1997; ZALESKI, Carol, Otherworld Journeys: Accounts of Near-Death Experience in Medieval and Modern Times, New York/Oxford 1987.
   Theological Positions: KNOTZINGER, Knut, "Zur Geschichte und Theologie der Unterscheidung der Geister," in: KHOURY, Adel Theodor (ed.), Zur Unterscheidung der Geister, Altenberge 1994, 30-72; RAHNER, Karl, Visionen und Prophezeiungen. Zur Mystik und Transzendenzerfahrung. Enlarged reedition of the 2ⁿᵈ ed. 1958, ed. by Josef SUDBRACK, Freiburg 1989 (¹1948/49).

→ *Channeling, Experience, Fantasy/Imagination, Hildegard of Bingen, Light/Enlightenment, Memory, Mysticism, Parapsychology, Perception/Sensory System, Private Religion, Projection, Psychopathology, Revelation, Shamanism, Stigmata/Stigmatics*

Hubert Mohr

Voodoo • 1957

Voodoo

1. Like the Afro-Brazilian religions Candomblé and Umbanda, or Cuban Santería, the Afro-Caribbean Voodoo religion is one of the African systems of religion that emerged in colonialism. These systems were brought to the 'New World' by enslaved members of African tribes, and there underwent an independent development. The word 'Voodoo' (variant, 'Hoodoo') is from the Haitian Creole French language (Fr., *vaudou*; Creole, *vaudoux*), where it originated in the language of the Ewe Fon, of West African Benin and Togo. In Haiti, it is used mostly as a denomination of foreigners across the board, and thus is applied to a large number of Haitian indigenous cults. In colonial, and Western Anglo-American, linguistic usage it is a (pejorative) synonym for 'black magic.' Ultimately the denomination is from *vodún*, the word for 'god' or 'worship' in the language of the Ewe Fon. Beginning in the seventeenth century, 'Voodoo' was used in the missionary literature that dealt with the Ewe Fon, who call an initiate in their religion a *vodúnsi* or *hunsi*, a 'bride of the deity,' a concept adopted by the Haitian Voodoo religion. In the Caribbean, in the South of the United States (Florida, Louisiana), and in parts of South America, 'Voodoo' can denote various phenomena. On the one hand, the concept refers to an *Afro-Catholic religion* that is widespread on the island of Hispaniola, especially in Haiti. The designation can also be applied synonymously with those of persons: for 'spell-worker' (*hoodoo doctor*) in the Southern states of the United States, for 'witch' (*bruja*) in Latin America. In the broad sense, 'Voodoo' can denote the religions and cults originating in regions of West Africa.

Concept

2. Haitian Voodoo is the religion of the former African slaves carried off from West Africa in the eighteenth century by the French colonialists, and put to work in the sugarcane fields. It has at times had an important political role: it was able to mobilize forces against the rulers, as at the close of the eighteenth century in the struggle for the abolition of slavery and the country's independence from France (1804). It gathered opposition to various Haitian regimes devoted to policies of their own interest. The last instance of the latter was under dictator 'Papa Doc' François Duvalier (ruled 1957–1971). Socially, there is a distinction between rural and urban forms of Voodoo. In rural areas, worship and belief are oriented to small farmers, and have their pillars of support in the traditional family alliances. Involvement with ancestors and farming stands at the center of religious practice. Voodoo believers in the cities have adapted their practice to relationships there. They simplify this practice, to an extent, and find a 'secondary family' in the temple communities.

Political Influence and Social Background

3. Like Candomblé and Umbanda in Brazil ($\rightarrow$ Afro-American Religions), Haitian Voodoo still manifests authentic African characteristics. Voodoo is a typical example of a $\rightarrow$ possession cult centered on divinities or groups of divinities (*loas*, from the *lwa* of the Yoruba linguistic groups, 'divinity,' or 'mystery'), and originating in the West African ethnic groups Yoruba and Fon. Voodoo's gods, or groups of gods, are called 'mysteries,' or 'saints.' According to Fon myth, there are three regions of the world, in which various gods reign: the sky, the earth, and in between, the clouds. The creator god (Yoruba, *Olorun*; Creole, *Bon Dieu Bon*) lives in the remote sky, and is not reverenced.

Divinities

Loas, the Gods or 'Mysteries' of Voodoo

Name	Rite / 'Nation'	Region of Action, Attributes	Signs of Possession	Symbols	Dwelling places	Region of the World	Sacrificial Gifts	Liturgical Color	Weekday	Christian Correspondence
Legba	Rada	Guardian of the home; intermediary between God and the human being; sentry at the gate, at intersections, and at streets; rival of Dambala	Brutality, strength, violence	Frail old man in shabby clothing	Gates, intersections, medicinal trees	Earth	Cassava, rice, smoked green bananas, piebald hen	Red	Friday, Saturday	St. Peter St. Anthony (lost articles)
Zaka	Rada	Loa of farming and fields, rural, mistrustful, cunning, greedy, hates cities	Looks like a farmer; large straw hat, blue shirt, blue pants, red necktie, straw purse or handbag	mabouya (small reptile)	Fields	Earth	Maize, bread, raw cane-sugar, liquor	Blue, Red, Green	Friday, Saturday	St. Isidore
Gédé	Rada, Petro	Protection from or attraction of harm; Loa of death	Obscene words and gestures, corpselike exterior	Dead, black cross, farm tools	Cemeteries and subterranean places	Earth	Black ram, black cock	Black, Violet, White	Monday, Friday	St. Expeditus
Baron Samdi	Rada Petro	Leader of Gédé (Loa of death)	Macabre, obscene	Tall, black clothing	Cross at the entrance to the cemetery	Earth	Salted Herring, black she-goat, black hen	Black, Violet	Saturday	—
Dambala	Rada	Principle of the good 107 wealth, happiness, prosperity	Serpentine movements	Rainbow snake	Springs and streams	Water	Anything white: chicken, rice, milk, eggs	White	Thursday	St. Patrick, in the expulsion of the snakes from Ireland
Aida Wedo	Rada	Wealth, happiness, prosperity; wife of Dambala	Serpentine movements	Rainbow snake	Springs and streams	Water	Anything white: chiken, rice, milk, eggs	Blue, White	Monday, Tuesday	Our Lady of the Immaculate Conception
Ezili	Rada	Love, beauty, graces, luxury, pleasure, promiscuity; coquette, sensual mulatto	Seductive exterior, provoking behavior, seeks perfume	Heart, mirror	Riverbanks	Water	Toilet articles, choice and elegant food, rice, chicken	Blue, Pink	Tuesday, Thursday	Virgin Mary
Ogu Feray	Rada	Battler of misfortune, warrior, soldier	Authoritarian, coarse language, barrack-room tone of voice	Sword plunged into the earth	Calabash tree, bamboo stalks	Fire	Red cock, bull	Red	Friday, Sunday, Monday	St. James the Great (Santiago)
Agwe	Rada	Protection of seafaring, of oceanic trade, of fishing; mulatto, with blond hair, and sea-green eyes, naval officer	Seeks water for diving and swimming	ship, oar	Sea	Water	White sheep, chicken, champagne	White, Green, Pink	Thursday	St. Ulrich
Simbi	Petro	Gift of clairvoyance, guardian of springs and ponds	Leaps into a pool or river	Water basin	Springs, caves, mountains	Water	Black or gray animals, swine, ram, guinea fowl, turkey cock, chicken	Black, Gray	Tuesday, Thursday, Friday	The Three Wise Men

Following Laënnec Hurbon, *Les mystères du Vaudou*, Paris 1993, pp. 140-143.

Through the influence of Catholicism, Voodoo believers also know the Christian God. But besides God and the Voodoo divinities, they also venerate two other kinds of spiritual beings: human souls that have become spirits of the dead, and spirits that have never been directly tied to matter. Voodoo gods live in the sea, waterfalls (including the famous Saut d'Eau, with the pilgrimage to Ezili Dantò, i.e. Our Lady of Mount Carmel), springs, forests, at intersections, cemeteries, piles of stones, and in saints' rooms that stand alongside the places of worship. Many gods of Voodoo possess a correspondence among the Catholic saints, on whose feast days they, too, are celebrated (see chart).

Gods and rites are divided into groups (Creole, *nanchon*), according to the regions of their origin. Thus, there are the Wangol (from Angola), the Ibo, and the Kogo. More important, however, are the *Rada* and the *Petro*, who are honored especially in urban areas. The word *Rada* derives from the name of the capital of the old Kingdom of Arada, near Abomey, in Benin, while the *Petro* cult, more orientated to the indigenous Creoles, refers to the name of a priest, Don Pedro, who, in the eighteenth century, introduced a variant of the Voodoo trance dance. Petro divinities and spirits are invoked especially for magical actions. Obviously, Voodoo priests may support both groups, and a believer is either Rada or Petro, but may likewise take part in ceremonies of the other type. — *The 'Nations'*

4. As with Candomblé in Brazil, and Santería in Cuba, so with the Voodoo cults is it a matter of a typical phenomenon of the fusion of African religions with Catholicism, spiritism, and the religious traditions of the American Indians. The religion of Voodoo, then, refers not to sacred scriptures, but to ritual practice (it can thus be described as a 'cult religion' in that sense). The latter concentrates on the animal rituals of a bloody sacrifice, as well as on → trance dances. Both are regarded as generating a bond with the gods. The rites are practiced by initiated members (*hunsi*), in cultic groups presided over by priests and priestesses (*hugan* or *mambo*). Initiands are introduced into the group by way of a complicated and rather spectacular ritual sequence. The centers of worship are sacred cabins, or city temples, that have an altar and a central post, which latter will enable the *loas* to descend to believers, and mount them in trance as their 'riding horses.' There exists, besides, a cult of the dead, with meticulous burial rites, and with the mythic figure of the Baron Sam[e]di as 'Lord of the Dead.' Thus the cemeteries become important places of assembly and worship. — *Worship*

5. The magical practices of Voodoo are renowned and maligned. It is the preferred cult of the lowest social class in Haiti—the small farmers and the urban (sub-) proletariat—although, today, persons of the upper class are also found here. Participants in the ceremonies seek deliverance from all of the difficulties of normal life. Diseases are seen as the effect of demonic spells. In the state of trance, body and soul find relief: Voodoo gods can break the influence of evil demons. Probably the magical practice best known in the West is the one performed with a small doll, through which certain magical actions are seen as being able to effect the injury of someone's health, or even their 'Voodoo death.' — *Magical Practices*

Reception

6. Little magical dolls, bloodcurdling rites, Voodoo death, the invocation of serpents, → zombies, and dismal nocturnal scenarios are the ingredients that have made the Voodoo religion a favorite staging of Western exoticism. Ever since R. Spencer St. John, with his 1884 adventure account *Hayita or the Black Republic*, new adventure sensations have continually sprung up in the underground of Western fantasy. Like the witches' Sabbath of yore, Haiti's Voodoo, its 'poor aesthetics' and mysterious aura have assumed for outsiders the shape of a hotch-potch of all of the practices tabooed or disparaged by Christianity: bloody sacrifices, trance dances, invocation of the dead (necromancy), dangerous 'black magic'. For thus the Voodoo religion, precisely via its cinematic exploitation, entered the aesthetic trivia of Western pictures: as a cheap staging of popular horror mythology (*James Bond—Live and Let Die*, 1973; *Angel Heart*, dir. Alan Parker, 1987).

A different social reality appears behind these fantasy images, however. Poverty (with seventy percent unemployment at the moment, the country currently ranks as the poorest in the Western hemisphere) and political instability have occasioned the emigration of many Haitians to North America. They have taken their native Voodoo religion along with them to the urban centers of this diaspora: to New York and Montreal, but especially to Miami and to New Orleans, where today there is a Historical Voodoo Museum. Voodoo today has also gained a foothold as a magical practice in the European scene, as well: Hamburg, for example, has its own Voodoo store. Whether all of this will exorcize the phantasm of the sinister, bloodcurdling cult, however, remains an open question.

Literature

Deren, Maya, Divine Horsemen: The Living Gods of Haiti, London 1953; Fleurant, Gerdès, Dancing Spirits: Rhythms and Rituals of Haitian Vodun, the Bada Rite, Westport 1996; Laguerre, Michel S., Voodoo and Politics in Haiti, Basingstoke 1989; McCarthy Brown, Karen, Mama Lola: A Vodou Priestess in Brooklyn, Berkeley ²2001 (¹1992); Métraux, Alfred, Voodoo in Haiti, New York 1972 (Fr. ¹1958); Pinn, Anthony B., Varieties of African American Religious Experience, Minneapolis 1998; Rosenthal, Judy, Possession, Ecstasy, and Law in Ewe Voodoo, Charlottesville 1998; Senn, Bryan, Drums of Terror: Voodoo in the Cinema, 1998.

→ *Afro-American Religions, Colonialism, North America (Traditional Religions), Possession, South America, Trance, Zombie*

Claudio Mattes

War / Armed Forces

War as a Social Institution

1. *Definition:* War is an organized carrying out of a → conflict between or among groups equipped with deadly weapons. Unlike the individual exercise of violence, war is therefore a societal institution that permits, indeed legally prescribes, the killing of other persons. Depending on the respective degree of organization and complexity of the societies involved, the profile of war can differ greatly. War presupposes the existence of at least a rudimentary military force and apparatus. Minimally organized, or non-organized applications of violence ought not to be called war, but pillage, raid,

incursion, or murder, perhaps vendetta, mounted as these efforts are on the basis of groups defined by kinship or location.

2. *Forms and Functions:* Since early modernity, a declaration of war on the part of the state has been considered to be a requirement for the beginning of a war. From a perspective of anthropology or politics, however, must be emphasized that there are stages of the escalation and de-escalation of war—with corresponding consequences for the lawfulness of the killing. Thus, Caplow distinguishes hostile contact, threat, mobilization, armed confrontation, escalation and counter-escalation, retreat, two-sided or one-sided appraisal, and reorganization.[1] Accordingly, war can be evaluated as the failure of nonviolent solutions for conflicts—in a spiral of escalation that, in principle, could have been interrupted at any stage. An effective mobilization is required in order to undertake a war of long duration, as it often is, between states. Thus, economic strength acquires great significance in the maintenance of an intensive war.

Spiral of Escalation

   b) Far more frequent than wars for the defeat of societies that are technologically inferior in principle (for the purpose of building an empire), are wars waged in regions characterized by the prolonged co-existence of more than one society. Military success, then, depends on capacity for coalition. Alliances of groups with different identities can find acceptance under the name of religion. Contractually and ritually constituted amphictyonies (Gk., 'unions of sacred politics') define the 'alliance situation' (→ Holy War). 'Wars of religion' can suddenly occasion the emergence of new alliances.

   c) Wars appear 'necessary' when, in materialistic categories (for example, in a refinement of Malthus's thesis of 1798), the management of 'population surplus' that would necessitate more or better 'living space' and resources, is emphasized as an achievement to be pursued. But wars happen culturally: they confirm societal structures and internal cultural legitimizations (male superiority, murder of female newborns). Individual psychology (aggression drive) or phylogenetic ('love or hatred'[2]) deductions explain the organized exercise of violence only to a small extent. By contrast, increasingly complex cost/benefit 'calculations'—oriented to received, group-specific, criteria—may be executed by elites. In that case, they gain in importance, to the extent that the agents cited are still capable of making decisions that are in any way rational. Indeed, against this same rationality, there is a pressure to maintain an adequate potential for defense (if not, indeed, for aggression). This pressure, in turn, bears down on the social organization, its military apparatus, and the economic orientation, an impulse to adaptation. Just as was verified once more at the end of the twentieth century, even in Central Europe, war belongs to the normality of social life. And it belongs there far more frankly than scholarly anthropological and sociological investigations into war and → peace (especially those initiated in the 1960s) wished to admit.

3. The general deficit that afflicts research on war and peace, also affects relationships between *religion and war*. War brings to a head individual and societal problems bound up with the function of religion: extreme hierarchies and inequality (army), experiences of alienation, loss, and contingency (exile, need, death). Three fields are of interest here: the religious, especially ritual accentuation and reintegration of the crisis conditions; motives for war; and consequences of war for the religions involved.

Religion and War

Ritual Accentuation

a) In many societies, the *beginning and end of a military expedition*, the departure and return of the → 'heroes,' the wounded, and the dead, are marked by special or accentuated → rituals. These regulate: the beginning and end of situations of social—and, for combatants—moral exception (legitimate killing, male society, hierarchies independent of usual social norms); the handling, distribution, annihilation or integration of booty and prisoners of war; and the translation of the prestige gained in these exceptional situations, that most of society at home has not even perceived, into everyday perception and admiration. Examples of large-scale rituals include the Roman triumph, the ritual murder of prisoners in ancient Mexico (→ Human Sacrifice), or when God—at least theoretically—is handed all of the booty, as in the 'Yahweh War' in Israel.

Motivation

b) Special promises of salvation to killed combatants (reward in Paradise) and a religious dramatizing of the conflict ('demonizing' of the adversary) are frequently introduced as important elements of war. In the 'totalizing' institution of the military, however, and among professional soldiers, the effect of motivation is easily overestimated. A more important function of religion in war, in all likelihood, is to preserve and extend the legitimacy of the conflict (which secures repeated escalation, as well) vis-à-vis non-participants, the unengaged, and even the losing party. The adversary acquires a different quality in becoming a part of a lasting struggle between 'good' and 'evil,' over and above the currently operative reasons, concerning which varying opinions can be held. → Myths and ritual demonstrations that explain victory over others in terms of superhuman means (miracles) are helpful in the management of defeats. A typical narrative structure is the reinterpretation of an irreversible defeat as part of a still open, or even oppositely observed, history, as with the cargo cults of the peoples subjected in imperialism, or in millenarian movements. Thus, war is secured in cultural memorial (→ Memory; Monument/Memorial Places).

Intensified Piety

Religious commitment in spectacular form, especially in the erection of new temples or churches, legitimizes military achievements (just as it does others). This capability is an important part of the decision about the public presence of particular cults, in the hands of the warring elite, which is not always identical with the religious elite. In modern Europe, intensifications, as well as polarizations (intensified rejections), have been observed in the religious practice of those involved in war.[3] For the outward effects (and correspondingly, for documentation), it may be important whether organized religions succeed—at least, temporarily—in channeling diffuse piety. In any case, religion offers combatants, as well as those at home, a medium and means for thematizing fears.

1. CAPLOW 1995, 6.
2. EIBL-EIBESFELDT 1986.
3. BOLL 1997.

Literature

BOLL, Friedhelm (ed.), Volksreligiosität und Kriegserleben, Münster 1997; CAPLOW, Theodore, Systems of War and Peace, Lanham 1995; CRÉPON, Pierre, Les religions et la guerre, Paris ²1991 (collection of sources); DUPUY, Trevor N. (ed.), International Military

Soldiers are often in psychically exceptional situations, and many wish for religious encouragement. Discussion in the churches shows various stances vis-à-vis military pastoral care. One element supports a pastoral duty. Another rejects any church engagement, regarding war in itself as violating the fundamental commandments of religion. Here, soldiers have gathered around a large table that has become an altar through the installation of certain sacred accoutrements. The leader of the divine service is distinguished from the other uniformed persons only by the stole around his shoulders. Field Mass and Eucharist are about to begin. (Christoph Auffarth)

and Defense Encyclopedia, 6 vols., Washington 1993; EIBL-EIBESFELDT, Irenäus, Krieg und Frieden aus der Sicht der Verhaltensforschung, Munich ²1986; GLADIGOW, Burkhard, "*Homo publice necans*. Kulturelle Bedingungen kollektiven Tötens," in: Saeculum 37 (1986), 150-165; JOHNSON, James Turner/KELSAY, John (eds.), Cross, Crescent, and Sword: The Justification and Limitation of War in Western and Islamic Tradition, New York 1990; KROENER, Bernhard R./PRÖVE, Ralf (eds.), Krieg und Frieden. Militär und Gesellschaft in der Frühen Neuzeit, Paderborn 1996; MOSSE, George L., Fallen Soldiers: Reshaping the Memory of the World Wars, New York 1990; VAN DER LINDEN, Marcel/MERGNER, Gottfried (eds.), Kriegsbegeisterung und mentale Kriegsvorbereitung. Interdisziplinäre Studien, Berlin 1991; VON STIETENCRON, Heinrich/RÜPKE, Jörg (eds.), Töten im Krieg, Freiburg 1995.

→ *Conflict/Violence, Hero/Heroism, Holy War, Jihad, Martial Arts, Monument/Memorial Places, Peace, Terrorism, Violence*

Jörg Rüpke

Water

1. Water is a prerequisite for any life, and determines the daily existence of all persons at all moments. It is as much as about sixty percent of our body, and covers three fourths of the earth's surface. We encounter it as sweet water—as a spring, a river, a waterfall, a lake, dew, rain, clouds, ice, and snow. We use it as we eat, bathe, or drink. It quenches thirst, freshens, cools, heals, cleans, flushes the old out and the new in. Where it is missing, as in the desert, the effect is as life-threatening as where it comes in the shape of floods or storms. As salt water of the oceans and seas, it conceals mighty nutritional resources, is a feared power of destruction, longed-for vacation place, and garbage dump of industrial society.

In religions, the importance and meaning of water is a matter of extremely multiple levels. In myths, it appears not only as a source of life, a generative and renewing power, but also as a dangerous, menacing power, with a

Uriella (Erika Bertschinger Eicke) is leader and prophetess of the Order *Fiat Lux* (Lat., "Let there be light"). Here, in Black Forest Ibach, she transforms ordinary faucet water into 'Athrum water.' She swirls the water to the left, counterclockwise, with her left hand. Through the left hand, according to Uriella, the 'Athrum ray' of life, love, and salvation flows into the water, and charges it. But, for example, in curing the sick, she draws negative elements from the body with her right hand. With *Fiat Lux*, a purifying lifestyle has a high value, in view of the proclaimed purification of earth and humanity. Believers ingest the saving water to cleanse all their organs, and to strengthen their forces of resistance to illness. For injuries, the water is applied externally. Fruit and vegetables, too, should be immersed to prevent damage, and even the effects of medical injections are supposed to be strengthened when this 'universal medicine' is taken along with them. Small wonder, then, if Uriella's followers bring canisters to Ibach, when they visit there, in order to take plenty of water home with them. Even before the foundation of the order, Erika Bertschinger's friendship circle, *Lichtquell Bethanien* ('Bethany Source of Light') chose as its emblem a shell, with a cross, flowing from the water, and surrounded with a garland of rays. Even today it embellishes the *Fiat Lux* Order's stationery, along with its newspaper, *Der reinste Urquell* ("The Purest Fountainhead"). (Benita von Behr and Kirsten Holzapfel)

violent potential for destruction. As an element presenting the human being with a largely unattainable, uncontrollable space of life, it stands for 'the other,' strange and mysterious, object at once of fascination and trembling. As a force of nature and bestower of life, persons encounter it only with a need to neutralize its effect on them, and to acquire a positive influence on the potential of water for benediction and peril, especially where persons' lifestyle is most powerfully dependent upon this element. The latter is the case in traditional agrarian societies (→ Agrarian Religion/Agrarian Magic), or in seafaring or river cultures (Mesopotamia on the Euphrates and Tigris, Egypt on the Nile), and in coastal regions, where fishing is the stuff of life. In worship, it is the indispensable medium of ritual cleansing, which, frequently, alone accomplishes the premise of standing in connection with the Holy (→ Purification/Hygiene/Bodily Grooming). Indeed, when ascribed transforming powers, water is the medium of the Holy itself. For believers, water is especially a means of intensive sensory experience. Water can be felt, heard, seen, smelled, and tasted. All of the qualities ascribed to it are experienced, 'felt,' with all of the senses. Religion is then a matter of corporeal experience (→ Perception/Sensory System).

2. As a space of life accessible to human beings only with difficulty, water is a vehicle of fascination and mystery, and to this very day a projection screen of collective fears and longings most fertile for the formation of myths: Leviathan, Nessie (→ New Myths/New Mythologies)—the notion of monsters living in the water— → Atlantis and the Titanic—the terrifying image of the destruction of civilization in a flood that swallows up everything whole—are just a few examples.

In myths of → origin, water often plays a key role, and frequently exists before the emergence of the world itself. It can represent the original state of formless, as yet unorganized, 'nothing'— → chaos—in which life develops only through the intervention of divine forces; or also, it can possess generative powers that favor or produce the emergence of life. In many cosmogonies, the inanimate original, inanimate flood is passive, and the creative process alone is a matter of the power of the divine will (→ Cos-

mology/Cosmogony); or, it comes forth by way of the intervention of divine powers, as in the Japanese *Kojiki* (collection of mythological texts), in which the divine pair, Izanagi and Izanami, thrust a lance into the sea, and when they withdrew it, its salty drops became the first land, the Island of Onogoro. Water can also be a medium of the emergence of new life, or of a new god—without itself actively producing them, as in the Hindu myth in which Brahma, creating himself, is born of a golden egg awash in the water (Manava Dharmasastra 1, 8-9). In the Babylonian myth of creation *Enuma Elish,* water itself possesses generating forces: both divinities, Apsu, the male sweet water ocean, and Tiamat, the female salty sea, mingle and generate new gods, the sky (*Ansar*), and the Earth (*Kisar*).

In its function as obligatory elixir of life, water stands for the life-bestowing, nourishing, and fertile principle. In Hindu mythology, for example, the water of the Ganges is associated with cow's milk, and addressed as *Ma* ('mother'). In the Johannine motif of the 'water of life,' or 'living [i.e. running, flowing] water,' in the Fourth Gospel and the Book of Revelation, water is the symbol of everlasting, inexhaustible life. Revelation 22:1-2 tells of a stream of 'living,' crystal-clear water, flowing from the throne of God and the Lamb, and surrounded by trees that bear fruit twelve times a year. Genesis itself (2:10-14) names a stream that flowed through the → Garden of Eden, split into four branches—Pishon, Gihon, Tigris, and Euphrates—and rendered the land fruitful.

Water also conceals a danger. In the Great Flood, God released the chaotic primeval floods in their devastating force (Gen 7). The sea appears in the Bible as inimical to life, and will no longer exist in the New Creation

Many villages of the Canary island of La Gomera celebrate the feast days of the locally venerated saints with exuberant *fiestas.* After Mass, figures of many of the saints ride out over the sea in boats. For Our Lady of Guadalupe, patron saint of the island, for Our Lady of Mount Carmel, patron of fishers, or, as here, for the feast day of Saint Peter, another patron saint of fishers, on June 29, processions of boats are held. In this fashion, the existential importance of the ocean for the inhabitants of the island is reflected in their local worship and festival culture. This meaning derives, of course, both from the island's geographical relation to the sea, and from the latter's economic importance (fishing and tourism).

(Rev 21:1). Yet God is ruler of water (cf. Exod 14:21). Jesus's walking on the water can be understood in this context (Mark 6:45-52).

The conception is very frequently encountered, that the world of the living is divided from that of the dead by water (→ Hereafter). In Greek mythology, the boatman Charon ferries souls to Hades across the river Acheron (in some versions, across the underworld river Styx), and lake of Acheron. In Sumerian belief, the dead cross the underworld river Chabur on their way to the land without return (*Kurnugea*). In ancient Egypt, it was in all actuality that the Nile divided the world of the living from that of the dead: all gravesites lay to the west of the river, in the direction of the wilderness, while cities were on the east side. In his "Dead Man" (USA and Germany, 1997), filmmaker Jim Jarmusch developed the theme of crossing the water as a North American Indian myth: At the conclusion, dying protagonist William Blake is cast adrift by Indians. In Christian culture, the expression 'to cross the Jordan' recalls similar conceptualizations. With the West African Ewe, the conceptualization is just the contrary: human beings cross a river before their birth. Frequently, water even marks the bounds of the universe, as in the ancient oriental and biblical notion (cf. Gen 1:6-8) of the water of a primeval sea, divided into an ocean in the sky and a sea under the earth, being kept over the firmament and under the disk of the earth.

Last but not least, water possesses mirroring qualities. It is proverbial that the young Narcissus, in the Greek myth, is bewitched by his own image on the surface of a body of water. In Japanese popular belief, the mirror of the water, with its images that reflect and captivate at once, is a means of magical attainment of influence (especially in the demonic spell). It affords a glimpse of the future, as comes to expression in accounts of springs and ponds near temples that withhold a mirror image from those on the brink of death.

Water Deities and Personifications of Water

3. Throughout the world, there are deities, spirits, and mythical or sacred beings—often, but not always, female—specially associated with water. The waters can be the flowing manifestation of a deity, whose residence and place of worship, or region of power, these waters are. The earmarks of cult are decisively dependent on the role played by water in human beings' manner of subsistence. In Catholic Christianity, in dealing with this moist element, reference is made to → saints of whom many are associated with forms in which the waters make their appearance. This reference often points to a particular connection with the saint's biography (death in the water). The list ranges from the patron saints of brooks (Sebastian), springs (Gangolf, Vitus), fishers (Peter, among others; see illus.), shippers and seamen (Christopher and others), to helpers in emergencies at sea (Nicholas of Myra), in searches for the drowned (Catherine of Alexandria), in floods and storms, or to those to be invoked for and against rain. Water deities and spirits may be associated (a) with a mythical or a concrete body of water, for example with a particular river or spring (Greek spring nymphs), (b) the sea, or even (c) with water in general.

a) Mythical, personified *rivers* include, for example, the Titan Oceanus, who was presented as the father of numerous rivers and springs in ancient Greece, and who surrounded the world as a ring-shaped sweet water river, or, again, Hindu river goddess Sarasvati. As real rivers in India, especially Ganga (the Ganges) and Yamuna are venerated as goddesses, while all rivers are regarded as sacred, and usually female. Places of the confluence of several streams are especially sacred, and favorite → pilgrimage destinations, such as the confluence of Ganga, Yamuna, and Sarasvati in Prayaga (Allahabad), where, every twelve years, the great bathing festival of Kumba Mela attracts millions of pilgrims (→ Feast and Celebrations, with ill.).

b) It is mainly in its function as a trade route, and as a source of nourishment, that the *sea* is brought into correlation with gods. In ancient Greece, the mighty and irascible god Poseidon ruled over the sea, which he could swirl with his trident and bring seamen into danger. In China, the Sea Goddess and Sky Queen Tin Hau, who can cut the wind to pieces with her sword, is venerated especially in the coastal regions. Ships carry her image in their cabins, along with three paper talismans, which show the goddess in different presentations. In distress at sea, they are burned, one after the other, to win her succor. In arctic religions, the myth of the female Inuit sea spirit Sedna (Nuliajuk) is widespread. She lives at the bottom of the ocean, and, as ruler over the animals, releases certain sea-animals to the hunt. In famine, it is the duty of the shaman to undertake a ritual journey to her, to comb from her long, fluffy hair the soil that symbolizes human misdeeds, and render her favorable once more. In the Afro-American religions, sea goddess Yemanja (→ Sacrifice, with ill.) is especially loved and revered.

c) Not all divinities and mythical beings can be clearly correlated with a certain type of water. The → 'Voodoo' goddess Nau Wata, for example, who is extremely popular in West Africa, lives in the sea, as well as in lagoons, rivers, and lakes. It is much the same with myths of European mermaids, who are regarded as living in rivers and lakes, as well as in the sea.

4. In worship, water can function as a medium of purification, transformation, and energy.

As a *purifying substance*, water is an important component of worship in many religions, representing an indispensable prerequisite for contact with the saints. Thus, for example, with ritual washing (*ghusl*) before prayer in Islam (→ Purification/Hygiene/Bodily Grooming, with ill.), or with the veneration of a god (*puja*) in Hinduism, water is of inestimable value for ritual cleansing. In India, bathing in sacred rivers, such as in the Ganga, apart from their material power of purification, is of the highest ritual and spiritual consequence. It is the same with → Shintô.

Functions in Workshop

As a *medium of transformation*, and symbol of a new beginning, water is used in Christianity for → baptism. To recall their baptism, Catholics sign themselves with holy water upon entering a church. The same water serves in the benediction of sacred images and utensils. Salt is added when the water is blessed for all of these uses, and the water receives further attention when it is to be employed on other occasions. Holy water for the consecration of a church or altar contains salt, oil, and wine. Baptismal water is consecrated at Easter and Pentecost.

The widespread conception of water as a *vessel of sacred, healing, and vitalizing qualities*, inspires numberless pilgrims, worldwide, to embark on their journeys. They travel with empty bottles, to fill with water and take home, sensing its need. The precious moisture is sent from Lourdes the world over, Ganges water is sold to the faithful in copper jars, Muslims draw water from the sacred spring *Tzamtzam*, in → Mecca, and carry it home: it is, of course, an especially precious gift. A container of water is dipped in Uriella's bathtub before mailing (see ill.). The concept is widespread in → New Age religion that ordinary water, although it has lost its original life force, can be 'energetically animated' by means of 'whirlers' and other activation apparatus, and restored to the condition of its primordial energy. Now 'in-formation', in the form of very fine matter, will have been conveyed to its field of energy. The notion goes back especially to V. Schauberger (1886–1958), J. Grander (b. 1930), and Wilhelm Reich's Orgone theory, but is also an application of 'Reiki' techniques.

Literature

ALLEY, Kelly D., On the Banks of the Ganga: When Wastewater Meets a Sacred River, Ann Arbor 2003; BREWSTER, Harry, The River Gods of Greece: Myths and Mountain Waters in the Hellenic World, London 1997; BRITTAIN, Robert, Rivers, Man and Myths: From Fish Spears to Water Mills, Garden City 1958; ECK, Diana L., "Rivers," in: Encyclopedia of Religion 12 (1987), 425-428; FELDHAUS, Anne, Water and Womanhood: Religious Meanings of Rivers in Maharashtra, New York 1995; JING, Anning, The Water God's Temple of the Guangsheng Monastery: Cosmic Function of Art, Ritual, and Theater, Leiden 2002; JONES, Francis, The Holy Wells of Wales, Cardiff 1954; PROPP, William Henry, Water in the Wilderness: A Biblical Motif and Its Mythological Background, Atlanta 1987; RUDHARDT, Jean, "Water," in: Encyclopedia of Religion 15 (1987), 350-358; WILD, Robert A., Water in the Cultic Worship of Isis and Sarapis, Leiden 1981.

→ *Baptism, Benares, Cosmology/Cosmogony, Materiality, Nature, Place (Sacred), Perception, Purification/Hygiene/Bodily Grooming, Purity*

Benita von Behr

Weber, Max

Biographical Sketch

Max Weber, born in Erfurt (Germany) in 1864, enrolled in 1882 in Heidelberg to study jurisprudence; in 1884 he carried on his studies in Berlin, where he received a doctorate for a work on trading societies in Italian cities. In 1892 he did a postdoctoral essay on the importance of Roman agrarian history for government and private rights. In 1893 Weber was appointed as professor of economics at Freiburg (Germany); three years later he got a similar chair in Heidelberg, where he lived until 1918—retired from his professorial duties for health reasons since 1903. In 1919 he accepted an appointment at the University of Munich, where he died in 1920.

Interest in Capitalist Economy

In 1891/1892 Weber did an empirical survey of the situation of farm-workers in East Prussia. In analyzing the data he recognized a dilemma of the estate owners: when becoming modern entrepreneurs producing for the market and hiring cheap Polish labor, they inadvertently undermined the German presence in that region. But when sticking to their traditional way of life, they were in danger of descending to the status of simple farmers (Weber 1984 [1892], 903). Weber's analysis witnessed a keen interest in the conditions, emergence, and consequence of a change to a capitalist economy.

The Case of Antiquity

Weber did not see the development of a capitalist economy as self-evident, as he explained 1896 in a lecture on the "Social Reasons for the Decline of Ancient Culture" (1924). Most scholars ascribed the Fall of Rome to the mass migrations; Weber in contrast saw it as an outcome of a gradual social change inside the Empire. Initially, ancient civic communities based their economies on slave labor. Because of their advantageous position on the coast, they engaged heavily in trade. After the second century CE, because of the *Pax Romana*, when the supply of slaves dried up and the economic focus shifted inland, a self-sufficient estate economy gradually displaced the trade and industry of the cities. When even government officials and soldiers could no longer cover their needs through taxes, but through barter, little remained of the capitalistic trade economy. At the end of Antiquity the cities disintegrated into villages, the culture once again became rural. It was this reversal of development that allowed the dramatic devastation of the mass migrations.

For a rising capitalist economy political conditions were necessary, as the ancient case shows. But they alone were not sufficient for the establishment of capitalism. The other necessary ingredient is the subject of Weber's famous essay, "The Protestant Ethic and the Spirit of Capitalism" (1904/5; see Weber 1992 and 2002). Weber was not the first to notice a connection between Protestant regions and capitalism; he was the first to give an explanation. Impending capitalism needed the support of an internal power, an ethos, because it first had to bring down a powerful opponent: *traditionalism*. "A person does not 'by nature' want to make more and more money, but simply to live—to live in the manner in which he is accustomed to live, and to earn as much as is necessary for this. Wherever capitalism has begun its work of increasing the 'productivity' of human labor by increasing its intensity, it has run up against the infinitely persistent resistance of this leitmotiv of precapitalist economic labor" (2002 [1904/5], 16]).

Protestantism and Capitalism

    This dogged resistance, which Weber almost ascribed to human nature, did not fade away by itself. It was broken by Puritanism, since that religion required from the believers a methodical pattern of working and abstention from consumption (→ Asceticism). It was this manner of life that pushed forward inadvertently the development of capitalism. Weber's thesis elicited a heated debate. Though a few scholars were critical, at the end Weber was convinced (Weber 1910 and 1978) that his argument had withstood all objections.

In order "to correct the isolation of this study and to place it in relation to the whole of cultural development" (1992 [1904/5], 284]), Weber turned to studying the religions of Confucianism, Hinduism, Buddhism, Judaism, and Islam, and investigated the relationship of these world religions to economic ethics. During this research Weber made an exciting discovery, recounted by Marianne Weber: "The process of *rationalization* dissolves magical notions and increasingly 'disenchants' the world and renders it godless. Religion changes from magic to doctrine. And now, after the disintegration of the primitive image of the world, there appear two tendencies: a tendency towards the *rational* mastery of the world on the one hand and one towards *mystical* experience on the other. But not only the religions receive their stamp from the increasing development of thought; the process of rationalization moves on several tracks, and its autonomous development encompasses all creations of civilization—the economy, the state, law, science, and art [. . .]. Weber regarded this recognition of the special character of occidental *rationalism* and the role it was given to play for Western culture as one of his most important discoveries. As a result, his original inquiry into the relationship between religion and economics expanded into an even

Economic Ethics in Comparative Perspective

more comprehensive inquiry into the *special nature of all of Western culture*" (Marianne Weber 1988 [1926], 333).

The 'Disenchantment' of the World

From this point onward, 'disenchantment,' understood as the development *not* of a godless world as Marianne Weber implies (→ Secularization), but of a world in which the gods had lost their ontological roots, became a concept that figured centrally in Weber's thinking about the rise and rationality of Western culture (→ Disenchantment/Reenchantment). Weber was not the only German social scientist at that time to link the analysis of modern Western culture to religious history (→ Modernity/Modern Age). And not only capitalism but other modern institutions too were regarded as in need of explanations that took into account the beliefs of the people involved.

Theory of Action

In order to introduce the history of religions into that analysis, Weber turned to the category of 'action' (1981 [1913]). He sharply distinguished a subjectively intended meaning from an objectively valid meaning. Action is intelligible behavior towards objects and requires a subjective meaning that may be more or less clear to the actor. Since meaning is not supplied by experiencing the reality of cosmos or history, religions have to provide them (→ Meaning/Signification). They alone can supply a world view and → ethics that is able to resist the opposite experience of a world devoid of any inherent meaning. Weber insisted that religious meanings differ from personal motivations, and that they are embodied in social interactions (→ Communication). Closely related to this distinction is the one between rational and correct action. An observer may judge an action as rational though it is oriented to assumptions that he regards as invalid. An action oriented toward conceptions of → magic, for example, is subjectively of a far more instrumental character than ethical or mystical religiosity. In *Economy & Society* the whole section on religion ("Sociology of Religion," or better: "Religious Communities") revolves around that distinction. In the beginning "only the things or events that actually exist or take place played a role in life." But this situation did not last. Early on an important change set in: "Magic is transformed from a direct manipulation of forces into a *symbolic activity*" (1978 [1921/2], 403). At the end of the process, "intellectualism suppresses belief in magic, the world's processes become disenchanted, lose their magical significance, and henceforth simply 'are' and 'happen' but no longer signify anything. As a consequence, there is a growing demand that the world and the total pattern of life be subject to an order that is significant and meaningful" (1978 [1921/2], 506). It was a religio-historical development that divested the world of inherent meaning and ultimately also transformed the form and validity of religions.

Professionalization of Religions

In Weber's view, the process of disenchantment went hand in hand with the emergence of religious → specialists—the magician, the → priest, the → prophet, and the intellectual (→ Intellectual Religion)—who conceived and controlled the mysterious powers in different manners. Historically, according to Weber, most religions have known only occasional associations of their adherents. Solely a few developed a full-fledged congregational religiosity: Buddhism, Judaism, Christianity, and Islam. Their congregations faced a major challenge, however, when religion took the direction of world-rejection as a means to → salvation. The more a religion of salvation developed, became systematized, and internalized as an ethics of commitment—in contrast to an ethics of compliance with laws—the more its adherents experienced 'tensions' with the world.

Weber sketched this analysis for the first time in chapter 11 of the religion section in *Economy & Society* written in 1913/14 (1978 [1921/2], 576-610). In 1915 he revised and expanded it in one of his essays on the "Economic Ethics of the World Religions" (Gerth/Mills 1946, 323-359). Religious congregations requiring brotherly love as an ethic of commitment engendered tensions with respect to the spheres of economics, politics, sexuality, science, and art—spheres that the adherents thus came to experience as autonomous and hostile. In these spheres, believers resolved their tensions by efforts either to 'flee' the world or to 'master' it—the former pathway constituting what Weber calls 'mysticism,' the latter 'asceticism.' In either case, new religious practices arose, practices that became integral to religion within the disenchanted world. *Contra* Marianne Weber, then, 'disenchantment' was, for Max Weber, not the development of a godless culture, but quite the opposite. An increasingly rational culture (→ Rationalism/Irrationalism), aware of the unethical character of the ruling social orders, stimulated the emergences of varied new forms of religiosity. Weber's exposition abounds in examples of this process. Thus, in his view, Calvinism, when it abandoned the prohibition of usury as a result of inherent economic forces, organized charity for orphans and cripples as an undertaking of its own (→ Charitable Organizations). Historically, mystical religions chose the opposite route and practiced, at least in principle, a loving self-surrender, not for the sake of the poor but for the sake of the surrender itself (→ Mysticism). Likewise, regarding the sphere of politics, congregational religiosity did not merely oppose military violence; it favored either a world-fleeing pacifism or active measures to fight the power of sin. Again and again, Weber emphasized the paradox that the same religious ethics that engendered awareness of social orders as ruled by hostile rational forces simultaneously generated new kinds of religiosity. Regarding the spheres of → sexuality and → art, he even observed the development of practices that entailed a re-enchantment of the world, practices comparable to those of world-rejection: → eroticism and art as means to escape the cold rationality of the modern world.

From this perspective, the less a modern rational culture denies inherent meanings in cosmos and → history, the more a quest for meaning devolves back onto the individual. Under these circumstances, the religions handed down from the past are becoming sources for principles of life conduct—albeit sources whose validity now rests solely on subjective individual decisions. In this 'disenchanted' context, the gods acquire a peculiar new life, as Weber declared in his speech "Politics as Vocation" (1919): "Today the routines of everyday life challenge religion. Many old gods ascend from their graves; they are disenchanted and hence take the form of impersonal forces. They strive to gain power over our lives and again they resume their eternal struggle with one another" (Gerth/Mills 1946, 149).

Paradoxes of Modern Culture

Literature

Works: GERTH, Hans H./MILLS, Charles Wright, From Max Weber: Essays in Sociology. Oxford 1946; WEBER, Max, Die Lage der Landarbeiter im ostelbischen Deutschland (1892), ed. M. RIESEBRODT, Max Weber Gesamtausgabe (MWG) I/3, 2 vols., Tübingen 1984; Idem, "Die sozialen Gründe des Untergangs der antiken Kultur" (1896), in: Gesammelte

Aufsätze zur Sozial- und Wirtschaftsgeschichte, Tübingen 1924, 289-311; Idem, The Protestant Ethic and the Spirit of Capitalism, trans. by Talcott PARSONS, London/New York 1992; Idem, The Protestant Ethic and the "Spirit" of Capitalism and other Writings, ed., trans., intro. by Peter BAEHR and Gordon C. WELLS, Harmondsworth 2002; Idem, "Anticritical Last Word on The Spirit of Capitalism" (1910), trans. and intro. by Wallace M. DAVIS, in: American Journal of Sociology 83 (1978), 1105-1131; Idem, "Some Categories of Interpretive Sociology" (1913), trans. by E. E. GRABER, in: The Sociological Quarterly 22 (1981), 151-180; Idem, Die Wirtschaftsethik der Weltreligionen. Konfuzianismus und Taoismus (1915–1920), ed. by Helwig SCHMIDT-GLINTZER in cooperation with P. KOLONKO (MWG I/19), Tübingen 1989; Idem, Die Wirtschaftsethik der Weltreligionen. Hinduismus und Buddhismus (1916–1920), ed. by Helwig SCHMIDT-GLINTZER in cooperation with K. H. GOLZIO (MWG I/20), Tübingen 1996; Idem, Wissenschaft als Beruf (1917/1919); Politik als Beruf (1919), ed. by W. J. MOMMSEN and W. SCHLUCHTER in cooperation with B. MORGENBROD (MWG I/17), Tübingen 1992; Idem, Gesammelte Aufsätze zur Religionssoziologie, 3 vols., Tübingen 1920; Idem, Wirtschaft und Gesellschaft, Teil I: Die Wirtschaft und die gesellschaftlichen Ordnungen und Mächte; Teil II: Typen der Vergemeinschaftung und Vergesellschaftung, ed. by Marianne WEBER (Grundriß der Sozialökonomik III. Abtlg.), Tübingen 1921/22; Idem, Wirtschaft und Gesellschaft. Vol. 2: Religiöse Gemeinschaften (MWG I/22-2), ed. by Hans G. KIPPENBERG together with Petra SCHILM and Jutta NIEMEIER, Tübingen 2001; Idem, Economy and Society: An Outline of Interpretive Sociology, edited by Günther ROTH and Claus WITTICH, Berkeley 1978; Idem, The Sociology of Religion, intro. by Talcott PARSONS, Boston 1993.

Secondary Literature: GAUCHET, Marcel, The Disenchantment of the World: A Political History of Religion, Princeton 1999; KIPPENBERG, Hans G., "Religious Communities and the Path to Disenchantment: The Origins, Sources, and Theoretical Core of the Religion Section," in: CAMIC, Charles et al. (eds.), Max Weber's *Economy and Society*: A Critical Companion, Stanford 2005, 164-182; LEHMANN, Hartmut/ROTH, Günther (eds.), Weber's Protestant Ethic: Origins, Evidence, Contexts, Cambridge 1993; SCHLUCHTER, Wolfgang, Rationalism, Religion, and Domination: A Weberian Perspective, Berkeley 1989; WEBER, Marianne, Max Weber. Ein Lebensbild, Tübingen 1926 (Engl. as: Max Weber: A Biography, New Brunswick/Oxford 1988).

→ *Asceticism, Disenchantment/Reenchantment, Economy, Enlightenment, European History of Religion, History, Meaning/Signification, Modernity/Modern Age, Protestantism, Rationalism/Irrationalism, Science, Society*

Hans G. Kippenberg

Wholeness / Holism

1. While the term 'whole' has been one of the fundamental concepts of Western philosophy and science from the outset, the concept of *wholeness*, as a scientific one, is a neologism, having come into use only toward the end of the nineteenth century. Here it is especially biology and psychology that give the concept the meaning that it still has today in scientific theory ('holism'), medicine ('holistic medicine'), or psychology ('holistic psychology').

Concepts and Theories of Wholeness: Goethe

2. The concept of wholeness has a close affinity with the German word *Gestalt* (originally, 'figure,' 'mold,' 'build,' 'fashion,' or 'shape'—the way in which something is 'contoured,' is 'settled into its space'). Here it was Goethe in particular, who gave this concept its specific meaning in his scientific studies. Thus, he connected with *Gestalt* the concept of morphological development in metamorphosis—that is, development of living beings as a transforma-

tion of *Gestalten*. Goethe's notion of *Gestalt* thereby introduces an essential aspect into the conception of totality, or wholeness: that of development. By contrast with the notion of 'form' (*forma* as the Latin translation of the Greek *morphé*), *Gestalt* indicates a movement of development towards the actual totality of the image of an organism. As 'living form,' *Gestalt* itself is always the expression of a life history. Here the life process is seen from the whole of a being's system and plan. Individual processes are viewed as elements of the production and reproduction of the whole, and not only the achievements of an order—therefore resembling the biological life-plan of a concrete mechanical biophysics—but also the expression of a free principle of *Gestaltung*, of 'shaping' or formation.

In *psychology*, the gestalt theory enunciated the totality of perception. Christian von Ehrenfels (1859–1932), in his *Über die Gestaltsqualitäten* (Ger., "On the Qualities of Gestalt"; 1890), presented an example that has since become a celebrated one: he showed the totality, or 'totality-ness' of perception by appealing to → music, where he pointed out that a melody is always perceived 'totally,' in totality, in its 'totality' or 'totalities,' even though it is only individual respective tones that sound. → Perception, insists Ehrenfels, is a gestalt perception—and thus, not a piecing together of individual values into an image, but the grasping, the 'comprehending,' of a gestalt, in the presence of, and by virtue of, individual traits. Here the microcosm is a reproduction of the macrocosm, and vice versa.

Psychology

   Totality, as the foundation of 'gestalting,' and of knowledge—of coming-to-know—is also to be found in the interpretation of history and in culture theory, especially with Oswald Spengler (1880–1936). In his influential *Der Untergang des Abendlandes* (Ger. 1920–1922; Eng. as "The Decline of the West"), Spengler attempted to demonstrate that the history of high cultures runs a 'gestalt-like course,' that makes it morphologically comparable. The character of cultures as totalities, Spengler holds, is the expression of a culture-forming force that is always typical in each phase of its development.

3. An important, if not as well known, direction of theories of totality is presented by *holism* (Gr., *to hólon*, 'the whole'). The notion goes back to South African statesman and researcher Jan C. Smuts (1870–1970) and his 1926 *Holism and Evolution*. The work's basic thought is the vitalist idea of a totality of the processes and events of life, but with a renunciation, and even the exclusion of, any concept of finality. Besides Smuts, especially John Scot Haldane, Adolf Meyer-Abich, Edgar Daché, and Ludwig Bertalanffy can be cited. The common interest pursued by these scientists was to overcome the contradictions between the 'mechanism' of classical physics, and vitalism, which had just found renewal by way of the works of Hans Driesch. This reconciliation was to be reached by the complete replacement of the concept of 'end/goal' with that of 'totality.' Unlike 'end,' totality no longer has a purpose or goal to which any course of nature would have to direct itself, or would be directed. This 'teleological,' goal-determined sort of scientific method still harbors a metaphysical remainder, or superfluity, also subjected to a purpose—and thus, although in the broad sense only, has a dependency on a theological concept of creation (→ Progress). For holists, the holistic concept is unencumbered by such metaphysical presuppositions. These scientists produce the notion or concept of totality in its pure functionality. This means that any natural process produces the totality of its

Holism and System-Thought

possibilities—or, for instance in the case of an injury, or some harm, returns itself to this totality, regenerates itself. Biologically, then, totality is first and foremost the maintenance of totality. This premise founds a fundamental law of living beings. The individual organism seeks to attain and to preserve that which is applied or invested in it as a totality. The general character of this notion is thereby at the same time its preference and prerogative, since unlike both 'mechanism' (cf. → body) and 'vitalism' (cf. → soul), it supplies nothing substantial.

From this conception of totality, Ludwig von Bertalanffy (*Theoretische Biologie*, Ger., "Theoretical Biology," 1932) developed the notion of *system*— which now has played an important role not only in biology (Humberto Maturana), but also, and especially, in the social sciences (Niklas Luhmann). Orders of totality, then, are self-forming, 'autopoietic,' systems. Accordingly, the conceptualization of totality not only overcomes an old problem of theory, the notion of purpose, but lays out an altogether new point of view— that of system, its inner structure, and its relation to its environment. This concept is consequently foundational for the ecological consideration of → nature. In ecology, nature is grasped with the help of the notion of system, and thereby seen as a totality.

Totality and Religion   4. Today once more, in modern → New Age beliefs, especially in physics-oriented approaches ('New Age Science'), totality or holism play a central role, also due to the influence of East Asian conceptions (Daoism and Zen), which help in constituting a foundation for holism becoming a religious movement. According to these holistic approaches, the assembling of units or objects creates a greater reality that is not analyzable with concepts. Gregory Bateson's notion of holism seeks to bridge the gap to the Cartesian scientific understanding. Thus, Bateson can be regarded as the forerunner of Fritjof Capra and Rupert Sheldrake.

For physicist *Fritjof Capra*, the pregnant trait of all Eastern *Weltanschauungen* is the experience of all of the phenomena of the world as a manifestation of a single basic reality as the manifestation of a single identity. Capra parallels this with physics, especially with modern quantum mechanics, and so sees both models of the interpretation of the world in a complementary 'togetherness' or composition. It is the whole that determines the relationship of the parts.

Biologist *Rupert Sheldrake* sees in holism—as developed by Bateson— an ordering principle in living systems. 'Morphogenetic fields' would thus stamp the form, development, and relationship of organisms, as well as the increase and growth of elementary structures (e.g., of crystals). At this point, climatologist *Jim Lovelock* enters the scene, with a scientific conception of the terrestrial ecosystem worked out by Lovelock and microbiologist Lynn Margolis under the mythic term GAIA (Gk., 'Earth,' and Goddess of Life). For both, the earth is an intelligent living being that guides itself to the optimum result.

Subsequently, *holistic medicine* now attempts to understand the totality of the person—body, spirit, and soul—in its complex interaction. In this fashion, it seeks to introduce a conceptualization of health through a consciousness-raising in the individual. Numerous new physical and mental techniques, or therapeutic experiments in holistic medicine, are based on age-old conceptions of the cooperation of body, spirit, and psyche (primarily from the Far East and Southern Asia). From the viewpoint of holistic medicine today, these are to be seen as methods to preserve health rather than as therapeutic techniques, and they always aim at the 'entire person,' who is also to be a 'new human being.'

Literature

Sources: BATESON, Gregory, Steps to an Ecology of Mind, New York 1972; Idem, Mind and Nature: A Necessary Unity, London 1979; BOHM, David, Wholeness and the Implicate Order, London 1980; CAPRA, Fritjof, The Tao of Physics, London 1975; Idem, The Turning Point: Science, Society, and the Rising Culture, New York 1982; Idem, The Web of Life: A New Scientific Understanding of Living Systems, New York 1996; Idem, The Hidden Connections, London 2002; HARMAN, Willis, Global Mind Change: The Promise of the 21st Century, [2]1998; LASZLO, Ervin, Systems View of the World: A Holistic Vision for Our Time, Cresskill 1996; LOVELOCK, James/MARGULIS, Lynn, Gaia: A New Look at Life on Earth, Oxford 1979; MEYER-ABICH, Adolf, Naturphilosophie auf neuen Wegen, Stuttgart 1948; ROGERS, Carl, Person to Person: The Problem of Being Human. A New Trend in Psychology, Lafayette 1967; SHELDRAKE, Rupert, A New Science of Life: The Hypothesis of Formative Causation, London 1981; Idem, The Rebirth of Nature: The Greening of Science and God, London 1990; SMUTS, Jan C., Holism and Evolution, London 1926.
Secondary Literature: ANTMANN, Rolf, Die Ganzheit in der europäischen Philosophie, Tübingen 1990; ASH, Mitchell G., Gestalt Psychology in German Culture, 1890–1967: Holism and the Quest for Objectivity, Cambridge 1995; BENCI, Vieri et al. (eds.), Determinism, Holism, and Complexity, New York 2003; CARUANA, Louis, Holism and the Understanding of Science: Integrating the Analytical, Historical and Sociological, Aldershot 2000; ESFELD, Michael, Holism in Philosophy of Mind and Philosophy of Physics, Dordrecht 2001; JOHNSON, David, Hume, Holism, and Miracles, Ithaca 1999; LAWRENCE, Christopher/WEISZ, George (eds.), Greater than the Parts: Holism in Biomedicine, 1920–1950, New York 1998; PHILIPPS, Denis C., Holistic Thought in Social Science, Stanford 1976.

→ *Environmentalism, Esalen Institute, Esotericism, Illness/Health, Mysticism, Nature, New Age, Science, Soul*

Stephan Grätzel

Will, Free

1. In general, 'will' (in Lat., *voluntas*; in Ger., *Wille*; in Fr., *volonté*) denotes the motivation of an acting subject in the direction of a particular goal. The subject of a will is not necessarily an individual human being, but, in the transferred sense, can also be a collectivity ('general will,' Fr. *volonté générale*), or a power conceived as transcendent, and as influencing the human being and the world (will of God). Insofar as the will is qualified as free, it presupposes the possible autonomy of the actor/agent. A distinction must then be made between freedom for self-motivation, and freedom for the choice of an end. In this connection, there are ethical issues. Can an action be ascribed to someone's own responsibility, or not? This question, as to whether there can be a willing act or a free choice, has been of importance for judicial findings ever since ancient Greek penal law. The state of affairs concealed behind the problem of free will points to the core of different concepts and problems of religious images of the human being and understandings of the world. Systems of belief do present systems of action, as

well, that, by way of morally qualified concepts, seek to motivate a particular activity.

The Human Being and God: Autonomy?

2. When the problem of the expounding of religious concepts steps front and center (in the literary genre of commentaries, or in dogmatic doctrinal systems), *explicit* questions arise concerning the motives, purposes, and possibilities/opportunities of human action (or transcendent action with respect to human beings), that were transferred, in Western tradition especially, to the question of human volitional freedom. Free will was discussed in the framework of the relationship of → God, the human being, and the world. The ancient Stoic view takes its point of departure in an order of reason that stands at the disposition of the human will. Through → Augustine's (354–430) doctrine on grace, reflection on the question of the freedom of the human will soared to a primary position in the Christian discussion of the relationship between human action and divine grace. In Augustine's writings, a deterministic conception of free will is more and more to be observed. He had once defended, against → Manichaeism, the freedom of the human will to choose between good and evil. In his later work he was still prepared to grant it when the will stood in harmony with the determining, super-ordinate will of God. This position, to the effect that the free will was dependent on the grace of God, which Augustine sought to see prevail over other Christian positions (e.g., against the will-directed anthropology of Pelagius), found its modern resumption in the conflict between Martin → Luther (1483–1546) and Erasmus of Rotterdam (1469–1536). The balanced and moderate position that Erasmus had presented in his *De Libero Arbitrio* (Lat., "On Free Choice"; 1524), in which he saw the superiority of human beings over animals in their power of decision, was rejected by Luther, in his 1525 treatise *De Servo Arbitrio* ("On Enslaved Choice"). For Luther, on grounds of Original → Sin and human → predestination, human works can contain no merit for the attainment of the grace of God. For him, freedom comes only from liberation in faith. The criticism, based on this position, of the granting of indulgences, became the occasion of the Reformation. In the nineteenth century, Schopenhauer's discussion of the will shaped a new dimension. The antagonism between will without knowledge, and reason without will, becomes the principle of the explanation of the world. Friedrich → Nietzsche's (1844–1900) aphoristic, indistinct use of 'will to power' would at first bring to expression a liberation, and a conquest of self vis-à-vis the pressures of the world—and an existential objection to God. Here Nietzsche sees a growing basic tendency of all living beings, and ultimately, a fundamental force of the universe. In the wake of Sigmund → Freud's (1856–1939) → psychoanalysis, the question of the attribution of will and reason to human action was transferred to a tension between conscious, reasoning ego and unconscious id, the latter being the locus of the drives, so that the question is then posed of the extent to which the human being can be 'master in his own house.'

Self-Determination

3. In the scientific discussion of the twentieth century, the conditioned status of the human act in terms of psychology, and of the history of society, became an object of inquiry. Now inserted into that larger concern was the question of the freedom of the will. The will, and the extent of its freedom, became a multiply-influenced part of the human constitution. Science discussed the question of the freedom of the will in the context of a world

and a human being conditioned by natural law. The theory of → chaos, and a return to propositions on probability, have recently tended to restore the freedom of human activity to its former scope. → Existentialism, in Sartre's (1905–1980) sense, is less against certain forms of determinism than against the fatalism of the human being. The will to freedom becomes the challenge to the individual. Finally, moments of Rousseau's collective will, and of Nietzsche's will to power, strike a connection in Leni Riefenstahl's "The Triumph of the Will," a Nazi propaganda film in the spirit of an aestheticizing religion. The self-extinction of the individual will in a collective will to victory, on the part of the 'body of the people' who are subjected to the Führer's will alone, becomes a popular, superficially Nietzschean, collective intoxication (→ Masses). Now the goal is the oneness of people, Reich, and Führer translated into a mass scene, and at the same time presented in a film. The dilemma of volitional self-determination now entered the political history of the twentieth century, and its quality as a problem was rendered more acute. In the discussion of phenomena such as the new religious movements (→ New Religions), or fundamentalist currents as well, the problem of freedom, and of the possible manipulation of the human will, abides as an explosive, controversial topic (→ Anti-Cult Movements).

4. The concept of volitional freedom is characteristic of Western culture and philosophy. But the question of the subject and the autonomy of human activity can be reconstituted as a fundamental problem of non-European belief systems, as well. In Islam, the freedom of the will is predetermined by the divine will, and by the intervention of God in the world. Human beings retain certain opportunities for choice: however, these are limited to (1) the 'obligations' (*taklīf*), and (2) the individually predetermined human 'capacities' (*qudra*) for free decision, that are stipulated in revelation. Besides the divine dependency, the will is also constrained by the religious community, which subjects it to the collective will, on the principle of the 'public welfare' (*maslaha*). *Islam*

In Buddhism, various conceptions of a human subject were developed, including the denial of its reality. On the one side, the 'I,' and the human will along with it, are regarded as illusions, to be overcome and 'quenched,' since they are responsible for one's clinging to this world, and are thereby responsible as well for the painful cycle of rebirths (*karma*). On the other side, a right decision, a right action, and therefore a 'right will' are necessary in order to travel the way that leads to the desired liberation. Volitional freedom is therefore necessary, at first, in order to be able to act ethically and religiously, but then is a hindrance to redemption. Thus, ultimately, it is itself to be overcome. *Buddhism*

Literature

ALEXANDER, Archibald, Theories of the Will in the History of Philosophy, Bristol 2002 (¹1898); ANDERSON, Pamela Sue, Ricoeur and Kant: Philosophy of the Will, Atlanta 1993; DIHLE, Albrecht, The Theory of Will in Classical Antiquity, Berkeley 1982; KENNY, Anthony, Aristotle's Theory of the Will, New Haven 1979; MORAN, Frances M., Subject and Agency in Psychoanalysis: Which Is to Be Master?, New York 1993; OVERHOFF, Jürgen, Hobbe's Theory of the Will: Ideological Reasons and Historical Circumstances, Lanham 2000; PETRIK, James, Descartes' Theory of the Will, Wakefield 1991; PINK, Thomas, The

Psychology of Freedom, Cambridge 1996; Pink, Thomas/Stone, M. W. F. (eds.), The Will and Human Action: From Antiquity to the Present Day, London 2004; Riley, Patrick, The General Will before Rousseau: The Transformation of the Divine into the Civic, Princeton 1986; Saarinen, Risto, Weakness of the Will in Medieval Thought: From Augustine to Buridan, Leiden 1994; Stent, Gunther S., Paradoxes of Free Will, Philadelphia 2002.

→ *Destiny/Fate, Determinism, Ethics/Morals, Fatalism, Predestination*

Jürgen Mohn

Witch / Persecution of Witches

Meaning of the Word and Determination of the Concept

1. 'Witch' (from Old English *wicce/wicca*, 'sorceress') denotes, generally, a female person who can use magic, sorcery, spells, and/or enchantment to evoke hurtful reactions and results. The concepts for 'witch' present in European languages and societies betray various accentuations of meaning, depending on different aspects of the person or her activity. In the Italian word *strega* (from Lat., *striga*, 'owl'), the witch is interpreted as a flying, child-abducting being. The French *sorcière* (from Lat., *sors*, 'lot') indicates witches' art of soothsaying. In content, a distinction must be made between the cultural pattern of interpretation (C. Honegger) stamped by Europe, and the pattern of behavior (to be found outside Europe, as well) that distinguishes *witchcraft* as injurious, or else useful, → magic. Anthropological objects such as → amulets and → Voodoo dolls are examples of the same magical 'reality' as meant by the witchcraft, of past and present, although, of course, not in their literal reality and operation. 'Witch crazes' and persecution of witches are phenomena of European and extra-European societies. Especially in Africa, the killing of persons on grounds of alleged witchcraft has taken on terrifying proportions. In Tanzania alone, between 1970 and 1984, more than 3,000 persons were murdered for allegedly practicing witchcraft (Behringer 1998).

2. Between 1430 and 1870 European persecution of witches occurred mainly in Germany, in the Holy Roman Empire of the German Nation, and in its neighboring regions, Poland, Eastern France, and Northern Italy, but comparatively less in the Ecclesiastical State and in Spain.

The Witch Paradigm

The witch paradigm at the root of these persecutions represents, as a fictitious schema of interpretation, a highly complex texture of popular and scholarly conceptualizations of faith. Scholarship in the area of witchcraft distinguishes the ancient and medieval conception of maleficent witches and sorcerers from the collective concept of 'witch,' which was developed around 1430 in Savoy, the Dauphiné, and Western Switzerland (Blauert 1989). In the latter concept, three principal complexes of thought were banded together: (1) older traditions of putting heretics and witches on trial (→ Heresy), (2) non-Christian ideas from popular faith (e.g., belief in fairies), and (3) scholarly theories on the power of the → Devil and → demons. The individual elements of the cumulative witchcraft offense—harmful spells, pacts with the Devil, sexual intercourse with the same, transformation of animals, flight through the air, the witches' Sabbath—ought not be thought of as a rigid schema, trimmed to fit each individual case. There were different kinds of harmful spells, with differing provenance: injury to crops, weather spells,

A ceremony of initiation into a Wicca coven, a ritual group of the new witches movement (→ Paganism/Neopaganism). High priestess Zsuszanna Budapest presents the initiand (right) with an amulet of feathers. That only women are present has its basis in the fact that Budapest is founder of the feministic direction of 'Dianic Wicca' (after Roman goddess of the hunt Diana), whose ritual groups accept women exclusively. Budapest, born in 1940 in the Hungarian capital, combines traditional techniques used by Eastern European female soothsayers and healers (her mother was a medium), and 'feminist spirituality,' a concept that, she declares, she herself coined. Since 1970, she had been in Los Angeles, and later was a women's liberation activist, reformulating the political tenets of radical feminism in religious concepts and terms. In 1975 she founded the first feminist Wicca coven, Susan B. Anthony Coven Number 1, which became the model in Dianic Wicca. Her *Feminist Book of Lights and Shadows* (1975; republished in 1989 as *The Holy Book of Women's Mysteries*) had the effect of creating a cult. In 1975, she was arrested for reading Tarot cards—which led to a paradigmatic trial, and ultimately, in 1983, to the abrogation of California's Law Against the Practice of Divination. Today Budapest moderates her own TV show ("Thirteenth Heaven"), and leads the Women's Spirituality Forum in San Francisco. (Hubert Mohr)

generation of illnesses, milk spells, witch dancing, came rather from a rural milieu; animal transformation, and flight, from medieval popular belief; the witches' Sabbath and love-making with the Devil, from scholastic theology, from stereotypes of processes against heretics (especially the Waldenses), and from anti-Jewish propaganda (→ Anti-Semitism).

Historical Survey

The first trials were held in 1415–1445 in the Dauphiné, in 1428 in Wallis, in 1438–1442 in the Diocese of Lausanne. The delict of witchcraft was punished by burning alive, both by the secular courts, where harmful spells were treated as grave capital offense, and by the → Inquisition as heresy and → apostasy, under the concept of apostatic service to the Devil. The procedure mounted against heretics by the Inquisition was whetted by persecutors to the shape of a special judicial process of its own. In this exceptional crime, the defense of the accused was no longer provided, evidence was simplified into the deposition of suspect instances, and the application of punishment was facilitated. The accused, then, especially in the processes of local secular courts, found themselves in a hopeless situation. In not a few cases, higher instances, such as the Paris Parliament in France, and the Imperial Chamber Court in Germany—or authoritative documents in university law departments—offered the only possibility of escaping the death penalty. Of the estimated 50,000 to 100,000 executions of witches between 1580 and 1620, some 25,000 occurred in Germany, and extended to Protestant and Catholic regions alike. The region of the most intensive persecution in Europe was Lorraine, with 2,700 executions between 1560 and 1620. The persecutions came in waves, and were of various duration and intensity in individual countries. The absolute climaxes of the 'witch hunts' were in the years between 1560 and 1630. Some 75-80% of those convicted and executed were women, often widowed and unmarried. Researchers have unanimously repudiated the notion that an above-average number of those found guilty of witchcraft were midwives and 'wise women.' Nor were those outside society more often accused than others. Even children could be victims of the witch trials.

Explanations

Plausible explanations for the witch hunts are crises of agriculture and famine, evoked by changes in climate ('Little Ice Age'), as well as the norms, fears, and fantasies of the witch persecutors. The role of the demonological literature—for example, Inquisitor Heinrich Kramer's *Malleus Maleficarum* (Lat., "Hammer of Witches"; 1487)—and of the popular notions of witches, has not yet been definitively explained. Numerous regional investigations attest that the pressure to persecution was exerted not from above, but, often, from below, by the broad masses, as means of the regulation of conflict. Opponents of the witch persecutions, as for example physician Johann Weyer (1515–1588), held a difficult position. At times, they appealed to moderate traditional ecclesiastical law; at other times—increasingly, in the seventeenth century—they discerned mentally ill or melancholic women, so that the demonological stereotype was transformed to a medical syndrome.

Witches in the Modern Age

3. In the Age of the Enlightenment, and in Romanticism, the negative appraisals of witches that had been made in the early modern age were turned into positive ones, by way of the formation of myths. Witches now came to be sacrifices of justice—of ecclesiastical and secular repression (Voltaire)—or 'wise women' (Jacob Grimm). Today's feminist (→ Women's Movement/

Spiritual Feminism) and new religious movements stylize the witch as a symbol of female self-determination, and of a cultic community of nature magic (e.g., Wicca cult in English-speaking regions; → Paganism/Neopaganism). In the United States alone, an estimated 250,000 'new witches' belong to various groups. The figure of the → fairytale witch lives on, in popular narratives of all cultures, as a supernatural being, who disposes of powers of enchantment both injurious and curative. In German folktales and sagas, she is encountered as a hideous old woman, who devours children, and can change herself into animals. The folkloric tradition includes the masking and witch-burnings of Carnival and Winter Solstice. The traditional, primarily rural, belief in witches of the present uses witches' spells for magical defense against bewitchment.

Plastic and pictorial art, poetry, and film attest a lively interest in witches. A case in point would be the witch images in the modern art of Alfred Kubin (1877–1959), Otto Dix (1891–1969), and Max Pechstein (1881–1955), or in the literature of Otfried Preussler (Ger., *Die Kleine Hexe*, "The Little Witch"; 1957), the best-known children's books about a witch, which has thus far been printed in over fifty editions. Arthur Miller's play *The Crucible* (1953), a historical parable of denunciation and mass insanity, was filmed in 1957 with the collaboration of Jean-Paul Sartre. John Updike's novel *The Witches of Eastwick* (1984), whose satirical subject is the battle of the sexes, became popular through the eponymous Hollywood film, with Jack Nicholson. The witch also appears as a mythic backdrop for the entertainment and consumer industries of the present. Magical abilities and utensils are offered, in newspaper advertisements, by commercial 'witches,' for the solution for the problems of life. Penny novels are available in all of the railroad-station magazine racks for creepy self-entertainment during a wait for a train. Leather witch-masks are sold on the sado-masochistic scene, thus rendering the witch a marketable sex object. In many places, tourism concepts have developed around witches. Consumer articles consciously make their concept of the witch a positive one, of the witch as a miraculous healer.

Literature

Sources: BEHRINGER, Wolfgang (ed.), Hexen und Hexenprozesse in Deutschland, Munich ²1993; BRESLAW, Elaine G. (ed.), Witches of the Atlantic World: A Historical Reader and Primary Sourcebook, New York/London 2000; SUMMERS, Montague (ed./trans.), The Malleus Maleficarum of Heinrich Kramer and James Sprenger, London 1928.

Secondary Literature: ANKARLOO, Bengt/HENNINGSEN, Gustav (eds.), Early Modern European Witchcraft: Centres and Peripheries, Oxford 1989; ANKARLOO, Bengt/CLARK, Stuart (eds.), History of Witchcraft and Magic in Europe, 6 vols., London 1999ff.; BAUER, D. R./LORENZ, Sönke (eds.), Das Ende der Hexenverfolgungen, Stuttgart 1995; BEHRINGER, Wolfgang, Hexen. Glaube, Verfolgung, Vermarktung, Munich 1998; Idem, Witches and Witch-Hunts: A Global History, Cambridge 2004; BLAUERT, Andreas, Frühe Hexenverfolgungen. Ketzer-, Zauberei- und Hexenprozesse des 15. Jahrhunderts, Hamburg 1989; BURNS, William E., Witch Hunts in Europe and America: An Encyclopedia, Westport 2003; CLARK, Stuart, Thinking With Demons: The Idea of Witchcraft in Early Modern Europe, Oxford 1997; COHN, Norman, Europe's Inner Demons: The Demonization of Christians in Medieval Christendom, rev. ed., Chicago 2000 (¹1975); GINZBURG, Carlo, The Night Battles: Witchcraft and Agrarian Cults in the Sixteenth and Seventeenth Centuries, Baltimore 1983 (It. ¹1966); Idem, Ecstasies: Deciphering the Witches' Sabbath, New York 1991 (It. ¹1989); GODBEER, Richard, Escaping Salem: The Other Witch Hunt of 1692, New York 2005; HONEGGER, Claudia (ed.), Die Hexen der Neuzeit. Studien zur Sozialgeschichte eines kulturellen Deutungsmusters, Frankfurt/M. 1978; LEVACK, Brian

P., The Witch-Hunt in Early Modern Europe, London ²1995 (¹1987); MacFarlane, Alan, Witchcraft in Tudor and Stuart England, New York 1970; Roper, Lyndal, Witch Craze: Terror and Fantasy in Baroque Germany, New Haven 2004; Waite, Gary K., Heresy, Magic, and Witchcraft in Early Modern Europe, Basingstoke 2003.

→ *Apostasy, Demon/Demonology, Fairytale, Gender Stereotypes, Heresy, Inquisition, Magic, Paganism/Neo-Paganism, Women's Movement/Spiritual Feminism*

Werner Tschacher

Women's Movement / Spiritual Feminism

1. As early as the mid-1970s, chronologically parallel to the emergence and spread/extension of → New Age religious movements, concepts of → magic and → spirituality acquired a greater importance. A spiritual feminism, as an umbrella concept for a multiplicity of forms of belief and expression, has emerged from the new, autonomous women's movement. It is a political, and religious and/or spiritual movement at the same time. The spectrum of subjects involved in an overview of female spirituality extends from the general critique of the political, private, and religious conditions of woman's life in the patriarchy in history and the present (→ Matriarchy/Patriarchy), to today's feminist spirituality in society and church, to feminist spirituality as the vision of a new, female way of life and culture—the quest for a genuinely female identity. The broader concept of spiritual feminism or feminist spirituality can comprise the most distinct groupings. There are as many opinions here as there are women who express themselves on this subject. Feminist spirituality goes out beyond the boundaries of traditional religious spaces, and yet presses into these spaces from without. Thus, Christian and Jewish women seek new paths, forms of expression, and content for female piety, within and without the Church and Judaism. Women belonging to political traditions of feminist 'separatism' find themselves together with liberal mothers and employees in search of both a cultural and spiritual homeland. Together they reverence the potential fullness of a 'Great Goddess.' Spiritual feminism thus represents the quest for the denomination of a multiplicity of currents and (self-) determinations, whose differing assessments depend on women's own respective outlooks.

Feminist Theories and Standpoints

2. The new women's movement in Western Europe and in the United States is one of the most important social movements since the end of the 1960s. It has gained 'revolutionary' and innovative influence in various areas and regions of society, along with initiating a new orientation in political ethics. In the → peace movement, in the → ecumenical movement, in the regions of science and higher education, in the trade unions, in politics, in the churches, their ideas and political demands have established themselves. The goals are change of social norms and institutions, and the rescission of the historically produced biologistic differentiation of the sexes, i.e., culturally conditioned essential definitions of femaleness and maleness (→ Gender Stereotypes), as well as the defeat of any form of sexist oppression and disadvantage. Today, the issue 'Women and Emancipation' has been received across all of the spectra of society. Three great directions are worthy of mention: (a) *Liberal feminism*, which represents a policy of equal rights

in the sense of universally valid rights, (b) *socialistic feminism* that sees the oppression of women as based in the structures of pan-societal power-relations, and (c) *radical feminism*, which regards equal rights, participation, and share in the organizations of existing society, as an insufficient goal for women. In this latter case feminism means a separate organizing movement, for the creation of autonomous woman-spaces, the psychological process of liberation of woman from identification with man, and a new definition, or new evaluation, of social problems by women. It explains the patriarchal organization of → sexuality and reproduction (→ Regeneration/Fertility) as the key reference point of male power. It is precisely here that the slogan, "The personal is political," becomes the central theme.

At the end of the 1970s, the interests of radical feminism split in two. A 'political' direction saw self-determination with regard to → body, spirit, and 'soul,' and the political 'struggle,' for example in the ecological and peace movement, as its goal. Thus, this element pursued a 'feminization' of the social system of norms and values. Meanwhile, another part raised demands for matriarchal life structures that would transcend current societal relations. This discussion was conducted within and outside of traditional religions.

3. Within radical feminism, theoretical confrontation with patriarchal values and norms began very quickly. Many women perceived a male-centeredness ('androcentrism'), and male sexism, in all areas of society. This construal of maleness promoted radical positions in feminist separatism. Out of their varying components, and over the intermediate positions of a 'cultural feminism,' they then built a bridge of 'spiritual feminism.' This feministic spiritual movement sees itself as a radical counter-sketch to a patriarchal society. In it, → utopias of new collective, cultural, and spiritual forms of female living are drawn up and tried out. Comprehensive, radical criticisms of the patriarchy and its institutions, in politics, culture, and religion, as well as the demand for a genuinely 'female counterculture,' are the earmarks of contributions to the project.

'Cultural Feminism'

a) Feminist authors such as Mary Daly, Herrad Schenk, Miriam Simos (alias Starhawk), and Caroline Merchant describe the demise of the patriarchal structure. A society directed by the 'male principle,' and the betrayal of moral principles, is made responsible for the political and social problems of the present. Feminist criticism of religion is here closely bound up with general criticism of patriarchy. Traditional monotheistic religions such as Judaism, Christianity, and Islam are regarded as patriarchal institutions, and stand for settled traditionalism, stamped by the exclusion of female worlds of experience and widespread gynophobia, on the part of male religious dignitaries. Former Catholic theologian and feminist philosopher Mary Daly sees in Christianity compulsion, mythologization, and therewith the eternalization of the sex-role stereotypes. For her, the image or symbol of a male → God is only one of patriarchy's many mechanisms of oppression. Others reproach the Christian Church for its destruction of sanctuaries of female mystery cults (→ Mysteries) and supposed matriarchal high religions. In their criticism of Judaism, a latent → anti-Semitism on the part of feminist theologians is sometimes discernable. To Judaism is ascribed the origin of patriarchal → monotheism, and therewith the beginning of all 'evil.' Many feminists can no longer wish to join themselves to a strong, mighty, authoritative Father,

Radical Religious and Cultural Critique of Patriarchy

nor do they wish to. He symbolizes abuse of power. Religion is then experienced as no more than a toolbox of patriarchy's control and oppression. The concepts of 'female identity' and 'alienation' are therefore central points of application: women's spirituality can realize itself only in holistic spiritual sisterhood (→ Wholeness/Holism).

Woman—Corporality—Nature

b) The foundational image of → nature as female principle offers a metaphorical approach, which has played a central role in the male concept of femaleness since the nineteenth century. At the beginning of the 1970s, it seemed to many eco-feminists that a solution to the environmental crisis was possible only by way of a revival of concepts emphasizing the special affinity of/between woman and nature. Nature was understood as a living organism, analogous with women (collectively), with both of them being exploited and 'violated' by patriarchy (→ Environmentalism). Here traditional patriarchal religions played a key role, with the hostile attitude toward → body and → sexuality of the Christian churches, and their tabooing and demonizing of female sexuality (menstrual cycle [→ Blood], contraception [→ Abortion/Contraception]).

Spiritual Feminism

4. Many currents within and without ('cultural') feminism make use of the concept of → *spirituality*. By contrast with traditional and → New Age religions alike, spiritual feminism represents the standpoint of the 'immanence' (→ Transcendence) realized in women's 'fusion' or 'blending' with the earth and nature, which are mythically embodied by the Great Goddess. Notions of a 'genuinely female spirituality' offer a wide spectrum: an all-encompassing, loving 'sisterhood' (meant as ideological as well as spiritual solidarity and community of women), the self-definition of female identity, 'reverence for life,' visions of spiritual freedom and self-determination. Here spirituality is immanent in the world, the spiritual healing of the world. In its most radical configuration, spirituality means self-acceptance, identity, independently of male acknowledgement—a spiritual, economic, and physical as well as psychic independence from 'man.' Spirituality becomes a concept of living.

Feminist Theology

5. Within the churches, the positions of spiritual feminism run a rather moderate course. Its roots reach back to the time of the first middle-class women's movement in the nineteenth century. In the United States, the first woman was admitted to the study of theology in 1847. In Prussia, on the other hand, women were permitted to study theology only in 1908. Women were long denied 'religions competencies,' and even today they are excluded from the priestly office in Catholicism (→ Priest/Priestess). In the ever intensifying lay movement in the Church, struggles for equal rights have been making progress ever since the beginning of the twentieth century. In the 1960s, demands for women's equality in church offices arose across the confessions. Influenced by American and African → liberation theologies, as well as by the budding women's movement, noted theologians, such as Dorothee Sölle, inquired into the place of woman in theology. Many went further, calling their own entire tradition into question (Daly, Mulak, Weiler), and questioning its meaningfulness for women. This spontaneous adoption of themes led to the debates cited above. With an eye to the Bible, and the history of the Church, attempts have been made to write female/feminine (salvation) history—HERstory instead of HIStory, 'thealogy' instead of 'theology.')

Discussions on the legitimacy of God as a male symbol have been conducted, and various new concepts of God have been developed. Resulting positions range from a theology of the figure of Jesus as an advocate for women, and thereby mediator between the sexes, and the sketch of a neuter spirit (Heb., *ruakh*), to the symbol of a triadic Goddess. Supra-confessionally, feminists today look for new spiritual signs, → symbols, and → rituals. Hostility to the body and the senses as manifested in the liturgy are now to be replaced by new, sensuous rituals—often removed from church buildings—with circle dances, music, song, colors, light, scents. Thus, the bloody mysteries inherent in the → Lord's Supper, which are especially problematic for women, ought to be reinterpreted and re-symbolized; the theological tradition of the sin and atonement of an innate female impurity could be countered with sensuous celebration, in memory of the communion with God. Many new points of criticism have arisen in recent years. Along with calls for women's ordination, the fundamental question has also been posed whether the churches are really the place where feminists feel welcome, and can develop spiritually. The answer is, for one, dependent on the men in these institutions—on their openness to criticism, and readiness for change. But it is also dependent on the individual preparedness of every individual woman to break with traditions, and, if necessary, to live and work even outside of the Church.

6. A discussion on the necessity and sense of genuinely female or feminine symbols, rituals, and images of God took place at the end of the 1970s, in connection with discussion and research on → matriarchy. For many spiritual women, the symbol of the male → God had outlived its usefulness, and it seemed that that of the Goddess bore the liberating principles of both sexes. This revival of the Goddess/goddesses is more the conscious expression of a political behavior than it is a religious emotion. The logic proceeds as follows. Let the Goddess become a necessary figure of identification for women. She symbolizes the rightness of female claim to authority and aspiration for power. Her sign serves for the evaluation of the female body, and she herself becomes 'Redeemer of the Earth.' The rapidly devised sacred doctrine of 'thea-logy' expresses the wish for a mythic foundation of the 'feminine principle.' Jutta Voss speaks of 'the sacred potency' of the feminine (female), as symbol of life, death, and never-ending rebirth.[1] The triple form of the Goddess represents the female body with its cycles, to which every woman along with the menstrual cycle is physically subject, fostering (1) the phase of youth, (2) that of maturity, and (3) that of age.

The Figure of the Great Goddess

Phases: Association	Youth	Maturity	Old Age
Female Type	Virgin	Mother	Wise Old
Mythical Figure	Diana, Aphrodite	Demeter, Inanna, Isis	Kali, Hecate, Percht
Color	White Goddess	Red Goddess	Black Goddess
Function/ Region	Youth, Erotics	Maturity, Fertility Creativity, Birth, Dispenser of Culture	Magic, Death, Beyond, [Old] Age, Rebirth, Healer
Lunar Phase	Quarter Moon	Full Moon	New Moon
Season	Spring	Summer	Fall, Winter
Directions [on compass]	East	South	West, North
Element	Air	Fire	Water, Earth

Mythological Schema of the 'Threefold Goddess'

Ritual Practice

Ritual practice is oriented, for the most part, to the cycles of → agrarian religions and astronomical reference points (→ Paganism/Neopaganism). In many rituals, celebrants make an effort to (re-) produce the unity and harmony of nature, cosmos, and everything that lives. They serve as the healing process of Gaia, the 'Mother Earth.' And so the Goddess symbolizes the concrete, sensible presence of the divine, in a concept of the world in which everything is living, dynamic, reticulated, and bound up, strengthened and reinforced by living energies, a living being (Starhawk 1999). The patriarchal, 'mechanistic' worldview is seen as just the opposite. It looks upon → nature as a dead object, exploiting it without inhibition or containment (H. Göttner-Abendroth, C. Merchant). The Goddess embodies the cyclical world picture of the genuinely feminine, the image so vehemently demanded by female researchers of matriarchy. Connected with the sanctification of the cyclical orbit of nature (and women), there is the hope of more attention, and social regard. Nature is threatened, to be sure, but ultimately nature is divine, as the 'reincarnation of the Goddess.' In matriarchal religion, she is bound up with a myth of 'celestial self-redemption,' and thus with the redemption of the female sex on earth.

Feminist 'Witches'

7. The 'witch' has become an identifying image of the women's movement (→ Witch/Persecution of Witches; Paganism/Neopaganism). At first, she was used only in demonstrations, as a counter-concept expressing the struggle against patriarchal norms and values. By the mid-1970s, however, she was already filled with mythologized ideological content. The ironic, provocative metaphor 'witch,' nevertheless, is consciously adopted only by a part of the women's movement, as by the feminist Wicca witches (see ill. at → Witch/Persecution of Witches). Many exponents of feminist spirituality see themselves rather as priestesses, healers, 'wise women,' or shamans, if indeed they are not simply indifferent to traditional concepts. The first feminist witch circles emerged in the United States. But they were mostly oriented to occult/magical witch paradigms of the Wicca movement that appeared in the England of the 1950s and have since socially established themselves. In the feminist witch movement, answers to questions of ecology, politics, life meaning, and religion, that in church and society have remained unsolved, are sought in varying manners. The ideology of modern witchcraft contains the following. (a) The feeling of homeland, a feeling that is to be attained by a life in 'sisterly' communities of experience and life; (b) a life in peace and harmony with nature (concept of immanence; → Nature Piety, → Wholeness/Holism); (c) the demand to engage oneself, politically as well as spiritually, in the rescue of the world's eco-systems (→ Environmentalism); (d) the formation of a spiritual 'women's culture' (women's communes, women's spiritual projects).

The image of the witch embraces the concept of → magic. Ideas of magic span an arc from therapeutic, to esoteric, to 'classic' ideas of magic (the spell; → Prayer/Curse). In this 'spiritually political' movement, magic/spirituality and witches/shamans are usually grouped at random, and their names applied as synonyms for the same thing. Magic (and → spirituality) have become umbrella concepts, in which a transformed world-image, and newly developed rituals mix together and coagulate. This concept, thus defined in anti-Enlightenment terms, stands for female wisdom and female spiritual power. It forms a wall against patriarchal → science and religion.

Some feminists appeal to magic as a designation for primitive, and now again current, practices of female spirituality. 'Magic rituals' stand for the respective groups that mean to connect with the universe, the elements, and nature (Luisa Francia, Ute Manan Schiran, Heide Göttner-Abendroth)—and therefore have shamanic and pantheistic features (→ Pantheism)—or else are connected with the Goddess as universal power (Anna Dinklmann, Starhawk, Zsuzsanna Budapest).

9. Feminist spirituality contains at once a critique of culture, and a quest for culture. The quest for → identity is at the same time a question concerning feminine self-understanding under the given conditions of the patriarchal society. However, the critique of patriarchy and its 'gods' has not been entirely satisfactory. The 'search for the divine', as a province of sense or meaning, is first and foremost connected with the wish for self-knowledge of what it is or can be 'to be a woman'. The concrete spiritual or religious concepts then follow. Here spirituality ought to create a commitment that relates to spiritual feeling, group identity, and the sacralization of 'feminine values'. It is the means to form the creators of women's own utopia of spiritual harmony, in the face of social and societal disharmony. Male dis-order is set against a female order (→ Chaos). But the formation of a female identity is not something that occurs only through the search for spirituality: it leads to the new discovery, and conquest, of the world, with all of its offers and opportunities, and participates in the epochal determination of a fundamental revolt. Thus, in other words, it is an attempt to accomplish, by way of religion, a social transformation.

1. Voss, Jutta, Das Schwarzmond-Tabu, Stuttgart 1988, 255.

Literature

Primary Sources: CARMODY, Denise Lardner, Seizing the Apple: A Feminist Spirituality of Personal Growth, New York 1984; DALY, Mary, Beyond God the Father: Toward a Philosophy of Women's Liberation, Boston 1973; GÖTTNER-ABENDROTH, Heide, Die Göttin und ihr Heros. Die matriarchalen Religionen in Mythos, Märchen und Dichtung, Munich 1980; JONES, Prudence/MATTHEWS, Caitlín (eds.), Voices from the Circle: The Heritage of Western Paganism, Hammersmith 1990; MATTHEWS, Caitlín (ed.), Voices of the Goddess: A Chorus of Sibyls, Wellingborough 1990; STARHAWK (MIRIAM SIMOS), The Spiral Dance: A Rebirth of the Ancient Religion of the Great Goddess, 20th anniversary ed., San Francisco 1999 ([1]1979); Eadem, Dreaming the Dark: Magic, Sex and Politics, Boston 1988 ([1]1982); WEILER, Gerda, Der enteignete Mythos. Eine feministische Revision der Archetypenlehre C. G. Jungs und Erich Neumanns, Frankfurt/M. 1991.

Secondary Literature: CARSON, Anne, Goddesses and Wise Women: The Literature of Feminist Spirituality, 1980–1992. An Annotated Bibliography, Freedom 1992; CHRIST, Carol P., Laughter of Aphrodite: Reflections on a Journey to the Goddess, San Francisco 1988; CHRIST, Carol P./PLASKOW, Judith (eds.), Womanspirit Rising, New York 1979; ELLER, Synthia, Living in the Lap of the Goddess: The Feminist Spirituality Movement in America, New York 1993; FRANKIEL, Tamar, The Voice of Sarah: Feminine Spirituality and Traditional Judaism, New York 1995; GRIFFIN, Wendy, Daughters of the Goddess: Studies of Healing, Identity, and Empowerment, Walnut Creek/Lanham 2000; KING, Ursula, Women and Spirituality, Houndsmill 1989; MEYER-WILMES, Hedwig, Rebellion on the Borders, Kampen 1995 (Ger. [1]1990); PAHNKE, Donate, Ethik und Geschlecht. Menschenbild und Religion in Patriarchat und Feminismus, Marburg 1991; SPRETNAK, Charlene (ed.), The Politics of Women's Spirituality, New York 1982; VAN DYKE, Annette J., The Search for a Woman-Centered Spirituality, New York 1992.

→ *Body, Environmentalism, Gender Stereotypes, Hierarchy, Magic, Matriarchy/Patriarchy, Nature, Nature Piety, New Age, Occultism, Paganism/Neopaganism, Sexuality, Spirituality, Witch/Persecution of Witches*

Angela Schenkluhn

Work

1. a) Work is human activity with the goal of producing what is necessary or useful for the existence of the individual and his or her kin. For this purpose, the working individual must enter into a conscious process of confrontation with nature, and thus, always alter natural circumstances. The simplest example to use for an explanation of this state of affairs is the production of tools. Thus, one of the most pregnant definitions of the human being is his and her specification as the 'tool-making animal.' In spite of this universal anthropological determination of work, an evaluation of work in terms of social and cultural history claims quite a broad spectrum, and this view precipitates out into religious history as well. Aside from a more or less natural division between male and female work—which occurred early in hunting and gathering societies—the division of 'head' and 'hand' labor is of special importance. This dichotomy, still prevailing in the division between 'mental' and 'physical' work, owes its origin to the fact that, by perfecting tools, it has been possible to diminish the amount of work necessary for the satisfaction of the elementary necessities of life.

The 'Tool-Making Animal'

Work as Punishment

b) All of the so-called historical religions—including the world religions—have formed during a time that knew a division between mental and manual labor. This genealogy is reflected in the world of religious concepts in a number of ways. (1) It is reflected in the widespread idea of a primordial paradise (→ Garden/Paradise), in whose condition human beings had the fruits of nature, for free enjoyment, in superfluity. The necessity of work has entered only through an event that has disturbed the harmony and leisure of this life, as recounted in, for example, the story of Original → Sin, in Gen 3. (2) The conceptions of gods and → God know nothing of working gods—gods can indeed battle, and thereby accomplish great deeds, but these acts are not understood as work; rather the gods feel disturbed by the noisy labors of human persons, as is so plainly depicted in the Babylonian Great Flood (Atramhasis) depicted. (3) Religious activity, for example in worship, is not conceptualized as work. In all religions that have ever known religious → specialists, the latter have been specifically exempted from physical labor. In extreme cases, this exemption can actually lead to the formation of a priestly caste, who need perform no manner of gainful labor, as with the Brahmans of ancient India. A necessary premise, in such a scenario, is the production of an economic surplus, and its appropriation by non-working groups in society.

Monks and Work

2. This distanced-to-negative attitude toward work is the contrary of another, likewise grounded in religion: a high esteem for simple work, especially for that of the farmer. This is encountered with many of the prophets of Israel, as in the Book of Amos, for example. This tension was rendered more

Doing the dishes in a Zen Buddhist monastery in Japan. In common, the young men busy themselves with their eating utensils. The Indian tradition of wandering ascetics engages these monks in a contemplative life without any means of their own subsistence. The members of Buddhist orders, whether they beg their maintenance in a daily quest for alms, or live on the landed property of the order, are entirely dependent on the labor of the laity for their life support. In Zen Buddhism, work is appraised not on the basis of its meaning as a profitable activity, but as the exercise of attention in daily actions. Zen monasteries receive contributions from their lay members, while garden and household work is part of the course of the day of a monk or nun. This approach finds its expression in the formula, "A day without work, a day without eating." (Kirsten Holzapfel)

acute in religions that originally had no cult personnel. It becomes particularly clear in the history of Christianity, where, as early as the first century, the duty to work was intensified—especially, it would seem, in regard to wandering preachers, who traveled from place to place, and lived at the expense of the community. Very soon, however, a condition formed in the Christian community, as is the general rule in the history of religions: a class of religious specialists formed who engaged in no gainful employment, and who lived on a system of contributions maintained by the communities. At one extreme, this development was propelled by an ascetic class (→ Asceticism), whose members, in conscious negation of the world, included work among the things they eschewed. Benedict of Nursia (480–547) turned this beginning of → monasticism, so little organized, in another direction. The principle of praying and working tended to create a new religious attitude toward work, which, however, could be maintained only with difficulty even in monasticism. The division between lay brothers and clerical monks, in the long term, allowed the separation of mental/spiritual work (*vita contemplativa*) and corporeal work (*vita activa*) to revive, with a higher evaluation of the former. The urban mendicant orders of the Middle Ages (Dominicans and Franciscans) limited themselves fully to preaching and cure of souls, and (at least theoretically) obtained the necessities of life by begging. Very soon, however, even here the vow of → poverty bound only the monk, not the monastery. Buddhism exhibits a similar phenomenon, especially in Theravada Buddhism, where, after the establishment of permanent monasteries, the monk was to obtain his sustenance himself by begging, although the monastery, by way of endowments, could have rich landed property at its disposal, worked by laity. As the monastic life is preferred in religion, a lower worth and value is then automatically ascribed to productive activity. The latter, it is true, is not directly rejected.

Work as Religious Obligation

3. It was almost automatically that this tendency arose, that qualified everyday work as being of lesser religious worth than a life dedicated entirely to religion. Thus, it could be assailed only where the division between laity and religious → specialists had been rescinded theoretically, as occurred in the sixteenth-century Reformation. Of course, neither → Luther nor Calvin entertained any high esteem for work performed for the sake of success. Rather, they regarded the essential thing as the fulfillment of one's duty. But in the view of equal value of all activities, in principle, regardless of whether they were spiritual or manual, in any case a new understanding of everyday work was perceptible vis-à-vis antiquity and the Middle Ages. However, in the background of the Reformers' new evaluation of everyday work, there was always their polemic against the special position and rank of the clergy. This was especially true in the case of the orders. In their appeal to the "Evangelical Counsels" (*Consilia Evangelica*) of chastity and poverty, the orders had come under suspicion of seeking to obtain a state of grace through works. The Reformers stressed, instead, that grace and salvation could be conferred on the human being even in a worldly state. This had never been questioned theoretically, but it was no longer clear in Catholic religious life.

The warning against idleness is known even from the Hebrew Bible, and then, by way of the New Testament, courses through all of church history. This admonition did not yet have the effect, however, of work being considered an end in itself. Only in the eighteenth century did a new evaluation of work enter the scene. The aspect of creativity then won out, over the aspects of difficulty and burden. The causes of this change in evaluation are disputed. Max → Weber, in his famous *Die protestantische Ethik und der Geist des Kapitalismus* (Ger., "The Protestant Ethic and the Spirit of Capitalism"), suggests that religious motives were critical. But even today, it is a subject of scientific discussion. A special role is played by the Calvinistic tenet of the double → predestination. Before the creation of the world, God established which human beings were to be destined for eternal life and which to eternal death. If such is the case, what importance or meaning can be ascribed to the activity of human beings? How, then, does the new emphasis on the duty to perform work function as an appropriate means to solve the doubt over one's own status in grace? How, then, has it come about that this accentuation, intended as a pastoral consideration, came thus to be reinterpreted in such a manner that now secular, worldly success (measurable in wealth) was a sign of election? It is at least as plausible to hypothesize that, in a society increasingly resting on work for pay, as was increasingly evident in the nineteenth century, besides being physically forced to work, ideological, that is, religious legitimation become popular. It should be kept in mind that in the nineteenth century it was argued that only a low compensation could motivate the worker to continuous labor.

The modern development is identifiable by the fact that, today, in all religions, a positive qualification of work prevails, so that this can be emphasized in the 'interreligious dialogue' as a common trait. Although it is considerably difficult to argue that the respective religious traditions are willing to attribute a high value to worldly work, theological acuity nevertheless has attempted to solve even this problem, by way of postulating a work ethic that will apply to all religions, corresponding to an economy that operates globally.

Literature

Klöckler, Michael/Tworuschka, Udo (eds.), Ethik der Religionen – Lehre und Leben, vol. 2: Arbeit, Göttingen 1985; Kehrer, Günter, "Arbeit," in: Handbuch religionswissenschaftlicher Grundbegriffe 2 (1990), 45-50; Marx, Karl, Capital: A Critique of Political Economy, 3 vols., New York 1977–1981 (Ger. [1]1867); Weber, Max, The Protestant Ethic and the Spirit of Capitalism, London/New York 1992 (Ger. [1]1904/05).

→ *Everyday Life, Economy, Marxism, Poverty, Protestantism, Weber*

Günter Kehrer

Writing

1. The point in time at which the human being began to register data in writing can be referred to some 3,000 years before Christ. Naturally, the act of writing was possible before the invention of writing—by scratching, painting, etc., individual signs—probably as early as the Paleolithic. But it is undisputed that only the invention and application of writing, as a comprehensive code and means of preservation—for the storing and expansion of speech-connected information—resulted in the formation and flourishing of the early civilizations (→ Memory). In Mesopotamia, the phenomenon occurred as cuneiform writing, in Egypt as hieroglyphics. The invention of mobile vehicles such as the clay tablet (ancient Near East), papyrus (Egypt), parchment (Asia Minor), and paper (China) played a decisive role in the propagation of writing. Another critical development was that of the codex and the → book, which became the binding and archiving units. Familiarity with writing, and writings themselves, were applied first and foremost for the registration of data in the political, socio-economic, and religious areas. The appropriation of writing had need of a special formation. Accordingly, the writer belonged to the foremost political or religious class. Competency for writing, then, rested especially with the political elite, so that writing functioned as a means of rule and primacy. This dimension did not change, in principle, until modern times, since only those who enjoyed special training could write. However, illiteracy has faded away in modern times, in the

Writing and Reading as Cultural Techniques

A Japanese Zen Master, a member of the Rinzai School (founded in China by Lin-chi I-hsüan), writes in calligraphy (in Jap., *Shodô*, 'Path of Writing'). He writes a Chinese letter, *qi* (in Jap., *ki*), meaning 'spirit,' 'mind,' 'spiritual' or 'mental power,' or 'inner energy.' In → Zen Buddhism, calligraphy is a means to prepare for meditation, or in itself applied meditation. For this practice, calm and composure are prerequisites. Another prerequisite is absorption in Nothing, and submersion in it. A Chinese author of the Sung Dynasty characterized Zen Buddhist calligraphy as *hsin yin* ('Seal of the Heart'). This spiritual attitude also appears in painting with watercolors, which, despite its simplicity, symbolically presents the religious dimensions both of human existence, and of the world.

process of the institutionalization of the modern ideal of education through universal obligatory education. In the nineteenth century, the mechanization of the art of writing (the typewriter) had, it is true, rather a negative effect on the popularization of writing at first (appearance of 'typists,' who had to be trusted with their newly developed writing art). But the rapid spread of the typewriter and—beginning in the 1980s—the 'personal computer' completely overtook this temporary reversal. Electronic development simplified writing, which became 'typing,' and thus the composition of writings, as well. It was on this account that writing generally lost its specific class privilege. Although it remains difficult to establish whether the book culture is entering its demise today, it is certain that the culture of writing and recording by hand in the new electronic forms of → communication, such as e-mail and Internet, will possess an ever more relevant value in the immediate future.

2. In the area of religion, as well, writing specialists were regarded as enjoying a special relevance. That is, writing was a privilege belonging to the elite class (priests, monks, theologians), and this ability led to the legitimization of their primacy. Fixation in writing of various sorts of religious data, and their storage, were the principal task of these specialists. The writing and composing of religious documents ('Holy Scripture,' hagiographies, books of law, prayer books, and even the exposition [exegesis] of commentaries on authoritative texts) excluded, in principle, participation by the laity. Therefore the ability to write contributed to a cementing of internal class differentiation within the group. However, it frequently made possible

the bond between religion and the key state instances that stabilized government (bureaucracy, royal chancery, ancient Eastern temples). Although, at present, writing is an activity open in principle to every person, it can still be recognized that a certain group of writers, especially in those traditions in which written (not printed) material possesses a high authority, play an important role in the community (e.g., copyist of the Torah; see also → Bible, with ill.).

3. In the religious colloquial, what is understood by 'scripture' is first and foremost 'the holy scripture(s),' that is, a corpus of texts that transmit religious information (messages). In most of the 'book religions,' the authorship of these scriptures is referred to God, or to the religious founder, which establishes their absolute → authority. Even though concrete historical persons, such as → Muhammad, can be identified as the authors, their writing activity does not take a central role, but only a passive, secondary one. God (or a spirit, an angel, etc.) dictates or writes, while human beings, at most inspired by God, or by beings resembling God, write down what has been heard or perceived (verbal inspiration). Writing in a condition of trance, as well, is frequently to be observed in other religions, as in Shamanism, or with written documents conveyed or prepared by persons with mediumistic talents (→ Spiritism; Channeling).

4. Ever since their appearance, 'sacred' or 'holy scriptures' have assumed a founding or differentiating function vis-à-vis their corresponding communities. *Interaction with Sacred Scriptures*

For the preservation of the 'correct' meaning of the texts, there appeared a special social class, which, even today, remains concerned primarily with the exposition of the texts (scripture scholars or theologians). The task of these → specialists is to explain the 'true' sense or meaning of the texts, or of the letters, respectively, either in function of societal constellations that are constantly being transformed over the course of history, or else from an 'unchangeable' universal perspective. In all of the scriptural religions this social class receives a privileged position and exercises a decisive influence when it comes to dogmatic controversies.

While laity in the scriptural religions (e.g., Protestantism, Islam, or Mahayana Buddhism) are not excluded from access to sacred scriptures in principle, it is also true that, in certain traditions, these are part of secret or mysterious knowledge ('arcanum'; → Esotericism), with which only the initiate may deal (Egyptian Book of the Dead).

A consequence of the concept that what is written in holy scriptures comes from supra-terrestrial beings, is the veneration or adoration or their physical form. A typical example is the holy book of the Sikh religion, Adi Granth, which enjoys a quasi-divine veneration. In the above-described behavior with the sacred writings in various rituals, the character of holy scripture as an object of veneration is clearly expressed: ritual honor to be accorded to the scriptures is attested in Catholicism (Bible), Buddhism, and Lamaism (Sutras), Judaism (Torah scrolls in the synagogue), and state Shintô (Imperial Educational Edict).

5. Specific characteristics of scripture in religion can be recognized in magical behavior with what has been written. If the idea of the supra-terrestrial and magical power of what is written moves into the foreground, then the character of scripture as the vehicle of magical power gains more strength (→ Magic; Amulet). If something written (or a small fragment of

That the cultural technique of writing and reading (and thus knowledge of antiquity) was maintained in Western and Central Europe at the dawn of the early Middle Ages was the merit of the Christian monastic culture. Tirelessly, its writing specialists copied more or less sacred texts, in scriptoria (from Lat., *scribere*, 'write'), as Umberto Eco so clearly depicts in his mystery novel *The Name of the Rose*. By way of example, Alcuin's scriptorium at Tours, at the beginning of the ninth century, annually produced two complete bibles. This ancient and venerable tradition has undergone an astonishing renaissance in the age of computers and the Internet. The Trappist monks of Holy Cross Monastery, for instance, in Berryville, Virginia, along with their traditional fruitcake production, have earned their living since 1990 by executing computer assignments for secular enterprises. Trappists, who follow a strict version of the Cistercian Rule, are much in demand for their writing abilities, as they are highly motivated, and in addition, are bound by a rule of silence, so that they can concentrate entirely on their assignments in their writing niches. For the development of their writing business, to which belong ambitious tasks like the development and maintenance of data banks as well, the monks have founded a flourishing commercial enterprise. Its name, incidentally, is *Electronic Scriptorium*. (Hubert Mohr)

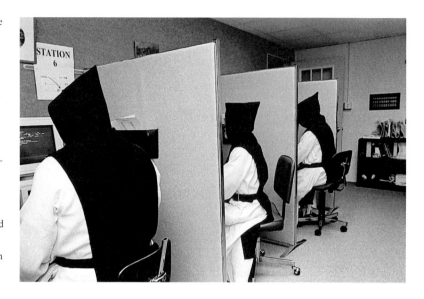

sacred scripture) is regarded as charged with power, then one can apply the power-laden writing for certain magical purposes. If what is written takes the form of a book, then this magical aspect shows itself in, for example, the practice of soothsaying from the book ('bibliomancy'), in which presages are ascribed to certain verses in the book, for instance, in the Sibylline books, Homer, or the → Bible. That a paper or piece of wood on which certain verses are written should be worn as an amulet or talisman, fastened on or applied for decoration, likewise offers an example of this practice. We need only recall the *mezuzah*, a small capsule on the front doors of Jewish houses and dwellings, which contains a handwritten fragment of the Torah (Deut 6:4-9; 11:13-21).

At the same time, it can be observed that certain letters, numerals, or formulas are ascribed special magical power, as with the letter or alphabetic mysticism of the → Kabbalah, and with magical formulae and 'syllables' (in Sanskrit, → *mantra*), in Brahmanism, → Tantra, and esoteric Buddhism. The conceptualization that certain letters incarnate physical or supra-terrestrial entities, can be recognized in, for example, Buddhist inscriptions, or → mandalas that, instead of the name of a Buddha or a picture of the Buddha, contain a letter (in Skt., *bija*) referring to the being and presence of the Buddha. In esoteric Buddhism, a written letter is often applied in meditation: here the first letter of the Sanskrit alphabet (*a-kara*), incarnating the cosmic being of time and space, is a special favorite.

The Oral Aspect: Expressions of What Is Written

6. Of course, the mystique and magic of the written must be considered in connection with the oral aspect (→ Oral Tradition). It is believed of mantras that their magic power develops only when they are actually pronounced in prescribed → rituals, and spoken precisely, and in such a way as to reproduce the sounds regarded as primordially supra-terrestrial, and as constituting the cosmos. Therefore the ritual relevance of the written ought not to be underestimated. After all, in community rituals, the oral or acoustical actions (reading, reading aloud, reciting, hearing; → Perception) play a role of the first importance, while, in the private practice of belief, the value of

the written is relatively great (meditation in the presence of written signs or symbols).

7. Religious use of the writing faculty is not exhausted in the writing down of, and the ritual attention to, holy scriptures. The latter must also—completely or in part—be multiplied. In certain traditions, besides, copying itself is ascribed a religious value. Thus, copying from sutras, as in Mahayana Buddhism, constitutes an important religious practice, which can lead to a better understanding of the text being copied, and at the same time to a better spiritual disposition.

Copying

8. That writing and copying made up an important part of religious practice, in some traditions relates to the fact that the writing technique had become an independent artistic capacity at the hands of writing specialists. The capacity or ability in question was the art of 'beautiful writing,' (the literal translation of the Greek) 'calligraphy.' In Islam, beyond its religious relevance, the practice of calligraphy contributed to the fact that, out of the potential for decoration inherent in signs for writing, the latter developed into general patterns for the adornment of Islamic architecture. The above-mentioned copies of Buddhist sutras as calligraphic works, at the same time belong to the realm of the architectural art. In the thirteenth century, the monks of Japanese → Zen Buddhism were the principal vehicles of artistic calligraphy, and they still maintain this tradition today.

Calligraphy: Writing as an Ornamental Art

9. In the electronic age, the meaning of writing, and of writings, is being transformed in the religions, as well. The blossoming of the information society makes possible the mass production of religious writings, and the latter, through the progressing electronic network, can be made available to all who are interested. Alongside 'old media,' such as electronic tapes or videotapes, in the future the computer could figure among the important vehicles of religious activities (→ Media). Approaches are recognizable in the private area of religious practice (Internet sale of consecrated Hosts, automated prayer service), although community rituals still exercise a greater power or attraction on the faithful. Even the formation of communities cannot escape this tendency. The fact that writings spread by the Internet do not have a concrete and limited circle of addressees, forces authors to address their messages to a potential audience unknown to them. The broad audience thereby assumes, first, a passive role (reading). Active writing (entering onto the Internet) can only follow for those willing to endorse virtual community. Today, it is difficult to establish the functionality of the act of writing, or that of the writings themselves, in the traditional schema.

Modern Mass Production

Literature

GAUR, Albertine, A History of Writing, London 1984; GOODY, Jack, The Logic of Writing and the Organization of Society, Cambridge 1986; Idem, The Interface between the Written and the Oral, Cambridge 1987; GRAHAM, William A., "Scripture," in: Encyclopedia of Religion 13 (1987), 139-145; Idem, Beyond the Written Word: Oral Aspects of Scripture in the History of Religion, Cambridge 1987; HOOKER, James T., Reading the Past: Ancient Writing from Cuneiform to the Alphabet, London 1990; LEVERING, Miriam (ed.), Rethinking Scripture: Essays from a Comparative Perspective, New York 1989; STEINER, Deborah Tarn, The Tyrant's Writ: Myths and Images of Writing in Ancient Greece, Princeton 1994.

→ *Bible, Book, Communication, Language, Literature, Media, Memory, Oral Tradition, Text/Textual Criticism*

Hiroshi Kubota

Yoga

Origins

The concept and practices of yoga come out of India (→ Indian Subcontinent). The Sanskrit word *yoga* is related to the English 'yoke.' In the ancient text of the Veda, accordingly, it meant first, the hitching (therefore, the 'yoking') of draught animals to a cart or plow.

Then, in the time of the Upanishads (from c. 900 BCE), as a systematic examination of human nature began in India, the concept was broadened to include a mental and religious dimension. A basic premise of the mystics of the days in question was that religious seekers must 'yoke' their senses and drives (constantly subjected, as they are, to transformation), that is, dominate them, in order to be able to venture an advance to their essential basis and ground—as eternally and changelessly apostrophized. Only thus, according to the teaching of the Upanishads, was 'liberation' (Skt., *moksha)* from the cycle of → 'rebirths' (samsara) to be attained. From such an allegorical comparison of human meaning with draught animals, the concept *yoga* in India gradually advanced to the status of an umbrella concept for the type of the praxis-oriented way of salvation.

Around the first centuries CE, the *yoga sutra*s (i.e. yoga verse) of *Patañjali* appeared, considered to be a basic text even today. In these maxims, a scant two hundred, yoga is defined as the "coming-to-rest of the activities of the human heart and soul," in the sense of a 'hitching up,' a yoking, of the mind and spirit. Here Patañjali teaches an eight-limbed "way of yogic practice," as follows.

- *yama:* general ethical commandments, such as nonviolence, truthfulness, not stealing, moderation, and not hoarding;
- *niyama:* specific ethical commandments, such as cleanliness, health, attention, self-study, and orientation to the immortal;
- *asama:* seating, and body position(s);
- *pranayama:* breathing exercises (→ Breathing);
- *pratyahara:* withdrawal of the senses inward;
- *dharana:* meditation;
- *samadhi:* immersion, being one. Yoga scholar Mircea → Eliade denotes the highest condition of yoga, *samadhi*, as 'entasy'—in the sense of a complete 'being at,' or 'being within' oneself, as distinguished from the frequently encountered religious → ecstasy, in the sense of a total 'being outside of oneself' (Eliade 1969).

Hatha Yoga

Besides the other kinds of yoga, beginning in the twelfth century CE, in India developed, on the spiritual foundation of tantrism (→ Tantra), *hatha yoga* (yoga of the 'power thrusts'), which valued the corporeal aspects of the 'way of the practice,' a differentiated physiology of its own. Here belongs, for example, the concept of *chakras*—thought of as delicate matter—a concept that today enjoys a growing popularity, especially in Western countries (→ New Age).

In the West, toward the end of the nineteenth century, yoga in its practical application was transmitted especially by the appearance of Indian Swami Vivekananda (1863–1902) at the World Congress of Religions (1893) in Chicago, and by the activities of the → Theosophical Society under Helena Petrovna Blavatsky (1831–1891) and Annie Besant (1847–1933). This first generation of Western adepts limited itself to yoga's concentrative and meditative practices. But, at the end of the 1930s, with the founding of the yoga schools of Boris Sacharov (1899–1959) in Berlin, and Selvarajan Yesudian (1916–1998) and Elisabeth Haich (1897–1994) in Budapest, the era of a Western yoga of a newer stamp began. This second phase in the development of yoga is characterized by the opening of instruction to a wider circle—unlike the exclusive guidance of a closed circle in the earlier phase of Theosophically marked yoga—as well as by a stronger orientation, during the exercises, toward psycho-physical events. Simultaneously, Western research offered its first verifications of the manners of operation of individual yoga exercises, as examined through medical and psychological studies.

Yoga in the West

Today, many of the courses in Yoga offered in the West are extensively dissevered from the original, unambiguously religious relation of Indian yoga, and especially pursue corporeal purposes of regeneration and therapeutic prophylaxis. Accordingly, in Western countries, on the occasion of investigations into the motives of a participation in yoga or yoga courses, it is 'relaxation' and 'physical fitness' that are cited as first on the list (Fuchs 1990, 239f.). Along with content and direction, the current Western forms of the transmission of yoga are specified. Thus, practitioners of yoga in Europe and North America are rather rarely—as in traditional India—instructed by → gurus, who expect a high degree of personal dedication, but by yoga teachers, who are usually active in a second occupation, and direct their instruction to the didactic principles of adult education. This Western development can therefore be designated, as a whole, *secularization of yoga*. In this connection, it is likewise interesting that eighty percent of those three million people practicing and teaching yoga in Germany are women (Fuchs 1990, 198 and 201), while, in India, yoga is still a clear domain of men.

Secularization

Literature

Sources: MALHOTRA, Ashok Kumar, An Introduction to Yoga Philosophy: An Annotated Translation of the Yoga Sutras, Aldershot 2001; PRASADA, Rama, Patanjali's Yoga Sutras, with the Commentary of Vyasa and the Gloss of Vachaspati Mishra, New Delhi 1978.
   Secondary Literature: DE MICHELIS, Elizabeth, A History of Modern Yoga: Patañjali and Western Esotericism, London 2004; ELIADE, Mircea, Yoga: Immortality and Freedom, New York ²1969 (Fr. ¹1954); FEUERSTEIN, Georg, The Philosophy of Classical Yoga, Manchester 1980; FUCHS, Christian, Yoga in Deutschland. Rezeption, Organisation, Typologie, Stuttgart 1990; JARRELL, Howard R., International Yoga Bibliography, 1950 to 1980, Metuchen 1981; WORTHINGTON, Vivian, A History of Yoga, London/Boston 1982.

→ *Body, Breathing, Guru, Hinduism, Indian Subcontinent, Meditation, Mysticism, New Age, Occultism, Theosophical/Anthroposophical Society*

Christian Fuchs

Zarathustra

No one knows exactly when and where Zarathustra, the 'founder' of → Zoro-astrianism, lived. In fact, it is not even certain whether Zarathustra repre-sents a historical individual at all. Even in the most ancient sources, the 'historical Zarathustra' appears as a remarkably nebulous figure, later to be repeatedly overlaid with mythology, theology, ritual, literature, iconogra-phy, and ideology.

The Gathas

The name Zarathustra (or Zarathushtra) appears in five very ancient hymns, the 'Gathas' ('songs'), composed in an ancient Iranian language. It is not cer-tain who it was who composed these songs—Zarathustra himself? The place and time of the emergence of the Gathas is disputed. Most scholars assume that they were composed at the latest in the eighth century BCE, and perhaps even in the middle of the second millennium BCE, while some scholars opt for a date in the sixth/fifth centuries BCE. (The date of the composition of the hymns implies the date for Zarathustra.) It is generally assumed that these hymns were composed somewhere east of the borders of today's → Iran. In these songs, Zarathustra makes his appearance as an exceptional figure, an especially close confederate of the dominant god Ahura Mazda with whom he communicates and who grants him support. Together with a group of like-minded people, he is haunted by their adversaries.

The Later (Standard) Avesta

The Gathas probably belonged to the oldest layers of a liturgical text called the 'Yasna' (that at the same time is the name of a ritual in the course of which this text is recited). The Yasna makes part of a collection of ritual texts known as the 'Avesta' (which is often, rather misleadingly, referred to as 'the sacred writings' of Zoroastrianism). In contrast to the Gathas, the major parts of these texts portray a rather schematic view of Zarathustra: he acts as a powerful enemy of the demons, as a companion of the gods and goddesses, and as a partisan of good order, religion, and ritual. Many Avestan texts are rhetorically devised as dialogs between Zarathustra and the god Ahura Mazda: Zarathustra asks a question and the god provides the answers.

Biographies

In the Avestan texts, Zarathustra occasionally appears in a mythological or legendary light. Materials of this sort were later worked up into veritable bio-graphies, in middle- and new Persian languages. Most episodes of those bio-graphies entwine around Zarathustra's conception, his mother's pregnancy, his birth and childhood. The key event in these biographies is his (ecstatic) encounter with the divine beings at the age of thirty. At forty, he is supposed to have converted a prince or king to his religion, miraculously overcoming the resistance of 'wicked' priests. In these biographies, Zarathustra's death is mentioned marginally. These texts proved useful not only for edification and apologetics, but also for the legitimization of certain ideas and institutions.

Pictorial Representation

It was presumably only by way of contact with the visual piety of Brit-ish Christians that, in the early nineteenth century, Indian followers of Zarathustra's religion, the Parsis (→ Zoroastrianism), developed the desire for a graphic representation of their 'prophet.' Consequently, a number of portraits of Zarathustra made their appearance, which nowadays play an important role in the everyday life and prayer life of the followers of Zarathustra. One of their favorite representations is the work of German painter Eduard J. D. Bendemann (1811–1889), and was originally prepared for the throne room of the Castle of Dresden.

Already in antiquity, there was a lively interest in Zarathustra (alias Zoroaster) in the West. The reports circulating concerning this Zoroaster include the biographical episode (also mentioned in the Iranian biographies) that he, alone among human beings, laughed at birth. Christian authors interpreted this as evidence either of his demonic character, or else of his special geniality. Similarly ambiguous was the report that it was Zoroaster who invented → magic and the liberal arts. Another influential tradition saw in Zoroaster a king, a successor of Noah. Furthermore, he was accounted a great astrologer and astronomer. *Zoroaster in the West*

    In the early modern age, along with Hermes Trismegistus, Zarathustra won prestige as representative of a very ancient, yet timeless, wisdom (*prisca theologia*; → Esotericism; Hermetism/Hermeticism), whose deciphering and 'renaissance' were to contribute to a renewal of religious life. Later, certain figures of the → Enlightenment looked on Zarathustra as the protagonist of a 'natural religion,' or 'religion of reason,' that looked as if it could shake Christianity to its foundations. Voltaire, in his struggle against the backward powers of superstition (*l'infâme*), appealed to Zoroaster.

Friedrich Nietzsche's *Thus Spoke Zarathustra* (part 1: 1883) produced a new Zarathustra discourse. In first drafts, → Nietzsche had used the Greek Heraclitus as his hero. Now, not without irony, he reached even further back, to the 'Persian,' Zarathustra. With Nietzsche's book, 'Zarathustra' received a new life of his own, and (like his creator) he became a cult figure for a new readership. To be sure, Zarathrustra's name could also unfold its charm without a careful reading of the book. There are several visual presentations of Nietzsche's Zarathustra, and with Richard Strauss's tone poem (1896) named after the book—which, in turn, straightway attained to cult status as music for Stanley Kubrik's "2001: A Space Odyssey" (1968)—Zarathustra even gained an acoustic presence. The fascination that shone in Nietzsche's book condensed in a number of sequels from the first third of the twentieth century. Nietzsche himself, in *Ecce Homo*, insisted that it had been the 'Persian Zarathustra' who had been the first to create the ominous error of the translation of morals into metaphysics. Therefore the confutation of this error had to come, once more, in the name of Zarathustra, the most truthful of all. *Nietzsche and Sequels*

His admirers hailed the founder of the Mazdasnan movement as a 'new Zarathustra.' The relation to Zarathustra is reflected in his very name: Dr. Otoman-Zar-Adusht (!) Ha'nish (1844–1939). The name of the religion likewise plays on the Zarathustric religion ('Mazdasnan' is derived from Ahura Mazda). There are also some further modern religious movements that, in some way or the other, claim a link to Zarathustra (such as with Osho [→ Osho Movement], OHASPE, Theosophists, and Anthroposophists [→ Theosophical/Anthroposophical Society]). *Mazdasnan*

While he was praised as an ancient sage in some esoteric currents, Zarathustra has for long centuries ranked in the Islamic East as an antagonist. In the *A Modern National Hero* vicinity of Persepolis, however, there is a remarkable ancient building that the vernacular, by association with the great stone cube of Mecca, called 'Zarathustra's Kaaba.' With the rise of modern Iranian nationalism, Zarathustra has come, in certain circles, to perform a positive political function. As the epitome of a pure, brilliant, ethically directed, ancient Aryan Iranian civilization, Zarathustra was stylized into a kind of proto-national hero. In recent decades, furthermore, Zarathustra has been 'discovered' by certain Central Asian intellectuals (e.g., in Tajikistan). Moreover, a number of Kurds are convinced that Zarathustra was one of their 'prophets.'

Literature

GNOLI, Gherardo, Zoroaster in History, New York 2000; KELLENS, Jean, Essays on Zarathustra and Zoroastrianism, Costa Mesa 2000; ROSE, Jenny, The Image of Zoroaster: The Persian Mage through European Eyes, New York 2000; STAUSBERG, Michael, Faszination Zarathushtra. Zoroaster und die Europäische Religionsgeschichte der Frühen Neuzeit. 2 vols, Berlin/New York 1998; Idem, Die Religion Zarathushtras: Geschichte—Gegenwart—Rituale, vol. 1, Stuttgart etc. 2002.

→ *European History of Religion, Esotericism, Iran, Reception, Zoroastrianism*

Michael Stausberg

Zen Buddhism

1. *Zen* is the Japanese designation for the Chinese *chan* (in Sanskrit, *dhyāna*, 'meditation,' 'immersion'), and denotes a tradition of Mahayana Buddhism for which the key religious practice is '→ meditation sitting' (in Jap., *zazen*). What is characteristic of Zen can be summarized in four brief enunciations: (1) Zen understands itself as a special tradition outside of orthodox teaching; it emphasizes (2) independence of the authority of sacred scriptures; (3) a transmission of the teaching 'from heart to heart,' from master to pupil; and (4) the sight and observation of one's own being (*kenshô*). Zen stresses the priority of an experience of enlightenment over intellectual confrontation with Buddhist teaching and the performance of a polished ritualistics, such as that obtained in the schools of esoteric Buddhism (Tendai, Shingon). Further, Zen interprets the concept of ritual in a new manner. Everyday activities, such as raking leaves, eating, and drinking tea, in a context of schooling in mindfulness, are performed with consciousness and attention, and in this consciousness, become the daily ritual.

Zen in China

2. a) The founder of Zen is the half-legendary figure of the eighteenth Indian patriarch, Bodhidharma (d. 532). At the beginning of the sixth century, Bodhidharma brought the Buddhist teaching to China. There it connected with Daoist elements, and developed a character of its own. Bodhidharma became the first Chinese Zen patriarch. The sixth patriarch, Hui-neng (638–713), composer of the Platform Sutras, enjoyed a far-reaching influence. Master Pai-chang (eighth patriarch, 720–814) introduced a stable monastic rule for monks, thereby bestowing on Zen its independence from other Buddhist schools. A surprising development was the imposition of the commandment of daily work: "A day without work is a day without eating."

The Zen Practice of the Tea Ritual (in Jap., Sarei*)*

The founder of Japanese Sôtô Zen, Dôgen (1200–1253), made tea drinking a substantial component of daily life in Zen monasteries. *Sarei*, the tea ritual, celebrated on certain occasions, serves as a stimulant, with the tea ingested before the phases of meditation (in Jap., *zazen*), and at the same time has a community-founding function. From the thirteenth to the fifteenth centuries, tea was prepared and consumed as a mixture of water and tea powder, produced from pulverized leaves of green tea, and beaten foamy with a bamboo brush. This is the form of tea preparation that we find today in the 'tea ceremony' ('Tea Way,' in Jap., *chadô*). The monks of the monastery gathered before the image of the Bodhidharma, and drank tea from a bowl, passing it around in a circle. In the sixteenth and seventeenth centuries, a new variant of the tea preparation came into style, influenced by the China of the Ming dynasty, and suppressing the tea-powder variant. Tea was prepared by brewing green-tea leaves in a bowl or pot of hot water; and the broth was then consumed. This variant of the tea preparation is still the common form today for the monastic Tea Ritual *Sarei*, daily celebrated in the meditation hall. This is the form familiar to people in the West, which has its origin in the fact that tea first came to Europe in the time of the Ming Dynasty.

The tea culture originates in China. Japanese monks, pursuing Buddhist studies in China in the twelfth century, became acquainted with tea—as a medicine, as a sacrifice, and as a drink—and carried seeds and seedlings back to Japan. The most celebrated monk to have introduced and promoted tea farming in Japan was Zen master Esai (1141–1215), founder of the Rinzai Zen school. Along with Buddhist studies, Esai concerned himself with Chinese medicine, and, in his *Kissayôjôki* ("Notes for Tea Drinking for Health"), emphasized the purpose of tea drinking indicated in his title. One of Zen's most basic concepts, which made it possible for the art of tea (in Jap., *chanoyu;* lit., 'hot water for tea') to develop outside the monastery walls, comes from Dôgen. From an originally religious ceremony in Buddhist monasteries, the art of tea then became an aesthetic spiritual discipline for laity. (The concept 'Tea Way'—in Jap., *chadô*—comes from Dôgen.) According to the understanding of Dôgen, no distinction obtains between the sacred and the profane. Each instant, each everyday action opens out toward the experience of the Absolute. "Reflect that the Buddha and the Patriarchs express their true 'self' in daily actions such as drinking tea and eating rice. Such acts are the entire life of the Buddha, as also that of the Patriarchs. Apart from it, there is no 'way of the Buddha'" (Dôgen, *Shôbôgenzô*, Zurich 1975, 1:129). Schooling in attentiveness and immersion, which the Buddhist monk traditionally exercises in monastic meditation, is translated by Dôgen into daily deeds. In a source book for the Tea Way from the seventeenth century, monk Jakuan Sôtaku's *Indications concerning Zen and Tea* (*Zencharoku*), we read: "Under the thought that tea can be brought into agreement with the essential points of the Way of the Buddha, the 'Way of the Tea' appeared. [...] In the genuine sense, the preparation of the Tea Ceremony, as Zen practice, is a mental, spiritual exercise, that is essential for a clear grasp of one's own being. [...] To possess a heart arrested by nothing, and thus to have in hand the utensils for the tea—this is the meaning of immersion. Even when it is a matter of nothing but the teaspoon, let one give one's heart without reserve to that teaspoon, and think of nothing else at all."

In the Tea Way, the Zen method of the schooling of the consciousness in the accomplishment or everyday actions, in the sense of an utter surrender to the moment, wins an artistic dimension. One of the great molders of the Tea Way is Sen Rikyû (1521–1591), Zen adept and 'cultural manager', as well as political adviser to Shogun Toyotomi Hideyoshi. With his design of the Tea Way, he contrived a new concept of human 'synanthropy' and ethics, oriented to Zen Buddhist principles. Here the foundational pillars represent the four virtues of harmony (in Jap., *wa*), attention (*kei*), purity (*sei*), and inner composure (*jaku*). The tea ceremony should realize at every moment artlessness, adaptation to circumstances, contentment, thankfulness, mindfulness, concentration, and the consciousness of transiency.

In this picture, European Zen pupils practice the rite of 'tea passing' at the beginning of a phase of meditation in the Meditation Hall of the *Bodhidharma Zendo*, the Zen Center founded in Vienna in 1979.

Sabine Bayreuther

Toward the time of the T'ang Dynasty (618–906), there arose five different Zen traditions—the 'Five Houses' (in Chinese, *wu-chia*)—with their respective peculiarities in understanding and schooling practice. During the time of the Kamakura dynasty, two of these lines, the Lin-chi (in Jap., *Rinzai*) and the Ts'ao-tung (in Jap., *Sôtô*) schools, found their way to Japan, and there they blossomed anew. In the late eighteenth century, Buddhism in China began an extensive retrenchment. In the T'ai-p'ing rebellion (1850–1865), the once flourishing monasteries lay abandoned, and Buddhist life was broadly paralyzed. At the beginning of the twentieth century, abbots and scholars undertook attempts at renewal, but these remained largely without effect. The general political and spiritual climate offered little space for religious activities. Buddhism's teachings were regarded as relics of China's 'feudal' past, and especially in the years of the Maoist Cultural Revolution (1966–1976), they were systematically repressed, while the monasteries' economic bases were widely destroyed. The consequences come down all the way into the present.

Zen in Japan

b) After the Gempei War of 1185, a political power switch occurred in Japan. The military nobility in → Kyôto repressed the court nobility, and assumed governmental power in the form of the shogunate. The seat of the military governors (Shogun) was Kamakura. The changed political situation favored the ascent of new Buddhist schools, especially the Zen schools, whose value concepts were so closely akin to Samurai ethics and Confucian virtues. Through Japanese Tendai monks, pursuing studies in Buddhist China, Zen teachings reached Japan. Eisai (1141–1215) founded the tradition of the Rinzai Zen in Japan, Dôgen those of Sôtô Zen. The principal temple of the Sôtô school is the Eiheiji, the Temple of Eternal Peace (Prefecture of Fukui), while the Rinzai line, by association with their Chinese exemplar, conceded special tasks and privileges to five large monasteries, the 'Five Mountains' (in Jap., *gosan*), in Kyôto and Kawakura. In the mid-seventeenth century, Chinese master Yin-yüan Lung-ch'i (in Jap., *Ingen Ryûki*) founded a third Zen school, the Ôbaku, with its principal monastery Mampukuji in Uja, in the vicinity of Kyôto. This parallel line of the Rinzai School retains little importance today.

At present, the Zen school in Japan has some ten million followers, slightly less than ten percent of the Japanese population. Actual Zen teaching and practice play a very subordinate role in the lives of lay Buddhists. The strict life of the Zen monasteries and the radical nature of Zen religious practice are quite unpopular among the population. This effect has been reinforced by the common practice, on the part of Japanese enterprises since the end or the 1950s, of obliging employees to undertake *zazen* schooling in Zen monasteries. The purpose is education in traditional Confucian virtues, such as discipline, respect, company loyalty, and readiness for commitment. Critics see in these practices a mere utilization of the Zen method, now reduced to the service of profit-oriented economic interests, for manipulating workers, and rendering them subservient. The aim, however, has nothing in common with the acquisition of knowledge, or with a spiritual life in the sense of the Buddhist ethic. One basis for the readiness of so many Zen temples to co-operate with company management may be, besides the financial aspect, a sharply declining interest on the part of the Japanese population in intensive Buddhist practice since the Second World War. The social function of Buddhist temples has been radically reduced (to the celebration of funerals and other offices of the dead). The structure of the Buddhist temple system in Japan provides that the eldest son of a priestly family become a monk, complete his religious formation in a monastery of the respective school-orientation, and take up the 'family temple.' This custom holds for Zen temples, as well. The motivation to go the Zen way as monk and priest is seldom based on a religious vocation, but is oriented to social advantages and traditions of legacy. This tends to deprive Zen of its depth in Japan.

3. Along with the exercise of *zazen*, the work ethic is one of the most important elements of Zen practice. "All activities are the activities of the Buddha" (Suzuki Shôzan, 1579–1655). Enlightenment (*satori*) can be achieved not only in the condition of meditative immersion, but also in dedication to daily tasks. Everyday life is the place of religious exercise. Especially in the Rinzai tradition, daily physical work (*samu*) plays an important role in the monks' regulated daily round. Observance of the maxim, "Practical action is more important than religious theory," leads to Zen's radical simplification of cult: renunciation of elaborate ceremonial, rituals, images, and symbolism, rejection of philosophical abstractions, as well as of any exaggerated apparatus of aids to piety. A determination not to cling to religious objects (or writings) led to aniconic tendencies. Sixth patriarch Hui-neng was accustomed to shred scrolls of sutras, Master Tianran (738–824) burned a wooden Buddha to keep warm in winter. Such acts also manifest the anarchical moment that typifies Zen. Reactions can depreciate into the vulgar, the obscene, the subversive, and turn against received hierarchical structures, empty traditions

Essential Traits of Zen

and habits of thought. The Zen monk slips into the role of the religious clown, fool, or provocateur. Many masters are shown in watercolors laughing uproariously.

Daily Life and Schooling Practices in the Monastery

4. Zen monasteries levy no taxes. The monastic community lives on donations, on begging rounds (money, rice, vegetables), on its own agricultural projects, and on stipends received for religious services (e.g., funeral ceremonies). The life of the monks is marked by hierarchical structures, rules, discipline, and a day organized down to the last detail. Besides physical labor, monks' tasks and duties include the daily recitation of Buddhist instructional texts (sutras), and weeklong meditations (*sesshin*), nocturnal *zazen*, begging (*takuhatsu*), and, in Rinzai monasteries, the practice of the *kôan*. In this latter practice they receive from the master a proposition or application, frequently paradoxical or rationally insoluble ("What is the sound of one hand clapping?"), by means of which they are to school themselves to move past rational thinking, and to attain to an experience of oneness. In Sôtô Zen monasteries, where the *kôan* is not practiced, the master affords the practitioners the opportunity to present their problems in special question sessions (*mondo*). In addition, a number of the more experienced monks hold certain offices. For example, the senior monk supervises the meditation hall and introduces the *zazen*. Others are the cook in the monastery kitchen, cantors at the recitation of the sutras, personal servants of the Zen Master, and the monks whose tasks are the reception and entertaining of guests, or seeing to the monastery's bookkeeping and financial management. Furniture in Zen monasteries, like the Zen life practiced there, is characterized by simplicity, parsimony, plainness, and severity, and the practitioner must be content with little. His acts are to be upright and artless. We encounter this aspect of Zen in Zen aesthetics: in the art of reduction, for example, in the form of monochrome watercolors, in the simplicity of an artistic flower arrangement, or in the style of a Japanese Zen-garden (→ Garden/Paradise). Daily activities such as garden maintenance become aestheticized, and serve as a locus of spiritual experience.

Zen in the West

5. The transmission of Zen to the West occurred first and foremost through Daisetzu Suzuki (1870–1966), who came to America at the beginning of the twentieth century with the purpose of collaborating in the publication of East Asian, and especially Zen Buddhist, writings. He gave numerous lectures and addresses in the cities of America and Europe. Another master, Shigetsu Sasaki Sokei-an (1882–1945), founder and Master of the First Zen Institute of America, in New York, lived and taught in the United States from 1906 until his death in 1945. The pioneer generation of Zen research in Germany includes religion scholars Hans Haas (1868–1934) and Wilhelm Gundert (1880–1971), and Protestant theologians Rudolf Otto (1869–1937) and Karl Heim (1874–1958). In 1925, for the first time, Zen texts were published, with detailed commentary, in German (August Faust, Shuhei Ohasama). With Jesuit Father Hugo M. Enomiya-Lassalle, the 'Christian Zen' movement began. In 1968, after twenty years' Zen practice under Japanese masters, the priest began to teach Zen in Germany.

In Europe and North America, numerous groups of Sôtô and Rinzai Zen were established, and are members of umbrella organizations of Buddhist communities. Dangers accompanying the implantation of Zen in the West are exoticization, and unreflective adoption of Japanese structures. The establishment of Zen in the West is a difficult tightrope-walk between a temperate adaptation to Western lifestyles, and preservation of the essence of Zen.

Literature

Sources: DESHIMARU, Taisen, Questions to a Zen Master, London 1991; DÔGEN ZENJI, A Primer of Sôtô Zen: A Trans. of Dôgen's Shôbôgenzô Zuimonki by REIHÔ MASUNGA, London 1978; ENOMIYA-LASSALLE, Hugo M., Zen Meditation for Christians, La Salle 1974; HEINE, Steven, Opening a Mountain: Kôans of the Zen Masters, Oxford 2002.
   Secondary Literature: ABE, Masao, Zen and Western Thought, London 1985; Idem, Zen and Comparative Studies, Honolulu 1997; ANDERSON, Jennifer L., An Introduction to Japanese Tea Ritual, Albany 1991; BARONI, Helen J., The Illustrated Encyclopedia of Zen Buddhism, New York 2002; BODIFORD, William M., Sôtô Zen in Medieval Japan, Honolulu 1993; DUMOULIN, Heinrich, Zen Buddhism: A History, 2 vols., New York 1988–1990; Idem, Zen Buddhism in the 20th Century, New York 1992; KAPLEAU, Philip, The Three Pillars of Zen: Teaching, Practice, and Enlightenment, New York ²⁵2000 (¹1965); KRAFT, Kenneth (ed.), Zen: Tradition and Transition, New York 1988.

→ *Buddhism, China/Japan/Korea, Esalen Institute, Kyôto, Martial Arts, New Age*

Sabine Bayreuther

Zionism

1. Zionism is a movement in → Judaism, appearing at the end of the nineteenth century, with the goal of the creation of a 'national homeland' for the Jews scattered through the → Diaspora. The designation is derived from 'Zion,' a hill in → Jerusalem, where there once stood the Jebusites' citadel that David overcame ('City of David'; 2 Sam 5:7). Even in the Bible, the name was extended to the Temple Mount, all of Jerusalem, and, finally, Israel. As a mythical place, Zion stands for the 'Mount of God,' after the exemplar of the 'mountain far to the north,' home of the gods of Phoenician mythology (Ps 48; cf. 2:6). After the destruction of the Temple (70 CE), Zion became the symbol of Jewish longing for a return to the ancient homeland. This hope of return found expression in the Jewish liturgy, as, for instance, in the blessing and farewell greeting, "Next year in Jerusalem!" However, the idea long remained joined to Messianic hopes. Only in the nineteenth century were plans developed for the creation of a Jewish homeland. Premises for the creation of a Jewish homeland were, for one, the extension of a racist → anti-Semitism that erased the success of the Jewish emancipation, and for another, the rise of a nationalism that favored the emergence of a Jewish national movement.

2. The first impetus for the Zionist movement came from Eastern Europe. In reaction to the pogroms of the early 1880s, in Russia, Leon Pinsker (1821–1891) composed his *Autoemanzipation*, in which he presented the necessity of the foundation of a Jewish homeland. Likewise under the pressure of the Russian pogroms, there arose, in Eastern Europe in 1882, the *Chibbat Zion* (Heb., 'Love for Zion') movement, whose goal was the promotion of Jewish settlement-movements in Palestine. The activities of the *Chibbat Zion* can

Zionist Movement before 1948

Commemorative post-
age stamp of the State of
Israel for the one-hun-
dredth jubilee of the first
Zionist Congress in Basle
in 1897, with the image
of Theodor Herzl, the
Basle Casino as the meet-
ing place of the first and
subsequent Congresses,
and the Israeli state flag.

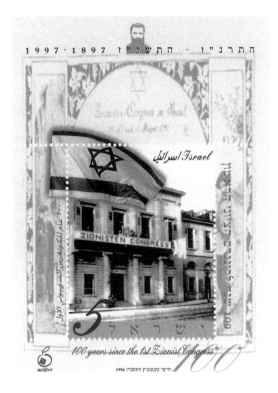

be denominated 'practical Zionism.' This direction met with sharp criticism from the side of the 'cultural Zionists,' especially Achid Haam (1856–
1927), who championed the creation of a cultural and spiritual center in
Palestine.

Theodor Herzl and
Political Zionism

The founder of political Zionism is journalist and author Theodor Herzl
(1860–1904). Under the pressure of the nationalistic strivings of Austria-
Hungary and the influence of the Dreyfus Affair in France—where he had
resided since 1891 as correspondent for Vienna's *Neue Freie Presse*—Herzl
developed his Zionist ideas. In 1896, he published *Der Judenstaat – Ver-*
such einer modernen Lösung der Judenfrage (Eng. as "The Jewish State:
An Attempt at a Modern Solution of the Jewish Question"). There, Herzl
represented the view that the 'Jewish question' could be solved only by the
concentration of the Jews in a particular region. He regarded the 'Jewish
question' not under a religious, but under a national aspect, and his piece
provoked intense reaction. On the Orthodox side, he was declared a heretic,
as his endeavors were deemed to stand in contradiction with the Messianic
promises—an argument still put forward by the extreme Orthodox today.
Assimilated Jews, too, turned against Herzl, as they feared that, with Zionism, any emancipation that had already been achieved would itself be in
jeopardy. In 1897, the first Jewish Congress took place in Basle, at which
Herzl founded the *Zionistische Weltorganisation* (Ger., "World Zionist Organization"), as an umbrella organization for the Zionist groups. Subsequently,
"World Zionist Congresses" have been held every two years—since 1961,
in Jerusalem. Herzl's diplomatic efforts to reach Zionist aims politically at
first met with no success. But Eastern European Zionists forged ahead with

the settlement of Palestine. Immigration (in Heb., *aliya*, 'ascent') became an important basis for the realization of Herzl's ideas. Between the beginning of the 1880s and the founding of the State of Israel, there were six waves of immigration. The Jewish population (*yishuv*, 'inhabited land') swelled from 25,000 to more than 600,000. Often, immigration was accompanied by the influx of a manual labor force. With respect to the latter, the wish was for the creation of a productive basis for the new society. In place of the often physically unprepared Jews of the Diaspora, a new generation of strong, able-bodied persons would now step forward. Among the immigrants in the time from 1905–1926, socialist tendencies prevailed. Beginning in 1909, and influenced by socialist idealism, *Kibbutzim* (pl. of Heb. *kibbutz*, a 'gathering') appeared. These were community settlements, based on rigorously socialist principles, extensively corresponding to the commune of an ideal type. The Kibbutzim played a decisive role in the settlement of the land, and in the political development of the Jewish community system. The socialist tendencies of this time are also responsible for the fact that it was the labor union *Histadrut*, founded in 1920, that set up state structures in many areas.

Political acknowledgment of Zionist goals materialized only as a result of the 1917 Balfour Declaration, in which Great Britain certified its support of the creation of a Jewish homeland in → Palestine. The proclamation of the State of Israel, to be sure, came only in 1948, after millions of Jews had been sacrificed to the National Socialist evil. After the → Shoah, a rejection of the State of Israel seemed inconceivable.

3. With the founding of the State of Israel, the supreme Zionist goal had been attained. Zionism then had to define its content anew, as many of its tasks had been assumed by the Israeli state. Concentration was then on the pro-Israeli work in the Diaspora, and care for new immigrants. From some 650,000 Jews at the founding of the state, the population grew by nine-fold by the turn of the century (1997: 5,836,000). *Zionism and the State of Israel*

The Six Days War of 1967 represents a turning point in the history of Zionism, in which Israel occupied East → Jerusalem, with Mount Zion and the Wailing Wall, the Sinai Peninsula, the area of West Jordan, the Golan Heights, and the Gaza Strip. By way of the additional regions won in the Six Days War, the Arab minority increased considerably in the Jewish state. This demographic change moved to the foreground the question of the relationship with the Arabs, who were creating an identity of their own, as 'Palestinians.' In addition, after this demonstration of Israeli strength Zionism found nearly complete pan-Jewish support. Many Jews saw the victory, with its conquest of the Old City of Jerusalem and the Temple Mount, as well as of the biblical focal point from Nablus/Sichem to Hebron, as a divine sign. A new 'settlement movement' sprang up, representing a fundamentalistic, national-religious (Neo-) Zionism, and introducing religious arguments for the annexation of the occupied territories. A religious variant of Zionism, that until now had played only a marginal role, grew in importance in the years after 1967, and traditional secular Zionism was overshadowed. This development reached its climax with the murder of Israeli Prime Minister Yitzhak Rabin by a fanatical religious Jew, in November 1995. *National Religious 'Neo-Zionism': The Settlers' Movement*

One result of this merging of (non-religious) political Zionism and religious messianic Zionism was the growth of the radical *Gush Emunim* movement *Gush Emunim and Protestant Zionism*

(Heb., 'Block of the Faithful'), still influential in Israeli politics today. In a strange alliance with North American pre-millennialist Protestant Zionists—who view the 'gathering of the people of Israel' in the 'Holy Land' and the Jews' subsequent conversion to Christianity as a birth pang of the Messianic age (→ Millenarianism/Chiliasm)—the religious charging of Zionism with Messianism changed the political landscape of the Near East.

Anti-Zionism

4. At the dawn of the twenty-first century, Zionism has numerous problems to combat. Immigration into Israel—after a powerful wave of immigration at the beginning of the 1990s, from the region of the former Soviet Union—is now shrinking, while the number of emigrants is climbing. The Zionist assumption that, with the existence of a Jewish state, enmity towards Jews would come to an end, has proved to be untenable. Not only in Arab space did Anti-Zionist attitudes spring up; the Soviet Union pilloried Israel, in the Cold War, as an outpost of United States imperialism, availing itself, as did other Eastern bloc countries, of anti-Semitic stereotypes. A similar argumentation was mounted by a large number of spokespersons from the 'Third World,' and, to an extent, by the leftist movements of the West, which alleged Israel's colonialist character, and criticized a racist dimension in Zionism. In 1975, a UN resolution (Nov. 10, 1975, no. 3379) even defined Zionism as a form of racism. The resolution was rescinded (Doc. No. A/RES/46/86, 74th plenary meeting of Dec. 16, 1991). However, this did not mean the end of anti-Zionism. Anti-Semitism, no longer respectable since the Shoah, here found its prolongation.

Zionism in Crisis

5. Since the 1980s, Zionism has itself been under academic discussion. 'New historians' Benny Morris, Han Pappe, Avi Schlaim, and Tom Segev, whose position is often the object of allusion, included the standpoint of the Palestinians in their consideration of Israeli history and society, and criticized various aspects of Zionism. Thus, they maintained their attitude against a background of the Intifada, and of the aporias of the Israeli occupation policy. The inclusion of their criticism in a new history textbook, from 1999, sparked a battle among Israelis. The pride with which the delegates of the Thirty-Seventh Zionist Congress looked back on the one hundred years gone by since the first Congress, cannot conjure away the crisis of the present.

Literature

Sources: HERZL, Theodor, Briefe und Tagebücher, ed. by Alex BEIN et al., 7 vols., Frankfurt/M. 1983–1996; SCHOEPS, Julius H. (ed.), Zionismus. Texte zu seiner Entwicklung, Dreieich 1983.

The 'New Historians': MORRIS, Benny, The Birth of the Palestinian Refugee Problem 1947–1949, Cambridge 1988; PAPPE, Ilan, The Making of the Arab-Israeli Conflict 1948–1951, London 1992; SEGEV, Tom, 1949—The First Israelis, New York 1992; Idem, The Seventh Million: The Israelis and the Holocaust, New York 1993.

Secondary Literature: AVINERI, Shlomo, The Making of Modern Zionism: The Intellectual Origins of the Jewish State, New York 1981; BERKOWITZ, Michael, Zionist Culture and West European Jewry before the First World War, Cambridge 1993; LAQUEUR, Walter, A History of Zionism, London 1972; MORRIS, Benny, Righteous Victims: A History of the Zionist-Arab Conflict, 1881–2001, new ed., New York 2001; SILBERSTEIN, Laurence J., The Postzionism Debates: Knowledge and Power in Israeli Culture, New York/London 1999; VITAL, David, The Origins of Zionism, Oxford 1975; Idem, Zionism: The Formative Years, Oxford 1982; Idem, Zionism: The Crucial Phase, Oxford 1987.

→ *Anti-Semitism, Diaspora, Jerusalem, Judaism, Millenarianism/Chiliasm, Palestine/Israel, Shoah*

Isabel Herkommer

Zombie

1. The word *zombi(e)*, or *zumbi*, comes from the Bantu languages (→ Africa), and means 'enslaved spirit.' Zombies are 'un-dead' or 'living corpses,' of whom it is supposed that they can be awakened to life for purposes of black magic. 'Zombie' can denote either: the spirit (of someone dead), as the soul separated from the body, or a 'living corpse,' a body without a soul. The zombie concept originated in the → Voodoo religion, but is also familiar in other parts of the Caribbean, and in Brazil.

    In order to understand the phenomenon, it is important to indicate that in no traditional African religion is there a contradiction between magical and religious practice. Magic, as an effort to reach a purpose (rain and fertility, wealth, a love object) by supernatural means, is part of regular religious practice. But in addition, there is a discourse concerning witchcraft—possibly also a practice of the same—centering on harmful spells and the conjuration of the dead (necromancy). In Haitian Voodoo, the conceptualization prevails that a 'black magician,' with magical knowledge and magical powers, can catch the souls of living, or even dead, creatures, human or beast, and contrive to have them serve him. By his magical power, the sorcerer entraps these spirits and keeps them under his control. He can even hold them prisoner in a magical doll. In the background is the belief, itself actually African, that the human body hosts two souls: one, the 'vital soul' (in Creole, *gros bon ange*), and the other, the 'shadow soul' (*petit bon ange*), which leaves the body during sleep, and, after death, wanders aimlessly through the world as a zombie. The practice of black magic consists, first, of catching the *petit bon ange*—at a 'vulnerable' moment, when the connection to the body, and thus with the *gros bon ange*, is interrupted—and reducing it to one's service. In Brazil, the word 'zombie' is used only of persons who retain their bodies, and are still in life, but who have lost their (shadow) souls and character through magic. Then, it is believed, they can no longer distinguish between good and evil. Far more spectacular is the other apprehension: that of a dead body that the soul spirits are deemed to have abandoned. In that case, it is widely believed, the sorcerer ought to 'zombify' someone, by giving him a poisoned drink, so that he falls into the rigidity of death. Then, during the night, the sorcerer exhumes the victim and drips a magical fluid on his grave. Now the corpse rises from the earth as a zombie, without a will, a body without a soul, who must obey his lord and sorcerer in all things, and must work bearing burdens, or in the field. As with human beings in former times under colonial law, a slave zombie can be purchased from a sorcerer and resold. Here, the zombie status can be perceived mythically, as a social code for slavery, and less as a real event—although Haiti has explicit laws against the fashioning of zombies, and zombification has been brought into connection, in recent years, with local secret societies, which are prohibited and punished by law.

    2. Especially under the influence of the American film industry, the zombie has become familiar the world over. This began with Jacques Tourneur's

Concept

With "I Walked with a Zombie" (1943, dir. Jacques Tourneur, prod. Val Lewton), after Victor Halperin's "White Zombi" (1932), Haiti's voodoo religion had conquered the cinemas of the Western world once and for all—granted, in the horror genre, as exotic trimming for a well-crafted spine-tingler. "Forbidden Voodoo secrets sensationally revealed," the poster advertised, and set the visitor reverentially a-shudder at such a prodigy of magical pagan gestation. The gentleman with blemished eyes, who obstructs the two ladies' way to the gathering place of the followers of Voodoo, in the middle of a sugar-cane field, is obviously on the scene to give the appearance of a zombie, one of the 'living dead.' True, he is called 'Carrefour' (Fr., 'Intersection'), and watches a crossroads—thus representing the god (Loa) Legba in his guise as Mâitre Carrefour. In Haitian Voodoo, however, the latter is represented as a feeble old graybeard, on crutches. The film develops the zombie theme purely in subordination to a story of whites: Jessica, wife of a plantation owner (left in the picture), is caught between two alienated half-brothers, and has been 'zombified.' Betsy (center), her nurse, attempts to heal her, but the project goes amiss. Finally, it is seen

horror classic, "I Walked with a Zombie" (1943), in which Haiti's Voodoo cult is used effectively for a movie scenario. Close on the heels of this piece followed a whole sub-genre of horror films, which promptly broke with the cultural roots of the zombie myth. The Western audience, shivering with delight, were here offered not so much tales of soul thievery, as modern versions (if rather exotically detached) of the old European fear of 'those who return' (the *revenants*; → Spirits/Ghosts/Revenants), and of the 'undead.' As B-movies, they belong today to the popular culture of the Western world and to its → new myths.

Literature

SLAYTER, Jay (ed.), Eaten Alive! Italian Cannibal and Zombie Movie, London 2002; WADE, Davis, Passage of Darkness: The Ethnobiology of the Haitian Zombie, Chapel Hill 1988.

→ *Afro-American Religions, Magic, New Myths/New Mythologies, Popular Culture, Spiritism, Spirits/Ghosts/Revenants, Voodoo*

Claudio Mattes

Zoroastrianism

Designations

'Zoroastrianism' is the modern designation (established in colonial times) for one of the oldest living religious traditions of mankind. The name refers to one of the Greek names of its 'founder' Zoroaster, known as Zarathushtra in the sources from ancient → Iran (→ Zarathustra). In antiquity, most Greek authors referred to the religion simply as 'the religion of the Persians,' while indigenous sources termed it as the 'good' or the 'mazda-worshipping' religion—the latter term focusing on the god Ahura Mazda ('the Wise Lord' or, alternatively, 'Lord Wisdom') who is venerated as the main god, the 'strongest' of the gods (their 'father' and 'fashioner') who has put the universe in good order.

Ancient History and Indigenous Historiography

Zoroastrianism is a religion of considerable historical importance. While its precise origins—both as to the questions of time and space—are a matter of ongoing academic dispute, it had reached the mainland of Persia at the very latest during the reign of the Achaemenian Dynasty, Persian kings who (from the late sixth century BCE onwards) created and ruled over the first world-empire in history, until they were defeated by Alexander and the last Achaemenian king (Darius III) was murdered in 330 BCE. Some Achaemenian kings heavily drew on Zoroastrianism as a source of legitimation for their construction of political empire. For instance, Darius I ('the Great') who is mainly known for his great building projects (Persepolis), his administrative genius and his failed attempt to conquer Greece referred to the 'will' (alternatively: the 'size') of Ahura Mazda as *the* source of his political success in his royal inscriptions. (The king had seized power from a rival and hence was in need of 'extra' legitimacy.) However, the glory and splendor of the Achaemenians (which is regularly displayed in exhibitions in major museums of the world) was all but forgotten by the later indigenous Zoroastrian historiography that would only remember the fatal onslaught of Alexander the 'accursed' who was blamed for a violent loss of religious traditions. In retrospect Alexander was accused of having murdered priests and scholars, having carried off writings and having them translated, having extinguished ritual fires and having destroyed temples (a somewhat anachronistic accusation since there probably were no fire-temples at the period in question).

While Zoroastrianism struggled under Hellenistic and Roman rule and flourished under the reign of the Arsacid dynasty that controlled large parts of Mesopotamia and Iran (generally known as the 'Parthian' empire) from the third century BCE through the early third century CE, the later Zoroastrian religious tradition praised the Sasanian kings (reigning from 224–651 CE) for powerfully reestablishing the religion. As a matter of fact, several Sasanian rulers highlighted Zoroastrianism on such official propagandistic media as inscriptions, reliefs, and coins. Some kings are reported to have gathered and strengthened the religious traditions. The Sasanian period saw the establishment of many fire-temples, powerful religious endowments, and the rise of a hierarchically differentiated professional priesthood. Occasionally, clashes occurred between different religions operating on Sasanian territory, and there were several instances of persecution of Christians. The very fact that Christianity was developing a powerful base in Iran is indicative of a plurality of competing religions and local cults and practices that tend to be marginalized by the often held idea that there was something like a 'Sasanian state church.' While the Sasanians present themselves as pious Zoroastrians and later sources celebrate some Sasanian kings as exemplary devout kings, among modern Iranian Zoroastrians the Sasanians are often held responsible for a decline of the religion and its misuse for political purposes that would pave the way for the downfall of the empire. As a matter of fact, the Sasanian empire was conquered by Arabic troops in the mid-seventh century CE. Still to this day, most Zoroastrians use the presumed

that the local Voodoo cult had been infiltrated and manipulated by a white female physician. Incidentally, the film was made directly after Haiti's last and most vigorous 'Campaign to Combat Superstition' (1940–1941). In the course of the latter, temples of the Voodoo religion were plundered and destroyed, cult objects were burned, and Voodoo priests were thrown into prison. Furthermore, every Catholic had to take a special oath, in which he or she abjured the 'diabolical cult of Voodoo.' (Hubert Mohr) date (631 CE) of the coronation of the last Sasanian ruler (Yazdgird III) as the beginning of their era (2005 CE = 1374 Y). There is no strictly religious era—one of the many signs of the ethnic character of the religion.

The Coming of Islam and Its Aftermath

The Arabic conquest marked the beginning of a process of Islamization of the country that would last over several centuries (→ Islam), but by the thirteenth century CE the Zoroastrians were reduced to an insignificant minority and they were concentrated in some small parts of the country only. In this way, the geographical outreach of the religion was severely reduced—both in Iran and neighboring regions such as Central Asia where it had developed varieties that were markedly different from the main Iranian tradition, for instance with respect to visual representations. (Already in the late third century, when king Tiridates had adopted Christianity in Armenia and had it imposed on the population, Zoroastrianism had declined in that region, but modern research has pointed to many Zoroastrian 'traces' in the religion of the Armenians.)

The deteriorating living conditions of the Iranian Zoroastrians led some to seek refuge at the Indian West coast (Gujarat) where pockets of Zoroastrians had probably by the twelfth century CE established lasting community structures (→ Indian Subcontinent). The Indian Zoroastrians came to be known as the 'Parsis' (an ethnic term presumably referring to their homeland). In the course of time, they developed a specific ethnic identity with a strong sense of shared history, a peculiar language (Parsi-Gujarati), particular rites, ceremonies, and ritual spaces (by law inaccessible to non-Parsis) and their own dress codes and culinary preferences (the latter two have by now mostly disappeared from every-day life but are carefully staged on 'auspicious occasions' such as initiations and weddings).

Colonialism, Diasporas, and Current Demographics

The Parsi communities blossomed during Mughal and British rule. In the collective memory of many Parsis the colonial age is still regarded as something like the 'golden age' of the community in terms of material wealth, social prestige, cultural achievements, and political influence. At the same time, the religion underwent considerable transformations building on economic, legal, spatial, and ideological changes. An unprecedented number of temples were built, most of them in urban Bombay (Mumbai), the modern stronghold of the religion. On the other hand, a number of practices and beliefs became less important (especially the once universal fear of demons had all but vanished). The socio-religious position of the clergy declined and lay leadership was firmly established (partly, but not fully, along democratic lines), and a new code of personal law was enforced (which, among other changes, for the first time consistently established women as autonomous subjects). Social and religious reform movements started to forge new identity-discourses (fighting against 'superstition' and advocating a return to what they regard as the pristine teaching of the prophet), and esoteric movements (building on doctrines of the → Theosophical Society) made an impact on conservative sections of the communities. Since the late nineteenth century, the question of the permissibility of conversion to Zoroastrianism and mixed marriages has been a topic of ongoing debates and (re-) negotiations about Zoroastrian, or Parsi, identities, sometimes involving secular courts. Conversions are still not permitted among the Parsis and while intermarriage is a reality in most families, it is still regarded as a taboo and the religious status of the persons concerned is a matter of dispute.

Some Parsis enthusiastically welcomed independence, but it created a trauma for many others. A rhetoric of crisis seems to pervade the Indian communities. The most visible sign of crisis is the continuous demographic decline that in the long run seems to threaten the very survival of the community in India. (The Indian communities now number less than 70,000.) Part of the explanation for this decline is a reluctance to procreate that is typical for certain sectors of modern societies, while it at the same time is clearly at odds with the exhortations to bear children which can be found throughout the religious literature.

In part, the demographic decline of the contemporary Parsis can also be explained by → migration abroad. Starting with the late eighteenth century, Parsis temporarily or permanently settled not only in different parts of the subcontinent (including what is now Pakistan), but also in distant points of the colonial global trading networks, including Japan, China, Burma, Ceylon, Arabia, Eastern and Southern Africa. While most of these settlements are in decline, migration to Europe (mainly Britain) continues. Since the 1960s, new waves of emigration brought Parsis to the United States and Canada, Australia and New Zealand, and the Gulf states. These developments have contributed a strongly diasporic dimension to modern Zoroastrianism (→ Diaspora).

In → Iran, at the end of the nineteenth century, Zoroastrianism had been reduced to a tiny minority of less than 10,000 who had to bear a wide range of harsh discriminatory practices from the dominant Muslim population. The intervention of their fellow-believers from India, labor migration to India, and substantial political and legal changes have ever since greatly improved the lot of the Iranian Zoroastrians (and led to a tripling of their number). Many Zoroastrians left agriculture, migrated to the modern capital Tehran (which is by now the main stronghold of the Iranian Zoroastrians), and went into the new middle-class professions. Just like in India, some even found great success.

Religious Transformations in Modern Iran

Modern Iranian Zoroastrianism has undergone fundamental changes. As Zoroastrians have been freed from many restrictions, so the religion has been reconceived as a message of freedom (the presumed essence of Zarathushtra's message). In many respects, the ceremonial system has been deliberately neglected, and many rules and rituals that are still carefully upheld by Indian priests have been all but abandoned by their Iranian colleagues. The Yasna, for example, which the Parsis regard as an important liturgy (it takes a pair of trained priests several hours to perform it), is nowadays only celebrated rarely and in a drastically reduced format by some Iranian priests. Most of the → purification rituals have been abandoned and—contrary to the Indians—the Iranians no longer use cow's urine as a purifying agent (and hence there is no more need to perform the elaborate ceremony to consecrate it). The professional priesthood has seen a sharp decline and the leading priests have joined the social and intellectual elite in a crusade to uproot ancient 'superstition,' including some female rituals, devotion to 'lesser' divinities such as Mithra and animal → sacrifice (that had already been abandoned in India some centuries back). The fear of being classified as 'fire-worshippers' led the priests and other spokespersons of the community to emphasize the 'symbolic' role of fire-worship; some new temples even house gas fires. Accordingly, ancient consecrated fires are no longer tended according to the rules that were followed in the past. However, in modern times a number of smaller shrines have emerged as places of memory and devotion.

In order to safeguard their place as a modernizing religion in a modernizing country, the so-called 'towers of silence'—walled funerary structures in which the corpses would be exposed to the sun and birds of prey (→ Funeral/Burial)—were abandoned during the twentieth century to be replaced by cemeteries, where, however, care was taken to protect the earth from direct contact with the corpses. (The 'towers of silence' were introduced in the centuries after the Islamic conquest, and were refined in India, where they are still in use, despite the fact that there are no more vultures to devour the corpses.)

Some varieties of modern Iranian nationalism sought to construct a non-Arabic national identity. In this discursive context Zoroastrianism has emerged as a national legacy, and in its reconfigured shape (the religion of freedom and morality representing the splendor of ancient Iran) it turned out to be an appealing ideological alternative for many Iranians, and some Iranians have actually converted to Zoroastrianism. Nowadays, an international organization based in California (the 'Zarathustrian Assembly') is actively promoting the religion (or their heavily revised version of it) and 'accepts' people willing to convert. This organization, however, is violently opposed by others, including a neo-traditionalist organization based in Bombay ('Zoroastrian Studies').

Conversion is out of the question in the Islamic Republic of Iran that was established in 1979. Many Zoroastrians have left the country since 1979 and settled in North America, Australia, and Europe (e.g. Britain, Sweden, and Germany) contributing their share to diasporic Zoroastrianism. In Iran itself the Islamic Republic has blown some wind into the sails of religion. Religious events are among the few accepted occasions for collective merriment and entertainment. Moreover, the Zoroastrian casualties of the first Gulf War (against Iraq, 1980–1988) are nowadays celebrated as Zoroastrian → 'martyrs,' a concept previously unknown in the Zoroastrian vocabulary.

Literature

Boyce, Mary, Zoroastrianism: Its Antiquity and Constant Vigour, Costa Mesa 1992; Choksy, Jamsheed K., Evil, Good and Gender: Facets of the Feminine in Zoroastrian Religious History, New York 2002; De Jong, Albert, Traditions of the Magi: Zoroastrianism in Greek and Latin Literature, Leiden/New York 1997; Hinnells, John, The Zoroastrian Diaspora, Oxford 2005; Kellens, Jean, Essays on Zarathustra and Zoroastrianism, Costa Mesa 2000; Kreyenbroek, Philip (in collaboration with Shehnaz Neville Munshi), Living Zoroastrianism: Urban Parsis Speak about Their Religion, Richmond 2001; Luhrmann, Tanya M., The Good Parsi: The Fate of a Colonial Elite in a Postcolonial Society, Cambridge 1996; Stausberg, Michael, Die Religion Zarathushtras: Geschichte—Gegenwart—Rituale, 3 vols, Stuttgart 2002–2004; Stausberg, Michael (ed.), Zoroastrian Rituals in Context, Leiden 2004.

→ *Indian Subcontinent, Iran, Islam, Zarathustra*

Michael Stausberg

At the celebration of the New Year, the Afro-Brazilian population offer sacrifice to the goddess Yemanjá, on the banks of the Rio de Janeiro: flowers, dolls, and other gifts especially dear to the goddess are committed to the sea. In their sacrificial prayers, believers beg of Yemanjá the granting of their requests and wishes. (J. Drexler)

A special sacrifice, under the all-seeing eyes of the Buddha, at the ornamented stupa of Bodnath (Katmandu, in Nepal). At this Tibetan Buddhist sanctuary, it is seen as spiritually meritorious to have limewater poured from the edge of the one-meter-high hemisphere by temple workers, in exchange for a monetary contribution. The action is performed several times a day, so that, in the some five centuries of its existence, the monument has materially expanded. A second form of ritual libation is more expensive: from the base of the hemisphere, in high bows, saffron water is cast up upon the limestone to make dark stains, from which emerges the pattern of a lotus blossom—a sacred symbol in Buddhism. (E. Stapelfeldt)

In many religions, the burning of sweet-scented essences (incense, rosin, sandalwood, aloes, myrrh, camphor, cedar, etc.) constitutes an important component of worship or cult. In Catholicism, for example, the burning of incense (or 'incensation') has been practiced since the fourth century, and stands as an image and symbol of the prayer that ascends to God. The sacrifice of smoke and fragrances serves for the consecration or dedication of places, for ritual purification, to dispel demons, and to rejoice the gods by the ascending fragrance. Especially in → Daoism, the burning of incense sticks plays an important role in ritual, and in the everyday practice of believers: the vessels for sacrifices of smoke are key components of the temple. Here a young mother in Hong Kong offers a bundle of incense sticks in a Daoist temple, dedicated to the gods Man and Mo. Both deities go back to persons who, according to legend, lived some 1,500 years ago. Man, the God of Literature, is the patron of government officials, while Mo, the God of Martial Arts, is venerated by both police officers and the criminal milieu. (Benita von Behr)

The village of Charazani celebrates the Feast of *Todos Santos* (Sp., 'All Saints'). Here, the Christian feasts of All Saints and All Souls, November 1 and 2, are connected with pre-Christian conceptualizations of the return of the dead (cf. → Death and Dying). In this region, loved ones return after their deaths as *almas nuevas* (Sp., 'new souls') for three feasts of All Saints, and visit the cabins in which they have lived. On November 2, the villagers go out to the cemetery, accompanied by music groups, whose flutes and drums have played uninterruptedly since the day before. Families with a 'new soul' bring gifts along. Days before, sugar-cane poles have been constructed, in their cabin, hung with breads and fruits, and standing on a richly draped table. Nor must bottles of whiskey be lacking. Many of the celebrants are already tipsy, since, after Mass on November 1, they have entered the homes in which the 'new souls' have paid a visit, spoken prayers, and conversed all night long, drinking alcohol. At the cemetery, the gifts are supposed to be placed at the graves. In what one might call the Quechua catechism, the position taken by the Catholic Church with regard to the usages of *Todos Santos* becomes ambivalent. Nevertheless, in the everyday ritual of the Bolivian Andes in the area of the usages pertaining to the dead, a contiguity of Christian and non-Christian religious elements is feasible. (Kirsten Holzapfel, following Ina Rösing)

How difficult it is, especially in the modern age, to distinguish religious characteristics from profane, entertainment from bestowal of meaning! This similarity is seen in many examples from today's team sports. The rituals of the opening and closing ceremonies of great presentations such as the → Olympic Games, or world championships, provide productive material. At the kickoff celebration of the world soccer championships in France, on June 9, 1998, four twenty-meter-tall "ethnofuturistic giants" (German Press Association dpa) float in a star march to Place de la Concorde in Paris, intended to symbolize the (soccer) cultures of Asia, Africa, Latin America, and Europe. The figures were escorted to their destination by balloon figures of (in order) musicians, dancers, in-line skaters, and speaking soccer-players. Hundreds of thousands of attendees lined the processional route. The closing ceremonies, to be seen here, remind those reared as Christians, of the 'dance around the golden calf' (the stylized soccer-ball goblet in the middle). A less critical sort can identify the spectacle with the motto *Seid umschlungen, Millionen!* (Ger., "Embrace, ye millions!"—Schiller, in the "Ode to Joy" of Beethoven's Ninth Symphony). That the scene is not simply to be divided into 'sacred' and 'profane,' but that it presents a multi-layered *civic ritual*, is suggested by a glance at the giants: they stand in the tradition of Baroque continent-allegories, as well as in the folkloristic magical festive custom of over-sized dolls, the *mannequins* (for example, in the Tarascon in Southern France). Third and finally, they can be ascribed among the figures of a modern hero-cult—after all, the ritual exaltation of sports stars into superhuman demigods is known from Greek antiquity. But does this now make them 'soccer gods'— → idols of a 'religion of the masses'? (Hubert Mohr)

On November 4, 1995, Israeli Prime Minister Yitzhak Rabin was murdered in Tel Aviv. In recognition of his work in negotiations between Israel and the Palestinians, he had received the Nobel Peace Prize in 1994, together with Yassir Arafat and Shimon Perez. During the weeks after the act of terror, persons, mainly youth, assembled at the square where he had been murdered, and they held protest vigils, carrying storm lanterns, flowers, and letters. The wall at the place of the crime was spontaneously filled with images and graffiti. The government offered its contribution only later, with a memorial plate in the soil and by officially naming the square "Rabin Place." The graffiti, of which the picture shows a section, were varnished, and kept as a historical memorial. In this time of terror, the graffiti writers adopted the Hebrew biblical expression, *Yakum Damo*—"His Blood Be Avenged!" Whether these words represent a petition to God or a challenge to human beings, remains ambiguous. The references to the Song of Moses (Deut 32:43), as well as that to Ps 79:10, indicate that the murder calls for the wrath of God, as it brought down a person who acted according to God's will, Yitzhak Rabin. The expression used at parting, *Shalom, Haver*—"Goodbye, Friend" (on the left, under the portrait)—originally an expression of sympathy, grief, and shock, has long since become a widespread saying. It was the last sentence in President Bill Clinton's address (otherwise in English) at the funeral ceremony. Meanwhile T-shirts and bumper stickers recall the deceased. Members of the Socialist Party use it to greet Rabin as a comrade. Partisans of the peace movement appeal to him as a person of like mind. And a fragment in the picture suggests the frequently applied verse *Ata Haser* ("We Miss You"). The greeting of peace has become a slogan, with which inhabitants of Israel express their support for the peace process. (A. Kleefeld and Kirsten Holzapfel)

An interesting form of the secularization of trance can currently be observed in Morocco. The cult actors of the Gnawa Brotherhood are disconnecting themselves from their old traditions, and broadening their opportunities. Selected by a Danish gallery director, some of them have even begun to paint pictures while in a trance, and thus to render visible their inner life. This process becomes extremely clear in a painting by Mohamed Tabal. Here Tabal expresses his own possession by the spirits of the water, and thereby alludes to the origin of Gnawa on the Niger River. One can see fish, but also camels, which represent the voyage from Nigeria to Morocco. The expression on his face is that of a person all in ineffable rapture and referring to a frenetic presentation of the spirits, who incite self-mutilation. (F. Welte)

The young Peronist who lights an altar candle in the meeting room of a local Peronist group of Buenos Aires, pays tribute to the founding couple of the Party, Juan Domingo Perón (1895–1974) and his wife, Eva ('Evita') Duarte (1919–1952). Perón led Argentina from 1946 to 1955 with an authoritarian presidential regime that had taken on the characteristics of a mass, social revolutionary, → political religion, such as that recognized in the European Fascism of the twentieth century. His wife 'Evita,' a singer and motion picture actress by profession, succeeded, in exultant scenes, in making herself and the regime advocates of the 'shirtless' poor (Span., *descaminados*) and women. Evita's early death from cancer, at the age of 33, contributed to her becoming the object of an enthusiastic cult of the dead, promoted by Perón's Labor Party (*Partido Laborista*). Her corpse was embalmed, and her mausoleum was preserved as a place of pilgrimage, while her office at union headquarters became a room for memorial and meditation. In modern political movements, the veneration of persons encourages an intentional eradication of the boundaries of nation, party, and salvation movement. The devotional shrine pictured here may serve as an example. It is at party headquarters, and features a Catholic altar furnished with missal, crucifix, and Madonna, but dominated by photographs of the 'holy couple,' Juan and Evita. The transition from commemorative picture to image for meditation (perhaps even divine idol) seems fleeting. Granted, charisma and veneration of persons cannot be planned, as was acrimoniously shown at the close of Perón's career. After his political comeback in 1973, Perón tried to 'clone' Evita, presenting his second wife, dancer María Estella Martínez (b. 1931), as 'Isabel,' the new popular leader. After Perón's death, Isabel did succeed him in the presidential chair, but did not possess the capacities for control of the masses that her predecessor had demonstrated, and in 1976 she was ingloriously overthrown by a military junta. (Hubert Mohr)

A ceremony of initiation into a Wicca coven, a ritual group of the new witches movement (→ Paganism/Neopaganism). High priestess Zsuszanna Budapest presents the initiand (right) with an amulet of feathers. That only women are present has its basis in the fact that Budapest is founder of the feministic direction of 'Dianic Wicca' (after Roman goddess of the hunt Diana), whose ritual groups accept women exclusively. Budapest, born in 1940 in the Hungarian capital, combines traditional techniques used by Eastern European female soothsayers and healers (her mother was a medium), and 'feminist spirituality', a concept that, she declares, she herself coined. Since 1970, she had been in Los Angeles, and later was a women's liberation activist, reformulating the political tenets of radical feminism in religious concepts and terms. In 1975 she founded the first feminist Wicca coven, Susan B. Anthony Coven Number 1, which became the model in Dianic Wicca. Her *Feminist Book of Lights and Shadows* (1975; republished in 1989 as *The Holy Book of Women's Mysteries*) had the effect of creating a cult. In 1975, she was arrested for reading Tarot cards—which led to a paradigmatic trial, and ultimately, in 1983, to the abrogation of California's Law Against the Practice of Divination. Today Budapest moderates her own TV show ("Thirteenth Heaven"), and leads the Women's Spirituality Forum in San Francisco. (Hubert Mohr)

LIST OF ENTRIES

Freemasonry
Freud, Sigmund
Friendship
Fundamentalism
Funeral / Burial

Gandhi, Mahatma
Garden / Paradise
Gender Stereotypes
Genetic Engineering
Genius
Ghetto / Ghettoization
Gnosticism
God / Gods / The Sacred
Golem
Government / Rule / Politics /
    State
Grave / Tomb
Group, Religious
Guilt
Guru

Hair
Handicapped
Hare Krishna Movement
    (ISKCON)
Hasidism
Heathen
Heaven / Sky
Hell
Hereafter
Heresy
Hermeneutics
Hermetism / Hermeticism
Hero / Heroism
Hierarchy
Hildegard of Bingen
Hinduism
History
Holocaust
Holy
Holy War
Homosexuality / Homoeroticism
House / Home
Humanism
Human Rights
Human Sacrifice

Icon
Identity
Ideology
Idol

Illness / Health
Image / Iconoclasm
Immortality
Indian Subcontinent
Indonesia
Industrial Society
Initiation
Inquisition
Insanity
Intellectual Religion
Interest
Intoxication / Drugs /
    Hallucinogens
Intuition
Iran
Islam
Israel → Palestine / Israel

Japan → China / Korea / Japan
Jehova's Witnesses
Jerusalem
Jesuits
Jesus
Jihad
Joan of Arc
Joke (Religious)
Judaism

Kabbalah
Khomeini
Kitsch, Religious
Korea → China / Korea / Japan
Ku Klux Klan
Kyôto

Labyrinth
Laicism
Lamaism
Landscape
Language
Late Antiquity
Law
Liberation Theology
Life Cycle
Light / Enlightenment
Literature
Liturgy / Dramaturgy
Local Devotion
Lord's Supper / Eucharist
Love
Luck / Happiness
Luther, Martin

Machine
Machu Picchu / Cuzco
Macrocosm
Magic
Mandala
Manichaeism
Mantra
Mao, Cult of
Marginality / Liminality
Marriage / Divorce
Martial Arts
Martyr
Marxism
Mary
Mask
Masses
Master / Pupil
Materiality
Matriarchy / Patriarchy
Meaning / Signification
Mecca
Media
Meditation
Mediterranean Region
Meister Eckhart
Memory
Metaphysics
Middle Ages
Migration
Millenarianism / Chiliasm
Minorities
Miracles
Mission
Modernity / Modern Age
Monarchy / Royalty
Monasticism
Money
Monotheism
Monument / Memorial Places
Mormons
Mountains (Five Sacred)
Mourning
Muhammad
Mummification
Museum
Music
Mysteries
Mysticism
Myth / Mythology

Name(s)
National Socialism

Nativism
Natural Science
Nature
Nature Piety
New Age
New Myths / New Mythologies
New Religions
New York
Nietzsche, Friedrich
Nihilism
Nirvana
North America
North America, Traditional
    Religions
Northern Eurasia / Circumpolar
    Region
Northern Ireland
Nudity
Number / Calculation

Occultism
Oedipus
Olympic Games
Oracle
Oral Tradition
Order / Brotherhoods
Orientalism / Exoticism
Orientation
Origin
Orthodox Churches
Orthodoxy / Orthopraxis
Osho Movement

Paganism / Neopaganism
Pain
Palestine / Israel
Pantheism
Papacy
Parapsychology
Peace
Penance / Penitent
Perception / Sensory System
Pietism
Pilgrimage
Place, Sacred
Platonism
Pluralism
Polemics
Political Religion
Polytheism
Popular Culture
Possession

LIST OF MAPS*

_____

* In square brackets: the title of the article to which the map belongs.

Volume 4

LIST OF ILLUSTRATIONS

LIST OF CHRONOLOGICAL TABLES

GENERAL INDEX

Terms that are covered by a single entry are marked **bold**.

Calvin   132, 509, 818, 950, 1308,
   1493, 1513, 1877, 1990
Calvinism / Calvinists   21, 32, 117,
   139, 254, 625, 652, 1459, 1501,
   1602, 1624, 1879, 1971
Camara, Dom Helder   444, 1096
Camare   272
Cameron, James   1131, 1472
Cameroon   58, 157, 337, 939, 1374
Campa   312
Campanella, Tommaso   1932
Camus, Albert   694, 840, 1171,
   1327, 1874
Canaan   535
Canada   23, 410, 514, 684, 790,
   1235, 1329, 1331, 1335, 1343-
   1344, 1348, 1352, 1588, 1831,
   1865, 2013
Cancik, Hubert   599
Candomblé   38-40, 580, 1273,
   1957, 1959
Cannabis   954-957, 1668
Cannibalism   248-250, 308, 772,
   893, 1176, 1288, 1575-1576,
   1774, 1851
Canon   119, 169-171, 198, 234,
   250-252, 721, 866, 1082-1083,
   1108, 1308, 1346, 1377, 1464,
   1510, 1533, 1830, 1869, 1924
Canonization   250-252, 327, 1108,
   1214, 1231-1233, 1616, 1923
Canterbury   282
Cantillation   1274
Capac, Huayna   306, 312
Cape Verde   21
Capital   56, 254, 518, 549, 652, 936,
   949-951, 1082, 1095, 1245,
   1250, 1347, 1500-1501
Capitalism   113-114, 253-254, 268,
   406, 549-550, 586, 652, 665,
   688, 950, 1020, 1161, 1244,
   1245, 1331, 1343, 1483, 1513,
   1577, 1591, 1716, 1750, 1820,
   1900, 1936, 1968-1970
Capital punishment   255-258,
   626, 1525, *see also* Execution
Caplow, Th.   1961
Capra, Fritjof   606, 947, 1974
Cardano, Girolamo   180
Cardenal, Ernesto   1096
Card-reading   1520, 1800
Cargo cult   428, 479, 499, 1796,
   1962
Caribbean   38, 41-42, 309, 1224,
   1477, 1774, 1957, 2009
Caricature   121
Caritas   327-328, 587

Carlisle, Belinda   840
Carlyle, Thomas   787, 852
Carnival   107, 259-260, 383, 478,
   581, 726, 748, 866, 1165, 1167,
   1509, 1634, 1711, 1756, 1774,
   1833, 1920-1921, 1981
Carolsfeld, J. Schnorr von   136
Carpocratians   793
Carpzov II, Johann Benedikt   1841
Carroll, Lewis   714
Carson, Rachel   596
Carter, Chris   1927
Carter, Howard   564
Carthage   85, 90, 153
Carthusians   1831
Carus, Carl Gustav   591, 1304,
   1539, 1626, 1647
Casas, Bartolomé de Las   395, 1335
Casaubon, Isaac   850
Cashibo   248
Casimir III   1042
Cassirer, Ernst   420, 607, 1183,
   1289
Castaneda, Carlos   301, 956, 1157,
   1906
Caste   198, 261-263, 338, 398-399,
   447, 478, 523, 709, 774, 824,
   826, 854, 855, 858, 862, 864-
   865, 866, 867, 916, 917, 918,
   928, 944, 1090, 1147, 1376,
   1378, 1447, 1608, 1610, 1699,
   1988
Castel, Robert   1546
Castelo Branco   1095
Castiglione, Baldasare   1623
Castoriadis, Cornelius   420
Castracani, Castruccio   1398
Castration   941
Çatal Hüyük (Huyuk)   83, 89, 535,
   560, 1177, 1490
Catalepsy   1914
Cathari / Cathars   512, 533, 583,
   616, 654, 658, 724, 753, 793,
   796, 846, 943, 1142, 1222,
   1497, 1602, 1700, 1707, 1800
Catharsis   263-265, 443, 724, 904,
   1542, 1665, 1772, 1873
Catherine of Siena   1283
Catholicism   6-8, 13, 21, 41-43, 86,
   87, 117, 126, 153-155, 170-171,
   199-200, 246-248, 250, 265-
   268, 274, 298, 301-302, 317,
   379, 428, 512, 533, 541, 552,
   602, 631, 635, 638-640, 644,
   646, 653, 661, 664-665, 667,
   697, 724-725, 731, 810-811,
   854, 878, 913, 937, 954, 1008,

   1022, 1097, 1102, 1153, 1155,
   1162-1163, 1238, 1243, 1321,
   1332, 1336, 1339-1340, 1356,
   1358-1359, 1427, 1437, 1454,
   1533, 1565, 1606, 1609, 1612,
   1621-1622, 1662, 1794, 1822,
   1832-1833, 1924-1945, 1947,
   1959, 1984, 1993
Cato   950
Caucasian   1575
Caucasus   538, 647
Causality   507, 510, 1138, 1688
Cave paintings   1076
Cave   67, 106, 125, 271-273, 303,
   579, 754, 815, 845, 1258, 1341,
   1444-1456, 1490, 1779, 1958
Celebes   932-935
Celibacy   137, 273-276, 483, 706,
   782, 818, 1025, 1073, 1153,
   1379, 1426, 1498, 1503,
   1563, 1668, 1711, 1715-1716,
   1894
Cellini, Benvenuto   180
Celts   276-279, 292, 638, 650, 1378,
   1456, 1492, 1521, 1576, 1589,
   1592, 1594, 1867
Cemetery   109, 115, 293, 295-297,
   351, 381, 845, 1116, 1213,
   1251-1252, 1267, 1823, 1958-
   1959, 2014
Central America   298, 300-303,
   325, 377, 395, 426, 499, 585,
   1069, 1095, 1322, 1341, 1381,
   1407, 1439, 1447, 1773, 1921
Cervantes   1082-1083
Cesare Beccaria   257
Ceylon   208, 1452, 2013, *see also*
   Sri Lanka
Chŏndogyo   376
Chabad-Lubavitcher   836
Chad   18
Chagall, Marc   911
Chahine, Youcuf   744, 746
Chakra   205, 868, 1484, 1846, 1996
Chamberlain, H. St.   288
Chambers, William   1587
Champollion, Jean François   554,
   564
Channeling   248, 318-320, 434,
   610, 1313, 1521, 1806, 1808,
   1927, 1950, 1993
Chaos   83, 321-322, 422, 595, 802,
   870, 1286, 1964, 1977, 1987
Chaos Theory   322
Chaplin, Charlie   1921
Chapman, Tracy   840
Charcot, Jean-Martin   760

Orthopraxis 1391, 1394, 1481
Orunmila 30
Orwell, George 704, 1933
Ôsaka 359
Oshanin, Lev 249
Osho 929, 1392, *see also* Bhagwan
    Shree Rajneesh
Osho Movement 143, 431, 582,
    826, 868, 1391-1392, 1527,
    1594, 1646, 1717, 1847, 1915,
    1999
Osiris 84, 558, 562, 568, 570, 1267,
    1540
Osmond, Humphrey 956
Ossianism 286
Ostwald, Wilhelm 589, 1459
Otherworld 1722
Otto, Nikolaus 1129
Otto, Rudolf 9-10, 141, 574, 579,
    722, 800, 803, 810, 876, 1211,
    1280-1281, 1295, 1312, 1480,
    1612, 1693, 2004
Otto, Walter F. 1289, 1403, 1469
Ottoman Empire 965, 1202, 1415,
    1417
Ottoman I 990
Ottomans 991
Our Lady of Guadalupe 301, 1454,
    1559
Ouroboros 623
Outer space 1691, 1933
Out-groups 816
Outsider 830, 881, 945, 1223,
    1391, 1515, 1614, 1852, 1908,
    1909, 1917, 1919-1920, 1946,
    1953
Ovates 531
Overbeck, Franz 136, 1323
Owen, Robert 432
Owls 74, 685

Pacelli, Eugenio 667
Pachacutic 1132
Pachomius 1242
Pacifism 139, 681, 775, 1250, 1431,
    1971
Páez Indians 313
Paganism 9, 24, 44, 46, 51, 82, 88,
    102-103, 110, 126, 184, 283,
    286, 288, 305, 312, 411, 497,
    530, 594-595, 650, 653, 655,
    665, 750, 794, 837, 879, 899,
    948, 1004, 1085, 1234, 1276-
    1277, 1307, 1309-1310, 1312,
    1324, 1331, 1366, 1393-1398,
    1401-1402, 1404-1405, 1466,
    1468-1470, 1575, 1587, 1593,

1625, 1678, 1811, 1840, 1852,
    1871-1873, 1882, 1933, 2010,
    see also Neopaganism
Pai-chang 2000
Pain 138, 174, 191, 194, 211, 672,
    747, 821, 951, 1174, 1260,
    1263, 1406-1408, 1435, 1437,
    1439, 1486, 1539, 1563, 1815,
    1817-1818, 1851
Painting 1490
Paisley, Ian 1359
Pakistan 217, 775, 880, 917-918,
    920, 929, 951, 961, 996-997,
    1142, 1265, 1560, 1738, 1741,
    1824, 1857, 1903, 1942, 2013
Paladino, Eusapia 1804
Palenque 305
Paleolithic Age 488, 1383, 1489,
    1490, 1851, 1991
Palestine Liberation Organization
    (PLO) 1411, 1419, 1422
Palestine 13, 62, 110, 158, 255,
    384, 471, 513, 535, 537-538,
    539, 988, 996-997, 1006, 1008,
    1030, 1046, 1159, 1241, 1247,
    1409, 1411-1412, 1415-1419,
    1753, 1836, 1863-1865, 2005-
    2008
Pan 512, 1309
Panama 298, 318, 1407, 1780
Pan-Arabism 965, 1417, 1419
Pan-Babylonism 564
Panchen Lama 1073, 1074
Pandora 1515, 1711
Panentheism 1424, 1648
Pan-Indianism 1344
Pan-Indian movements 1345
Pan-Islamism 965
Panpsychism 1537
Pan-Slavism 645, 1594
Pantheism 88, 298, 510, 594, 596,
    609-610, 655, 699, 834, 987-
    988, 1211, 1280, 1281, 1283,
    1304-1305, 1312, 1326-1327,
    1423-1424, 1466, 1624, 1987
Pantheon 60, 85, 99, 168, 333,
    481, 483, 506, 557, 560, 727,
    863, 922-923, 1457, 1469,
    1890
Pantokrator 1014
Panturanism 1736, 1738
Papacy 28, 157, 266, 379, 846,
    1086, 1389, 1425, 1426, 1501,
    1653
Pappas, Irene 745
Pappe, Han 2008
Pappenheim, Bertha 264

Papua New Guinea 690, 783, 1166,
    1791, 1795-1796
Papus 1365
Paracelsus 618, 794, 955, 1365,
    1399
Paradise 33, 84, 141, 303, 476, 533,
    542, 586, 603-604, 717, 738,
    750, 762, 777-778, 802, 837,
    839-841, 845, 854, 871, 903,
    913, 1003, 1016, 1067, 1125,
    1131, 1160, 1171, 1258-1259,
    1287, 1308, 1361-1362, 1385,
    1431, 1474, 1570-1571, 1623,
    1672, 1715, 1797, 1823, 1881,
    1933, 1962, 1739, 1988, *see also*
    Eden, Garden
Paraguay 66, 310, 398, 1774, 1780
Parakkamabahu 228
Paranoia 945
Parapsychology 696, 1427-1429,
    1542, 1603, 1804-1805, 1808
Paratext 1869
Paris 424, 602, 631, 1528
Park, Mungo 1591
Parker, Alan 1960
Parks, Rosa 1339
Parliament of World Religions 553
Parmenides 91
Parousia 1691
Parsi / Parsees 6, 553,773, 859,
    919, 926, 959, 1248, 1998,
    2012-2013
Parsifal 288
Parsons, Talcott 1506, 1761
Part, Arvo 1275
Parvati 71, 864
Pascal, Blaise 1079, 1685, 1706
Pasolini, Pier Paolo 735-736, 738
Pasqually, Martines de 796
Passion 301, 737, 1282-1283, 1406,
    1439, 1508, 1530, 1813-1815
Passion plays 735, 743, 977, 1160,
    1167, 1194, 1434
Passover 726, 727, 835, 1013,
    1041, 1118, 1162, 1731, 1757
Patagonia 1773
Patanjali 1199, 1996
Path 483, 1509, 1640, 1644-1645
Pathocentrism 174
Pathology 1550
Patriarchy 675, 688, 706, 829,
    1150, 1177-1179, 1514, 1528,
    1769, 1982-1984, 1987
Patricide 1514
Patrilocality 1149
Patriotism 1727, 1854
Patroclus 762

Patronage 1207-1209, 1605
Pauen, Michael 795
Paul 124, 192-193, 196, 256, 275,
    318, 323, 384, 408, 497, 548,
    551, 802, 810, 812, 878, 887,
    913, 1116-1118, 1524, 1528-
    1529, 1613, 1644, 1652-1653,
    1699, 1739, 1941
Paul III 943, 1010
Paul IV 1043
Paul VI 1012
Paulicians 616, 1142
Pausanias 1904
Pax Christi 1432
Pax Romana 1431
Peace 208, 214, 239, 443, 445,
    454, 447, 475, 553, 595, 650,
    890, 1006, 1009, 1012, 1081,
    1156, 1178-1179, 1240, 1359,
    1372-1373, 1421, 1430-1432,
    1474, 1608, 1654, 1705, 1749,
    1862, 1923, 1929, 1948, 1961,
    1986
Peace movements 1431-1432,
    1531, 1982, 1983
Peace of Westphalia 661
Peak experiences 946, 956
Pearl Harbor 367
Pechstein, Max 1381, 1981
Pedagogy 823, 848-849, 1272,
    1757, 1934
Pederasty 878
Pedro I 311
Peisistratos 520
Péladan, Joséphin 1365
Pelagianism 154
Pelagius 1976
Pen, Jean-Marie Le 1020
Penalty 147
Penance / Penitent 59, 441-442,
    581, 679, 747, 803, 824, 902,
    943, 962, 1107, 1120, 1160,
    1216, 1241, 1406-1407, 1433-
    1434, 1439, 1447, 1449, 1579,
    1738, 1881
Penderecki, Krzysztof 1275
Penn, William 1331, 1335
Penner, Hans 1919
Pennsylvania 1331
Pentecost 46, 727, 1298, 1967
Pentecostal churches 1273
Pentecostal communities 23, 37
Pentecostalism 248, 317, 324, 327,
    537, 1322, 1779
Pentecostal movements 24, 265,
    582, 1332, 1474, 1744
Penthesilea 53-54

People's Temple 79, 473, 684, 946,
    1552, 1825, 1865
Perception 13, 127, 271, 424, 434,
    438, 466, 697-698, 716, 907,
    1435, 1437, 1439-1441, 1444-
    1446, 1496, 1498, 1536-1537,
    1539-1540, 1581, 1612, 1621,
    1828, 1896, 1913, 1916, 1924,
    1950-1953, 1955, 1964, 1973,
    1994
Percivale 737
Perec, Georges 1112
Perennial philosophy 699
Perez, Shimon 1862
Performance 130, 479, 1109, 1214-
    1215, 1454, 1474, 1503, 1635,
    1638, 1872
Pergamon Altar 1271
Periboia 1369
Perls, Fritz 606
Perón, Juan Domingo 1944
Perrault, Charles 702
Persecution of witches 1978, *see
    also* Witch(es)
Persecution 122, 163
Persepolis 2000, 2011
Persia 151, 321, 385, 387, 389,
    393-394, 561, 653, 1041, 1105,
    1134, 1142, 1575
Persians 92, 870, 1247-1248, 1381
Persinger, Michael 700
Person / Personhood 496, 625,
    822, 1167, 1173, 1348, 1406,
    1536, 1540, 1545, 1553
Personality cult 150, 179, 345,
    347, 377, 1105, 1145-1146,
    1268, 1607, 1943, 1945, *see also*
    Veneration of persons
Personality disorder 1542
Peru 306, 310, 426, 878, 1132,
    1268, 1773, 1774, 1779, 1780
Pesach 1051
Pesach Haggadah 726
Pétain, Marshal 1019
Peter of Spain 1681
Petersen, Johann Wilhelm 843,
    1449
Peterson, Erik 87, 1465
Petitean, Bernard-Thadée 365
Petrarch 1077, 1308, 1904
Petrus Venerabilis 1573
Peyote 954-956, 1176, 1344, 1595
Peyote religion 1125
Pfefferkorn, Johannes 1841
Pfister, Oskar 1545
Phallus 863, 867, 1642, 1920
Phantasms 1950

Pharisees 110, 1036, 1566
Phenomenology (of religion) 9-10,
    518, 810, 876, 1484, 1540, 1627
Phersu 96
Philae 28
Philanthropy 588
Philhellenism 1587
Philippines 364, 377, 725, 747,
    1129, 1322, 1530, 1791
Philistines 1409
Philo of Alexandria 170, 848, 1246
Philology 9, 1080, 1869
Philosophia occulta 1365
Philosophia perennis 607-608,
    611, 849, 1280
Philosophy of life 322, 958, 1512,
    1582, 1584
Philosophy of nature 176, 1304,
    1309, 1424, 1458, 1585, *see also*
    Nature
Philosophy 8-10, 83, 86, 88,
    91, 101-112, 122, 125-126,
    135-136, 141, 143, 149-151,
    154, 169, 173-175, 214, 252,
    380, 385, 454, 467, 474, 501,
    507, 510, 524, 531, 533, 573,
    575, 591, 608-609, 613, 615,
    623, 627-628, 664, 693-694,
    699, 724, 763, 768, 794-795,
    803-804, 810, 823, 826, 843,
    847, 849, 857, 867, 874, 884,
    965-966, 980-981, 987, 1039-
    1041, 1045, 1080-1081, 1119,
    1123-1124, 1184, 1210-1211,
    1216, 1218-1219, 1236, 1283,
    1290, 1304, 1324-1325, 1385,
    1399, 1448, 1456, 1458, 1468,
    1481, 1513, 1517-1518, 1528,
    1582-1583, 1594, 1623, 1625,
    1681, 1684, 1687, 1690, 1778,
    1815, 1819, 1822, 1845, 1853,
    1880, 1882-1883, 1890, 1934,
    1972, 1977
Phoenicia / Phoenicians 85, 90,
    535, 1527
Photography 128, 129, 191, 911,
    1195-1196
Physico-theology 571
Physics 126, 509, 576, 1364, 1485,
    1685-1686, 1689, 1973-1974
Physiocentrism 174, 1309-1310
Phytomorphism 800
Piaget, Jean 1755, 1935
Picatrix 1625
Pico della Mirandola, Giovanni
    573, 590, 617, 849, 1399, 1624,
    1626

851, 1104, 1401, 1515-1518, 1663, 1711, 1920-1921
Promiscuity   688, 1149, 1177, 1527, 1958
Promise Keepers   1712
Propaganda   737, 1191, 1464
Prophecy   23, 62, 119, 325, 415, 582, 592, 809-810, 841, 952-953, 1056, 1226, 1297, 1373, 1377, 1519-1521, 1523-1524, 1659, 1720, 1800, 1889, 1914, *see also* Divination, Prophet
Prophet   17, 23, 42, 91, 111, 156, 170, 178, 195-196, 251, 413, 419, 434, 727, 732, 763, 820, 836, 873, 948, 950, 962, 966-968, 972, 1055, 1108, 1142, 1187, 1193, 1215, 1248, 1264-1266, 1347, 1373, 1377, 1503-1504, 1522-1524, 1551, 1571, 1615, 1645, 1751, 1757, 1798, 1829, 1910, 1913, 1950, 1954, 1970, 2000, 2012, *see also* Prophecy
Prophetess   1478, 1522
Prophetism   1522, 1524
Proselytes   649, 1525
Proskynesis   1438, 1446, 1487, 1525-1526
Prostitution   602, 1154, 1505, 1527-1529, 1559, 1711, 1781
Prostration   802, 1438, 1487, 1526
Protagoras   149
Protest   141, 445, 1095, 1159, 1530-1531, 1554, 1824, 1851-1852
Protestantism   7, 8, 22, 41, 81, 112, 138-139, 162, 170, 179, 247, 253-254, 259, 266, 268, 289, 302, 379, 397-398, 437, 439, 453, 502, 528, 631, 635, 638, 640, 647, 652, 660, 667, 678, 854, 880, 910, 937, 1008, 1022, 1116, 1127, 1150, 1153, 1232, 1237, 1321-1322, 1331-1332, 1336-1340, 1356, 1358-1359, 1449, 1483, 1513, 1533-1535, 1597, 1682, 1700, 1708, 1715, 1779, 1793-1794, 1822, 1871, 1900, 1924, 1929, 1993
Protocols of the Elders of Zion   114
Proudhon, Pierre Joseph   56
Providence   413, 465, 507, 1124, 1307-1308, 1369
Prussia   113-114, 148, 662, 1153
Psellos   849
Pseudepigrapha   171

Psi phenomena   1427, 1429, *see also* Parapsychology
Psyche   146, 204, 264, 422-423, 461, 717, 1023, 1200, 1283, 1427, 1485, 1536, 1538-1541, 1545, 1549, 1637, 1693, 1771, 1951-1952, 1974
Psychiatry   583, 696, 1263, 1545, 1695, 1771
Psychic Disorders   1541
Psychic illnesses   1550
Psychoanalysis   146, 263-264, 335, 443, 524-525, 604, 625, 705, 717, 760, 823, 1130, 1278, 1369, 1470, 1476, 1495, 1539, 1543-1547, 1637, 1902, 1976
Psychokinesis   1428
Psychology   12, 79, 127, 146, 180, 335, 579, 582-584, 621, 684, 723, 855, 897, 905, 946, 1123, 1134, 1212, 1272, 1314, 1392, 1408, 1439, 1470, 1476, 1485, 1495, 1506, 1511, 1514, 1536, 1539, 1541-1543, 1545-1546, 1550, 1635, 1637-1638, 1695, 1739, 1771-1772, 1805, 1817, 1902, 1911, 1934, 1950-1951, 1961, 1972-1973, 1976
Psychopathology   466-467, 696, 717-718, 823, 1476, 1506, 1548, 1551, 1723, 1823, 1928, 1952
Psychosis   696, 945, 1548, 1551, 1823, 1952
Psychotherapy   956, 1263, 1392, 1542-1543, 1546
Ptah   570
Ptolemy, Claudius   144, 614
Ptolemy II Philadelphos   170
Puberty   332, 336, 338, 464, 880, 906, 938, 1070, 1553-1555, 1598, 1712, 1954
Publicity   134, 176, 185, 412, 440, 518, 679, 727, 780, 1160, 1193, 1251, 1253, 1505, 1508, 1555-1558, 1923
Pueblo   522
Puerto Rico   43
Puja   207, 859, 865, 925, 1144, 1967
Punics   85, 90
Punishment   186, 255, 581, 625, 690, 723, 771, 812, 822-823, 841-843, 1149, 1378, 1407-1408, 1433, 1453, 1517, 1570, 1579, 1602, 1604, 1738, 1750, 1815, 1823-1824, 1835, 1840, 1873, 1879, 1881
Punjab   919, 929

Punk   829
Pupil   825-826, 1173-1174, 1375, 1800, 1945, *see also* Master
Purāṇas   863
Purgatory   623, 842, 854, 913, 1222, 1565, 1807, 1951
Purification   67, 107, 161, 181, 263-265, 415, 485, 532, 747, 828, 844, 854, 866, 904-905, 913, 942, 951-952, 1104, 1107, 1143, 1157, 1175, 1276, 1294, 1434, 1443, 1446-1447, 1486-1487, 1538, 1558-1561, 1563-1565, 1579, 1598, 1662, 1728-1729, 1799, 1815, 1964, 1967, 2013
Purim   1051
Puritanism   179, 254, 398, 442, 1331, 1333, 1335, 1445, 1969
Purity   114, 187, 262-263, 275, 338, 398, 410-411, 416, 441, 528, 768, 802, 853, 867, 967, 1016, 1178, 1215, 1328, 1343, 1361, 1447, 1488, 1528, 1538, 1558-1560, 1562-1565, 1598, 1711, 1726, 1728, 1745, 1819, 1840, 1843, 2002
Purna-kumbha   729
Pye, Michael   1621
Pygmies   1740
Pylades   762
Pyramid   26, 298, 301, 305, 414-415, 488, 554-558, 563, 1076, 1213, 1259, 1266, 1383-1384, 1447, 1802, 1926
Pythagoras   608, 611, 613, 1274, 1602, 1665, 1771, 1937
Pythagoreanism   803, 1364, 1772, 1937
Pythia   1079, 1373

Qadariyya / Qadiriya   15, 31, 33, 721
Qadi   967, 1091
Qarmats   1186, 1188
Qawwali   1741
Qi   1259
Qiddush ha-shem   1824
Qippa   415
Quakers   254, 328, 448, 763, 1331, 1335, 1337-1338, 1431, 1444, 1447
Quantum mechanics   510, 1314, 1364, 1974
Quebec   1335-1336
Quechua   308, 311-312
Queneau, Raymond   1112
Quesada   309